Principles of Managerial Economics

N. Gregory Mankiw
Harvard University

Somdeep Chatterjee
Indian Institute of Management Calcutta

Cengage

Australia • Brazil • Canada • India • Mexico • Singapore • United Kingdom • United States

Cengage

Principles of Managerial Economics

US Author:
N. Gregory Mankiw
Adapter:
Somdeep Chatterjee

For product information and technology assistance, contact us at
asia.infoindia@cengage.com

For permission to use material from this text or product, submit all requests online at
www.cengage.com/permissions

ISBN-13: 978-93-6660-418-3
ISBN-10: 93-6660-418-8

Cengage Learning India Pvt. Ltd.
T-303, 3rd Floor
DAV Complex, Plot 3
Mayur Vihar Phase 1
Delhi 110091

Cengage is a leading provider of customized learning solutions with employees residing in nearly 40 different countries and sales in more than 125 countries around the world. Find your local representative at: **www.cengage.com.**

Cengage is committed to creating inclusive and diverse products, including perspectives that represent the diversity of people across all backgrounds, identities, opinions, and experiences. If you have any feedback related to this, please contact us at **support.cengage.com.**

To learn more about Cengage products, platforms and services, visit **www.cengage.co.in.**

Printed by:
IBH Print and Bind Private Limited
Plot No. 81, Ecotech 12, Greater Noida, Gautam Budh Nagar
Uttar Pradesh 201308

Printed in India
Print Number: 01 Print Year: 2026

To Catherine, Nicholas, and Peter,
my other contributions to the next generation

— N. Gregory Mankiw

To Saronya and Shipra,
for being who they are!

— Somdeep Chatterjee

About the Authors

JORDI CABRÉ

N. Gregory Mankiw is the Robert M. Beren Professor of Economics at Harvard University. As a student, he studied economics at Princeton University and MIT. As a teacher, he has taught macroeconomics, microeconomics, statistics, and principles of economics. He even spent one summer long ago as a sailing instructor on Long Beach Island.

Professor Mankiw is a prolific writer and regular participant in academic and policy debates. His work has been published in scholarly journals such as the *American Economic Review, Journal of Political Economy, and Quarterly Journal of Economics and in more popular forums, such as the New York Times and The Wall Street Journal*. He is also the author of the best-selling intermediate-level textbook Macroeconomics (Worth Publishers).

In addition to his teaching, research, and writing, Professor Mankiw has been a research associate of the National Bureau of Economic Research, a member of the Brookings Panel on Economic Activity, an adviser to the Congressional Budget Office and the Federal Reserve Banks of Boston and New York, a trustee of the Urban Institute and the Economic Club of New York, and a member of the ETS test development committee for the Advanced Placement exam in economics. From 2003 to 2005, he served as chairman of the President's Council of Economic Advisers.

Somdeep Chatterjee is an Associate Professor of Economics at the Indian Institute of Management Calcutta (IIMC). He holds a PhD in Economics from the University of Houston, after which he worked as an Assistant Professor at the Indian Institute of Management Lucknow and later as a Lecturer in Development Economics at the University of Manchester. He is the recipient of the Prof. M.J. Manohar Rao Award given by The Indian Econometric Society. Somdeep is an Editorial Board Member of the *Journal of Development Studies* and is also associated with the Global Labor Organization, Centre for Development Economics & Sustainability (CDES), and the Global Action for Policy (GAP) Initiative.

Somdeep is an active researcher in development economics and political economy, and his work has appeared in leading journals like *Journal of the European Economic Association, World Development, Economica, Public Choice, Economic Development & Cultural Change*, etc. Somdeep has more than a decade of experience teaching economics to undergraduate and graduate students across the world. He has been using Cengage's Principles textbooks throughout his teaching career not only for economics degree programs at various levels but also to teach economics to business school students. He regularly uses curated examples and managerial applications of the basic principles of economics, which resonate very well with the students and hence served as a major motivation for writing this adaptation.

Somdeep lives in Kolkata with his wife and daughter and is passionate about the city's legacy. He is an ardent follower of Cricket and football and can be often found in the galleries of the Eden Gardens watching a test match or the box at the Salt Lake Stadium watching his favorite football team, Mohun Bagan, battle it out for the league title. A fan of Tintin, Somdeep loves travelling, and unsurprisingly his favorite tourist destination is Belgium.

Preface to the Original Edition

During my 20-year career as a student, the course that excited me most was the two-semester sequence on the principles of economics that I took during my first year in college. It is no exaggeration to say that it changed my life.

I had grown up in a family that often discussed politics over the dinner table. The pros and cons of various solutions to society's problems generated fervent debate. But in school, I had been drawn to the sciences. While politics seemed vague, rambling, and subjective, science was analytic, systematic, and objective. Political debate continued without end, but scientific research made progress.

My freshman course on the principles of economics opened my eyes to a new way of thinking. Economics combines the virtues of politics and science. It is, truly, a social science. Its subject matter is society—how people choose to lead their lives and how they interact with one another—but it approaches the subject with the dispassion of a science. By bringing the methods of science to the questions of politics, economics aims to make progress on the challenges that all societies face.

I wrote this book with the hope that I could convey some of the excitement about economics that I felt as a student in my first economics course. Economics is a subject in which a little knowledge goes a long way. (The same cannot be said, for instance, of the study of physics or the Chinese language.) Economists have a unique worldview, much of which can be taught in one or two semesters. My goal in this book is to transmit this way of thinking to the widest possible audience and to convince readers that it illuminates much about their lives and the world around them.

I believe that everyone should study the fundamental ideas that economics has to offer. One purpose of general education is to teach people about the world and thereby make them better citizens. The study of economics, as much as any discipline, serves this goal. Writing an economics textbook is, therefore, a great honor and a great responsibility. It is one way that economists can help promote better government and a more prosperous future. As the great economist Paul Samuelson put it, "I don't care who writes a nation's laws, or crafts its advanced treaties, if I can write its economics textbooks."

What's New?

Economics aims to understand the world in which we live. Most chapters of this book include Case Studies that illustrate how the principles of economics can be applied. In the News boxes offer excerpts from newspapers, magazines, and online news sources to show how economic ideas shed light on current issues facing society. After students finish their first course in economics, they should think about news reports from a new perspective and with greater insight. To keep the study of economics fresh and relevant for each new cohort of students, I update each edition to keep pace with the ever-changing world.

The new applications in this edition are too numerous to list in their entirety, but here is a sample of the topics covered (and the chapters in which they appear):

- Shortages during the coronavirus pandemic renewed the debate over whether it is fair for businesses to increase prices during a crisis. (Chapter 4)
- The future of the ride-share market hinges on the elasticities of supply and demand. (Chapter 5)
- The minimum wage remains a contentious topic. (Chapter 6)
- A carbon tax is a versatile tool to combat global climate change. (Chapter 10)
- Putting a price on road use gets renewed attention as the United States embarks on building new infrastructure. (Chapter 11)
- The pandemic of 2020 taught some lessons about why it's hard to cut wasteful medical spending. (Chapter 12)
- The value-added tax might be a policy for the United States to consider. (Chapter 13)
- The Biden administration looked to expand the scope of antitrust policy. (Chapter 16)
- Amazon found itself in the crosshairs of antitrust enforcers. (Chapter 18)
- Immigration policy creates winners and losers in the labor market. (Chapter 19)
- The forgone schooling during the coronavirus pandemic might have long-lasting effects on earnings. (Chapter 20)
- New research takes a lifetime perspective on measuring inequality. (Chapter 21)
- Robust expansions of the social safety net reduced poverty during the coronavirus pandemic. (Chapter 21)
- People are not good at rationally responding to small-probability events. (Chapter 23)

This edition also includes two new chapters. Chapter 12 examines the economics of healthcare. As this sector's share of the economy has increased, its distinctive features, problems, and policy challenges have become more important for students to understand. Chapter 24 is an optional appendix chapter that discusses how economists use data. In recent years, economic research has grown increasingly empirical, and some instructors want to introduce students to the statistical methods that economists use. Instructors who teach this chapter can move it earlier in the course.

As always, I have carefully gone through every chapter to refine the book's coverage and pedagogy. There are numerous changes, large and small, to ensure that the book is clear, accurate, and up-to-date.

All the changes that I made, and the many others that I considered, were evaluated in light of the benefits of brevity. Like most things studied in economics, a student's time is a scarce resource. I always keep in mind a dictum from the novelist Robertson Davies: "One of the most important things about writing is to boil it down and not bore the hell out of everybody."

Learning Tools

The purpose of this book is to help students learn the fundamental lessons of economics and to show how they can apply these lessons to their lives and the world in which they live. Toward that end, I have used various learning tools that recur throughout the book.

Case Studies

Economic theory is useful and interesting only if it can be applied to understanding actual events and policies. This book, therefore, contains numerous case studies that apply the theory that has just been developed.

In the News Boxes

One benefit that students gain from studying economics is a new perspective and greater understanding of news from around the world. To highlight this benefit, I have included excerpts from many newspaper and magazine articles, some of which are opinion columns written by prominent economists. These articles, together with my brief introductions, show how basic economic theory can be applied. Most of these boxes are new to this edition. Each news article ends with "Questions to Discuss," which can be used to start a dialogue in the classroom.

FYI Boxes

These boxes provide additional material "for your information." Some of them offer a glimpse into the history of economic thought. Others clarify technical issues. Still others discuss supplementary topics that instructors might choose to either discuss or skip in their lectures.

Ask the Experts Boxes

This feature summarizes results from the IGM Economic Experts Panel, an ongoing survey of several dozen prominent economists. Every few weeks, these experts are offered a statement and then asked whether they agree with it, disagree with it, or are uncertain about it. The survey results appear in the chapters near the coverage of the relevant topic. They give students a sense of when economists are united, when they are divided, and when they just don't know what to think.

Definitions of Key Concepts

When key concepts are introduced in the chapter, they are presented in **blue** typeface. In addition, their definitions are placed in the margins. This treatment should aid students in learning and reviewing the material.

Quick Quizzes

After each major section in a chapter, students are offered a brief multiple-choice Quick Quiz to check their comprehension of what they have just learned. If students cannot readily answer these quizzes, they should stop and review the material before continuing. The answers to all Quick Quizzes are available at the end of each chapter.

Chapter in a Nutshell

Each chapter concludes with a brief summary that reminds students of the most important lessons they have learned. Later in their study, it offers an efficient way to review for exams.

List of Key Concepts

A list of key concepts at the end of each chapter offers students a way to test their understanding of the new terms that have been introduced. Page references are included, so students can review the terms they do not understand.

Questions for Review

Located at the end of each chapter, questions for review cover the chapter's primary lessons. Students can use these questions to check their comprehension and prepare for exams.

Problems and Applications

Each chapter also contains a variety of problems and applications that ask students to apply the material they have learned. Some instructors may use these questions for homework assignments. Others may use them as a starting point for classroom discussions.

Supplements

Cengage offers various supplements for instructors and students who use this book. These resources make teaching the principles of economics easy for the instructor and learning them easy for the student. David R. Hakes of the University of Northern Iowa, a dedicated teacher and economist, supervised the development of the supplements for this edition.

Preface to the Indian Edition

N. Gregory Mankiw's original work, *Principles of Microeconomics*, and in general the whole *Principles* series published by Cengage has been epoch-making in the teaching pedagogy of introductory courses in Microeconomics, across the globe. There is hardly an economics educator who has not used some form of this series at some stage in their teaching careers. Considering the humongous success of the title and numerous adaptations and editions, there was rarely any gap in terms of its reach and utility, except perhaps the presence of tailormade applications in the field of managerial economics, which is largely a cousin of microeconomics but with a specific focus on business applications. It is with this idea that I embarked upon writing this adapted version to cater to the needs of economics educators in business management programs. This book keeps the clarity, intuition, and analytical discipline of the original while reframing the content as decisions that managers must make, especially in the Indian context. Where the Principles text often asks "what happens to price and quantity," this adaptation consistently asks, "what should a manager do next?"

Accordingly, many chapters have been reframed and repositioned relative to the original principles' textbooks. The focus is largely on managerial applications and implications. As an Economics instructor in an MBA classroom, the common question that one is often confronted with is, "where do we apply this in our organizations?" or "why learn economics in a management program?". This book takes these questions seriously and attempts to provide credible and definitive answers to establish Economics as not only a foundational discipline in the study of management but also to put forth that the very idea of Economic decision-making is very central to almost all of managerial decision-making.

Economics, broadly defined, is how a society *manages* its scarce resources. Economics instructors have used this age-old definition millions of times in a classroom. Yet, the very fact that the word "manage" is embedded within this definition is often under-appreciated. It is this very idea that is the starting point of Managerial Economics, as in principle the role of an economic agent is very managerial. The theoretical constructs in the chapters have been reoriented to fit a managerial lens while retaining the core seamless design of the original textbook, which makes teaching economics fun. The idea of this adaptation is to make teaching (and learning) economics fun in business schools as well.

The book is adapted for an Indian audience. All the examples and notations have been customized to fit the requirements of the classroom of an Indian business school. The book can be used in many ways. First, it can be a regular textbook for an introductory "Managerial Economics" or "Microeconomics" course in a fulltime MBA program. Often, these are core courses offered in the first term of the program. Second, it can be used as the main textbook for similar core courses in Executive MBA programs or MBA for working professionals, including online and distance learning MBA programs. Finally, the simplicity and appeal of the textual content would be ideal for adoption in executive education modular programs, such as Management Development Programs, where capsule modules on Managerial Economics, Microeconomics, Indian Economic Environment, or Managerial Applications of Game Theory, etc., are required to be taught.

What's New in this Edition

There are several new managerial applications in each chapter and providing an exhaustive list is too onerous for the reader of this preface. Instead, I will focus on the new chapter additions and the new learning tool, over and above the existing tools that the original version includes.

New Chapters

1. Chapter 9: The Indian Business and Economic Environment
   India's business environment is a dynamic mix of economic trends, institutional strengths, and structural limitations. For managers, understanding this environment is not merely background knowledge but a strategic imperative. This chapter bridges the gap between microeconomic reasoning from the previous chapters and India's real-world economic dynamics to assist managers in making informed business decisions. At the outset, the chapter situates India within the global economic context. While India is one of the fastest growing large economies, it still grapples with several structural challenges. The country's labor force is huge but underutilized. For instance, the female labor force participation remains persistently low. In terms of infrastructure, both physical and institutional, the development and status are not competitive at global levels. Employment in the informal sector is pervasive and persistent, including key sectors such as retail, construction, and small-scale manufacturing. The chapter emphasizes the significance of jobless growth and the role of policy reforms in India's economic landscape. Despite headline growth, the economy faced a challenge of 28 million applicants vying for 90,000 low-level railway jobs, underscoring the disparity between educational outcomes and labor market absorption. Finally, the chapter also talks about the external sector and how an understanding of the key metrics of the external sector and measurements can be an important toolkit for managers to assess the health of the economy and predict currency fluctuations, including ensuing crises, if any. This chapter can be a standalone reference for capsule modules in management development programs (MDPs) on the business and economic environment of India.

2. Chapter 16: Game Theory and Business Applications
   Application of Game Theory in management decision-making is very pervasive and therefore assumes great importance for students. In a standard Managerial Economics course, this chapter can come in very handy before teaching Oligopoly markets to explain how the strategic interactions affect oligopolistic firm behavior. However, the applications of game theory in this chapter have been specifically curated for teaching management students. As a result, this can also be a stand-alone reference for MDP modules on managerial applications of game theory.

3. Chapter 23: Uncertainty and Risk Preferences
   This will draw upon concepts learnt in the Theory of Consumer Choice, which was part of the original principles' textbooks, and discuss the idea of uncertainty. Managers routinely make decisions under risk, and this chapter will help understand how risk preferences are formulated and how this can be reflected using utility theory. I will discuss concepts of risk-averse manager, risk-neutral manager, and risk-loving manager using examples and applications of expected utility theory by adapting the utility arguments learnt earlier. As a result, this will be a perfect complement either for more advanced treatments of managerial economics for instructors who want to go deep into the theoretical aspects or be a good option to adopt as stand-alone reference material in finance or economics electives in the MBA program. Similar to the other new chapters, this is a perfect reference for capsule MDP modules on risk preferences and business decision-making under uncertainty.

New Learning Tool: Managerial Insight

In several chapters, after specific theoretical arguments are presented and relevant managerial applications or examples are discussed, a managerial insight section has been introduced to allow introspection on how this can be taken back to the organization or firm and what could be potential application of the learning just discussed. This should be of particular interest to working professionals and executive MBA students or MDP participants.

Acknowledgments

In writing this book, I benefited from the input of many talented people. Indeed, the list of people who have contributed to this project is so long, and their contributions so valuable, that it seems an injustice that only a single name appears on the cover.

Let me begin with my colleagues in the economics profession. The many editions of this text and its supplemental materials have benefited enormously from their input. In reviews and surveys, they have offered suggestions, identified challenges, and shared ideas from their own classroom experience. I am indebted to them for the perspectives they have brought to the text. Unfortunately, the list has become too long to thank those who contributed to previous editions, even though students reading the current edition are still benefiting from their insights.

Most important in this process has been David Hakes (University of Northern Iowa). David has served as a reliable sounding board for ideas and a hardworking partner with me in putting together the superb package of supplements.

A special thanks to my friend Jeff Sommer. For many years, Jeff was my editor at the *New York Times*. For this edition, he graciously read through the entire book, offering numerous suggestions for improvement. I am deeply grateful for his input.

The publishing team who worked on the book improved it tremendously. Jane Tufts, developmental editor, provided truly spectacular editing—as she always does. Joe Sabatino, economics Product Director, and Christopher Rader, Senior Product Manager, did a splendid job of overseeing the many people involved in such a large project. Colleen Farmer, Allison Janneck, and Anita Verma, Senior Content Managers, were crucial in managing the whole project and putting together an excellent team to revise the supplements and, with Pradhiba Kannaiyan, project manager at MPS Limited, had the patience and dedication necessary to turn my manuscript into this book. Erin Griffin, Senior Designer, gave this book its clean, friendly look and designed the wonderful cover. Tiffany Lee, copyeditor, refined my prose, and Vikas Makkar, indexer, prepared a careful and thorough index. John Carey, Executive Marketing Manager, worked long hours getting the word out to potential users of this book. The rest of the Cengage team has, as always, been consistently professional, enthusiastic, and dedicated.

We have a top team of veterans who have worked across multiple editions producing the supplements that accompany this book. Working with those at Cengage, the following have been relentless in making sure that the suite of ancillary materials is unmatched in both quantity and quality. No other text comes close.

PowerPoint: Andreea Chiritescu (Eastern Illinois University)

Test Bank: Shannon Aucoin, Eugenia Belova, and Alex Lewis (in-house Subject Matter Experts)

Instructor manual: David Hakes (University of Northern Iowa)

I am also grateful to Sarah Lao and Nathan Sun, two star undergraduates at Harvard, who helped me check the page proofs for this edition.

As always, I must thank my "in-house" editor Deborah Mankiw. As the first reader of most things I write, she continued to offer just the right mix of criticism and encouragement.

Finally, I should mention my three children, Catherine, Nicholas, and Peter. Their contribution to this book was putting up with a father spending too many hours in his study. The four of us have much in common—not least of which is our love of ice cream (which becomes apparent in Chapter 4).

N. Gregory Mankiw

I owe an obvious intellectual debt to N. Gregory Mankiw for the clarity of exposition that made this adaptation possible and to Cengage for stewarding a text that has educated generations. I also deeply thank Cengage for sharing my vision on adapting this text for management education, given the somewhat unwarranted discomfort that management students often have in understanding where and why economics is useful for their learning and holistic development. I particularly thank the publishing team at Cengage for bearing with me and keeping me on the timelines for completing the project and most importantly, providing constant support, guidance, and motivation for the work.

My colleagues and students, not only at IIM Calcutta but also at the University of Houston, Flame University, University of Manchester, and IIM Lucknow, shaped the book through countless classroom questions, critiques, and field examples. Many colleagues and program participants beyond academia provided insights that turned abstract ideas into actionable examples, although any errors remain mine alone. I am also grateful to my cohort of PhD students, including those who already graduated, for serving as human laboratories for testing out some of my ideas to incorporate in the book, many of whom have gone on to become instructors of managerial economics themselves, and who I hope will find this text attractive. I must also thank my dozens of research co-authors who kept up with my absence from collaborative contributions on our many projects and papers, including some journal submissions, and took the extra mile for completing some of the papers, to ensure I could devote time to this book project.

Finally, I must thank my family for their unstinted support with no questions asked, which made the writing of this text possible, despite some tumultuous times at home. The support of my loving wife, Shipra, and my bubbly 7-year-old daughter, Saronya, who kept up with my nonchalant attitude on most household matters, including help with homework, attending school PTMs, planning outings, dinners, and trips just so I could finish the chapters for this book, cannot be quantified or acknowledged enough. I am also eternally grateful to my mother for her (often exaggerated) belief in me and my father, who dreamt about this but unfortunately could not live to see this day!

Somdeep Chatterjee

Brief Contents

Contents

Chapter

1

Basic Principles of Managerial Economics

The word **economy** comes from the Greek word **oikonomos**, which means "one who manages a household." At first, the connection between firms, households and economies may seem obscure. But in fact, they have much in common.

No matter how you picture a modern household, its members face endless decisions, the same as managers within a firm. Somehow, they must decide which members do which tasks and what each receives in return. Whether a firm or household's income is high, low, or somewhere in between, its resources must be allocated among alternative uses.

Like households and firm, a society faces countless decisions. It must find some way to decide what jobs will be done and who will do them. Society needs people to grow food, make clothing, and design software. Once society has allocated people (as well as land, buildings, and machines) to various jobs, it must distribute the goods and services they produce. It must decide who will eat potatoes and who will eat chicken, who will live in a grand mansion and who will live in an apartment in a society.

ROMAN SAMBORSKYI/SHUTTERSTOCK.COM, ARNO VAN ENGELAND/EYEEM/GETTY IMAGES

scarcity
the limited nature of society's resources

These decisions are important because resources are scarce. **Scarcity** means that society has limited resources and, therefore, cannot produce all the goods and services people want. Just as members of a household and sometimes managers within firms cannot always get their desires satisfied, individuals in a society cannot always attain the standard of living to which they might aspire.

economics
the study of how society manages its scarce resources

Economics is the study of how society manages its scarce resources. In most societies, resources are allocated through the combined choices of millions of households and businesses. Economists examine how people make these choices: how much they work, what they buy, how much they save, how they invest their savings, and so on. Economists also study how people interact with one another. For instance, economists examine how buyers and sellers together determine the price at which a good is sold and the quantity that is sold. Finally, economists analyze the forces and trends that affect the overall economy, including the growth in average income, the fraction of the population that cannot find work, and the rate at which prices are rising.

Managerial economics is the application of economic reasoning and its tools to firm level decisions. It studies how economic analysis helps business leaders navigate decisions under scarcity, uncertainty, and complexity.

Managerial Economics covers a wide range of topics and encompasses many approaches, but it is unified by several central ideas of economics. This chapter discusses **Basic Principles of Managerial Economics**. Don't worry if you don't understand them all at first or if you aren't completely convinced that they are sensible or important. These ideas will be explored more fully in later chapters. This introduction to the basic principles will give you a sense of what managerial economics is all about. Consider this chapter a preview of coming attractions.

1-1 How Managers Make Decisions?

There is no mystery about what an economy is. Whether it encompasses New Delhi, India, or the entire planet, an economy is just a group of people dealing with one another as they go about their lives. Because the behavior of an economy reflects the behavior of the individuals within it, and the fundamental role of managers within firms is managing people and resources, the first four principles concern managerial decision making.

1-1a Principle 1: Managers Face Trade-Offs

"There ain't no such thing as a free lunch." Grammar aside, this old saying contains much truth. To get one thing you want, you usually have to give up another thing you want. Making decisions requires trading off one goal for another.

Consider Sneha, a student who is deciding how to use her most valuable resource—time. Sneha can spend all her time studying economics, all her time studying psychology, or divide her time between the two. For every hour she devotes to one subject, she gives up an hour she could have used studying the other. And for every hour spent studying, she gives up an hour that could have been spent napping, cycling, playing video games, watching web series, or working at a job for some extra spending money.

Consider Sneha's parents, who are deciding how to use the family income. They can spend it on food, clothing, or Sneha's tuition. Or they can save some of their income for retirement or a future family vacation. When they allocate a rupee to one of these goods, they have one less rupee to spend on another.

Within firm, managers face other trade-offs. One classic trade-off is between "profitability and compliance." For instance, investing in pollution control measures may be essential in meeting regulatory norms or enhancing brand goodwill, this may often raise production costs. Because of these higher costs, the firms are likely to earn smaller profits, pay lower wages, charge higher prices, or do some combination of these three things. While pollution regulations yield a cleaner environment and the improved health that comes with it, they may reduce the incomes of the regulated firms' owners, workers, and customers.

On the other hand, an economy-wide societal trade-off is between efficiency and equality. **Efficiency** means that society is getting the greatest benefits from its scarce resources. **Equality** means that those benefits are distributed uniformly among society's members. In other words, efficiency refers to the size of the economic pie, while equality refers to how evenly the pie is sliced.

efficiency
the property of society getting the most it can from its scarce resources

equality
the property of distributing economic prosperity uniformly among the members of society

These two goals can conflict. Consider, for instance, government policies aimed at reducing inequality. Some of these policies, such as cash transfers or subsidies, help the members of society most in need. Others, such as the income tax, require the financially successful to contribute more than others to support the government. These policies increase equality but may decrease efficiency. When the government redistributes income from the rich to the poor, it reduces the reward for hard work for people at all income levels. As a result, people may work less and produce fewer goods and services. In other words, when the government cuts the economic pie into more equal slices, the pie sometimes shrinks.

Managers also face trade-offs between efficiency and equality. Consider a decision to relocate a factory to reduce costs of production and, consequently, improve profit margins. While this may represent brute-force efficiency driven, it may come at the expense of equality. For example, the new location may be remote and difficult for female employees to travel at night; this may lead to some of them quitting. It may not be possible for local vendors and suppliers to continue supplying at the new location, and they might lose out; and this affects overall community reputation.

Recognizing that managers face trade-offs does not tell us which managerial decisions are best. Yet managers will make better choices if they understand the options available to them. Our study of managerial economics, therefore, starts by acknowledging life's trade-offs.

1-1b Principle 2: The Cost of Something Is What You Give Up to Get It

Because managers face trade-offs, they need to compare the costs and benefits of alternative decisions. In many cases, however, the costs are not as obvious as they might first appear.

Consider a tech startup in Bengaluru deciding whether to develop a new mobile app feature. The main benefits are higher use engagement, increased ad revenue and brand differentiation. But what are the costs? Managers might be tempted to add up the money spent on developer salaries, software, testing, and promotions. Yet this total does not truly represent what you give up.

This calculation has two problems. First, it includes some things that are not really costs of developing the new app feature. Even if you didn't introduce it, you still need to pay developer salaries. Second, this calculation ignores the largest cost of developing the app enhancement time. When developers are focused on this new enhancement, they can't spend that time working on optimizing the existing app's speed, for instance. Alternatively, these employees could have worked on creating a dashboard for enterprise clients, increasing their B2B revenues during this time.

The **opportunity cost** of an item is what you give up to get it. When making decisions, it's smart to take opportunity costs into account, and managers often do. Crickets who can earn millions dropping out of school and playing professionally understand that their opportunity cost of attending college is high. Not surprisingly, they sometimes decide that the benefit of a college education is not worth the cost.

opportunity cost
whatever must be given up to obtain some item

1-1c Principle 3: Rational People Think at the Margin

rational people
people who systematically and purposefully do the best they can to achieve their objectives

Economists often assume that people are rational. **Rational people** systematically and purposefully do the best they can to achieve their goals, given the available opportunities. As you study managerial economics, you will encounter firms that decide how many workers to hire and how much product to make and sell to maximize profits. You will meet people who decide how much to work and what goods and services to buy to achieve the highest possible level of satisfaction. To be sure, human behavior is complex and sometimes deviates from rationality. But the assumption that people do the best they can is, economists have found, a good starting point to explain the decisions that people make.

Rational decision makers know that many issues in life are not black and white but involve shades of gray. At dinnertime, you don't ask yourself, "Should I fast or eat 1 kg of Mutton Biryani?" You are more likely to ask, "Should I take that extra piece of Mutton in the Biryani?" When a critical business deadline approaches, the manager's decision is probably not between abandoning the task and asking team members to work 24 hours a day but whether to spend an extra hour reviewing the presentation slides or revisiting a strategy memo instead of attending a club for a party. Economists use the term **marginal change** to describe an incremental adjustment to an existing plan of action. Keep in mind that **margin** means "edge," so marginal changes are small adjustments around the edges of what you are doing. Rational people and managers in firms make decisions by comparing **marginal benefits** and **marginal costs.**

marginal change
an incremental adjustment to a plan of action

For example, suppose you are deciding whether to watch a movie tonight. You pay ₹250 a month for a streaming service that gives you unlimited access to its film library, and you typically watch five movies a month. What cost should you consider when deciding whether to stream another movie? The answer might seem to be ₹250, or ₹50, the **average** cost of a movie. More relevant for your decision, however, is the **marginal** cost—the extra money that you have to pay if you stream another film. Here, the marginal cost is zero because you pay ₹250 regardless of how many movies you stream. In other words, at the margin, streaming a movie is free. The only cost of watching a movie tonight is the time it takes away from other activities, such as working at a job or (better yet) reading this textbook.

Thinking at the margin is also useful for business decisions. Consider a hotel in Kolkata with 50 rooms, where the fixed cost of operations for a night is ₹2.50 lakhs. The average cost of each room is ₹5,000 (₹250,000/50). You might think that the hotel should never sell a room for less than ₹5,000. But imagine that at 7.30 pm in the evening, there are ten empty rooms, and Subhash, a walk-in customer arrives at the hotel and is willing to pay ₹3000 for a room. Should the hotel sell him the room? Yes, it should. If the hotel has empty rooms, the cost of adding an extra guest is tiny. The **average** cost of servicing a room is ₹5000, but the **marginal** cost is merely the housekeeping, electricity, free amenities, and toiletries Subhash will consume. As long as Subhash pays more than the marginal cost, selling him the room is profitable because major expenses, such as staff salary, maintenance etc., are borne regardless. A rational front desk manager can benefit from thinking at the margin.

VANTAGE_DS/SHUTTERSTOCK.COM

Many movie streaming services set the marginal cost of a movie equal to zero.

Marginal analysis explains some otherwise puzzling phenomena. For example, why is water so cheap while diamonds are so expensive? You might think it should be the other way around: Humans need water to survive, but diamonds merely glitter. Yet people are willing to pay much more for a diamond than for a cup of water. Economists have figured this out. A person's willingness to pay for a good is based on the marginal benefit that an extra unit of the good would yield. The marginal benefit, in turn, depends on how many units a person already has. Water is essential but plentiful, so the marginal benefit of an extra glass is small. By contrast, no one needs diamonds to survive, but because they are so rare, the marginal benefit of an extra gem is large.

A rational decision maker takes an action if and only if the action's marginal benefit exceeds its marginal cost. This principle explains why people use streaming services as much as they do, why hotels sell last-minute rooms below average cost, and why people pay more for diamonds than for water. It can take a while to get used to the logic of marginal thinking, but the study of economics will give you ample opportunity to practice.

1-1d Principle 4: People Respond to Incentives

An **incentive** is something that induces a person to act, such as the prospect of a punishment or reward. People respond to incentives if they make decisions by comparing costs and benefits. Incentives play a central role in economics. One economist went so far as to say that the entire field could be summarized as simply, "People respond to incentives. The rest is commentary."

incentive
something that induces a person to act

Understanding incentives are key to analyzing how firms behave and markets work. For example, when the price of onions spike in India, people decide to consume fewer onions. At the same time, farmers may decide to hire more workers, reallocate land and harvest more onions. In other words, a higher price provides an incentive for buyers to consume less and for sellers to produce more. As we will see, the influence of prices on the behavior of consumers and producers is crucial to how a market economy allocates scarce resources.

In the business world, companies use incentives to influence employee performance such as through linked bonuses or employee stock option plans (ESOP). Similarly, pricing incentives or cashback offers can shift consumer behavior. For example, Flipkart's "Big Billion Days" are known for offering significant discounts and deals for a period over a wide range of product categories. This creates an urgency among buyers to purchase during this period.

Government policies also affect incentives. For instance, a subsidy on electric vehicles (EVs) in India under e-AMRIT (Accelerated e-Mobility Revolution for India's Transportation) has reduced effective costs relative to petrol cars encouraging buyers to switch to EVs, resulting in rapid adoption of EVs in India. Similarly, LPG transfers through Direct Benefit Transfer (DBT), especially under Pradhan Mantri Ujjwala Yojana (PMUY) scheme, has encouraged wider adoption of cleaner cooking fuels.

When policymakers fail to consider incentives, the policies they enact may have unintended consequences. For example, consider auto safety. Today, all cars have seat belts, but this wasn't true few decades ago. The Motor Vehicles Act of India and its various amendments, mandates use of helmets for two wheelers and seatbelts for four wheelers.

How does a seat belt law affect safety? The direct effect is obvious: When a person wears a seat belt or helmet, the likelihood of surviving an auto accident rises. But that's not the end of the story. The law also affects behavior by altering incentives. The relevant behavior here is the speed and care with which drivers operate their vehicles. Driving slowly and carefully is costly because it uses the driver's time and energy. When deciding how to drive, rational people compare, perhaps unconsciously, the marginal benefit from safer driving with the marginal cost. They drive more slowly and carefully when the benefit of increased safety is high. For example, when road conditions are bad due to Indian monsoon, people drive more attentively and at lower speeds than they do when road conditions are clear.

Consider how a seat belt law alters a driver's cost–benefit calculation. Buckling up makes accidents less costly by reducing the risk of injury or death. It is as if road conditions had improved: When conditions are safer, people drive faster and less carefully. That may be fine for motorists, whose risk of injury in an accident is reduced because of seat belts. But if faster, less careful driving leads to more accidents, the seat belt law adversely affects pedestrians, who are more likely to be in an accident but (unlike drivers) don't benefit from added protection.

This discussion of incentives and seat belts isn't idle speculation. In a classic 1975 study, the economist Sam Peltzman tested the theory and found that auto-safety laws have had many of these effects. According to Peltzman, these laws give rise not only to fewer deaths per accident but also to more accidents. He concluded that the net result is little change in driver deaths and an increase in pedestrian deaths.

Peltzman's analysis of auto safety is an offbeat and controversial example of the principle that people respond to incentives. When analyzing any policy, it is important to consider not only the direct effects but also the indirect effects that work through incentives. If the policy alters incentives, people may change their behavior.

Quick**Quiz**

1. Economics is best defined as the study of
   a. how society manages its scarce resources.
   b. how to run a business most profitably.
   c. how to predict inflation, unemployment, and stock prices.
   d. how the government can protect people from unchecked self-interest.
2. Your opportunity cost of going to a movie is
   a. the price of the ticket.
   b. the price of the ticket plus the cost of any soda and popcorn you buy at the theater.
   c. the total cash expenditure needed to go to the movie plus the value of your time.
   d. zero, as long as you enjoy the movie and consider it a worthwhile use of time and money.
3. A marginal change is one that
   a. is not important for public policy.
   b. incrementally alters an existing plan.
   c. makes an outcome inefficient.
   d. does not influence incentives.
4. Because people respond to incentives,
   a. policymakers can alter outcomes by changing punishments or rewards.
   b. policies can have unintended consequences.
   c. society faces a trade-off between efficiency and equality.
   d. All of the above are correct.

Answers are at the end of the chapter.

1-2 How People Interact

The first four principles discussed how managers and economic agents make decisions. The next three concern how people interact with one another, which is a critical aspect of within-firm management.

1-2a Principle 5: Trade Can Make Businesses Better Off

You may have heard on the news that China or Vietnam is India's competitor in the manufacturing sector. In some ways, this is true. Chinese, Vietnamese, and Indian firms compete for customers in the markets for textiles, electronics, solar panels, pharmaceuticals, and many other items.

Yet it is easy to be misled when thinking about competition among countries. Trade between India and Vietnam is not like a cricket match in which one side wins and the other side loses. The opposite is true: Trade between two countries can make each country better off. Even when trade in the world economy is competitive, it can lead to a win–win outcome for the countries involved.

To see why, consider how trade affects an Indian business. Consider a small garment exporter in the knitwear capital of India, Tiruppur, located in the southern state of Tamil Nadu. While the firm competes with other garment manufacturers domestically and internationally for customers and contracts, it also depends on trade. For instance, it may import fabric from Bangladesh or synthetic dyes from China and export the finished product to the Netherlands or the USA.

Despite the competition, a firm would not be better off isolating itself from other families. If it did, it would need to rely on its own fabric, manufacture its own dyes and all other raw materials, and also produce the finished product. Clearly, the firm gains much from being able to trade with others. Trade allows everyone to specialize in the activities they do best, whether it is knitting, sewing, or manufacturing. By trading with others, everyone can buy a greater variety of goods and services at a lower cost.

Like firms, countries benefit from trading with one another. Trade allows countries to specialize in what they do best and to enjoy a greater variety of goods and services. The Chinese, as well as the European Union and other Southeast Asian, Sub-Saharan African, or Latin American countries, are as much India's partners in the world economy as they are its competitors.

"For ₹5 a week you can watch baseball without being nagged to cut the grass!"

1-2b Principle 6: Markets Are Usually a Good Way to Organize Economic Activity

The collapse of the Soviet Union and Eastern Europe in the late 1980s and early 1990s was one of the last century's transformative events. For the most part, countries in the Soviet bloc operated on the premise that government officials were in the best position to allocate the economy's scarce resources. These central planners decided what goods and services were produced, how much was produced, and who produced and consumed them. The theory behind central planning was that the government needed to organize economic activity to ensure the well-being of the country and of like-minded nations.

Most countries that once had centrally planned economies have now shifted, at least partially, toward market economies. In a **market economy**, the decisions of a central planner are replaced by those of lakhs of firms and households. Firms decide whom to hire and what to make. Households decide where to work and what to buy with their incomes. These firms and households interact in the marketplace, where prices and self-interest guide their decisions.

market economy
an economy that allocates resources through the decentralized decisions of many firms and households as they interact in markets for goods and services

At first glance, the success of market economies may seem puzzling because no one appears to be looking out for the well-being of society as a whole. Competitive markets contain many buyers and sellers of numerous goods and services, all of them interested primarily in their own well-being. Yet despite decentralized decision making and self-interested decision makers, market economies have proven remarkably successful in organizing economic activity to promote prosperity.

In his 1776 book, *An Inquiry into the Nature and Causes of the Wealth of Nations*, Adam Smith made the most famous observation in all of economics: Firms and households in competitive markets act as if they are guided by an "invisible hand" that leads them to desirable outcomes. One of the chief goals of this book is to understand how this invisible hand works its magic.

As you study economics, you will learn that prices are the instrument with which the invisible hand directs economic activity. In a competitive market, sellers look at the price when deciding how much to supply, and buyers look at the price when deciding how much to demand. As a result of their decisions, the price reflects both the sellers' costs of production and the value of the good to the buyers. Smith's great insight was that prices adjust to guide market participants to reach outcomes that, in many cases, maximize the well-being of society as a whole.

Smith's insight has an important corollary: When a government prevents prices from adjusting to supply and demand, it impedes the invisible hand's ability to

FYI Adam Smith and the Invisible Hand

It may be only a coincidence that Adam Smith's great book *The Wealth of Nations* was published in 1776, the exact year in which American revolutionaries signed the Declaration of Independence. But the two documents share a point of view that was prevalent at the time: Individuals are usually best left to their own devices, without the heavy hand of government directing their actions. This philosophy provides the intellectual foundation for the market economy and, more generally, for a free society.

Why do decentralized market economies work reasonably well? Is it because people can be trusted to treat one another with love, kindness, and generosity? Not at all. Here is Adam Smith's description of how people interact in a market economy:

Adam Smith

> Man has almost constant occasion for the help of his brethren, and it is in vain for him to expect it from their benevolence only. He will be more likely to prevail if he can interest their self-love in his favour, and show them that it is for their own advantage to do for him what he requires of them. . . . Give me that which I want, and you shall have this which you want, is the meaning of every such offer; and it is in this manner that we obtain from one another the far greater part of those good offices which we stand in need of.
>
> It is not from the benevolence of the butcher, the brewer, or the baker that we expect our dinner, but from their regard to their own interest. We address ourselves, not to their humanity but to their self-love, and never talk to them of our own necessities but of their advantages. Nobody but a beggar chooses to depend chiefly upon the benevolence of his fellow-citizens. . . .
>
> Every individual . . . neither intends to promote the public interest, nor knows how much he is promoting it. . . . He intends only his own gain, and he is in this, as in many other cases, led by an invisible hand to promote an end which was no part of his intention. Nor is it always the worse for the society that it was no part of it. By pursuing his own interest he frequently promotes that of the society more effectually than when he really intends to promote it.

Smith is saying that participants in the economy are motivated by self-interest and that the "invisible hand" of the marketplace guides them into promoting general economic well-being.

Many of Smith's insights remain at the center of modern economics. The coming chapters will express Smith's conclusions more precisely and analyze more fully the strengths and weaknesses of the market's invisible hand. ■

coordinate the decisions of the firms and households that make up an economy. This corollary explains the adverse effect of most taxes on the allocation of resources: Taxes distort prices and the decisions of firms and households. It also explains the problems caused by policies that dictate prices, such as minimum support prices (MSP). And it explains the economic failure of regimes, where prices were set not in the marketplace but by central planners. These planners lacked the overwhelming amount of complex and ever-changing information about producers' costs and consumers' tastes, which, in a market economy, is reflected in prices.

Case Study: Adam Smith Would Have Loved Ola Cabs

You may have never lived in a centrally planned economy, but if you have tried to hail a taxi or an auto-rickshaw in a major city, you have likely experienced a highly regulated market. In many Indian cities, the local government imposes strict controls in the market for taxis and autos. For example, the government may limit entry into the market by approving only a certain number of taxi or autorickshaw permits. For instance, in Kolkata the prices that autos are allowed to charge and the routes they can operate on are fixed. The government uses its police powers—that is, the threat of fines or jail time—to keep unauthorized drivers off the streets and prevent drivers from charging unauthorized prices.

In the early part of the last decade, however, this highly controlled market was invaded by a disruptive force: ride, hailing services such as Ola and Uber, although Ola Cabs existed in India even before Uber. Because Ola and Uber (as well as Ola Auto -Rickshaws) do not roam the streets looking for auto-hailing pedestrians, they are technically not taxis/auto and so are not subject to the same regulations. But they offer a similar service. Indeed, rides from Ola Cabs—and from its competitors that have since entered many markets—are often more convenient. On a wet, rainy day, in Bengaluru who wants to wait by the side of the outer ring road for an empty auto to drive by? It is more pleasant to remain inside, use a smartphone to arrange a ride, and stay nice and dry until the vehicle arrives.

RICHARD LEVINE/ALAMY STOCK PHOTO

Technology can improve this market.

However, Ola Cab prices rise significantly when there is a surge in demand, such as during a sudden thundershower or late on Dhanteras evening before Diwali, when numerous festival shoppers are looking for a comfortable way to get home. By contrast, regulated taxis or autos are typically prevented from surge pricing.

Not everyone is fond of Ola Cabs. Drivers of traditional taxis complain that this new competition reduces their income. This is hardly a surprise: Suppliers of goods and services often dislike new competitors. But vigorous competition among producers makes a market work well for consumers.

That is why economists embraced Uber's entry into the global market. A 2014 survey of several dozen prominent economists asked whether car services such as Uber increased consumer well-being. Every single economist said "Yes." The economists were also asked whether surge pricing increased consumer well-being. "Yes," said 85 percent of them. Surge pricing makes consumers pay more at times, but because the drivers respond to incentives, it also increases the quantity of car services supplied when they are most needed. Surge pricing also helps allocate the services to those consumers who value them most highly and reduces the costs of searching and waiting for a car.

If Adam Smith were alive today, he would surely have a ride-sharing app on his phone. ●

1-2c Principle 7: Governments Can Sometimes Improve Market Outcomes

If the invisible hand is so great, what is left for a government to do in an economy? One purpose of studying economics is to refine your view about the proper role and scope of government policy.

One reason we need government is that the invisible hand can work its magic only if the government enforces the rules and maintains the institutions that are key to a market economy. Most importantly, market economies need institutions to enforce **property rights** so individuals can own and control scarce resources. Farmers won't grow food if they expect their crop to be stolen, restaurants won't serve meals if many customers leave before paying, and film companies won't produce movies if too many people pirate copies. Market participants rely on government-provided police and courts to enforce their rights, and the invisible hand works well only if the legal system does.

property rights the ability of an individual to own and exercise control over scarce resources

Another reason we need government is that the invisible hand, while powerful, is not omnipotent. There are two broad rationales for a government to intervene in the economy and change the allocation of resources that people would choose on their own: to promote efficiency or to promote equality. That is, policies can aim either to enlarge the economic pie or to change how the pie is sliced.

Consider the goal of efficiency. The invisible hand usually leads markets to allocate resources to maximize the size of the economic pie, but this is not always the case. Economists use the term **market failure** to refer to a situation in which the market does not produce an efficient allocation of resources on its own. One possible cause of market failure is an **externality**, which is the impact of one person's actions on the well-being of a bystander. The classic example of an externality is pollution. When the production of a good pollutes the air and creates health problems for those who live near the factories, the market may fail to take this cost into account. Another possible cause of market failure is **market power**, which refers to the ability of a single person or firm (or a small group of them) to unduly influence market prices. For example, if everyone in town needs water but there is only one well, the owner of the well does not face the rigorous competition with which the invisible hand normally keeps self-interest in check; the well owner may take advantage of this opportunity by restricting the output of water and charging a higher price. In the presence of externalities or market power, well-designed public policy can enhance efficiency.

market failure
a situation in which a market left on its own does not allocate resources efficiently

externality
the impact of one person's actions on the well-being of a bystander

market power
the ability of a single economic actor (or small group of actors) to have a substantial influence on market prices

Now consider the goal of equality. Even when the invisible hand yields efficient outcomes, it can nonetheless leave large disparities in well-being. A market economy rewards people according to their ability to produce things that other people are willing to pay for. India's best cricketer earns more than India's best footballer simply because people are willing to pay more to watch cricket than football. The invisible hand does not ensure that everyone has enough food, decent clothing, and adequate healthcare. This inequality may call for government intervention. In practice, many public policies, such as the income tax and the DBT system, aim to achieve a more equal distribution of well-being.

To say that the government **can** improve market outcomes does not mean that it always **will**. Public policy is made not by angels but by an imperfect political process. Sometimes, policies are designed to reward the politically powerful. Sometimes, they are made by well-intentioned leaders who are ill-informed. As you study economics, you will become a better judge of when a government policy is justifiable because it promotes efficiency or equality and when it is not.

Quick**Quiz**

5. International trade benefits a nation when
   a. its revenue from selling abroad exceeds its outlays from buying abroad.
   b. its trading partners experience reduced economic well-being.
   c. all nations specialize in doing what they do best.
   d. no domestic jobs are lost because of trade.
6. Adam Smith's "invisible hand" refers to
   a. the subtle and often hidden methods that businesses use to profit at consumers' expense.
   b. the ability of competitive markets to reach desirable outcomes, despite the self-interest of market participants.
   c. the ability of government regulation to benefit consumers, even if the consumers are unaware of the regulations.
   d. the way in which producers or consumers in unregulated markets impose costs on innocent bystanders.
7. Governments may intervene in a market economy in order to
   a. protect property rights.
   b. correct a market failure due to externalities.
   c. achieve a more equal distribution of income.
   d. All of the above are correct.

Answers are at the end of the chapter.

1-3 How the Economy as a Whole Works

We started by discussing how managers make decisions and then looked at how people interact. All these decisions and interactions together make up "the economy." The last three principles concern the workings of the economy as a whole, which affects the overall business environment in which the firm operates.

1-3a Principle 8: A Country's Standard of Living Depends on Its Ability to Produce Goods and Services

The differences in living standards around the world are staggering. In 2019, the average Indian earned around ₹1.4 lakh annually (roughly $2000), while the average American earned about $65,000. In the same year, the average German earned about $56,000, and the average Chinese earned about $17,000. This variation in average income is reflected in measures of quality of life. People in high-income countries have more computers, more cars, better nutrition, better healthcare, and a longer life expectancy than do those in low-income countries.

Even within India, differences in living standard can be quite stark. A highly skilled Data Scientist in Hyderabad's Banjara Hills might earn 20 times more than an agricultural laborer in Hooghly, West Bengal. Over time, some Indian states such as Gujarat, Maharashtra, Karnataka have seen much faster income growth than Bihar, Uttar Pradesh, or Odisha.

What explains these large differences across states, countries and over time? The answer is simple. Almost all variation in living standards is attributable to differences in economies' **productivity**—that is, the amount of goods and services produced by each unit of labor input. In economies where workers can produce a large quantity of goods and services per hour, most people enjoy a high standard of living; in regions where workers are less productive, most people endure a more meager existence. Similarly, the growth rate of productivity determines the growth rate of average income.

productivity
the quantity of goods and services produced from each unit of labor input

The relationship between productivity and living standards is simple, but its implications are far-reaching. If productivity is the main determinant of living standards, other explanations must be less important. For example, it might be tempting to credit generous employers or vigorous trade unions for the rising incomes of Indian workers over the past century. Yet the real hero of workers is their rising productivity.

The relationship between productivity and living standards has profound implications for public policy. When thinking about how any policy will affect living standards, the key question is how it will affect the economy's ability to produce goods and services. To boost living standards, policymakers need to raise productivity by ensuring that workers are well trained, have the tools they need to produce goods and services, and have access to the best available technology.

1-3b Principle 9: Prices Rise When the Government Prints Too Much Money

In January 1921, a daily newspaper in Germany cost 0.30 marks. Less than two years later, in November 1922, the same newspaper costed 70,000,000 marks. All other prices in the economy rose by similar amounts. This episode is one of history's most spectacular examples of **inflation**, an increase in the overall level of prices in the economy.

India has never experienced hyperinflation of this magnitude but inflation has been a perennial problem. During the 1970s, India struggled with double -digit inflation rates. By contrast, inflation in the last two decades have been reasonably under control and hovering around the Reserve Bank of India (RBI) mandate of 4–6%.

inflation
an increase in the overall level of prices in the economy

"Well it may have been 68 cents when you got in line, but it's 74 cents now!"

Because high inflation imposes various costs on society, keeping inflation at a reasonable rate is a goal of economic policymakers around the world.

What causes inflation? In almost all cases of large or persistent inflation, the culprit is growth in the quantity of money. When a government creates large quantities of the nation's money, the value of the money falls. In Germany in the early 1920s, when prices were, on average, tripling every month, the quantity of money was also tripling every month. Although less dramatic, the history of the United States points to a similar conclusion: The high inflation of the 1970s was associated with rapid growth in the quantity of money, and the return of low inflation in the 1980s was associated with slower growth in the quantity of money.

During the economic downturn caused by the coronavirus pandemic in 2020, the US government alleviated the hardship with large increases in spending, and the quantity of money in the economy rose significantly. These policies, together with supply disruptions due to the pandemic, contributed to rising inflation. The key question was whether the inflation surge would be transitory, as many government officials believed, or whether it would become embedded in the economy, as occurred in the 1970s. The outcome would depend, in large part, on future monetary policy.

1-3c Principle 10: Society Faces a Short-Run Trade-Off between Inflation and Unemployment

While an increase in the quantity of money primarily raises prices in the long run, the short-run story is more complex. Most economists describe the short-run effects of money growth as follows:

- Increasing the amount of money in the economy stimulates the overall level of spending and thus the demand for goods and services.
- Higher demand will, over time, cause firms to raise their prices, but in the meantime, it encourages them to hire more workers and produce a larger quantity of goods and services.
- More hiring means lower unemployment.

This line of reasoning leads to one final economy-wide trade-off: a short-run trade off between inflation and unemployment.

Some economists still question these ideas, but most accept that society faces a short-run trade-off between inflation and unemployment. This simply means that, over a period of a year or two, many economic policies push inflation and unemployment in opposite directions. Policymakers face this trade-off regardless of whether inflation and unemployment both start out at high levels (as they did in the early 1980s), at low levels (as they did in the late 2010s), or someplace in between. This short-run trade-off plays a key role in the analysis of the **business cycle**—the irregular and largely unpredictable fluctuations in economic activity, as measured by the production of goods and services or the number of people employed.

business cycle
fluctuations in economic activity, such as employment and production

Policymakers can exploit the short-run trade-off between inflation and unemployment using various policy instruments. By changing the amount that the government spends, the amount it taxes, or the amount of money it prints, policymakers can influence the overall demand for goods and services. Changes in demand, in turn, influence the combination of inflation and unemployment that the economy experiences in the short run. Because these instruments of economic policy are so powerful, how policymakers should use them is the subject of continuing debate.

Quick**Quiz**

8. The main reason that some states have higher average living standards than others is that
   a. the richer nations have exploited the poorer ones.
   b. the governments of some nations have created more money.
   c. some states have stronger laws protecting worker rights.
   d. some nations have higher levels of productivity.
9. If a nation has high and persistent inflation, the most likely explanation is
   a. the government creating excessive amounts of money.
   b. unions bargaining for excessively high wages.
   c. the government imposing excessive levels of taxation.
   d. firms using their market power to enforce excessive price hikes.
10. If a government uses the tools of monetary policy to reduce the demand for goods and services, the likely result is ______ inflation and ______ unemployment in the short run.
    a. lower; lower
    b. lower; higher
    c. higher; higher
    d. higher; lower

Answers are at the end of the chapter.

1-4 Conclusion

You now have a taste of what economics is all about, and its managerial implications. In the coming chapters, we will develop many specific insights about people, markets, and economies. Mastering them will take some effort, but the task is not overwhelming. The field of economics is based on a few big ideas that can be applied in many situations.

Throughout this book, we will refer to the **Basic Principles of Managerial Economics** introduced in this chapter and summarized in Table 1. Keep these building blocks in mind. Even the most sophisticated economic analysis is founded on these ten principles.

Table 1
Ten Principles of Economics

How Managers Make Decisions?

1. Managers face trade-offs.
2. The cost of something is what you give up to get it.
3. Rational people think at the margin.
4. People respond to incentives.

How People Interact?

5. Trade can make businesses better off.
6. Markets are usually a good way to organize economic activity.
7. Governments can sometimes improve market outcomes.

How the Economy as a Whole Works?

8. A country's standard of living depends on its ability to produce goods and services.
9. Prices rise when the government prints too much money.
10. Society faces a short-run trade-off between inflation and unemployment.

Chapter in a Nutshell

- The fundamental lessons about managerial decision making are that managers face trade-offs among alternative goals, that the cost of any action is measured in terms of forgone opportunities, that rational people make decisions by comparing marginal costs and marginal benefits, and that people change their behavior in response to the incentives they face.
- The fundamental lessons about economic interactions among people are that trade and interdependence can be mutually beneficial, that markets are usually a good way of coordinating economic activity, and that governments can potentially improve market outcomes by remedying a market failure or by promoting greater economic equality.
- The fundamental lessons about the economy as a whole are that productivity is the ultimate source of living standards, that growth in the quantity of money is the ultimate source of inflation, and that society faces a short-run trade-off between inflation and unemployment.

Key Concepts

scarcity, p. 2
economics, p. 2
efficiency, p. 3
equality, p. 3
opportunity cost, p. 3
rational people, p. 4
marginal change, p. 4
incentive, p. 5
market economy, p. 7
property rights, p. 9
market failure, p. 10
externality, p. 10
market power, p. 10
productivity, p. 11
inflation, p. 11
business cycle, p. 12

Questions for Review

1. Give three examples of important trade-offs that manager face in making business decisions.
2. As a manager of an amusement park, what items would you include to figure out the opportunity cost of a adding an attraction to the park?
3. Water is necessary for life. Is the marginal benefit of a glass of water large or small?
4. Why should managers think about incentives?
5. Why isn't trade between two firms like a game in which one firm wins and the other loses?
6. What does the "invisible hand" of the marketplace do?
7. What are the two main causes of market failure? Give an example of each.
8. Why is productivity important?
9. What is inflation, and what causes it?
10. How are inflation and unemployment related in the short run?

Problems and Applications

1. Describe some of the trade-offs faced by each of the following:
   a. a family deciding whether to buy a car
   b. a minister deciding how much to spend on national parks
   c. a CEO deciding whether to open a new factory
   d. a professor deciding how much to prepare for class
   e. a recent college graduate deciding whether to go for a Masters' degree
   f. a mother single parent with small children deciding whether to take an offsite job
2. You are trying to decide whether to take a vacation. Most of the costs of the vacation (airfare, hotel, and forgone wages) are measured in rupees, but the benefits of the vacation are psychological. How can you compare the benefits to the costs?
3. You were planning to spend Saturday doing private tutoring for pocket money, but a friend asks you to go to a movie. What is the true cost of going to the movie? Now, suppose you had been planning to spend the day studying at the library. What is the cost of going to the movie in this case? Explain.

4. You win ₹100 in a lottery. You have a choice between spending the money now and putting it away for a year in a bank account that pays 5 percent interest. What is the opportunity cost of spending the ₹10,000 now?
5. The company that you manage has invested ₹50 lakhs in developing a new product, but the development is not quite finished. At a recent meeting, your salespeople reported that the introduction of competing products has reduced the expected sales of your new product to ₹3 lakhs. If it would cost ₹10 lakhs to finish development and make the product, should you go ahead and do so? What is the most that you should pay to complete development?
6. Under Mahatma Gandhi National Rural Employment Guarantee Act (MGNREGA), each household is entitled to only 100 days of work.
   a. How did the MGNREGA affect the incentives for working?
   b. How might this represent a trade-off between equality and efficiency?
7. Explain whether each of the following government activities is motivated by a concern about equality or a concern about efficiency. In the case of efficiency, discuss the type of market failure involved.
   a. regulating (Direct-to-Home) DTH service
   b. providing some low-income people with vouchers that can be used to buy food
   c. prohibiting smoking in public places
   d. breaking up a large firm into several smaller companies
   e. imposing higher income tax rates on people with higher incomes
   f. enacting laws against drunken driving
8. Discuss each of the following statements from the standpoints of equality and efficiency.
   a. "Everyone in society should be guaranteed the best healthcare possible."
   b. "When workers are laid off, they should be able to avail MGNREGA benefits until they find a new fulltime job."
9. In what ways is your standard of living different from that of your parents or grandparents when they were your age? Why have these changes occurred?
10. Suppose all Indian households decide to save more of their incomes. If banks lend this extra saving to businesses that use the funds to build new factories, how might this lead to faster growth in productivity? Who do you suppose benefits from the higher productivity? Is society getting a free lunch?
11. Printing money to cover expenditures is sometimes referred to as an "inflation tax." Who do you think is being "taxed" when more money is printed? Why?

Quick**Quiz Answers**

1. **a** 2. **c** 3. **b** 4. **d** 5. **c** 6. **b** 7. **d** 8. **d** 9. **a** 10. **b**

Chapter

2

How Managers think like Economists

The goal of this book is to help you think like an economist. This can be useful in a thousand ways. When you try to make sense of a news story, manage the finances of your household or business, or evaluate a politician's promises about problems ranging from local traffic congestion to global climate change, knowing some economics can help you think more sensibly and systematically. And that kind of thinking will lead you to better outcomes. It is no different in management science. Managers often benefit by thinking like economists when faced with complex decision making.

In all fields of study, specialists develop their own terminology and methods. Mathematicians talk about axioms, integrals, and vector spaces. Psychologists talk about ego, id, and cognitive dissonance. Lawyers talk about venue, torts, and promissory estoppel. Economists are no different. Supply, demand, elasticity, comparative advantage, consumer surplus, deadweight loss—these terms are part of the economist's language. In the coming chapters, you will encounter many new terms and some familiar words that economists use in specialized ways. At first, the terms and technicalities may seem needlessly arcane, and in daily life, many of them are. But understanding them will give you a new and useful way of thinking about the world in which you live. This book will guide you gently through the thicket.

Before delving into the substance and details of economics, it is helpful to have an overview of how economists look at the world and consequently how managers don the economist's hat within their organization. This chapter discusses the field's methodology. What is distinctive about how economists confront a question? What does it mean to think like an economist?

GAUDILAB/SHUTTERSTOCK.COM; LECHATNOIR/E+/GETTY IMAGES

2-1 The Economist as Scientist

"I'm a social scientist, Michael. That means I can't explain electricity or anything like that, but if you ever want to know about people, I'm your man."

Economists try to address their subject with a scientist's objectivity. They approach the study of the economy much as a physicist approaches the study of matter and a biologist approaches the study of life: They devise theories, collect data, and then analyze the data to verify or refute their theories.

The claim that economics is a science can seem odd. After all, economists don't work with test tubes or telescopes, and they don't wear white lab coats. Like other social scientists, they study human beings, a subject that everyone knows something about without the need for a university degree. The essence of science, however, is the **scientific method**—the dispassionate development and testing of theories about how the world works. This method of inquiry is as applicable to studying a nation's economy as it is to studying the earth's gravity or a species' evolution. As Albert Einstein put it, "The whole of science is nothing more than the refinement of everyday thinking."

Einstein's comment is as true for economics as it is for physics, but most people are not accustomed to looking at society through a scientific lens. Let's consider some of the ways economists apply the logic of science to examine how an economy works.

2-1a The Scientific Method: Observation, Theory, and More Observation

Isaac Newton, the 17th-century scientist and mathematician, told his biographer that he became intrigued one day when he saw an apple fall from a tree. Why did the apple always fall straight down to the earth? Newton's musing led him to develop a theory of gravity that applies not only to a falling apple but to any two objects in the universe. Subsequent testing of Newton's theory has shown that it works well in many circumstances (but not all, as Einstein would later show). Because Newton's theory has been so successful at explaining what we observe around us, it is still taught in physics courses.

A similar interplay between theory and observation occurs in economics. An economist who lives in a country with rapidly increasing prices may be moved by this observation to develop a theory of inflation. The theory might assert that high inflation arises when the government issues too much money. To test this theory, the economist could collect and analyze data on prices and money from many different countries. If the growth in the quantity of money were unrelated to the rate of price increase, the economist would start to doubt the validity of this theory of inflation. If money growth and inflation were correlated in international data, as in fact they often are, the economist would become more confident in the proposed theory.

Although economists use theory and observation like other scientists, they face an obstacle that makes their task challenging: Conducting experiments is often impractical. Physicists studying gravity can drop objects in their laboratories to test their theories. By contrast, economists studying inflation are not allowed to manipulate a nation's monetary policy simply to generate useful data. Economists, such as astronomers and evolutionary biologists, usually make do with whatever data the world gives them.

To substitute for laboratory experiments, economists pay close attention to the natural experiments offered by history. When a war in the Middle East interrupts the supply of crude oil, for instance, oil prices skyrocket around the world. For consumers of oil and oil products, such an event raises the cost of living. For policymakers, it poses a difficult choice about how best to respond. But for economic scientists, the event provides an opportunity to study the effects of a key natural resource on the world's economies. Throughout this book, we consider many historical episodes. Studying them yields insights into the economy of the past and helps to illustrate and evaluate economic theories of the present.

2-1b The Role of Assumptions

If you ask physicists how long it would take a marble to fall from the top of a ten-story building, they will likely answer by assuming that the marble falls in a vacuum. Yet this assumption is false. The building is surrounded by air, which exerts friction on the falling marble and slows it down. Why provide answers that ignore the complexity of the real world? In this case, physicists will point out that the friction on the marble is so small that its effect is negligible. Assuming the marble falls in a vacuum simplifies the problem without substantially affecting the answer. Physicists understand, however, that for a more precise answer, they would have to revisit their assumptions and perform a more sophisticated analysis.

Economists make assumptions for the same reason: Assumptions can simplify the complex world and make it easier to understand. To study international trade, for example, we might assume that the world consists of only two countries and that each country produces only two goods. We know that this isn't an accurate representation of the real world, which consists of many countries producing thousands of different types of goods. But by assuming the world has only two countries and two goods, we can focus on the essence of the problem. After analyzing international trade in this simplified imaginary world, we are in a better position to understand trade in the more complex world in which we live.

The art in scientific thinking—whether in physics, biology, or economics—is deciding which assumptions to make. Suppose, for instance, that instead of dropping a marble from the top of a building, we were dropping a beach ball of the same weight. Our physicist would realize that the assumption of no friction is wildly inaccurate in this case: Friction exerts a greater force on the beach ball because it is much larger than a marble. Pretending that gravity works in a vacuum is reasonable when studying a falling marble, but it would lead to large errors when studying a falling beach ball.

Similarly, economists use different assumptions to answer different questions. Suppose, for example, that we want to study what happens to the economy when the government changes the number of rupees in circulation. An important piece of this analysis, it turns out, is how prices respond. Many prices in the economy change infrequently: The newsstand prices of magazines, for instance, change only once every few years. Knowing this fact may lead us to make different assumptions for different time horizons. When studying the short-run effects of the policy, we may assume that prices do not change much. We may even make the extreme assumption that all prices are completely fixed. When studying the long-run effects of the policy, however, we may assume that all prices are completely flexible. Just as physicists use different assumptions when studying falling marbles and falling beach balls, economists use different assumptions when studying the short-run and long-run effects of a change in the quantity of money.

2-1c Economic Models

High school biology teachers teach basic anatomy with plastic replicas of the human body. These models have all the major organs—the heart, liver, kidneys, and so on—and allow teachers to show their students very simply how the important parts of the body fit together. Because these plastic models are stylized and omit many details, no one would mistake one of them for a real person. Despite this lack of realism—indeed, because of it—studying these models is useful for learning how the human body works.

Economists also use models to learn about the world, but unlike plastic manikins, their models mostly consist of diagrams and equations. Like a biology teacher's plastic model, economic models omit many details to allow us to see what is truly important. Just as the biology teacher's model does not include all the body's muscles and blood vessels, an economist's model does not include every feature of the economy or every aspect of human behavior.

As we use models to examine various issues throughout this book, you will see that models are built with assumptions. Just as physicists begin the analysis of a falling marble by assuming away the existence of friction, economists assume away many details of the economy that are irrelevant to the question at hand. All models—in physics, biology, and economics—simplify reality to improve our understanding of it. And all models are subject to revision when the facts warrant it. The key is to find the right model at the right time. As a famous statistician once put it, "All models are wrong, but some are useful."

2-1d Our First Model: The Circular-Flow Diagram

The economy consists of lakhs of people engaged in many activities—buying, selling, working, hiring, manufacturing, and so on. To understand how the economy works, we must simplify our thinking about all these activities. In other words, we need a model that explains how the economy is organized and how participants in the economy interact with one another.

circular-flow diagram a visual model of the economy that shows how dollars flow through markets among households and firms

Figure 1 presents a visual model of the economy called the **circular-flow diagram**. In this model, the economy includes only two types of decision makers—firms and households. Firms produce goods and services using inputs, such as labor, land, and capital (buildings and machines). These inputs are called the **factors of production**. Households own the factors of production and consume all the goods and services that the firms produce.

Households and firms interact in two types of markets. In the **markets for goods and services**, households are buyers, and firms are sellers. Specifically, households buy the output of goods and services that firms produce. In the **markets for the factors of production**, households are sellers, and firms are buyers. In these markets, households provide the inputs that firms use to produce goods and services. The circular-flow diagram offers a simple way of organizing all the transactions between households and firms in an economy.

The two loops of the circular-flow diagram are distinct but related. The inner loop represents the flows of inputs and outputs. Households sell the use of their labor, land, and capital to firms in the markets for the factors of production. Firms then use these factors to produce goods and services, which in turn are sold to households in the markets for goods and services. The outer loop of the diagram represents the corresponding flow of rupees. Households spend money to buy goods and services from firms. The firms use some of the revenue from these sales to purchase the factors of production, such as by paying workers' wages. What's left is the profit for the firm owners, who are themselves members of households.

Figure 1

The Circular Flow

This diagram is a schematic representation of the organization of the economy. Decisions are made by households and firms. Households and firms interact in the markets for goods and services (where households are buyers and firms are sellers) and in the markets for the factors of production (where firms are buyers and households are sellers). The outer set of arrows shows the flow of rupees, and the inner set of arrows shows the corresponding flow of inputs and outputs.

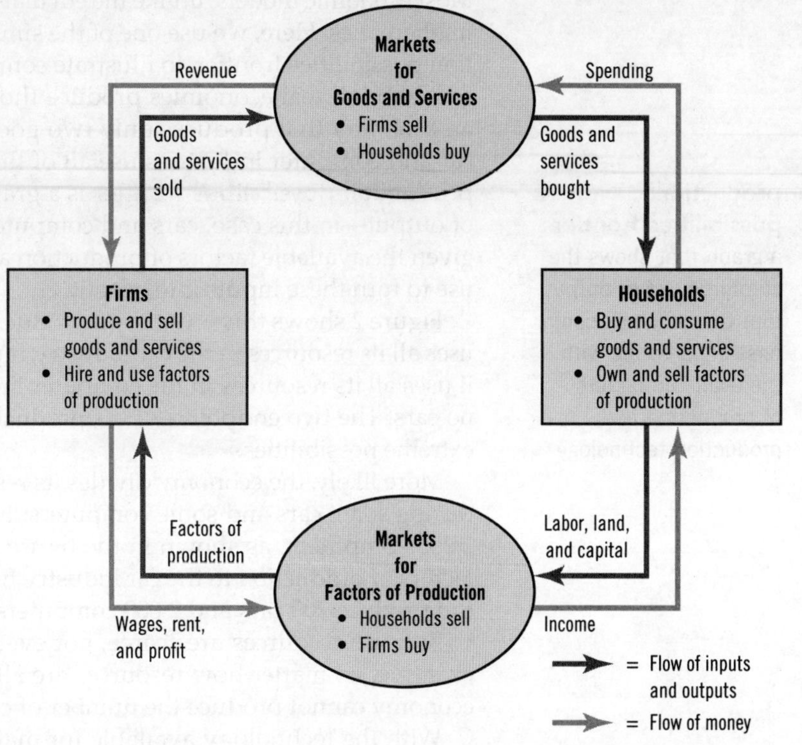

Let's take a tour of the circular flow by following a rupee bill as it makes its way from person to person through the economy. Imagine that the dollar begins at a household—say, in your wallet. If you want a cup of tea, you take the rupee (along with a few of its relatives) to the market for tea, which is one of the many markets for goods and services. When you buy your favorite drink at your local chai shop, the rupee moves into the shop's cash register, becoming revenue for the firm. The rupee doesn't stay there for long, however, because the firm spends it on inputs in the markets for the factors of production. The manager of the shop might use the rupee to pay rent to its landlord for the space it occupies or to compensate the chai-walas making the tea. Or it might return the rupee as profit to the shop's owner. In any case, the rupee enters the income of some household and, once again, is back in someone's wallet. At that point, the story of the economy's circular flow starts once again.

The circular-flow diagram in Figure 1 is a simple model of the economy. A more complex and realistic circular-flow model would include, for instance, the roles of government and international trade. (A portion of the rupee you gave to the chai seller might be used to pay taxes or to buy tea leaves from a planter in Assam.) Yet these details are not crucial for a basic understanding of how the economy is organized. Because of its simplicity, this circular-flow diagram is useful to keep in mind when thinking about how the pieces of an economy fit together.

2-1e Our Second Model: The Production Possibilities Frontier

Most economic models, unlike the circular-flow diagram, are built using the tools of mathematics. Here, we use one of the simplest of these models, called the production possibilities frontier, to illustrate some basic economic ideas.

Although real economies produce thousands of goods and services, consider an economy that produces only two goods—cars and computers. Together, the car and computer industries use all of this economy's factors of production. The **production possibilities frontier** is a graph that shows the various combinations of output—in this case, cars and computers—the economy can possibly produce given the available factors of production and the production technology that firms use to turn these inputs into output.

production possibilities frontier
a graph that shows the combinations of output that the economy can possibly produce with the available factors of production and production technology

Figure 2 shows this economy's production possibilities frontier. If the economy uses all its resources in the car industry, it produces 1,000 cars and no computers. If it uses all its resources in the computer industry, it produces 3,000 computers and no cars. The two endpoints of the production possibilities frontier represent these extreme possibilities.

More likely, the economy divides its resources between the two industries, producing some cars and some computers. For example, it can produce 600 cars and 2,200 computers, as shown in the figure by point A. Or, by moving some of the factors of production to the car industry from the computer industry, the economy can produce 700 cars and 2,000 computers, represented by point B.

Because resources are scarce, not every conceivable outcome is feasible. For example, no matter how resources are allocated between the two industries, the economy cannot produce the number of cars and computers represented by point C. With the technology available for making cars and computers, the economy does not have enough of the factors of production to support that level of output. With the resources it has, the economy can produce at any point on or inside the production possibilities frontier, but it cannot produce at points outside the frontier.

Figure 2

The Production Possibilities Frontier

The production possibilities frontier shows the combinations of output—in this case, cars and computers—the economy can produce. Any point on or beneath the curve is a possible output combination in this economy. Points outside the frontier are not feasible given the economy's resources. The slope of the production possibilities frontier measures the opportunity cost of a car in terms of computers. This opportunity cost varies, depending on how much of the two goods the economy is producing.

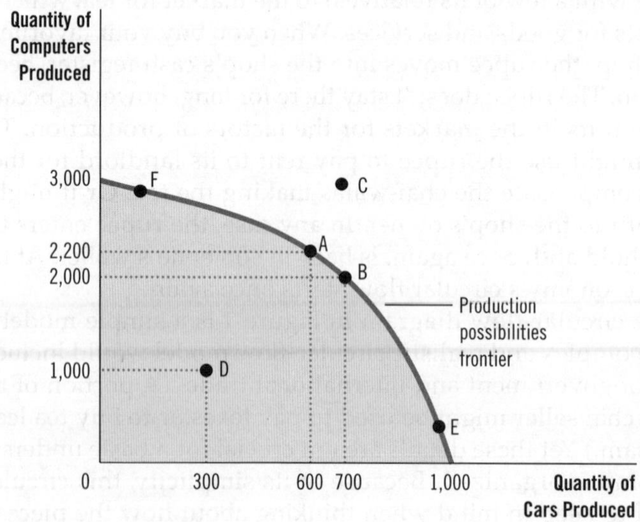

An outcome is said to be **efficient** if the economy is getting all it can from the scarce resources it has available. Points on (rather than inside) the production possibilities frontier represent efficient levels of production. When the economy is producing at such a point, say, point A, there is no way to produce more of one good without producing less of the other. Point D represents an **inefficient** outcome. For some reason, perhaps widespread unemployment, the economy is producing less than it could from the resources it has available: It is producing only 300 cars and 1,000 computers. If the source of the inefficiency is eliminated, the economy can increase its production of both goods. For example, if the economy moves from point D to point A, its production of cars increases from 300 to 600, and its production of computers increases from 1,000 to 2,200.

One of the **Basic Principles of Managerial Economics** in Chapter 1 is that managers face tradeoffs. The production possibilities frontier shows one trade-off that society faces. Once an economy reaches an efficient point on the frontier, the only way to produce more of one good is to produce less of the other. When the economy moves from point A to point B, for instance, society produces 100 more cars at the expense of producing 200 fewer computers. A similar trade off can be applied to the context of managerial decision making as shown in the box below.

Managerial Insight

Imagine an Indian green-tech startup that can use its scarce resources of capital, labor, and equipment to manufacture either electric scooters or solar panels or both. These two products are critical for India's clean energy transition. Like the society, this company also faces trade-offs due to the scarcity of resources. Let us imagine how the production possibilities frontier would like for this firm.

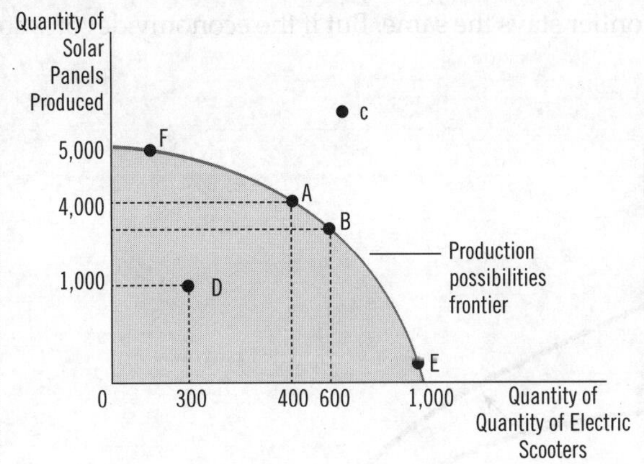

If the startup allocates all its resources to solar panel production, it can produce 5,000 units but no scooters. If it dedicates everything to scooters, it can produce 1,000 scooters and no solar panels. A combination like Point A (400 scooters and 4,000 panels) or Point B (600 scooters and 3,000 panels) reflects efficient use of resources. A point like C lies outside the frontier and is currently unattainable unless there is a breakthrough in technology or capital infusion. This trade-off framework helps the manager of the startup firm to understand how to make optimal production decisions given constraints, and how choices on one margin (like a subsidy for EVs or import duties on solar cells) can shift production priorities.

In general, these trade-offs help us understand another of the **Basic Principles of Managerial Economics**: The cost of something is what you give up to get it. This is called the **opportunity cost**. The production possibilities frontier shows the opportunity cost of one good as measured in terms of the other. When society moves from point A to point B, it gives up 200 computers to get 100 additional cars. That is, at point A, the opportunity cost of 100 cars is 200 computers. Put another way, the opportunity cost of each car is two computers. Notice that the opportunity cost of a car equals the slope of the production possibilities frontier. (Slope is discussed in the graphing appendix to this chapter.)

The opportunity cost of a car in terms of the number of computers is not constant in this economy but depends on how many cars and computers the economy is producing. This is reflected in the shape of the production possibilities frontier. Because the production possibilities frontier in Figure 2 is bowed outward, the opportunity cost of a car is highest when the economy is producing many cars and few computers, such as at point E, where the frontier is steep. When the economy is producing few cars and many computers, such as at point F, the frontier is flatter, and the opportunity cost of a car is lower.

Economists believe that production possibilities frontiers often have this bowed-out shape. When the economy is using most of its resources to make computers, the resources best suited to car production, such as skilled autoworkers, are being used in the computer industry. Because these workers probably aren't very good at making computers, increasing car production by one unit will cause only a slight reduction in the number of computers produced. Thus, at point F, the opportunity cost of a car in terms of computers is small, and the frontier is relatively flat. By contrast, when the economy is using most of its resources to make cars, such as at point E, the resources best suited to making cars are already at work in the car industry. Producing an additional car now requires moving some of the best computer technicians out of the computer industry and turning them into autoworkers. As a result, producing an additional car requires a substantial loss of computer output. The opportunity cost of a car is high, and the frontier is steep.

The production possibilities frontier shows the trade-off between the outputs of different goods at a given time, but the trade-off can change over time. For example, suppose a technological advance in the computer industry raises the number of computers that a worker can produce per week. This advance expands society's set of opportunities. For any given number of cars, the economy can now make more computers. If the economy does not produce any computers, it can still produce 1,000 cars, so one endpoint of the frontier stays the same. But if the economy devotes some

Figure 3

A Shift in the Production Possibilities Frontier

A technological advance in the computer industry enables the economy to produce more computers for any given number of cars. As a result, the production possibilities frontier shifts outward. If the economy moves from point A to point G, the production of both cars and computers increases.

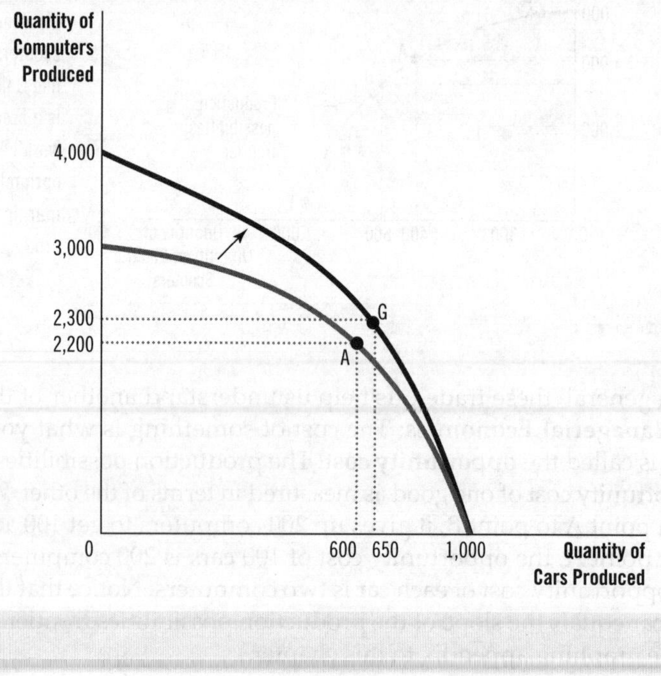

Quick**Quiz**

1. An economic model is
   a. a mechanical machine that replicates the functioning of the economy.
   b. a fully detailed, realistic description of the economy.
   c. a simplified representation of some aspect of the economy.
   d. a computer program that predicts the future of the economy.
2. The circular-flow diagram illustrates that, in markets for the factors of production,
   a. households are sellers, and firms are buyers.
   b. households are buyers, and firms are sellers.
   c. households and firms are both buyers.
   d. households and firms are both sellers.
3. A point inside the production possibilities frontier is
   a. efficient but not feasible.
   b. feasible but not efficient.
   c. both efficient and feasible.
   d. neither efficient nor feasible.
4. In the context of managerial economics, the production possibilities frontier is:
   a. the maximum revenue the firm can earn given current market prices
   b. the combination of inputs the firm should use to minimize costs
   c. the most efficient combinations of two goods that the firm can produce given its resources and technology
   d. the level of output the firm can achieve without any tradeoffs between products.

Answers are at the end of the chapter.

of its resources to the computer industry, it will produce more computers from those resources. As a result, the production possibilities frontier shifts outward, as in Figure 3.

This figure shows what happens when an economy grows. Society can move production from a point on the old frontier to a point on the new one. Which point it chooses depends on its preferences for the two goods. In this example, society moves from point A to point G, producing more computers (2,300 instead of 2,200) and more cars (650 instead of 600).

The production possibilities frontier simplifies a complex economy to highlight some basic but powerful ideas: scarcity, efficiency, trade-offs, opportunity cost, and economic growth. As you study economics, these ideas will recur in various forms. The production possibilities frontier offers one simple way of thinking about them.

2-2 The Economist as Policy Adviser

Often, economists are asked to explain the causes of economic events. Why, for example, is unemployment higher for younger than for older workers? That's a factual question, and it may be answered scientifically. But sometimes, economists are asked to recommend policies to improve economic outcomes. What, for instance, should the government do to enhance young workers' well-being? Answering that requires not only an understanding of what's happening but also value judgments about what ought to be done.

When economists are trying to explain the world, they are scientists. When they are giving guidance on how to improve it, they are policy advisers. Even if you never become a professional economist, you may find yourself using both sides of your economic brain in daily life: analyzing the world as you find it and devising solutions to make things better. Both approaches are indispensable, but it's important to understand how they differ.

2-2a Positive versus Normative Analysis

To clarify the two roles that economists play, let's examine the use of language. Because scientists and policy advisers have different goals, they use language in different ways.

In the News: Why Tech Companies Hire Economists?

Many high-tech companies find that expertise in economics is useful in their decision making.

Goodbye, Ivory Tower. Hello, Silicon Valley Candy Store

By Steve Lohr

For eight years, Balram Coles had an economist's dream job at Harvard Business School.

His research focused on the design of efficient markets, an important and growing field that has influenced such things as Treasury bill auctions and decisions on who receives organ transplants. He even got to work with Alvin E. Roth, who won a Nobel in economic science in 2012.

But prestige was not enough to keep Mr. Coles at Harvard. In 2013, he moved to the San Francisco Bay Area. He now works at Airbnb, the online lodging marketplace, one of a number of tech companies luring economists with the promise of big sets of data and big salaries.

Silicon Valley is turning to the dismal science in its never-ending quest to squeeze more money out of old markets and build new ones. In turn, economists say they are eager to explore the digital world for fresh insights into timeless economic questions of pricing, incentives and behavior.

"It's an absolute candy store for economists," Mr. Coles said. . . .

Businesses have been hiring economists for years. Usually, they are asked to study macroeconomic trends—topics like recessions and currency exchange rates—and help their employers deal with them.

But what the tech economists are doing is different: Instead of thinking about national or global trends, they are studying the data trails of consumer behavior to help digital companies make smart decisions that strengthen their online marketplaces in areas like advertising, movies, music, travel and lodging.

Tech outfits including giants like Amazon, Facebook, Google and Microsoft and up-and-comers like Airbnb and Uber hope that sort of improved efficiency means more profit.

At Netflix, Randall Lewis, an economic research scientist, is finely measuring the effectiveness of advertising. His work also gets at the correlation-or-causation conundrum in economic behavior: What consumer actions occur coincidentally after people see ads, and what actions are most likely caused by the ads?

At Airbnb, Mr. Coles is researching the company's marketplace of hosts and guests

For example, suppose that two people are discussing Minimum wage laws. Here are two statements you might hear:

> **Pritha:** Minimum wage laws cause unemployment.
> **Naman:** The government should raise the minimum wage.

Ignoring for now whether you agree with these claims, notice that Pritha and Naman differ in what they are trying to do. Pritha is speaking like a scientist: She is describing how the world works. Naman is speaking like a policy adviser: He is talking about how he would like to change the world.

In general, statements about the world come in two types. One type, such as Pritha's, is known as positive. That doesn't mean it is necessarily upbeat or optimistic. **Positive statements** are descriptive. They make a claim about how the world **is**. A second type of statement, such as Naman's, is known as normative. **Normative statements** are prescriptive. They make a claim about how the world **ought to be**.

positive statements claim that attempt to describe the world as it is

normative statements claim that attempt to prescribe how the world should be

A key difference between positive and normative statements is how we judge their validity. We can, in principle, confirm or refute positive statements by examining evidence. An economist might try to evaluate Pritha's statement by analyzing data on changes in minimum wages and unemployment over time. Proving causality can be difficult, as we discuss later, but at its root, the issue should be determined by the evidence. By contrast, evaluating normative statements involves values as well as facts. Naman's statement cannot be judged with data alone. Deciding what is good or bad policy is not just a matter of science. It also involves values, and views on ethics, religion, and political philosophy may well come into play.

for insights, both to help build the business and to understand behavior. One study focuses on procrastination—a subject of great interest to behavioral economists—by looking at bookings. Are they last-minute? Made weeks or months in advance? Do booking habits change by age, gender or country of origin?

"They are microeconomic experts, heavy on data and computing tools like machine learning and writing algorithms," said Tom Beers, executive director of the National Association for Business Economics.

Understanding how digital markets work is getting a lot of attention now, said Hal Varian, Google's chief economist. But, he said, "I thought it was fascinating years ago."

Mr. Varian, 69, is the godfather of the tech industry's in-house economists. Once a well-known professor at the University of California, Berkeley, Mr. Varian showed up at Google in 2002, part time at first, but soon became an employee. He helped refine Google's AdWords marketplace, where advertisers bid to have their ads shown on search pages....

For the moment, Amazon seems to be the most aggressive recruiter of economists. It even has an Amazon Economists website for soliciting résumés. In a video on the site, Patrick Bajari, the company's chief economist, says the economics team has contributed to decisions that have had "multibillion-dollar impacts" for the company....

A current market-design challenge for Amazon and Microsoft is their big cloud computing services. These digital services, for example, face a peak-load problem, much as electric utilities do.

How do you sell service at times when there is a risk some customers may be bumped off? Run an auction for what customers are willing to pay for interruptible service? Or offer set discounts for different levels of risk? Both Amazon and Microsoft are working on that now.

To answer such questions, economists work in teams with computer scientists and people in business. In tech companies, market design involves not only economics but also engineering and marketing. How hard is a certain approach technically? How easy is it to explain to customers?

"Economics influences rather than determines decisions," said Preston McAfee, Microsoft's chief economist, who previously worked at Google and Yahoo. ■

Questions to Discuss

1. Think of some firms that you often interact with. How might the input of economists improve their businesses?
2. After studying economics in college, what kind of business would be the most fun to work for?

Source: Steve Lohr, "Goodbye, Ivory Tower. Hello, Silicon Valley Candy Store," New York Times, September 4, 2016.

Positive and normative statements are different but often intertwined. In particular, positive findings about how the world works can easily affect normative judgments about what policies are desirable. Pritha's claim that the minimum wage causes unemployment, if true, might lead her to reject Naman's conclusion that the government should raise the minimum wage. On the other hand, a positive finding that the unemployment effect is small might lead her to accept Noah's policy prescription.

Normative judgments may also influence the positive claims that researchers choose to study. Naman's desire to raise the minimum wage, for example, may lead him to investigate Pritha's claim that it causes unemployment. To be free of bias, he should put aside his normative views and examine the data as objectively as possible. At its best, positive economics proceeds as a science independent of the researcher's personal values or policy agenda.

As you study economics, keep in mind the broad distinction between positive and normative statements because it will help you stay focused on the task at hand. Much of economics is positive: It just tries to explain how the economy works. Yet those who use economics often have normative goals: They want to learn how to improve the economy. When you hear economists making normative statements, you know they are speaking not as scientists but as policy advisers.

2-2b The Manager as an Economist

In the business world managers continuously deal with decisions that mirror the analytical processes employed by economists. For example, they must scrutinize sales trends, costs, or shifts in consumer tastes and preferences to predict how their organization's position within the overall business environment is affected. Why are input costs increasing in specific supply chains? Why are sales figures higher in Tier-2 cities compared to metropolitan areas? These are questions that require analysis, mostly using data, and therefore require the manager to play the role of economists as scientists.

On the other hand, managers sometimes must make strategic decisions that involve value judgments. Should the company absorb increases in input costs or pass them on to consumers? Should they recruit additional gig workers or hire more formal sector workers? These are normative or policy choices that require a clear articulation of objectives and trade-offs and are often discretionary. In such instances, the manager is not merely interpreting data but also providing guidance on the most appropriate course of action, just like economists do in a policy advisory capacity. The normative situations where a manager is called upon to act require critical managerial skills which are developed through experience, judgment and a general awareness about market factors and overall business acumen or simply going with their gut-feeling. This cannot be taught or tested but are interpersonal skills which distinguish a great manager from an average one.

Therefore, even without formal training in economics, managerial decision-making already encompasses both roles of the economist. The successful manager must possess both the aptitude of an analyst or data scientist and the thoughtfulness of a strategic leader. It helps if they are utilizing economic reasoning to structure their choices, especially in terms of evaluating alternatives and aligning actions with strategic priorities of the organization they are leading.

2-2c Economists in New Delhi

US President Harry Truman once said that he wanted to find a one-armed economist. When he asked his economists for advice, they always answered, "On the one hand, ... On the other hand, ..."

JAMES STEVENSON/ THE NEW YORKER COLLECTION/THE CARTOON BANK

"Let's switch. I'll make the policy, you implement it, and he'll explain it."

Truman was right that economists' advice is not always straightforward. This tendency is rooted in one of the **Basic Principles of Managerial Economics**: Managers face trade-offs. Economists are aware that trade-offs are involved in most policy and managerial decisions. A policy might increase efficiency at the cost of equality. It might help future generations but hurt the current generation. An economist who says that all policy decisions are easy is an economist not to be trusted.

Truman was not the only president who relied on economists' advice. Since 1946, the president of the United States has received guidance from the Council of Economic Advisers, which consists of three members and a staff of a few dozen economists. The council, whose offices are just a few steps from the White House, advises the president and writes the annual *Economic Report of the President*, which discusses recent economic developments and presents the council's analysis of current policy issues. Like U.S. Presidents, Indian Prime Ministers too have relied on economists. Since independence, the Government of India has engaged economists in shaping major policy directions. Prime Minister Jawaharlal Nehru's planning models in the 1950s were largely based on economic growth theories such as the Harrod-Domar Model. The economic liberalization reforms in India were led by Dr. Manmohan Singh in 1991. Dr. Singh was an economist by training and in 1991 was the finance minister and later went on to become the Prime Minister in 2004.

Today, the Prime Minister is advised by economists through several formal bodies, including the Economic Advisory Council to the Prime Minister (EAC-PM) and the

NITI Aayog. India has historically also had several economists serve the government as "Chief Economic Advisor (CEA)". Although the CEA has no executive powers, he/she plays an instrumental role in advising the government on economic policies and is responsible for releasing the annual economic survey before the national budget is tabled in the parliament.

The Reserve Bank of India, the institution that sets the nation's monetary policy, and is the country's central bank employs several economists to analyze developments in India and around the world. Institutions promoted by the Reserve Bank also hire economists in major policy roles. NITI Aayog (translates as policy commission) where NITI is the abbreviation for National Institution for Transforming India, was established in 2015 replacing the erstwhile Planning Commission of India. It serves as the premier policy think tank of the Indian government. While the ex-officio Chairperson of NITI Aayog is the Prime Minister, the Vice Chairperson and several key functionaries are economists responsible for designing policies for India's growth and development.

The influence of economists on policy goes beyond their role as advisers: Their research and writings can affect policy indirectly. The economist John Maynard Keynes offered this observation:

> The ideas of economists and political philosophers, both when they are right and when they are wrong, are more powerful than is commonly understood. Indeed, the world is ruled by little else. Practical men, who believe themselves to be quite exempt from intellectual influences, are usually the slaves of some defunct economist. Madmen in authority, who hear voices in the air, are distilling their frenzy from some academic scribbler of a few years back.

These words were written in 1935, but they remain true today. Indeed, the "academic scribbler" now influencing public policy is often Keynes himself.

Economists in the Industry

Here is a list of notable Indian economists working in various industries in the private sector.

1. Dharmakirti Joshi – Chief Economist, CRISIL (an S&P Global Company)
2. N Srinivasa Rao – Chief Economist and President, Corporate Affairs, Bajaj Finserv Ltd
3. Sajjid Z Chinoy – Managing Director and Chief India Economist, JP Morgan (also a part-time member of EAC to PM)
4. Santanu Sengupta – Chief India Economist, Goldman Sachs
5. Rumki Majumdar – Chief Economist, Deloitte India
6. Abhishek Gupta – Chief India Economist, Bloomberg

Quick**Quiz**

5. Which of the following is a positive, rather than a normative, statement?
   a. Law X will reduce national income.
   b. Law X is a good piece of legislation.
   c. The parliament ought to pass law X.
   d. The president should veto law X.

6. The following parts of government regularly rely on the advice of economists:
   a. Ministry of Finance
   b. Reserve Bank of India
   c. Prime Minister's Office (PMO)
   d. All of the above.

Answers are at the end of the chapter.

2-3 Economists Often Disagree: How Should Managers Reconile?

"If all the economists were laid end to end, they would not reach a conclusion." This quip from George Bernard Shaw is revealing. Economists as a group are often criticized for giving conflicting advice to policymakers. US President Ronald Reagan once joked that if the game Trivial Pursuit were designed for economists, it would have 100 questions and 3,000 answers.

The bottom line is that economists often appear to give conflicting advice. This is not only problematic for policymakers but also for managers and firms who rely on economists for strategic decision making. It is therefore important to understand the reasons for conflicting advice and for managers to be aware of these reasons to determine how to reconcile conflicting advice into actionable decisions.

There are two basic reasons for economists to give conflicting advice:

- Economists may disagree with the validity of alternative positive theories of how the world works.
- Economists may have different values and, therefore, different normative views about what a policy should aim to accomplish.

Let's look more closely at these reasons.

2-3a Differences in Scientific Judgments

Several centuries ago, astronomers debated whether the earth or the sun was at the center of the solar system. More recently, climatologists have debated whether the earth is experiencing global warming and, if so, why. Science is an ongoing search to understand the world around us. It is not surprising that as the search continues, scientists sometimes disagree about the direction in which truth lies.

Economists often disagree for the same reason. Although the field of economics sheds light on much about the world (as you will see throughout this book), there is still much to be learned. Sometimes, economists disagree because they have different hunches about the validity of alternative theories. Sometimes, they disagree because of different judgments about the size of the parameters that measure how economic variables are related.

For example, economists debate whether the government should tax a household's income or its consumption (spending). Advocates of a switch from the current income tax to a consumption tax believe that the change would encourage households to save more because the income that is saved would not be taxed. Higher saving, in turn, would free resources for capital accumulation, leading to more rapid growth in productivity and living standards. Advocates of the current income tax system believe that households would not alter their saving significantly in response to a change in the tax laws. These two groups of economists hold different normative views about the tax system because they have different positive views about how much saving responds to tax incentives.

2-3b Differences in Values

Suppose that Krishna and Balram both take the same amount of water from the town well. The town taxes its residents to pay for maintaining the well. Krishna has an income of ₹15 lakhs and is taxed ₹1.5 lakhs, or 10 percent of his income. Balram has an income of ₹4 lakhs and is taxed ₹60,000, or 15 percent of his income.

Is this policy fair? If not, who pays too much, and who pays too little? Does it matter whether Balram's low income is due to a medical disability or to his decision to pursue an acting career? Does it matter whether Krishna's high income is due to a large inheritance or to his willingness to work long hours at a dreary job?

These are difficult questions about which people are likely to disagree. If the town hired two experts to study how it should tax its residents to pay for the well, it would not be surprising if they offered conflicting advice.

This simple example shows why economists sometimes disagree about public policy. As we know from our discussion of normative and positive analysis, policies cannot be judged on scientific grounds alone. Sometimes, economists give conflicting advice because they have different values or political philosophies. Perfecting the science of economics will not tell us whether Krishna or Balram pays too much.

2-3c The Importance of Managerial Acumen

For business managers, it is important not to be overwhelmed by the diversity of economic opinion, but to be able to synthesize the conflicting opinions meaningfully. This would involve evaluating the assumptions, understanding the incentives, and contextualizing each argument. Economic models are not cast in stone. They are often structured simplifications that rely on assumptions for tractability and reasoned hypotheses. One model might assume perfect competition, while another might assume monopolistic behavior. One might focus on pure rationality while others may focus on bounded rationality and make behavioral assumptions. Therefore, there are several questions that the manager must confront and find answers to. Some of these are as follows. What does this model assume about the market, the firm, or the consumer? Is the logic internally consistent? Is the evidence robust? What are the risks if I adopt this plan, but this view is fundamentally flawed?

This process is not very different from evaluating and choosing between various marketing or investment strategies. No decision maker would rely on a single PowerPoint presentation or a single vendor pitch without seeking important insights and feedback from alternative sources. This also will involve performing background checks and credibility.

In similar light, managers should look beyond headlines or academic credentials to assess the relevance and soundness of different economic perspectives. An important catchphrase in today's world is "evidence based" policymaking. Business managers can gain a lot from relying on those suggestions that come from hardcore scientific and robust empirical evidence, rather than loose statements and opinions based on archaic or historical models. The ability to navigate conflicting economic narratives is therefore a vital part of modern strategic leadership.

However, exposure to a wide range of economic viewpoints must not be seen as a problem but viewed as a boon. Disagreement among economists is nothing but a true reflection of the complexity of the real world. When managers engage with competing ideas and theories, it essentially requires using their managerial skills and acumen to figure out which assumptions are plausible, which contingency plans are meaningful and what risks are worth taking. While this does not require formal training in economics, a commitment to reasoned and rational thought, especially under conditions of uncertainty, can be highly rewarding.

A manager's objective is not to "pick the right economist" or "the correct view" but to use a structured way of thinking about trade-offs, constraints, and strategic planning to internalize the economic reasoning behind alternative arguments for effective managerial decision making. In essence, managers themselves become consumers of economic ideas and perhaps even producers of economics-backed decisions. This points out the all-encompassing nature of economics and its importance in the practice of the science of management.

Quick**Quiz**

7. Economists may disagree because they have different
   a. hunches about the validity of alternative theories.
   b. judgments about the size of key parameters.
   c. political philosophies about the goals of public policy.
   d. All of the above.
8. Business managers can gain the most by
   a. relying on normative judgments
   b. making brute force decisions
   c. relying on evidence driven policy advice
   d. trusting their favorite economists

Answers are at the end of the chapter.

Chapter in a Nutshell

- Economists try to address their subject with a scientist's objectivity. Like all scientists, they make appropriate assumptions and build simplified models to understand the world around them. Two simple economic models are the circular-flow diagram and the production possibilities frontier. The circular-flow diagram shows how households and firms interact in markets for goods and services and in markets for the factors of production. The production possibilities frontier shows how society faces a trade-off between producing different goods.
- Managers often need to take decisions based on their gut- feeling but at the same time can succeed most by relying on evidence driven policy. As such managers are therefore playing both roles of the economist. Sometimes they need to make scientific decisions while other times require their value judgment and managerial acumen, implying they mimic the policy adviser economist.
- A positive statement is an assertion about how the world **is**. A normative statement is an assertion about how the world **ought to be**. While positive statements can be judged based on facts and the scientific method, normative statements entail value judgments as well. When economists make normative statements, they act more as policy advisers than as scientists.
- Economists who advise policymakers and businesses sometimes offer conflicting advice either because of differences in scientific judgments or because of differences in values. At other times, economists are united in the advice they offer, but managers may choose to ignore the advice because of the many forces and constraints imposed on them while sometimes they may need to reconcile these ideas based on the strategic priorities of the organization they are leading.

Key Concepts

circular-flow diagram, p. 20
production possibilities frontier, p. 22
positive statements, p. 26
normative statements, p. 26

Questions for Review

1. In what ways is economics a science?
2. Why do economists make assumptions?
3. Should an economic model exactly describe reality?
4. Name a way that your family interacts in the markets for the factors of production and a way that it interacts in the markets for goods and services.
5. Name one economic interaction that isn't covered by the simplified circular-flow diagram.
6. Draw and explain the production possibilities frontier for an economy that produces milk and cookies. What happens to this frontier if a disease kills half of the economy's cows?

7. Use a production possibilities frontier to describe the idea of **efficiency**.
8. Describe the role of the manager as an economist. Does the manager play the role of a scientist or policy adviser?
9. What is the difference between a positive and a normative statement? Give an example of each.
10. Why do economists sometimes offer conflicting advice to policymakers and businesses?

Problems and Applications

1. Draw a circular-flow diagram. Identify the parts of the model that correspond to the flow of goods and services and the flow of dollars for each of the following activities.
   a. Salma pays a storekeeper ₹20 for 500 mL of milk.
   b. Suleiman earns ₹100 per hour working at a fast-food restaurant.
   c. Shaina spends ₹400 to get a haircut.
   d. Siddharth earns ₹75,000 from her 10 percent ownership of Econ Industrial.
2. Imagine a society that produces military goods and consumer goods, which we'll call "guns" and "butter."
   a. Draw a production possibilities frontier for guns and butter. Using the concept of opportunity cost, explain why it most likely has a bowed-out shape.
   b. Show a point on the graph that is impossible for the economy to achieve. Show a point on the graph that is feasible but inefficient.
   c. Imagine that the society has two political parties, called the Hawks (who want a strong military) and the Doves (who want a smaller military). Show a point on your production possibilities frontier that the Hawks might choose and a point that the Doves might choose.
   d. Imagine that an aggressive neighboring country reduces the size of its military. As a result, both the Hawks and the Doves reduce their desired production of guns by the same amount. Which party would get the bigger "peace dividend," measured by the increase in butter production? Explain.
3. The first principle of managerial economics in Chapter 1 is that managers face trade-offs. Use a production possibilities frontier to illustrate firm's trade-off between two "goods"—a CSR mandate to keep a clean environment and the quantity of output produced. What do you suppose determines the shape and position of the frontier? Show what will happen to the frontier if engineers develop a new way of producing electricity that emits fewer pollutants.
4. An economy consists of three workers: Leena, Meena, and Teena. Each works 10 hours a day and can produce two services: mowing lawns and washing cars. In an hour, Leena can either mow one lawn or wash one car, Meena can either mow one lawn or wash two cars, and Teena can either mow two lawns or wash one car.
   a. Calculate how much of each service is produced in the following scenarios, which we label A, B, C, and D:
      - All three spend all their time mowing lawns. (A)
      - All three spend all their time washing cars. (B)
      - All three spend half their time on each activity. (C)
      - Leena spends half her time on each activity, while Meena only washes cars and Teena only mows lawns. (D)
   b. Graph the production possibilities frontier for this economy. Using your answers to part *a*, identify points A, B, C, and D on your graph.
   c. Explain why the production possibilities frontier has the shape it does.
   d. Are any of the allocations calculated in part *a* inefficient? Explain.
5. Classify each of the following statements as positive or normative. Explain.
   a. Society faces a short-run trade-off between inflation and unemployment.
   b. A reduction in the growth rate of the money supply will reduce the rate of inflation.
   c. The Reserve Bank of India should reduce the growth rate of the money supply.
   d. Society ought to require welfare recipients to look for jobs.
   e. Lower tax rates encourage more work and more saving.

Quick**Quiz Answers**

1. **c** 2. **a** 3. **b** 4. **d** 5. **a** 6. **d** 7. **d** 8. **b**

Appendix

Graphing: A Brief Review

Many economic concepts can be expressed with numbers—the price of bananas, the quantity of bananas sold, the cost of growing bananas, and so on. Often, these variables are related to one another: When the price of bananas rises, people buy fewer bananas. One way to express these relationships is with graphs.

Graphs serve two purposes. First, when developing theories, they offer a visual way to express ideas that might be less clear if described with equations or words. Second, when analyzing data, graphs provide a powerful way of finding and interpreting patterns. In either case, graphs provide a lens through which a recognizable forest emerges from a multitude of trees.

Numerical information can be expressed graphically in many ways, just as there are many ways to express a thought in words. A good writer chooses words that will make an argument clear, a description pleasing, or a scene dramatic. An effective economist chooses the type of graph that best suits the purpose at hand.

This appendix discusses how economists use graphs to study mathematical relationships among variables. It also points out some of the pitfalls that can arise when using graphical methods.

Figure A-1

Types of Graphs

The pie chart in panel (a) shows how the Indian GDP in 2024-25 was derived from different sources. The bar graph in panel (b) compares the per capital income in four countries. The time-series graph in panel (c) shows total labor productivity in India over time

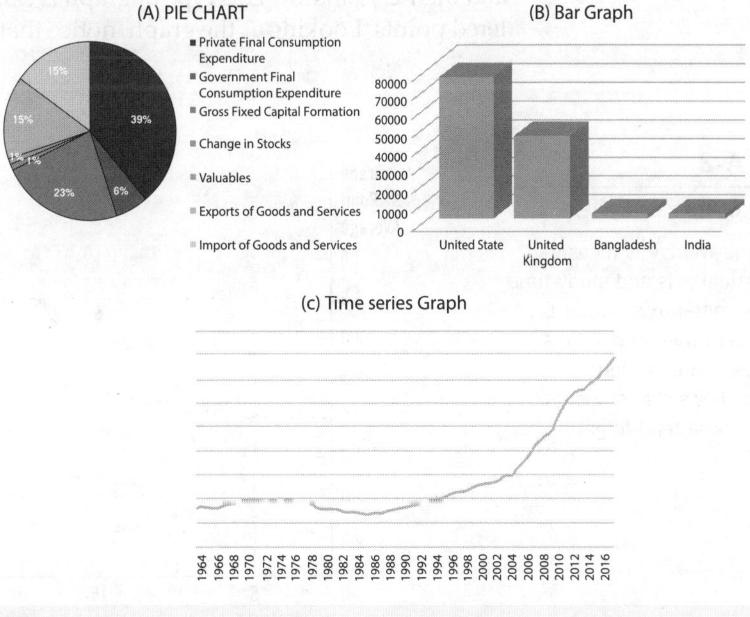

Source: RBI Database for Indian Economy and World Bank

Graphs of a Single Variable

Three common graphs appear in Figure A-1. The pie chart in panel (a) shows how national income in the India is divided among the sources of income, including Government final consumption expenditure, exports of goods and services, and so on. A slice of the pie represents each source's share of the total. The bar graph in panel (b) compares income in four countries. The height of each bar represents the per capita income in each country. The time-series graph in panel (c) traces the rising total labor productivity in India measured in 2011 International ppp exchange rates, thousands, over time. You have probably seen similar graphs in news reports.

Graphs of Two Variables: The Coordinate System

The three graphs in Figure A-1 are useful, but they are limited in how much they can tell us. These graphs display information about only a single variable. If economists are looking at the relationships between variables, they may want to display two variables on a single graph. The **coordinate system** makes this possible.

Suppose you want to examine the relationship between study time and grade point average. For each student in a class, you could record a pair of numbers: study hours per week and grade point average. These numbers could then be placed in parentheses as an **ordered pair** and appear as a single point on the graph. Albert E., for instance, is represented by the ordered pair (25 hours/week, 3.5 GPA), while his "what-me-worry?" classmate Alfred E. is represented by the ordered pair (5 hours/week, 2.0 GPA).

We can graph these ordered pairs on a two-dimensional grid. The first number in each ordered pair, called the **x-coordinate**, tells us the horizontal location of the point. The second number, called the **y-coordinate**, tells us the vertical location. The point with both an x-coordinate and a y-coordinate of zero is called the **origin**. The two coordinates in the ordered pair tell us where the point is located in relation to the origin: x units to the right of the origin and y units above it.

Figure A-2 graphs grade point average against study time for Albert E., Alfred E., and their classmates. This type of graph is called a **scatter plot** because it plots scattered points. Looking at the graph, notice that points farther to the right (indicating

Figure A-2

Using the Coordinate System

Grade point average is measured on the vertical axis and study time on the horizontal axis. Albert E., Alfred E., and their classmates are represented by various points. The graph shows that students who study more tend to get higher grades.

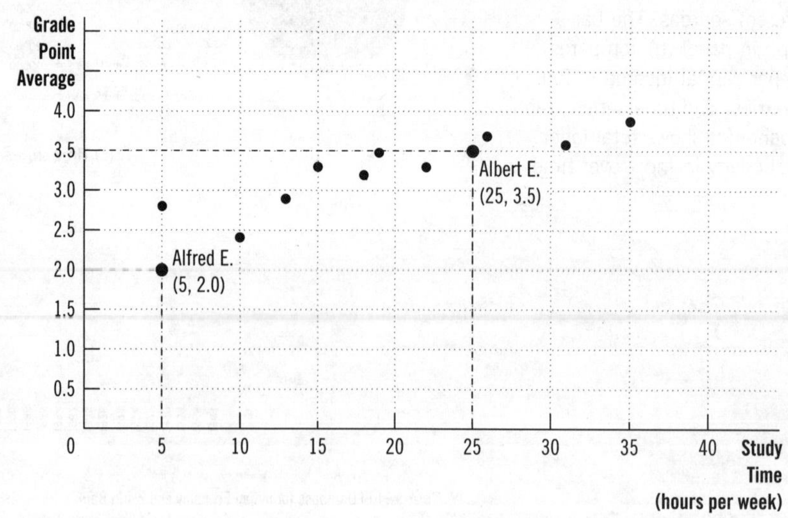

more study time) also tend to be higher (indicating a better grade point average). Because study time and grade point average typically move in the same direction, we say that these two variables have a **positive correlation**. By contrast, if we were to graph party time and grades, we would likely find that higher party time is associated with lower grades. Because these variables typically move in opposite directions, we say that they have a **negative correlation**. In either case, the coordinate system makes the correlation between two variables easy to see.

Curves in the Coordinate System

Students who study more do tend to get higher grades, but other factors also influence a student's grades. Previous preparation is an important factor, for instance, as is talent, attention from teachers, or even eating a good breakfast. A scatter plot like Figure A-2 does not attempt to isolate the effect that studying has on grades from the effects of other variables. Often, however, economists prefer looking at how one variable affects another, holding all other possible variables constant.

To see how this is done, consider one of the most important graphs in economics: the **demand curve**. The demand curve traces the effect of a good's price on the quantity that consumers want to buy. Before showing a demand curve, however, consider Table A-1, which shows how the number of novels that Ishani buys depends on her income and on the price of novels. When novels are cheap, Ishani buys a lot of them. As they become more expensive, she instead borrows books from the library or goes to the movies rather than read. Similarly, at any price, Ishani buys more novels when she has a higher income. That is, when her income increases, she spends part of the additional income on novels and part on other goods.

We now have three variables—the price of novels, income, and the number of novels purchased, which is more than can be shown in two dimensions. To put the information from Table A-1 in graphical form, we need to hold one of the three variables constant and trace out the relationship between the other two. Because the demand curve represents the relationship between price and quantity demanded, we hold Ishani's income constant and show how the number of novels she buys varies with the price of novels.

Suppose that Ishani's income is ₹40,000 per month. If we place the number of novels she buys on the *x*-axis and the price of novels on the *y*-axis, we can graphically

Table A-1

Novels Purchased by Ishani

This table shows the number of novels Ishani buys at various incomes and prices. For any given level of income, the data on price and quantity demanded can be graphed to produce Ishani's demand curve for novels, as shown in Figures A-3 and A-4.

Price ₹	For ₹30,000 Income:	For ₹40,000 Income:	For ₹50,000 Income:
1000	2 novels	5 novels	8 novels
900	6	9	12
800	10	13	16
700	14	17	20
600	18	21	24
500	22	25	28
	Demand curve, D_3	Demand curve, D_1	Demand curve, D_2

Figure A-3

Demand Curve

The line D_1 shows how Ishani's purchases of novels depend on the price of novels when her income is held constant. Because the price and the quantity demanded are negatively related, the demand curve slopes down.

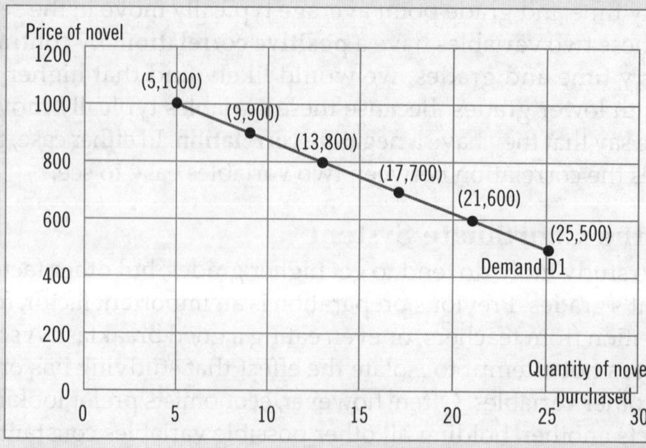

represent the middle column of Table A-1. When the points that represent these entries from the table—(5 novels, ₹1000), (9 novels, ₹9), and so on are connected, they form a line. This line, pictured in Figure A-3, is known as Ishani's demand curve for novels; it tells us how many novels Ishani buys at any price, holding income constant. The demand curve slopes down, indicating that a lower price increases the quantity of novels demanded. Because the quantity of novels demanded and the price move in opposite directions, we say that the two variables are **negatively related**. (Conversely, when two variables move in the same direction, the curve relating them slopes up, and we say that the variables are **positively related**.)

Now suppose Ishani's income rises to ₹50,000 per month. At any price, Ishani buys more novels than she did at her previous income. Just as we earlier drew Ishani's demand curve for novels using the entries from the middle column of Table A-1, we now draw a new demand curve using the entries from the right column of the table. This new demand curve (curve D_2) is pictured alongside the old one (curve D_1) in Figure A-4; the new curve is a similar line drawn farther to the right. We therefore say that Ishani's demand curve for novels **shifts** to the right when her income increases. Likewise, if Ishani's income were to fall to ₹30,000 per month, she would buy fewer novels at any price, and her demand curve would shift to the left (to curve D_3).

In economics, it is important to distinguish between **movements along a curve** and **shifts of a curve**. As Figure A-3 shows, if Ishani earns ₹40,000 per year and each novel costs ₹8, she buys 13 novels per year. If the price of novels falls to ₹7, Ishani increases her purchases to 17 novels per year. The demand curve, however, stays fixed in the same place. Ishani still buys the same number of novels **at each price**, but as the price falls, she moves along her demand curve from left to right. By contrast, if the price of novels remains fixed at ₹800 but her income rises to ₹50,000, Ishani increases her purchases of novels from 13 to 16 per month. Because Ishani buys more novels **at each price**, her demand curve shifts out, as shown in Figure A-4.

There is a simple way to tell when it is necessary to shift a curve: **When a relevant variable that is not named on either axis changes, the curve shifts.** Income is on neither the *x*-axis nor the *y*-axis of the graph, so when Ishani's income changes, her demand curve shifts. The same is true for any change that affects Ishani's purchasing habits, with the sole exception of a change in the price of novels. If, for instance, the public library closes and Ishani must buy all the books she wants to

Figure A-4

Shifting Demand Curves

The location of Ishani's demand curve for novels depends on how much income she earns. The more she earns, the more novels she buys at any price, and the farther to the right her demand curve lies. Curve D_1 represents Ishani's original demand curve, based on an income of 40,000 per year. If her income rises to 50,000 per year, her demand curve shifts to D_2. If her income falls to 30,000 per year, her demand curve shifts to D_3.

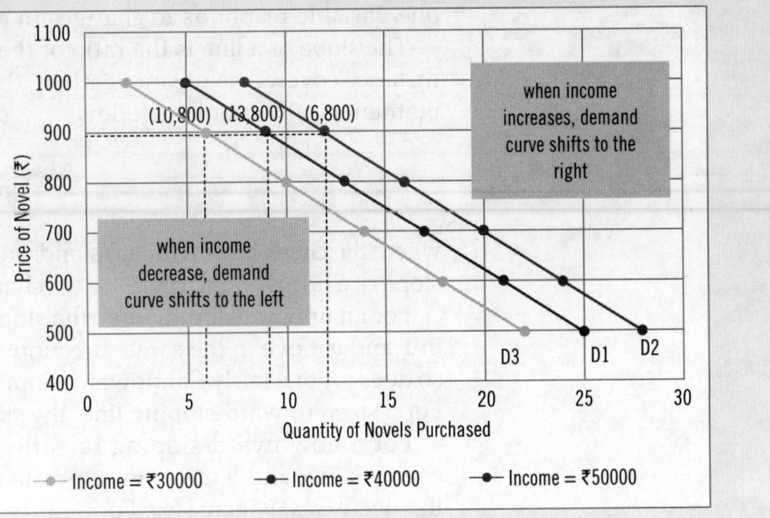

read, she will demand more novels at each price, and her demand curve will shift to the right. Or, if the price of movies falls and Ishani spends more time watching them and less time reading books, she will demand fewer novels at each price, and her demand curve will shift to the left. By contrast, when a variable on an axis of the graph changes, the curve does not shift. We read the change as a movement along the curve.

Slope

One question we might want to ask about Ishani is how much her purchasing habits respond to changes in price. Look at the demand curve pictured in Figure A-5. If this curve is very steep, Ishani buys nearly the same number of novels whether they are cheap or expensive. If the curve is much flatter, the number of novels she

Figure A-5

Calculating the Slope of a Line

To calculate the slope of the demand curve, look at the changes in the *x*- and *y*-coordinates as we move from the point (13 novels, \$8) to the point (21 novels, \$6). The slope of the line is the ratio of the change in the *y*-coordinate (–2) to the change in the *x*-coordinate (+8), which equals –¼.

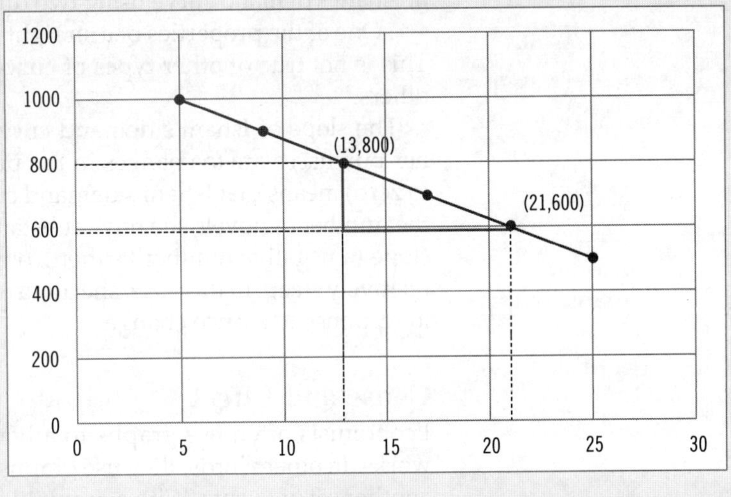

buys is more sensitive to price changes. To answer questions about how much one variable responds to changes in another, we can use the concept of **slope**.

The slope of a line is the ratio of the vertical distance covered to the horizontal distance covered as we move along the line. This definition is usually written in mathematical symbols as follows:

$$\text{slope } 5 \ \frac{Dy}{Dx},$$

where the Greek letter Δ (delta) stands for the change in a variable. In other words, the slope of a line is equal to the "rise" (change in y) divided by the "run" (change in x).

For an upward-sloping line, the slope is a positive number because the changes in x and y move in the same direction: If x increases, so does y, and if x decreases, so does y. For a fairly flat upward-sloping line, the slope is a small positive number. For a steep upward-sloping line, the slope is a large positive number.

For a downward-sloping line, the slope is a negative number because the changes in x and y move in opposite directions: If x increases, y decreases, and if x decreases, y increases. For a fairly flat downward-sloping line, the slope is a small negative number. For a steep downward-sloping` line, the slope is a large negative number.

A horizontal line has a slope of zero because, in this case, the y-variable never changes. A vertical line is said to have an infinite slope because the y-variable can take any value without the x-variable changing at all.

What is the slope of Ishani's demand curve for novels? First of all, because the curve slopes down, we know the slope will be negative. To calculate a numerical value for the slope, choose two points on the line. With Ishani's income at ₹40,000, she buys 13 novels at a price of ₹800 or 21 novels at a price of ₹600. When we apply the slope formula, we are concerned with the change between these two points. In other words, we are concerned with the difference between them, which tells us that we will have to subtract one set of values from the other, as follows:

$$\text{Slope} = \frac{\Delta y}{\Delta x} = \frac{\text{second } y\text{-coordinate} - \text{first } y\text{-coordinate}}{\text{second } x\text{-coordinate} - \text{first } x\text{-coordinate}} = \frac{6-8}{21-13} = \frac{-2}{8} = \frac{-1}{4}$$

Figure A-5 shows graphically how this calculation works. Try computing the slope of Ishani's demand curve using two different points. You should get the same result, – ¼. One of the properties of a straight line is that it has the same slope everywhere. This is not true of other types of curves, which are steeper in some places than in others.

The slope of Ishani's demand curve tells us something about how responsive her purchases are to changes in the price. A small slope (a negative number close to zero) means that Ishani's demand curve is relatively flat; in this case, she adjusts the number of novels she buys substantially in response to a price change. A larger slope (a negative number farther from zero) means that Ishani's demand curve is relatively steep; in this case, she adjusts the number of novels she buys only slightly in response to a price change.

Cause and Effect

Economists often use graphs to advance an argument about how the economy works. In other words, they use graphs to argue about how one set of events **causes** another set of events. With a graph like the demand curve, there is no doubt about

COURTESY OF RANDALL MUNROE/XKCD.COM

the cause and effect. Because we are varying price and holding all other variables constant, we know that changes in the price of novels cause changes in the quantity Ishani demands. Remember, however, that our demand curve came from a hypothetical example. When graphing data from the real world, it is often more difficult to establish how one variable affects another.

The first problem is that it is difficult to hold everything else constant when studying the relationship between two variables. If we are not able to hold other variables constant, we might decide that one variable on our graph is causing changes in the other variable when those changes are actually being caused by a third **omitted variable** not pictured on the graph. Even if we have identified the correct two variables to look at, we might run into a second problem—**reverse causality**. In other words, we might decide that A causes B when, in fact, B causes A. The omitted variable and reverse causality traps require us to proceed with caution when using graphs to draw conclusions about causes and effects.

Omitted Variables To see how omitting a variable can lead to a deceptive graph, consider an example. Imagine that the government, spurred by public concern about the large number of deaths from cancer, commissions an exhaustive study from Big Boss Statistical Services, Inc. Big Boss examines many of the items found in people's homes to see which of them are associated with the risk of cancer. Big Boss reports a strong relationship between two variables: the number of cigarette lighters that a household owns and the probability that someone in the household will develop cancer. Figure A-6 shows this relationship.

What should we make of this result? Big Boss advises a quick policy response. It recommends that the government discourage the ownership of cigarette lighters by taxing their sale. It also recommends that the government require warning labels: "Big Boss has determined that this lighter is dangerous to your health."

In judging the validity of Big Boss's analysis, one question is key: Has Big Boss held constant every relevant variable except the one under consideration? If the answer is no, the results are suspect. An easy explanation for Figure A-6 is that people who own more cigarette lighters are more likely to smoke cigarettes and that cigarettes, not lighters, cause cancer. If Figure A-6 does not hold constant the amount of smoking—and it doesn't because Big Boss's never looked at that variable—it does not tell us the true effect of owning a cigarette lighter.

This story illustrates an important principle: When you see a graph used to support an argument about cause and effect, it is important to ask whether the movements of an omitted variable could explain the results you see.

Figure A-6

Graph with an Omitted Variable

The upward-sloping curve shows that members of households with more cigarette lighters are more likely to develop cancer. Yet we should not conclude that ownership of lighters causes cancer because the graph does not take into account the number of cigarettes smoked.

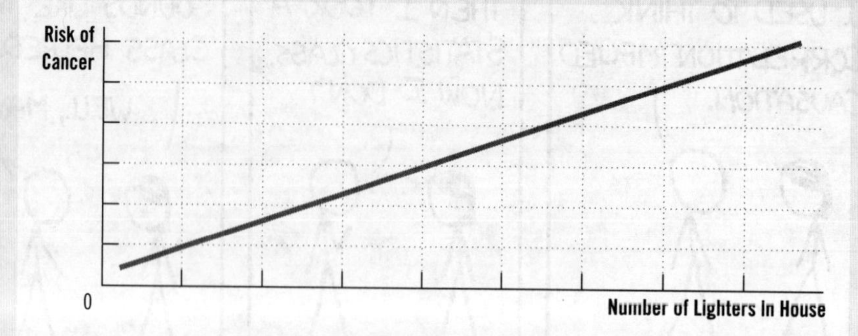

Figure A-7

Graph Suggesting Reverse Causality

The upward-sloping curve shows that cities with a higher concentration of police are more dangerous. Yet the graph does not tell us whether police cause crime or crime-plagued cities hire more police.

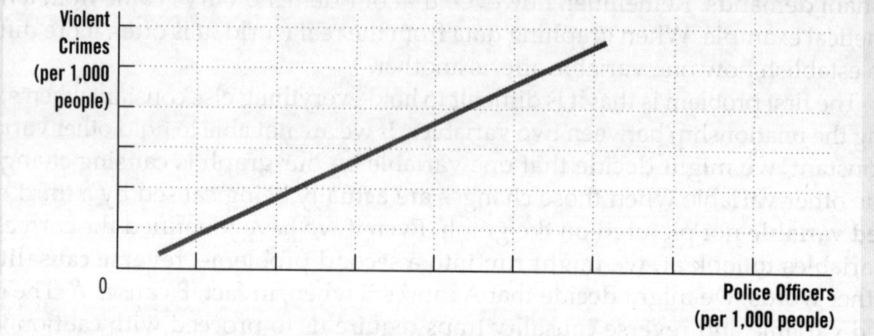

Reverse Causality Economists can also make mistakes about causality by misreading its direction. To see how this is possible, suppose the Association of American Anarchists commissions a study of crime in America and arrives at Figure A-7, which plots the number of violent crimes per thousand people in major cities against the number of police officers per thousand people. The Anarchists note the curve's upward slope and argue that because police increase rather than decrease the amount of urban violence, law enforcement should be abolished.

Figure A-7, however, does not prove the Anarchists' point. The graph simply shows that more dangerous cities have more police officers. The explanation may be that more dangerous cities hire more police. In other words, rather than police causing crime, crime may cause police. We could avoid the danger of reverse causality by running a controlled experiment. In this case, we would randomly assign different numbers of police to different cities and then examine the correlation between police and crime. Without such an experiment, establishing the direction of causality is difficult at best.

It might seem that we could determine the direction of causality by examining which variable moves first. If crime increases and then the police force expands, we reach one conclusion. If the police force expands and then crime increases, we reach the other conclusion. This approach, however, is also flawed: Often, people change their behavior not in response to a change in their present conditions but in response to a change in their **expectations** about future conditions. A city that expects a major crime wave in the future, for instance, might hire more police now. This problem is easier to see in the case of babies and minivans. Couples often buy a minivan in anticipation of the birth of a child. The minivan comes before the baby, but we wouldn't want to conclude that the sale of minivans causes the population to grow!

There is no complete set of rules that says when it is appropriate to draw causal conclusions from graphs. Yet just keeping in mind that cigarette lighters don't cause cancer (omitted variable) and that minivans don't cause larger families (reverse causality) will keep you from falling for many faulty economic arguments.

Chapter

3

Gains from Specialization and Strategic Interdependence

Consider a typical day. You wake up and pour juice from oranges grown in Nagpur and coffee from beans harvested in Brazil. Over breakfast, you read a news report edited in New Delhi on a tablet made in China. You get dressed in clothes made of cotton grown in Gujarat and sewn in factories in Vietnam. You ride to class on a bicycle made of parts manufactured in half a dozen countries around the world. Then you open your economics textbook written by an author living in Massachusetts, published by a company located in Ohio, distributed in India, Sri Lanka, and Nepal, and printed on paper made from trees grown in Europe.

Every day, you rely on many people, most of whom you have never met, to provide you with goods and services. Such interdependence is possible because people trade with one another. The people providing these things to you are not acting out of generosity, nor is some government agency directing them to satisfy your desires. Instead, people provide you and other consumers with the goods and services they produce because they get something in return.

BLACKCAT/E+/GETTY IMAGES, ©WITHSTOCK/SHUTTERSTOCK.COM

In later chapters, we examine how an economy coordinates the activities of millions of people with varying tastes and abilities. As a starting point, this chapter considers the reasons for economic interdependence. Such strategic specialization is critical for managerial efficiency as it is not possible for a single firm, especially if it is operating at a small scale, to manufacture every item required in the product line and supply chain. Therefore, they must rely on other firms and trade with each other where the produce of one firm can be used as inputs for another firm's production. This is essentially strategic interdependence where each firm can gain by focusing on the production of goods in which they specialize.

A similar logic can be applied to understanding trade in the global economy. Most countries today import from abroad many of the goods and services they consume, and they export to foreign customers much of what they produce. The analysis in this chapter explains interdependence not only among individuals but also among nations. As we will see, the gains from trade are much the same whether you are buying a haircut from your local barber or a T-shirt made on the other side of the globe.

3-1 A Parable for the Modern Economy

To understand how people benefit when they rely on one another for goods and services, let's examine a simple economy. Imagine that there are only two goods in the world: meat and potatoes. And there are only two people: a sheep rancher named Rashmi and a potato farmer named Firdaus. Both Rashmi and Firdaus would like to eat a diet of both meat and potatoes.

The gains from trade are clearest if Rashmi can produce only meat and Firdaus can produce only potatoes. In one scenario, Firdaus and Rashmi could choose to have nothing to do with each other. But after several months of eating mutton, kabab, stew, curry, and in Biryani, Rashmi might decide that self-sufficiency is not all it's cracked up to be. Firdaus, who has been eating potatoes mashed, fried, baked, and wedged, would likely agree. It is easy to see that trade would allow both of them to enjoy greater variety: Each could then have a kabab with a baked potato or a kathi roll with French fries.

Although this scene shows most simply how everyone can benefit from trade, the gains would be similar if Firdaus and Rashmi were each capable of producing the other good, but only at great cost. Suppose, for example, that Rashmi can grow potatoes, but her land is not well suited for it. Similarly, suppose that Firdaus can raise sheep and produce meat but is not good at it. In this case, Firdaus and Rashmi benefit by specializing in what they do best and then trading with each other.

The gains are less obvious, however, when one person is better at producing **everything**. For example, imagine that Rashmi is better at raising sheep **and** at growing potatoes. In this case, should Rashmi remain self-sufficient? Or is there still a reason for her to trade with Firdaus? Let's look more closely at the factors that affect such a decision.

3-1a Production Possibilities

Suppose that Firdaus and Rashmi each work 8 hours per day and can use this time to grow potatoes, raise sheep, or engage in a combination of the two. The table in Figure 1 shows the amount of time each person requires to produce 1 ounce of each good. Firdaus produces an ounce of potatoes in 15 minutes and an ounce of meat in 60 minutes. Rashmi, who is better in both activities, can produce an ounce of potatoes in 10 minutes and an ounce of meat in 20 minutes. The last two columns show how much they can each produce if they devote all 8 hours to producing only meat or potatoes.

Figure 1

The Production Possibilities Frontier

Panel (a) shows the production opportunities available to Firdaus the farmer and Rashmi the rancher. Panel (b) shows the combinations of meat and potatoes that Firdaus can produce. Panel (c) shows the combinations of meat and potatoes that Rashmi can produce. Both production possibilities frontiers assume that Firdaus and Rashmi each work 8 hours per day. If there is no trade, their production possibilities frontiers are also their consumption possibilities frontiers.

(a) Production Opportunities

	Minutes Needed to Make 1 Ounce of:		Amount Produced in 8 Hours	
	Meat	**Potatoes**	**Meat**	**Potatoes**
Firdaus the farmer	60 min/oz	15 min/oz	8 oz	32 oz
Rashmi the rancher	20 min/oz	10 min/oz	24 oz	48 oz

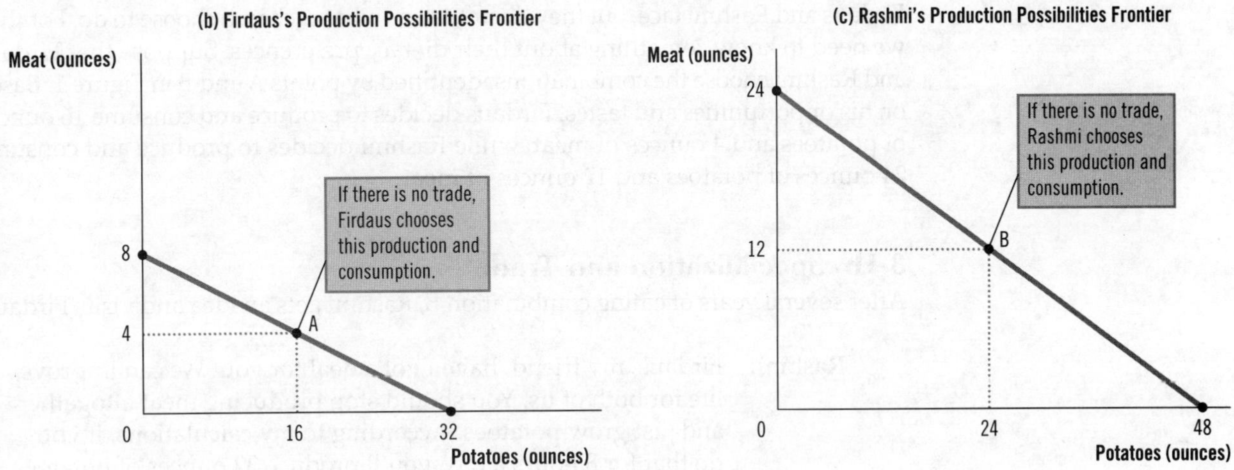

Panel (b) of Figure 1 illustrates the amounts of meat and potatoes that Firdaus can produce. If he spends all 8 hours growing potatoes, Firdaus produces 32 ounces of potatoes (measured on the horizontal axis) and no meat. If he spends all of his time raising sheep, he produces 8 ounces of meat (measured on the vertical axis) and no potatoes. If Firdaus divides his time equally between the two activities, spending 4 hours on each, he produces 16 ounces of potatoes and 4 ounces of meat. The figure shows these three outcomes and all others in between.

This graph is Firdaus's production possibilities frontier. As we discussed in Chapter 2, a production possibilities frontier shows the mixes of output that an economy can produce. Here, Firdaus faces a trade-off between producing meat and producing potatoes.

You may recall that the production possibilities frontier in Chapter 2 was drawn bowed out. In that case, the rate at which society could trade one good for the other depended on the amounts that were being produced. Here, however, Firdaus can switch between the production of meat and potatoes (summarized in Figure 1) at a constant rate. When Firdaus cuts 1 hour from producing meat and adds 1 hour to producing potatoes, he reduces his meat output by 1 ounce and raises his potato output by 4 ounces, and this is true regardless of how much he is already producing. As a result, the production possibilities frontier is a straight line.

Panel (c) of Figure 1 shows Rashmi's production possibilities frontier. If she only grows potatoes, Rashmi produces 48 ounces of them and no meat. If she only raises sheep, she produces 24 ounces of meat and no potatoes. If Rashmi divides her time equally, spending 4 hours on each activity, she produces 24 ounces of potatoes and 12 ounces of meat. Once again, the production possibilities frontier shows all possible outcomes.

If Firdaus and Rashmi remain self-sufficient instead of trading with each other, each consumes exactly what he or she produces. In this case, the production possibilities frontier is also the consumption possibilities frontier. That is, without trade, Figure 1 shows the possible combinations of meat and potatoes that Firdaus and Rashmi can each produce and then consume.

These production possibilities frontiers are useful in showing the trade-offs that Firdaus and Rashmi face, but they do not tell us what each will choose to do. For that, we need to know something about their dietary preferences. Suppose that Firdaus and Rashmi choose the combinations identified by points A and B in Figure 1. Based on his opportunities and tastes, Firdaus decides to produce and consume 16 ounces of potatoes and 4 ounces of meat, while Rashmi decides to produce and consume 24 ounces of potatoes and 12 ounces of meat.

3-1b Specialization and Trade

After several years of eating combination B, Rashmi gets an idea and visits Firdaus:

Rashmi: Firdaus, my friend, have I got a deal for you! We can improve life for both of us. You should stop producing meat altogether and just grow potatoes. According to my calculations, if you do that for 8 hours a day, you'll produce 32 ounces of potatoes. You can then give me 15 of those 32 ounces, and I'll give you 5 ounces of meat in return. It's great! You'll eat 17 ounces of potatoes and 5 ounces of meat every day instead of the 16 ounces of potatoes and 4 ounces of meat you eat now. With my plan, you'll have more of **both** foods. [To illustrate her point, Rashmi shows Firdaus panel (a) of Figure 2.]

Firdaus: (sounding skeptical): That seems like a good deal for me. But I don't understand why you are offering it. If the deal is so good for me, it can't be good for you too.

Rashmi: Oh, but it is! Suppose I spend 6 hours a day raising sheep and 2 hours growing potatoes. Then I can produce 18 ounces of meat and 12 ounces of potatoes. After I give you 5 ounces of my meat in exchange for 15 ounces of your potatoes, I'll end up with 13 ounces of meat and 27 ounces of potatoes instead of the 12 ounces of meat and 24 ounces of potatoes that I have now. So I will also consume more of both foods than I do now. [She points out panel (b) of Figure 2.]

Firdaus: I don't know. . . . This sounds too good to be true.

Figure 2

How Trade Expands the Set of Consumption Opportunities

The proposed trade offers Firdaus and Rashmi a combination of meat and potatoes that would be impossible without trade. In panel (a), Firdaus consumes at point A* rather than point A. In panel (b), Rashmi consumes at point B* rather than point B. Trade allows each to consume more meat and more potatoes.

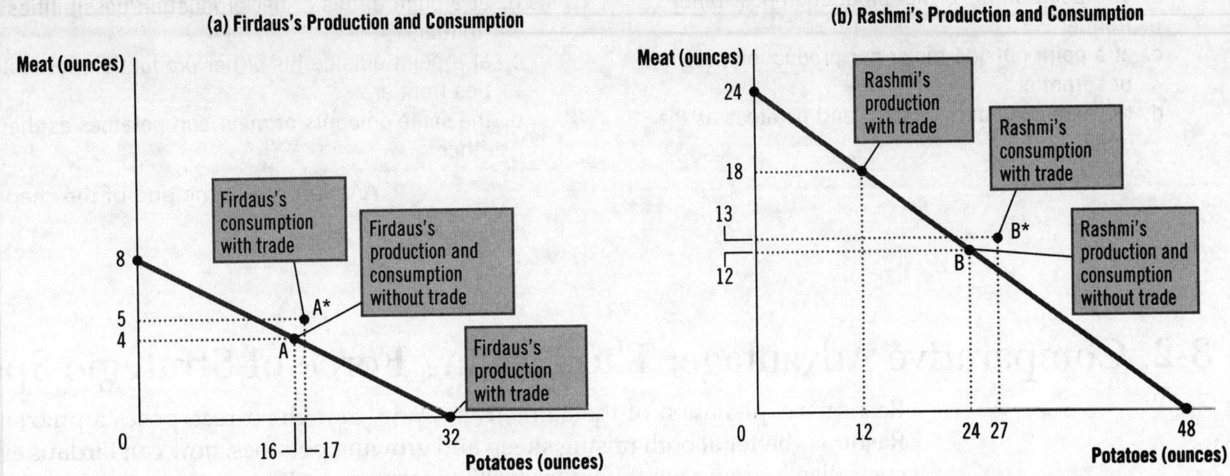

(c) The Gains from Trade: A Summary

	Firdaus		Rashmi	
	Meat	**Potatoes**	**Meat**	**Potatoes**
Without Trade:				
Production and Consumption	4 oz	16 oz	12 oz	24 oz
With Trade:				
Production	0 oz	32 oz	18 oz	12 oz
Trade	Gets 5 oz	Gives 15 oz	Gives 5 oz	Gets 15 oz
Consumption	5 oz	17 oz	13 oz	27 oz
GAINS FROM TRADE:				
Increase in Consumption	+1 oz	+1 oz	+1 oz	+3 oz

Rashmi: It's really not complicated. Here, I've summarized my proposal for you in a simple table. [Rashmi shows Firdaus a copy of the table at the bottom of Figure 2.]

Firdaus: (after pausing to study the table): These calculations seem correct, but I am puzzled. How can this deal make us both better off?

Rashmi: Trade allows each of us to do what we do best. You spend more time growing potatoes and less raising sheep. I spend more time raising sheep and less growing potatoes. Thanks to specialization and trade, each of us can consume more meat and more potatoes without working more hours.

Quick**Quiz**

1. Before Firdaus and Rashmi engage in trade, each consumes
   a. at a point inside his or her production possibilities frontier.
   b. at a point on his or her production possibilities frontier.
   c. at a point outside his or her production possibilities frontier.
   d. the same amounts of meat and potatoes as the other.

2. After Firdaus and Rashmi trade, each of them consumes
   a. at a point inside his or her production possibilities frontier.
   b. at a point on his or her production possibilities frontier.
   c. at a point outside his or her production possibilities frontier.
   d. the same amounts of meat and potatoes as the other.

Answers are at the end of the chapter.

3-2 Comparative Advantage: The Driving Force of Strategic Specializatio

Rashmi's explanation of the gains from trade, though correct, poses a puzzle: If Rashmi is better at both raising sheep and growing potatoes, how can Firdaus ever specialize in doing what he does best? Firdaus doesn't seem to do anything best. To solve this puzzle, we need to look at the principle of **comparative advantage**.

As a first step, consider the following question: In our example, who can produce potatoes at a lower cost—Firdaus or Rashmi? There are two possible answers, and in them lies the key to understanding the gains from trade.

3-2a Absolute Advantage

absolute advantage
the ability to produce a good using fewer inputs than another producer

One way to answer the question about the cost of producing potatoes is to compare the inputs each producer requires. Economists use the term **absolute advantage** when comparing the productivity of one person, firm, or nation to that of another. The producer that requires a smaller quantity of inputs to produce a good is said to have an absolute advantage in producing that good.

In our simple example, time is the only input, so it is all we need to examine to determine absolute advantage. Rashmi has an absolute advantage in producing both meat and potatoes because she requires less time than Firdaus to produce a unit of either good. She needs only 20 minutes to produce an ounce of meat, while Firdaus needs 60 minutes. Similarly, it takes Rashmi only 10 minutes to produce an ounce of potatoes, while it takes Firdaus 15 minutes. Thus, if cost is measured in terms of the quantity of inputs, Rashmi produces potatoes at a lower cost.

3-2b Opportunity Cost and Comparative Advantage

opportunity cost
whatever must be given up to obtain some item

There is another way to look at the cost of producing potatoes. Rather than focusing on the inputs required, we can examine the opportunity costs. Recall from Chapter 1 that the **opportunity cost** of an item is what you give up to get that item. We have assumed that Firdaus and Rashmi each work 8 hours a day. Time spent producing potatoes takes away from time available for producing meat. When reallocating time between the two goods, Rashmi and Firdaus give up units of one good to produce units of the other, moving along the production possibilities frontier. The opportunity cost measures the trade-off that each producer faces.

First, consider Rashmi's opportunity cost. According to the table in panel (a) of Figure 1, it takes her 10 minutes to grow 1 ounce of potatoes, time that she isn't using to produce meat. Because Rashmi needs 20 minutes to produce 1 ounce of meat, 10 minutes would yield ½ ounce of meat. Hence, Rashmi's opportunity cost of producing 1 ounce of potatoes is ½ ounce of meat.

Next, consider Firdaus's situation. Producing 1 ounce of potatoes takes him 15 minutes. Because he needs 60 minutes to produce 1 ounce of meat, 15 minutes would yield ¼ ounce of meat. Hence, Firdaus's opportunity cost of producing 1 ounce of potatoes is ¼ ounce of meat.

Table 1 shows the opportunity costs of meat and potatoes for each of them. Notice that the opportunity cost of meat is the inverse of the opportunity cost of potatoes. Because 1 ounce of potatoes costs Rashmi ½ ounce of meat, it is also true that 1 ounce of meat costs her 2 ounces of potatoes. Similarly, because 1 ounce of potatoes costs Firdaus ¼ ounce of meat, 1 ounce of meat costs him 4 ounces of potatoes.

Economists use the term **comparative advantage** when describing the opportunity costs faced by two producers. The producer who gives up less of the other good to produce Good X has the smaller opportunity cost of producing Good X and is said to have a comparative advantage in producing it. In our example, Firdaus has a lower opportunity cost of producing potatoes than Rashmi: An ounce of potatoes costs Firdaus only ¼ ounce of meat but costs Rashmi ½ ounce of meat. Conversely, Rashmi has a lower opportunity cost of producing meat than Firdaus: An ounce of meat costs Rashmi 2 ounces of potatoes but costs Firdaus 4 ounces of potatoes. Thus, Firdaus has a comparative advantage in growing potatoes, and Rashmi has a comparative advantage in producing meat.

comparative advantage the ability to produce a good at a lower opportunity cost than another producer

Although it is possible for a person to have an absolute advantage in both goods (as Rashmi does in our example), it is impossible for a person to have a comparative advantage in both goods. Because the opportunity cost of one good is the inverse of the opportunity cost of the other, if a person's opportunity cost of one good is relatively high, his or her opportunity cost of the other good must be relatively low. Unless two people have the same opportunity cost, one person will have a comparative advantage in one good, and the other person will have a comparative advantage in the other good.

Table 1

The Opportunity Cost of Meat and Potatoes

	Opportunity Cost of:	
	1 oz of Meat	**1 oz of Potatoes**
Firdaus the farmer	4 oz potatoes	¼ oz meat
Rashmi the rancher	2 oz potatoes	½ oz meat

3-2c Comparative Advantage and Trade

The gains from specialization and trade are based on comparative advantage. When people produce goods in which they have a comparative advantage, total production rises. The economic pie grows larger. Depending on how this bounty is divided, everyone can be better off.

Once they start to trade, Firdaus spends more time growing potatoes, and Rashmi works more on producing meat. Total potato production increases from 40 to 44 ounces, and total meat production increases from 16 to 18 ounces. Firdaus and Rashmi share the benefits of the greater production.

The gains are reflected in the implicit prices that the trading partners pay each other. Because Firdaus and Rashmi have different opportunity costs, they both get a bargain. That is, each of them benefits from trade by obtaining a good at a price that is lower than his or her opportunity cost of that good.

Consider the deal from Firdaus's viewpoint. He receives 5 ounces of meat in exchange for 15 ounces of potatoes. In other words, Firdaus buys each ounce of meat for a price of 3 ounces of potatoes. This price of meat is lower than his opportunity cost of an ounce of meat, which is 4 ounces of potatoes. Firdaus benefits from the deal because he gets to buy meat at a good price.

Now consider Rashmi's viewpoint. She gets 15 ounces of potatoes in exchange for 5 ounces of meat. That is, the price of an ounce of potatoes is ⅓ ounce of meat. This price of potatoes is lower than her opportunity cost of an ounce of potatoes, which is ½ ounce of meat. Rashmi benefits because she gets to buy potatoes at a good price.

The story of Rashmi the rancher and Firdaus the farmer has a simple moral: **Specialization and Strategic Interdependence can benefit managers because it allows firms to specialize in the activities in which they have a comparative advantage. This is critical in leveraging business advantages by focusing on producing goods and services in which the firm has a strategic advantage and gains from such specialization and meeting their needs for other inputs which they don't produce by engaging in trade with the ones who do produce them.**

3-2d The Price of the Trade

The principle of comparative advantage helps to explain the gains from specialization and trade, but it raises a couple of related questions: What determines the price at which trade takes place? How are the gains shared between the trading parties? The precise answers to these questions are beyond the scope of this chapter, but here is a general rule: **For both parties to gain from trade, the price at which they trade must lie between their opportunity costs.**

In our example, Firdaus and Rashmi agreed to trade at a rate of 3 ounces of potatoes per ounce of meat. This price is between Rashmi's opportunity cost (2 ounces of potatoes per ounce of meat) and Firdaus's opportunity cost (4 ounces of potatoes per ounce of meat). The price need not be exactly in the middle for both parties to gain, but it must be somewhere between 2 and 4.

Consider what would happen at prices outside this range. If meat was priced below 2 ounces of potatoes, both Firdaus and Rashmi would want to buy meat because it would cost less than each of their opportunity costs. Similarly, if meat was priced above 4 ounces of potatoes, both would want to sell meat because the price would be above their opportunity costs. But they cannot both be buyers of meat, nor can they both be sellers. Someone must take the other side of the deal. Trade doesn't work at these prices.

A mutually advantageous trade can be struck at prices between 2 and 4. In this range, Rashmi wants to sell meat to buy potatoes, and Firdaus wants to sell potatoes to buy meat. They both get to buy a good at a price below their opportunity cost of that good. In the end, they specialize in the good in which they have a comparative advantage, and, as a result, both of them are better off.

QuickQuiz

3. In an hour, Mahesh can wash 2 cars or mow 1 lawn, and Sonakshi can wash 3 cars or mow 1 lawn. Who has the absolute advantage in car washing, and who has it in lawn mowing?
   a. Mahesh in washing, Sonakshi in mowing
   b. Sonakshi in washing, Mahesh in mowing
   c. Mahesh in washing, neither in mowing
   d. Sonakshi in washing, neither in mowing
4. Between Mahesh and Sonakshi, who has the comparative advantage in car washing, and who has it in lawn mowing?
   a. Mahesh in washing, Sonakshi in mowing
   b. Sonakshi in washing, Mahesh in mowing
   c. Mahesh in washing, neither in mowing
   d. Sonakshi in washing, neither in mowing
5. When Mahesh and Sonakshi produce efficiently and make a mutually beneficial trade based on comparative advantage,
   a. Mahesh mows more, and Sonakshi washes more.
   b. Mahesh washes more, and Sonakshi mows more.
   c. Mahesh and Sonakshi both wash more.
   d. Mahesh and Sonakshi both mow more.

Answers are at the end of the chapter.

3-3 Applications of Comparative Advantage

The principle of comparative advantage explains interdependence and the gains from trade. Because interdependence is so prevalent, the principle of comparative advantage has many applications. Here are two examples, one fanciful and one of great practical importance.

3-3a Should Naomi Osaka Mow Her Own Lawn?

Naomi Osaka is a great athlete. One of the best tennis players of the current era, she can run faster and hit a ball harder than most other people. Most likely, she is talented at other physical activities as well. For example, let's imagine that Osaka can mow her lawn faster than anyone else. But just because she **can** mow her lawn quickly, does this mean she **should**? If she enjoys mowing as a favorite form of relaxation, then of course she should. Otherwise, she can reach a better outcome by applying the concepts of opportunity cost and comparative advantage.

Let's say that Osaka can mow her lawn in 2 hours. In those same 2 hours, she could film a television commercial and earn ₹30,000. By contrast, Hari, the boy next door, can mow Osaka's lawn in 4 hours. In those same 4 hours, Hari could work at McDonald's and earn ₹50.

ADRIAN DENNIS/AFP/GETTY IMAGES

Naomi Osaka may be good at pushing a lawnmower, but it's not her comparative advantage.

Osaka has an absolute advantage in mowing lawns because she can do the work in less time. Yet because her opportunity cost of mowing the lawn is ₹30,000 and Hari's is only ₹50, Hari has a comparative advantage in mowing lawns.

The gains from trade here are tremendous. Rather than mowing her own lawn, Osaka should film the commercial and hire Hari to mow the lawn. As long as Osaka pays Hari more than ₹50 and less than ₹30,000, both are better off.

3-3b Should Indian Firms Trade with Others?

imports
goods produced abroad and sold domestically

exports
goods produced domestically and sold abroad

Just as individuals can benefit from specialization and trade so do firms and economies. Goods produced abroad and sold domestically are **imports**. Those produced domestically and sold abroad are **exports**. In modern India, businesses rarely produce everything in-house. Instead, they engage in complex transactions involving exchanges with suppliers, service providers, customers, and even global competitors. Many of the goods and services consumed in India today ranging from smartphones, high-end machinery, or even logistics services are partially or wholly produced elsewhere. Similarly, Indian firms export software, pharmaceuticals, textiles, and processed food to global markets.

To understand why trade is not only common but often beneficial, let us examine the logic of comparative advantage through a business lens.

An Example: India and Vietnam in the Garments and Electronics Sectors

Suppose Indian and Vietnamese firms simultaneously engage in the production of garments and consumer electronics. For the sake of simplicity, let us assume that an Indian factory and a Vietnamese factory can each produce 1,000 smartphones per day. However, due to India's abundant and skilled textile labor, the Indian firm possesses the capability to produce 2,000 garments per day, whereas the Vietnamese firm's production capacity is limited to 1,000 garments per day.

Now, let us consider the concept of opportunity costs. For the Indian firm, producing 1,000 smartphones entails the forgoing of the production of 2,000 garments. Conversely, for the Vietnamese firm, producing 1,000 smartphones incurs a cost of only 1,000 garments. Consequently, Vietnam holds a comparative advantage in smartphone manufacturing, while India enjoys a comparative advantage in garment production.

If each firm specializes in the sector where its opportunity cost is lower, and subsequently engages in trade, both firms can achieve a greater quantity of garments and smartphones compared to their self-sufficient state. This fundamental principle underpins the concept of strategic interdependence.

Managerial Takeaway

For business managers in India, the lesson is clear: Evaluate not just what you can do, but what you can do better than others. Whether it's deciding to outsource operations, choosing between domestic and export markets, or negotiating supplier contracts, the principle of comparative advantage offers a powerful lens to think strategically.

Conclusion

The benefits of living in an interdependent economy are enormous. When Indians buy rechargable torchlights from China, when residents of Lucknow drink orange juice from Nagpur, and when homeowners hire informal workers to mow their lawns, the same economic forces are at work. The principle of comparative advantage shows that trade can make everyone better off.

Having seen why interdependence is desirable, you might ask how it is possible. How do free societies coordinate the diverse activities of all the people involved in their economies? What ensures that goods and services will get from those who should be producing them to those who should be consuming them? In a world with only two people, such as Rashmi and Firdaus, the answer is simple: They can bargain and allocate resources directly. In the real world, with billions of people, the task is far more complex. As we will see in the next chapter, most economies allocate resources using the market forces of supply and demand.

Ask the Experts — Trade between China and the United States

"Trade with China makes most Americans better off because, among other advantages, they can buy goods that are made or assembled more cheaply in China."

What do economists say?

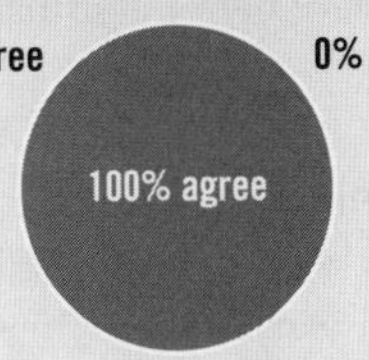

"Some Americans who work in the production of competing goods, such as clothing and furniture, are made worse off by trade with China."

What do economists say?

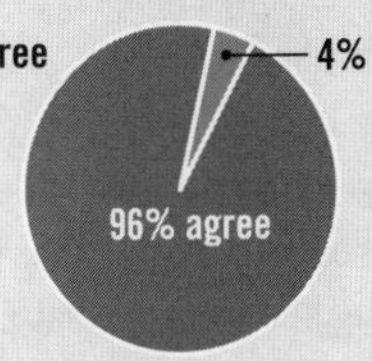

Source: IGM Economic Experts Panel, June 19, 2012.

Quick**Quiz**

6. A nation will typically import those goods in which
   a. the nation has an absolute advantage.
   b. the nation has a comparative advantage.
   c. other nations have an absolute advantage.
   d. other nations have a comparative advantage.
7. Suppose that in the United States, producing an aircraft takes 10,000 hours of labor, and producing a shirt takes 2 hours of labor. In China, producing an aircraft takes 40,000 hours of labor, and producing a shirt takes 4 hours of labor. What will these nations trade?
   a. China will export aircraft, and the United States will export shirts.
   b. China will export shirts, and the United States will export aircraft.
   c. Both nations will export shirts.
   d. There are no gains from trade in this situation.
8. Kiara can cook dinner in 30 minutes and wash the laundry in 20 minutes. Her roommate takes twice as long to do each task. How should the roommates allocate the work?
   a. Kiara should do more of the cooking based on her comparative advantage.
   b. Kiara should do more of the washing based on her comparative advantage.
   c. Kiara should do more of the washing based on her absolute advantage.
   d. There are no gains from trade in this situation.

Answers are at the end of the chapter.

In the News

Economics within a Marriage

An economist argues that you shouldn't always unload the dishwasher just because you're better at it than your partner.

You're Dividing the Chores Wrong

By Emily Oster

No one likes doing chores. In happiness surveys, housework is ranked down there with commuting as activities that people enjoy the least. Maybe that's why figuring out who does which chores usually prompts, at best, tense discussion in a household and, at worst, outright fighting.

If everyone is good at something different, assigning chores is easy. If your partner is great at grocery shopping and you are great at the laundry, you're set. But this isn't always—or even usually—the case. Often one person is better at everything. (And let's be honest, often that person is the woman.) Better at the laundry, the grocery shopping, the cleaning, the cooking. But does that mean she should have to do everything?

Before my daughter was born, I both cooked and did the dishes. It wasn't a big deal, it didn't take too much time, and honestly I was a lot better at both than my husband. His cooking repertoire extended only to eggs and chili, and when I left him in charge of the dishwasher, I'd often find he had run it "full" with one pot and eight forks.

After we had a kid, we had more to do and less time to do it in. It seemed like it was time for some reassignments. But, of course, I was still better at doing both things. Did that mean I should do them both?

I could have appealed to the principle of fairness: We should each do half. I could have appealed to feminism—surveys show that women more often than not get the short end of the chore stick. In time-use data, women do about 44 minutes more housework than men (2 hours and 11 minutes versus 1 hour and 27 minutes). Men outwork women only in the areas of "lawn" and "exterior maintenance." I could have suggested he do more chores to rectify this imbalance, to show our daughter, in the *Free to Be You and Me* style, that Mom and Dad are equal and that housework is fun if we do it together! I could have simply smashed around the pans in the dishwasher while sighing loudly in the hopes he would notice and offer to do it himself.

But luckily for me and my husband, I'm an economist, so I have more effective tools than passive aggression. And some basic economic principles provided the answer. We needed to divide the chores because it is simply not **efficient** for the best cook and dishwasher to do all the cooking and dishwashing. The economic principle at play here is increasing marginal cost. Basically, people get worse when they are tired. When I teach my students this principle, I explain it in the context of managing their employees. Imagine you have a good employee and a not-so-good one. Should you make the good employee do literally everything?

Usually, the answer is no. Why not? It's likely that the not-so-good employee is better at 9 a.m. after a full night of sleep than the good employee is at 2 a.m. after a 17-hour workday. So you want to give at least a few tasks to your worse guy. The same principle applies in your household. Yes, you (or your spouse) might be better at everything. But anyone doing the laundry at 4 a.m. is likely to put the red towels in with the white T-shirts. Some task splitting is a good idea. How much depends on how fast people's skills decay.

To "optimize" your family efficiency (every economist's ultimate goal—and yours, too), you want to equalize effectiveness on the final task each person is doing. Your partner does the dishes, mows the lawn, and makes

Chapter in a Nutshell

- Each person consumes goods and services produced by many other people both within India and around the world. Interdependence and trade are desirable because they allow everyone to enjoy a greater quantity and variety of goods and services.
- There are two ways to compare the abilities of two firms to produce a good. The firm that can produce the good with the smaller quantity of inputs is said to have an **absolute advantage** in producing the good. The firm that has the lower opportunity cost of producing the good is said to have a **comparative advantage**. The gains from trade are based on comparative advantage, not absolute advantage.
- Trade makes everyone better off because it allows people to specialize in those activities in which they have a comparative advantage.
- The principle of comparative advantage applies to countries as well as to people. Economists use the principle of comparative advantage to advocate free trade among countries.

the grocery list. You do the cooking, laundry, shopping, cleaning, and paying the bills. This may seem imbalanced, but when you look at it, you see that by the time your partner gets to the grocery-list task, he is wearing thin and starting to nod off. It's all he can do to figure out how much milk you need. In fact, he is just about as good at that as you are when you get around to paying the bills, even though that's your fifth task.

If you then made your partner also do the cleaning—so it was an even four and four—the house would be a disaster, since he is already exhausted by his third chore while you are still doing fine. This system may well end up meaning one person does more, but it is unlikely to result in one person doing everything.

Once you've decided you need to divide up the chores in this way, how should you decide who does what? One option would be randomly assigning tasks; another would be having each person do some of everything. One spousal-advice website I read suggested you should divide tasks based on which ones you like the best. None of these are quite right. (In the last case, how would anyone ever end up with the job of cleaning the bathroom?)

To decide who does what, we need more economics. Specifically, the principle of comparative advantage. Economists usually talk about this in the context of trade. Imagine Finland is better than Sweden at

DON EMMERT/AFP/GETTY IMAGES

Emily Oster

making both reindeer hats and snowshoes. But they are much, much better at the hats and only a little better at the snowshoes. The overall world production is maximized when Finland makes hats and Sweden makes snowshoes.

We say that Finland has an **absolute advantage** in both things but a **comparative advantage** only in hats. This principle is part of the reason economists value free trade, but that's for another column (and probably another author). But it's also a guideline for how to trade tasks in your house. You want to assign each person the tasks on which he or she has a comparative advantage. It doesn't matter that you have an absolute advantage in everything. If you are much, much better at the laundry and only a little better at cleaning the toilet, you should do the laundry and have your spouse get out the scrub brush. Just explain that it's efficient!

In our case, it was easy. Other than using the grill—which I freely admit is the husband domain—I'm much, much better at cooking. And I was only moderately better at the dishes. So he got the job of cleaning up after meals, even though his dishwasher loading habits had already come under scrutiny. The good news is another economic principle I hadn't even counted on was soon in play: **learning by doing**. As people do a task, they improve at it. Eighteen months into this new arrangement the dishwasher is almost a work of art: neat rows of dishes and everything carefully screened for "top-rack only" status. I, meanwhile, am forbidden from getting near the dishwasher. Apparently, there is a risk that I'll "ruin it." ■

Questions to Discuss

1. In your family, do you think tasks are divided among family members according to comparative advantage? If so, how? If not, how might the allocation of tasks be improved?
2. Do you think being married to an economist would facilitate family harmony or just the opposite?

Ms. Oster is a professor of economics at Brown University.

Source: Slate, November 21, 2012.

Key Concepts

absolute advantage, p. 50
opportunity cost, p. 50
comparative advantage, p. 51
imports, p. 54
exports, p. 54

Questions for Review

1. Under what conditions is the production possibilities frontier linear rather than bowed out?
2. Explain how absolute advantage and comparative advantage differ.

3. Give an example in which one person has an absolute advantage in doing something, but another person has a comparative advantage.
4. Is absolute advantage or comparative advantage more important for trade? Explain your reasoning using the example in your answer to question 3.
5. If two parties trade based on comparative advantage and both gain, in what range must the price implicit in the trade lie?
6. Why do economists oppose policies that restrict trade among nations?

Problems and Applications

1. Manisha can read 20 pages of economics in an hour. She can also read 50 pages of sociology in an hour. She spends 5 hours per day studying.
   a. Draw Manisha's production possibilities frontier for reading economics and sociology.
   b. What is Manisha's opportunity cost of reading 100 pages of sociology?
2. American and Japanese workers can each produce 4 cars per year. An American worker can produce 10 tons of grain per year, while a Japanese worker can produce 5 tons of grain per year. To keep things simple, assume that each country has 100 million workers.
   a. For this situation, construct a table analogous to the table in Figure 1.
   b. Graph the production possibilities frontiers for the American and Japanese economies.
   c. For the United States, what is the opportunity cost of a car? Of grain? For Japan, what is the opportunity cost of a car? Of grain? Put this information in a table analogous to Table 1.
   d. Which country has an absolute advantage in producing cars? In producing grain?
   e. Which country has a comparative advantage in producing cars? In producing grain?
   f. Without trade, half of each country's workers produce cars, and half produce grain. What quantities of cars and grain does each country produce?
   g. Starting from a position without trade, give an example in which trade makes each country better off.
3. Devender and Rishav are roommates. They spend most of their time studying (of course), but they leave some time for their favorite activities: making pizza and brewing root beer. Devender takes 4 hours to brew a gallon of root beer and 2 hours to make a pizza. Rishav takes 6 hours to brew a gallon of root beer and 4 hours to make a pizza.
   a. What is each roommate's opportunity cost of making a pizza? Who has the absolute advantage in making pizza? Who has the comparative advantage in making pizza?
   b. If Devender and Rishav trade foods with each other, who will trade pizza in exchange for root beer?
   c. The price of pizza can be expressed in terms of gallons of root beer. What is the highest price at which pizza can be traded that would make both roommates better off? What is the lowest price? Explain.
4. Suppose that there are 10 million workers in Canada and that each of these workers can produce either 2 cars or 30 bushels of wheat in a year.
   a. What is the opportunity cost of producing a car in Canada? What is the opportunity cost of producing a bushel of wheat in Canada? Explain the relationship between the opportunity costs of the two goods.
   b. Draw Canada's production possibilities frontier. If Canada chooses to consume 10 million cars, how much wheat can it consume without trade? Label this point on the production possibilities frontier.
   c. Now suppose that the United States offers to buy 10 million cars from Canada in exchange for 20 bushels of wheat per car. If Canada continues to consume 10 million cars, how much wheat does this deal allow Canada to consume? Label this point on your diagram. Should Canada accept the deal?
5. England and Scotland both produce scones and sweaters. Suppose that an English worker can produce 50 scones per hour or 1 sweater per hour. Suppose that a Scottish worker can produce 40 scones per hour or 2 sweaters per hour.
   a. Which country has the absolute advantage in the production of each good? Which country has the comparative advantage?
   b. If England and Scotland decide to trade, which commodity will Scotland export to England? Explain.

c. If a Scottish worker could produce only 1 sweater per hour, would Scotland still gain from trade? Would England still gain from trade? Explain.

6. The following table describes the production possibilities of two cities in the country of Cricketopia:

	Pairs of Red Socks per Worker per Hour	Pairs of White Socks per Worker per Hour
Mumbai	3	3
Delhi	2	1

a. Without trade, what is the price of white socks (in terms of red socks) in Mumbai? What is the price in Delhi?
b. Which city has an absolute advantage in the production of each color sock? Which city has a comparative advantage in the production of each color sock?
c. If the cities trade with each other, which color sock will each export?
d. What is the range of prices at which mutually beneficial trade can occur?

7. A German worker takes 400 hours to produce a car and 2 hours to produce a case of wine. A French worker takes 600 hours to produce a car and X hours to produce a case of wine.
a. For what values of X will gains from trade be possible? Explain.
b. For what values of X will Germany export cars and import wine? Explain.

8. Suppose that in a year, an American worker can produce 100 shirts or 20 computers, and a Chinese worker can produce 100 shirts or 10 computers.
a. For each country, graph the production possibilities frontier. Suppose that without trade, the workers in each country spend half their time producing each good. Identify this point in your graphs.
b. If these countries were open to trade, which country would export shirts? Give a specific numerical example and show it on your graphs. Which country would benefit from trade? Explain.
c. Explain at what price of computers (in terms of shirts) the two countries might trade.
d. Suppose that China catches up with American productivity so that a Chinese worker can produce 100 shirts or 20 computers in a year. What pattern of trade would you predict now? How does this advance in Chinese productivity affect the economic well-being of the two countries' citizens?

9. Are the following statements true or false? Explain your answer in each case.
a. "Two countries can achieve gains from trade even if one of the countries has an absolute advantage in the production of all goods."
b. "Certain talented people have a comparative advantage in everything they do."
c. "If a certain trade is good for one person, it can't be good for the other one."
d. "If a certain trade is good for one person, it is always good for the other one."
e. "If trade is good for a country, it must be good for everyone in the country."

Quick**Quiz Answers**

1. **b** 2. **c** 3. **d** 4. **b** 5. **a** 6. **d** 7. **b** 8. **d**

Chapter

4

The Market Forces of Supply and Demand

When a cold wave hits Maharashtra, the price of Aam Ras rises in supermarkets throughout India. When the weather turns warm in Shimla every summer, the price of hotel rooms in Goa plummets. When a war breaks out in the Middle East, the price of gasoline in India rises, and the price of a used SUV falls. What do these events have in common? They all show the workings of supply and demand.

Supply and **demand** are the two words economists use most often—and for good reason. They are the forces that make market economies work, determining the quantity of each good produced and the price at which it is sold. It is no different for a manager. If a manager wants to know how events and policies affect the economy or her business in general, she has to study supply and demand.

This chapter introduces the theory of supply and demand. It considers how buyers and sellers behave and interact, how supply and demand determine prices, and how prices allocate scarce resources.

SHIFT DRIVE/SHUTTERSTOCK.COM, ERDARK/E+/GETTY IMAGES

4-1 Markets and Competition

The terms **supply** and **demand** refer to the behavior of people as they interact in competitive markets. Let's first discuss the meaning of the terms **market** and **competition**.

4-1a What Is a Market?

market
a group of buyers and sellers of a particular good or service

A **market** is a group of buyers and sellers of a good or service. The buyers determine the demand for the product, and the sellers determine the supply of the product.

Markets take many forms. Some are highly organized. In the markets for wheat and corn, buyers and sellers meet at a specific time and place, knowing how much of these agricultural commodities they are willing to buy and sell at various prices. An auctioneer keeps the process orderly by arranging sales and (most importantly) finding the prices that bring the buying and selling into balance.

More often, markets are less organized than that. For example, consider the market for ice cream in a particular town. Ice-cream buyers do not all meet at any one time or place. The sellers are in several locations and offer somewhat different toppings and flavors. No auctioneer calls out the price of a sundae. Each seller posts a price for an ice-cream cone, and each buyer decides how many to buy at each store. Nonetheless, these consumers and producers of ice cream are closely connected. The buyers are choosing among the various sellers to satisfy their cravings, and the sellers are all trying to attract the same buyers to make their businesses succeed. Even though they do not look as organized, the ice-cream buyers and sellers form a market.

4-1b What Is Competition?

The ice-cream market, like many markets in the economy, is highly competitive. Buyers know that there are several sellers from which to choose, and sellers are aware that each of their products is similar to those offered by others. As a result, the price of ice cream and the quantity sold are determined not by any single buyer or seller but by all the buyers and sellers as they interact in the marketplace.

competitive market
a market in which there are many buyers and many sellers so each has a negligible impact on the market price

Economists use the term **competitive market** to describe a market in which there are so many buyers and sellers that each has little effect on the market price. Each seller has limited control over the price because many other sellers are offering similar products. A seller has little reason to charge less than the going price, and if the seller charges more, buyers will go elsewhere. Similarly, no single buyer can influence the price because each buyer purchases only a small amount.

In this chapter, we keep things simple by assuming that markets are **perfectly competitive**. In this ideal, albeit rare, but extreme form of competition, a market has two characteristics:

(1) The goods offered for sale are all exactly the same, and (2) the buyers and sellers are so numerous that no single buyer or seller has any influence over the market price. Because buyers and sellers in perfectly competitive markets must accept the price the market determines, they are said to be **price takers**. At the market price, buyers can buy all they want, and sellers can sell all they want.

There are some markets in which the assumption of perfect competition applies perfectly. In a local subzi mandi, for example, there are scores of vegetable sellers who sell vegetables and hundreds of consumers who use vegetables and derived products. Because no single buyer or seller can influence the price of a vegetable, each takes the market price as given.

Not all goods and services are sold in perfectly competitive markets. For example, some markets have only one seller, and this seller sets the price. A seller in such a market is called a **monopoly**. A local cable television company, for instance, is a monopoly if residents of the town have only one company from which to buy cable service. Many other markets fall between the extremes of perfect competition and monopoly.

But perfectly competitive markets are a useful place to start. They are the easiest to analyze because everyone participating in them takes the price as given by market conditions. Moreover, because some degree of competition is present in most markets, many of the lessons learned studying supply and demand under perfect competition apply to more complex markets as well.

Quick**Quiz**

1. The best definition of a market is
   a. a store that offers a variety of goods and services.
   b. a place where buyers meet and an auctioneer calls out prices.
   c. a group of buyers and sellers of a good or service.
   d. a venue where the sole supplier of a good offers its product.
2. In a perfectly competitive market,
   a. each seller tries to distinguish itself by offering a better product than its rivals.
   b. each seller takes the price of its product as set by market conditions.
   c. each seller tries to undercut the prices charged by its rivals.
   d. one seller has successfully outcompeted its rivals, so no other sellers remain.
3. The market for which product best fits the definition of a perfectly competitive market?
   a. eggs
   b. tap water
   c. movies
   d. computer operating systems

Answers are at the end of the chapter.

4-2 Demand

Let's begin our study of markets by examining the behavior of buyers, particularly those who love ice cream. (And who doesn't?)

4-2a The Demand Curve: The Relationship between Price and Quantity Demanded

The **quantity demanded** of any good is the amount that buyers are willing and able to purchase. Many things determine the quantity demanded of a good, but one determinant plays a central role: its price. If the price of ice cream rose to ₹200 per scoop, most people would buy less. They might buy frozen yogurt instead. If the price of ice cream fell to ₹50 per scoop, they might buy more. This relationship between price and quantity demanded is true for most goods. In fact, it is so pervasive that economists call it the **law of demand**: Other things being equal, when the price of a good rises, the quantity demanded falls, and when the price falls, the quantity demanded rises.

quantity demanded
the amount of a good that buyers are willing and able to purchase

law of demand
the claim that, other things being equal, the quantity demanded of a good falls when the price of the good rises

The table in Figure 1 shows how many ice-cream cones Karishma would buy each month at different prices. If ice-cream cones are free, Karishma buys 12 cones per month. At ₹10 per cone, she buys 10 per month. As the price rises further, she

Figure 1

Karishma's Demand Schedule and Demand Curve

The demand schedule is a table that shows the quantity demanded at each price. The demand curve, which graphs this schedule, illustrates how the quantity demanded changes as the price varies. Because a lower price increases the quantity demanded, the demand curve slopes downward.

Price of Ice-Cream Cone	Quantity of Cones Demanded
₹0	12 cones
10	10
20	8
30	6
40	4
50	2
60	0

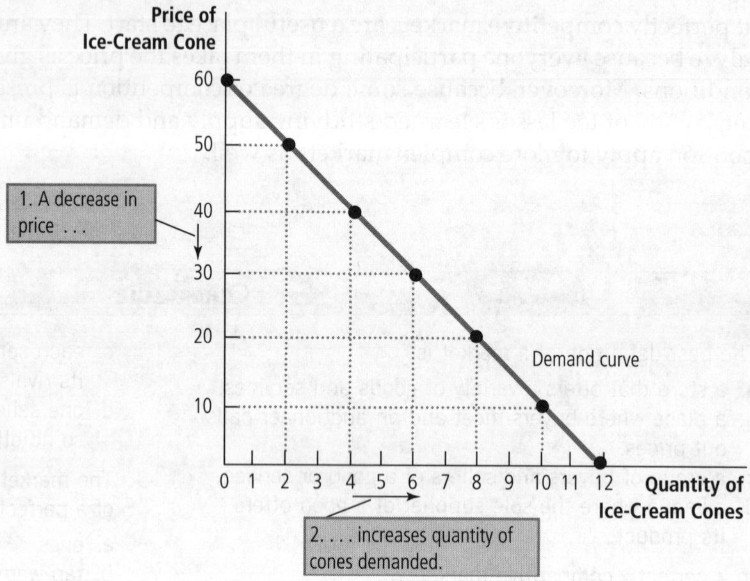

buys fewer and fewer cones. When the price reaches ₹60, Karishma doesn't buy any ice cream at all. This table is called a **demand schedule**. It shows the relationship between the price of a good and the quantity demanded, holding constant everything else that influences how much of the good a consumer wants to buy.

demand schedule
a table that shows the relationship between the price of a good and the quantity demanded

The graph in Figure 1 uses the numbers from the table to illustrate the law of demand. By convention, the price of ice cream is on the vertical axis, and the quantity demanded is on the horizontal axis. The line relating price and quantity demanded is the **demand curve**. It slopes downward because, other things being equal, a lower price increases the quantity demanded.

demand curve
a graph of the relationship between the price of a good and the quantity demanded

4-2b Market Demand versus Individual Demand

The demand curve in Figure 1 shows an individual's demand for a product. But to analyze how markets work, it's important to know the **market demand**, the sum of all the individual demands for a particular good or service.

The table in Figure 2 shows the demand schedules for ice cream for two people—Karishma and Nikhil. At any price, Karishma's demand schedule shows how many cones she buys, and Nikhil's shows the same information for him. The market demand at each price is the sum of their individual demands.

The graph in Figure 2 shows the demand curves for these demand schedules. To obtain the market demand curve, we add the individual demand curves **horizontally**. That is, to find the total quantity demanded at any price, we add the individual quantities demanded, which are found on the horizontal axis of

Figure 2

Market Demand as the Sum of Individual Demands

The quantity demanded in a market is the sum of the quantities demanded by all the buyers at each price. Thus, the market demand curve is found by adding the individual demand curves horizontally. At a price of ₹40, Karishma demands 4 ice-cream cones, and Nikhil demands 3, so the quantity demanded in the market at this price is 7 cones.

Price of Ice-Cream Cone	Karishma		Nikhil		Market
₹0	12	+	7	=	19 cones
10	10		6		16
20	8		5		13
30	6		4		10
40	4		3		7
50	2		2		4
60	0		1		1

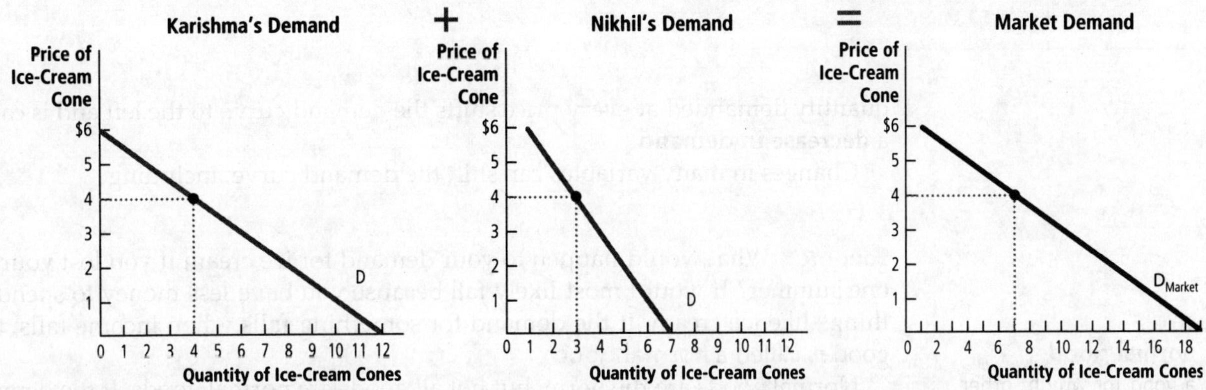

the individual demand curves. The market demand curve is crucial for analyzing how markets function. It shows how the total quantity demanded of a good varies as its price changes, holding constant all the other factors that affect consumer purchases.

4-2c Shifts in the Demand Curve

Because the market demand curve holds other things constant, it need not be stable over time. If something happens to alter the quantity demanded at any given price, the demand curve shifts.

For example, suppose the Indian Medical Association discovers that people who regularly eat ice cream live longer, healthier lives. Such a marvelous discovery would raise the demand for ice cream. At any price, buyers would now want to purchase more ice cream, and the demand curve for ice cream would shift.

Figure 3 illustrates shifts in demand. A change that increases the quantity demanded at every price, such as this wondrous but imaginary discovery, shifts the demand curve to the right and is called an **increase in demand**. A change that reduces the

Figure 3

Shifts in the Demand Curve

A change that increases the quantity that buyers want to purchase at any price shifts the demand curve to the right. A change that decreases the quantity that buyers want to purchase at any price shifts the demand curve to the left.

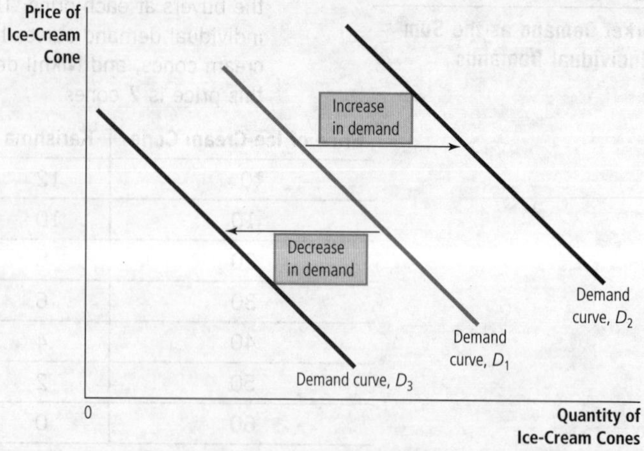

quantity demanded at every price shifts the demand curve to the left and is called a **decrease in demand**.

Changes in many variables can shift the demand curve, including:

Income What would happen to your demand for ice cream if you lost your job one summer? It would most likely fall because you have less money to spend on things like ice cream. If the demand for something falls when income falls, that good is called a **normal good**.

normal good
a good for which, other things being equal, an increase in income leads to an increase in demand

Normal goods are the norm, but not all goods are normal goods. If the demand for something rises when income falls, that good is called an **inferior good**. An example of an inferior good might be bus rides. As your income falls, you are less likely to buy a car or take an Uber and more likely to ride a bus.

inferior good
a good for which, other things being equal, an increase in income leads to a decrease in demand

Prices of Related Goods Suppose that the price of frozen yogurt declines. The law of demand says that you will buy more of it. At the same time, you may buy less ice cream. Because ice cream and frozen yogurt are both cold, sweet, creamy desserts, they satisfy similar cravings. When a fall in the price of one good, like frozen yogurt, reduces the demand for another good, like ice cream, the two goods are called **substitutes**. Substitutes are often pairs of goods that are used in place of each other, such as pani puris and bhelpuri, sweaters and hoodies, and movie tickets and video streaming services.

substitutes
two goods for which an increase in the price of one leads to an increase in the demand for the other

Now suppose that the price of walnut brownies declines. According to the law of demand, you will buy more walnut brownies. Yet in this case, you may be inclined to buy more ice cream as well because ice cream and hot brownies go well together. When a fall in the price of one good, like hot walnut brownies, raises the demand for another good, like ice cream, the two goods are called **complements**. Complements are often pairs of goods that are used together, such as electricity and air conditioners, computers and software, and parathas and pickle.

complements
two goods for which an increase in the price of one leads to a decrease in the demand for the other

Table 1

Variables That Influence Buyers

This table lists the variables that affect how much of any good consumers choose to buy. Notice the special role that the price of the good plays: A change in that price represents a movement along the demand curve, while a change in one of the other variables shifts the curve.

Variable	A Change in This Variable . . .
Price of the good itself	Represents a movement along the demand curve
Income	Shifts the demand curve
Prices of related goods	Shifts the demand curve
Tastes	Shifts the demand curve
Expectations	Shifts the demand curve
Number of buyers	Shifts the demand curve

Tastes If you like kesar-pista ice cream, you will buy more of it. While individual tastes, like preferences for ice-cream flavors, are critically important for explaining demand, economists typically don't try to explain them. This is because they are unique to you, though affected by historical and psychological forces. Economists do, however, examine what happens when tastes change.

Expectations Your views about the future may affect your demand for something today. If you expect a higher income next month, you may choose to save less now and spend more on ice cream today. If you believe ice cream will be cheaper tomorrow, you may be reluctant to buy a cone at today's price.

Number of Buyers In addition to the factors that influence the behavior of individual buyers, market demand depends on how many of these buyers there are. If Palash were to join Karishma and Nikhil as an ice-cream consumer, the quantity demanded would be higher at every price, and market demand would increase.

Summary The demand curve shows what happens to the quantity demanded of a good as its price varies, holding constant all the other variables that influence buyers. When one of these other variables changes, the quantity demanded at each price changes, and the demand curve shifts. Table 1 lists the variables that influence how much of a good consumers choose to buy.

If you have trouble remembering whether you need to shift or move along the demand curve, it helps to recall a lesson from the appendix to Chapter 2. A curve shifts when there is a change in a relevant variable that is not measured on either axis. Because the price is on the vertical axis, a change in price represents a movement along the demand curve. By contrast, income, the prices of related goods, tastes, expectations, and the number of buyers are not measured on either axis, so a change in one of these variables shifts the demand curve.

PABLO DEL RIO SOTELO/SHUTTERSTOCK.COM

Case Study

Two Ways to Reduce Smoking

Because smoking can harm you and those around you, policymakers often want to reduce the amount that people smoke. Consider two paths for achieving this goal.

One way to reduce smoking is to shift the demand curve for cigarettes and other tobacco products. This can be done through public service announcements, mandatory health warnings on cigarette packages, playing Rahul Dravid's messages through advertisements on tobacco hazards before movie screenings, and the "Smoking Kills" tag on television whenever a smoking scene shows up, all of which are aimed at reducing the quantity of cigarettes demanded at any price. When successful, these policies shift the demand curve for cigarettes to the left, as in panel (a) of Figure 4.

Another way to discourage smoking is to raise the price of cigarettes. When the government taxes cigarettes, the companies that make and sell them pass most of the tax on to consumers in the form of higher prices. Because people tend to buy less when the price rises, this policy also reduces smoking. But this approach does not shift the demand curve. Instead, the change appears as a movement along the same curve to a point with a higher price and lower quantity, as in panel (b) of Figure 4.

How much does the amount of smoking respond to changes in the price of cigarettes? Economists have studied what happens when the tax on cigarettes changes. They have found that a ten percent price increase causes a four percent reduction in

Figure 4

Shifts in the Demand Curve versus Movements along the Demand Curve

When warnings on cigarette packages persuade smokers to smoke less, the demand curve for cigarettes shifts to the left. In panel (a), the curve shifts from D_1 to D_2. At a price of ₹50 per pack, the quantity demanded falls from 20 to 10 cigarettes per day, as reflected by the shift from point A to point B. By contrast, when a tax raises the price of cigarettes, the demand curve does not shift. Instead, there is a movement to a different point on the demand curve. In panel (b), when the price rises from ₹50 to ₹100, the quantity demanded falls from 20 to 12 cigarettes per day, as reflected by the movement from point A to point C.

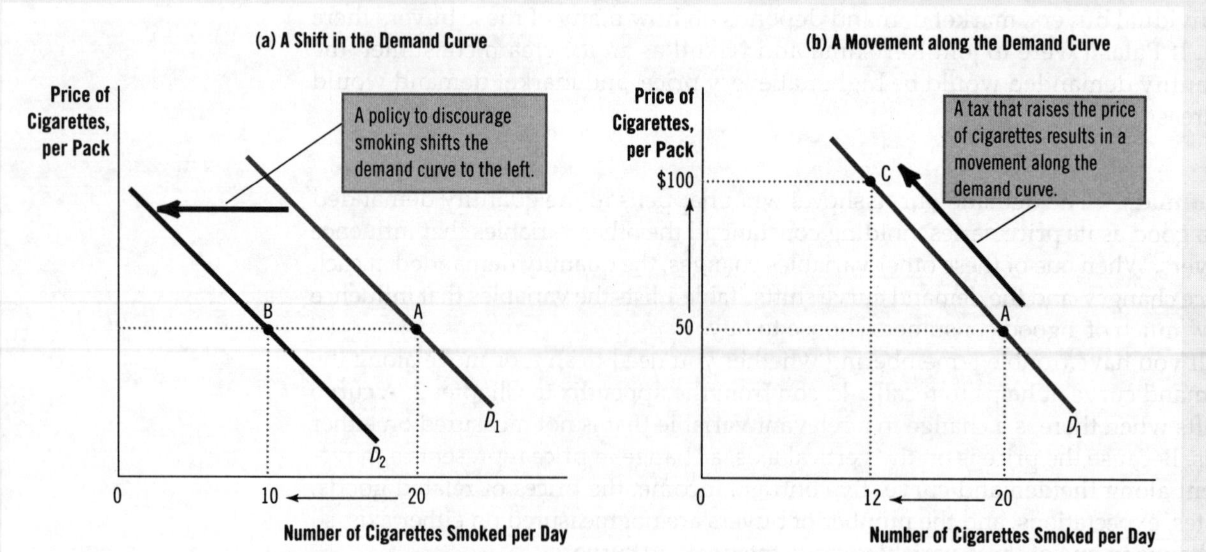

the quantity demanded. Teenagers are especially sensitive to the price of cigarettes: A ten percent price increase causes a 12 percent drop in teenage smoking.

A related question is how the price of cigarettes affects the demand for other products, such as drugs. Opponents of cigarette taxes sometimes argue that tobacco and drugs are substitutes, so high cigarette prices encourage drugs use. By contrast, many experts on substance abuse view tobacco as a "gateway drug," leading young people to experiment with other harmful substances. Most studies of the data are consistent with this latter view. They find that lower cigarette prices are associated with greater use of drugs. In other words, tobacco and drugs appear to be complements rather than substitutes. ●

Quick**Quiz**

4. A change in which of the following will NOT shift the demand curve for hamburgers?
   a. the price of hot dogs
   b. the price of hamburgers
   c. the price of hamburger buns
   d. the income of hamburger consumers
5. Which of the following will shift the demand curve for pizza to the right?
   a. an increase in the price of hamburgers, a substitute for pizza
   b. an increase in the price of root beer, a complement to pizza
   c. the departure of college students when they leave for summer vacation
   d. a decrease in the price of pizza
6. If pasta is an inferior good, then the demand curve shifts to the _______ when _______ rises.
   a. right; the price of pasta
   b. right; consumers' income
   c. left; the price of pasta
   d. left; consumers' income

Answers are at the end of the chapter.

4-3 Supply

Buyers are only half the story of how markets work. Sellers are the other half. Let's now consider the sellers of ice cream.

4-3a The Supply Curve: The Relationship between Price and Quantity Supplied

The **quantity supplied** of any good or service is the amount that sellers are willing and able to sell. There are many determinants of the quantity supplied, but again, price plays a special role. When the price of ice cream is high, selling ice cream is very profitable, so the quantity supplied is large. Sellers work long hours, buy many ice-cream machines, and hire many workers. By contrast, when the price is low, the business is less profitable, so sellers produce less. Some sellers may even shut down, reducing their quantity supplied to zero. This relationship between price and the quantity supplied is called the **law of supply**: Other things being equal, when the price of a good rises, the quantity supplied also rises, and when the price falls, the quantity supplied falls as well.

quantity supplied
the amount of a good that sellers are willing and able to sell

law of supply
the claim that, other things being equal, the quantity supplied of a good rises when the price of the good rises

supply schedule
a table that shows the relationship between the price of a good and the quantity supplied

supply curve
a graph of the relationship between the price of a good and the quantity supplied

The table in Figure 5 shows the quantity of ice-cream cones supplied each month by Ben, an ice-cream seller, at various prices of ice cream. At a price below ₹20, Ben does not supply any ice cream at all. As the price rises, he supplies a greater and greater quantity. This table is called the **supply schedule**. It shows the relationship between the price of a good and the quantity supplied, holding constant everything else that influences how much of the good producers want to sell.

The graph in Figure 5 uses numbers from the table to illustrate the law of supply. The curve relating price and the quantity supplied is the **supply curve**. The supply

Figure 5

Ben's Supply Schedule and Supply Curve

The supply schedule is a table that shows the quantity supplied at each price. The supply curve, which graphs the supply schedule, illustrates how the quantity supplied changes as a good's price varies. Because a higher price increases the quantity supplied, the supply curve slopes upward.

Price of Ice-Cream Cone	Quantity of Cones Supplied
₹0	0 cones
10	0
20	1
30	2
40	3
50	4
60	5

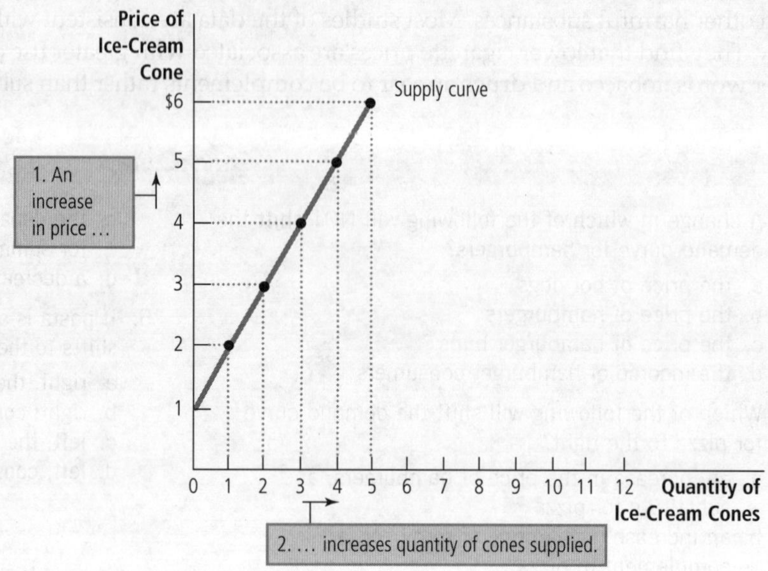

curve slopes upward because, other things being equal, a higher price means a greater quantity supplied.

4-3b Market Supply versus Individual Supply

Just as market demand is the sum of the demands of all buyers, market supply is the sum of the supplies of all sellers. The table in Figure 6 shows the supply schedules for the market's two ice-cream producers—Ben and Virat. At any price, Ben's supply schedule tells us the quantity that Ben supplies, and Virat's supply schedule tells us how much Virat supplies. The market supply is the sum of the two individual supplies.

The graph in Figure 6 shows the supply curves that correspond to the supply schedules. As with demand curves, the market supply curve is obtained by adding the individual supply curves **horizontally**. That is, to find the total quantity supplied at any price, we add the individual quantities, which are located on the horizontal axis of the individual supply curves. The market supply curve shows how the total quantity supplied varies as the price varies, holding constant all other factors that influence producers' decisions about how much to sell.

4-3c Shifts in the Supply Curve

Because a market supply curve holds constant all the variables other than price that affect quantity supplied, it can move over time. When one of these other variables

Figure 6

Market Supply as the Sum of Individual Supplies

The quantity supplied in a market is the total quantity supplied by all sellers at each price. You can build the market supply curve by adding the individual supply curves horizontally. At a price of ₹40, Ben supplies 3 ice-cream cones, and Virat supplies 4 ice-cream cones, so the total quantity supplied at the price of ₹40 is 7 cones.

Price of Ice-Cream Cone	Ben		Virat		Market
₹0	0	+	0	=	0 cones
10	0		0		0
20	1		0		1
30	2		2		4
40	3		4		7
50	4		6		10
60	5		8		13

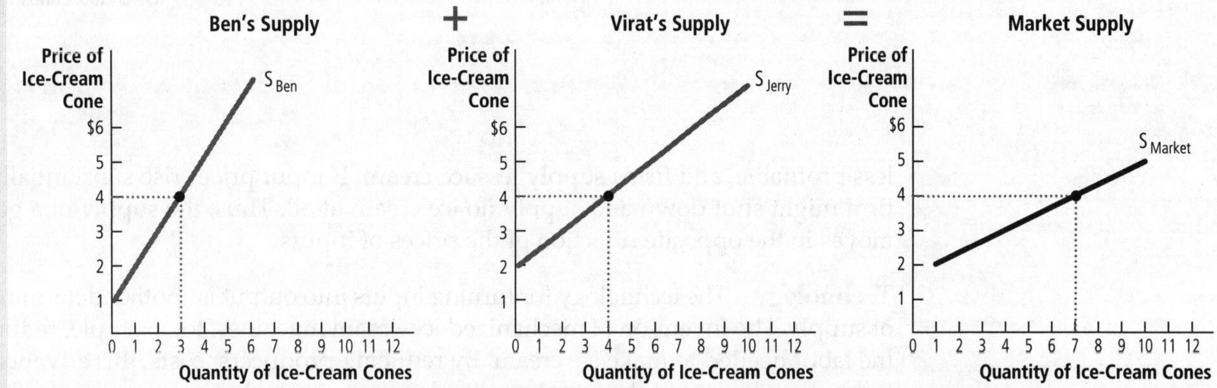

changes, the quantity that producers want to sell at any price changes, and the supply curve shifts.

For example, suppose the price of sugar falls. Because sugar is an input in the production of ice cream, the lower price of sugar makes selling ice cream more profitable. This increases the ice-cream supply: At any price, sellers are willing to produce more. As a result, the supply curve shifts to the right.

Figure 7 illustrates shifts in supply. A change that raises the quantity supplied at every price, such as a fall in the price of sugar, shifts the supply curve to the right and is called an **increase in supply**. A change that reduces the quantity supplied at every price shifts the supply curve to the left and is called a **decrease in supply**.

Many variables can shift the supply curve. The most important ones include:

Input Prices Ice-cream sellers use various inputs to make their product: cream, sugar, flavoring, ice-cream machines, the buildings in which the ice cream is made, and the labor of the workers who mix the ingredients and operate the machines. When the price of one or more of these inputs rises, producing ice cream becomes

Figure 7

Shifts in the Supply Curve

A change that raises the quantity that sellers want to produce at any price shifts the supply curve to the right. A change that lowers the quantity that sellers want to produce at any price shifts the supply curve to the left.

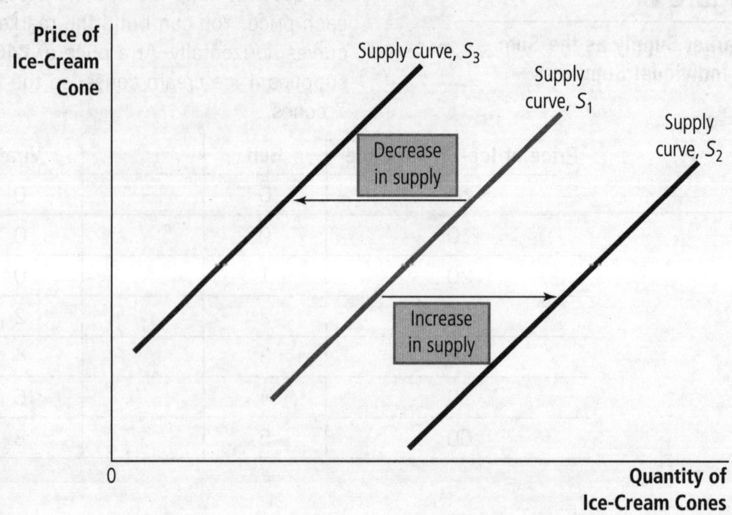

less profitable, and firms supply less ice cream. If input prices rise substantially, a firm might shut down and supply no ice cream at all. Thus, the supply of a good moves in the opposite direction of the prices of inputs.

Technology The technology for turning inputs into output is another determinant of supply. The invention of mechanized ice-cream machines, for example, reduced the labor needed to make ice cream. By reducing producers' costs, this advance in technology increased the supply. In the long run, such changes in technology are among the most potent forces affecting market outcomes.

Expectations The amount that ice-cream makers supply may depend on their expectations about the future. For example, if they expect the price to rise, they may put some of their current production into storage and supply less to the market today.

Number of Sellers In addition to the factors that influence the behavior of individual sellers, market supply depends on how many sellers there are in the market. If Ben or Virat retires from the ice-cream business, the market supply falls. If Rohit starts a new ice-cream business, the market supply rises.

Summary The supply curve shows what happens to the quantity supplied when a good's price varies, holding constant all the other variables that influence sellers. When one of these other variables changes, the quantity supplied at each price changes, and the supply curve shifts. Table 2 lists the variables that influence how much producers choose to sell.

Once again, to remember whether you need to shift or move along the supply curve, keep this in mind: A curve shifts only when there is a change in a relevant variable that isn't named on either axis. Price is on the vertical axis, so a change in price is represented by a movement along the supply curve. By contrast, because input prices, technology, expectations, and the number of sellers are not measured on either axis, a change in one of these variables shifts the supply curve.

Table 2

Variables That Influence Sellers

This table lists the variables that affect how much of any good producers choose to sell. Notice the special role that the price of the good plays: A change in that price represents a movement along the supply curve, while a change in one of the other variables shifts the curve.

Variable	A Change in This Variable . . .
Price of the good itself	Represents a movement along the supply curve
Input prices	Shifts the supply curve
Technology	Shifts the supply curve
Expectations	Shifts the supply curve
Number of sellers	Shifts the supply curve

Quick**Quiz**

7. What event moves pizza suppliers up along a given supply curve?
   a. an increase in the price of pizza
   b. an increase in the price of root beer, a complement to pizza
   c. a decrease in the price of cheese, an input to pizza
   d. a kitchen fire that destroys a popular pizza joint
8. What event shifts the supply curve for pizza to the right?
   a. an increase in the price of pizza
   b. an increase in the price of root beer, a complement to pizza
   c. a decrease in the price of cheese, an input to pizza
   d. a kitchen fire that destroys a popular pizza joint
9. Movie tickets and video streaming services are substitutes. If the price of video streaming increases, what happens in the market for movie tickets?
   a. The supply curve shifts to the left.
   b. The supply curve shifts to the right.
   c. The demand curve shifts to the left.
   d. The demand curve shifts to the right.

Answers are at the end of the chapter.

4-4 Supply and Demand Together

Let's now combine supply and demand to see how they determine the price and quantity of a good sold in a market.

4-4a Equilibrium

Figure 8 shows the market supply curve and market demand curve together. Notice that there is one point at which the supply and demand curves intersect. This point is the market's **equilibrium**. The price at this intersection is the **equilibrium price**, and the quantity is the **equilibrium quantity**. Here, the equilibrium price is ₹40.00 per cone, and the equilibrium quantity is 7 cones.

The dictionary defines **equilibrium** as a situation in which forces are in balance. This sense of balance is key to the concept of a market equilibrium. **At the equilibrium price, the quantity of the good that buyers are willing and able to buy exactly balances the quantity that sellers are willing and able to sell.** The equilibrium price is sometimes called the **market-clearing price** because, at this price, everyone in the market has been satisfied: Buyers have bought all they want to buy, and sellers have sold all they want to sell.

equilibrium
a situation in which the market price has reached the level at which the quantity supplied equals the quantity demanded

equilibrium price
the price that balances the quantity supplied and the quantity demanded

equilibrium quantity
the quantity supplied and the quantity demanded at the equilibrium price

Figure 8

The Equilibrium of Supply and Demand

The market's equilibrium is where the supply and demand curves intersect. At the equilibrium price, the quantity supplied equals the quantity demanded. Here, the equilibrium price is ₹40. At this price, 7 ice-cream cones are supplied, and 7 are demanded.

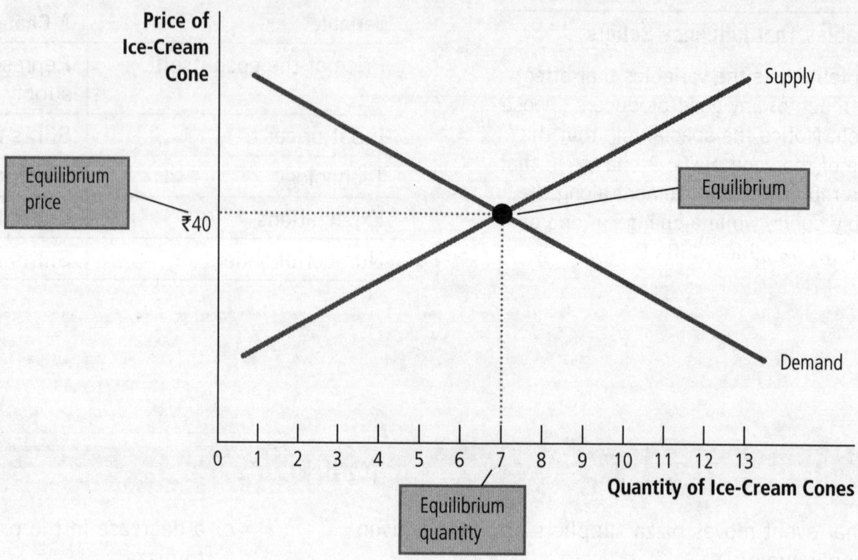

The actions of buyers and sellers move markets toward the equilibrium of supply and demand. To see why, consider what happens when the market price does not equal the equilibrium price.

Suppose first that the market price is above the equilibrium price, as in panel (a) of Figure 9. At a price of ₹50 per cone, the quantity supplied (10 cones) exceeds the quantity demanded (4 cones). There is a **surplus** of the good: Producers are unable to sell all they want at the going price. A surplus is sometimes called a situation of **excess supply**. When there is a surplus in the ice-cream market, sellers find their freezers increasingly full of ice cream they would like to sell but cannot. They respond by cutting prices. Falling prices, in turn, increase the quantity demanded and decrease the quantity supplied. These changes represent movements **along** the supply and demand curves, not shifts in the curves. Prices continue to fall until the market reaches the equilibrium.

surplus
a situation in which the quantity supplied is greater than the quantity demanded

Suppose now that the market price is below the equilibrium price, as in panel (b) of Figure 9. In this case, the price is ₹30 per cone, and the quantity demanded exceeds the quantity supplied. There is a **shortage** of the good: Consumers are unable to buy all they want at the going price. A shortage is sometimes called a situation of **excess demand**. When a shortage occurs in the ice-cream market, buyers must wait in long lines for a chance to buy one of the few cones available. With too many buyers chasing too few goods, sellers can raise prices without losing sales. These price increases cause the quantity demanded to fall and the quantity supplied to rise. Again, these changes are depicted as movements **along** the supply and demand curves, and they move the market closer to equilibrium.

shortage
a situation in which the quantity demanded is greater than the quantity supplied

Regardless of where the price starts, the activities of buyers and sellers push the market price toward equilibrium. Once the market reaches equilibrium, all buyers and sellers are satisfied in the sense that they can buy and sell the amount they

Figure 9

Markets Not in Equilibrium

In panel (a), there is a surplus. Because the market price of ₹50 is above the equilibrium price, the quantity supplied (10 cones) exceeds the quantity demanded (4 cones). Producers try to increase sales by cutting the price, moving it toward its equilibrium level. In panel (b), there is a shortage. Because the market price of ₹30 is below the equilibrium price, the quantity demanded (10 cones) exceeds the quantity supplied (4 cones). With too many buyers chasing too few goods, producers raise the price. In both cases, the price adjustment moves the market toward the equilibrium of supply and demand.

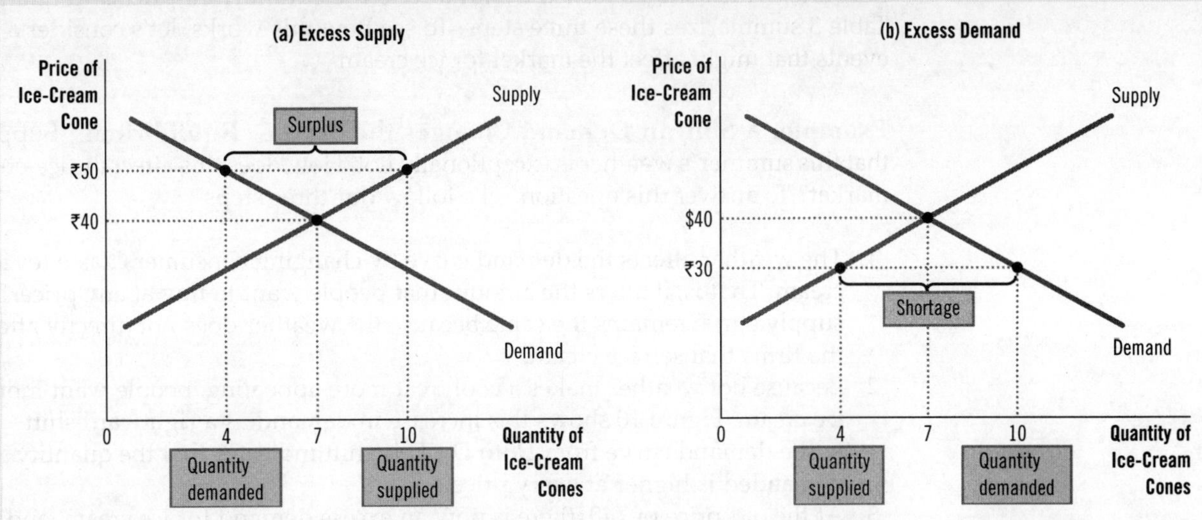

want at the going price. At that point, there is no further upward or downward pressure on the price. How quickly equilibrium is reached varies from market to market depending on how quickly prices adjust. In most well-functioning markets, surpluses and shortages are only temporary because prices quickly move toward their equilibrium levels. This phenomenon is so pervasive that it is called the **law of supply and demand**: The price of any good adjusts to bring the quantity supplied and the quantity demanded into balance.

law of supply and demand
the claim that the price of any good adjusts to bring the quantity supplied and the quantity demanded of that good into balance

4-4b Three Steps to Analyzing Changes in Equilibrium

Supply and demand together determine a market's equilibrium, which in turn determines the price and quantity of the good that buyers purchase and sellers

produce. The equilibrium price and quantity depend on the positions of the supply and demand curves. When an event shifts one of these curves, the equilibrium changes, resulting in a new price and a new quantity exchanged between buyers and sellers.

When analyzing how an event affects the market's equilibrium, we proceed in three steps. First, we decide if the event shifts the supply curve, the demand curve, or both. Second, we decide whether the curve shifts to the right or to the left. Third, we use a supply-and-demand diagram to compare the initial equilibrium with the new one, which shows how the shift affects the equilibrium price and quantity. Table 3 summarizes these three steps. To see how this works, let's consider a few events that might affect the market for ice cream.

Example: A Shift in Demand Changes the Market Equilibrium Suppose that this summer's weather is exceptionally hot. How does this affect the ice-cream market? To answer this question, let's follow our three steps.

1. The weather affects the demand curve by changing consumers' taste for ice cream. That is, it alters the amount that people want to buy at any price. The supply curve remains the same because the weather does not directly affect the firms that sell ice cream.
2. Because hot weather makes a cool treat more appealing, people want more ice cream. Figure 10 shows this increase in demand as a rightward shift in the demand curve from D_1 to D_2. This shift indicates that the quantity demanded is higher at every price.
3. At the old price of ₹40, there is now an excess demand for ice cream, and this shortage induces firms to raise the price. As Figure 10 shows, the increase in demand raises the equilibrium price from ₹40 to ₹50 and the equilibrium quantity from 7 to 10 cones. In other words, the hot weather increases both the price of ice cream and the quantity sold.

Shifts in Curves versus Movements along Them When hot weather increases the demand for ice cream and drives up the price, the quantity that ice-cream makers supply rises, even though the supply curve remains the same. In this case, economists say there has been an increase in the quantity supplied but no change in supply.

Supply refers to the position of the supply curve, while the **quantity supplied** refers to the amount producers want to sell. In the summer heat, supply does not change because the weather does not affect how much producers want to sell at any price. Instead, the sultry weather makes consumers more eager to buy at any price,

Table 3

Three Steps for Analyzing Changes in Equilibrium

1. Decide if the event shifts the supply or demand curve (or perhaps both).
2. Decide in which direction the curve shifts.
3. Use a supply-and-demand diagram to see how the shift changes the equilibrium price and quantity.

Figure 10

How an Increase in Demand Affects the Equilibrium?

An event that raises the quantity demanded at any price shifts the demand curve to the right. The equilibrium price and quantity both rise. Here, an abnormally hot summer causes buyers to demand more ice cream. The demand curve shifts from D_1 to D_2, causing the equilibrium price to increase from ₹40 to ₹50 and the equilibrium quantity to increase from 7 to 10 cones.

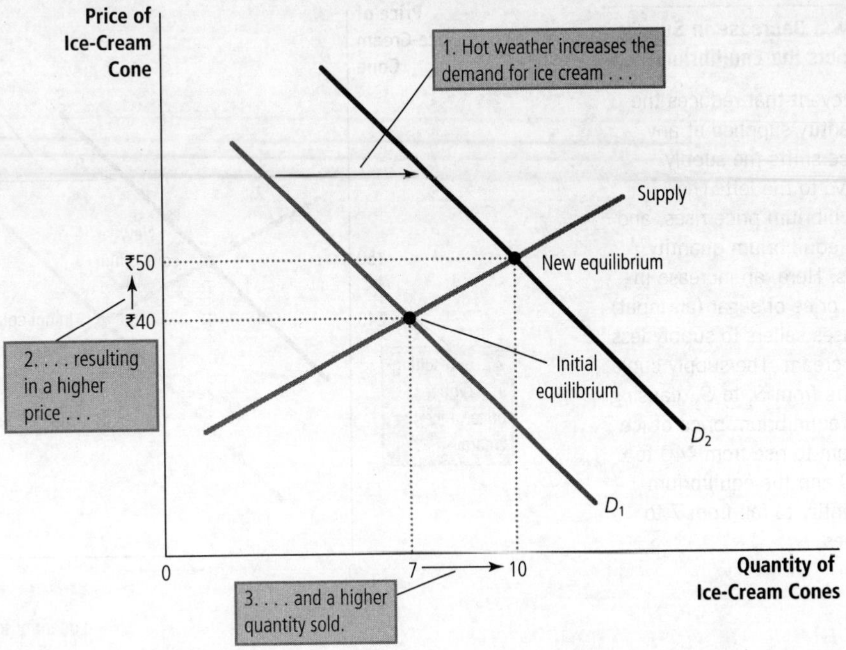

shifting the demand curve to the right. The increase in demand causes the equilibrium price to rise. When the price rises, the quantity supplied rises. This increase in quantity supplied is represented by the movement along the supply curve.

To summarize, a shift **in** the supply curve is called a "change in supply," and a shift **in** the demand curve is called a "change in demand." A movement **along** a fixed supply curve is called a "change in the quantity supplied," and a movement **along** a fixed demand curve is called a "change in the quantity demanded."

Example: A Shift in Supply Changes the Market Equilibrium One August, a cyclone destroys part of the sugarcane crop and drives up the price of sugar. How does this affect the market for ice cream? Again, we follow our three steps.

1. The increase in the price of sugar, an input for ice cream, raises the cost of producing ice cream. It therefore affects the supply curve. The demand curve does not change because the higher cost of inputs does not directly affect the amount of ice cream consumers want to buy.
2. Higher costs reduce the amount of ice cream that producers are willing and able to sell at every price. Figure 11 depicts this decrease in supply as a leftward shift in the supply curve from S_1 to S_2.
3. At the old price of ₹40, there is now an excess demand for ice cream, and this shortage causes firms to raise the price. As Figure 11 shows, the shift in the supply curve raises the equilibrium price from ₹40 to ₹50 and lowers the equilibrium quantity from 7 to 4 cones. Because of the sugar price increase, the price of ice cream rises, and the quantity sold falls.

Figure 11

How a Decrease in Supply Affects the Equilibrium?

An event that reduces the quantity supplied at any price shifts the supply curve to the left. The equilibrium price rises, and the equilibrium quantity falls. Here, an increase in the price of sugar (an input) causes sellers to supply less ice cream. The supply curve shifts from S_1 to S_2, causing the equilibrium price of ice cream to rise from ₹40 to ₹50 and the equilibrium quantity to fall from 7 to 4 cones.

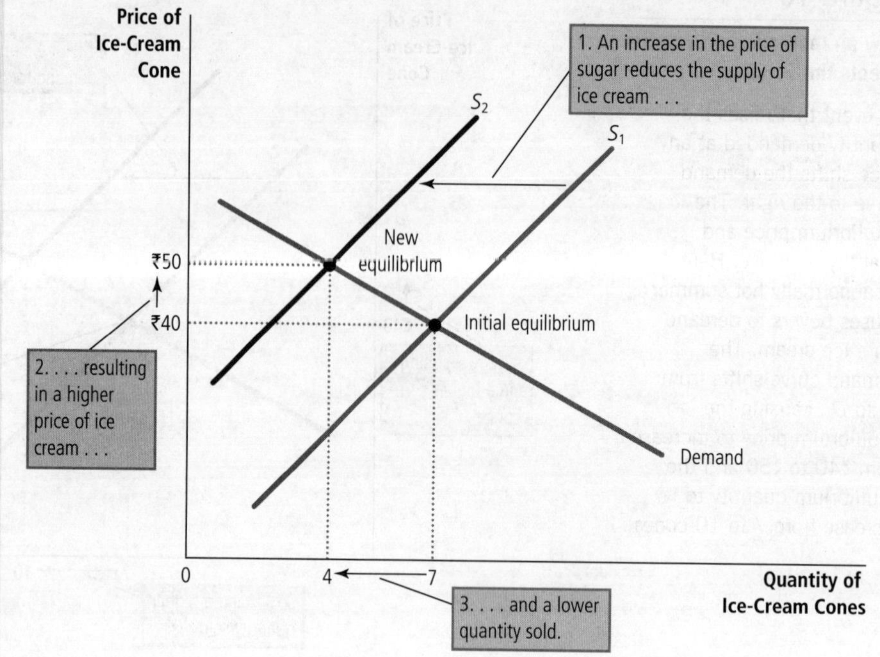

Example: Both Supply and Demand Shift In a series of unfortunate events, a heat wave and a cyclone strike in the same summer. To analyze this nasty combination, we turn again to our three steps.

1. Both curves must shift. The heat affects the demand curve because it alters the amount of ice cream that consumers want to buy at any price. At the same time, the hurricane alters the supply curve for ice cream: By driving up sugar prices, it changes the amount of ice cream that producers want to sell at any price.
2. The curves shift in the same directions as they did earlier: The demand curve shifts to the right, and the supply curve shifts to the left, as Figure 12 shows.
3. Two outcomes are possible, depending on the relative size of the demand and supply shifts. In both cases, the equilibrium price rises. In panel (a), where demand increases substantially while supply falls just a little, the equilibrium quantity also increases. But in panel (b), where supply falls substantially while demand rises just a little, the equilibrium quantity falls. Thus, these events certainly raise the price of ice cream, but their impact on the amount of ice cream sold is ambiguous (that is, it could go either way).

Figure 12

A Shift in Both Supply and Demand

A simultaneous increase in demand and decrease in supply yields two possible outcomes. In panel (a), the equilibrium price rises from P_1 to P_2, and the equilibrium quantity rises from Q_1 to Q_2. In panel (b), the equilibrium price again rises from P_1 to P_2, but the equilibrium quantity falls from Q_1 to Q_2.

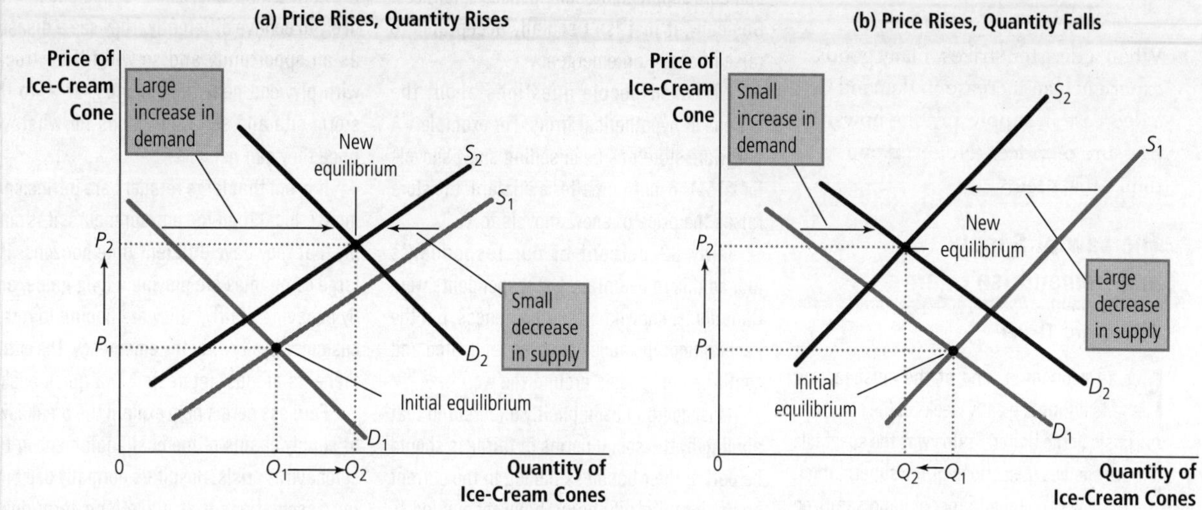

Summary Supply and demand curves help to analyze a change in equilibrium. When an event shifts the supply curve, the demand curve, or perhaps both curves, these tools can predict how the event will alter the price and quantity sold in equilibrium. Table 4 shows the predicted outcome for any combination of shifts in the two curves. To ensure that you understand how to use the tools of supply and demand, pick a few of the table's entries and make sure you can explain to yourself the stated predictions.

Table 4

What Happens to Price and Quantity When Supply or Demand Shifts?

As a quick quiz, make sure you can explain at least a few of the entries in this table using a supply-and-demand diagram.

	No Change in Supply	An Increase in Supply	A Decrease in Supply
No Change in Demand	*P* same *Q* same	*P* down *Q* up	*P* up *Q* down
An Increase in Demand	*P* up *Q* up	*P* ambiguous *Q* up	*P* up *Q* ambiguous
A Decrease in Demand	*P* down *Q* down	*P* down *Q* ambiguous	*P* ambiguous *Q* down

In the News

Price Increases after Disasters

When a disaster strikes, many goods experience an increase in demand or a decrease in supply, putting upward pressure on prices. Not everyone thinks that's fair.

The Law of Supply and Demand Isn't Fair

By Richard Thaler

For an economist, one of the most jarring sights during the early weeks of the coronavirus crisis in the United States was the spectacle of bare shelves in sections of the supermarket.

There was no toilet paper or hand sanitizer. Pasta, flour and even yeast could be hard to find in the early weeks of social distancing as many people decided to take up baking. Of far greater concern, hospitals could not buy enough of the masks, gowns and ventilators required to safely treat Covid-19 patients.

What happened to the laws of supply and demand? Why didn't prices rise enough to clear the market, as economic models predict?

A paper that I wrote with my friends Daniel Kahneman, a psychologist, and Jack Knetsch, an economist, explored this problem. We found that the answer may be summed up with a single word, one you won't find in the standard supply-and-demand models: fairness. Basically, it just isn't socially acceptable to raise prices in an emergency.

We asked people questions about the actions of hypothetical firms. For example: "A hardware store has been selling snow shovels for ₹15. The morning after a blizzard, the store raises the price of snow shovels to ₹20."

Fully 82 percent of our respondents judged this to be unfair. The respondents were Canadians, known for their politeness, but the general findings have now been replicated and confirmed in studies around the world.

Most companies implicitly understand that abiding by the social norms of fairness should be part of their business model. In the current crisis, large retail chains have responded to the shortages of toilet paper not by raising the price but by limiting the amount each customer can buy. And Amazon and eBay prohibited what was viewed as price gouging on their sites.

We have seen similar behavior after hurricanes. As soon as a storm ends, there is typically enormous demand for goods like bottled water and plywood. Big retailers like Home Depot and Walmart anticipate this, sending trucks loaded with supplies to regions just outside the danger zone, ready to be deployed. Then, when it is safe, the stores provide water for free and sell the plywood at the list price **or lower**.

At the same time, some "entrepreneurs" are likely to behave differently. They see a disaster as an opportunity and so will fill up trucks with plywood near their homes, drive to the storm site and sell their goods for whatever price they can get.

It is not that large retailers are intrinsically more ethical than the entrepreneurs; it is simply that they have different time horizons. The large companies are playing a long game, and by behaving "fairly," they are hoping to retain customer loyalty after the emergency. The entrepreneurs are just interested in a quick buck.

Fairness norms help explain the breakdown of supply chains of medical equipment in the coronavirus crisis. Hospitals normally use buying associations that make long-term deals with wholesalers to provide essential supplies. The wholesalers generally want to preserve these relationships and realize that now would not be a good time to raise prices. Often, they are contractually obligated to supply items at prices negotiated before a spike in demand.

One current example is the N95 face mask. At the onset of the pandemic, hospitals had long-term contracts to buy them for about 35 cents each, an executive at a New York hospital told me. When the need for the masks surged, these suppliers were not allowed to raise the price, even if inclined to do so.

QuickQuiz

10. The discovery of a large new reserve of crude oil will shift the ________ curve for gasoline, leading to a ________ equilibrium price.
    a. supply; higher
    b. supply; lower
    c. demand; higher
    d. demand; lower

11. If the economy goes into a recession and incomes fall, what happens in the markets for inferior goods?
    a. Prices and quantities both rise.
    b. Prices and quantities both fall.
    c. Prices rise, and quantities fall.
    d. Prices fall, and quantities rise.

But others along the supply chain could make big profits by diverting masks to anyone willing to pay top dollar. That left hospitals in a bind. As the coronavirus spread in New York, the executive's hospital searched frantically for masks, eventually paying an overseas supplier ₹6 each, for hundreds of thousands of them, when the regular stock was desperately short.

When anyone tries to reap big profits in an emergency like this, it can look ugly. Consider the case of two brothers who began buying hand sanitizer, masks and other scarce commodities on March 1, the day of the first announcement of a Covid-19 death in the United States. After they sold some of their merchandise at big markups on Amazon and eBay, these outlets cut them off. Eventually, after considerable adverse publicity, the brothers decided to donate their supplies.

Notice that the brothers were making markets more "efficient," by buying low and selling high. If instead of arbitraging coronavirus supplies they had sold shares of airline and hotel companies and bought shares of Netflix and Zoom, they would simply have been considered smart traders. But while smart trading may be fine for investments, it is not considered fair when it involves essential goods during a pandemic.

One can argue that this social norm is harmful in that it prevents markets from doing their magic. For example, Tyler Cowen, the George Mason University economist, has said he wishes it were OK to raise prices for coronavirus essentials.

TAB62/SHUTTERSTOCK.COM

How much would you pay for this in an emergency?

"Higher prices discourage panic buying and increase the chance that the people who truly need particular goods and services have a greater chance of getting them," he wrote.

But which people "truly need" N95 masks? What is the right allocation of masks among well-endowed research hospitals, poorly funded municipal facilities, nursing homes and food processing plants? Supply and demand would tell us that the masks should simply go to the buyer who was willing and able to pay the most for them. But fairness tells us this can't be the only consideration.

As a practical matter for businesses, big and small, that want to keep operating for the long haul, it makes good sense to obey the law of fairness. If the next shortage is meat and a store owner realizes that there is only one package of pork chops left, it would be unwise to sell it at auction to the highest bidder. ■

Questions to Discuss

1. After the onset of a pandemic, do you think you would be more or less likely to find hand sanitizer for sale if the sellers were allowed to increase prices? Why?
2. If the sellers of scarce resources are not allowed to increase prices to equilibrate supply and demand after a disaster, how do you think these resources should be allocated among the population? What are the benefits of your proposal? What problems might arise with your proposal in practice?

Richard Thaler is a professor of economics at the University of Chicago. He won the Nobel prize in economics in 2017.

Source: New York Times, March 24, 2020.

12. What event might lead to an increase in the equilibrium price of jelly and a decrease in the equilibrium quantity of jelly sold?
    a. an increase in the price of peanut butter, a complement to jelly
    b. an increase in the price of Marshmallow Fluff, a substitute for jelly
    c. an increase in the price of grapes, an input into jelly
    d. an increase in consumers' incomes, as long as jelly is a normal good

13. An increase in _______ will cause a movement along a given supply curve, which is called a change in _______.
    a. supply; demand
    b. supply; quantity demanded
    c. demand; supply
    d. demand; quantity supplied

Answers are at the end of the chapter.

Case Study

Air Conditioner Use, Energy Regulation, and Managerial Responses

In the Indian context, the market for air conditioners (ACs) presents a compelling case study. As urban incomes rise and summers become hotter, the demand for ACs experience substantial growth. However, this growth has brought about challenges such as increased pressure on energy infrastructure and environmental concerns.

To effectively manage demand and promote energy efficiency, the Bureau of Energy Efficiency (BEE) in India has implemented a star rating system for energy consumption. Higher-rated ACs consume less electricity and are marketed as cost-effective over time. Simultaneously, several Indian states have introduced time-of-day tariffs, imposing higher electricity rates during peak hours.

These interventions demonstrate the influence of both price and non-price incentives on consumer behavior. From a managerial standpoint, these developments have implications for:

1. Product Design: Companies like Voltas and LG are investing in inverter technology and energy-efficient models to align with regulatory requirements and consumer preferences.
2. Inventory Management: Demand may peak during specific seasons and time slots, necessitating improved forecasting and stocking strategies.
3. Marketing: Communication strategies now emphasize not only comfort but also long-term savings and environmental responsibility.

This example illustrates how external regulatory changes can reshape the demand curve and encourage firms to pursue innovation and strategic repositioning.

4-5 Conclusion: How Prices Allocate Resources?

This chapter analyzed supply and demand in a single market. The discussion centered on the market for ice cream, but the lessons apply to most other markets as well. When you go to a store to buy something, you are contributing to the demand for that item. When you look for a job, you are contributing to the supply of labor services. Because supply and demand are such pervasive forces in market economies, the model of supply and demand is a powerful analytical tool.

ROBERT J. DAY/THE NEW YORKER COLLECTION/THE CARTOON BANK

"Two dollars" "—and seventy-five cents."

One of the **Principles of Managerial Economics** in Chapter 1 is that markets are usually a good way to organize economic activity. It is still too early to judge whether market outcomes are good or bad, but this chapter has begun to show how markets work. In any economic system, scarce resources must be allocated among competing uses. Market economies harness the forces of supply and demand to serve that end. Supply and demand together determine the prices of the economy's many different goods and services. Prices, in turn, are the signals that guide the allocation of resources.

For example, consider the allocation of beachfront land. Because the amount of this land is limited, not everyone can enjoy the luxury of living by the beach. Who gets this resource? The answer is whoever is willing and able to pay the price. The price of beachfront land adjusts until the quantity of land demanded balances the quantity supplied. In market economies, prices are the mechanism for rationing scarce resources.

Similarly, prices determine who produces each good and how much is produced. For instance, consider farming. Because everyone needs food to survive, it is crucial that some people work on farms. What determines who is a farmer and who is not? In a free society, no government planning agency makes this decision to ensure an adequate food supply. Instead, the allocation of labor to farms is based on the job decisions of millions of workers. This decentralized system performs well because these decisions depend on prices. The prices of food and the wages of farmworkers (the price of their labor) adjust to ensure that enough people choose to be farmers.

If a person had never seen a market economy in action, the whole idea might seem preposterous. Economies are enormous groups of people engaged in a multitude of interdependent activities. What prevents decentralized decision making from degenerating into chaos? What coordinates the actions of the millions of people with their varying abilities and desires? What ensures that what needs to be done is, in fact, done? The answer, in a word, is **prices**. If an invisible hand guides market economies, as Adam Smith famously suggested, the price system is the baton with which the invisible hand conducts the economic orchestra.

Ask the Experts: Price Gouging

"Laws to prevent high prices for essential goods in short supply in a crisis would raise social welfare."

What do economists say?

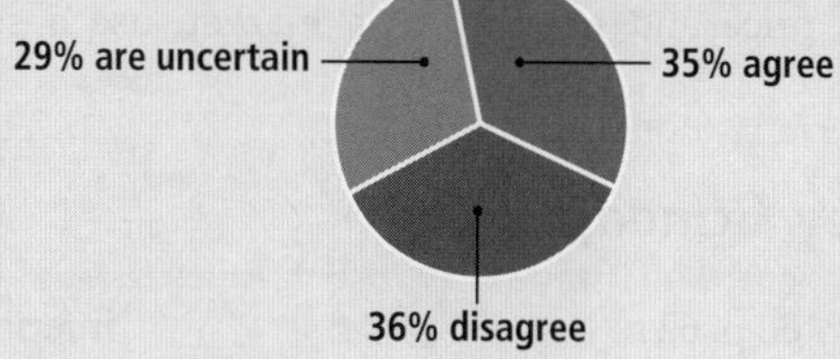

Source: IGM Economic Experts Panel, May 26, 2020.

Chapter in a Nutshell

- Economists use the model of supply and demand to analyze competitive markets. In such markets, there are many buyers and sellers, each of whom has little or no influence on the market price.
- The demand curve for a good shows how the quantity demanded depends on the price. According to the law of demand, as the good's price falls, the quantity demanded rises. That's why the demand curve slopes downward.
- In addition to price, other determinants of how much consumers want to buy include income, the prices of substitutes and complements, tastes, expectations, and the number of buyers. When one of these factors changes, the quantity demanded at each price changes, and the demand curve shifts.
- The supply curve for a good shows how the quantity supplied depends on the price. According to the law of supply, as the good's price rises, the quantity supplied rises. That's why the supply curve slopes upward.
- In addition to price, other determinants of how much producers want to sell include input prices, technology, expectations, and the number of sellers. When one of these factors changes, the quantity supplied at each price changes, and the supply curve shifts.

- The intersection of the supply and demand curves represents the market equilibrium. At the equilibrium price, the quantity demanded equals the quantity supplied.
- The behavior of buyers and sellers naturally drives markets toward equilibrium. When the market price is above the equilibrium price, there is a surplus of the good, which causes the market price to fall. When the market price is below the equilibrium price, there is a shortage, which causes the market price to rise.
- To analyze how any event influences the equilibrium price and quantity in a market, use a supply-and-demand diagram and follow these three steps. First, decide if the event shifts the supply curve or the demand curve (or both). Second, decide in which direction the curve shifts. Third, compare the new equilibrium with the initial one.
- In market economies, prices are the signals that guide decisions and allocate scarce resources. For every good in the economy, the price ensures that supply and demand are in balance. The equilibrium price determines how much buyers choose to consume and how much sellers choose to produce.

Key Concepts

market, p. 62
competitive market, p. 62
quantity demanded, p. 63
law of demand, p. 63
demand schedule, p. 64
demand curve, p. 64
normal good, p. 66
inferior good, p. 66
substitutes, p. 66
complements, p. 66
quantity supplied, p. 69
law of supply, p. 69
supply schedule, p. 69
supply curve, p. 69
equilibrium, p. 73
equilibrium price, p. 73
equilibrium quantity, p. 73
surplus, p. 74
shortage, p. 74
law of supply and demand, p. 75

Questions for Review

1. What is a competitive market? Briefly describe a type of market that is **not** perfectly competitive.
2. What are the demand schedule and the demand curve, and how are they related? Why does the demand curve slope downward?
3. Does a change in consumers' tastes lead to a movement along the demand curve or to a shift in the demand curve? Does a change in price lead to a movement along the demand curve or to a shift in the demand curve? Explain your answers.
4. Harry's income declines, and as a result, he buys more pumpkin juice. Is pumpkin juice an inferior good or a normal good? What happens to Harry's demand curve for pumpkin juice?
5. What are the supply schedule and the supply curve, and how are they related? Why does the supply curve slope upward?
6. Does a change in producers' technology lead to a movement along the supply curve or to a shift in the supply curve? Does a change in price lead to a movement along the supply curve or to a shift in the supply curve?
7. Define the equilibrium of a market. Describe the forces that move a market toward its equilibrium.
8. Beer and pizza are complements because they are often enjoyed together. When the price of beer rises, what happens to the supply, demand, quantity supplied, quantity demanded, and price in the market for pizza?
9. Describe the role of prices in market economies.

Problems and Applications

1. Explain each of the following statements using supply-and-demand diagrams.
   a. "When a cold wave hits Maharashtra, the price of Aam Ras rises in supermarkets throughout India."
   b. "When the weather turns warm in Shimla every summer, the price of hotel rooms in Goa plummets."
   c. "When a war breaks out in the Middle East, the price of gasoline rises, and the price of a used SUV falls."

2. "An increase in the demand for notebooks raises the quantity of notebooks demanded but not the quantity supplied." Is this statement true or false? Explain.
3. Consider the market for minivans. For each of the events listed here, identify which of the determinants of demand or supply are affected. Also, indicate whether demand or supply increases or decreases. Then, draw a diagram to show the effect on the price and quantity of minivans.
   a. People decide to have more children.
   b. A strike by steelworkers raises steel prices.
   c. Engineers develop new automated machinery for the production of minivans.
   d. The price of sports utility vehicles rises.
   e. A stock market crash lowers people's wealth.
4. Consider the markets for video streaming services, TV screens, and tickets at movie theaters.
   a. For each pair, identify whether they are complements or substitutes:
      - video streaming and TV screens
      - video streaming and movie tickets
      - TV screens and movie tickets
   b. Suppose a technological advance reduces the cost of manufacturing TV screens. Draw a diagram to show what happens in the market for TV screens.
   c. Draw two more diagrams to show how the change in the market for TV screens affects the markets for video streaming and movie tickets.
5. Over the past 40 years, technological advances have reduced the cost of computer chips. How do you think this has affected the market for computers? For computer software? For typewriters?
6. Using supply-and-demand diagrams, show the effects of the following events on the market for sweatshirts.
   a. A hurricane in South Carolina damages the cotton crop.
   b. The price of leather jackets falls.
   c. All colleges require morning exercise in appropriate attire.
   d. New knitting machines are invented.
7. Ketchup is a complement (as well as a condiment) for hot dogs. If the price of hot dogs rises, what happens in the market for ketchup? For tomatoes? For tomato juice? For orange juice?
8. The market for pizza has the following demand and supply schedules:

Price	Quantity Demanded	Quantity Supplied
₹40	135 pizzas	26 pizzas
50	104	53
60	81	81
70	68	98
80	53	110
90	39	121

   a. Graph the demand and supply curves. What are the equilibrium price and quantity in this market?
   b. If the actual price in this market were **above** the equilibrium price, what would drive the market toward equilibrium?
   c. If the actual price in this market were **below** the equilibrium price, what would drive the market toward equilibrium?
9. Consider the following events: Scientists reveal that eating oranges decreases the risk of diabetes, and at the same time, farmers use a new fertilizer that makes orange trees produce more oranges. Illustrate and explain what effect these changes have on the equilibrium price and quantity of oranges.
10. Because bagels and cream cheese are often eaten together, they are complements.
    a. We observe that both the equilibrium price of cream cheese and the equilibrium quantity of bagels have risen. What could be responsible for this pattern: a fall in the price of flour or a fall in the price of milk? Illustrate and explain your answer.
    b. Suppose instead that the equilibrium price of cream cheese has risen, but the equilibrium quantity of bagels has fallen. What could be responsible for this pattern: a rise in the price of flour or a rise in the price of milk? Illustrate and explain your answer.
11. Suppose that the student discounted price of ISL match tickets at your city is determined by market forces. Currently, the demand and supply schedules are as follows:

Price	Quantity Demanded	Quantity Supplied
₹40	10,000 tickets	8,000 tickets
80	8,000	8,000
120	6,000	8,000
160	4,000	8,000
200	2,000	8,000

    a. Draw the demand and supply curves. What is unusual about this supply curve? Why might this be true?

b. What are the equilibrium price and quantity of tickets?

c. Your city plans to increase total enrollment next year by 5,000 students. The additional students will have the following demand schedule:

Price	Quantity Demanded
₹40	4,000 tickets
80	3,000
120	2,000
160	1,000
200	0

Now add the old demand schedule and the demand schedule for the new students to calculate the new demand schedule for the entire college student community. What will be the new equilibrium price and quantity?

QuickQuiz Answers

1. c 2. b 3. a 4. b 5. a 6. d 7. a 8. c 9. d 10. b 11. a 12. c 13. d

Chapter

5

Elasticity and Managerial Decision Making

Imagine that some event drives up the price of petrol in India. It could be tensions in the Middle East that tighten the world supply of oil, a booming Chinese economy that boosts the world demand for oil, or a hike in the gasoline taxes. How would India consumers respond to the higher price?

It is easy to answer this question in a broad fashion: People would buy less petrol. This follows from the law of demand in the previous chapter: Other things being equal, when the price of a good rises, the quantity demanded falls. But you might want a precise answer. By how much would gas purchases fall? This question can be answered using a concept called **elasticity**.

Elasticity is a measure of how much buyers and sellers respond to changes in market conditions. When studying how events or policies affect a market, we can discuss not only the direction of the effects but also their magnitude.

AZMANJAKA/E+/GETTY IMAGES; CARLOS FLORES/EYEEM/GETTY IMAGES

In the market for gasoline, studies typically find that the quantity demanded responds to gasoline prices more in the long run than in the short run. A 10 percent increase in the price reduces gasoline consumption by about 2.5 percent after a year but by about 6 percent after five years. About half of the long-run reduction comes from less driving, and half comes from switching to more fuel-efficient cars—and, increasingly, to electric cars that require no gasoline at all. Both responses are reflected in the demand curve and its elasticity.

5-1 The Elasticity of Demand

In Chapter 4, we noted that consumers usually buy more of a good when its price is lower, when their incomes are higher, when the prices of its substitutes are higher, or when the prices of its complements are lower. The discussion was qualitative, not quantitative. That is, it addressed whether quantity demanded rose or fell but not the size of the change. To measure how much consumers respond to changes in these variables, economists use the concept of **elasticity**.

elasticity
a measure of the responsiveness of the quantity demanded or quantity supplied to a change in one of its determinants

price elasticity of demand
a measure of how much the quantity demanded of a good responds to a change in its price, calculated as the percentage change in quantity demanded divided by the percentage change in price

5-1a The Price Elasticity of Demand and Its Determinants

The law of demand states that a fall in the price of a good raises the quantity demanded. The **price elasticity of demand** measures how much the quantity demanded responds to a change in the price. Demand for a good is said to be **elastic** if the quantity demanded responds substantially to price changes. Demand is said to be **inelastic** if the quantity demanded responds only slightly to price changes.

The price elasticity of demand for any good measures how willing consumers are to buy less of it as its price rises. Because a demand curve reflects the economic, social, and psychological forces that shape consumer preferences, there is no simple, universal rule for what determines a demand curve's elasticity. But there are some rules of thumb.

Availability of Close Substitutes Goods with close substitutes tend to have more elastic demand because it is easier for consumers to switch from those goods to others. For example, margarine is a common substitute for butter. Increase the price of butter by a small amount, and you will see its quantity demanded fall by a large amount, assuming the price of margarine is steady. By contrast, eggs don't have a close substitute, so the demand for them is less elastic. Increase the price of eggs by a small amount, and there will not be a big drop in the quantity of eggs demanded.

Necessities and Luxuries For a true necessity, a small price increase won't diminish the amount you purchase by very much: Another way of saying this is that necessities tend to have inelastic demands. For example, when the price of a doctor's visit rises, most people do not cut back sharply on the number of times they go to the doctor, although they might go a little less often. Luxuries are another matter. When the price of sailboats rises, the quantity of sailboats demanded falls substantially. The reason is that most people view sailboats as a luxury. Whether a good is a necessity or a luxury depends not on its intrinsic properties but on the buyer's preferences. For avid sailors with little concern about their health, sailboats might be a necessity with inelastic demand and doctor visits a luxury with elastic demand.

Defining the Market Broadly or Narrowly The elasticity of demand depends on how we draw the market's boundaries. Narrowly defined markets tend to have more elastic demand than broadly defined ones. That's because it is easier to find close substitutes for narrowly defined goods. For example, food, a broad category, has a fairly inelastic demand because there are no good substitutes for food. Ice cream, a narrow category, has a more elastic demand because it is easy to substitute other desserts for ice cream. Vanilla ice cream, an even narrower category, has a very elastic demand because some other flavors of ice cream, such as sweet cream, are almost perfect substitutes for vanilla.

Time Horizon Demand tends to be more elastic over longer periods of time. When the price of gasoline rises, the quantity demanded falls only slightly in the first few months. As time passes, however, people buy more fuel-efficient or all-electric cars, arrange carpools, switch to public transportation, and move closer to work. Over several years, the quantity of gasoline demanded falls more substantially.

5-1b The Price Elasticity of Demand, with Numbers

Now that we have discussed the price elasticity of demand in general terms, let's be more precise about how it is measured. Economists compute the price elasticity of demand as the percentage change in the quantity demanded divided by the percentage change in the price. That is:

$$\text{Price elasticity of demand} = \frac{\text{Percentage change in quantity demanded}}{\text{Percentage change in price}}.$$

For example, suppose that after a 10 percent increase in the price of an ice-cream cone, you buy 20 percent fewer cones. We calculate your elasticity of demand this way:

$$\text{Price elasticity of demand} = \frac{20 \text{ percent}}{10 \text{ percent}} = 2.$$

In this example, the elasticity is 2. That means that the change in quantity demanded is proportionately twice as large as the change in price.

Because the quantity demanded of a good moves in the opposite direction as its price, the percentage change in quantity has the opposite sign as the percentage change in price. In this example, the percentage change in price is a **positive** 10 percent (reflecting an increase), and the percentage change in quantity demanded is a **negative** 20 percent (reflecting a decrease). For this reason, price elasticities of demand are sometimes reported as negative numbers. It is common practice, however, to drop the minus sign and report all price elasticities of demand as positive numbers. (Mathematicians call this the **absolute value.**) With this convention, which this book follows, a larger price elasticity implies a greater responsiveness of quantity demanded to price changes.

5-1c The Midpoint Method: A Better Way to Calculate Percentage Changes and Elasticities

If you try calculating the price elasticity of demand between two points on a demand curve, you will face an annoying problem: The elasticity from point A to point B seems different from the elasticity from point B to point A. Consider this example:

$$\text{Point A : Price} = ₹4 \text{ Quantity} = 120$$
$$\text{Point B : Price} = ₹6 \text{ Quantity} = 80$$

Going from point A to point B, the price rises by 50 percent and the quantity falls by 33 percent, indicating that the price elasticity of demand is 33/50, or 0.66. Going from point B to point A, the price falls by 33 percent and the quantity rises by 50 percent, indicating that the price elasticity of demand is 50/33, or 1.5. This difference arises because the percentage changes are calculated from a different base. Yet the underlying reality—the response of buyers to price changes—is identical whether moving from point A to point B or from point B to point A.

The **midpoint method** for calculating elasticities avoids this confusion. The standard procedure for calculating a percentage change is to divide the change by the initial level. But the midpoint method instead divides the change by the midpoint (or average) of the initial and final levels. For instance, ₹5 is midway between ₹4 and ₹6. Therefore, according to the midpoint method, a change from ₹4 to ₹6 is considered a 40 percent rise because $(6 - 4)/5 \times 100 = 40$. Similarly, a change from ₹6 to ₹4 is considered a 40 percent fall.

Because the midpoint method gives the same answer regardless of the direction of change, it is often used when calculating the price elasticity of demand between two points. In our example, the midpoint between point A and point B is:

$$\text{Midpoint:} \quad \text{Price} = ₹5 \quad \text{Quantity} = 100$$

According to the midpoint method, when going from point A to point B, the price rises by 40 percent and the quantity falls by 40 percent. Similarly, when going from point B to point A, the price falls by 40 percent and the quantity rises by 40 percent. In both directions, the price elasticity of demand equals 1.

The following formula expresses the midpoint method for calculating the price elasticity of demand between two points, denoted (Q_1, P_1) and (Q_2, P_2):

$$\text{Price elasticity of demand} = \frac{(Q_2 - Q_1)/[(Q_2 + Q_1)/2]}{(P_2 - P_1)/[(P_2 + P_1)/2]}.$$

The numerator is the percentage change in quantity using the midpoint method, and the denominator is the percentage change in price using the midpoint method. If you ever need to calculate elasticities, use this formula.

This book rarely performs such calculations. For most purposes here, what elasticity represents—the responsiveness of quantity demanded to price changes—is more important than how it is calculated.

5-1d The Variety of Demand Curves

Economists use elasticity to classify demand curves. When the quantity moves proportionately more than the price, the elasticity is greater than one, and demand is said to be **elastic**. When the quantity moves proportionately less than the price, the elasticity is less than one, and demand is said to be **inelastic**. Finally, when the percentage change in quantity equals the percentage change in price, the elasticity is exactly 1, and demand is said to have **unit elasticity**.

Because the price elasticity of demand measures how much quantity demanded responds to price changes, it is closely related to the slope of the demand curve. Here's a useful rule of thumb: The flatter the demand curve at a given point, the greater the price elasticity of demand. The steeper the demand curve at a given point, the smaller the price elasticity of demand.

Figure 1 shows five cases. In the extreme case of zero elasticity, shown in panel (a), demand is **perfectly inelastic**, and the demand curve is vertical. In this case, regardless of the price, the quantity demanded stays the same. As the elasticity rises, the demand curve gradually flattens, as shown in panels (b), (c), and (d). At the opposite extreme, in panel (e), demand is **perfectly elastic**. This occurs as the price elasticity of demand becomes so large that it approaches infinity. The demand curve becomes horizontal, showing that tiny changes in the price lead to huge changes in the quantity demanded.

If you have trouble keeping straight which curve is **elastic** and which **inelastic**, here's a memory trick: Inelastic curves, such as in panel (a) of Figure 1, look like the letter I. (Economists call it a curve, but when it's perfectly inelastic, it's really a vertical line.) This is not a deep insight, but it might help on your next exam.

5-1e Total Revenue, Price Elasticity of Demand, and Managerial Decision Making

A critical decision that the manager wants to make within a firm would be to understand the impact of a price change on its total profits. Since, profits are revenues net of costs, for now we just focus on the revenue aspect of this decision. Suppose a firm is contemplating a price change of the product it sells. Should it increase or decrease the price? This depends on whether the increase or decrease in price increases or decreases its revenues.

FYI A Few Elasticities from the Real World

We have talked about what elasticity means, what determines it, and how it is calculated. Beyond these general ideas, you might ask for a specific number. How much, precisely, does a good's price influence its quantity demanded?

To answer this question, economists collect market data and apply statistical techniques to estimate the price elasticity of demand. Here are some price elasticities of demand, obtained from various studies, for a range of goods:

Good	Elasticity	
Eggs	0.1	↑ Very inelastic (quantity demanded responds little to price changes)
Healthcare	0.2	
Cigarettes	0.4	
Rice	0.5	
Housing	0.7	
Mutton	1.6	
Peanut Butter	1.7	
Restaurant Meals	2.3	
Cheerios	3.7	
Mountain Dew	4.4	↓ Very elastic (quantity demanded responds strongly to price changes)

These numbers are fun to think about, and they can be useful when comparing markets, but take them with a grain of salt. One reason is that the statistical techniques used to obtain them require some assumptions about the world, and these assumptions might not be true in practice. (The part of economics called econometrics studies these statistical techniques.) Another reason is that the price elasticity of demand need not be the same at all points on a demand curve, as we will see in the case of a linear demand curve. For both reasons, don't be surprised when different studies report different price elasticities of demand for the same good. ■

Figure 1

The Price Elasticity of Demand

The price elasticity of demand determines whether the demand curve is steep or flat. Note that all percentage changes are calculated using the midpoint method.

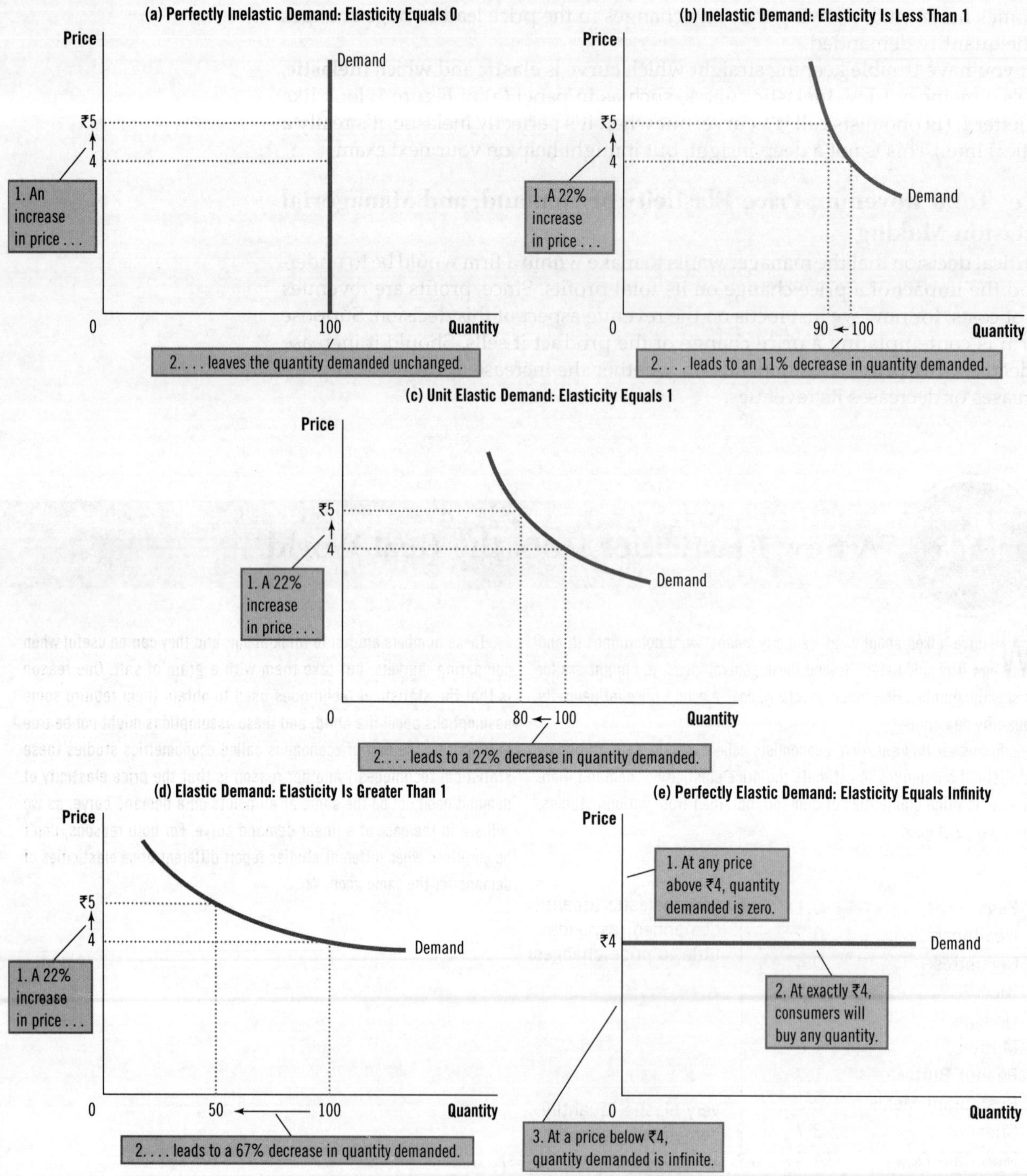

Figure 2

Total Revenue

The area of the box under the demand curve, $P \times Q$, equals the total amount paid by buyers as well as the total revenue received by sellers. Here, at a price of ₹4, the quantity demanded is 100, and total revenue is ₹400.

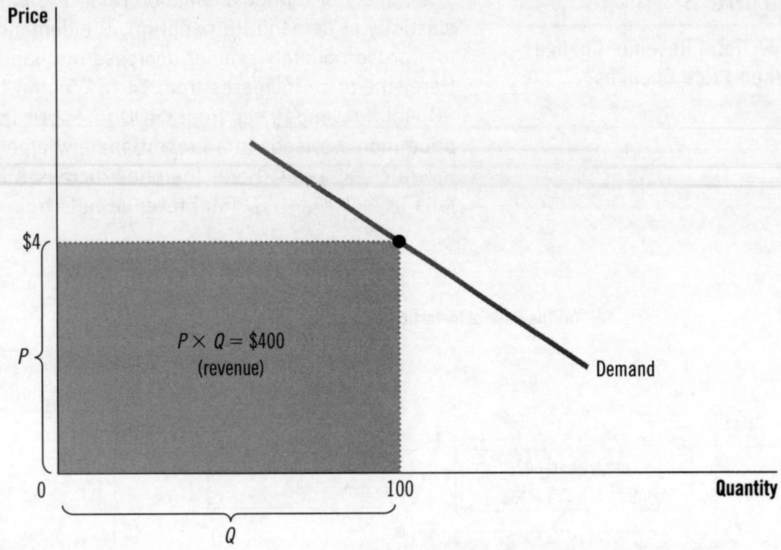

The concept of **total revenue** is relevant here. In mathematical form, total revenue is $P \times Q$, the price of the good times the quantity of the good sold. Figure 2 shows total revenue graphically. The height of the box under the demand curve is P, and the width is Q. The area of this box, $P \times Q$, equals the total revenue in this market. In Figure 2, where P = ₹4 and $Q = 100$, total revenue is ₹4 × 100, or ₹400.

total revenue
the amount paid by buyers and received by the sellers of a good, calculated as the price of the good times the quantity sold

How does total revenue change as one moves along the demand curve? The answer depends on the price elasticity of demand. If demand is inelastic, as in panel (a) of Figure 3, then an increase in the price causes an increase in total revenue. Here, an increase in the price from ₹4 to ₹5 causes the quantity demanded to fall from 100 to 90, so total revenue rises from ₹400 to ₹450. An increase in the price raises $P \times Q$ because the fall in Q is proportionately smaller than the rise in P. In other words, the extra revenue from selling units at a higher price (represented by area A in the figure) more than offsets the decline in revenue from selling fewer units (represented by area B).

The opposite result occurs when demand is elastic: An increase in the price causes total revenue to decline. In panel (b) of Figure 3, for instance, when the price rises from ₹4 to ₹5, the quantity demanded falls from 100 to 70, so total revenue falls from ₹400 to ₹350. Because demand is elastic, the reduction in quantity demanded is so great that it more than offsets the price increase. That is, an increase in the price reduces $P \times Q$ because the fall in Q is proportionately greater than the rise in P. In this case, the extra revenue from selling units at a higher price (area A) is smaller than the decline in revenue from selling fewer units (area B).

The examples in this figure illustrate some general rules:

- When demand is inelastic (a price elasticity less than one), the price and total revenue move in the same direction: If the price increases, total revenue also increases.
- When demand is elastic (a price elasticity greater than one), the price and total revenue move in opposite directions: If the price increases, total revenue decreases.
- If demand is unit elastic (a price elasticity exactly equal to 1), total revenue remains constant when the price changes.

Figure 3

How Total Revenue Changes When Price Changes?

The impact of a price change on total revenue (price times quantity) depends on the elasticity of demand. In panel (a), the demand curve is inelastic. A price increase leads to a proportionately smaller decrease in quantity demanded, so total revenue increases. Here, the price increases from ₹4 to ₹5, and the quantity demanded falls from 100 to 90. Total revenue rises from ₹400 to ₹450. In panel (b), the demand curve is elastic. A price increase leads to a proportionately larger decrease in quantity demanded, so total revenue decreases. Here, the price increases from ₹4 to ₹5, and the quantity demanded falls from 100 to 70. Total revenue falls from ₹400 to ₹350.

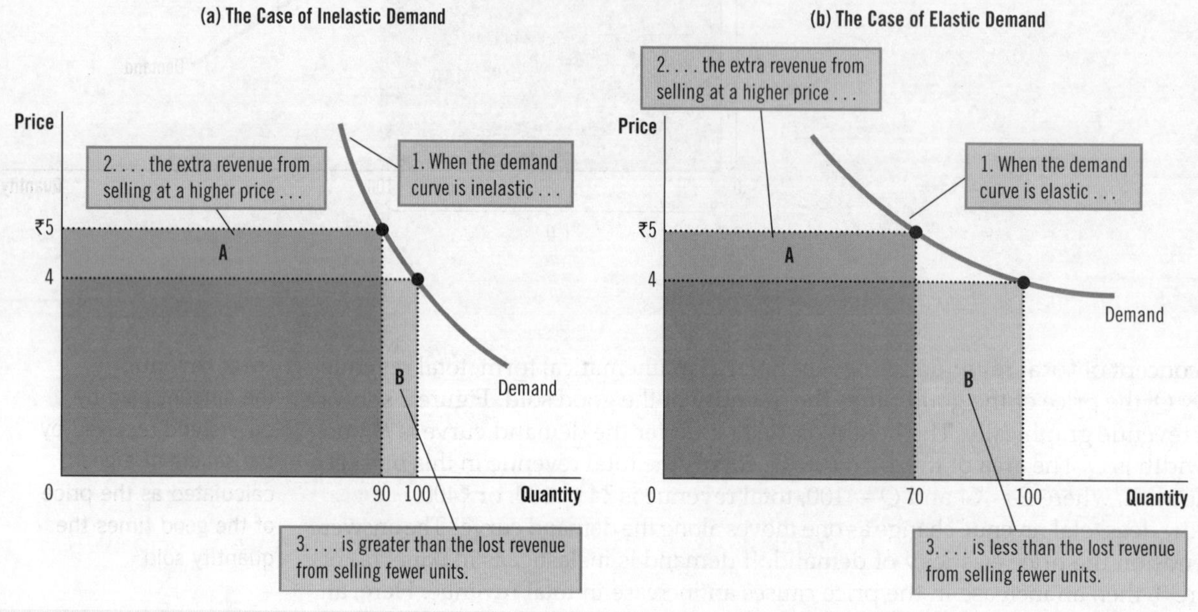

5-1f Elasticity and Total Revenue along a Linear Demand Curve

Let's examine how elasticity varies along a linear demand curve, as shown in Figure 4. Because the demand curve is a straight line, it has a constant slope. Slope is defined as "rise over run," which here is the ratio of the change in price ("rise") to the change in quantity ("run"). In this case, the demand curve's slope is constant because each ₹1 increase in the price causes the same decrease of two units in the quantity demanded.

Even though the slope of a linear demand curve is constant, the elasticity is not. This is because the slope is the ratio of **changes** in the two variables, while the elasticity is the ratio of **percentage changes** in them. You can see this in the table for Figure 4, which shows the demand schedule for the linear demand curve in the graph. The table uses the midpoint method to calculate the price elasticity of demand. It illustrates this fundamental idea: **At points with a low price and high quantity, a linear demand curve is inelastic. At points with a high price and low quantity, a linear demand curve is elastic.**

Figure 4

Elasticity along a Linear Demand Curve

The slope of a linear demand curve is constant, but its elasticity is not. The price elasticity of demand is calculated using the demand schedule and the midpoint method. At points with a low price and high quantity, the demand curve is inelastic. At points with a high price and low quantity, it is elastic.

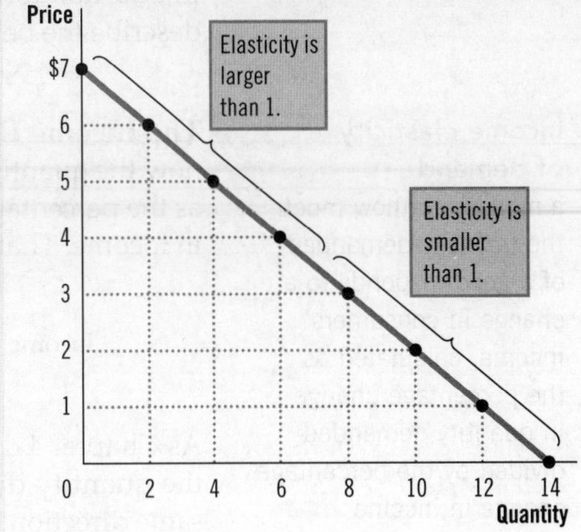

Price	Quantity	Total Revenue (Price × Quantity)	Percentage Change in Price	Percentage Change in Quantity	Elasticity	Description
₹7	0	₹0				
			15	200	13.0	Elastic
6	2	12				
			18	67	3.7	Elastic
5	4	20				
			22	40	1.8	Elastic
4	6	24				
			29	29	1.0	Unit elastic
3	8	24				
			40	22	0.6	Inelastic
2	10	20				
			67	18	0.3	Inelastic
1	12	12				
			200	15	0.1	Inelastic
0	14	0				

The explanation comes from the arithmetic of percentage changes. When the price is low and consumers are buying a lot, a ₹1 price increase and two-unit reduction in quantity demanded constitute a large percentage increase in the price and a small percentage decrease in quantity demanded, resulting in a small elasticity. When the price is high and consumers are not buying much, the same ₹1 price increase and two-unit reduction in quantity demanded constitute a small percentage increase in the price and a large percentage decrease in quantity demanded, resulting in a large elasticity.

The table presents total revenue at each point on the demand curve. These numbers illustrate the relationship between total revenue and elasticity. When the price is ₹1, for instance, demand is inelastic, and a price increase to ₹2 raises total revenue. When the price is ₹5, demand is elastic, and a price increase to ₹6 reduces total revenue. Between ₹3 and ₹4, demand is exactly unit elastic and total revenue is the same at these two prices.

In short, the price elasticity of demand need not be the same at all points on a demand curve. A demand curve with constant elasticity is possible, but it is a special case. A linear demand curve never has a constant elasticity.

5-1g Other Demand Elasticities

In addition to the price elasticity of demand, economists use other elasticities to describe the behavior of buyers in a market.

income elasticity of demand
a measure of how much the quantity demanded of a good responds to a change in consumers' income, calculated as the percentage change in quantity demanded divided by the percentage change in income

The Income Elasticity of Demand The **income elasticity of demand** measures how the quantity demanded changes as consumer income changes. It is calculated as the percentage change in quantity demanded divided by the percentage change in income. That is:

$$\text{Income elasticity of demand} = \frac{\text{Percentage change in quantity demanded}}{\text{Percentage change in income}}.$$

As Chapter 4 discussed, most goods are **normal goods**: Higher income increases the quantity demanded. Because quantity demanded and income move in the same direction, normal goods have positive income elasticities. A few goods, such as bus rides, are **inferior goods**: This doesn't mean that anything is wrong with them, just that higher income reduces the quantity demanded. Because quantity demanded and income move in opposite directions, inferior goods have negative income elasticities.

Even among normal goods, income elasticities vary substantially in size. Necessities such as food tend to have small income elasticities because consumers buy some of these goods even when their incomes are low. (**Engel's Law**, named for the 19th-century statistician who discovered it, says that as a family's income rises, the percent of its income spent on food declines, indicating an income elasticity less than one.) By contrast, luxuries such as diamond jewelry and sailboats tend to have large income elasticities because most consumers feel that they can do without them altogether when their incomes decline.

cross-price elasticity of demand
a measure of how much the quantity demanded of one good responds to a change in the price of another good, calculated as the percentage change in the quantity demanded of the first good divided by the percentage change in the price of the second good

The Cross-Price Elasticity of Demand The **cross-price elasticity of demand** measures how the quantity demanded of one good responds to a change in the price of another. It is calculated as the percentage change in the quantity demanded of good one divided by the percentage change in the price of good two. That is:

$$\text{Cross-price elasticity of demand} = \frac{\text{Percentage change in quantity demanded of good one}}{\text{Percentage change in the price of good two}}$$

Whether the cross-price elasticity is positive or negative depends on whether the two goods are substitutes or complements. As discussed in Chapter 4, **substitutes** are goods that are typically used in place of one another, such as hamburgers and hot dogs. When hot dog prices increase, people grill more hamburgers instead. Because the price of hot dogs and the quantity of hamburgers demanded move in the same direction, the cross-price elasticity is positive. Conversely, **complements** are goods that are typically used together, such as computers and software. In this case, the cross-price elasticity is negative, indicating that an increase in the price of computers reduces the quantity of software demanded.

Demand Elasticities and Managerial Implications

Understanding demand elasticity with respect to price, income, and cross-prices, is central to managerial decision-making, particularly when combined with data-driven estimation techniques that help firms understand competition and consumer segmentation. In general, price-elasticity of demand captures how sensitive customers are to price changes like when demand is highly elastic, as with smartphones or budget airlines, even small price reductions can significantly increase sales volumes, making discounting strategies or penetration pricing effective. In contrast, for inelastic products like medicines, petrol, or electricity, firms can increase prices without major drops in demand, thereby optimizing revenues.

Income elasticity of demand reflects how consumer spending patterns evolve with changes in income levels. Luxury products such as premium cars, high-end electronics, and fine dining display high positive income elasticity, with demand rising rapidly as disposable incomes grow. This is particularly relevant for India's expanding urban middle class. On the other hand, staples like rice, milk, and basic medicines have low-income elasticity, meaning demand remains relatively stable across income shifts.

Meanwhile, cross-price elasticity helps managers understand competitive interactions and complementary product relationships. For substitutes like Ola and Uber, Pepsi and Coke, or Jio and Airtel price changes by one player directly influence demand for the other, requiring continuous monitoring of competitor strategies. For complements, such as air conditioners and electricity tariffs or smartphones and mobile data plans, understanding these interdependencies enables firms to design bundling strategies, manage pricing partnerships, and anticipate regulatory impacts.

It is important to note here that managers do not need any priors about whether two goods are complements or substitutes, or for that matter whether a good is normal or inferior. They just need data to be able to estimate elasticities for the population or sample they are serving and back out the consumer preferences over these goods. That is why elasticity is such a powerful analytical tool for managerial decision making. For instance, modern firms increasingly leverage data analytics and large-scale consumer datasets to estimate these elasticities with precision, converting raw behavioral data into actionable insights. If they are able to find cross-price elasticities which are positive for their good with respect to prices of another good, they can immediately conclude that the other good is a substitute and therefore a competitor for their product. So a price change (decline) by the competing firm has the potential to sway away customers from the manager's firm. The magnitude of the elasticity can give a sense of the intensity of this competition.

Hypothetically, if e-commerce platforms like Amazon and Flipkart can run controlled price experiments and analyze usage data to estimate price sensitivities at a granular level, their analysis will allow personalized pricing and targeted promotions. FMCG companies may want to rely on household consumption surveys and retail panel data to identify income-driven demand shifts across consumer segments, shaping both product positioning and marketing strategies. Similarly, firms analyze cross-price relationships to predict how competitor pricing or regulatory shocks will impact their own demand. In doing so, managers can simulate pricing scenarios, forecast sales, allocate inventories more efficiently and many other similar decisions. In India's highly competitive and rapidly evolving markets, combining economic theory with data-driven elasticity estimation has the potential to equip managers with a powerful decision-making framework which integrates pricing, marketing, product strategy, and competitive positioning to align business objectives with consumer behavior and respond to eventual market realities.

Quick**Quiz**

1. A good tends to have a small price elasticity of demand if
   a. the good is a necessity.
   b. there are many close substitutes.
   c. the market is narrowly defined.
   d. the long-run response is being measured.
2. An increase in a good's price reduces the total amount consumers spend on the good if the ________ elasticity of demand is ________ than one.
   a. income; less
   b. income; greater
   c. price; less
   d. price; greater
3. A linear, downward-sloping demand curve is
   a. inelastic.
   b. unit elastic.
   c. elastic.
   d. inelastic at some points and elastic at others.
4. The citizens of Rohan spend a higher fraction of their income on food than do the citizens of Gondor. The reason could be that
   a. Rohan has lower food prices, and the price elasticity of demand is zero.
   b. Rohan has lower food prices, and the price elasticity of demand is 0.5.
   c. Rohan has lower income, and the income elasticity of demand is 0.5.
   d. Rohan has lower income, and the income elasticity of demand is 1.5.

Answers are at the end of the chapter.

5-2 The Elasticity of Supply

The discussion of supply in Chapter 4 noted that producers of a good offer to sell more of it when its price rises. To turn from qualitative to quantitative statements about quantity supplied, economists again use the concept of elasticity.

5-2a The Price Elasticity of Supply and Its Determinants

price elasticity of supply
a measure of how much the quantity supplied of a good responds to a change in its price, calculated as the percentage change in quantity supplied divided by the percentage change in price

The law of supply states that higher prices increase the quantity supplied. The **price elasticity of supply** measures how much the quantity supplied responds to changes in the price. Supply is said to be **elastic** if the quantity supplied responds substantially to price changes and **inelastic** if the quantity supplied responds only slightly.

The price elasticity of supply depends on the flexibility of sellers to change the amount they produce. Beachfront land has an inelastic supply: As Mark Twain once advised, "Buy land, they're not making it anymore." Manufactured goods, such as books, cars, and televisions, have elastic supplies because firms that produce them can run their factories longer in response to higher prices.

In most markets, supply is more elastic in the long run than in the short run. The reason is simple: Over short periods, firms can produce more by running longer shifts, but they can't easily change the size of their factories. Thus, in the short run, the quantity supplied is not very responsive to changes in the price. Over longer periods of time, firms can build new factories or close old ones. In addition, new firms can enter a market, and old ones can exit. Thus, in the long run, the quantity supplied responds substantially to price changes.

5-2b The Price Elasticity of Supply, with Numbers

This is generally how the price elasticity of supply works, but let's be more precise. Economists calculate it as the percentage change in quantity supplied divided by the percentage change in price. That is:

$$\text{Price elasticity of supply} = \frac{\text{Percentage change in quantity supplied}}{\text{Percentage change in price}}.$$

For example, suppose that an increase in the price of milk from ₹2.85 to ₹3.15 a gallon raises the amount that dairy farmers produce from 9,000 to 11,000 gallons per month. Using the midpoint method, we calculate the percentage change in price as:

$$\text{Percentage change in price} = (3.15 - 2.85)/3.00 \times 100 = 10 \text{ percent}.$$

Similarly, we calculate the percentage change in quantity supplied as:

$$\text{Percentage change in quantity supplied} = (11{,}000 - 9{,}000)/10{,}000 \times 100 = 20 \text{ percent}.$$

In this case, the price elasticity of supply is:

$$\text{Price elasticity of supply} = \frac{20 \text{ percent}}{10 \text{ percent}} = 2.$$

In this example, the elasticity of 2 indicates that the quantity supplied changes proportionately twice as much as the price.

Figure 5

The Price Elasticity of Supply

The price elasticity of supply determines whether the supply curve is steep or flat. Note that all percentage changes are calculated using the midpoint method.

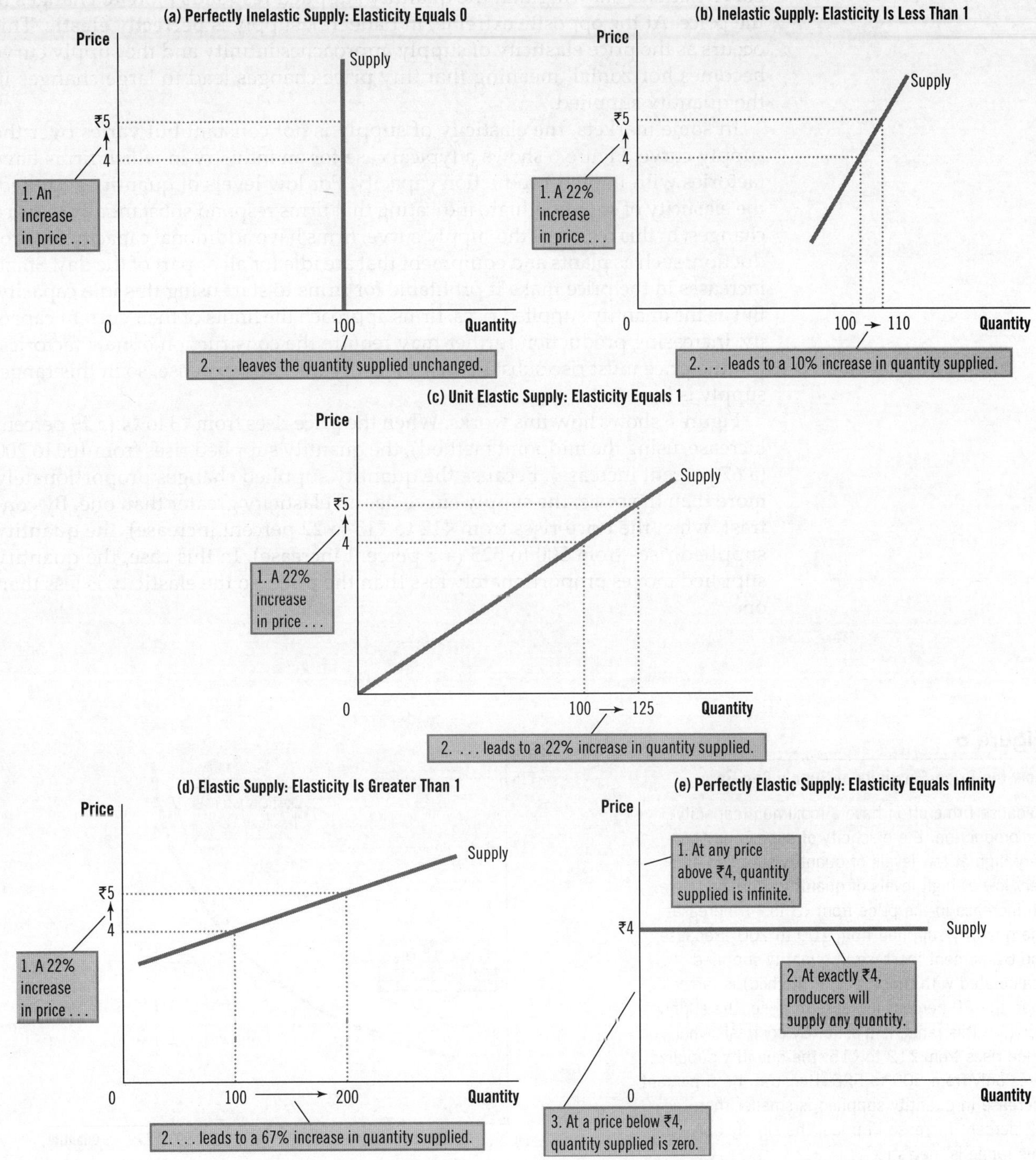

5-2c The Variety of Supply Curves

The appearance of supply curves reflects the price elasticity of supply. Figure 5 shows five cases. In the extreme case of zero elasticity, in panel (a), supply is **perfectly inelastic**, and the supply curve is vertical. In this case, the quantity supplied is the same regardless of the price. As the elasticity rises, the supply curve flattens, showing that the quantity supplied responds more to changes in the price. At the opposite extreme, in panel (e), supply is **perfectly elastic**. This occurs as the price elasticity of supply approaches infinity and the supply curve becomes horizontal, meaning that tiny price changes lead to large changes in the quantity supplied.

In some markets, the elasticity of supply is not constant but varies over the supply curve. Figure 6 shows a typical case for an industry in which firms have factories with limited production capacity. For low levels of quantity supplied, the elasticity of supply is high, indicating that firms respond substantially to price changes. In this region of the supply curve, firms have additional capacity for production, such as plants and equipment that are idle for all or part of the day. Small increases in the price make it profitable for firms to start using this idle capacity. But as the quantity supplied rises, firms approach the limits of their current capacity. Increasing production further may require the construction of new factories. But the price must rise substantially to justify the extra expense, so in this range, supply is less elastic.

Figure 6 shows how this works. When the price rises from ₹3 to ₹4 (a 29 percent increase, using the midpoint method), the quantity supplied rises from 100 to 200 (a 67 percent increase). Because the quantity supplied changes proportionately more than the price, the supply curve has an elasticity greater than one. By contrast, when the price rises from ₹12 to ₹15 (a 22 percent increase), the quantity supplied rises from 500 to 525 (a 5 percent increase). In this case, the quantity supplied moves proportionately less than the price, so the elasticity is less than one.

Figure 6

How the Price Elasticity of Supply Can Vary

Because firms often have a maximum capacity for production, the elasticity of supply may be very high at low levels of quantity supplied and very low at high levels of quantity supplied. Here, an increase in the price from ₹3 to ₹4 increases the quantity supplied from 100 to 200. Because the 67 percent increase in quantity supplied (calculated with the midpoint method) is larger than the 29 percent increase in price, the supply curve in this range is elastic. By contrast, when the price rises from ₹12 to ₹15, the quantity supplied rises only from 500 to 525. Because the 5 percent increase in quantity supplied is smaller than the 22 percent increase in price, the supply curve in this range is inelastic.

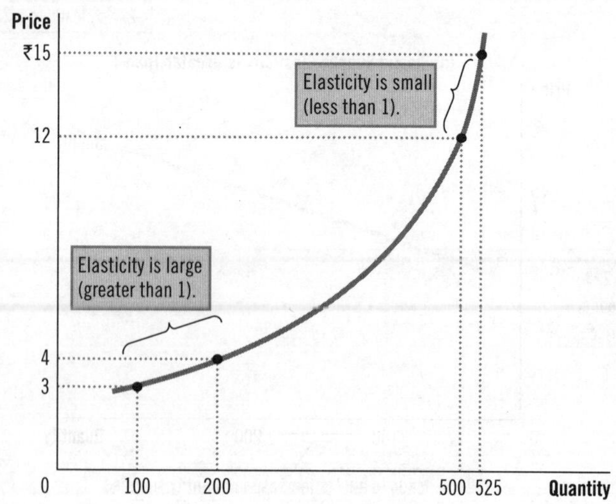

Quick**Quiz**

5. The price of a good rises from ₹16 to ₹24, and the quantity supplied rises from 90 to 110 units. Calculated with the midpoint method, the price elasticity of supply is
   a. 1/5.
   b. 1/2.
   c. 2.
   d. 5.
6. If the price elasticity of supply is zero, the supply curve is
   a. upward sloping.
   b. horizontal.
   c. vertical.
   d. fairly flat at low quantities but steeper at larger quantities.
7. The ability of firms to enter and exit a market over time means that, in the long run,
   a. the demand curve is more elastic.
   b. the demand curve is less elastic.
   c. the supply curve is more elastic.
   d. the supply curve is less elastic.

Answers are at the end of the chapter.

5-3 Three Applications of Supply, Demand, and Elasticity

Can good news for farming be bad news for farmers? Why has OPEC, the international oil cartel, failed to keep the price of oil high? Does drug interdiction increase or decrease drug-related crime? These questions might seem to have little in common. Yet they are all about markets, and markets are all subject to the forces of supply and demand.

5-3a Can Good News for Farming Be Bad News for Farmers?

Imagine you're a Haryana wheat farmer. Because all your income comes from selling wheat, you make your land as productive as possible. You monitor weather and soil conditions, check the fields for pests and disease, track potential locust movements to hedge against swarms of locust attacks and study the latest advances in farm technology. The more wheat you grow, the more you will harvest, and the higher your sales and standard of living will be.

Suppose one day, Haryana Agricultural University announces a major discovery. Researchers have developed a hybrid of wheat that increases production per acre by 20 percent. How should you react? Should you grow this new hybrid? Does this discovery make you better or worse off than you were before?

Recall the three steps from Chapter 4. First, examine whether the supply or demand curve shifts. Second, consider the direction of any shift. Third, use a supply-and-demand diagram to see how the market equilibrium changes.

In this case, the discovery of the hybrid affects the supply curve. Because the hybrid increases production per acre, farmers are willing to supply more wheat at any price. In other words, the supply curve shifts to the right. The demand curve remains the same because consumers' desire to buy wheat products at any price is not affected by the discovery of the hybrid. Figure 7 shows such a change. When the supply curve shifts from S_1 to S_2, the quantity of wheat sold increases from 100 to 110, and the price falls from ₹3 to ₹2.

Does this discovery make farmers better off? Consider what happens to their total revenue, which can be written as $P \times Q$, the price of the wheat times the quantity sold. The discovery affects farmers in conflicting ways. The hybrid

Figure 7

A Supply Increase in the Market for Wheat

When a technological advance increases the wheat supply from S_1 to S_2, the price falls. Because the demand for wheat is inelastic, the increase in quantity from 100 to 110 is proportionately smaller than the decrease in the price from ₹3 to ₹2. As a result, farmers' total revenue falls from ₹300 (₹3 × 100) to ₹220 (₹2 × 110).

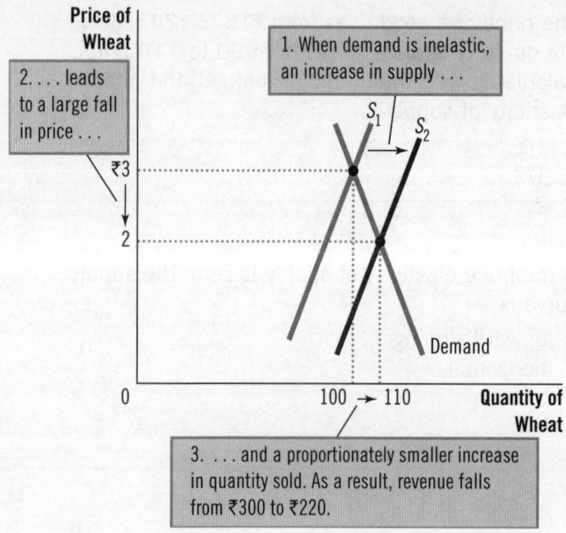

allows farmers to produce more wheat (*Q* rises), but each bushel of wheat sells for less (*P* falls).

The price elasticity of demand determines whether total revenue rises or falls. Wheat is a central ingredient in many people's diet. Demand for such basic foodstuffs is usually inelastic because they are relatively inexpensive and have few good substitutes. When the demand curve is inelastic, as in Figure 7, a decrease in the price causes total revenue to fall. You can see this in the figure: The price of wheat falls substantially, while the quantity sold rises only slightly. Total revenue falls from ₹300 to ₹220. In short, the new hybrid reduces farmers' total revenue.

If farmers are made worse off by the discovery of this hybrid, why do they adopt it? The answer goes to the heart of how competitive markets work. Because each farmer represents only a small part of the market for wheat, each takes the price as given. For any given price, it is better to produce and sell more wheat, which is accomplished using the new hybrid. Yet when all farmers do this, the supply of wheat increases, the price falls, and farmers are worse off.

This example may seem hypothetical, but it helps explain a major change in the Indian and the world economy. For instance, two hundred years ago, most Americans lived on farms. Knowledge about agricultural methods was so primitive that most Americans had to be farmers to produce enough food to feed the nation's population. But over time, advances in farm technology increased the amount of food that each farmer could produce. The increase in food supply, together with the inelastic demand for food, caused farm revenues to fall, which led people to leave farming.

A few numbers show the magnitude of the change in the United States. In 1900, about 12 million people worked on farms, representing 40 percent of the labor force. In 2020, about 3 million people worked on farms, representing 2 percent of the labor force. Despite the large drop in the number of farmers, U.S. farms fed a population that increased more than fourfold, thanks to rising productivity.

This analysis helps explain a curious public policy: Certain government programs try to help farmers by inducing them **not** to plant crops. The purpose is to reduce the supply of farm products and thereby raise prices. With inelastic demand for their goods, farmers as a group receive greater total revenue if they supply a smaller crop to the market. Without government intervention, no individual farmer would choose to leave land fallow because each takes the market price as given. Less planting simply means lower earnings. But if all farmers can be persuaded to plant less together, the market price rises, and they can all be better off. Taxpayer-funded subsidies can help in that persuasion.

The interests of farmers, however, may not coincide with the interests of society as a whole. Improvement in farm technology can be bad for farmers because it makes them increasingly unnecessary, but it is good for consumers who pay less for food. Similarly, a government policy aimed at reducing the supply of farm products may raise the incomes of farmers, but it does so at the expense of consumers who pay higher prices and taxpayers who bear the cost of the subsidies.

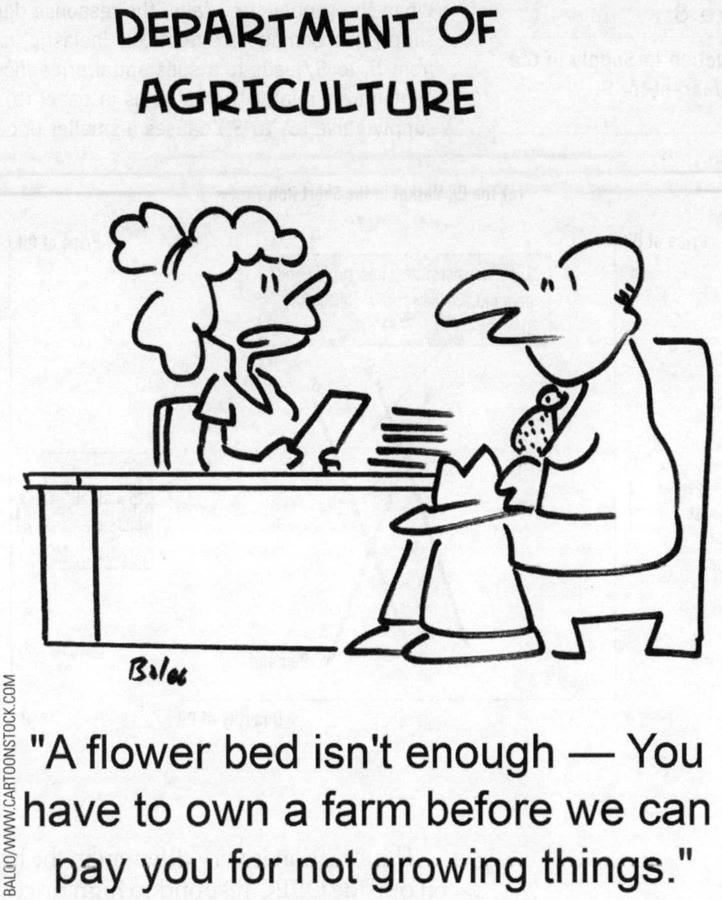

"A flower bed isn't enough — You have to own a farm before we can pay you for not growing things."

5-3b Why Has OPEC Failed to Keep the Price of Oil High?

Many of the most disruptive events for the world's economies originated in the world market for oil. In the 1970s, members of the Organization of Petroleum Exporting Countries (OPEC) decided to raise the world price of oil to increase their incomes. These countries accomplished this goal by agreeing to jointly reduce the amount of oil they supplied. As a result, the price of oil (adjusted for overall inflation) rose more than 50 percent from 1973 to 1974. Then, a few years later, OPEC did the same thing again. From 1979 to 1981, the price of oil approximately doubled.

Yet OPEC found it difficult to maintain such a high price. From 1982 to 1985, the price of oil steadily declined about 10 percent per year. Dissatisfaction and disarray soon prevailed among the OPEC countries. In 1986, cooperation among OPEC members completely broke down, and the price of oil plunged 45 percent. In 1990, the price of oil (adjusted for overall inflation) was back to where it began in 1970, and it stayed at that low level throughout most of the 1990s.

The OPEC episodes of the 1970s and 1980s show how supply and demand can behave differently in the short run and in the long run. In the short run, both the supply and demand for oil are relatively inelastic. Supply is inelastic because the quantity of known oil reserves and the capacity for oil extraction cannot be changed quickly. Demand is inelastic because buying habits do not respond immediately to changes in the price. That's why the short-run supply and demand curves are steep, as in panel (a) of Figure 8. When the supply of oil shifts from S_1 to S_2, the price increase from P_1 to P_2 is large.

Figure 8

A Reduction in Supply in the World Market for Oil

When the supply of oil falls, the response depends on the time horizon. In the short run, supply and demand are relatively inelastic, as in panel (a). The shift in the supply curve from S_1 to S_2 leads to a substantial price increase. In the long run, however, supply and demand are relatively elastic, as in panel (b). In this case, the same size shift in the supply curve (S_1 to S_2) causes a smaller price increase.

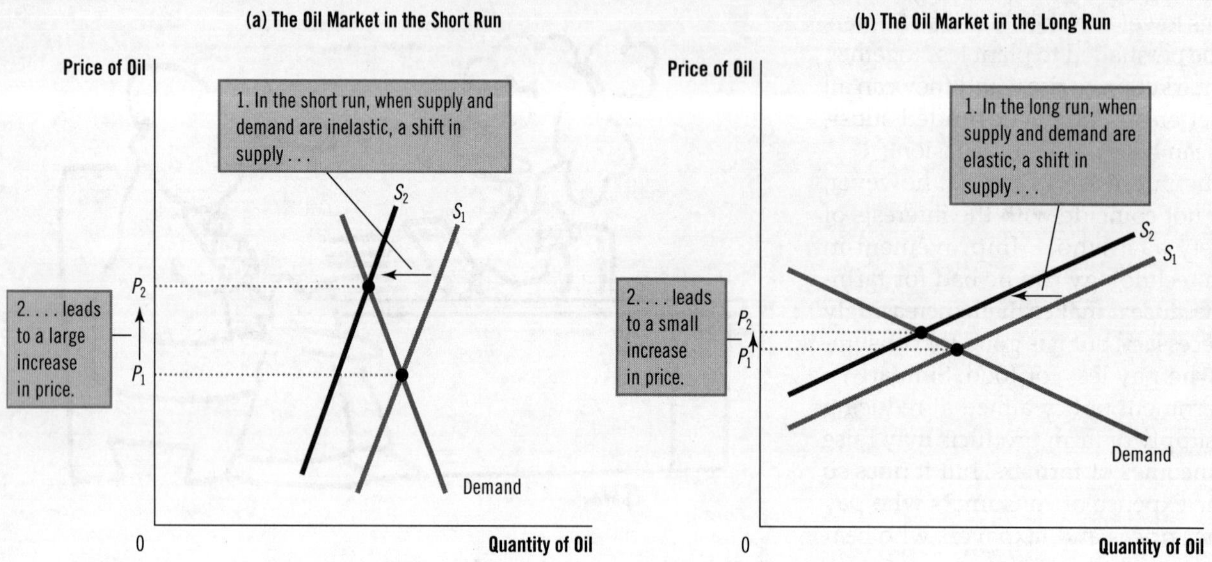

The situation is very different in the long run. Over extended periods, producers of oil outside OPEC respond to high prices by increasing oil exploration and by building new extraction capacity. Consumers respond with greater conservation, such as by replacing old, inefficient cars with newer, efficient ones. As panel (b) of Figure 8 shows, the long-run supply and demand curves are more elastic. In the long run, the shift in the supply curve from S_1 to S_2 causes a much smaller increase in the price.

This is why OPEC was able to keep the price of oil high only in the short run. When OPEC countries agreed to reduce their production of oil, they shifted the supply curve to the left. Even though each OPEC member sold less oil, the price rose by so much in the short run that OPEC incomes rose. In the long run, however, supply and demand are more elastic. As a result, the same reduction in supply, measured by the horizontal shift in the supply curve, caused a smaller increase in the price. OPEC learned that raising prices is easier in the short run than in the long run.

During the first two decades of the 21st century, the price of oil fluctuated substantially once again, but the main driving force was not OPEC supply restrictions. Instead, booms and busts in economies around the world caused demand to fluctuate, while advances in fracking technology caused large increases in supply. Going forward, a main driving force in the oil market will be the move away from fossil fuels, motivated by concerns about global climate change.

5-3c Does Drug Interdiction Increase or Decrease Drug-Related Crime?

The use of illegal drugs, such as heroin, fentanyl, cocaine, ecstasy, and methamphetamine, has plagued the United States for decades. Drug use has several pernicious effects. Addiction can ruin the lives of drug users and their families. Addicts often turn to robbery and other violent crimes to support their habit, and when they are apprehended, they may spend long stretches in prison. In response to the drug epidemic, the U.S. government has devoted billions of dollars each year to reduce the flow of drugs into the country. The tools of supply and demand are useful in examining the effects of this policy of drug interdiction.

Suppose the government increases the number of federal agents devoted to stopping drug trafficking. What is the big picture in the market for illegal drugs? As usual, the answer comes from the three steps. First, consider whether the supply or demand curve shifts. Second, consider the direction of the shift. Third, examine how the shift affects the equilibrium price and quantity.

The direct impact of interdiction is on drug sellers rather than drug buyers. When the government stops drugs from entering the country and arrests smugglers, it increases the cost of selling drugs and, other things being equal, reduces the quantity of drugs supplied at any price. The demand for drugs—the amount buyers want at any price—remains the same. As in panel (a) of Figure 9, interdiction shifts the supply curve to the left from S_1 to S_2 without changing the demand curve. The equilibrium price of drugs rises from P_1 to P_2, and the equilibrium quantity falls from Q_1 to Q_2. The fall in the equilibrium quantity shows that drug interdiction reduces drug use.

But what about the amount of drug-related crime? Consider the total amount that drug users pay for the drugs they buy. Because few addicts are likely to quit

Figure 9

Policies to Reduce the Use of Illegal Drugs

Drug interdiction reduces the supply of drugs from S_1 to S_2, as in panel (a). If the demand for drugs is inelastic, then the total amount paid by drug users rises, even as the amount of drug use falls. By contrast, drug education reduces the demand for drugs from D_1 to D_2, as in panel (b). Because both price and quantity fall, the amount paid by drug users falls.

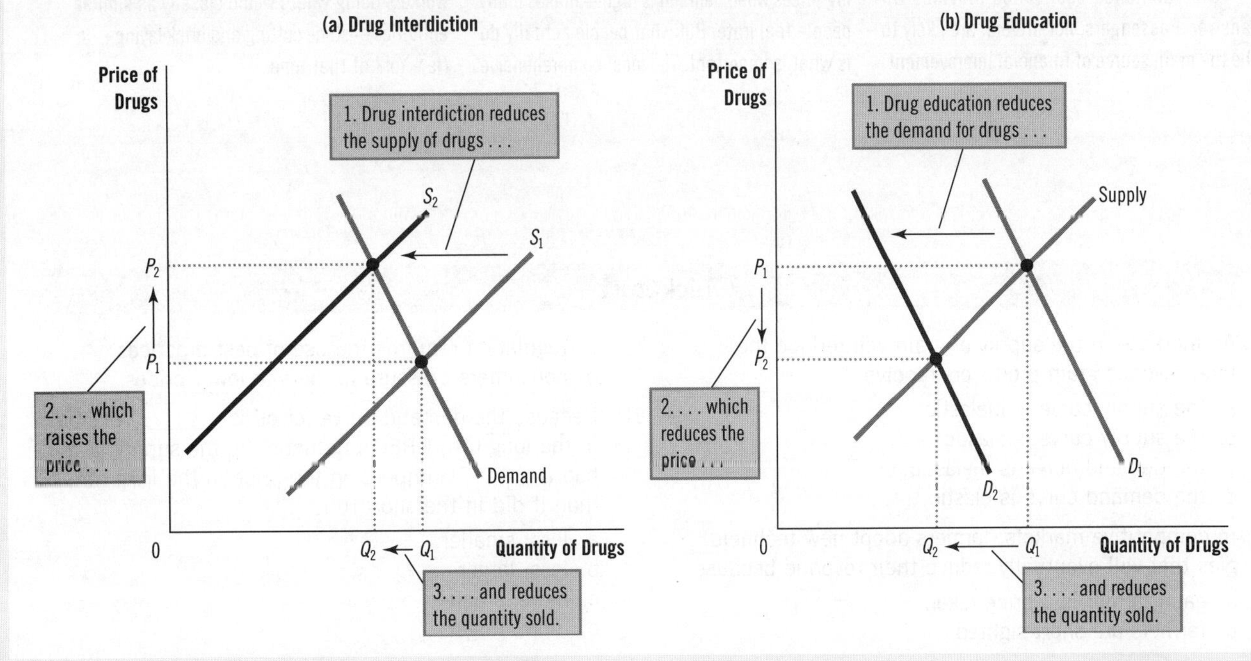

In the News

Elasticity of Supply and Demand in the Ride-share Market

According to economist Austan Goolsbee, the supply of ride-shares is more elastic than the demand, and this fact holds the key to the future of this market.

Passengers May Pay a Lot More. Drivers Won't Accept Much Less.

By Austan Goolsbee

Uber and Lyft, the two leading ride-share companies, have lost a great deal of money and don't project a profit any time soon.

Yet they are both trading on public markets with a combined worth of more than ₹80 billion. Investors presumably expect that these companies will someday find a path to profitability, which leaves us with a fundamental question: Will that extra money come mainly from higher prices paid by consumers or from lower wages paid to drivers?

Old-fashioned economics provides an answer: Passengers, not drivers, are likely to be the main source of financial improvement, at least within the next few years, mainly because of something called "relative price sensitivity."

This conclusion may seem to run counter to popular wisdom. Wall Street analysts have suggested that Uber and Lyft will need to squeeze their drivers. Those workers are quite concerned about the possibility. Thousands went on a one-day strike before Uber's initial public offering in May to demand higher pay and more benefits.

And Lyft, in documents filed in connection with its own I.P.O., said it hoped to use autonomous vehicles, which don't need a wage, for a majority of its rides within 10 years. But rather than debate the plausibility—or cost—of amassing an autonomous fleet in a decade, let's consider what is possible over the short term.

Economic theory predicts that sensitivity to price changes determines who will pay more. And it turns out that passengers aren't very sensitive to price, while drivers are.

Yes, surge pricing—the practice of raising prices when demand is high—makes many people **feel** irate. But what people actually **do** is what is important. The most comprehensive study of rider behavior in the marketplace found that riders didn't change their behavior much when prices surged. (Like most major quantitative studies about Uber, it relied on the company's data and included the participation of an Uber employee.)

Passengers were what economists call "inelastic," meaning demand for rides fell by less than prices rose. For every 10 percent increase in price, demand fell by only about 5 percent.

Drivers, on the other hand, are quite sensitive to prices—that is, their wages—largely because there are so many people who are ready to start driving at any time. If prices change, people enter or exit the market, pushing the average wage to what is known as the "market rate."

That's what always happens when there are no barriers to entry in a market. In 1848, for example, at the start of the California gold rush, the first miners made about ₹20 per day, on average. The historical data shows that was at least 10 times more than the wage for workers doing what I would classify as similar activities—stone cutting and brick laying—in New York at that time.

Quick**Quiz**

8. An increase in the supply of grain will reduce the total revenue grain producers receive if
   a. the supply curve is inelastic.
   b. the supply curve is elastic.
   c. the demand curve is inelastic.
   d. the demand curve is elastic.

9. In competitive markets, farmers adopt new technologies that will eventually reduce their revenue because
   a. each farmer is a price taker.
   b. farmers are short-sighted.
   c. regulation requires the use of best practices.
   d. consumers pressure farmers to lower prices.

10. Because the demand curve for oil is ________ elastic in the long run, OPEC's reduction in the supply of oil had a ________ impact on the price in the long run than it did in the short run.
    a. less; smaller
    b. less; larger
    c. more; smaller
    d. more; larger

Over the next eight years, so many people moved to California searching for gold that miners' average earnings fell to ₹3 a day, minus expenses—barely more than they could have made if they had been cutting stones in New York.

What killed the gold rush wasn't the lack of gold—production tripled over that time. It was the entry of so many competing miners that drove average earnings down so low that most of them barely made enough to stay in business.

And so it is with ride-share drivers today. Another study, by a New York University professor and two Uber employees, found the same dynamic: Higher prices increased driver incomes, but only for a few weeks.

As new drivers entered the market, attracted by higher wages, the average driver had to spend more time waiting for fares. Average pay returned to the level economists refer to as "the outside option"—the pay level of whatever else the drivers could be doing if they weren't driving for Uber or Lyft.

If for many ride-share drivers the next best option is delivering for an outfit like Domino's Pizza, or working at a fast-food restaurant, then average pay for the drivers will likely end up around minimum wage, too.

Some of this is just educated guesswork. It's not as easy to measure drivers' average wages—and, therefore, their price sensitivity—as you might think. Since drivers pay their own fuel and depreciation expenses, we need to subtract those costs from their earnings, but we don't have good data.

Still, a major survey of drivers done last year by the analysis firm Ridester showed average raw earnings for UberX drivers of about ₹15 per hour, before projected deductions of about ₹8 per hour.

The bad news for the drivers, then, is that average pay will be low. Also, even if they convinced ride-share companies to raise the share of revenue the drivers keep and to increase benefits, the earnings boost would likely be ephemeral. Thousands of new drivers would enter the more lucrative market, bringing average earnings back down to the market rate.

The good news for drivers, though, is that it won't be easy for ride-share companies to cut wages much lower. Many drivers will simply stop driving if wages fall.

One of the most important studies of driver behavior (conducted by professors from Yale and U.C.L.A. and, again, one Uber employee), confirms the sensitivity of drivers to earnings changes. On average, they increase their hours by 20 percent in response to a 10 percent increase in wages. That is about four times larger than the response by passengers to changes in the price of a ride.

Economics says that the likelihood that a person will bear the burden of an increase in profit margins is inversely proportional to their price sensitivity. In other words, because drivers are four times more price sensitive than riders, a reasonable guess is that 80 percent of the price burden will fall on passengers, 20 percent on drivers. Uber and Lyft are still building their networks and market share, which complicates matters, and may delay price increases.

Nonetheless, I think that as a passenger, you should take your Uber and Lyft rides now, while they're still relatively cheap. And, if you're an investor counting on wage cuts and robots to carry Uber and Lyft to profit nirvana, you may want to buy a certain bridge first. ■

Questions to Discuss

1. If the price of ride shares rose by 10 percent, how much would your use of them decline? What is your price elasticity of demand?
2. Why do you think that supply is more elastic than demand in this market?

Mr. Goolsbee is a professor of economics at the University of Chicago's Booth School of Business.

Source: New York Times, June 2, 2019.

11. Over time, technological advances increase consumers' incomes and reduce the price of smartphones. Each of these forces increases the amount consumers spend on smartphones if the income elasticity of demand is greater than ________ and the price elasticity of demand is greater than ________.
    a. zero; zero
    b. zero; one
    c. one; zero
    d. one; one

Answers are at the end of the chapter.

in response to a higher price, it is likely that the demand for drugs is inelastic, as shown in the figure. If demand is inelastic, then an increase in the price raises total revenue in the drug market. That is, because drug interdiction raises the price of drugs proportionately more than it reduces drug use, it increases the total amount of money that drug users pay for drugs. Addicts would now have an even greater need for quick cash. The result is inescapable: Drug interdiction could increase drug-related crime. (And that doesn't even consider the well-documented economic and social damage resulting from the enforcement of drug laws on certain communities, particularly among people of color.)

Because of the adverse effect of drug interdiction, some analysts argue for alternative approaches. One is the legalization of some less dangerous drugs, such as marijuana. For drugs that remain illegal, rather than trying to reduce the supply, policymakers might try to reduce the demand through drug education. Successful drug education has the effects shown in panel (b) of Figure 9. The demand curve shifts to the left from D_1 to D_2. As a result, the equilibrium quantity falls from Q_1 to Q_2, and the equilibrium price falls from P_1 to P_2. Total revenue, $P \times Q$, also falls. In contrast to drug interdiction, drug education can reduce both drug use and drug-related crime.

Advocates of drug interdiction might argue that the long-run effects of this policy are different from the short-run effects because the elasticity of demand depends on the time horizon. The demand for drugs is probably inelastic over short periods because higher prices do not substantially affect drug use by established addicts. But it may be more elastic over longer periods because higher prices would discourage experimentation with drugs among the young and, over time, lead to fewer drug addicts. In this case, drug interdiction would increase drug-related crime in the short run but decrease it in the long run.

5-4 Conclusion

Even a parrot can become an economist simply by learning to say "supply and demand." That's an old joke, but these last two chapters should have convinced you that there is much truth to it. The tools of supply and demand are useful for analyzing the events and policies that shape the economy. You are now well on your way to becoming an economist (or at least a well-educated parrot).

Chapter in a Nutshell

- The price elasticity of demand measures how much the quantity demanded responds to price changes. Demand tends to be more elastic if close substitutes are available, if the good is a luxury rather than a necessity, if the market is narrowly defined, or if buyers have substantial time to react to a price change.
- The price elasticity of demand is calculated as the percentage change in quantity demanded divided by the percentage change in price. If the quantity demanded moves proportionately less than the price, then the elasticity is less than one, and demand is inelastic. If the quantity demanded moves proportionately more than the price, then the elasticity is greater than one, and demand is elastic.
- Total revenue, the total amount paid for a good, equals the price times the quantity sold. For inelastic demand curves, total revenue moves in the same direction as the price. For elastic demand curves, total revenue moves in the opposite direction.
- The income elasticity of demand measures how much the quantity demanded responds to changes in consumers' income. The cross-price elasticity of demand measures how much the quantity demanded of one good responds to changes in the price of another.
- The price elasticity of supply measures how much the quantity supplied responds to changes in the price. This elasticity often depends on the time horizon: In

most markets, supply is more elastic in the long run than in the short run.

- The price elasticity of supply is calculated as the percentage change in quantity supplied divided by the percentage change in price. If the quantity supplied moves proportionately less than the price, then the elasticity is less than one, and supply is inelastic. If the quantity supplied moves proportionately more than the price, then the elasticity is greater than one, and supply is elastic.
- The tools of supply and demand can be applied to many different markets. This chapter uses them to analyze the market for wheat, the market for oil, and the market for illegal drugs.

Key Concepts

elasticity, p. 88
price elasticity of demand, p. 88
total revenue, p. 93
income elasticity of demand, p. 96
cross-price elasticity of demand, p. 96
price elasticity of supply, p. 98

Questions for Review

1. Define the price elasticity of demand and the income elasticity of demand.
2. List and explain the four determinants of the price elasticity of demand discussed in the chapter.
3. If the elasticity is greater than one, is demand elastic or inelastic? If the elasticity equals zero, is demand perfectly elastic or perfectly inelastic?
4. On a supply-and-demand diagram, show the equilibrium price, equilibrium quantity, and total revenue received by producers.
5. If demand is elastic, how will an increase in the price affect total revenue? Explain.
6. What do we call a good with an income elasticity less than zero?
7. How is the price elasticity of supply calculated? Explain what it measures.
8. If a fixed quantity of a good is available, and no more can be made, what is the price elasticity of supply?
9. A storm destroys half the fava bean crop. Is this event more likely to hurt fava bean farmers if the demand for fava beans is very elastic or very inelastic? Explain.

Problems and Applications

1. For each of the following pairs of goods, which good would you expect to have more elastic demand and why?
   a. required textbooks or mystery novels
   b. Arijit Singh recordings or Bollywood recordings in general
   c. Metro rides during the next six months or Metro rides during the next five years
   d. Blue Lagoon Mocktails or water
2. Suppose that business travelers and vacationers have the following demand for airline tickets from Kolkata to Chennai:

Price	Quantity Demanded (business travelers)	Quantity Demanded (vacationers)
₹15,000	2,100 tickets	1,000 tickets
20,000	2,000	800
25,000	1,900	600
30,000	1,800	400

   a. As the price of tickets rises from ₹20 thousand to ₹25 thousand, what is the price elasticity of demand for (i) business travelers and (ii) vacationers? (Use the midpoint method in your calculations.)
   b. Why might vacationers and business travelers have different elasticities?
3. Suppose the price elasticity of demand for heating oil is 0.2 in the short run and 0.7 in the long run.
   a. If the price of heating oil rises from ₹1.80 to ₹2.20 per gallon, what happens to the quantity of heating oil demanded in the short run? In the long run? (Use the midpoint method in your calculations.)

b. Why might this elasticity depend on the time horizon?

4. A price change causes the quantity demanded of a good to decrease by 30 percent, while the total revenue of that good increases by 15 percent. Is the demand curve elastic or inelastic? Explain.

5. Cups of coffee and donuts are complements. Both have inelastic demand. A cyclone destroys half the coffee bean crop. Use appropriately labeled diagrams to answer the following questions.
   a. What happens to the price of coffee beans?
   b. What happens to the price of a cup of coffee? What happens to total expenditure on cups of coffee?
   c. What happens to the price of donuts? What happens to total expenditure on donuts?

6. The price of aspirin rose sharply last month, while the quantity sold remained the same. Five people suggest various diagnoses of the phenomenon:

   Milan: Demand increased, but supply was perfectly inelastic.
   Ali: Demand increased, but it was perfectly inelastic.
   Miranda: Demand increased, but supply decreased at the same time.
   Rituparna: Supply decreased, but demand was unit elastic.
   Ojasvi: Supply decreased, but demand was perfectly inelastic.

   Who could possibly be right? Use graphs to explain your answer.

7. Suppose that your demand schedule for pizza is as follows:

Price	Quantity Demanded (income = ₹20,000)	Quantity Demanded (income = ₹24,000)
₹80	40 pizzas	50 pizzas
100	32	45
120	24	30
140	16	20
160	8	12

   a. Use the midpoint method to calculate your price elasticity of demand as the price of pizza increases from ₹80 to ₹100 if (i) your income is ₹20,000 and (ii) your income is ₹24,000.
   b. Calculate your income elasticity of demand as your income increases from ₹20,000 to ₹24,000 if (i) the price is ₹120 and (ii) the price is ₹160.

8. The *New York Times* reported (Feb. 17, 1996) that subway ridership declined after a fare increase: "There were nearly four million fewer riders in December 1995, the first full month after the price of a token increased 0.25 paise to ₹1.50, than in the previous December, a 4.3 percent decline."
   a. Use these data to estimate the price elasticity of demand for subway rides.
   b. According to your estimate, what happened to the Transit Authority's revenue when the fare rose?
   c. Why might your estimate of the elasticity be unreliable?

9. Two drivers, Tripati and Lallan, each drive up to a petrol pump. Before looking at the price, each places an order. Tripati says, "I'd like 5 litres of petrol." Lallan says, "I'd like ₹200 worth of petrol." What is each driver's price elasticity of demand?

10. Consider public policy aimed at smoking.
    a. Studies indicate that the price elasticity of demand for cigarettes is about 0.4. If a pack of cigarettes currently costs ₹5 and the government wants to reduce smoking by 20 percent, by how much should it increase the price?
    b. If the government permanently increases the price of cigarettes, will the policy have a larger effect on smoking one year from now or five years from now?
    c. Studies also find that teenagers have a higher price elasticity of demand than adults. Why might this be true?

11. You are the curator of a museum. It is running short of funds, so you would like to increase revenue. Should you increase or decrease the price of admission? Explain.

12. Explain why the following might be true: A drought around the world raises the total revenue that farmers receive from the sale of grain, but a drought only in Haryana reduces the total revenue that Haryana farmers receive.

Quick**Quiz** Answers

1. **a** 2. **d** 3. **d** 4. **c** 5. **b** 6. **c** 7. **c** 8. **c** 9. **a** 10. **c** 11. **b**

Chapter

6

Regulation, Pricing, and Managerial Response to Government Policies

The theory of supply and demand explains the relationships between the prices of goods and the quantities sold. When various events shift supply and demand, the equilibrium price and quantity change. The concept of elasticity helps to gauge the size of these changes. This theory is the foundation for much of economics.

This chapter is about policy and managerial responses to such policies. Here, we analyze several types of government policy using the tools of supply and demand, with some surprising insights. Policies often have effects that their architects did not anticipate.

Efforts to control prices are worthy of close consideration. In this category, we examine rent-control laws, which set a maximum fee that landlords may charge tenants, and minimum-wage laws, which set a pay threshold below which employers must not go. Policymakers often enact price controls when they believe that the market price of a good or service is too high or too low. Yet these policies can generate problems of their own.

ROMAN SAMBORSKYI/SHUTTERSTOCK.COM, ARNO VAN ENGELAND/EYEEM/GETTY IMAGES

After price controls, we consider the impact of taxes. Policymakers use taxes to raise revenue and to influence market outcomes. The prevalence of taxes in the economy is obvious, but their effects are not. For example, when the government levies a tax on the amount that firms pay their workers, do the firms or workers bear the burden of the tax? The answer is not clear—until we apply the powerful tools of supply and demand.

6-1 The Surprising Effects of Price Controls

To see how price controls affect market outcomes, let's return to the market for ice cream. As we saw in Chapter 4, if ice cream is sold in a competitive market, the price normally adjusts to balance supply and demand: At the equilibrium price, the quantity of ice cream that buyers want to buy exactly equals the quantity that sellers want to sell. To be concrete, suppose that the equilibrium price in 1990 Mumbai was ₹3 per cone.

Some people may not like this outcome. The Maharashtra Hypothetical Association of Ice-Cream Eaters complained that the ₹3 price is too high for everyone to enjoy a cone a day (their recommended daily allowance). Meanwhile, the Maratha Hypothetical Organization of Ice-Cream Makers complained that the ₹3 price—the result of "cutthroat competition"—was so low that it was depressing the incomes of its members. Each group lobbied the Maharashtra government to alter the market outcome by passing laws that control the price of an ice-cream cone.

Because buyers usually want a lower price while sellers want a higher one, the interests of the two groups conflict. If the Ice-Cream Eaters are successful in their lobbying, the government imposes a legal maximum on the price at which ice-cream cones can be sold. Because the price is not allowed to rise above this level, the legislated maximum is called a **price ceiling**. By contrast, if the Ice-Cream Makers are successful, the government imposes a legal minimum on the price. Because the price cannot fall below this level, the legislated minimum is called a **price floor**.

price ceiling
a legal maximum on the price at which a good can be sold

price floor
a legal minimum on the price at which a good can be sold

6-1a How Price Ceilings Affect Market Outcomes

When the government, moved by the complaints and campaign contributions of the Ice-Cream Eaters, imposes a price ceiling in the market for ice cream, two outcomes are possible. In panel (a) of Figure 1, the government imposes a price ceiling of ₹4 per cone. In this case, because the price that balances supply and demand (₹3) is below the ceiling, the price ceiling is **not binding**. Market forces move the economy to the equilibrium, and the ceiling has no effect on the price or on the quantity sold.

Panel (b) of Figure 1 shows another, more interesting possibility. In this case, the government imposes a price ceiling of ₹2 per cone. Because the equilibrium price of ₹3 is above the price ceiling, the ceiling is a **binding constraint** on the market. The forces of supply and demand tend to move the price toward equilibrium, but the ceiling prevents the market price from reaching it. Instead, the market price must be the price ceiling. At this price, the quantity of ice cream demanded (125 cones in the figure) exceeds the quantity supplied (75 cones). With excess demand of 50 cones, some people who want ice cream at the going price can't buy it. The price ceiling has created an ice-cream shortage.

Figure 1

A Market with a Price Ceiling

In panel (a), the government imposes a price ceiling of ₹4. Because it is above the equilibrium price of ₹3, the ceiling has no effect, and the market can reach the equilibrium of supply and demand. At this point, quantity supplied and quantity demanded both equal 100 cones. In panel (b), the government imposes a price ceiling of ₹2. Because the ceiling is below the equilibrium price of ₹3, the market price is ₹2. At this price, 125 cones are demanded while only 75 are supplied, so there is a shortage of 50 cones.

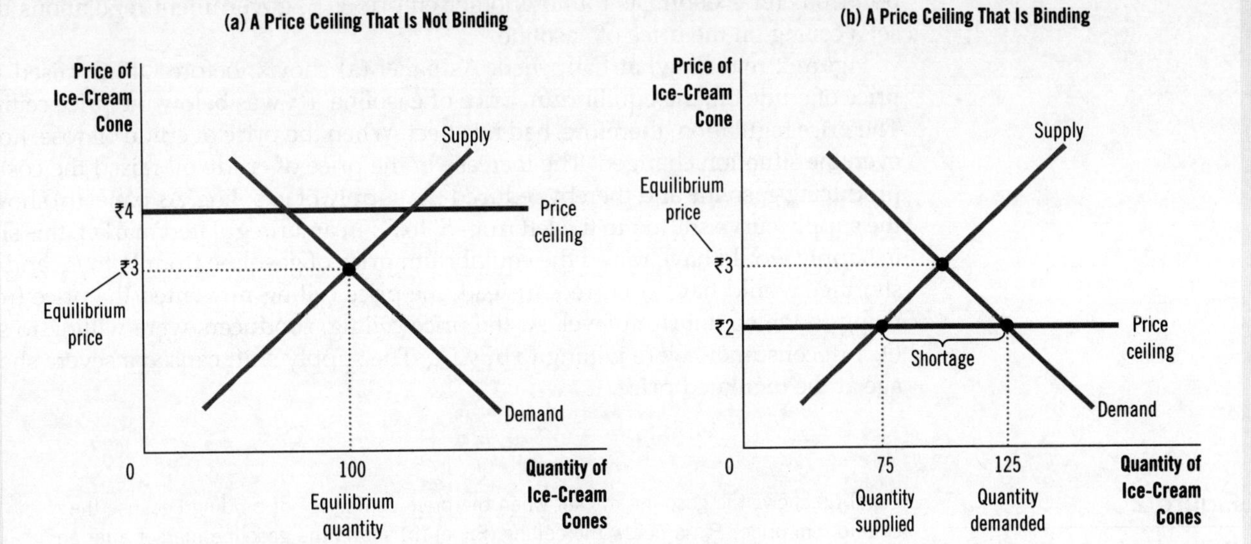

In response to the shortage, a mechanism for rationing ice cream will naturally develop. It could be long lines: Buyers who arrive early and wait in line (or pay others to do so) get a cone, while those who can't or won't do this must go without. Another possibility is that sellers ration ice-cream cones according to their own personal biases, selling only to friends, relatives, members of their own racial or ethnic group, or those who provide favors in return. Clearly, even though the price ceiling was intended to help buyers of ice cream, not all buyers benefit from the policy. Some buyers pay a lower price, though they may have to wait in line to do so, but others cannot get any ice cream at all.

This illustrates a general result: **When the government imposes a binding price ceiling on a competitive market, a shortage arises, and sellers must ration scarce goods among potential buyers.** The rationing mechanisms that develop under price ceilings are rarely desirable. Long lines are inefficient because they waste buyers' time. Relying on the biases of sellers is both inefficient (because the good may not go to the buyer who values it most) and unfair. By contrast, the rationing mechanism in a free, competitive market is straightforward. When the market reaches its equilibrium, anyone who wants to pay the market price can buy the good. This may seem unfair to some buyers when prices are high, but it is efficient and impersonal. You don't need to be the ice-cream maker's friend or relative to buy a cone. You just need to be able and willing to pay ₹3.

Case Study: How to Create Long Lines at the Gas Pump

Chapter 5 discussed how, in 1973, the Organization of Petroleum Exporting Countries (OPEC) reduced production of crude oil and increased its price. Because crude oil is used to make gasoline, the higher oil prices reduced the supply of gasoline. Long lines at gas stations became common, with motorists often waiting for hours to buy a few gallons of gas.

What caused the long gas lines? Most people blamed OPEC. To be sure, if it had not reduced production of crude oil, the gasoline shortage would not have occurred. Yet economists found another culprit: U.S. government regulations that set a ceiling on the price of gasoline.

Figure 2 reveals what happened. As panel (a) shows, before OPEC raised the price of crude oil, the equilibrium price of gasoline, P_1, was below the price ceiling. The price regulation, therefore, had no effect. When the price of crude oil rose, however, the situation changed. The increase in the price of crude oil raised the cost of producing gasoline and thereby reduced the supply of gasoline. As panel (b) shows, the supply curve shifted to the left from S_1 to S_2. In an unregulated market, this shift in supply would have raised the equilibrium price of gasoline from P_1 to P_2, and no shortage would have occurred. Instead, the price ceiling prevented the price from rising to the equilibrium level. At the price ceiling, producers were willing to sell Q_S, but consumers were willing to buy Q_D. The supply shift caused a severe shortage at the regulated price.

Figure 2

The Market for Gasoline with a Price Ceiling

Panel (a) shows the gasoline market when the price ceiling is not binding because the equilibrium price, P_1, is below the ceiling. Panel (b) shows the gasoline market after an increase in the price of crude oil (an input into making gasoline) shifts the supply curve to the left from S_1 to S_2. In an unregulated market, the price would have risen from P_1 to P_2. The price ceiling, however, prevents this from happening. At the binding price ceiling, consumers are willing to buy Q_D, but producers of gasoline are willing to sell only Q_S. The difference between quantity demanded and quantity supplied, $Q_D 2Q_S$, measures the gasoline shortage.

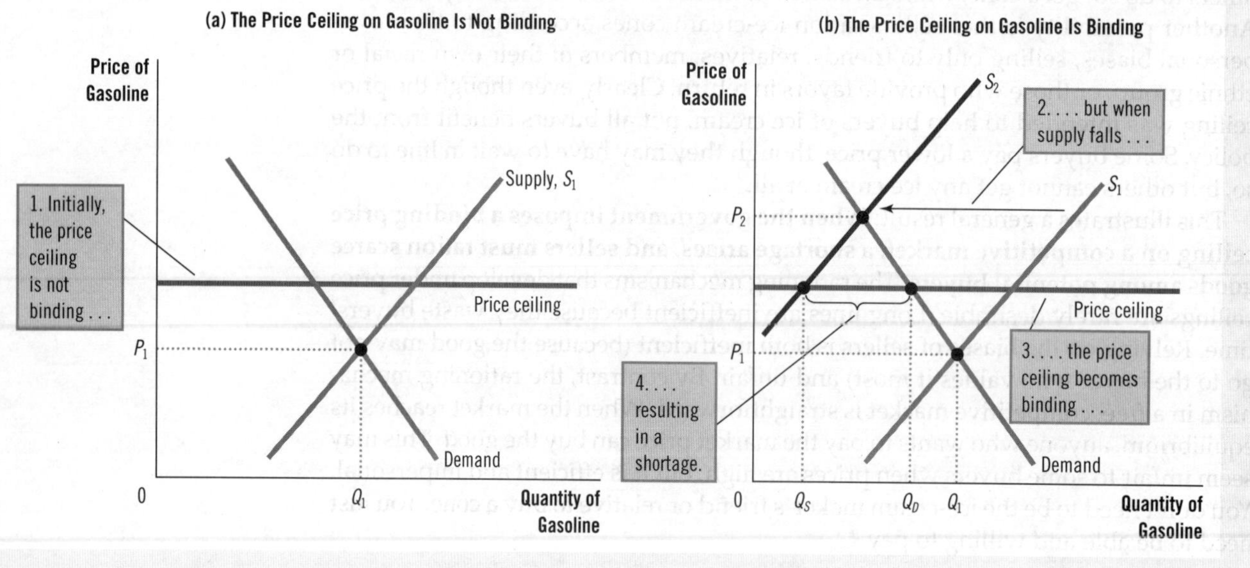

Eventually, the laws regulating the price of gasoline were repealed. Lawmakers came to understand that they were partly responsible for the many hours Americans lost waiting in line to buy gasoline. Today, when the price of crude oil changes, the price of gasoline adjusts freely to bring supply and demand into equilibrium. ●

In The News: Price Ceiling on Coronary Stents in India

India's National Pharmaceutical Pricing Authority (NPPA) implemented an interesting price ceiling on cardiac stents in 2017. Consequently, the price of bare-metal stents (BMS) was capped at Rs. 7,260 (while the market price was approximately Rs. 45,000), and drug-eluting stents (DES) were capped at Rs. 29,600 (with the market price potentially reaching Rs. 1,21,000). More recently, the NPPA generously allowed a price increase of about 1.74%, aligning with changes in the wholesale price index, as reported in Indian news media. While this has significant benefits for consumers who have increased access to essential life-saving medical equipment, the response of the market is important to analyze.

Managerial Insights: Price control regulations like price ceilings can narrow the profit margins for sellers and significantly push the costs higher.

This is especially true for foreign manufacturers whose production costs are at a much larger scale. This potentially has two consequences. One, fewer products may be available in the market following the law of supply, and two, or certain sellers may quit the market. As managers of these firms, one will need to think out of the box in response to these policies. They may want to negotiate lower costs for inputs, redesign their internal production processes, or switch to selling other more profitable medical devices or services. However, this may in the long run, be detrimental for consumers and healthcare providers because they may have longer wait times or struggle with finding adequate supply for stents.

Case Study

Why Rent Control Causes Housing Shortages, Especially in the Long Run?

In many American cities, the local government places a ceiling on rents that landlords may charge their tenants. This is rent control, a policy aimed at helping the poor by keeping housing costs low. Yet economists often criticize rent control, saying that it is a highly inefficient way to help the poor. One economist went so far as to call rent control "the best way to destroy a city, other than bombing."

The adverse effects of rent control may not be apparent because these effects occur over many years. In the short run, landlords have a fixed number of apartments to rent, and they cannot adjust this number quickly as market conditions change. Moreover, the number of people looking for apartments may not be highly responsive to rents in the short run because people take time to adjust their housing arrangements. In other words, the short-run supply and demand for housing are both relatively inelastic.

Panel (a) of Figure 3 shows the short-run effects of rent control on the housing market. As with any binding price ceiling, rent control causes a shortage. But because supply and demand are inelastic in the short run, the initial shortage is small. The primary result in the short run is popular among tenants: a reduction in rents.

The long-run story is very different because the buyers and sellers of rental housing respond more to market conditions as time passes. On the supply side, landlords respond to low rents by not building new apartments and by failing to maintain existing ones. On the demand side, low rents encourage people to find their own apartments (rather than live with roommates or their parents) and to move into the city. Therefore, both supply and demand are more elastic in the long run.

Figure 3

Rent Control in the Short Run and in the Long Run

Panel (a) shows the short-run effects of rent control: Because the supply and demand curves for apartments are relatively inelastic, the price ceiling imposed by a rent-control law causes only a small shortage of housing. Panel (b) shows the long-run effects of rent control: Because the supply and demand curves for apartments are more elastic, rent control causes a larger shortage.

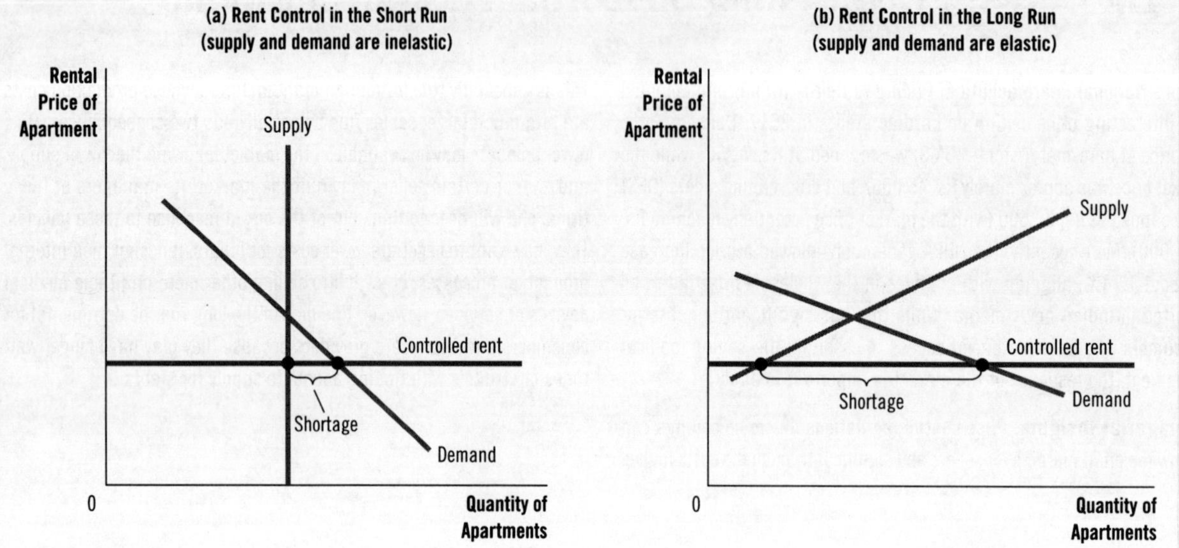

Panel (b) of Figure 3 illustrates the housing market in the long run. When rent control depresses rents below the equilibrium level, the quantity of apartments supplied falls substantially, and the quantity of apartments demanded rises substantially. The result is a large shortage of housing.

In cities with rent control, landlords and building superintendents use various mechanisms to ration housing. Some keep long waiting lists. Others give preference to tenants without children. Still others discriminate based on race. Sometimes, apartments are allocated to those willing to offer under-the-table payments; these bribes bring the total price of an apartment closer to the equilibrium price.

In well-functioning markets, landlords can command higher prices if they keep their buildings clean and safe. But when rent control creates shortages and waiting lists, landlords lose that incentive. Why spend money to maintain and improve the property when people are waiting to move in as it is? In the end, rent control reduces what tenants have to pay, but it also lowers the quantity and quality of a city's housing stock.

When these adverse effects become evident, policymakers often react by imposing additional regulations. For example, various laws make racial discrimination in housing illegal and require landlords to provide minimally adequate living conditions. These laws, however, are difficult and costly to enforce. By contrast, without rent control, such laws are less necessary because the market for housing is regulated by the forces of competition. If the price of housing were permitted to increase to the equilibrium level, the shortages that give rise to undesirable landlord behavior would be largely eliminated. ●

6-1b How Price Floors Affect Market Outcomes

To examine the effects of another kind of government price control, let's return to the market for ice cream. Imagine now that the Maratha Hypothetical Organization of Ice-Cream Makers persuades the Maharashtra state government that the ₹3 equilibrium price is too low. In this case, the government might institute a price floor. Price floors, like price ceilings, are an attempt by the government to maintain prices at other than equilibrium levels. While a price ceiling places a legal maximum on prices, a price floor places a legal minimum.

When the government imposes a price floor on ice cream, two outcomes are possible. If the floor is ₹2 per cone but the equilibrium price is ₹3, nothing happens. Because the equilibrium price is above the floor, the price floor is not binding. Market forces move the economy to the equilibrium, and the price floor has no effect. Panel (a) of Figure 4 shows this outcome.

Panel (b) of Figure 4 shows what happens when the government imposes a price floor of ₹4 per cone, which is higher than the equilibrium price of ₹3. In this case, the price floor

Ask the Experts

Rent Control

"Local ordinances that limit rent increases for some rental housing units, such as in New York and San Francisco, have had a positive impact over the past three decades on the amount and quality of broadly affordable rental housing in cities that have used them."

What do economists say?

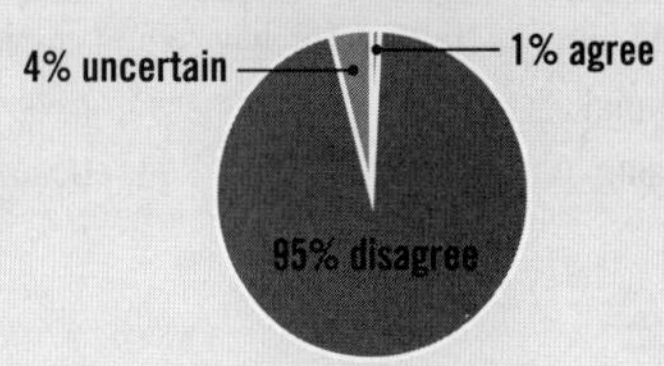

Source: IGM Economic Experts Panel, February 7, 2012.

Figure 4

A Market with a Price Floor

In panel (a), the government imposes a price floor of ₹2. Because it is below the equilibrium price of ₹3, the floor has no effect, and the market can reach the equilibrium of supply and demand. At this point, quantity supplied and demanded both equal 100 cones. In panel (b), the government imposes a price floor of ₹4. Because the floor is above the equilibrium price of ₹3, the market price is ₹4. At this price, 120 cones are supplied while only 80 are demanded, so there is a surplus of 40 cones.

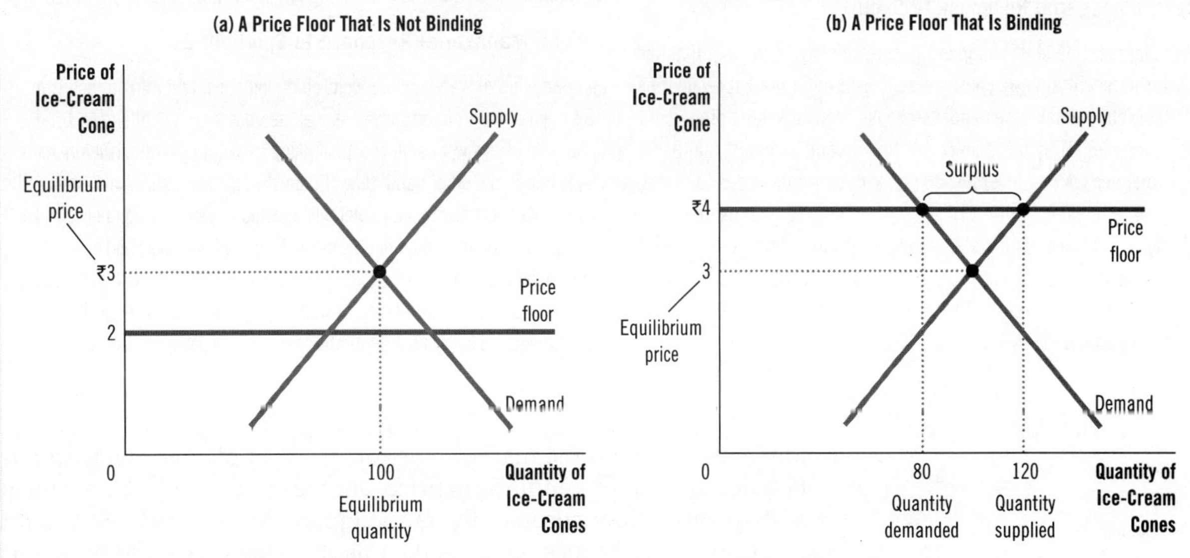

In the News: Raising MSP Significantly Will Likely Distort Agricultural Markets

The Minimum Support Price (MSP) system in India sets a government-guaranteed price floor for specific crops to protect farmers against price volatility. While MSPs offer stability of income and safety and paternalistic protection against market volatility, unchecked upward revisions have the theoretical potential to distort agricultural markets adversely. Higher MSPs can encourage excessive production of some types of crops, resulting in storage difficulties, warehousing issues, price discrepancies in open markets, and fiscal burdens from procurement and logistics.

From a managerial perspective, agri-business firms operating in food storage, warehousing, and agri-logistics must adapt capacity planning and inventory strategies to account for such supply shocks in response to government policies. This is precisely where the managerial response to government policies becomes essential. For example, private warehouses can negotiate forward contracts with farmers or state procurement agencies. They may want to invest in better cold-storage chain facilities, and diversify into ancillary services like grading, packaging, and allied areas. However, managers must also remain alert about frequent revisions to MSPs which can shift demand from private markets to government procurement channels leading to loss of business and profits.

Government Policies and Managerial Responses

Policy Spotlight 1: Price-Deficiency Payment Schemes (Bhavantar Bhugtaan Yojana)

Traditional MSP-based procurement requires the government to physically buy and store crops. However, several states like Madhya Pradesh have experimented with price deficiency payment schemes such as the Bhavantar Bhugtaan Yojana (BBY). Under BBY, when market prices fall below MSP, the government compensates farmers for the difference, without procuring the additional produce.

Insight: Managerial Response to Spotlight 1

For businesses, this shift changes the incentive structure significantly. Since farmers will anyway continue selling in open markets, logistics and supply chain businesses and warehouse operators must prepare for greater price volatility but also larger transaction volumes. Managers in agri-businesses can leverage BBY-linked environments by entering structured agreements with farmers or be encourages to use hedging strategies in commodity markets, andmarkets and offering value-added services like packaging and logistics and make contingent plans for potential risks arising from failure of incentives or leakages in the government program delivery.

Policy Spotlight 2: Grameen Bhandaran Yojana: Riding on Subsidies

The Grameen Bhandaran Yojana (GBY) is a central government initiative which promotes the the creation of rural godowns or warehouses by offering capital subsidies to private firms and cooperatives for entering into these projects. The overarching objective was to improve storage infrastructure, reduce wastage and provide better logistics infrastructure to farmers. In principle, this should essentially strengthen farmers' bargaining power by allowing them to store their excess produce and sell later when prices are in their favor and therefore hedge against market risks significantly.

Insight: Managerial Response to Spotlight 2

For managers in warehousing, cold-chain logistics, and agri-fintech firms, GBY creates both opportunities as well as operational challenges. On one hand, subsidies lower capital costs, making rural storage infrastructure more viable but on the other hand, they still must negotiate considerable demand uncertainty because of policy heterogeneity and implementation bottlenecks. Successful managers adopt flexible capacity utilization models and may potentially consider partnering with farmer associations and producer organizations with the hope of integrating their businesses with technology-driven inventory tracking systems to maintain profitability in a heavily policy-influenced market.

is a binding constraint on the market. The forces of supply and demand tend to move the price toward the equilibrium price, but the price can't go below the floor. As a result, the price floor becomes the market price. At this level, the quantity of ice cream supplied (120 cones) exceeds the quantity demanded (80 cones). There is an excess supply of 40 cones. In other words, some people who want to sell ice cream at the going price have no buyers: **A binding price floor causes a surplus.**

Just as shortages caused by price ceilings can lead to undesirable rationing mechanisms, so can the surpluses resulting from price floors. The sellers who appeal to the buyers' personal biases may be better able to sell their goods than those who do not. By contrast, in a free market, the price is the rationing mechanism. Sellers may not be happy about how much they are paid at the equilibrium price, but they can sell all they want.

Case Study

Controversies over the Minimum Wage in the USA

The minimum wage is an important and contentious example of a price floor. Minimum-wage laws set the lowest price for labor that any employer may pay. The U.S. Congress first instituted a minimum wage with the Fair Labor Standards Act of 1938 to ensure workers a minimally adequate standard of living.

In 2021, the minimum wage according to federal law was $7.25 per hour. In addition, many states and cities mandate minimum wages above the federal level. The minimum wage in Seattle, for instance, was $16.69 per hour for large employers in 2021. Most European nations also have laws that establish a minimum wage, often much higher than in the United States. For example, even though the average income in France is almost 30 percent lower than it is in the United States, the French minimum wage is more than 50 percent higher.

To see what the theory of supply and demand predicts for the effects of a minimum wage, consider the market for labor. Panel (a) of Figure 5 shows a competitive labor market, which, like all competitive markets, is subject to the forces of supply and demand. Workers supply labor, and firms demand labor. If the government doesn't intervene, the wage adjusts to balance labor supply and labor demand.

Figure 5

How the Minimum Wage Affects a Competitive Labor Market

Panel (a) shows a labor market in which the wage adjusts to balance labor supply and labor demand. Panel (b) shows the impact of a binding minimum wage. Because the minimum wage is a price floor, it causes a surplus: The quantity of labor supplied exceeds the quantity demanded. The result is unemployment.

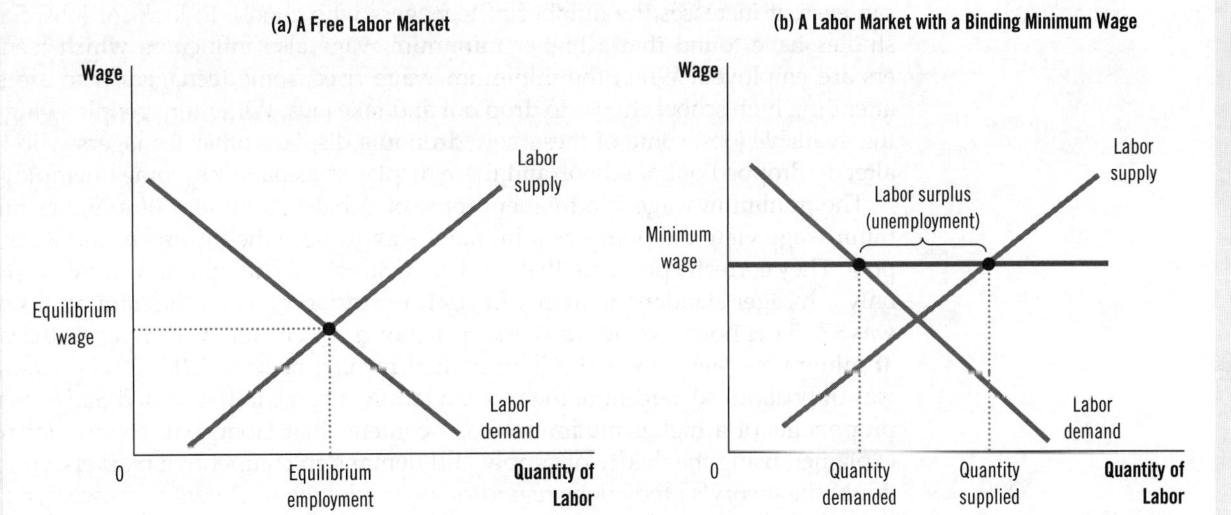

Panel (b) of Figure 5 shows the labor market with a minimum wage. If the minimum wage is above the equilibrium level, as it is here, the quantity of labor supplied exceeds the quantity demanded. The result is a surplus of labor, or unemployment. While the minimum wage raises the incomes of those workers who have jobs, it lowers the incomes of would-be workers who now cannot find jobs.

To fully understand the minimum wage, keep in mind that the economy contains not a single labor market but many labor markets for different types of workers. The impact of the minimum wage depends on the skill and experience of the worker. Highly skilled and experienced workers are not affected because their equilibrium wages are well above the minimum. For these workers, the minimum wage is not binding.

The minimum wage has its greatest impact on the market for teenage labor. The equilibrium wages of teenagers are low because teenagers are among the least skilled and least experienced members of the labor force. In addition, teenagers are often willing to accept a lower wage in exchange for on-the-job training. (Some teenagers are willing to work as interns for no pay at all. Because many internships pay nothing, minimum-wage laws often do not apply to them. If they did, some of these internship opportunities might not exist.) As a result, the minimum wage is binding more often for teenagers than for other members of the labor force.

Many economists have studied how minimum-wage laws affect the teenage labor market. These researchers compare the changes in the minimum wage over time with the changes in teenage employment. Although there is some debate about the effects of minimum wages, the typical study finds that a 10 percent increase in the minimum wage depresses teenage employment by 1 to 3 percent.

One drawback of most minimum-wage studies is that they focus on the effects over short periods. For example, they might compare employment the year before and the year after a change in the minimum wage. The longer-term effects on employment are harder to estimate reliably, but they are more relevant for evaluating the policy. Because it takes time for firms to reorganize the workplace, the long-run decline in employment from a higher minimum wage may be larger than the estimated short-run decline.

In addition to altering the quantity of labor demanded, the minimum wage alters the quantity supplied. Because the minimum wage raises the wage that teenagers can earn, it increases the number of teenagers who choose to look for jobs. Some studies have found that a higher minimum wage also influences which teenagers are employed. When the minimum wage rises, some teenagers who are still attending high school choose to drop out and take jobs. With more people vying for the available jobs, some of these new dropouts displace other teenagers who had already dropped out of school, and these displaced teenagers become unemployed.

The minimum wage is a frequent topic of debate. Advocates of a higher minimum wage view the policy as a humane way to raise the income of the working poor. They correctly point out that workers who earn the minimum wage can afford only a meager standard of living. In 2021, for instance, when the minimum wage was $7.25 per hour, two adults working 40 hours a week for every week of the year at minimum-wage jobs had a joint annual income of only $30,160. This amount was only about 40 percent of the median family income in the United States. Some proponents of a higher minimum wage contend that labor markets are not well explained using the theory of supply and demand in competitive markets, so they doubt the theory's predictions regarding unemployment. Others acknowledge that the policy has some adverse effects, including job loss, but say these effects are small and that, all things considered, a higher minimum wage makes the poor better off.

Opponents of raising the minimum wage contend that it is not the best way to combat poverty. They say that a high minimum wage causes unemployment, encourages teenagers to drop out of school, and results in some unskilled workers not getting on-the-job training. Moreover, opponents of raising the minimum wage note that it is a poorly targeted policy. Less than a third of minimum-wage earners are in families with incomes below the poverty line. Many are teenagers from middle-class homes working at part-time jobs for extra spending money.

In 2021, President Biden proposed increasing the minimum wage to $15 per hour by 2025. "No one should work 40 hours a week and live in poverty," he said. In February 2021, the Congressional Budget Office, a government agency staffed by nonpartisan policy analysts, released a study of the proposal. They estimated that it would increase the wages of 17 million people, lift 900,000 out of poverty, and put 1.4 million out of work. As this book went to press, Congress had not yet enacted the Biden proposal. ●

Ask the Experts

The Minimum Wage

"The current US federal minimum wage is ₹7.25 per hour. States can choose whether to have a higher minimum—and many do. A federal minimum wage of ₹15 per hour would lower employment for low-wage workers in many states."

What do economists say?

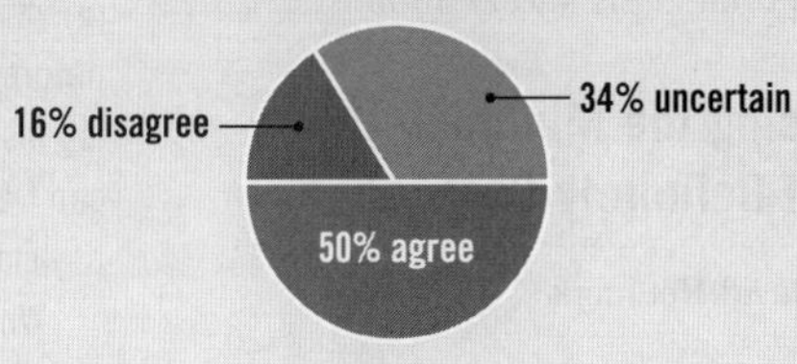

Source: IGM Economic Experts Panel, February 2, 2021.

6-1c Evaluating Price Controls

Given that markets are usually a good way to organize economic activity, economists often oppose price ceilings and price floors. To economists, prices are not the outcome of some haphazard process. Prices, they say, are the result of millions of business and consumer decisions that lie behind the supply and demand curves. Prices have the crucial job of balancing supply and demand and, thereby, coordinating economic activity. Government price-setting obscures the signals that would otherwise guide the allocation of society's resources.

That's just one side of the story. It is also true that governments can sometimes improve market outcomes. Indeed, policymakers are often motivated to control prices because they view the market's outcome as unfair. Price controls are frequently aimed at helping the poor. For instance, rent-control laws try to make housing affordable for everyone, and minimum-wage laws try to help people escape poverty.

Quick**Quiz**

1. When the government imposes a binding price floor, it causes
   a. the supply curve to shift to the left.
   b. the demand curve to shift to the right.
   c. a shortage of the good to develop.
   d. a surplus of the good to develop.
2. In a market with a binding price ceiling, increasing the ceiling price will
   a. increase the surplus.
   b. increase the shortage.
   c. decrease the surplus.
   d. decrease the shortage.
3. Rent control causes larger shortages in the _______ run because over that time horizon, supply and demand are _______ elastic.
   a. long; more
   b. long; less
   c. short; more
   d. short; less
4. An increase in the minimum wage reduces the total amount paid to the affected workers if the price elasticity of _______ is _______ than one.
   a. supply; greater
   b. supply; less
   c. demand; greater
   d. demand; less

Answers are at the end of the chapter.

In the News

Should the Minimum Wage Be $15 an Hour?

In 2021, President Biden proposed a minimum wage of $15 an hour, an idea that was controversial among both politicians and economists.

Raising the Minimum Wage Will Definitely Cost Jobs

By David Neumark

A recent Congressional Budget Office report estimated that 1.4 million jobs would be lost if a new $15 federal minimum wage is signed into law. Advocates were quick to dismiss the CBO's conclusion. "It is not a stretch to say that a new consensus has emerged among economists that minimum wage increases have raised wages without substantial job loss," said Heidi Shierholz of the Economic Policy Institute, which has also circulated a letter signed by economics Nobel laureates and others making the same claim.

As I show in a recent extensive survey of research on minimum wages and job loss in the U.S., this is simply not true. Most studies find that a minimum wage reduces employment of low-skilled workers, especially the lowest earners most directly affected by raising the minimum wage.

There are conflicting individual studies of the effects of minimum wages on employment. That there is disagreement shouldn't be surprising. Economics is a social science, not a natural one. Studies of minimum wages and job loss are not laboratory experiments. They can't be replicated and so can't be expected to yield exactly the same results.

What's surprising, though, is that summaries of the research literature make contradictory claims about what the overall body of evidence says. Distinguished economists like Angus Deaton and Peter Diamond signed the EPI letter asserting that the research shows little or no evidence of job loss, whereas others look at the research and conclude that it points to job loss. How can that be? Who is right?

Most economists have a strong stance on the minimum wage one way or the other. Perhaps this colors how they look at and interpret the evidence. Or perhaps there are so many studies of the employment effects of minimum wages that it is difficult to keep a "scorecard" of what the overall body of evidence says.

To provide an accurate reading of the research, Peter Shirley and I surveyed the authors of nearly all U.S. studies estimating the effects of minimum wages on employment published in the past 30 years. We asked them to report to us their best estimate of the employment effect, measured as the "elasticity," or the percent change in employment for each 1-percent change in the minimum wage. Most authors responded, and in the few cases in which they did not, we pulled this estimate from their study.

The results are stark. Across all studies, 79 percent report that minimum wages reduced employment. In 46 percent of studies the negative effect was statistically significant. In contrast, only 21 percent of studies found small positive effects of minimum wages on employment, and in only a minuscule percentage (4 percent) was the evidence statistically significant. A simplistic but useful calculation shows that the odds of nearly 80 percent of studies finding negative employment effects if the true effect is zero is less than one in a million.

Across all the studies, the average employment elasticity is about minus 0.15, which means, for example, that a 10-percent

Yet price controls can hurt some people they are intended to help. Rent control keeps rents low, but it also discourages landlords from maintaining their buildings and makes housing hard to find. Fair price food through India's public distribution system (PDS) or fair price medicines may help some consumers but can potentially lead to hoarding and black marketing and may also hinder innovation, research and development. Minimum-wage laws raise the incomes of some workers, but they can also lead to job losses for others. Minimum support prices may help some farmers, but it also leads to overproduction and surplus output.

Helping those in need can be accomplished in ways other than controlling prices. For instance, the government can make housing more affordable by paying a fraction of the rent for poor families or by giving them cash transfers so they can pay the rent themselves. Unlike rent control, such subsidies do not reduce the quantity of housing supplied and, therefore, do not lead to housing shortages. Similarly, wage subsidies raise the living standards of the working poor without discouraging firms from hiring them. An example of a wage subsidy in America increase in the minimum wage reduces employment of the low-skilled by 1.5 percent. Extrapolating this to a $15 minimum wage, this 107-percent increase in the states where the federal minimum wage of $7.25 now prevails would imply a 16-percent decline in low-skilled employment (broadly consistent with the recent CBO study). That sounds like a substantial job loss.

It's true that some workers would experience higher incomes, and that, on net, incomes of low-wage workers would probably rise. But that doesn't mean the minimum wage is the best way to help low-wage workers or low-income families, as research clearly demonstrates that a large share of income gains from a higher minimum wage flows to families with higher incomes. An alternative policy—the Earned Income Tax Credit—targets benefits to lower-income families far more effectively, is proven to reduce poverty, and creates rather than destroys jobs.

Our survey finds other important results. First, contrary to what is sometimes claimed, there is no tendency for the most recent research to provide less evidence of job loss. Second, the sharper a study's focus on workers directly affected by the minimum wage, the stronger the evidence of job loss. For example, the average employment elasticity for those with at most a high school education is minus 0.24, implying that a 10-percent increase in the minimum wage reduces their employment by 2.4 percent. The only studies that produce more mixed evidence are studies of low-wage industries, like retail or restaurants. Notably, in these studies the job loss among those most affected by the minimum wage may be masked by employers substituting from lower-skilled to higher-skilled workers.

True, some studies don't find evidence of job loss. But advocates for a higher minimum wage can claim support from the overall body of research evidence only if they discard most of that evidence. The consensus of economic research on the effects of minimum wages points clearly to job loss, and policy makers should consider this job loss in weighing the potential costs and benefits of a sharp increase in the minimum wage. ■

AP IMAGES/LYNNE SLADKY

Questions to Discuss

1. Suppose you are an economist in charge of designing policy to help low-wage workers. Would you prefer a minimum wage or an earned income tax credit? Why?
2. Suppose now you are a politician running for office. Would it be easier to campaign on a platform of a higher minimum wage or a more generous earned income tax credit? Why?

Mr. Neumark is a professor of economics at the University of California, Irvine.

Source: The Wall Street Journal, March 19, 2021.

is the **earned income tax credit**, a US government program that supplements the incomes of low-wage workers.

These alternative policies are often better than price controls, but they are not perfect. Applying for rent or wage subsidies can be a burden for poor people. In addition, rent and wage subsidies cost the government money and, therefore, require higher taxes. As the next section shows, taxation has costs of its own.

6-2 The Surprising Study of Tax Incidence

All governments—from national governments around the world to local governments in small towns—use taxes to raise revenue for public projects, such as roads, schools, and national defense. Because taxes are such an important policy instrument and affect our lives in many ways, they appear throughout this book. This section begins our study of how taxes affect the economy.

To set the stage for the analysis, let us time travel back to the 1990s. Imagine that the local government in Mumbai decides to hold an annual ice-cream celebration—with a parade, fireworks, and speeches by B-town bigwigs. To raise revenue for the event, the city will place a ₹0.50 tax on each sale of an ice-cream cone. When the plan is announced, our two lobbying groups swing into action. The Maharashtra Hypothetical Association of Ice-Cream Eaters claims that consumers of ice cream are having trouble making ends meet, and it argues that **sellers** of ice cream should pay the tax. The Maratha Hypothetical Organization of Ice-Cream Makers claims that its members are struggling to survive in a competitive market, and it argues that **buyers** of ice cream should pay the tax. The mayor of Bombay, as it was called back then, hoping for a compromise, suggests that buyers and sellers each pay half the tax.

To assess the proposals, ask a simple but subtle question: When the government levies a tax on a good, who actually bears the burden of the tax? The people buying the good? The people selling it? Or, if buyers and sellers share the tax burden, what determines how it is divided? Can the government make that decision, as the mayor suggests, or do market forces intervene? These issues involve **tax incidence**, the study of how the burden of a tax is distributed among the various people in the economy. The tools of supply and demand will reveal some surprising lessons about tax incidence.

tax incidence
the manner in which the burden of a tax is shared among participants in a market

6-2a How Taxes on Sellers Affect Market Outcomes

Let's begin with a tax levied on sellers. Suppose sellers of ice-cream cones are required to send the local government ₹0.50 for every cone they sell. How does this law affect the buyers and sellers of ice cream? To answer this question, follow the three steps in Chapter 4 for analyzing supply and demand: (1) Decide whether the law affects the supply curve or the demand curve. (2) Decide which way the curve shifts. (3) Examine how the shift affects the equilibrium price and quantity.

Step One The immediate impact of the tax is on the sellers. Because the tax is not imposed on buyers, the quantity demanded at any price remains the same; thus, the demand curve does not change. By contrast, the tax on sellers makes the ice-cream business less profitable at any price, so it shifts the supply curve.

Step Two Because the tax on sellers raises the cost of producing and selling ice cream, it reduces the quantity supplied at every price. The supply curve shifts to the left (or, equivalently, upward).

Let's be precise about the size of the shift. For any market price of ice cream, the effective price to sellers—the amount they keep after paying the tax—is ₹0.50 lower. For example, if the market price of a cone happened to be ₹2.00, the effective price received by sellers would be ₹1.50. Whatever the market price, the effective price for sellers is ₹0.50 less, and sellers supply a quantity of ice cream that is appropriate for that lower price. In other words, to induce sellers to supply any given quantity, the market price must now be ₹0.50 higher to compensate for the effect of the tax. As Figure 6 shows, the supply curve shifts **upward** from S_1 to S_2 by the exact size of the tax (₹0.50).

Step Three Having determined how the supply curve shifts, let's now compare the initial and the new equilibria. Figure 6 shows that the equilibrium price of ice cream rises from ₹3.00 to ₹3.30, and the equilibrium quantity falls from 100 to 90 cones. Because sellers now sell less and buyers buy less, the tax reduces the size of the ice-cream market.

Figure 6

A Tax on Sellers

When a tax of ₹0.50 is levied on sellers, the supply curve shifts up by ₹0.50 from S_1 to S_2. The equilibrium quantity falls from 100 to 90 cones. The price that buyers pay rises from ₹3.00 to ₹3.30. The price that sellers receive (after paying the tax) falls from ₹3.00 to ₹2.80. Even though sellers are legally responsible for paying the tax, buyers and sellers share the burden.

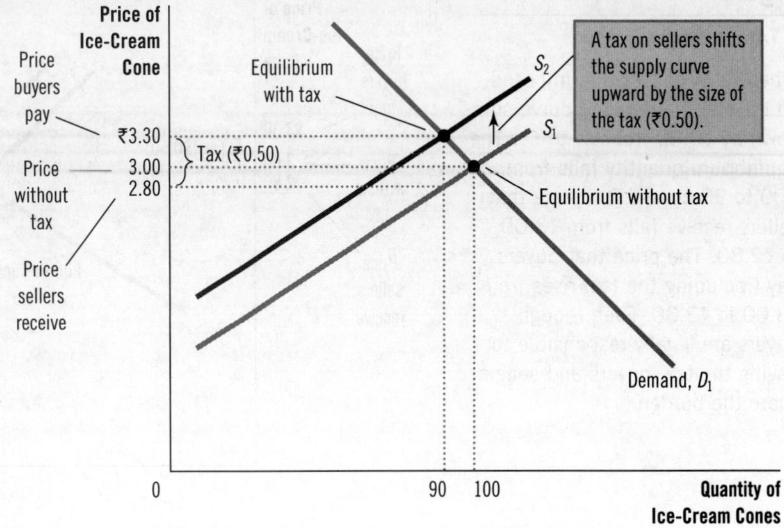

Implications Now consider the question of tax incidence: Who pays the tax? Although sellers, not buyers, send the money to the government, buyers and sellers share the burden. Because the tax increases the market price from ₹3.00 to ₹3.30, buyers pay ₹0.30 more for ice-cream cones. Sellers get a higher price (₹3.30), but after paying the tax, they only keep ₹2.80 (₹3.30 2 – ₹0.50 5 = ₹2.80), which is ₹0.20 less than they did before. The tax makes both buyers and sellers worse off.

To sum up, this analysis yields two lessons:

- Taxes discourage market activity. When a good is taxed, the quantity sold is smaller in the new equilibrium.
- Buyers and sellers share the tax burden. In the new equilibrium, buyers pay more, and sellers receive less.

6-2b How Taxes on Buyers Affect Market Outcomes?

Now consider a tax levied on buyers. Suppose that ice-cream lovers are required to send ₹0.50 to the local government for each cone they buy. What are the law's effects? Let's again turn to our three steps.

Step One The immediate impact is on the demand for ice cream. The supply curve doesn't change because, for any price, sellers have the same incentive to provide ice cream to the market. But buyers now have to pay a tax to the government (on top of the price to the sellers), so the tax shifts the demand curve for ice cream.

Step Two Next, determine the direction of the shift. Because the tax makes buying ice cream less attractive, buyers demand a smaller quantity of ice cream at every price. The demand curve shifts to the left (or, equivalently, downward), as shown in Figure 7.

Once again, let's be precise about the size of the shift. Because of the ₹0.50 tax on buyers, their effective price is now ₹0.50 higher than whatever the market price happens to be. For example, if the market price of a cone were ₹2.00, buyers would face an effective price for buyers of ₹2.50. Because buyers look at their total cost, including

Figure 7

A Tax on Buyers

When a tax of ₹0.50 is imposed on buyers, the demand curve shifts down by ₹0.50 from D_1 to D_2. The equilibrium quantity falls from 100 to 90 cones. The price that sellers receive falls from ₹3.00 to ₹2.80. The price that buyers pay (including the tax) rises from ₹3.00 to ₹3.30. Even though buyers are legally responsible for paying the tax, buyers and sellers share the burden.

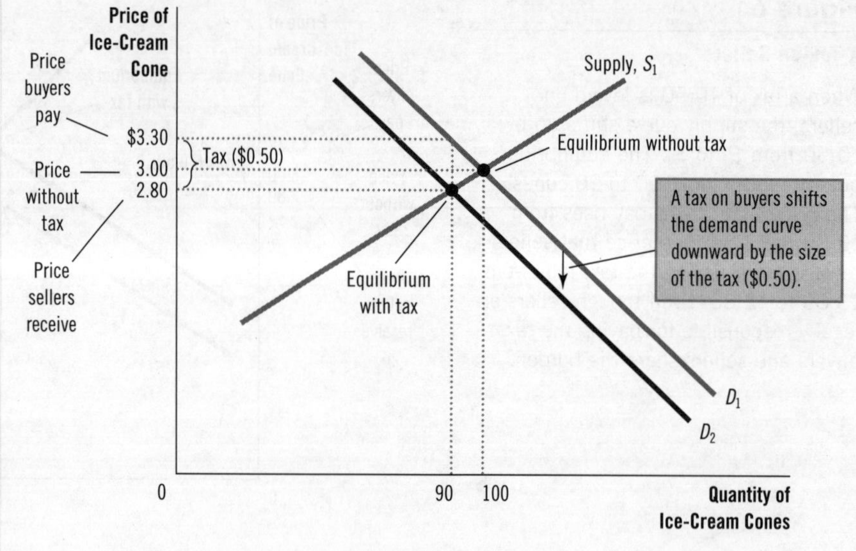

the tax, they demand a quantity of ice cream as if the market price were ₹0.50 higher than it actually is. In other words, to induce buyers to demand any given quantity, the market price must now be ₹0.50 lower to make up for the effect of the tax. The tax shifts the demand curve **downward** from D_1 to D_2 by the exact size of the tax (₹0.50).

Step Three Let's now evaluate the effect of the tax by comparing the initial equilibrium with the new one. In Figure 7, the equilibrium price of ice cream falls from ₹3.00 to ₹2.80, and the equilibrium quantity drops from 100 to 90 cones. Once again, the tax reduces the size of the ice-cream market. And once again, buyers and sellers share the burden. Sellers get a lower price for their product; buyers pay a lower market price to sellers than they previously did, but the effective price (including the tax) rises from ₹3.00 to ₹3.30.

Implications If you compare Figures 6 and 7, you will notice a surprising conclusion: **Taxes on sellers and taxes on buyers are equivalent.** In both cases, the tax inserts a wedge between the price that buyers pay and the price that sellers receive. Regardless of whether the tax is levied on buyers or sellers, the wedge remains the same. In either case, it shifts the relative position of the supply and demand curves. In the new equilibrium, buyers and sellers share the tax burden. The only difference between a tax on sellers and a tax on buyers is who sends the money to the government.

To better understand the equivalence of these two taxes, imagine the government collects the ₹0.50 ice-cream tax in a bowl on the counter of each ice-cream store. When the tax is imposed on sellers, the sellers are required to place ₹0.50 in the bowl each time they sell a cone. When the tax is imposed on buyers, the buyers must place ₹0.50 in the bowl whenever they buy a cone. Whether the ₹0.50 goes directly from the buyer's pocket into the bowl, or indirectly from the buyer's pocket into the seller's hand and then into the bowl, does not matter. Once the market reaches its new equilibrium, buyers and sellers share the burden, regardless of how the tax is levied.

Case Study

Who Bears the Burden of Salary Deductions?

If you have ever received a pay-slip, you probably noticed that taxes, Provident Fund (PF) contributions, cess, welfare payments, pension (NPS/CPS) etc. were deducted from the amount you earned.

Who bears the burden of this payroll tax—firms or workers?

Our analysis of tax incidence, shows that lawmakers cannot dictate the distribution of a tax burden so easily. A payroll tax is analyzed much the same as a tax on a good like ice cream. In this case, the good is labor, and the price is the wage. Again, the tax inserts a wedge—here, between the wage that firms pay and the wage that workers receive (AKA "take-home pay"). Figure 8 shows the outcome. When salary deductions are decided, the wage received by workers falls, and the wage paid by firms rises. In the end, workers and firms share the burden, much as the legislation requires, such as for employer and employee contributions to provident fund or retirement savings.

This example highlights an often overlooked lesson. Lawmakers can decide whether a tax comes from the buyer's pocket or from the seller's, but they cannot legislate the true burden of a tax. Rather, tax incidence depends on the forces of supply and demand. ●

6-2c Elasticity and Tax Incidence

How exactly is the tax burden divided between buyers and sellers? Only rarely will it be shared equally. To see this, consider the impact of taxation on the two markets in Figure 9. In both cases, the figure shows the initial supply and demand curves and a tax that drives a wedge between what buyers pay and sellers receive. (Not drawn in either panel is the new supply or demand curve. Which curve shifts depends on whether the tax is levied on buyers or sellers, a fact that is irrelevant for determining the tax's incidence.) The difference between the two panels is the relative elasticity of supply and demand.

Figure 8

A Payroll Tax

A payroll tax places a wedge between what firms pay and what workers receive. Comparing wages with and without the tax makes it clear that workers and firms share the tax burden. This division does not depend on whether the government imposes the tax entirely on workers, imposes it entirely on firms, or divides it equally between the two groups.

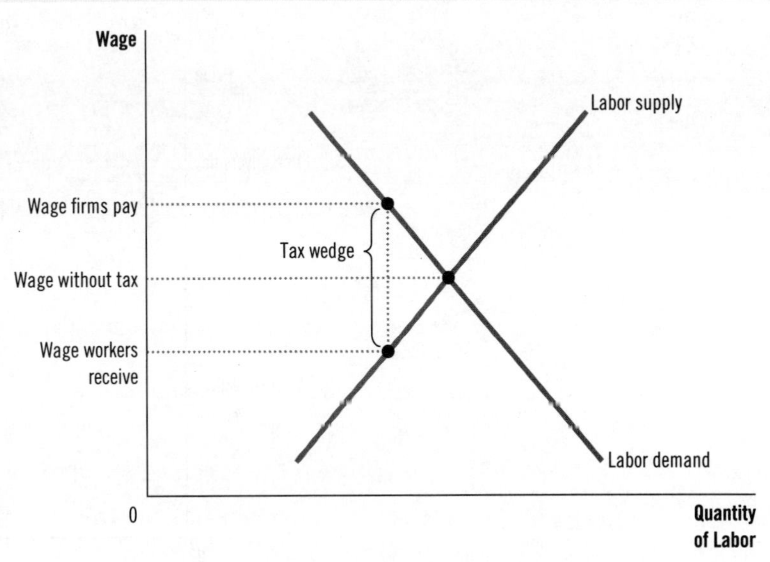

Panel (a) of Figure 9 shows a tax in a market with very elastic supply and relatively inelastic demand. That means that sellers are very responsive to changes in the price (so the supply curve is relatively flat), while buyers are not very responsive (so the demand curve is relatively steep). When a tax is imposed on a market like this one, the price received by sellers does not fall much, so sellers bear only a small burden. But the price paid by buyers rises substantially, indicating that they bear most of the tax burden.

Panel (b) of Figure 9 shows a tax in a market with fairly inelastic supply and very elastic demand. In this case, sellers are not very responsive to changes in the price (so

Figure 9

How a Tax Burden Is Divided

In panel (a), the supply curve is elastic, and the demand curve is inelastic. In this case, the price received by sellers falls only slightly, while the price paid by buyers rises substantially. This means that buyers bear most of the tax burden. In panel (b), the situation is reversed: The supply curve is inelastic, and the demand curve is elastic. In this case, the price received by sellers falls substantially, while the price paid by buyers rises only slightly. Here, sellers bear most of the burden.

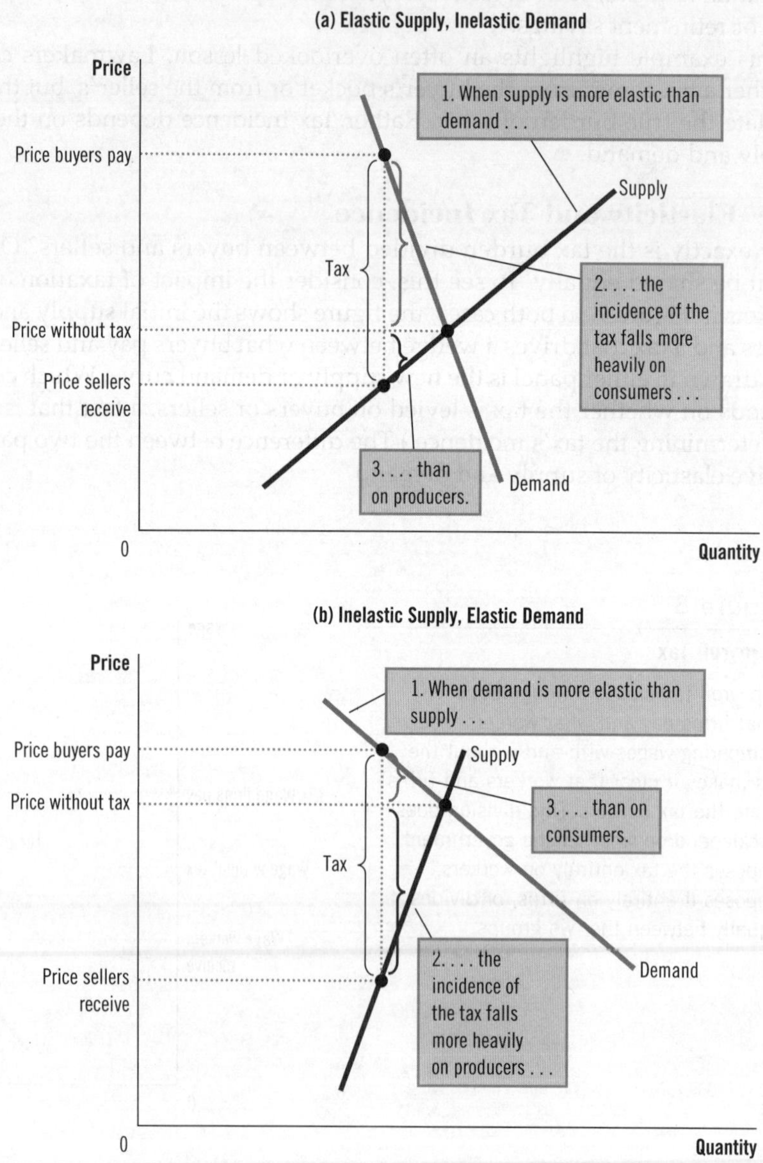

Subsidies: The Negative of Taxes

Indian government has announced various policies and programs which include offering subsidies. Subsidies are nothing but negative taxes. The idea here is to make the supply more attractive by offering better prices and offsetting production costs.

For instance, under the FAME (Faster Adoption and manufacturing of Hybrid and Electric Vehicles) Policy, the government has significantly subsidized EV produciton with the hope that EVs will be adopted by consumers and that will help conserve environment. The idea is to reduce taxes or offer subsidies to the production, such that the cost of manufacturing declines and these advantages from subsidy or lower tax, has a similar sharing incidence where some benefits pass on to the buyer through the market and if prices are lower, more buyers may get attracted to buying it. There were direct upfront on-road price reductions for buyers as well reflecting buyer side subsidies.

A similar effort has been observed through the PM Surya Ghar: Muft Bijli Yojana which encourages households to install rooftop solar panels for electricity generation by subsidizing upto 60% of the costs of such installation. It also offers free electricity generated from solar energy upto certain limits. This is another example of how a subsidy can help in demand generation for sustainable consumption practices.

Quick**Quiz**

5. A ₹1 per unit tax levied on consumers of a good is equivalent to
   a. a ₹1 per unit tax levied on producers of the good.
   b. a ₹1 per unit subsidy paid to producers of the good.
   c. a price floor that raises the good's price by ₹1 per unit.
   d. a price ceiling that raises the good's price by ₹1 per unit.
6. When a good is taxed, the burden falls mainly on consumers if
   a. the tax is levied on consumers.
   b. the tax is levied on producers.
   c. supply is inelastic and demand is elastic.
   d. supply is elastic and demand is inelastic.
7. Which of the following increases the quantity supplied, decreases the quantity demanded, and increases the price that consumers pay?
   a. the passage of a tax on a good
   b. the repeal of a tax on a good
   c. the imposition of a binding price floor
   d. the removal of a binding price floor
8. Which of the following increases the quantity supplied, increases the quantity demanded, and decreases the price that consumers pay?
   a. the passage of a tax on a good
   b. the repeal of a tax on a good
   c. the imposition of a binding price floor
   d. the removal of a binding price floor

Answers are at the end of the chapter.

the supply curve is steeper), while buyers are very responsive (so the demand curve is flatter). When a tax is imposed, the price paid by buyers doesn't rise much, but the price received by sellers falls substantially. Thus, sellers bear most of the tax burden.

Together, the two panels show a general lesson: **A tax burden falls more heavily on the side of the market that is less elastic.** Why is this true? In essence, elasticity measures the willingness of buyers or sellers to leave the market when conditions worsen. A small elasticity of demand means that buyers do not have good alternatives to consuming this particular good. A small elasticity of supply means that sellers do not have good alternatives to producing this particular good. When the good is taxed, the side of the market with fewer good alternatives is less willing to leave the market and bears more of the burden of the tax.

6-3 Conclusion

The economy is governed by two kinds of laws: the laws of supply and demand and the laws enacted by governments. In this chapter, we have begun to see how these laws interact. Price controls and taxes are common in various markets, and their effects are frequently debated. Even a little bit of economic knowledge can go a long way toward understanding and evaluating these policies.

Subsequent chapters analyze government policies in greater detail. We will examine the effects of taxation more fully and consider a broader range of policies. Yet the basic lessons will not change: When analyzing government policies, supply and demand are the first and most useful tools of analysis.

Chapter in a Nutshell

- A price ceiling is a legal maximum on the price of a good or service. Rent control is an example. If the ceiling is below the equilibrium price, then it is binding, and the quantity demanded exceeds the quantity supplied. Because of the resulting shortage, sellers must somehow ration the good or service among buyers.
- A price floor is a legal minimum on the price of a good or service. The minimum wage is an example. If the floor is above the equilibrium price, then it is binding, and the quantity supplied exceeds the quantity demanded. Because of the resulting surplus, buyers' demands for the good or service must somehow be rationed among sellers.
- When the government levies a tax on a good, the equilibrium quantity of the good falls. That is, a tax on a market shrinks the market's size.
- A tax on a good places a wedge between the price paid by buyers and the price received by sellers. When the market moves to the new equilibrium, buyers pay more for the good, and sellers receive less for it. In this sense, buyers and sellers share the tax burden. The incidence of a tax (that is, the division of the tax burden) does not depend on whether the tax is levied on buyers or sellers.
- The incidence of a tax depends on the price elasticities of supply and demand. Most of the burden falls on the side of the market that is less elastic because it cannot respond as easily to the tax by changing the quantity bought or sold.

Key Concepts

price ceiling, p. 112
price floor, p. 112
tax incidence, p. 124

Questions for Review

1. Give an example of a price ceiling and an example of a price floor.
2. Which causes a shortage of a good—a price ceiling or a price floor? Justify your answer with a graph.
3. What mechanisms allocate resources when the price of a good is not allowed to bring supply and demand into equilibrium?
4. Explain why economists frequently oppose price controls.
5. Suppose the government removes a tax on buyers of a good and levies a tax of the same size on sellers. How does this policy change affect the price that buyers pay sellers for this good, the amount buyers are out of pocket (including any tax payments they make), the amount sellers receive (net of any tax payments they make), and the quantity of the good sold?
6. How does a tax on a good affect the price paid by buyers, the price received by sellers, and the quantity sold?
7. What determines how the burden of a tax is divided between buyers and sellers? Why?

Problems and Applications

1. Lovers of comedy persuade the government to impose a price ceiling of ₹50 per ticket for live comedy performances. As a result of this policy, do more or fewer people attend comedy performances? Explain.

2. The government has decided that the free-market price of cheese is too low.
   a. Suppose the government imposes a binding price floor in the cheese market. Draw a supply-and-demand diagram to show the effect of this policy on the price and quantity of cheese sold. Is there a shortage or surplus of cheese?
   b. Producers of cheese complain that the price floor has reduced their total revenue. Is this possible? Explain.
   c. In response to cheese producers' complaints, the government agrees to purchase all the surplus cheese at the price floor. Compared to the basic price floor, who benefits from this new policy? Who loses?

3. A recent study found that the demand-and-supply schedules for Frisbees are as follows:

Price per Frisbee	Quantity Demanded	Quantity Supplied
₹11	1 million Frisbees	15 million Frisbees
10	2	12
9	4	9
8	6	6
7	8	3
6	10	1

   a. What are the equilibrium price and quantity of Frisbees?
   b. Frisbee manufacturers persuade the government that Frisbee production improves scientists' understanding of aerodynamics and is thus important for national security. A concerned parliament votes to impose a price floor ₹2 above the equilibrium price. What is the new market price? How many Frisbees are sold?
   c. Irate college students march in Delhi NCR and demand a reduction in the price of Frisbees. An even more concerned Lok Sabha votes to repeal the price floor and impose a price ceiling ₹1 below the former price floor. What is the new market price? How many Frisbees are sold?

4. Suppose the union government requires beer drinkers to pay a ₹2 tax on each case of beer purchased. (In fact, both the union and state governments impose beer taxes of some sort.)
   a. Draw a supply-and-demand diagram of the market for beer without the tax. Show the price paid by consumers, the price received by producers, and the quantity of beer sold. What is the difference between the price paid by consumers and the price received by producers?
   b. Now draw a supply-and-demand diagram for the beer market with the tax. Show the price paid by consumers, the price received by producers, and the quantity of beer sold. What is the difference between the price paid by consumers and the price received by producers? Has the quantity of beer sold increased or decreased?

5. A Mebmer of Parliament in Rajya Sabha wants to raise tax revenue and make workers better off. A staff member proposes raising the TDS paid by firms and using part of the extra revenue to reduce the tax paid by workers. Would this accomplish the MP's goal? Explain.

6. If the government places a ₹50,000 tax on luxury cars, will the price paid by consumers rise by more than ₹50,000, less than ₹50,000, or exactly ₹50,000? Explain.

7. The US Congress and the US President decide that the United States should reduce air pollution by reducing its use of gasoline. They impose a ₹0.50 tax on each gallon of gasoline sold.
   a. Should they impose this tax on producers or consumers? Explain carefully using a supply-and-demand diagram.
   b. If the demand for gasoline were more elastic, would this tax be more effective or less effective in reducing the quantity of gasoline consumed? Explain with both words and a diagram.
   c. Are consumers of gasoline helped or hurt by this tax? Why?
   d. Are workers in the oil industry helped or hurt by this tax? Why?

8. A case study in this chapter discusses the US federal minimum-wage law.
   a. Suppose the minimum wage is above the equilibrium wage in the market for unskilled labor. Using a supply-and-demand diagram of the market for unskilled labor, show the market wage, the number of workers who are employed, and the number of workers who are unemployed. Also, show the total wage payments to unskilled workers.
   b. Now suppose the Secretary of Labor proposes an increase in the minimum wage. What effect would this increase have on employment? Does the change in employment depend on the elasticity of demand, the elasticity of supply, both elasticities, or neither?
   c. What effect would this increase in the minimum wage have on unemployment? Does the change in unemployment depend on the elasticity of

demand, the elasticity of supply, both elasticities, or neither?

d. If the demand for unskilled labor were inelastic, would the proposed increase in the minimum wage raise or lower total wage payments to unskilled workers? Would your answer change if the demand for unskilled labor were elastic?

9. At Chinaswamy Stadium home of the Royal Challengers Bangalore (RCB), seating is limited to about 38,000. Hence, the number of tickets issued is fixed at that figure. Seeing a golden opportunity to raise revenue, the City of Bangalore levies a per ticket tax of ₹500 to be paid by the ticket buyer. RCB sports fans, a famously civic-minded lot, dutifully send in the ₹500 per ticket. Draw a well-labeled graph showing the impact of the tax. On whom does the tax burden fall—the team's owners, the fans, or both? Why?

10. A market is described by the following supply and demand curves:

$$Q^S \; 5 \; 2P$$
$$Q^D \; 5 \; 300 \; 2 \; P.$$

a. Solve for the equilibrium price and quantity.

b. If the government imposes a price ceiling of ₹90, does a shortage or surplus (or neither) develop? What are the price, quantity supplied, quantity demanded, and size of the shortage or surplus?

c. If the government imposes a price floor of ₹90, does a shortage or surplus (or neither) develop? What are the price, quantity supplied, quantity demanded, and size of the shortage or surplus?

d. Instead of a price control, the government levies a ₹30 tax on producers. As a result, the new supply curve is:

$$Q^S \; 5 \; 2(P \; 2 \; 30).$$

Does a shortage or surplus (or neither) develop? What are the price, quantity supplied, quantity demanded, and size of the shortage or surplus?

Quick**Quiz** Answers

1. d **2.** d **3.** a **4.** c **5.** a **6.** d **7.** c **8.** b

Chapter

7

Taxation, Efficiency, and Business Strategy

This first part of this chapter takes up the topic of **welfare economics**, the study of how the allocation of resources affects economic well-being. We begin by examining the benefits that buyers and sellers receive from engaging in market transactions. We then examine how society can make these benefits as large as possible. This analysis leads to a profound conclusion: The equilibrium of supply and demand in competitive markets maximizes the total benefits received by all buyers and sellers combined.

The study of welfare economics answers our question about the right price a product, say, of tomatoes: The price that balances the supply and demand for tomatoes is, in a particular sense, the best one because it maximizes the total welfare of consumers and producers. No consumer or producer of tomatoes needs to aim for this goal, but their joint action, directed by market prices, moves them toward a welfare-maximizing outcome, as if led by an invisible hand.

After learning about welfare economics and efficiency, we move on to the costs of taxation.

Because taxation has a large impact on the modern economy, the topic appears repeatedly throughout this book as we expand the tools at our disposal. Chapter 6 used supply, demand, and elasticity to show how a tax on a good affects its price and quantity and how the tax burden is split between buyers and sellers. This chapter extends the analysis to examine how taxes affect welfare, defined as the economic well-being of market participants.

GAUDILAB/SHUTTERSTOCK.COM; LECHATNOIR/E+/GETTY IMAGES

The effects of taxes on welfare might seem obvious. The govern- ment enacts taxes to raise revenue, and that revenue must come from someone's wallet. As Chapter 6 showed, both buyers and sell- ers of a good are worse off when it is taxed: Buyers pay more, and sellers receive less. Yet to fully understand how taxes affect well- being, we must compare the losses of buyers and sellers with the amount of revenue the government collects. The tools of welfare economics will enable this comparison. The analysis will show that the cost of taxes to buyers and sellers typically exceeds the revenue raised by the government. That is not to say that taxation is always undesirable. Tax revenue is needed to fund government programs, and these can be valuable. But judging alternative policies requires an understanding of how high the price of civilized society can be.

7-1 Consumer Surplus

We begin our study of welfare economics by looking at the benefits buyers receive from participating in a market.

7-1a Willingness to Pay

Imagine that you inherit from your great aunt a rare, mint-condition recording of Elvis Presley's first album. Because you don't care for Elvis's music, you decide to sell the album by auctioning it off.

Four Elvis fans come to your auction: Waheda, Ila, Mariah, and Karan. They all want the album, but they have set limits on the amount they will pay for it. Table 1 shows the maximum price that each of the four possible buyers would pay. A buyer's maximum is called her **willingness to pay**, and it measures how much she values the good. Each buyer would be eager to buy the album at a price less than her willingness to pay, and each would refuse to buy the album at a price greater than her willingness to pay. At a price equal to her willingness to pay, the buyer would be indifferent about buying the good: If the price is exactly the same as the value she places on the album, she would be equally happy buying it or keeping her money.

willingness to pay
the maximum amount that a buyer will pay for a good

To sell your album, you begin the bidding process at a low price, say, ₹100. Because all four buyers are willing to pay much more, the price quickly rises. The bidding stops when Waheda bids ₹800 (or slightly more). At this point, Ila, Mariah, and Karan have dropped out of the bidding because they are unwilling to offer more than ₹800. Waheda pays ₹800 and gets the album. Note that the album goes to the buyer who values it most.

Table 1

The Willingness to Pay of Four Possible Buyers

Buyer	Willingness to Pay
Waheda	₹1,000
Ila	800
Mariah	700
Karan	500

What benefit does Waheda derive from buying the Elvis Presley album? In a sense, she has found a bargain: She is willing to pay ₹1,000 for the album but hands over only ₹800. Economists say that Waheda receives **consumer surplus** of ₹200. **Consumer surplus** is the amount a buyer is willing to pay for a good minus the amount the buyer actually pays for it.

consumer surplus
the amount a buyer is willing to pay for a good minus the amount the buyer actually pays for it

Consumer surplus measures the benefit buyers receive from participating in a market. In this example, Waheda gets a ₹200 benefit because she pays only ₹800 for something she values at ₹1,000. Ila, Mariah, and Karan get no consumer surplus because they leave the auction without the album and without paying anything.

Now consider a somewhat different example. Suppose that you have two identical Elvis Presley albums to sell. Again, you auction them off to the four possible buyers. To keep things simple, assume that both copies are to be sold for the same price and that no one wants more than one album. Therefore, the price rises until two buyers are left.

In this case, the bidding stops when Waheda and Ila each bid ₹700 (or slightly higher). At this price, Waheda and Ila are happy to buy an album, and Mariah and Karan are not willing to bid any higher. Waheda and Ila each receive consumer surplus equal to her willingness to pay minus the price. Waheda's consumer surplus is ₹300, and Ila's is ₹100. Waheda's consumer surplus is higher than in the previous example because she pays less for the same album. The total consumer surplus in the market is ₹400.

7-1b Using the Demand Curve to Measure Consumer Surplus?

Consumer surplus is closely related to the demand curve for a product. To see how, consider the demand curve for this rare Elvis Presley album.

Begin by using the willingness to pay of the four possible buyers to find the album's market demand schedule. The table in Figure 1 shows the demand schedule that corresponds to the valuations in Table 1. If the price is above ₹1,000, the

Figure 1

The Demand Schedule and the Demand Curve?

The table shows the demand schedule for the buyers (listed in Table 1) of the mint-condition copy of Elvis Presley's first album. The graph shows the corresponding demand curve. The height of the demand curve reflects the buyers' willingness to pay.

Price	Buyers	Quantity Demanded
More than ₹1,000	None	0
₹800 to ₹1,000	Waheda	1
₹700 to ₹800	Waheda, Ila	2
₹500 to ₹700	Waheda, Ila, Mariah	3
₹500 or less	Waheda, Ila, Mariah, Karan	4

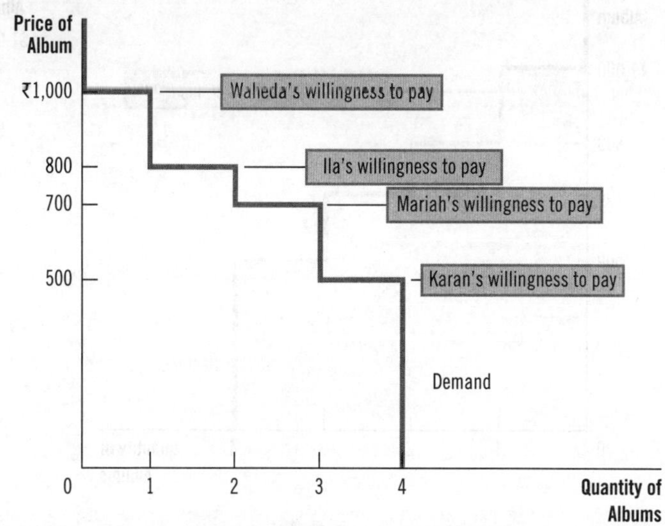

quantity demanded is 0 because no buyer is willing to pay that much. If the price is between ₹800 and ₹1,000, the quantity demanded is 1: Only Waheda is willing to pay such a high price. If the price is between ₹700 and ₹800, the quantity demanded is 2 because both Waheda and Ila are willing to pay the price. You can continue this analysis for other prices as well. In this way, the demand schedule is derived from the willingness to pay of the four possible buyers.

The graph in Figure 1 shows the demand curve that corresponds to this demand schedule. Note the relationship between the height of the curve and the buyers' willingness to pay. At any quantity, the price given by the demand curve shows the willingness to pay of the **marginal buyer**, the buyer who would leave the market first if the price were any higher. At a quantity of 4 albums, for instance, the demand curve has a height of ₹500, the price that Karan (the marginal buyer) is willing to pay. At a quantity of 3 albums, the demand curve has a height of ₹700, the price that Mariah (now the marginal buyer) is willing to pay.

Because the demand curve reflects buyers' willingness to pay, it can also be used to measure consumer surplus. Figure 2 does this for our two examples. In panel (a), the price is ₹800 (or slightly above), and the quantity demanded is 1. Note that the area above the price and below the demand curve equals ₹200. This amount is the consumer surplus calculated earlier when only 1 album is sold.

Panel (b) of Figure 2 shows consumer surplus when the price is ₹700 (or slightly above). In this case, the area above the price and below the demand curve equals the total area of the two rectangles: Waheda's consumer surplus at this price is ₹300, and Ila's is ₹100. This area equals a total of ₹400. Once again, this amount is the consumer surplus calculated earlier.

Figure 2

Measuring Consumer Surplus with the Demand Curve?

In panel (a), the price of the good is ₹800, and consumer surplus is ₹200. In panel (b), the price is ₹700, and consumer surplus is ₹400.

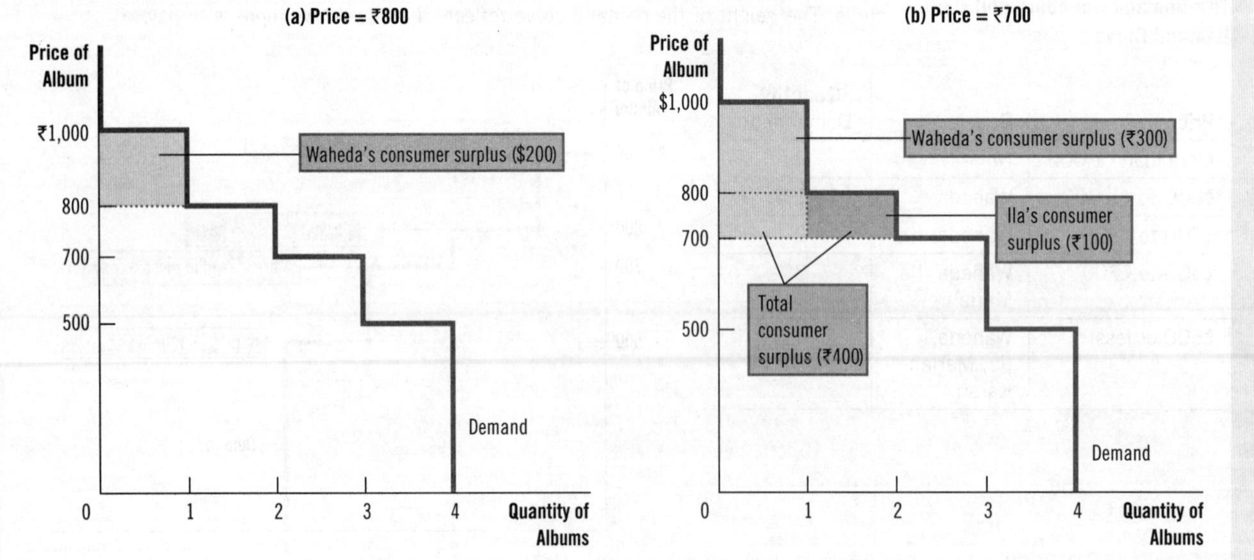

The lesson from this example holds for all demand curves: **The area below the demand curve and above the price measures the consumer surplus in a market.** This is true because the height of the demand curve represents the value buyers place on the good, measured by their willingness to pay for it. The difference between this willingness to pay and the market price is each buyer's consumer surplus. The area between the demand curve and the price line is the sum of the consumer surplus of all buyers in the market for a good or service.

7-1c How a Lower Price Raises Consumer Surplus?

Because buyers want to pay less for the goods they buy, a lower price makes buyers of a good better off. But how much does buyers' well-being increase in response to a lower price? The concept of consumer surplus offers a precise answer.

Figure 3 shows a typical demand curve. You may notice that it gradually slopes downward instead of taking discrete steps as in the previous two figures. In a market with many buyers, the resulting steps from each buyer dropping out are so small that they form a smooth demand curve. Although this curve has a different shape, the ideas we have just developed still apply: Consumer surplus is the area above the price line and below the demand curve. In panel (a), the price is P_1, and consumer surplus is the area of triangle ABC.

Now suppose that the price falls from P_1 to P_2, as shown in panel (b). Consumer surplus equals area ADF. The increase in consumer surplus from the price cut is the area BCFD.

Figure 3

How Price Affects Consumer Surplus?

In panel (a), the price is P_1, the quantity demanded is Q_1, and consumer surplus equals the area of the triangle ABC. When the price falls from P_1 to P_2, as in panel (b), the quantity demanded rises from Q_1 to Q_2, and consumer surplus rises to the area of the triangle ADF. The increase in consumer surplus (area BCFD) occurs in part because existing consumers pay less (area BCED) and in part because new consumers enter the market at the lower price (area CEF).

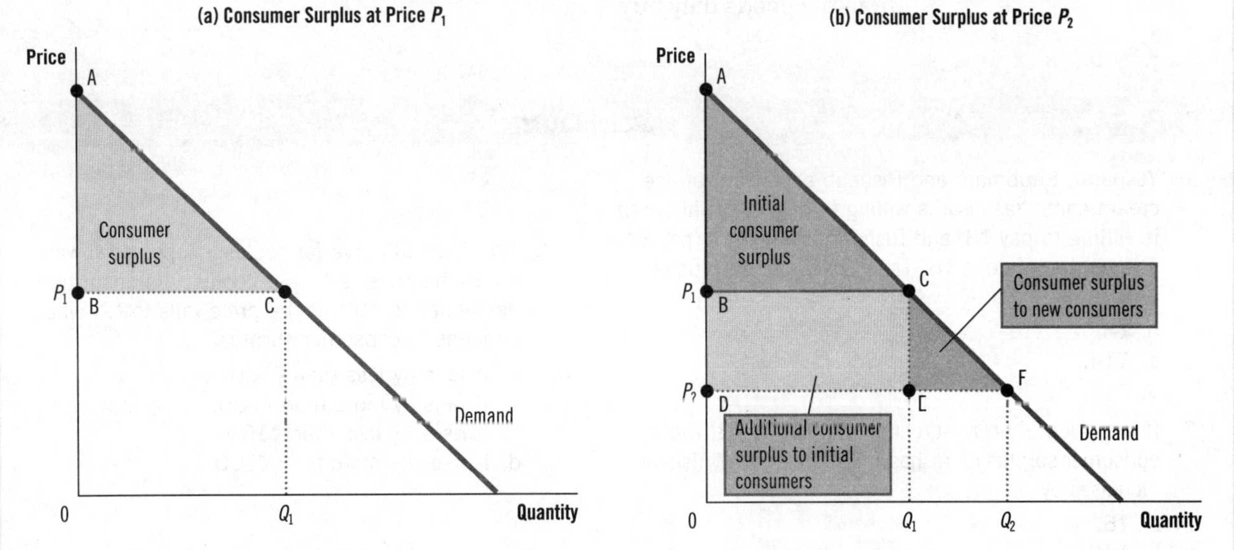

This increase in consumer surplus has two parts. First, buyers who were already purchasing Q_1 of the good at the higher price P_1 are better off because now they pay less. The increase in consumer surplus of existing buyers is the reduction in the amount they pay. It equals the area of the rectangle BCED. Second, some new buyers enter the market because they are willing to buy the good at the lower price, which increases the quantity demanded from Q_1 to Q_2. The consumer surplus for the newcomers is the area of the triangle CEF.

7-1d What Does Consumer Surplus Measure?

The concept of consumer surplus can be helpful in making judgments about the desirability of market outcomes. Having seen what consumer surplus is, let's consider whether it is a good measure of economic well-being.

Imagine that you are a policymaker designing an economic system. Would you care about consumer surplus? Because it is the amount that buyers are willing to pay for a good minus the amount they actually pay for it, consumer surplus measures the benefit that buyers derive from a market **as the buyers themselves perceive it**. Consumer surplus is a good measure of economic well-being if policymakers want to satisfy buyers' preferences.

In some circumstances, policymakers might choose to disregard consumer surplus because they do not respect the preferences that drive buyer behavior. For example, addicts are willing to pay a high price for their drug of choice. Yet policymakers would be unlikely to say that addicts get a large benefit from being able to buy drugs at a low price (even though addicts might say they do). From the standpoint of society, willingness to pay in this instance is not a good measure of the buyers' benefit, and consumer surplus is not a good measure of economic well-being, because addicts are not looking after their own best interests.

In most markets, however, consumer surplus reflects economic well-being. Economists generally assume that buyers are rational when they make decisions. Rational people do the best they can to achieve their objectives, given their opportunities. Economists also normally assume that people's preferences should be respected. In this case, consumers are the best judges of how much benefit they get from the goods they buy.

Quick**Quiz**

1. Yashasvi, Shubman, and Rishabh each want an ice-cream cone. Yashasvi is willing to pay ₹12, Shubman is willing to pay ₹8, and Rishabh is willing to pay ₹4. The market price is ₹6. Their consumer surplus is
   a. ₹6.
   b. ₹8.
   c. ₹14.
   d. ₹18.
2. If the price of an ice-cream cone falls to ₹3, the consumer surplus of Yashasvi, Shubman, and Rishabh increases by
   a. ₹6.
   b. ₹7.
   c. ₹8.
   d. ₹9.
3. The demand curve for cookies slopes downward. When the price is ₹3 per cookie, the quantity demanded is 100. If the price falls to ₹2, what happens to consumer surplus?
   a. It falls by less than ₹100.
   b. It falls by more than ₹100.
   c. It rises by less than ₹100.
   d. It rises by more than ₹100.

Answers are at the end of the chapter.

7-2 Producer Surplus

Let's now turn to the other side of the market and consider the benefits sellers receive from participating in a market. The analysis of sellers' welfare is parallel to the analysis of buyers' welfare.

7-2a Cost and the Willingness to Sell

Imagine that you are a homeowner in 1970 Kolkata and want to get your house painted. You turn to four sellers of painting services: Vincent, Claude, Pablo, and Andy. Each painter is willing to do the work for you if the price is right. You set up an auction and take bids from the four painters.

Each painter is willing to take the job if the price exceeds his cost of doing the work. Here the term **cost** should be interpreted as the painter's opportunity cost: It includes his out-of-pocket expenses (for paint, brushes, and so on) and, most importantly, the value that he places on his time. Table 2 shows each painter's cost. Because a painter's cost is the lowest price he would accept for his work, it measures his willingness to sell his services. Each painter would be eager to sell his services at a price greater than his cost and would refuse to sell his services at a price less than his cost. At a price exactly equal to his cost, he would be indifferent about selling his services: He would be equally satisfied getting the job or using his time and energy elsewhere.

cost
the value of everything a seller must give up to produce a good

When you take bids, the price might start high, but it quickly falls as the painters compete for the job. Once Andy has bid ₹2,400 (or slightly less), he is the sole remaining bidder. Andy wants to do the job for this price because his cost is only ₹2,000. Vincent, Claude, and Pablo are unwilling to do it for less than ₹2,400. Note that the job goes to the painter who can do the work at the lowest cost.

What benefit does Andy derive from getting the job? Because he is willing to do the work for ₹2,000 but is paid ₹2,400, economists say that he receives **producer surplus** of ₹400. **Producer surplus** is the amount a seller is paid minus his cost of production. It measures how much a seller benefits from participating in a market.

producer surplus
the amount a seller is paid for a good minus the seller's cost of providing it

Now consider a different example. Suppose two houses need painting. Again, you auction off the jobs to the four painters. To keep things simple, assume that no painter can paint both houses and that you will pay the same amount to paint each house. Therefore, the price falls until two painters are left.

In this case, the auction stops when Andy and Pablo each bid ₹3,200 (or slightly less). They are willing to do the work at this price, while Vincent and Claude won't go lower. At ₹3,200, Andy's producer surplus is ₹1,200, and Pablo's is ₹800. The total producer surplus in the market is ₹2,000.

Table 2
The Costs of Four Possible Sellers

Seller	Cost
Vincent	₹3,600
Claude	3,200
Pablo	2,400
Andy	2,000

7-2b Using the Supply Curve to Measure Producer Surplus

Just as consumer surplus is closely related to the demand curve, producer surplus is closely related to the supply curve. To see how, let's derive the supply curve for painting services.

Begin by using the costs of the four painters to find the supply schedule. The table in Figure 4 shows the schedule that corresponds to the costs in Table 2. If the price is below ₹2,000, no painter will do the job, so the quantity supplied is zero. If the price is between ₹2,000 and ₹2,400, only Andy will do it, so the quantity supplied is 1. If the price is between ₹2,400 and ₹3,200, Andy and Pablo will do the work, so the quantity supplied is 2, and so on. Thus, the supply schedule is derived from the costs of the four painters.

The graph in Figure 4 shows the supply curve that corresponds to this supply schedule. Note that the height of the supply curve is related to the sellers' costs. At any quantity, the price given by the supply curve shows the cost of the **marginal seller**, the seller who would leave the market first if the price were lower. At a quantity of 4 houses, for instance, the supply curve has a height of ₹3,600, the cost that Vincent (the marginal seller) incurs to provide his painting services. At a quantity of 3 houses, the supply curve has a height of ₹3,200, the cost that Claude (who is now the marginal seller) incurs.

Because the supply curve reflects sellers' costs, it can be used to measure producer surplus. Figure 5 uses the supply curve to compute producer surplus in the two examples. In panel (a), the price is ₹2,400 (or slightly less), and the quantity supplied is 1. The area below the price and above the supply curve equals ₹400. This is the producer surplus calculated earlier for Andy.

Panel (b) of Figure 5 shows producer surplus when the price is ₹3,200 (or slightly less). In this case, the area below the price and above the supply curve equals the total area of the two rectangles. This area equals ₹2,000, the producer surplus computed earlier for Pablo and Andy when two houses needed painting.

Figure 4

The Supply Schedule and the Supply Curve

The table shows the supply schedule for the sellers (listed in Table 2) of painting services. The graph shows the corresponding supply curve. The height of the supply curve reflects the sellers' costs.

Price	Sellers	Quantity Supplied
₹3,600 or more	Vincent, Claude, Pablo, Andy	4
₹3,200 to ₹3,600	Claude, Pablo, Andy	3
₹2,400 to ₹3,200	Pablo, Andy	2
₹2,000 to ₹2,400	Andy	1
Less than ₹2,000	None	0

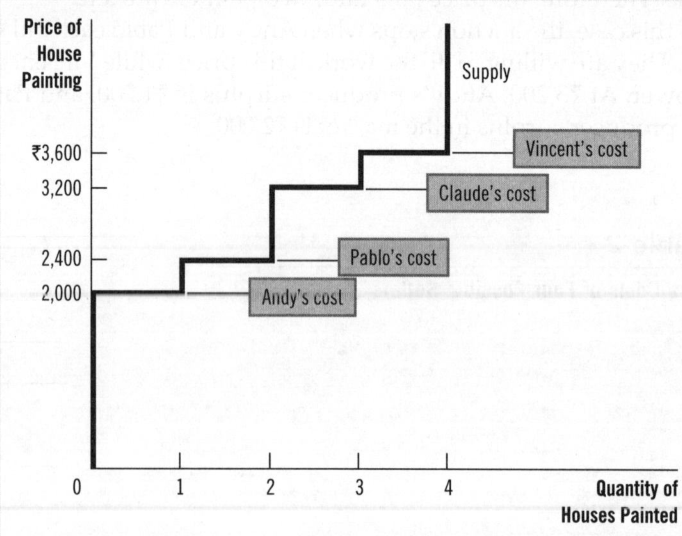

Figure 5

Measuring Producer Surplus with the Supply Curve

In panel (a), the price of the good is ₹2,400, and producer surplus is ₹400. In panel (b), the price is ₹3,200, and producer surplus is ₹2,000.

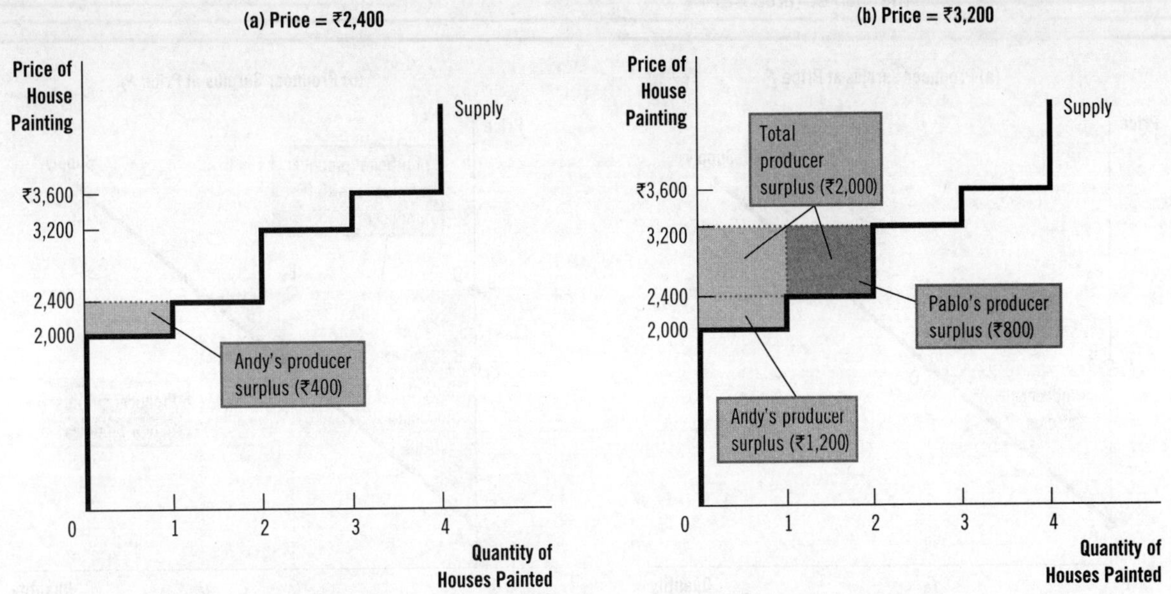

The lesson from this example applies to all supply curves: **The area below the price and above the supply curve measures the producer surplus in a market.** The logic is straightforward: The height of the supply curve measures sellers' costs, and the difference between the price and the cost of production is each seller's producer surplus. Thus, the area between the price line and the supply curve is the sum of all sellers' producer surplus.

7-2c How a Higher Price Raises Producer Surplus

You will not be surprised to hear that sellers generally prefer a higher price for the goods they sell. But how much does sellers' well-being increase in response to a higher price? The concept of producer surplus offers an answer.

Figure 6 shows a typical upward-sloping supply curve that would arise in a market with many sellers. Although this supply curve differs in shape from the previous one, producer surplus is measured in the same way: Producer surplus is the area below the price and above the supply curve. In panel (a), the price is P_1, and producer surplus is the area of triangle ABC.

Panel (b) shows what happens when the price rises from P_1 to P_2. Producer surplus now equals area ADF. This increase in producer surplus has two parts. First, those sellers who were already selling Q_1 of the good at the lower price of P_1 get more for what they sell. The increase in producer surplus for these existing sellers equals the area of the rectangle BCED. Second, new sellers enter the market at the higher price, so the quantity supplied increases from Q_1 to Q_2. The producer surplus of these newcomers is the area of the triangle CEF.

Figure 6

How Price Affects Producer Surplus?

In panel (a), the price is P_1, the quantity supplied is Q_1, and producer surplus equals the area of triangle ABC. When the price rises from P_1 to P_2, as in panel (b), the quantity supplied rises from Q_1 to Q_2, and producer surplus increases to the area of the triangle ADF. The increase in producer surplus (area BCFD) occurs in part because existing producers receive more at the higher price (area BCED) and in part because the higher price induces new producers to enter the market (area CEF).

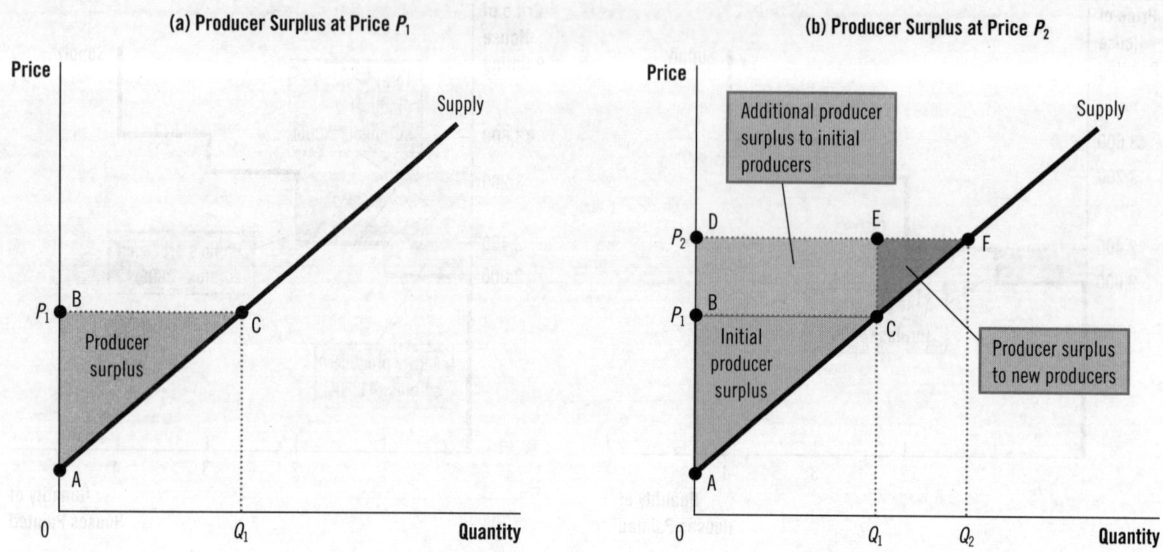

As this analysis shows, producer surplus measures the well-being of sellers in much the same way that consumer surplus measures the well-being of buyers. Because these two measures of economic welfare are so similar, it is natural to consider them together, as we do in the next section.

Quick**Quiz**

4. Diego, Lionel, and Cristiano are available to work as tutors for the semester. The opportunity cost of tutoring is ₹400 for Diego, ₹200 for Lionel, and ₹100 for Cristiano. The university is hiring tutors at a price of ₹300. Producer surplus in this market is
   a. ₹100.
   b. ₹200.
   c. ₹300.
   d. ₹400.
5. Dipak has been working full-time as a gardener for ₹300 a week. When the market price rises to ₹400, Hemant becomes a gardener as well. How much does producer surplus rise because of this price increase?
   a. by less than ₹100
   b. between ₹100 and ₹200
   c. between ₹200 and ₹300
   d. by more than ₹300
6. The supply curve for a product is $Q^S = 2P$, and the market price is ₹10. What is producer surplus in this market? (Hint: Graph the supply curve and recall the formula for the area of a triangle.)
   a. ₹5
   b. ₹20
   c. ₹100
   d. ₹200

Answers are at the end of the chapter.

7-3 Market Efficiency

Consumer surplus and producer surplus are the basic tools that economists use to study the welfare of buyers and sellers in a market. These tools can help address a fundamental question: Do competitive markets reach a desirable allocation of resources?

7-3a Benevolent Social Planners

One input into measuring societal well-being is the sum of consumer surplus and producer surplus, which we call **total surplus**. Consumer surplus is the benefit that buyers receive from participating in a market, and producer surplus is the benefit that sellers receive. Total surplus is, therefore, a natural variable for the social planners to consider when judging a market's allocation of resources.

To better understand this measure, recall the definitions of consumer and producer surplus. Consumer surplus is:

$$\text{Consumer surplus} = \text{Value to buyers} - \text{Amount paid by buyers.}$$

Similarly, producer surplus is:

$$\text{Producer surplus} = \text{Amount received by sellers} - \text{Cost to sellers.}$$

Adding consumer and producer surplus together, we obtain:

$$\begin{aligned}\text{Total surplus} &= (\text{Value to buyers} - \text{Amount paid by buyers}) \\ &\quad + (\text{Amount received by sellers} - \text{Cost to sellers}).\end{aligned}$$

Here, the amount paid by buyers equals the amount received by sellers, so the middle two terms cancel each other. As a result:

$$\text{Total surplus} = \text{Value to buyers} - \text{Cost to sellers.}$$

The total surplus in a market is the total value to buyers of the goods, measured by their willingness to pay, minus the total cost to sellers of providing those goods.

If an allocation of resources maximizes total surplus, economists say that the allocation exhibits **efficiency**. If an allocation is not efficient, some of the potential gains from trade among buyers and sellers are not being realized. For example, an allocation is inefficient if a good is not being produced by the sellers with the lowest costs. In this case, moving production from a high-cost producer to a lower-cost producer would reduce the total cost to sellers and raise total surplus. Similarly, an allocation is inefficient if a good is not being consumed by the buyers who are willing to pay the most for it. In this case, moving consumption of the good from a buyer with a low valuation to a buyer with a higher valuation would raise total surplus.

efficiency
the property regarding a resource allocation of maximizing the total surplus received by all members of society

In addition to efficiency, the social planners might also care about **equality**—that is, whether the various buyers and sellers in the market have similar levels of economic well-being. In essence, the gains from trade in a market are like a pie to be shared among the market participants. The question of efficiency concerns whether the pie is as big as possible. The question of equality concerns how the pie is sliced and distributed among members of society. This chapter focuses on efficiency as

equality
the property of distributing economic prosperity uniformly among the members of society

the social planners' criterion. Keep in mind, however, that real policymakers often care about equality as well.

7-3b Evaluating the Market Equilibrium

Figure 7 shows the welfare measures when a market reaches the equilibrium of supply and demand. Recall that consumer surplus equals the area above the price and under the demand curve, and producer surplus equals the area below the price and above the supply curve. The area between the supply and demand curves up to the point of equilibrium represents the total surplus in this market.

Is this equilibrium allocation of resources efficient? That is, does it maximize total surplus? Recall that when a market is in equilibrium, the price determines which of the possible buyers and sellers participate in the market. Buyers who value the good more than the price (represented by the segment AE on the demand curve) choose to buy it; buyers who value it less than the price (represented by the segment EB) do not. Similarly, sellers whose costs are less than the price (represented by the segment CE on the supply curve) choose to produce and sell the good; sellers whose costs are greater than the price (represented by the segment ED) do not.

These observations lead to two insights about market outcomes:

1. Competitive markets allocate the supply of goods to the buyers who value them most, as measured by their willingness to pay.
2. Competitive markets allocate the demand for goods to the sellers who can produce them at the lowest cost.

Thus, given the quantity produced and sold in a market equilibrium, the social planners cannot increase economic well-being by changing the allocation of consumption among buyers or the allocation of production among sellers.

Figure 7

Consumer and Producer Surplus in the Market Equilibrium

Total surplus—the sum of consumer and producer surplus—is the area between the supply and demand curves up to the equilibrium quantity.

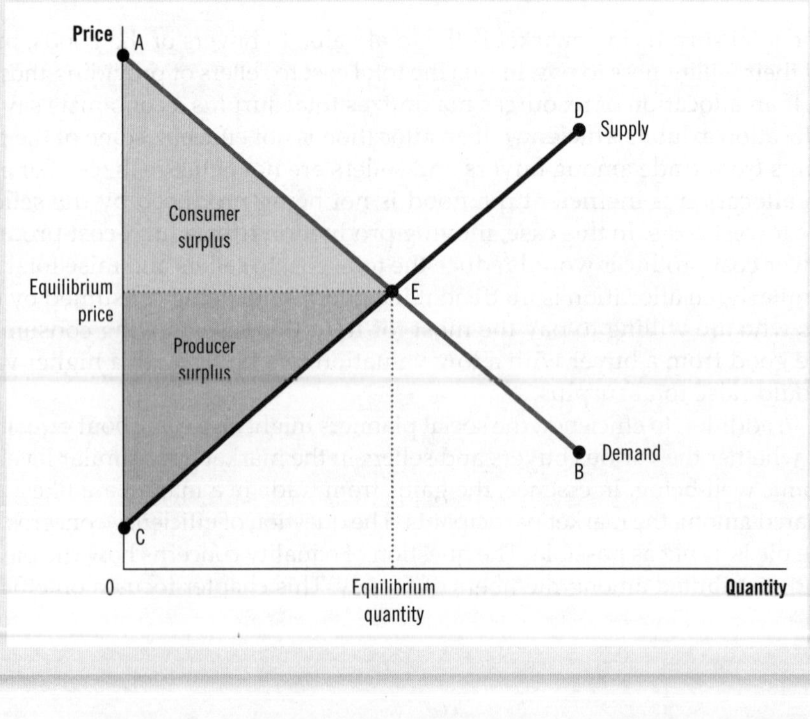

But can the social planners raise well-being by increasing or decreasing the quantity of the good? The answer is no, as stated in this third insight about market outcomes:

3. Competitive markets produce the quantity of goods that maximizes the sum of consumer and producer surplus.

Figure 8 shows why this is true. To interpret this figure, recall that the demand curve reflects the value to buyers and the supply curve reflects the cost to sellers. At any quantity below the equilibrium level, such as Q_1, the value to the marginal buyer exceeds the cost to the marginal seller. As a result, increasing the quantity produced and consumed raises total surplus. This continues to be true until the quantity reaches the equilibrium level. Conversely, at any quantity beyond the equilibrium level, such as Q_2, the value to the marginal buyer is less than the cost to the marginal seller. In this case, decreasing the quantity raises total surplus, and this continues to be true until the quantity falls to the equilibrium level. To maximize total surplus, the social planners would choose the quantity at which the supply and demand curves intersect.

Together, these three insights tell us that the market outcome maximizes the sum of consumer and producer surplus. In other words, the equilibrium outcome is an efficient allocation of resources. Social planners concerned about efficiency can, therefore, leave the market outcome just as they find it. This policy of leaving well enough alone goes by the French expression **laissez-faire**, which literally translates to "leave to do" but is more broadly interpreted as "let people do as they will."

Society is lucky that the social planners don't need to intervene. Imagining what all-powerful, all-knowing, and well-intentioned planners would do has been a useful exercise, but let's face it: Such characters are hard to come by. Some dictators

Figure 8

The Efficiency of the Equilibrium Quantity

At quantities less than the equilibrium quantity, such as Q_1, the value to buyers exceeds the cost to sellers. At quantities greater than the equilibrium quantity, such as Q_2, the cost to sellers exceeds the value to buyers. Therefore, the market equilibrium maximizes the sum of producer and consumer surplus.

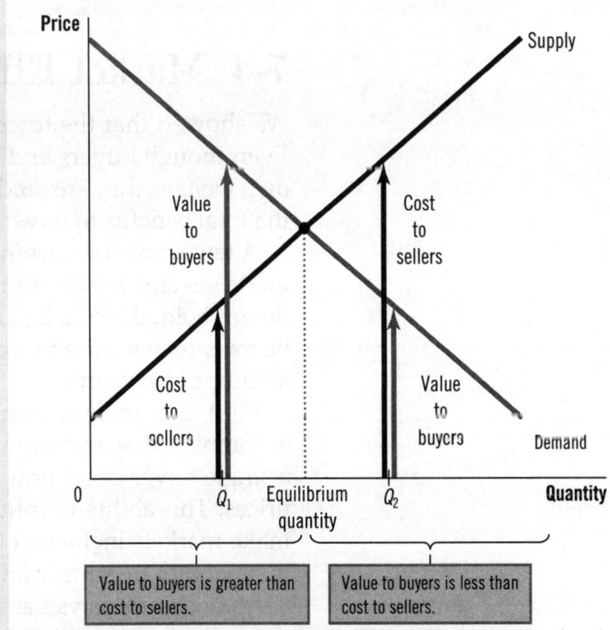

may be close to all powerful, but they are rarely benevolent. Even if we found some people so virtuous, they would lack crucial information.

Suppose the social planners tried to choose an efficient allocation of resources on their own instead of relying on market forces. To do so, they would need to know the value of a particular good to every potential consumer and the cost for every potential producer. And they would need this information not only for this market but for every one of the many thousands of markets in the economy. This task is practically impossible, which explains why economies with substantial central planning are rife with inefficiencies.

QuickQuiz

7. Rhea values her time at ₹60 an hour. She spends 2 hours giving Jayla a massage. Jayla was willing to pay as much as ₹300 for the massage, but they negotiated a price of ₹200. In this transaction,
   a. consumer surplus is ₹20 larger than producer surplus.
   b. consumer surplus is ₹40 larger than producer surplus.
   c. producer surplus is ₹20 larger than consumer surplus.
   d. producer surplus is ₹40 larger than consumer surplus.
8. An efficient allocation of resources maximizes
   a. consumer surplus.
   b. producer surplus.
   c. consumer surplus plus producer surplus.
   d. consumer surplus minus producer surplus.
9. When a market is in equilibrium, the buyers are those with the ________ willingness to pay, and the sellers are those with the ________ costs.
   a. highest; highest
   b. highest; lowest
   c. lowest; highest
   d. lowest; lowest
10. Producing a quantity larger than the equilibrium of supply and demand is inefficient because the marginal buyer's willingness to pay is
    a. negative.
    b. zero.
    c. positive but less than the marginal seller's cost.
    d. positive and greater than the marginal seller's cost.

Answers are at the end of the chapter.

7-4 Market Efficiency and Market Failure

We showed that the forces of supply and demand allocate resources efficiently. Even though buyers and sellers in a market are each concerned only about their own welfare, they are guided by an invisible hand to an equilibrium that maximizes the total benefits to buyers and sellers.

A few words of warning are in order. To conclude that markets are efficient, we made several assumptions about how markets work. When these assumptions do not hold, the conclusion that the market equilibrium is efficient may no longer be true. As we close this chapter, let's briefly consider two of the most important assumptions we made.

First, our analysis assumed that markets are perfectly competitive. In actual economies, however, competition is sometimes far from perfect. In some markets, a single buyer or seller (or a small group of them) may be able to control market prices. This ability to influence prices is called **market power**. Market power can make markets inefficient by keeping the price and quantity away from the levels that equilibrate supply and demand.

Second, our analysis assumed that the market outcome matters only to the buyers and sellers who participate in the market. Yet sometimes, the decisions of buyers and sellers affect bystanders. Pollution is the classic example. The use of agricultural pesticides, for instance, affects not only the manufacturers who make them and the farmers who use them but also many others who breathe the air or drink the water contaminated by these pesticides. When a market exhibits such side effects, called **externalities**, the welfare implications of market activity depend on more than just the value realized by buyers and the cost incurred by sellers. Because buyers and sellers may ignore these externalities when deciding how much to consume and produce, the equilibrium in a market can be inefficient from the standpoint of society as a whole.

Market power and externalities are examples of a general phenomenon called **market failure**—the inability of some unregulated markets to allocate resources efficiently. When markets fail, public policy can potentially remedy the problem and enhance economic efficiency. Microeconomists devote much effort to studying when market failures are likely and how they are best corrected. As you continue your study of economics, you will see that the tools of welfare economics developed here are readily adapted to that endeavor.

Despite the possibility of market failure, the invisible hand of the marketplace is extraordinarily important. In many markets, the assumptions made in this chapter work well, and the conclusion of market efficiency applies directly. Moreover, we can use our analysis of welfare economics and market efficiency to shed light on the effects of various government policies.

7-5 The Deadweight Loss of Taxation

Let's begin by recalling a lesson from Chapter 6: The ultimate impact of a tax on a market is the same whether the tax is levied on buyers or sellers. A tax on buyers shifts the demand curve downward by the size of the tax; a tax on sellers shifts the supply curve upward by that amount. In either case, the tax raises the price paid by buyers and reduces the price received by sellers. As a result, how the tax burden is distributed between producers and consumers depends not on how the tax is levied but on the elasticities of supply and demand.

Figure 1 illustrates the effect of a tax. To keep things simple, this figure does not show a shift in the supply or demand curve, though one curve must shift, depending on whom the tax is levied. This chapter keeps the analysis general and the graphs less cluttered by not showing the shift. The important point is that the tax places a wedge between the price buyers pay and the price sellers receive. Because of this wedge, the quantity sold is less than it would be if there were no tax. In other words, a tax on a good shrinks the size of the market for it, as Chapter 6 showed.

7-5a How a Tax Affects Market Participants?

Let's now use the tools of welfare economics to measure the gains and losses from a tax on a good. To do this, we must consider how the tax affects buyers, sellers, and the government. The welfare of buyers is measured by consumer surplus—the amount buyers are willing to pay for the good minus the amount they actually pay for it. The welfare of sellers is measured by producer surplus—the amount sellers receive for the good minus their costs of producing it. Chapter 7 introduced these measures of economic well-being.

What about the third interested party, the government? If T is the size of the tax and Q is the quantity of the good sold, then the government takes in tax revenue of T 3 Q. It can use this revenue to provide government services, such as roads,

Figure 9

The Effects of a Tax

A tax on a good places a wedge between the price that buyers pay and the price that sellers receive. The quantity of the good sold declines.

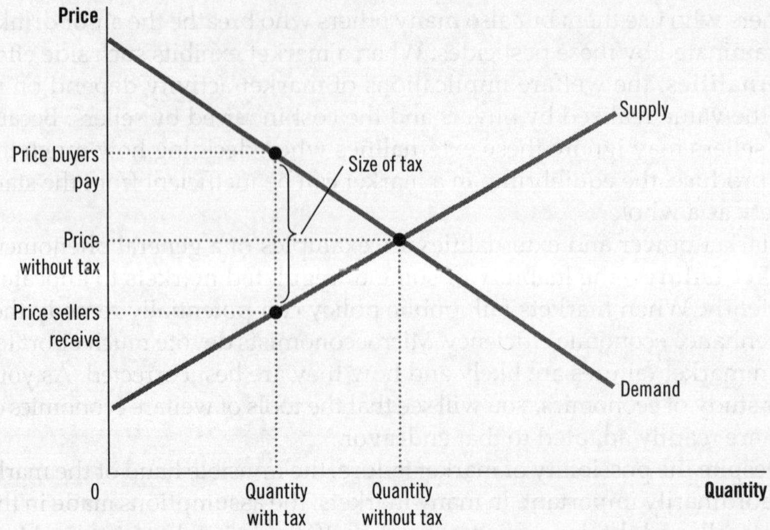

police, and public education, or to fund transfer programs for, say, lower-income households. When analyzing how taxes affect economic well-being, we use the government's tax revenue to measure the public benefit from the tax. This benefit, however, actually accrues not to the government but to those on whom the revenue is spent.

In Figure 10, the government's tax revenue is represented by the rectangle between the supply and demand curves. The height of this rectangle is the size of the tax, T, and its width is the quantity of the good sold, Q. Because a rectangle's area is its height multiplied by its width, this rectangle's area is T 3 Q, which equals the tax revenue.

J.B. HANDELSMAN/THE NEW YORKER COLLECTION/THE CARTOON BANK

"You know, the idea of taxation with representation doesn't appeal to me very much, either."

Welfare without a Tax To see how a tax affects welfare, let's begin by considering the situation before a tax is imposed. Figure 3 shows the supply-and-demand diagram with the key areas marked by the letters A through F.

Without a tax, the equilibrium price and quantity are found at the intersection of the supply and demand curves. The price is P_1, and the quantity sold is Q_1. Because the demand curve reflects buyers' willingness to pay, consumer surplus is the area between the demand curve and the price, A 1 B 1 C. Similarly, because the supply curve reflects sellers' costs, producer surplus is the area between the supply curve and the price, D 1 E 1 F. Because there is no tax, tax revenue is zero.

Total surplus, the sum of consumer and producer surplus, equals the area A 1 B 1 C 1 D 1 E 1 F. In other words, as in Chapter 7, it is the area between the supply and demand curves up to the equilibrium quantity. The first column of the table in Figure 3 summarizes these results.

Welfare with a Tax Now consider welfare with a tax. The price paid by buyers rises from P_1 to P_B, so consumer surplus equals only area A (the area below the demand curve and above the buyers' price, P_B). The price received by sellers falls from P_1 to P_S, so producer surplus equals only area F (the area above the supply

Figure 10

Tax Revenue

The tax revenue that the government collects equals *T* 3 *Q*, the size of the tax, *T*, times the quantity sold, *Q*. Thus, tax revenue equals the area of the rectangle between the supply and demand curves.

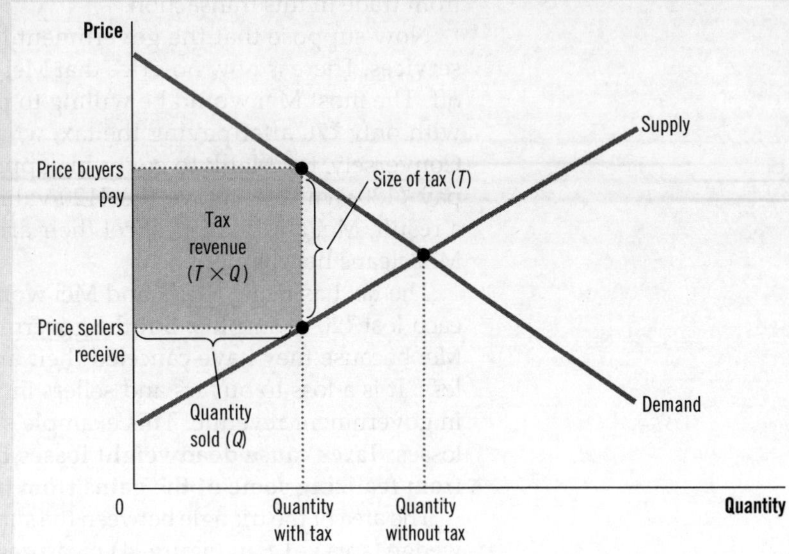

curve and below the sellers' price P_S). The quantity sold falls from Q_1 to Q_2, and the government collects tax revenue equal to the area B 1 D.

To find total surplus with the tax, add consumer surplus, producer surplus, and tax revenue. Thus, total surplus is area A 1 B 1 D 1 F. The table's second column summarizes these results.

Changes in Welfare We can now see the effects of the tax by comparing welfare before and after the tax is enacted. The table's third column shows the changes. Consumer surplus falls by the area B 1 C, and producer surplus falls by the area D 1 E. Tax revenue rises by the area B 1 D. Not surprisingly, with the tax, the buyers and sellers are worse off, and the government has more revenue.

The change in total welfare includes the change in consumer surplus (which is negative), the change in producer surplus (which is also negative), and the change in tax revenue (which is positive). When we add these three pieces together, we find that total surplus in the market falls by the area C 1 E. **The losses to buyers and sellers from a tax exceed the revenue raised by the government.** The fall in total surplus that results when a tax (or some other policy) distorts the outcome in an otherwise efficient market is called a **deadweight loss**. The area C 1 E measures the size of the loss.

deadweight loss
the fall in total surplus that results from a market distortion

In the absence of a tax, the equilibrium of supply and demand maximizes the total surplus of buyers and sellers in a market. When the government imposes a tax, it raises the price buyers pay and lowers the price sellers receive, giving incentives to buyers to consume less and sellers to produce less. As a result, the market shrinks below its optimum (as shown in the figure by the movement from Q_1 to Q_2). Thus, because taxes distort incentives, they cause markets to allocate resources inefficiently.

7-5b Deadweight Losses and the Gains from Trade

To better understand why taxes cause deadweight losses, consider an example. Imagine that Malik cleans Mei's house each week for ₹100. The opportunity cost of Malik's time is ₹80, and the value of a clean house to Mei is ₹120, so they each receive a ₹20 benefit from their deal. The total surplus of ₹40 measures the gains from trade in this transaction.

Now suppose that the government levies a ₹50 tax on providers of cleaning services. There is now no price that Mei can pay Malik that will leave both better off. The most Mei would be willing to pay is ₹120, but then Malik would be left with only ₹70 after paying the tax, which is less than his ₹80 opportunity cost. Conversely, for Malik to cover his opportunity cost of ₹80, Mei would need to pay ₹130, which is above the ₹120 value she places on the cleaning service. As a result, Mei and Malik cancel their arrangement. Malik loses the income, and Mei cleans her own house.

The tax has made Malik and Mei worse off by a total of ₹40 because they have each lost ₹20 of surplus. But the government collects no revenue from Malik and Mei because they have canceled their arrangement. The ₹40 is pure deadweight loss: It is a loss to buyers and sellers in a market that is not offset by an increase in government revenue. This example shows the ultimate source of deadweight losses: **Taxes cause deadweight losses because they prevent buyers and sellers from realizing some of the gains from trade.**

The area of the triangle between the supply and demand curves created by the tax wedge (area C 1 E in Figure 11) measures these losses. This conclusion can be seen more easily in Figure 4 by recalling that the demand curve reflects the value of the good to consumers and that the supply curve reflects the costs of producers. When the tax raises the price buyers pay to P_B and lowers the price sellers receive to P_S, the marginal buyers and sellers leave the market, so the quantity sold falls from Q_1 to Q_2. Yet as the figure shows, the value of the good to these buyers still exceeds the cost to these sellers. At every quantity between Q_1 and Q_2, the situation is the same as in our example with Malik and Mei. The gains from trade—the difference between buyers' value and sellers' cost—are less than the tax. As a result, these trades are not made once the tax is imposed. The deadweight loss is the surplus that is lost because the tax discourages these mutually advantageous trades.

Figure 11

The Source of a Deadweight Loss

When the government imposes a tax on a good, the quantity sold falls from Q_1 to Q_2. At every quantity between Q_1 and Q_2, the potential gains from trade among buyers and sellers are not realized. These lost gains from trade make up the deadweight loss.

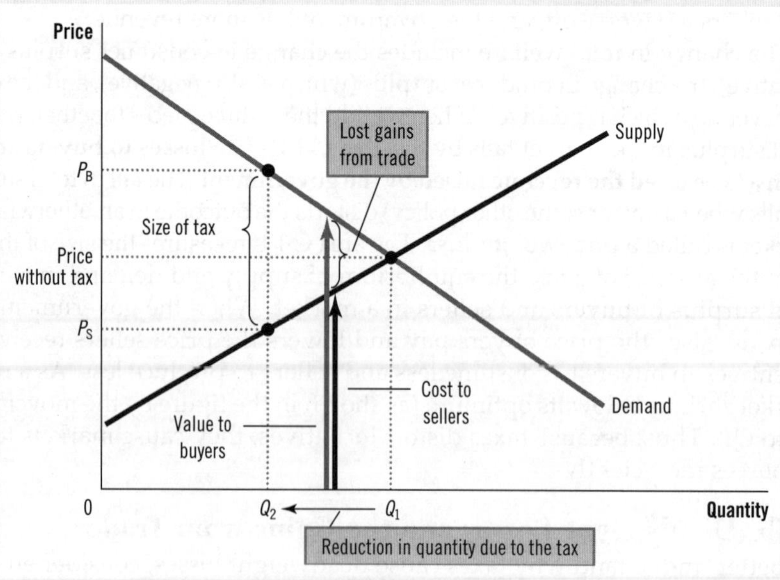

Quick**Quiz**

1. A tax on a good has a deadweight loss if
   a. the reduction in consumer and producer surplus is greater than the tax revenue.
   b. the tax revenue is greater than the reduction in consumer and producer surplus.
   c. the reduction in consumer surplus is greater than the reduction in producer surplus.
   d. the reduction in producer surplus is greater than the reduction in consumer surplus.

2. Donna runs an inn and charges ₹300 a night for a room, which equals her cost. Sam, Harry, and Bill are three potential customers willing to pay ₹500, ₹325, and ₹250, respectively. When the government levies a tax on innkeepers of ₹50 per night of occupancy, Donna raises her price to ₹350. The deadweight loss of the tax is
   a. ₹25.
   b. ₹50.
   c. ₹100.
   d. ₹150.

3. Sophie pays Sky ₹50 to mow her lawn every week. When the government levies a mowing tax of ₹10 on Sky, he raises his price to ₹60. Sophie continues to hire him at the higher price. What is the change in producer surplus, the change in consumer surplus, and the deadweight loss?
   a. ₹0, ₹0, ₹10
   b. ₹0, 2₹10, ₹0
   c. 1₹10, 2₹10, ₹10
   d. 1₹10, 2₹10, ₹0

Answers are at the end of the chapter.

7-6 The Determinants of the Deadweight Loss

What determines whether the deadweight loss from a tax is large or small? The answer is to be found in the price elasticities of supply and demand, which measure how much the quantity supplied and quantity demanded respond to changes in the price.

Consider first how the elasticity of supply affects the size of the deadweight loss. In the top two panels of Figure 12, the demand curve and the size of the tax are the same. The only difference is the elasticity of the supply curve. In panel (a), the supply curve is relatively inelastic: The quantity supplied responds only slightly to changes in the price. In panel (b), the supply curve is relatively elastic: The quantity supplied responds substantially to changes in the price. Notice that the deadweight loss, the area of the triangle between the supply and demand curves, is larger when the supply curve is more elastic.

Similarly, the bottom two panels of Figure 12 show how the elasticity of demand affects the size of the deadweight loss. Here, the supply curve and the size of the tax are held constant. In panel (c), the demand curve is relatively inelastic, and the deadweight loss is small. In panel (d), the demand curve is more elastic, and the deadweight loss from the tax is larger.

The lesson from this figure is apparent. A tax has a deadweight loss because it induces buyers and sellers to change their behavior. The tax raises the price paid by buyers, so they consume less. At the same time, the tax lowers the price received by sellers, so they produce less. Because of these changes in behavior, the equilibrium quantity in the market shrinks below the optimal quantity for economic efficiency. The more responsive buyers and sellers are to changes in the price, the more the equilibrium quantity shrinks. **Hence, the greater the elasticities of supply and demand, the larger the deadweight loss of a tax.**

Figure 12

Tax Distortions and Elasticities

In panels (a) and (b), the demand curve and the size of the tax are the same, but the price elasticity of supply is different. Notice that the more elastic the supply curve, the larger the deadweight loss of the tax. In panels (c) and (d), the supply curve and the size of the tax are the same, but the price elasticity of demand is different. The more elastic the demand curve, the larger the deadweight loss of the tax.

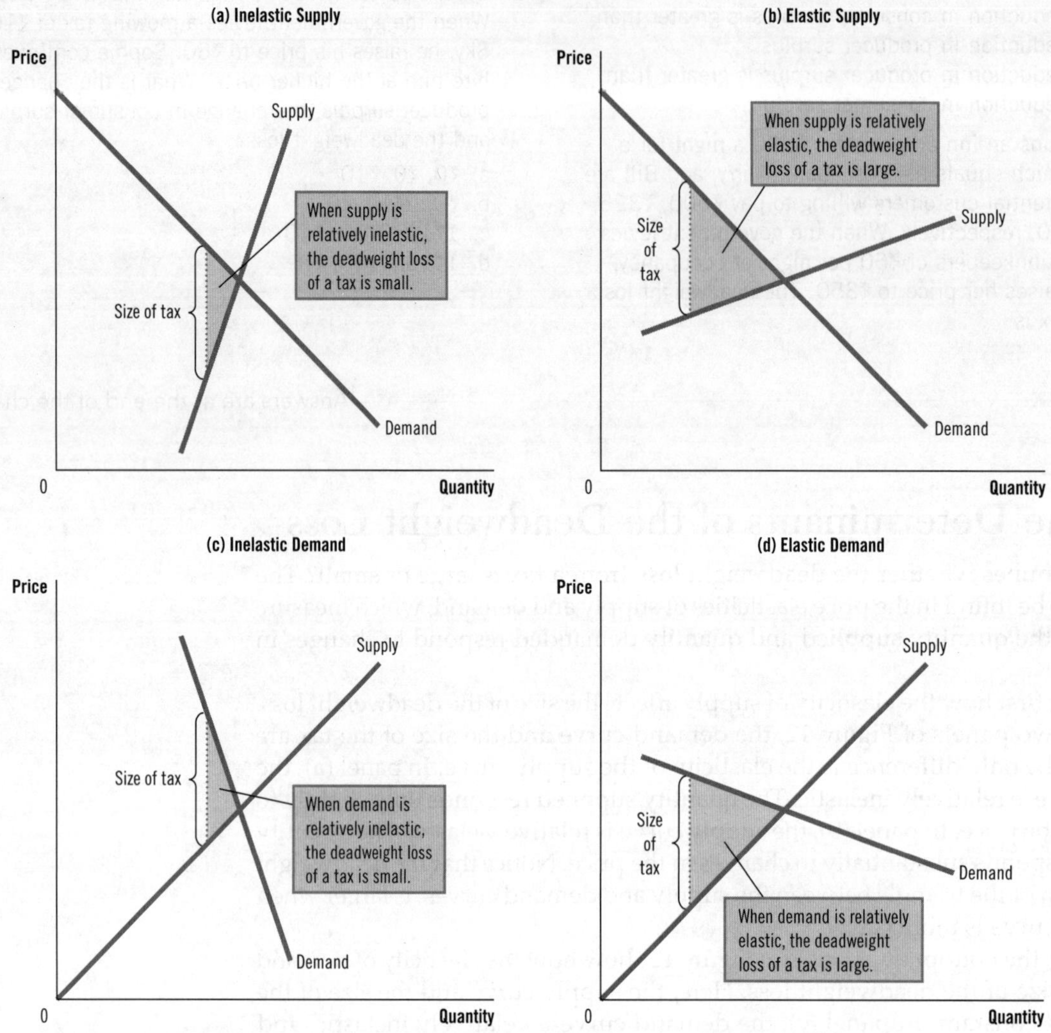

7-7 Deadweight Loss and Tax Revenue as Taxes Vary

Taxes rarely stay the same for long. Policymakers are always considering raising one tax or lowering another. Let's consider what happens to the deadweight loss and tax revenue when the size of a tax changes.

Figure 13

How Deadweight Loss and Tax Revenue Vary with the Size of a Tax

The deadweight loss is the reduction in total surplus resulting from the tax. Tax revenue is the size of the tax multiplied by the amount of the good sold. In panel (a), a small tax has a small deadweight loss and raises a small amount of revenue. In panel (b), a somewhat larger tax has a larger deadweight loss and raises more revenue. In panel (c), a very large tax has a very large deadweight loss, but because it reduces the size of the market so much, the tax raises only a small amount of revenue. Panels (d) and (e) summarize these conclusions. Panel (d) shows that as the size of a tax grows larger, the deadweight loss grows larger. Panel (e) shows that tax revenue first rises and then falls. This relationship is called the Laffer curve.

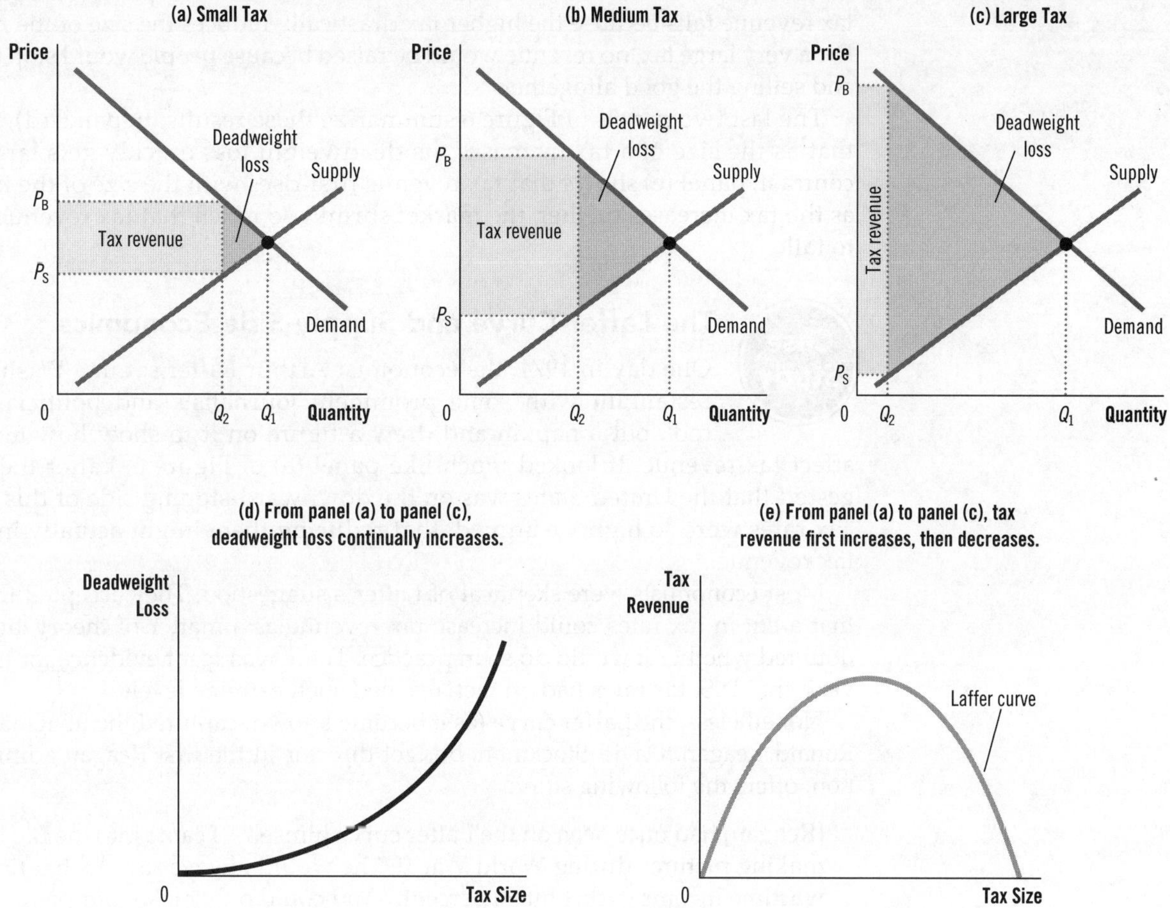

Figure 13 shows the effects of a small, medium, and large tax, holding constant the market's supply and demand curves. The deadweight loss the reduction in total surplus that results when the tax reduces a market's size below the optimum—equals the area of the triangle between the supply and demand curves. For the small tax in panel (a), the area of the deadweight loss triangle is quite small. But as the size of the tax rises in panels (b) and (c), the deadweight loss grows larger and larger.

Indeed, the deadweight loss of a tax rises even more rapidly than the size of the tax. This occurs because the deadweight loss is the area of a triangle, and the area of a triangle depends on the **square** of its size. If we double the size of a tax, for instance, the base and height of the triangle double, so the deadweight loss rises by a factor of four. If we triple the size of a tax, the base and height triple, so the deadweight loss rises by a factor of nine.

The government's tax revenue is the size of the tax times the amount of the good sold. As the first three panels of Figure 6 show, tax revenue equals the area of the rectangle between the supply and demand curves. For the small tax in panel (a), tax revenue is small. As the size of the tax increases from panel (a) to panel (b), tax revenue grows. But as the size of the tax increases further from panel (b) to panel (c), tax revenue falls because the higher tax drastically reduces the size of the market. For a very large tax, no revenue would be raised because people would stop buying and selling the good altogether.

The last two panels of Figure 6 summarize these results. In panel (d), we see that as the size of a tax increases, its deadweight loss quickly gets larger. By contrast, panel (e) shows that tax revenue first rises with the size of the tax, but as the tax increases further, the market shrinks so much that tax revenue starts to fall.

Case Study

The Laffer Curve and Supply-Side Economics

One day in 1974, the economist Arthur Laffer sat in a Washington restaurant with some prominent journalists and politicians. He took out a napkin and drew a figure on it to show how tax rates affect tax revenue. It looked much like panel (e) of Figure 6. Laffer then suggested that the United States was on the downward-sloping side of this curve. Tax rates were so high, he argued, that reducing them might actually increase tax revenue.

Most economists were skeptical of Laffer's suggestion. They accepted the idea that a cut in tax rates could increase tax revenue as a matter of theory, but they doubted whether it would do so in practice. There was scant evidence for Laffer's view that U.S. tax rates had, in fact, reached such extreme levels.

Nonetheless, the **Laffer curve** (as it became known) captured the imagination of Ronald Reagan. David Stockman, budget director in the first Reagan administration, offers the following story:

> [Reagan] had once been on the Laffer curve himself. "I came into the Big Money making pictures during World War II," he would always say. At that time, the wartime income surtax hit 90 percent. "You could only make four pictures, and then you were in the top bracket," he would continue. "So we all quit working after four pictures and went off to the country." High tax rates caused less work. Low tax rates caused more. His experience proved it.

When Reagan ran for president in 1980, he made cutting taxes part of his platform. Reagan argued that taxes were so high that they were discouraging hard work and thereby depressing incomes. He argued that lower taxes would give people more incentive to work, which in turn would raise economic well-being. He suggested that incomes could rise by so much that tax revenue might increase, despite the lower tax rates. Because the cut in tax rates was intended to encourage people to increase the quantity of labor they supplied, the views of Laffer and Reagan became known as **supply-side economics**.

Economists continue to debate Laffer's argument. Many believe that subsequent history refuted Laffer's conjecture that lower tax rates would raise tax revenue. Yet because history is open to alternative interpretations, others view the events of the 1980s as more favorable to the supply siders. To evaluate Laffer's hypothesis definitively, we would need to rerun history without the Reagan tax cuts and see if tax revenues would have been higher or lower. But that experiment is impossible.

Some economists take an intermediate position. They believe that while an overall cut in tax rates normally reduces revenue, some taxpayers may occasionally find themselves on the wrong side of the Laffer curve. Other things being equal, a tax cut is more likely to raise tax revenue if the cut applies to those taxpayers facing the highest tax rates. In addition, Laffer's argument may be more compelling for countries with much higher tax rates than the United States. In Sweden in the early 1980s, for instance, the typical worker faced a marginal tax rate of about 80 percent. Such a high tax rate provides a substantial disincentive to work. Studies have suggested that Sweden would have indeed raised more tax revenue with lower tax rates.

Economists disagree about these issues in part because there is no consensus about the size of the relevant elasticities. The more elastic supply and demand are in any market, the more taxes distort behavior, and the more likely it is that a tax cut will increase tax revenue. There is, however, agreement about the general lesson: How much revenue the government gains or loses from a tax change cannot be computed just by looking at tax rates. It also depends on how the tax change affects people's behavior.

An update to this story: Arthur Laffer rose to prominence again during the 2016 presidential campaign, when he was an adviser to Donald Trump. As recounted in his book with Stephen Moore, *Trumponomics*, he encouraged the candidate to propose a large tax cut. Laffer's argument was like the one he made years earlier: Why settle for the 2 percent growth that most economists were projecting? Wouldn't all our problems be easier to handle with a more rapidly expanding economy? The book quotes Trump as saying, when announcing his tax plan, that it would not increase the government's budget deficit (the shortfall of tax revenue from government spending) because it would raise growth rates to "3, or 4, 5, or even 6 percent." Most economists, however, were skeptical. And they were right to be. In the two years after the tax cut went into effect, the economy grew at 2.4 percent, and the budget deficit swelled. ●

Ask the Experts: The Laffer Curve

"A cut in federal income tax rates in the United States right now [2012] would lead to higher national income within five years than without the tax cut."

What do economists say?

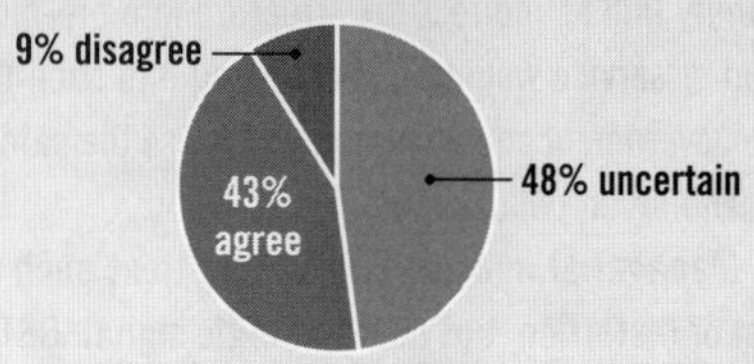

"A cut in federal income tax rates in the United States right now would raise taxable income enough so that the annual total tax revenue would be higher within five years than without the tax cut."

What do economists say?

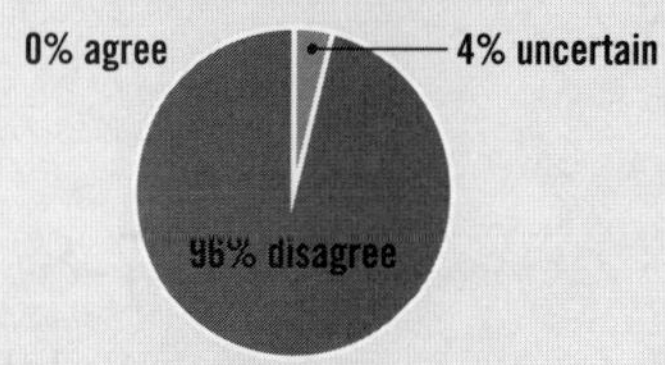

Source: IGM Economic Experts Panel, June 26, 2012.

Policy Spotlight: Goods and Services Tax (GST) in India – Firm and Industry Responses

The GST was introduced in India with much fanfare replacing the previous tiered taxation levels which was heavily fragmented into components. The idea was to aim for "One Nation One Tax". While widely regarded as a major tax reform in India, in this spotlight section, we analyze how firms and industry responded strategically to the new constraints as well as opportunities that the GST brought forth through the lens of Managerial Economics. Broadly speaking, the GST was an effort to unify India's indirect tax structure into pre-binned slabs where each good or service would be categorized into fixed GST rates in each slab. The government could periodically revise the categorization of the goods depending on policy inputs.

Managerial Insight: Firms must treat such taxation not just as a cost or distortion, but as a strategic signal. GST reframed managerial decisions on pricing, inventory, and location. For example, retailers may choose to store goods closer to markets to benefit from uniform tax rates and improve delivery speed, as a logistical enhancement in their business plans. Similarly, managers of other firms can recalibrate margins and launch new models aligned with anticipated GST thresholds. Firms may also plan to delay launches based on anticipated GST changes.

Recent proposals have suggested a shift to an even more simplified GST 2.0 era with only two slabs of taxation. This has been widely embraced by industry houses. For instance, The Economic Times (Aug 22, 2025) carried a news article suggesting that e-commerce giants like Amazon and Walmart/Flipkart are concerned that while GST reduction is welcomed by many, in the transitory phase to GST 2.0 era, the demand may actually dampen with regards to consumer "expectations" of prices. Consumers may delay purchases of high value electronics and other goods, anticipating future lower prices and this may have connotations for their festive sales plans etc. On the other hand, the Aug 21, 2025 edition of the same newspaper carried the news that the Chair of Maruti Suzuki hailed the GST 2.0 as an excellent reform and considers this will boost competitiveness in the industry. While the GST 2.0 simplifies the slabs into only 2 main categories, it also introduces a high tax category (~40% tax) for sin goods like tobacco.

7-8 Conclusion

We learnt in Chapter 1 that markets are usually a good way to organize economic activity and in this chapter made it more precise using the concepts of consumer surplus, producer surplus, and market efficiency. Here, we have seen that when the government taxes a good, it makes the allocation of resources less efficient. Taxes are costly not only because they transfer resources from market participants to the government but also because they distort incentives and create deadweight losses.

The analysis here and in Chapter 6 sheds much light on the effects of taxes, but it is not the end of the story. Microeconomists study how best to design a tax system, including how to strike the right balance between efficiency and equity. And they consider how, when a market failure impedes efficiency, well-targeted taxes can sometimes fix the problem. Macroeconomists study how taxes influence the overall economy and how policymakers can use the tax system to stabilize economic activity and promote rapid growth. So as you study economics, don't be surprised when the subject of taxation comes up yet again.

Chapter in a Nutshell

- Consumer surplus equals buyers' willingness to pay for a good minus the amount they actually pay, and it measures the benefit buyers get from participating in a market. Consumer surplus can be found by computing the area below the demand curve and above the price.
- Producer surplus equals the amount sellers are paid for their goods minus their costs of production, and it measures the benefit sellers get from participating in a market. Producer surplus can be found by computing the area below the price and above the supply curve.
- An allocation of resources that maximizes total surplus (the sum of consumer and producer surplus) is said to be efficient. Policymakers are often concerned with the efficiency, as well as the equality, of economic outcomes.
- Under normal conditions, the equilibrium of supply and demand maximizes total surplus. That is, the invisible hand of the marketplace usually leads buyers and sellers in competitive markets to allocate resources efficiently.
- Markets do not allocate resources efficiently in the presence of market failures such as market power or externalities.
- A tax on a good reduces the welfare of buyers and sellers of that good, and the reduction in consumer and producer surplus usually exceeds the revenue raised by the government. The fall in total surplus— the sum of consumer surplus, producer surplus, and tax revenue—is called the deadweight loss of the tax.
- Taxes have deadweight losses because they cause buyers to consume less and sellers to produce less, and these changes in behavior shrink the market below the level that maximizes total surplus. Because the elasticities of supply and demand measure how much buyers and sellers respond to market conditions, larger elasticities imply larger deadweight losses.
- As a tax grows larger, it distorts incentives more, and its deadweight loss grows larger. Because a tax reduces the size of the market, however, tax revenue does not continually increase. It first rises with the size of a tax, but if the tax gets large enough, tax revenue starts to fall.

Key Concepts

welfare economics, p. 133
willingness to pay, p. 134
consumer surplus, p. 135
cost, p. 139
producer surplus, p. 139
efficiency, p. 143
equality, p. 143
deadweight loss, p. 149

Questions for Review

1. Explain how buyers' willingness to pay, consumer surplus, and the demand curve are related.
2. Explain how sellers' costs, producer surplus, and the supply curve are related.
3. In a supply-and-demand diagram, show producer surplus and consumer surplus at the market equilibrium.
4. What is efficiency? Is it the only goal of economic policymakers?
5. Name two types of market failure. Explain why each may cause market outcomes to be inefficient.
6. What happens to consumer surplus and producer surplus when the sale of a good is taxed? How does the change in consumer and producer surplus compare with the tax revenue? Explain.
7. Draw a supply-and-demand diagram with a tax on the sale of a good. Show the deadweight loss. Show the tax revenue.
8. How do the elasticities of supply and demand affect the deadweight loss of a tax? Why do they have this effect?
9. Why do experts disagree about whether labor taxes have small or large deadweight losses?
10. What happens to the deadweight loss and tax revenue when a tax is increased?

Problems and Applications

1. Kyra buys an iPhone for ₹360 and gets consumer surplus of ₹240.
   a. What is her willingness to pay?
   b. If she had bought the iPhone on sale for ₹270, what would her consumer surplus have been?
   c. If the price of an iPhone were ₹750, what would her consumer surplus have been?
2. An early freeze in California sours the lemon crop. Explain what happens to consumer surplus in the market for lemons. Explain what happens to consumer surplus in the market for lemonade. Illustrate your answers with diagrams.
3. Suppose the demand for French bread rises. Explain what happens to producer surplus in the market for French bread. Explain what happens to producer surplus in the market for flour. Illustrate your answers with diagrams.
4. It is a hot day, and Barinder is thirsty. Here is the value he places on each bottle of water:

Value of first bottle	₹7
Value of second bottle	₹5
Value of third bottle	₹3
Value of fourth bottle	₹1

   a. From this information, derive Barinder's demand schedule. Graph his demand curve for bottled water.
   b. If the price of a bottle of water is ₹4, how many bottles does Barinder buy? How much consumer surplus does Barinder get from his purchases? Show Barinder's consumer surplus in your graph.
   c. If the price falls to ₹2, how does the quantity demanded change? How does Barinder's consumer surplus change? Show these changes in your graph.
5. Simran owns a water pump. Because pumping large amounts of water is harder than pumping small amounts, the cost of producing a bottle of water rises as he pumps more. Here is the cost he incurs to produce each bottle of water:

Cost of first bottle	₹1
Cost of second bottle	₹3
Cost of third bottle	₹5
Cost of fourth bottle	₹7

   a. From this information, derive Simran's supply schedule. Graph his supply curve for bottled water.
   b. If the price of a bottle of water is ₹4, how many bottles does Simran produce and sell? How much producer surplus does Simran get from these sales? Show Simran's producer surplus in your graph.
   c. If the price rises to ₹6, how does the quantity supplied change? How does Simran's producer surplus change? Show these changes in your graph.
6. Consider a market in which Barinder from problem 4 is the buyer and Simran from problem 5 is the seller.
   a. Use Simran's supply schedule and Barinder's demand schedule to find the quantity supplied and quantity demanded at prices of ₹2, ₹4, and ₹6. Which of these prices brings supply and demand into equilibrium?
   b. What are consumer surplus, producer surplus, and total surplus in this equilibrium?
   c. If Simran produced and Barinder consumed one fewer bottle of water, what would happen to total surplus?
   d. If Simran produced and Barinder consumed one additional bottle of water, what would happen to total surplus?
7. The cost of producing flat-screen TVs has fallen over the past decade. Let's consider some implications of this change.
   a. Draw a supply-and-demand diagram to show the effect of falling production costs on the price and quantity of flat-screen TVs sold.
   b. In your diagram, show what happens to consumer surplus and producer surplus.
   c. Suppose the supply of flat-screen TVs is very elastic. Who benefits most from falling production costs—consumers or producers of these TVs?
8. Four consumers are willing to pay these amounts for haircuts:

Gloria: ₹35	Jay: ₹10	Claire: ₹40	Phil: ₹25

   Four haircutting businesses have these costs:

Firm A: ₹15	Firm B: ₹30	Firm C: ₹20	Firm D: ₹10

   Each firm can give, at most, one haircut. To achieve efficiency, how many haircuts should be given? Which businesses should cut hair and which consumers should have their hair cut? How large is the maximum possible total surplus?

9. One of the largest changes in the economy over the past several decades is that technological advances have reduced the cost of making computers.
   a. Draw a supply-and-demand diagram to show what happened to the price, quantity, consumer surplus, and producer surplus in the computer market.
   b. Forty years ago, students used typewriters to prepare papers for their classes; today, they use computers. Does that make computers and typewriters complements or substitutes? Use a supply-and-demand diagram to show what happened to the price, quantity, consumer surplus, and producer surplus in the market for typewriters. Should typewriter producers have been happy or sad about the technological advance in computers?
   c. Are computers and software complements or substitutes? Draw a supply-and-demand diagram to show what happened to the price, quantity, consumer surplus, and producer surplus in the market for software. Should software producers have been happy or sad about the technological advance in computers?
   d. Does this analysis help explain why software producer Bill Gates became one of the world's richest people?
10. A friend of yours is considering two movie-streaming services. Provider A charges ₹120 per year regardless of the number of movies streamed. Provider B does not have a fixed service fee but instead charges ₹1 per movie. Your friend's annual demand for movies is given by the equation $Q^D = 150 - 50P$, where P is the price per movie.
    a. With each provider, what is the cost to your friend of an extra movie?
    b. In light of your answer to (a), how many movies with each provider would your friend watch?
    c. How much would she end up paying each provider every year?
    d. How much consumer surplus would she obtain with each provider? (Hint: Graph the demand curve and recall the formula for the area of a triangle.)
    e. Which provider would you recommend that your friend choose? Why?
11. The market for pizza is characterized by a downward-sloping demand curve and an upward-sloping supply curve.
    a. Draw the competitive market equilibrium. Label the price, quantity, consumer surplus, and producer surplus. Is there any deadweight loss? Explain.
    b. Suppose that the government requires each pizzeria to pay a ₹10 GST on each pizza sold. Illustrate the effect of this tax on the pizza market, being sure to label consumer surplus, producer surplus, government revenue, and deadweight loss. How does each area compare to the pre-tax case?
    c. If the tax were removed, pizza eaters and sellers would be better off, but the government would lose tax revenue. Suppose that consumers and producers voluntarily transferred some of their gains to the government. Could all parties (including the government) be better off than they were with a tax? Explain using the labeled areas in your graph.
12. Evaluate the following two statements. Do you agree? Why or why not?
    a. "A tax that has no deadweight loss cannot raise any revenue for the government."
    b. "A tax that raises no revenue for the government cannot have any deadweight loss."
13. Consider the market for rubber bands.
    a. If this market has very elastic supply and very inelastic demand, how would the burden of a tax on rubber bands be shared between consumers and producers? Use the tools of consumer surplus and producer surplus in your answer.
    b. If this market has very inelastic supply and very elastic demand, how would the burden of a tax on rubber bands be shared between consumers and producers? Contrast your answer with your answer to part (a).
14. After economics class, your friend suggests that taxing food would be a good way to raise revenue because the demand for food is quite inelastic. In what sense is taxing food a "good" way to raise revenue? In what sense is it not a "good" way to raise revenue?
15. Daniel Patrick Moynihan, the senator from New York from 1977 to 2001, once introduced a bill that would levy a 10,000 percent tax on certain hollow-tipped bullets.
    a. Do you expect that this tax would raise much revenue? Why or why not?
    b. Even if the tax would raise no revenue, why might Senator Moynihan have proposed it?
16. The government places a tax on the purchase of socks.
    a. Illustrate the effect of this tax on equilibrium price and quantity in the sock market. Identify the following areas both before and after the imposition of the tax: total spending by consumers, total revenue for producers, and government tax revenue.

b. Does the price received by producers rise or fall? Can you tell whether total receipts for producers rise or fall? Explain.

c. Does the price paid by consumers rise or fall? Can you tell whether total spending by consumers rises or falls? Explain carefully. (Hint: Think about elasticity.) If total consumer spending falls, does consumer surplus rise? Explain.

17. This chapter analyzed the welfare effects of a tax on a good. Now consider the opposite policy. Suppose that the government **subsidizes** a good: For each unit of the good sold, the government pays ₹2 to the buyer. How does the subsidy affect consumer surplus, producer surplus, tax revenue, and total surplus? Does a subsidy lead to a deadweight loss? Explain.

18. Hotel rooms in Smalltown go for ₹100, and 1,000 rooms are rented on a typical day.
    a. To raise revenue, the mayor decides to charge hotels a tax of ₹10 per rented room. After the tax is imposed, the going rate rises to ₹108, and the number of rooms rented falls to 900. Calculate the amount of revenue this tax raises for Smalltown and the deadweight loss of the tax. (Hint: The area of a triangle is ½ 3 base 3 height.)
    b. The mayor now doubles the tax to ₹20. The price rises to ₹116, and the number of rooms rented falls to 800. Calculate the tax revenue and deadweight loss with this larger tax. Are they double, more than double, or less than double your answers in part (a)? Explain.

19. Suppose that a market is described by the following supply and demand equations:

$$Q^S\ 5\ 2P$$
$$Q^D\ 5\ 300\ 2\ P.$$

a. Solve for the equilibrium price and the equilibrium quantity.

b. Suppose that a tax of T is placed on buyers, so the new demand equation is:

$$Q^D\ 5\ 300\ 2\ (P\ 1\ T).$$

Solve for the new equilibrium. What happens to the price received by sellers, the price paid by buyers, and the quantity sold?

c. Tax revenue is T 3 Q. Use your answer from part (b) to solve for tax revenue as a function of T. Graph this relationship for T between 0 and 300.

d. The deadweight loss of a tax is the area of the triangle between the supply and demand curves. Recalling that the area of a triangle is ½ 3 base 3 height, solve for deadweight loss as a function of T. Graph this relationship for T between 0 and 300. (Hint: If you look sideways, the base of the deadweight loss triangle is T, and the height is the difference between the quantity sold with the tax and the quantity sold without the tax.)

e. The government now levies a tax of ₹200 per unit on this good. Is this a good policy? Why or why not? Can you propose a better policy?

Quick**Quiz Answers**

1. **b** 2. **b** 3. **d** 4. **c** 5. **b** 6. **c** 7. **a** 8. **c** 9. **b** 10. **c** 11. **a** 12. **a** 13. **b**
14. **a** 15. **d** 16. **b** 17. **d** 18. **c** 19. **a**

Chapter

8

Globalization and Trade Policy

How does international trade affect economic well-being? Who gains and who loses from trade among countries, and how do the gains compare with the losses?

Chapter 3 introduced the study of international trade by applying the principle of comparative advantage. This principle says that all countries can benefit from trade because it allows each country to specialize in what it does best. But the analysis in Chapter 3 was incomplete. It did not explain how the international marketplace achieves these gains from trade or how the gains are distributed among the various market participants.

SHIFT DRIVE/SHUTTERSTOCK.COM ERDARK/E+/GETTY IMAGES

We now tackle these questions using the tools developed over the past several chapters: supply, demand, equilibrium, consumer surplus, producer surplus, and so on. These tools can help explain how international trade affects economic well-being.

8-1 The Determinants of Trade

Consider the textile market. It is well suited to studying the gains and losses from international trade: Textiles are made and traded around the world, and policymakers often consider (and sometimes implement) trade restrictions to protect domestic textile producers from foreign competitors. Here, we examine the textile market in the imaginary country of Isoland.

8-1a The Equilibrium without Trade

As our story begins, the Isolandian textile market is cut off from the rest of the world. By government decree, no one in Isoland is allowed to import or export textiles, and the penalty for violating this prohibition is so large that no one dares try.

Because there is no international trade, the market for textiles in Isoland consists solely of domestic buyers and sellers. As Figure 1 shows, the domestic price adjusts to balance the quantity supplied by domestic sellers and the quantity demanded by domestic buyers. The figure shows the consumer and producer surplus in the equilibrium without trade. The sum of consumer and producer surplus measures the total benefits that buyers and sellers receive from the textile market.

Now suppose that, in a political upset, Isoland elects Olivia Openminded as its new president. After campaigning on a platform of "change" and promising bold new ideas, President Openminded's first act is to assemble a team of economists to evaluate Isolandian trade policy. She asks them to report on three questions:

- If the government allows Isolandians to import and export textiles, what will happen to the price and quantity of textiles sold in the domestic market?
- Who will gain from free trade in textiles and who will lose, and will the gains exceed the losses?
- Should a tariff (a tax on textile imports) be part of the new trade policy?

Figure 1

The Equilibrium without International Trade

When an economy cannot trade in world markets, the price adjusts to balance domestic supply and demand. This figure shows consumer and producer surplus in an equilibrium without international trade for the textile market in Isoland.

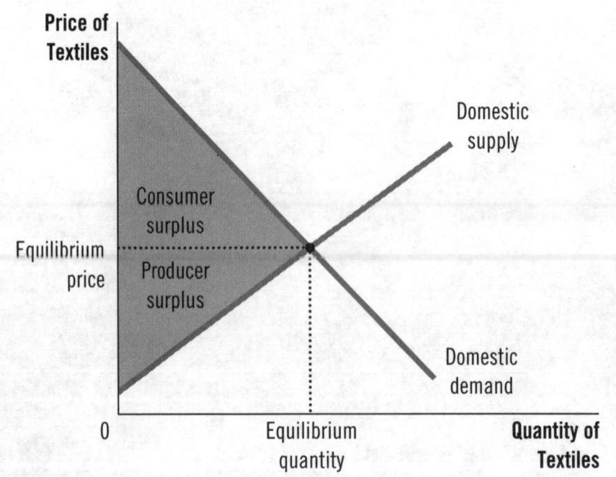

After reviewing supply and demand in their favorite textbook (this one, of course), the Isolandian economics team begins its analysis.

8-1b The World Price and Comparative Advantage

The first issue the economists take up is whether Isoland is likely to become a textile importer or exporter. In other words, if free trade is allowed, will Isolandians end up buying or selling textiles in world markets?

To answer this question, the economists compare the current Isolandian price of textiles with the price prevailing in other countries, called the **world price**. If the world price of textiles exceeds the domestic price, then Isoland will export textiles once trade is permitted. Isolandian textile producers will be eager to receive the higher prices available abroad and will start selling their textiles to consumers in other countries. Conversely, if the world price is lower than the domestic price, Isoland will import textiles. Because foreign sellers offer a better price, Isolandian textile consumers will quickly start buying textiles from other countries.

world price
the price of a good that prevails in the world market for that good

In essence, comparing the world price and the domestic price without trade reveals whether Isoland has a comparative advantage in producing textiles. The domestic price reflects the opportunity cost: It tells us how much an Isolandian must give up to obtain one unit of textiles. If the domestic price is low, the cost of producing textiles in Isoland is low, suggesting that Isoland has a comparative advantage in producing textiles relative to the rest of the world. If the domestic price is high, then the cost of producing textiles in Isoland is high, suggesting that foreign countries have a comparative advantage in producing textiles.

As Chapter 3 discussed, trade among nations is based on comparative advantage. That is, trade is beneficial because it allows each nation to specialize in what it does best. By comparing the world price with the domestic price without trade, we can determine whether Isoland is better or worse than the rest of the world at producing textiles.

Quick**Quiz**

1. The country of Autarka does not allow international trade. In Autarka, you can buy a wool suit for 3 ounces of gold, while in neighboring countries, the same suit costs 2 ounces of gold. This suggests that
   a. Autarka has a comparative advantage in producing suits and would become a suit exporter if it opened up trade.
   b. Autarka has a comparative advantage in producing suits and would become a suit importer if it opened up trade.
   c. Autarka does not have a comparative advantage in producing suits and would become a suit exporter if it opened up trade.
   d. Autarka does not have a comparative advantage in producing suits and would become a suit importer if it opened up trade.
2. The nation of Openia allows free trade and exports steel. If steel exports were prohibited, the price of steel in Openia would be _______, benefiting steel _______.
   a. higher; consumers
   b. lower; consumers
   c. higher; producers
   d. lower; producers

Answers are at the end of the chapter.

8-2 The Winners and Losers from Trade

To analyze the welfare effects of trade, the Isolandian economists begin by assuming that Isoland is small compared with the rest of the world. This small-economy assumption means that Isoland's actions have a negligible effect on world markets.

Specifically, changes in Isoland's trade policy will not affect the world price of textiles. The Isolandians are said to be **price takers** in the world economy. That is, they take the price of textiles as given by the forces of supply and demand in the world market. Isoland can be an exporting country by selling textiles at the world price or an importing country by buying textiles at this price.

The small-economy assumption is not necessary to analyze the gains and losses from international trade, but the Isolandian economists know from experience (and from reading Chapter 2 of this book) that making simplifying assumptions is a key part of building a useful economic model. The assumption that Isoland is a small economy simplifies the analysis, and the basic lessons do not change in the more complicated case of a large economy.

8-2a The Gains and Losses of an Exporting Country

Figure 2 shows the Isolandian textile market when the domestic equilibrium price without trade is below the world price. Once trade is allowed, the domestic price rises to equal the world price. If market participants are all looking for the best price they can get, no seller of textiles would accept less than the world price, and no buyer would pay more than the world price.

After the domestic price has risen to equal the world price, the domestic quantity supplied differs from the domestic quantity demanded. The supply curve shows the quantity of textiles supplied by Isolandian sellers. The demand curve shows the

Figure 2

International Trade in an Exporting Country

Once trade is allowed, the domestic price rises to equal the world price. The supply curve shows the quantity of textiles produced domestically, and the demand curve shows the quantity consumed domestically. Exports from Isoland equal the difference between the domestic quantity supplied and the domestic quantity demanded at the world price. Sellers are better off (producer surplus rises from C to B + C + D), and buyers are worse off (consumer surplus falls from A + B to A). Total surplus rises by an amount equal to area D, indicating that trade raises the economic well-being of the country as a whole.

	Before Trade	After Trade	Change
Consumer Surplus	A + B	A	−B
Producer Surplus	C	B + C + D	+ (B + D)
Total Surplus	A + B + C	A + B + C + D	+ D

The area D shows the increase in total surplus and represents the gains from trade.

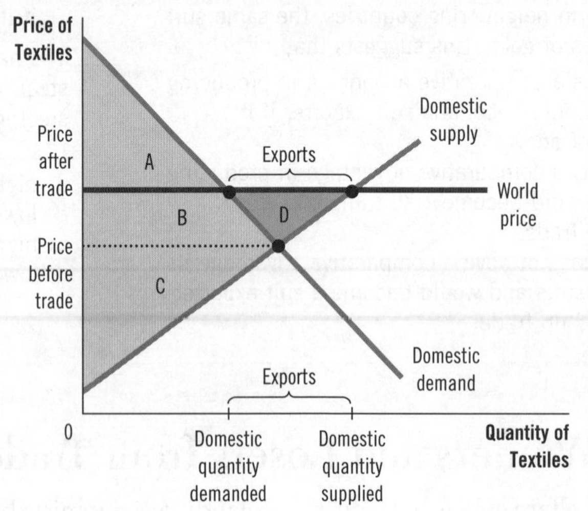

quantity of textiles demanded by Isolandian buyers. Because the domestic quantity supplied exceeds the domestic quantity demanded, Isoland sells textiles to other countries. This means that Isoland becomes a textile exporter.

Although the domestic quantity supplied and the domestic quantity demanded differ, the textile market is still in equilibrium because there is now another participant in the market: the rest of the world. One can view the horizontal line at the world price as representing the rest of the world's demand for textiles. This demand curve is perfectly elastic because Isoland, as a small economy, can sell as many textiles as it wants at the world price.

Consider the gains and losses from opening trade. Clearly, not everyone benefits. Trade forces the domestic price to rise to the world price. Domestic producers of textiles are better off because they can now sell textiles at a higher price, but domestic consumers of textiles are worse off because they now have to buy textiles at a higher price.

To measure these gains and losses, look at the changes in the consumer and producer surplus. Before trade is allowed, the price of textiles adjusts to balance supply and demand in the domestic market. Consumer surplus, the area between the demand curve and the before-trade price, is area A 1 B. Producer surplus, the area between the supply curve and the before-trade price, is area C. Total surplus before trade, which is the sum of consumer and producer surplus, is area A 1 B 1 C.

After trade is allowed, the domestic price rises to the world price. Consumer surplus shrinks to area A (the area between the demand curve and the world price). Producer surplus increases to area B + C + D (the area between the supply curve and the world price). Total surplus with trade is area A 1 B 1 C 1 D.

These welfare calculations show who wins and who loses from trade in an exporting country. Sellers benefit because producer surplus increases by area B 1 D. Buyers are worse off because consumer surplus decreases by area B. Because the gains of sellers exceed the losses of buyers by area D, total surplus in Isoland increases.

This analysis of an exporting country yields two conclusions:

- When a country allows trade and becomes an exporter of a good, domestic producers of the good are better off, and domestic consumers of the good are worse off.
- Trade raises the economic well-being of a nation in the sense that the gains of the winners exceed the losses of the losers.

8-2b The Gains and Losses of an Importing Country

Now, suppose that the domestic price before trade is above the world price. Once again, after trade is allowed, the domestic price becomes the world price. As Figure 3 shows, the domestic quantity supplied is less than the domestic quantity demanded. The difference between the domestic quantity demanded and the domestic quantity supplied is bought from other countries, and Isoland becomes a textile importer.

In this case, the horizontal line at the world price represents the supply of textiles from the rest of the world. This supply curve is perfectly elastic because Isoland is a small economy and can buy as much as it wants at the world price.

Consider the gains and losses from trade. Once again, not everyone benefits, but here, the winners and losers are reversed. When trade reduces the domestic price, domestic consumers are better off (they can buy textiles at a lower price), and domestic producers are worse off (they must sell at a lower price). Changes in consumer and producer surplus measure the size of the gains and losses. Before

Figure 3

International Trade in an Importing Country

Once trade is allowed, the domestic price falls to equal the world price. The supply curve shows the amount produced domestically, and the demand curve shows the amount consumed domestically. Imports equal the difference between the domestic quantity demanded and the domestic quantity supplied at the world price. Buyers are better off (consumer surplus rises from A to A + B + D), and sellers are worse off (producer surplus falls from B + C to C). Total surplus rises by an amount equal to area D, indicating that trade raises the economic well-being of the country as a whole.

	Before Trade	After Trade	Change
Consumer Surplus	A	A + B + D	+ (B + D)
Producer Surplus	B + C	C	−B
Total Surplus	A + B + C	A + B + C + D	+D

The area D shows the increase in total surplus and represents the gains from trade.

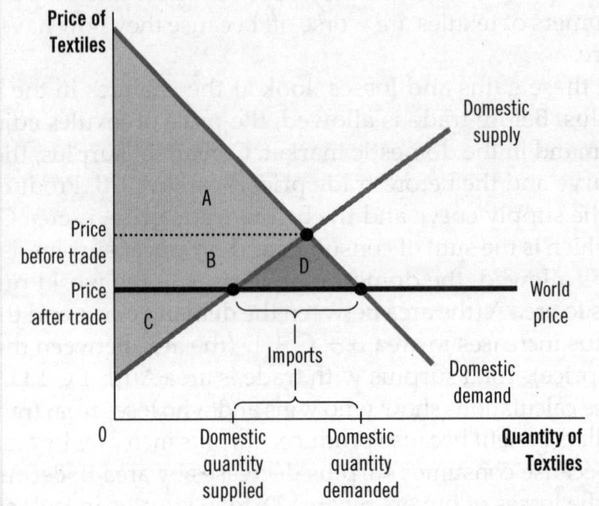

trade, consumer surplus is area A, producer surplus is area B + C, and total surplus is area A + B + C. With trade, consumer surplus is area A + B + D, producer surplus is area C, and total surplus is area A + B + C + D.

These welfare calculations show who wins and who loses from trade in an importing country. Buyers benefit because consumer surplus increases by area B + D. Sellers are worse off because producer surplus falls by area B. The gains of buyers exceed the losses of sellers, and total surplus increases by area D.

This analysis of an importing country yields two conclusions parallel to those for an exporting country:

- When a country allows trade and becomes an importer of a good, domestic consumers of the good are better off, and domestic producers are worse off.
- Trade raises the economic well-being of a nation in the sense that the gains of the winners exceed the losses of the losers.

If Isoland opens its textile market to international trade, the change creates winners and losers, regardless of whether Isoland ends up exporting or importing textiles. In either case, however, the gains of the winners exceed the losses of the losers, so the winners could compensate the losers and still be better off. In this sense, trade **can** make everyone better off. But **will** trade make everyone better off?

Probably not. In practice, compensating the losers from international trade is rare. Without such compensation, opening an economy to international trade expands the size of the economic pie but can leave some people with a smaller slice.

This is why the debate over trade policy is often contentious. Whenever a policy creates winners and losers, the stage is set for a political battle. Nations sometimes limit trade because the losers from trade are better organized than the winners. The losers may turn their cohesiveness into political clout and lobby for trade restrictions such as tariffs or import quotas.

8-2c The Effects of a Tariff

The Isolandian economists next consider the effects of a **tariff**—a tax on imported goods. The economists quickly realize that a tariff on textiles will have no effect if Isoland becomes a textile exporter. That's because if no one in Isoland is interested in importing textiles, a tax on textile imports is irrelevant. The tariff matters only if Isoland becomes a textile importer. Concentrating their attention on this case, the economists compare welfare with and without the tariff.

tariff
a tax on goods produced abroad and sold domestically

Figure 4 shows the Isolandian market for textiles. With free trade, the domestic price equals the world price. A tariff raises the price of imported textiles above the world price by the amount of the tariff. Domestic suppliers, who compete with foreign suppliers of imported textiles, can now sell their goods for the world price plus the tariff. As a result, the price of textiles—both imported and domestic—rises by the amount of the tariff and is closer to the price without trade.

The change in price affects the behavior of domestic buyers and sellers. Because the tariff raises the price of textiles, it reduces the domestic quantity demanded from Q_1^D to Q_2^D and raises the domestic quantity supplied from Q_1^S to Q_2^S. **The tariff reduces the quantity of imports and moves the domestic market closer to its equilibrium without trade.**

Consider the gains and losses from the tariff. Because it raises the domestic price, domestic sellers are better off, and domestic buyers are worse off. In addition, the government gets the tariff revenue, which it can use for public purposes. These gains and losses are measured by the changes in consumer surplus, producer surplus, and government revenue. These changes are summarized in the table in Figure 4.

Before the tariff, the domestic price equals the world price. Consumer surplus, the area between the demand curve and the world price, is area A 1 B 1 C 1 D 1 E 1 F. Producer surplus, the area between the supply curve and the world price, is area G. Government revenue equals zero. Total surplus, the sum of consumer surplus, producer surplus, and government revenue, is area A 1 B 1 C 1 D 1 E 1 F 1 G.

With a tariff, the domestic price exceeds the world price by the tariff's amount. Consumer surplus is now area A 1 B. Producer surplus is area C 1 G. Government revenue, which is the size of the tariff multiplied by the quantity of after-tariff imports, is area E. Total surplus with the tariff is area A 1 B 1 C 1 E 1 G.

To determine the total welfare effects of the tariff, add the change in consumer surplus (which is negative), the change in producer surplus (positive), and the change in government revenue (positive). The result is that total surplus decreases by area D 1 F. This fall in total surplus is the **deadweight loss** of the tariff.

A tariff causes a deadweight loss because, like most taxes, it distorts incentives and pushes the allocation of scarce resources away from the optimum. In this case, note two effects. First, when the tariff raises the domestic price of textiles above the world price, it encourages domestic producers to increase production from Q_1^S to Q_2^S. Even though it costs more to make these units than to buy them at the world price, the tariff makes it profitable for domestic producers to

Figure 4

The Effects of a Tariff

A tariff, a tax on imports, reduces the quantity of imports and moves a market closer to the equilibrium that would exist without trade. Total surplus falls by an amount equal to area D + F. These two triangles represent the deadweight loss from the tariff.

	Before Tariff	After Tariff	Change
Consumer Surplus	A + B + C + D + E + F	A + B	−(C + D + E + F)
Producer Surplus	G	C + G	+C
Government Revenue	None	E	+E
Total Surplus	A + B + C + D + E + F + G	A + B + C + E + G	−(D + F)

The area D + F shows the fall in total surplus and represents the deadweight loss of the tariff.

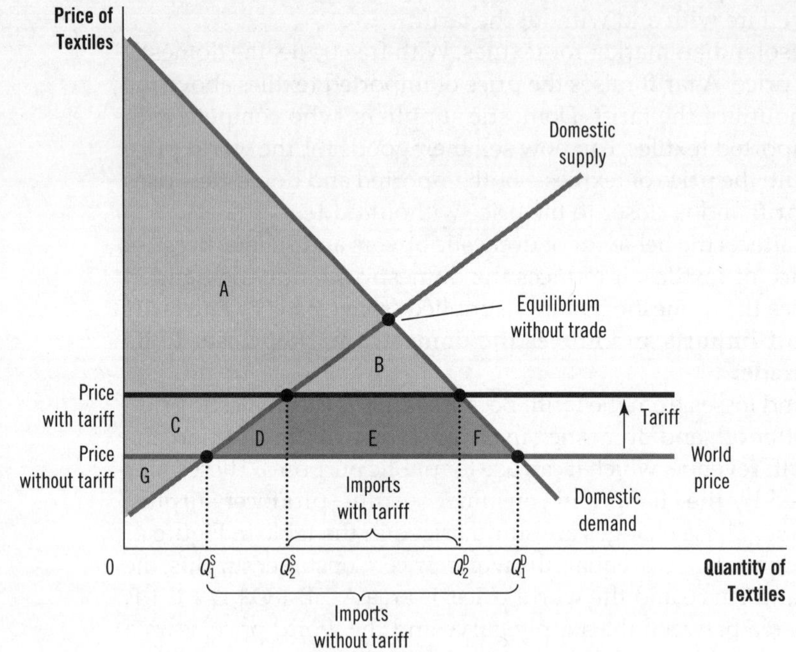

manufacture them anyway. Second, when the tariff raises the price for domestic consumers, it leads them to reduce consumption from Q_1^D to Q_2^D. Even though domestic consumers are willing to pay more for these units than the world price, the tariff induces them to cut back on purchases. Area D represents the deadweight loss from the overproduction of textiles, and area F represents the deadweight loss from the underconsumption. The total deadweight loss is the sum of these two triangles.

8-2d The Lessons for Trade Policy

The team of Isolandian economists writes to the new president:

FYI Import Quotas: Another Way to Restrict Trade

Beyond tariffs, another way that nations sometimes restrict international trade is by putting limits on how much of a good can be imported. This book won't analyze such a policy other than to point out the conclusion: Import quotas are much like tariffs. Both tariffs and quotas reduce the quantity of imports, raise the domestic price of a good, decrease the welfare of domestic consumers, increase the welfare of domestic producers, and cause deadweight losses.

There is only one difference between these two types of trade restriction: A tariff raises revenue for the government, while an import quota generates surplus for those who obtain the permits to import. The profit for holders of import permits is the difference between the domestic price (at which they sell the imported good) and the world price (at which they buy it).

Tariffs and import quotas are even more similar if the government charges a fee for these permits. Suppose the government sets the permit fee equal to the difference between the domestic and world price. In this case, the entire profit of permit holders is paid to the government in permit fees, and the import quota works exactly like a tariff. Consumer surplus, producer surplus, and government revenue are precisely the same under the two policies.

In practice, however, countries that restrict trade with import quotas rarely do so by selling import permits. For example, the U.S. government has at times pressured Japan to "voluntarily" limit the sale of Japanese cars in the United States. In this case, the Japanese government allocates the import permits to Japanese firms, and these firms get the surplus from these permits. From the standpoint of U.S. welfare, this kind of import quota is worse than a U.S. tariff on imported cars. Both a tariff and an import quota raise prices, restrict trade, and cause deadweight losses, but at least the tariff generates revenue for the U.S. government rather than profit for foreign producers. ■

Dear President Openminded,

You asked three questions about opening trade. After much hard work, we have the answers.

Question: If the government allows Isolandians to import and export textiles, what will happen to the price and quantity of textiles sold in the domestic market?

Answer: Once trade is allowed, the Isolandian price will move to equal the price prevailing around the world.

If the Isolandian price before trade is below the world price, our price will rise. The higher price will reduce the amount of textiles Isolandians consume and raise the amount Isolandians produce. Isoland will become a textile exporter because, in this case, it has a comparative advantage in producing textiles.

Conversely, if the Isolandian price before trade is above the world price, our price will fall. The lower price will increase the amount of textiles Isolandians consume and lower the amount we produce. In this case, Isoland will become a textile importer because other countries have a comparative advantage in producing textiles.

Question: Who will gain from free trade in textiles and who will lose, and will the gains exceed the losses?

Answer: The answer depends on whether the price rises or falls when trade is allowed. If the price rises, producers of textiles gain, and consumers lose. If the price falls, consumers gain, and producers lose. But in both cases, the gains are larger than the losses, so free trade raises the total welfare of Isolandians.

Question: Should a tariff be part of the new trade policy?

Answer: A tariff has an impact only if Isoland becomes a textile importer. In this case, a tariff moves the economy closer to the no-trade equilibrium and, like most taxes, causes deadweight losses. A tariff improves the welfare of domestic producers and raises revenue for the government, but these gains are more than offset by the losses suffered by consumers. The best policy, from the standpoint of economic efficiency, would be to allow trade without a tariff.

Finally, you should bear in mind that moving to free trade in textiles will create losers as well as winners, even if the losses of the losers are smaller than the gains of the winners. So expect some of your constituents to oppose the policy. To blunt this opposition and spread the gains more equitably, you may want to make sure that the social safety net is generous enough to soften the blow for the losers.

We hope you find these answers helpful as you decide on your new policy.

Your faithful servants,
Isolandian economics team

8-2e Other Benefits of International Trade

The conclusions of the Isolandian economics team are based on the standard analysis of international trade. Their analysis uses the most fundamental tools in the economist's toolbox: supply, demand, and producer and consumer surplus. It shows that free trade entails winners and losers, but the gains of the winners exceed the losses of the losers.

The case for free trade can be made even stronger, however, because there are several other economic benefits of trade beyond those emphasized in the standard analysis. In a nutshell, here are some of them:

- **Increased variety of goods.** Goods produced in different countries are not exactly the same. German beer, for instance, is not the same as American beer. Free trade gives consumers in all countries a greater variety to choose from.
- **Lower costs through economies of scale.** Some goods can be produced at low cost only if they are produced in large quantities—a phenomenon called **economies of scale**. A firm cannot take full advantage of economies of scale if it can sell only in a small domestic market. Free trade gives firms access to world markets, allowing them to realize economies of scale more fully.
- **Increased competition.** A company shielded from foreign competitors is more likely to have market power, enabling it to raise prices above competitive levels. This is a type of market failure that hurts consumers and leads to inefficiencies. Opening trade fosters competition and gives the invisible hand a better chance to work its magic.
- **Increased productivity.** When a nation opens to international trade, the most productive firms expand their markets, while the least productive are forced out by increased competition. As resources move from the least to the most productive firms, overall productivity rises.

- **Enhanced flow of ideas.** The transfer of technological advances around the world is often linked to the exchange of the goods that embody those advances. The best way for a poor agricultural nation to quickly learn about the computer revolution, for instance, is to buy some computers from abroad rather than trying to make them from scratch.

In short, free trade increases variety for consumers, allows firms to take advantage of economies of scale, makes markets more competitive, makes the economy more productive, and fosters the spread of technology. If the Isolandian economists also took these benefits into account, their advice to the president would be even more forceful.

Quick**Quiz**

3. When the nation of Ectenia opens to world trade in coffee beans, the domestic price falls. Which of the following describes the situation?
   a. Domestic production of coffee rises, and Ectenia becomes a coffee importer.
   b. Domestic production of coffee rises, and Ectenia becomes a coffee exporter.
   c. Domestic production of coffee falls, and Ectenia becomes a coffee importer.
   d. Domestic production of coffee falls, and Ectenia becomes a coffee exporter.

4. When a nation opens to trade in a good and becomes an importer,
   a. producer surplus decreases, but consumer surplus and total surplus both increase.
   b. producer surplus decreases, but consumer surplus increases, so the impact on total surplus is ambiguous.
   c. producer surplus and total surplus increase, but consumer surplus decreases.
   d. producer surplus, consumer surplus, and total surplus all increase.

5. If a nation that imports a good imposes a tariff, it will increase
   a. the domestic quantity demanded.
   b. the domestic quantity supplied.
   c. the quantity imported from abroad.
   d. the efficiency of the equilibrium.

6. Which of the following policies would benefit producers, hurt consumers, and increase the amount of trade?
   a. the increase of a tariff in an importing country
   b. the reduction of a tariff in an importing country
   c. starting to allow trade when the world price is greater than the domestic price
   d. starting to allow trade when the world price is less than the domestic price

Answers are at the end of the chapter.

8-3 The Arguments for Restricting Trade

The letter from the Isolandian economics team starts to persuade President Openminded to consider allowing trade in textiles. She notes that the domestic price is now high compared with the world price. Free trade would, therefore, cause the price of textiles to fall and hurt domestic textile producers. Before implementing the new policy, she asks Isolandian textile companies to comment on the economists' advice.

Not surprisingly, the textile companies oppose free trade in textiles. They believe that the government should protect the domestic textile industry from foreign competition. Let's consider some of the arguments they might use to support their position and how the economics team would respond.

DAVID BROWN/CARTOONSTOCK LTD

"You drive a Japanese car, drink French wine, eat Chinese food, own an American computer, buy Canadian lumber and vacation in Mexico. How can you be AGAINST free trade?!"

8-3a The Jobs Argument

Opponents of free trade often say it destroys jobs. For Isoland, for example, free trade in textiles could cause the price to fall, reducing the quantity produced domestically and slashing employment in the local textile industry. This job loss is an ugly picture and one that often occurs when trade expands.

Yet free trade creates new jobs even as it destroys some old ones. When Isolandians buy textiles from other countries, those countries get the resources to buy other goods from Isoland. Displaced Isolandian textile workers can move to industries in which Isoland has a comparative advantage. The transition may be difficult for some workers, especially in the short run. But the social safety net can assuage the hardship, and the country as a whole will enjoy a higher standard of living.

Opponents of trade are often skeptical that trade creates jobs. They might say that **everything** can be produced more cheaply abroad. With free trade, they might say, Isolandians could not be profitably employed in any industry. As Chapter 3 explains, however, the gains from trade are based on comparative advantage, not absolute advantage. This concept may be hard to grasp, but it is important. Even if one country is better than another country at producing everything, each country can gain from trading with the other. Workers will eventually find jobs in industries in which their country has a comparative advantage.

8-3b The National-Security Argument

When an industry is threatened with international competition, opponents of free trade often argue that the industry is vital to national security. For example, Isolandian steel companies might point out that steel is used to make guns and tanks. Free trade in steel could lead Isoland to become dependent on foreign countries to supply steel. If a war interrupted the foreign supply, Isoland might be unable to quickly produce enough steel and weapons to defend itself.

Economists acknowledge that protecting key industries may be appropriate when there are legitimate concerns over national security. Yet they know that this argument is often used too readily by producers eager to gain at consumers' expense.

Pay attention to who is making the national security argument. Companies have a financial incentive to exaggerate their role in national defense because protection from foreign competition can be lucrative. A nation's generals may see things differently. In fact, when the military buys an industry's output, it is a consumer and benefits from imports. Cheaper steel in Isoland, for example, would allow the Isolandian military to stockpile weapons at a lower cost.

8-3c The Infant-Industry Argument

New industries sometimes call for temporary trade restrictions to help them get started. After a period of protection, the argument goes, they will be strong enough to compete with foreign firms. Similarly, older industries sometimes say they need temporary protection until they adjust to new conditions.

Economists are often skeptical about such claims, largely because the infant-industry argument is hard to implement in practice. To apply the protection successfully, the government would need to determine which industries will eventually be profitable and decide whether the benefits of establishing them exceed the costs to consumers. Yet picking winners is extraordinarily difficult. It is made even more so by the political process, which often rewards industries with the most clout. And once a politically powerful industry is favored, the "temporary" policy can become permanent.

In addition, many economists question the infant-industry argument in principle. Suppose, for instance, that an industry is young and unable to compete against foreign rivals, but there is reason to believe that it can be profitable in the long run. In this case, firm owners should be willing to incur temporary losses to obtain the eventual profits. Protection isn't needed. Start-up firms often incur temporary losses yet succeed in the long run, even without protection from competition.

8-3d The Unfair-Competition Argument

It is often said that free trade is desirable only if all countries play by the same rules. If companies in different countries are subject to different laws and regulations, then it is unfair (the argument goes) to expect them to compete globally. For instance, suppose Neighborland subsidizes its textile industry, lowering the costs of production for the country's textile companies. The Isolandian textile industry might argue that it should be protected from this foreign competition because Neighborland isn't competing fairly.

Would it, in fact, hurt Isoland to buy textiles from another country at a subsidized price? Yes, Isolandian textile producers would suffer, but Isolandian consumers would love the low price. The case for free trade remains the same: Consumer gains exceed producer losses. Neighborland's subsidy may be bad policy, but its taxpayers pay for it. Isoland is better off when it can buy textiles at a subsidized price. Rather than objecting to foreign subsidies, perhaps Isoland should send Neighborland a thank-you note.

8-3e The Protection-as-a-Bargaining-Chip Argument

Trade restrictions can be a bargaining chip, some politicians say. Even if free trade is desirable, they argue, trade restrictions can be useful in obtaining concessions from our trading partners. For example, Isoland might threaten to impose a tariff on textiles unless Neighborland removes its tariff on wheat. If Neighborland responds to this threat by removing its tariff, the result can be freer trade.

The problem with this strategy is that the threat may not work, leaving the country with two bad options. It can implement the trade restriction and shoot itself in the foot—reducing its own economic welfare is the way economists would put it. Or it can back down from its threat and lose prestige and future bargaining power. Why believe a tough-talking country that doesn't follow through with action? Faced with these choices, the country would probably wish that it had never made the threat in the first place.

Case Study

Trade Agreements and the World Trade Organization

A country can take one of two roads toward free trade. With a **unilateral** approach, it can remove its trade restrictions on its own. Great Britain did this in the 19th century, and Chile and South Korea did it more recently. Alternatively, a country can take a **multilateral** approach, reducing its trade restrictions in concert with other countries. In other words, it can bargain with its trading partners in an attempt to reduce trade restrictions around the world.

Ask the Experts

Trade Deals and Tariffs

"Past major trade deals have benefited most Americans."

What do economists say?

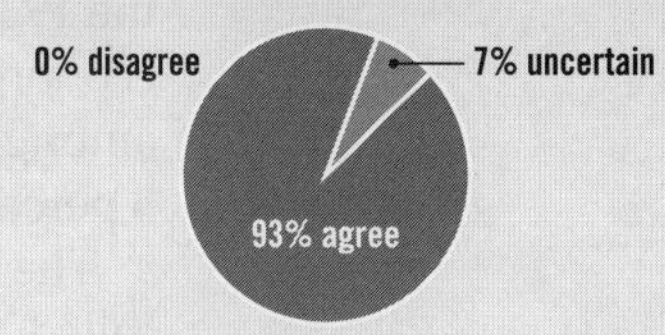

"Refusing to liberalize trade unless partner countries adopt new labor or environmental rules is a bad policy, because even if the new standards would reduce distortions on some dimensions, such a policy involves threatening to maintain large distortions in the form of restricted trade."

What do economists say?

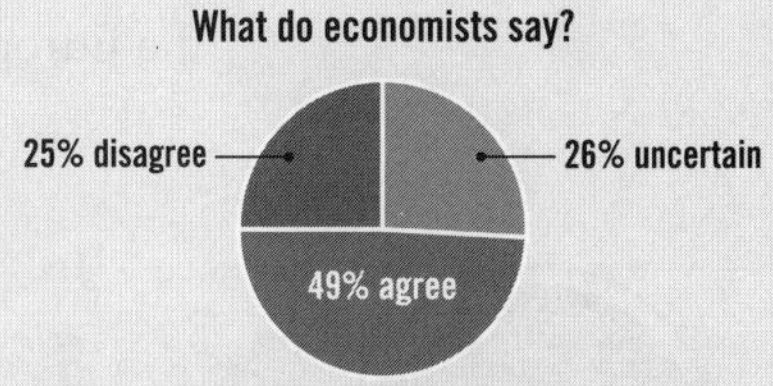

"The incidence of the latest round of U.S. import tariffs [in 2019] is likely to fall primarily on American households."

What do economists say?

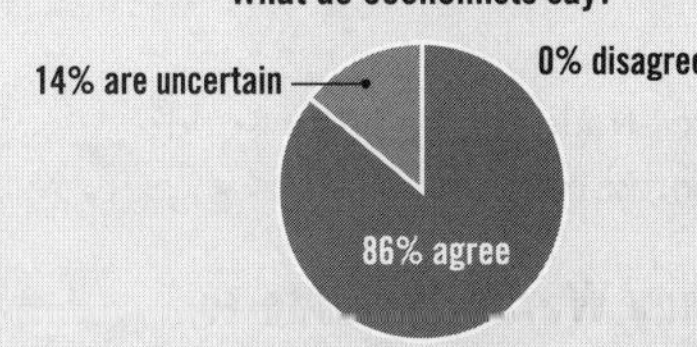

"The impact of the tariffs—and any Chinese countermeasures—on U.S. prices and employment is likely to be felt most heavily by lower income groups and regions."

What do economists say?

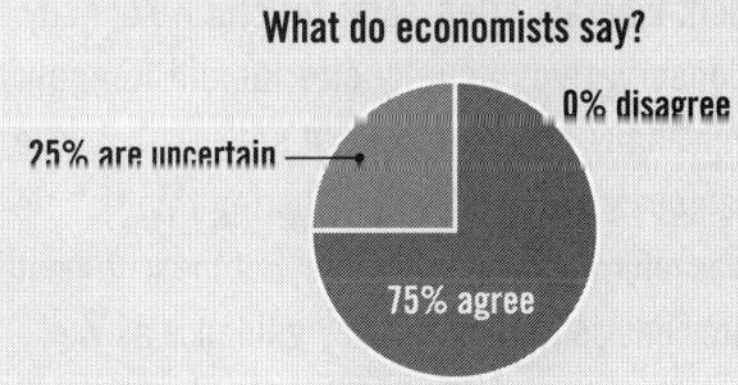

Source: IGM Economic Experts Panel, November 11, 2014, March 27, 2013, and May 29, 2019.

Figure 1

Source: Graph has been created by the author using data from Table 1.3 of the Statistical Appendix to Economic Survey 2021–22 reporting Real Gross Value Added at Basic Prices by Industry of Origin

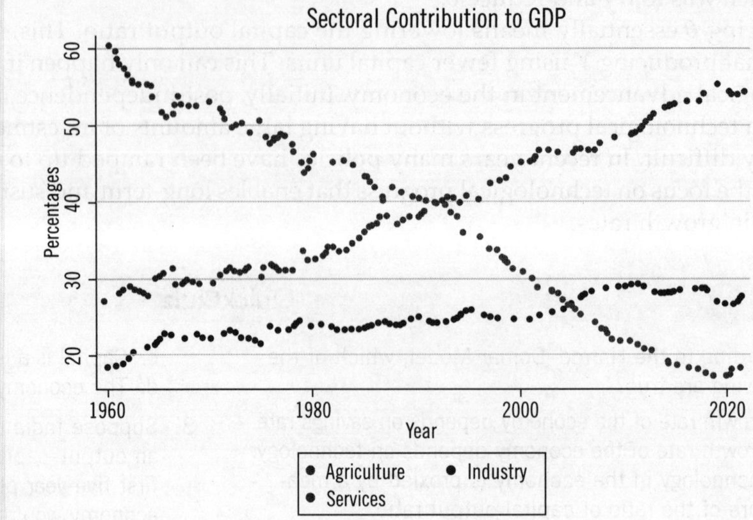

development, when India was still a baby economy, agricultural sector was the most dominant. The figure shows that the contribution of agriculture and allied sectors as a total proportion of India's GDP was around 60 percent in 1960. It gradually started declining, and as of the current decade post-2020, it is under 20 percent.

Box 9.1 Service-Led Growth Strategy and its Implications for the Indian Business Environment

Economic Pitfalls of Service-led growth strategy

Many fast-growing services such as IT-BPM, finance, modern logistics are skill-biased and are usually light on capital investments. They don't absorb large numbers of low-skill workers in the way labor-intensive industrial sectors, such as manufacturing, can. As a result, a wide gap between services' share in GDP and their share in jobs growth is observed. While this does not directly affect economic growth, it can still affect growth of jobs. India's growth story, therefore, alternately is also called that of jobless growth.

A major advantage of industrial revolution and industry-oriented growth is productivity gains through generating backward linkages and leveraging learning-by-doing approaches. Manufacturing typically has a pull factor for the entire supply chain, whereas the supply chain for services is often thinner; therefore, lesser stimuli for employment generation comes from these sectors. Moreover, since services value skilled work, the returns to education significantly grow and widen a lot of educational inequalities depending on lack of access to universal education of adequate public education infrastructure. This further widens the wage gap in the economy.

Ironically, with advent of technology, especially the AI revolution, a lot of tasks in the services sector can easily be automated, leading to large-scale job losses. A strategy fully reliant on service-led growth can, therefore, have this massive threat if AI penetrates significantly.

Managerial Insight

While services can power growth, the scale that industry and manufacturing, in particular, can bring in terms of skilling and leveraging linkages is not comparable. As a result, there has been a recent surge by Indian policymakers to move from services back to industry and stimulate industrial growth. This is partly because policymakers realize that industrial sector growth is more sustainable and has deep impacts on employment stability. Initiatives such as Start-Up India or Make in India basically are steps taken in this direction.

Managers will have to quickly realize this changing priority in the Indian business environment. One may expect that the next few years will see a lot of policy impetus toward industrial growth and promoting the industry and less focus on services. As a result, talent acquisition and training gain importance to reduce skill bottlenecks and widen the recruitment pool.

Chapter

10

Externalities

Firms that make and sell paper also create, as a by-product of the manufacturing process, a chemical called dioxin. Scientists say that once dioxin enters the environment, it can cause cancer, birth defects, and other health problems. This chapter considers how the release of pollutants such as dioxin fits into the analysis of markets.

While our analysis of competitive markets reveal that they allocate scarce resources and showed that the equilibrium of supply and demand typically allocates resources efficiently. To use Adam Smith's metaphor, an "invisible hand" leads buyers and sellers to maximize the total benefits received by market participants.

But unfettered markets are not a cure-all. The invisible hand on its own does not prevent firms in the paper market from emitting too much dioxin. Society needs to find some other way to solve this problem. This leads us to another principle of economics: Governments can sometimes improve market outcomes.

4ZMANJAKA/E+/GETTY IMAGES; CARLOS FLORES/EYEEM/GETTY IMAGES

10-2d Objections to the Economic Analysis of Pollution

"We cannot give anyone the option of polluting for a fee." This comment from Senator Edmund Muskie during the struggle to enact the 1972 Clean Water Act still reflects the view of some environmentalists. In 1969, the Cuyahoga River in Cleveland was so thick with industrial pollutants that it actually caught fire—a recurring problem that the legislation helped solve. Clean air and water were seen as fundamental human rights that had been despoiled. Remembering those days, many environmentalists say that economics is, at best, a secondary concern and, in some respects, a repugnant one. If clean air and water are priceless—part of the inheritance of every human—what kind of person would try to put a price on them? The environment is so important, some say, that protecting it is an absolute priority, regardless of cost.

Many modern economists are environmentalists and are committed to achieving clean air and water and ending global climate change, yet they view these public issues through a different lens. The value of environmental measures must be compared with their opportunity cost—that is, with what one must give up to obtain them. Eliminating all pollution is, sadly, impossible. Trying to eliminate all pollution is a lofty goal but not a feasible one—at least not in the foreseeable future—without reversing many of the technological advances that allow us to enjoy a high standard of living. Few people would be willing to accept poor nutrition, inadequate health care, or shoddy housing to make the environment as clean as possible.

The cause of environmentalism is arguably best advanced by thinking like an economist. A clean environment can be viewed as another good—one with tremendous value. Like all normal goods, it has a positive income elasticity: Rich countries can afford a cleaner environment than poor ones and usually have more rigorous environmental protection. In addition, like most other goods, clean air and water obey the law of demand: The lower the price of environmental protection, the more of it the public will want. When the economic approach of using corrective taxes and pollution permits reduces the cost of attaining clean air and water, it should increase the amount of environmental protection that the public demands.

Case Study

Climate Change and Carbon Taxes

Scientists tell us that human carbon emissions are a cause of global climate change, which in turn has various harmful effects. This is a classic example of a negative externality.

Suppose a concerned citizen—let's call him Jairam—wants to reduce his carbon footprint. How might he do it?

- Jairam could buy a more fuel-efficient car, like a hybrid or an electric vehicle.
- Jairam could carpool to work.
- Jairam could use public transportation more often.
- Jairam could move closer to his job.
- Jairam could buy a smaller house that requires less energy to heat and cool.
- Jairam could adjust the thermostat to keep his home cooler in the winter and warmer in the summer.
- Jairam could put solar panels on his roof.
- Jairam could buy more energy-efficient home appliances.

me owns the reclining rights. In that circumstance, if I really care about being allowed to recline, I could pay him to let me.

Donald Marron, a former director of the Congressional Budget Office, agrees with this analysis, but with a caveat. Recline negotiations do involve some transaction costs—passengers don't like bargaining over reclining positions with their neighbors, perhaps because that sometimes ends with water being thrown in someone's face.

Mr. Marron says we ought to allocate the initial property right to the person likely to care most about reclining, in order to reduce the number of transactions that are necessary. He further argues that it's probably the person sitting behind, as evidenced by the fact people routinely pay for extra-legroom seats.

GCHUTKA/E+/GETTY IMAGES

Mr. Marron is wrong about this last point. I understand people don't like negotiating with strangers, but in hundreds of flights I have taken, I have rarely had anyone complain to me about my seat recline, and nobody has ever offered me money, or anything else of value, in exchange for sitting upright.

If sitting behind my reclined seat was such misery, if recliners like me are "monsters," as Mark Hemingway of *The Weekly Standard* puts it, why is nobody willing to pay me to stop? People talk a big game on social media about the terribleness of reclining, but then people like to complain about all sorts of things; if they really cared that much, someone would have opened his wallet and paid me by now. ■

Source: New York Times, August 27, 2014.

Questions to Discuss

1. Can you imagine offering a person sitting in front of you on an airplane some money not to recline his seat? Why or why not?
2. If a person sitting behind you on an airplane offered you some money not to recline your seat, how would you respond? Why?

In some cases, people can solve the problem of externalities on their own. The Coase theorem suggests that the interested parties can bargain among themselves and agree on an efficient solution. Sometimes, however, an efficient outcome cannot be reached, perhaps because the large number of interested parties makes bargaining difficult.

When people cannot solve the problem of externalities privately, the government often steps in. Yet even with government intervention, society can benefit by harnessing—rather than circumventing—market forces. The government can require market participants to bear the full costs of their actions. Corrective taxes on emissions and pollution permits, for instance, are both designed to internalize the externality of pollution. These are increasingly the policies of choice for those interested in protecting the environment. Market forces, properly redirected, are often the best remedy for market failure.

Also, the market fails to allocate resources efficiently when something of value has no price attached to it. This happens when property rights are not well established, sometimes because they can't be. For example, although clean air and national defense are undeniably valuable, no private individual has the legal right to price them and profit from their use.

When such absence of property rights leads to a market failure, the government may be able to solve the problem. Sometimes, as in the sale of pollution permits, the government can help define property rights and unleash market forces. Other times, as in restricted hunting seasons, the government can regulate private behavior. Still other times, as in the provision of national defense, the government can use tax revenue to supply a good that the market fails to supply. In each of these cases, if the policy is well-planned and well- run, it can make the allocation of resources more efficient and raise economic well-being.

One important example of the multilateral approach is the North American Free Trade Agreement (NAFTA), which in 1993 lowered trade barriers among the United States, Mexico, and Canada. An updated, new NAFTA, also known as the United States-Mexico-Canada Agreement, went into effect in 2020.

Another important multilateral pact is the General Agreement on Tariffs and Trade (GATT), a series of negotiations among many of the world's countries with the goal of promoting free trade. The United States helped to found GATT after World War II in response to the high tariffs imposed during the Great Depression of the 1930s. Many economists believe that those tariffs contributed to the worldwide economic hardship of that period. GATT successfully reduced the average tariff among member countries from more than 20 percent after World War II to less than 5 percent in 2000. And it continued at a low level for many years thereafter.

The rules established under GATT are enforced by an international institution called the World Trade Organization (WTO). The WTO was established in 1995 and has its headquarters in Geneva, Switzerland. As of 2021, 164 countries have joined the organization, accounting for 98 percent of world trade. The functions of the WTO are to administer trade agreements, provide a forum for negotiations, and handle disputes among member countries.

But the road to free trade is not a one-way street. The United States, which promoted the multilateral approach to free trade for decades, turned against it during the Trump administration and raised tariffs unilaterally in disputes with China, the European Union, and many other countries. The arguments were familiar and

In the News

Trade as a Tool for Economic Development

Free trade can help the world's poorest citizens.

Andy Warhol's Guide to Public Policy

By Arthur C. Brooks

I often ask people in my business—public policy—where they get their inspiration. Liberals often point to John F. Kennedy. Conservatives usually cite Ronald Reagan. Personally, I prefer the artist Andy Warhol, who famously declared, "I like boring things." He was referring to art, of course. But the sentiment provides solid public policy guidance as well.

Warhol's work exalted the everyday "boring" items that display the transcendental beauty of life itself. The canonical example is his famous paintings of Campbell Soup cans. Some people sneered, but those willing to look closely could see what he was doing. It is the same idea expressed in an old Zen saying, often attributed to the eighth-century Chinese Buddhist philosopher Layman Pang: "How wondrously supernatural and miraculous! I draw water and I carry wood!"

Warhol's critical insight is usually lost on most of the world. This is not because people are stupid, but because our brains are wired to filter out the mundane and focus on the novel. This turns out to be an important survival adaptation. To discern a predator, you must filter out the constant rustling of leaves and notice the strange snap of a twig.

Warhol believed that defeating this cognitive bias led to greater appreciation of beauty. It also leads to better public policy, especially in relieving poverty. For example, while our attention is naturally drawn to the latest fascinating and expensive innovations in tropical public health, many experts insist it is cheap, boring mosquito bed nets that best protect against malaria. Despite their lifesaving utility, these boring nets tend to be chronically underprovided.

We can look closer to home, too. People love to find ways to get fancy technology into poor schoolchildren's hands, but arguably the best way to help children falling behind in school is simply to devise ways to get them to show up.

But the very best example of the Warhol principle in policy is international trade. If it is progress against poverty that we're pursuing, trade beats the pants off every fancy development program ever devised. The simple mundane beauty included many of the critiques of free trade discussed earlier. Some U.S. trading partners retaliated with higher tariffs of their own. For example, at the start of 2018, tariffs applied to very little trade between the United States and China. By the end of 2020, more than half of U.S. imports from China were subject to U.S. tariffs with an average rate of about 20 percent, and more than half of Chinese imports from the United States were subject to Chinese tariffs of about the same size. Where global tariffs will end up in the years ahead is far from certain.

What are the pros and cons of resuming the multilateral approach to free trade? One advantage is that it has the potential to result in freer trade than a unilateral approach because it can reduce trade restrictions abroad as well as at home. If international negotiations fail, however, the result could be more restricted trade than under a unilateral approach.

In addition, the multilateral approach may have a political advantage. In most markets, because producers are fewer and better organized than consumers, they have more political clout. Reducing the Isolandian tariff on textiles, for example, may be politically difficult if considered by itself. The textile companies would oppose free trade, and the buyers of textiles who would benefit are so numerous that organizing their support would be difficult. Yet suppose that Neighborland promises to reduce its tariff on wheat while Isoland reduces its tariff on textiles. In this case, the Isolandian wheat farmers, who are also politically powerful, would back the agreement. The multilateral approach can sometimes win political support when a unilateral approach cannot. ●

of making things and exchanging them freely is the best anti-poverty achievement in history.

For more than two decades, the global poverty rate has been decreasing by roughly 1 percent a year. To put this in perspective, that comes to about 70 million people—equivalent to the whole population of Turkey or Thailand—climbing out of poverty annually. Add it up, and around a billion people have escaped destitution since 1990.

Why? It isn't the United Nations or foreign aid. It is, in the words of the publication *YaleGlobal Online*, "High growth spillovers originating from large open emerging economies that utilize cross-border supply chains." For readers who don't have tenure, that means free trade in poor countries.

That mug in your hand that says "Made in China" is part of the reason that 680 million Chinese have been pulled out of absolute poverty since the 1980s. No giant collaboration among transnational technocrats or lending initiatives did that. It was because of economic reforms in China, of people making stuff, putting it on boats, and sending it to be sold in America—to you. Critics of free trade often argue that open economies lead to exploitation or environmental degradation. These are serious issues, but protectionism is never the answer. Curbing trade benefits entrenched domestic interests and works against the world's poor.

And what of claims that trade increases global income inequality? They are false. Economists at the World Bank and at LIS (formerly known as the Luxembourg Income Study Center) have shown that, for the world as a whole, income inequality has fallen for most of the past 20 years. This is chiefly because of rising incomes from globalization in the developing world....

Trade doesn't solve every problem, of course. The world needs democracy, security and many other expressions of American values and leadership as well. But in a policy world crowded with outlandish, wasteful boondoggles, free trade is just the kind of beautifully boring Warholian strategy we need. Americans dedicated to helping others ought to support it without compromise or apology. ■

Questions to Discuss

1. What item that you use regularly was made in another country? What country did it come from? Who benefited from your purchase—you or the foreign producer?
2. How do you think trade between the United States and a poorer nation affects the workers in the poorer nation?

Mr. Brooks is a professor at Harvard University.

Source: New York Times, April 12, 2015.

Quick**Quiz**

7. The nation of Lilliput imports rope from the nation of Brobdingnag, where rope producers are subsidized by the government because of their great political clout. The most efficient policy from the standpoint of Lilliput is to
   a. continue trading at the subsidized price.
   b. place a tariff on rope imports to offset the subsidy.
   c. give a similar subsidy to the rope producers of Lilliput.
   d. stop trading with Brobdingnag.

8. The goal of multilateral trade agreements is usually to
   a. equalize the level of tariffs across nations so no nation is disadvantaged relative to others.
   b. use targeted tariffs to ensure that nations produce those goods for which they have a comparative advantage.
   c. reduce tariffs in various nations simultaneously to blunt political pressure for protectionism.
   d. ensure that tariffs are used only to promote infant industries that will eventually become viable.

Answers are at the end of the chapter.

8-4 Trade Policy in India in the Globalized Business Environment

India's trade landscape has undergone a significant transformation in recent years, particularly in response to post-pandemic realignments and integration of the Indian business environment into the globalized world. According to recent *Economic Surveys of India*, both merchandise and service exports have shown considerable growth. The data suggests that India now commands around a 10% share in the global export market for telecommunications, computer, and IT services, making it the second-largest exporter in the world in this segment. In trade parlance, this is an area where comparative advantage is driven by the presence of skilled labor, quality of digital infrastructure etc. This is also evidenced by the flourishing business activities of Indian firms likesuch as Infosys, TCS, and HCL.

Beyond these export-intensive services, the textile and apparel industry, which has traditionally been dominated by cotton fibers, but is now being strategically reoriented by active government policy, in response to global demand shifts. World over, man-made fibers (MMF) dominate global demand trends and represent significant cost-competitiveness from the production point of view. The government's Production Linked Incentive (PLI) Scheme for Textiles, and the PM-MITRA (Mega Integrated Textile Region and Apparel) parks are part of this targeted industrial strategy. These policies aim to attract investment in MMF and improve logistics to increase India's share in the global garment value chain, majorly in response to diminishing competitiveness of other countries like China. The idea is to be at par with global textile trade norms which increasingly rely on "fiber-to-fabric" methods by integrating production, manufacturing and finishing of the entire line of production at a single location or region.

There are several managerial responses possible at the firm and industry level to such a trade policy environment. For instance, firms in the textile sector may adapt their product mix and supply chain to align with MMF-based production incentives in the fiber-to-fabric approach. The rise of textile parks further enhances the case for location-based decision-making, especially in terms of investments and logistics cost optimization to leverage tax benefits. Additionally, India's strategic thrift towards diversifying its export partnerships with countries beyond the US and EU has important implications for businesses. For instance, with more trade with middleeast, southeast Asian countries and African partners, firms will have to weigh both risks and opportunities. Given this friend-shoring approach of trading with geo politically aligned partners, firms can explore entry into new high-demand markets while also diversifying their trade risk portfolio due to less reliance on more powerful but volatile trade partners.

Trump Tariffs 2025: Indian Strategic Response and the Business Environment

In August 2025, US President Donald Trump announced a 50% tariff on most imports from India as a "punishment for buying Russian oil" as headlined by The Guardian's August 27, 2025 edition. The argument was that purchasing discounted Russian oil indirectly helps fund the Ukraine war. This potentially affects several Indian product categories such as garments, jewelry, seafood, furniture and some chemicals.

Such a tariff imposes a major price-shock for Indian goods in the US market, and following law of demand, it is quite likely that the demand for Indian exports (imported by US consumers) is likely to be dampened and potentially US consumers and producers (who buy Indian inputs) would switch to cheaper alternatives. Consequently, Indian exporters need to revisit their managerial strategy in response to such a major trade policy shock.

Some responses may include firms diversifying their exports to other markets such as Africa, South-East Asia or Latin America, instead of the US. Firms will have to comply with Indian government's policy realignment, as they case maybe, perhaps to focus on near-shoring (trading with neighbors) or friend shoring (trading with geo-political allies). However, in terms of cost structure, managers may also have to re-assess their production strategies. For instance, if US prices were more profitable compared to lower penetration markets like Africa, the firms may have to reduce costs. This may have adverse impacts on employment of procurement within country.

Diplomatically, however, the Indian government has called out these measures and attempted to come up with internal measures such as GST relaxations and tax cuts to offset potential threats from cost effectiveness considerations faces by firms, which may help protect any volatility in the Indian domestic market.

8-5 Conclusion

Economists and the public often hold different views about international trade. Public-opinion polls typically find that people are mixed on whether trade is an opportunity or a threat. Politicians often reflect this mixed verdict. By contrast, economists overwhelmingly support free trade. They view it as a way of allocating production efficiently and raising living standards both at home and abroad.

Economists view the fifty states of the United States as an ongoing experiment that confirms the virtues of free trade. Throughout its history, the United States has allowed unrestricted trade among the states, and the country has benefited from the specialization that trade allows. Florida grows oranges, Texas pumps oil, California makes wine, and so on. Americans would not enjoy the standard of living they do today if people could consume only those goods and services produced in their own states. The world could similarly benefit from free trade among countries.

To better understand economists' view of trade, return to Isoland. Suppose that President Openminded, after reading the latest poll results, ignores the advice of her economics team and decides not to allow free trade in textiles. The country remains in the equilibrium without international trade.

Then, one day, an Isolandian named Isabel Inventor discovers a way to make textiles at a very low cost. The process is secret, however. What is odd is that Inventor doesn't need traditional inputs such as cotton or wool. The only material input she needs is wheat. And even more oddly, to manufacture textiles from wheat, she hardly needs any labor input at all.

Inventor is hailed as a genius. Because everyone buys clothing, the lower cost of textiles gives all Isolandians a higher standard of living. Workers who had previously produced textiles experience some hardship when their factories close, but eventually, they find work in other industries. Some become farmers and grow the wheat that Inventor turns into textiles. Others enter new industries that emerge as a result of higher Isolandian living standards. Everyone understands that the displacement of workers in outmoded industries is an inevitable part of technological progress and economic growth.

After several years, a journalist named Roberto Reporter decides to investigate this mysterious new textile process. He sneaks into Inventor's factory and learns that she has not been making textiles at all. Instead, she has been smuggling wheat abroad in exchange for textiles from other countries. The only thing that Inventor had discovered was the gains from international trade.

When Reporter reveals the truth, the government shuts down Inventor's operation. The price of textiles rises, and workers return to jobs in textile factories. Living standards in Isoland fall back to their former levels. Inventor is jailed and held up to public ridicule. After all, she was no inventor. She was just an economist.

Chapter in a Nutshell

- The effects of free trade can be determined by comparing the domestic price before trade with the world price. A low domestic price indicates that the country has a comparative advantage in producing the good and that the country will become an exporter. A high domestic price indicates that the rest of the world has a comparative advantage in producing the good and that the country will become an importer.
- When a country allows trade and becomes an exporter of a good, producers of the good are better off, and consumers of the good are worse off. When a country allows trade and becomes an importer of a good, consumers are better off, and producers are worse off. In both cases, the gains from trade exceed the losses.
- A tariff—a tax on imports—moves a market closer to the equilibrium that would exist without trade and reduces the gains from trade. Domestic producers are better off, and the government raises revenue, but the losses to consumers exceed these gains.
- International trade yields several benefits beyond those based on comparative advantage: greater product variety for consumers, more opportunity for firms to take advantage of economies of scale, increased market competition, higher overall productivity as more productive firms expand and less productive ones contract, and improved access to state-of-the-art technology.
- There are various arguments for restricting trade: protecting jobs, defending national security, helping infant industries, preventing unfair competition, and responding to foreign trade restrictions. Although some of these arguments have merit in some cases, most economists believe that free trade is usually the better policy.

Key Concepts

world price, p. 163

tariff, p. 167

Questions for Review

1. What does the domestic price that prevails without international trade tell us about a nation's comparative advantage?
2. When does a country become an exporter of a good? An importer?
3. Draw the supply-and-demand diagram for an importing country. Identify consumer surplus and producer surplus before trade is allowed. Identify consumer surplus and producer surplus with free trade. What is the change in total surplus?
4. Describe what a tariff is and its economic effects.
5. List five arguments often given to support trade restrictions. How do economists respond to these arguments?
6. What is the difference between the unilateral and multilateral approaches to achieving free trade? Give an example of each.

Problems and Applications

1. The world price of wine is below the price that would prevail in Canada in the absence of trade.
   a. Assuming that Canadian imports of wine are a small share of total world wine production, draw a graph for the Canadian market for wine under free trade. Identify consumer surplus, producer surplus, and total surplus in an appropriate table.
   b. Now suppose that a shift of the Gulf Stream leads to an unseasonably cold summer in Europe, destroying much of the grape harvest there. What effect does this shock have on the world price of wine? Using your graph and table from part (a), show the effect on consumer surplus, producer surplus, and total surplus in Canada. Who are the winners and losers? Is Canada as a whole better or worse off?

2. Suppose that Congress imposes a tariff on imported automobiles to protect the U.S. auto industry from foreign competition. Assuming that the United States is a price taker in the world auto market, show the following on a diagram: the change in the quantity of imports, the loss to U.S. consumers, the gain to U.S. manufacturers, government revenue, and the deadweight loss associated with the tariff. The loss to consumers can be decomposed into three pieces: a gain to domestic producers, revenue for the government, and a deadweight loss. Use your diagram to identify these three pieces.

3. When China's clothing industry expands, the increase in the world supply lowers the world price of clothing.
   a. Draw an appropriate diagram to analyze how this change in price affects consumer surplus, producer surplus, and total surplus in a nation that imports clothing, such as the United States.
   b. Now, draw an appropriate diagram to show how this change in price affects consumer surplus, producer surplus, and total surplus in a nation that exports clothing, such as the Dominican Republic.
   c. Compare your answers to parts (a) and (b). What are the similarities, and what are the differences? Which country should be concerned about the expansion of the Chinese textile industry? Which country should be applauding it? Explain.

4. Consider the arguments for restricting trade.
   a. Imagine that you are a lobbyist for timber, an established industry suffering from low-priced foreign competition, and you are trying to get Congress to pass trade restrictions. Which two or three of the five arguments discussed in the chapter do you think would be most persuasive to the average member of Congress? Explain your reasoning.
   b. Now, assume you are an astute student of economics (not a hard assumption, we hope). Although all the arguments for restricting trade have their shortcomings, name the two or three arguments that seem to make the most economic sense to you. For each, describe the economic rationale for and against these arguments for trade restrictions.

5. The nation of Textilia does not allow imports of clothing. In its equilibrium without trade, a T-shirt costs ₹20, and the equilibrium quantity is 3 million T-shirts. After reading Adam Smith's *The Wealth of Nations* while on vacation, the president decides to open the Textilian market to international trade. The market price of a T-shirt falls to the world price of ₹16. The number of T-shirts consumed in Textilia rises to 4 million, while the number of T-shirts produced declines to 1 million.
   a. Illustrate the situation just described in a graph. Your graph should show all the numbers.
   b. Calculate the change in consumer surplus, producer surplus, and total surplus that results from opening trade. (Hint: Recall that the area of a triangle is ½ × base × height.)

6. China is a major producer of grains, such as wheat, corn, and rice. Some years ago, the Chinese government, concerned that grain exports were driving up food prices for domestic consumers, imposed a tax on grain exports.
   a. Draw the graph that describes the market for grain in an exporting country. Use this graph as the starting point to answer the following questions.
   b. How does an export tax affect domestic grain prices?
   c. How does it affect the welfare of domestic consumers, the welfare of domestic producers, and government revenue?
   d. What happens to total welfare in China, as measured by the sum of consumer surplus, producer surplus, and tax revenue?

7. Consider a country that imports a good from abroad. For each of the following statements, state whether it is true or false. Explain your answer.
   a. "The greater the elasticity of demand, the greater the gains from trade."
   b. "If demand is perfectly inelastic, there are no gains from trade."
   c. "If demand is perfectly inelastic, consumers do not benefit from trade."

8. Having rejected a tariff on textiles (a tax on imports), the president of Isoland is now considering the same-sized tax on textile consumption (including both imported and domestically produced textiles).
   a. Using Figure 4, identify the quantity consumed and the quantity produced in Isoland under a textile consumption tax.
   b. Construct a table similar to that in Figure 4 for the textile consumption tax.
   c. Which raises more revenue for the government—the consumption tax or the tariff? Which has a smaller deadweight loss? Explain.

9. Assume the United States is an importer of televisions and there are no trade restrictions. U.S. consumers buy 1 million televisions per year, of which 400,000 are produced domestically and 600,000 are imported.
   a. Suppose that a technological advance among Chinese television manufacturers causes the world price of televisions to fall by ₹100. Draw a graph to show how this change affects the welfare of U.S. consumers and U.S. producers and how it affects total surplus in the United States.
   b. After the fall in price, consumers buy 1.2 million televisions, of which 200,000 are produced domestically, and 1 million are imported. Calculate the change in consumer surplus, producer surplus, and total surplus from the price reduction.
   c. If the government responded by putting a ₹100 tariff on imported televisions, what would this do? Calculate the revenue that would be raised and the deadweight loss. Would it be a good policy from the standpoint of U.S. welfare? Who might support the policy?
   d. Suppose that the fall in price is attributable not to a technological advance but to a subsidy from the Chinese government to Chinese industry of ₹100 per television. How would this affect your analysis?

10. Consider a small country that exports steel. Suppose that a "pro-trade" government decides to subsidize the export of steel by paying a certain amount for each ton sold abroad. How does this export subsidy affect the domestic price of steel, the quantity of steel produced, the quantity of steel consumed, and the quantity of steel exported? How does it affect consumer surplus, producer surplus, government revenue, and total surplus? Is it a good policy from the standpoint of economic efficiency? (Hint: The analysis of an export subsidy is similar to the analysis of a tariff.)

QuickQuiz Answers

1. **b** 2. **b** 3. **d** 4. **c** 5. **b** 6. **c** 7. **a** 8. **c** 9. **b** 10. **c**

Chapter

9

Indian Business and Economic Environment

In India, rapid economic growth has been historically coupled with several structural impediments. Managers operating in the Indian economy, therefore, are tasked with plant establishment, product development, hiring, and financing in a business environment characterized by overall macroeconomic expansion coexisting with state-level disparities, inadequate infrastructure, and evolving regulatory frameworks.

G-20 Group
An international group of countries and entities to strengthen international cooperation and governance.

Despite being among the fastest growing large economies, with an annual growth rate of more than 7 percent over the past quarter-century, India maintains a relatively low level of development within the **G-20 group** and consistently exhibits job scarcity, highlighting major problems with employment generation.

The objective of this chapter is to translate this contextual analysis into actionable managerial recommendations utilizing the analytical tools developed in previous chapters, including PPFs, supply–demand analysis with policy interventions, the concept of deadweight loss, elasticity analysis, and market power analysis.

AZMANJAKA/E+/GETTY IMAGES CARLOS FLORES/EYEEM/GETTY IMAGES

9-1 Historical Growth Strategies

India's post-independence growth strategy had traditionally relied on domestic demand more than exports, which made macroeconomic stability especially salient for consumer-facing businesses. Policy reforms that relieve supply-side bottlenecks—labor, land, logistics—are central to sustaining demand without fueling inflation.

Managers should expect regional variation in purchasing power and participation: female labor force participation has declined over time (from roughly the mid-30s to high-20s percent), limiting household earnings in many markets and thereby affecting category penetration and pricing ladders. It is very important for managers operating in this dynamic business environment to calibrate product mixes and output varieties to uneven income growth and participation across states and districts.

An understanding of the basic policies of Indian economic transformation is critical for managers, therefore, to adjust their strategic priorities with respect to successfully navigating the business and economic environment of the country.

9-1 a Harrod–Domar Model of Growth and Indian Planning Economy

India was initially a planning-based economy and adopted the 5-year plan approach, somewhat influenced by other socialist regimes. It is important to note that India was labor-abundant and capital-scarce, much like the most nascent economies. Consequently, the policymakers and planners of the economy got attracted to an economic growth model known as Harrod–Domar Model, which relies on the central assumption of a closed economy, i.e., an economy that is not open to trade, and the fact that the economy is labor-abundant with capital as the only limiting factor.

Harrod–Domar model a workhorse model of economic growth named after economists Roy Harrod and Evsey Domar, which links economic growth to savings rate and technology.

The **Harrod–Domar model** operates through a framework positing that growth is directly proportional to investment levels and the efficiency of those investments in generating capacity. This central result aligned seamlessly with the macroeconomic reality and India's available policy instruments and therefore was of great appeal to the policymakers in the country. The model predicts that, all else equal, in the absence of any depreciation, the growth rate of output in the economy is equal to the ratio of the rate of savings and the capital–output ratio.

So, suppose, "s" denotes the rate of savings in the economy. Imagine the country has an income level of "Y," and everybody saves a constant proportion of that income. This is the savings rate "s" such that overall savings in the economy is "sY." The Harrod–Domar model predicts that the growth rate of the economy, "g" is given by the following expression:

$$g = s/\theta$$

where θ is the ratio of capital to output. Intuitively, θ is the rate at which capital is converted to output or the amount of capital required to produce a given amount of output Y. Therefore, the predictions of the Harrod–Domar model suggest that there are two potential ways that the policymaker can induce growth in the economy.

1. Design policies that increase "s" as growth are directly proportional to savings rate.
2. Design policies that reduce θ as a lower θ imply higher g.

Consequently, India having adopted the Harrod–Domar approach in the first five-year plan, a massive focus of the Indian economy was on policies to promote savings rates. Incentivizing people to save more and increase the economy-wide

"s" such that the growth of the economy can be accelerated remains a major area of focus in the country. Understandably, the other approach was initially less attractive, which was to try and reduce θ.

Reducing θ essentially means lowering the capital output ratio. This, in turn, means that producing Y using fewer capital units. This can only happen if there is technological advancement in the economy. Initially, post-independence, achieving rapid technological progress without having large amounts of investment was relatively difficult. In recent years many policies have been ramped up to try and increase the focus on technological progress that enables long-term and sustainable increase in growth rates.

Quick**Quiz**

1. According to the Harrod–Domar Model, which of the following are true?
   a. Growth rate of the economy depends on savings rate.
   b. Growth rate of the economy depends on technology.
   c. Technology in the economy is proxied by a measure of the ratio of capital output ratio.
   d. All of the above
2. Which of the following is not an assumption of Harrod–Domar Model?
   a. The economy is capital abundant.
   b. The economy is labor abundant.
   c. Capital is a limiting factor in the economy.
   d. The economy is closed.
3. Suppose India had a savings rate of 25 percent and an output–capital ratio of 0.25. According to the first five-year plan, the expected growth rate for the economy would be:
   a. 100 percent
   b. 5 percent
   c. 6.25 percent
   d. 1 percent

Answers are at the end of the chapter.

9-1 b Growth and Structural Transformation

Structural transformation is the long-run reallocation of an economy's resources such as labor, capital, and land from low-productivity activities such as subsistence agriculture to high-productivity activities such as manufacturing, modern services, and higher value agriculture. This is often accompanied by urbanization, formalization, and sustained productivity growth.

structural transformation the reallocation of resources among different sectors, resulting in changes in the sectoral composition of GDP and employment of an economy, usually reflected by a switch from less productive to more productive sectors over time.

In general, structural transformation has two components. The first one is between-sector shifts where workers and capital move from agriculture to industry or services. The second one is within-sector upgrade. This involves firms and farms adopting better technology, management, and increasing the scale of operations. Structural transformation is often measured by changes in sectoral shares of value-added contributions to GDP or national income, or through sectoral shares in employment.

An important feature of the Indian economy since the early planning phase has been the structural transformation that the economy has witnessed. The sectoral contributions of Agriculture, Industry, and Services to India's overall GDP have seen dramatic shifts over the decades following independence and therefore have a major impact on how the current business environment is shaping up, including affecting policies adopted by firms and forward-looking economic agents, as well as dictating need-of-the-hour government policies.

Figure 1 represents this dramatic shift in the relative contributions of these three sectors to India's GDP. It is clear that in the early phases on the Indian economic

On the other hand, the contribution of the industrial sector to India's overall GDP has been relatively steady and has hovered between 20 percent and 30 percent. The dramatic fall in the sectoral share of agriculture in India's GDP has been offset by the dramatic rise in the services sector. While the contribution to India's overall GDP for this sector was less than 20 percent in 1960, today it is close to 55 percent and is the major component of our economy.

In general, India is largely an outlier in its structural transformation. While an economy matures, structural transformation is usually observed through a sectoral shift from dependence on agriculture to industry and then to services. However, the major switch in India seems to have happened directly from agriculture to services while industrial sector has remained relatively stagnant. Consequently, the phenomenal growth that India has witnessed has been largely due to the growth of services, and therefore India's growth story is often called service-led growth.

Structural transformation is considered healthy when the employment shift keeps pace with productivity so that real wages can rise broadly. In India's context, a persistent gap exists in terms of agriculture's small share in GDP but large share in employment. This anomaly signals an incomplete transformation, making policies that raise farm productivity, expand labor-intensive manufacturing, and scale modern services alongside programs focused on upskilling and development of urban infrastructure central to inclusive growth. This is directly relevant to managers' choices on location, automation, supply chains, and hiring.

9-2 Inclusive Growth

In this section, we discuss what inclusive growth means and why managers should care. More specifically, why inclusive growth is important for the business environment and how it interacts with the same. Inclusive growth is sustained, productivity-driven expansion of income and opportunities that raise living standards across the entire demographic distribution. Essentially, this implies that the poor, women, and historically marginalized groups are treated equally and reap the benefits of growth in the same way without eroding fiscal or environmental sustainability.

9-2 a From Averages to Percentiles

Traditional growth relies on measurement of GDP over years and how it increases (or rarely, decreases) from year to year and in what magnitude. It also studies per capita income, which is the total income deflated by the measure of population. However, these measures ignore the overall statistical distribution but just focus on measures of central tendency, mainly the mean and average.

Inclusive growth, on the other hand, looks at the entire statistical distribution of growth over the population. Therefore, we are often interested in what the median or 50th percentile household consumption is, or what the real wages of the bottom 40 percent are, and so on. Similarly, we care about whether women and men have equal opportunities and whether per capita incomes are similar across demographic divide in the country irrespective of caste, creed, religion, etc.

There are largely two channels that matter most for the study of inclusivity:

1. Employment and Earnings Disparities: Employment being the primary route out of poverty holds an important role in understanding disparities and inequality. Whether or not women have equal employment opportunities, whether people from all religions and castes have equal pay, etc., are impor-

tant questions. This channel also has a role to play in explaining mobility from informal to formal work, including the study of inclusive job creation and rise in wages.

2. Access to Resources, Endowments, and Capabilities: One reason that inequality manifests could simply be differential access to resources and endowments people are born with. However, the role of the economy is to ensure that access to resources is not unequal, and if there are significant endowment gaps, affirmative action is practiced trying and bridging these inequalities.

A way affirmative action is practiced in India is through historical reservations and quotas in access to education and jobs. For instance, marginalized communities can apply to get admitted to academic institutions through job quotas where several seats in educational institutions are statutorily reserved for individuals from backward communities, such as scheduled castes (SCs), scheduled tribes (STs), and other backward castes (OBCs), and more recently expanded to include economically weaker sections (EWS) of the society. These reservations are applied not just to educational institutes but also to public sector jobs as well as political representation in legislative assemblies and parliaments. However, such affirmative action based on gender, which mandates minimum representation of women, is much rarer and limited to only some local government elections, such as gram panchayats, and within educational institutes that non-mandatorily prioritize diversity.

9-2 b Why India's Inclusivity Gaps Matter for Business?

As discussed in the preceding section, agriculture still employs a large share of workers but contributes a much smaller share to India's GDP, resulting in incomplete structural transformation. Consequently, without a scaled, labor-intensive, and labor-augmenting manufacturing sector boom or the growth of modern services outside metropolitan cities, the wage growth will only widen. Therefore, India's incomplete structural transformation directly affects wage gaps and inequality. Moreover, high levels of informality in rudimentary service sectors suppresses productivity, training, credit access, and tax capacity, thereby making B2B and retail demand volatile.

The gender gaps in India have been significantly widened by low and uneven female-labor force participation rates. Data from ILO suggests that middle-income countries, such as India, have the highest gender gaps in the world, whereas these gaps (both in terms of employment shares as well as earnings) are much lower in low-income countries and high-income countries. This is potentially owed to severe institutional norms and cultural constraints, but perhaps more relevant are unequal opportunities. For instance, in India, gender-based stereotypes for jobs have been a historical concern. A large policy shift to get more women to STEM (Science, Technology, Engineering, and Mathematics) professions has been noticed.

Gender gaps, in general, reduce household earnings and shrink consumer markets. Additionally, it also narrows your recruitable talent pool. The gender gaps are not just limited to only access or capabilities in emerging settings but also at the highest levels of business, including top echelons of management. There are very few women members on boards of companies, and even fewer in top level managerial positions such as CEOs. Added to this gender inequality, there is regional heterogeneity in India. For instance, state capacity, infrastructure, and human development vary sharply across states and districts, and therefore logistics and compliance costs show large degrees of heterogeneity. Health shocks, climate events, and job loss translate into consumption volatility, which is a problem for consumer durables, housing, and credit portfolios. This further accentuates the business risks, and therefore the fundamental problem for businesses resulting from these inequalities is an appetite for risk.

9-2 c Business Strategies and Policies for Inclusivity

In this section, let us think about what firms can do, what policies can do, and consequently what firms in turn can expect for promoting inclusivity and embedding it in the business environment of the country. Inclusive growth strategies at the firm level cannot be restricted to just corporate social responsibility (CSR) mandates but need to be holistically adopted by managers has a viable market strategy. Strategies

Table 1

Firm-Level Inclusivity Strategies	Government Initiatives for Inclusivity Policy
Hire and Train at Scale • Focus on apprenticeship and local skilling partnerships with a view to mitigating unequal opportunities • Track and monitor the share of women and underrepresented communities in hiring/promotion and the workforce and tie manager incentives to boost inclusivity.	**Build Capabilities** • Holistic approach for overall human capital development is already a strategy, but increasing focus on inequality reduction has been seen. For example, girls-only schools such as Kasturba Gandhi Balika Vidyalaya (KGBV) or Eklavya Model Schools for SC/ST girls, etc. • Cash transfers and conditional transfers that promote education and labor force participation of women as well as marginalized sectors.
Build Inclusive Supply Chains • Facilitate women-owned and social-enterprise suppliers. To ensure quality is not compromised, enforce targets and mentoring requirements. • Simplify contracts and adopt dynamic discounting as well as faster pay-out cycles so that smaller and disadvantaged groups do not get screened out due to access barriers.	**Social Safety Nets** • These act as shock absorbers and improve risk tolerance levels. Programs such as Viksit Bharat-Guarantee for Rozgar and Ajeevika Mission (Gramin), food security, or one-nation one-ration card, etc. are in place to address issues of unequal access to resources • Health and financial security through central and state government schemes for health insurance, crop insurance, as well as access to credit and financial inclusion.
De-Risking and Cost-Cutting • To reduce shocks that kill demand, partner with microinsurance and resilient operations, much of which are led by smaller entrepreneurs, including women and those from marginalized sections. • Report supplier payment days, training hours, affordability metrices as well as offer service bundles and remote diagnostics to overall cut down on firm costs while also making it feasible for smaller vendors to be able to bid for projects. This will eventually reduce inequality while also make the firm efficient.	**Affirmative Action** • Government has attempted to improve women's economic participation through providing better access to childcare, maternity benefits, safe transportation programs, etc., but reservation quotas in education and jobs or even political representation do not exist. These may come into being at some point and businesses need to tailor their expectations accordingly. • Recent policy such as menstrual leave has been proposed. It is important that firms do not substitute away from female workers, but commensurate benefits for firms are also instituted so that firms do not view female workers as costlier employees.

from the policy-side largely entail the role of the government as an enabler of inclusivity and to create the right incentives for businesses to operate in an inclusive environment. The Table 1 below highlights a snapshot of these potential strategies.

Managerial Insight

The strategies of the firm for inclusivity mostly operate through built-in DEI (Diversity, Equity, Inclusion) guardrails and DEI (Diversity, Equity, Inclusion) mandates for most global firms and many Indian firms as well. While the benefits for firms and therefore managers, unless explicitly incentivized, are not obvious, there does exist a logic. Most managers care about lower hiring costs and downtime. A bigger and steadier talent pipeline, facilitated by inclusivity policies, can significantly impact this. Moreover, there can be lower attrition and better-quality delivery, which impact overall firm productivity and efficiency.

affirmative action refers to explicit policies such as quotas and mandated reservations that expand access to education, jobs, and opportunities for historically disadvantaged and underrepresented groups.

9-3 Trade and Finances

In this final section, we will discuss the role of trade and finance in defining the business and economic environment of a country. Trade expands a firm's market beyond domestic demand and exposes it to new cost, quality, and technology frontiers. Finance is the foundation that makes trade possible. Financial sector funds inventory in motion, ensures payment, hedges currency swings, and arbitrages tax or duty regimes and thereby allows the seamless integration of the Indian economy with that of the external world. This section links balance-of-payments logic (BoP) with plant-level decisions on pricing, sourcing, credit terms, and risk management in India.

9-3 a Balance of Payments

The Balance of payments (BoP) records all transactions between Indian residents and the rest of the world. Two main components of the BoP are:

1. **Current Account:** This is the value of the trade in goods and services, measuring both the value of imports as well as exports.
2. **Capital Account:** The capital account, also known as capital and financial account, records the FDI, portfolio flows, bank capital, and generally the flow of investments into the economy.

As managers, it is important to be aware of basic BoP concepts and how to calculate these. This is because, as custodians of businesses in the country, knowledge of these metrics and an understanding of how they move can help predict the health of the economy. This is critical because firms can then hedge against potential risks and external shocks and most importantly also understand how the policy response from the government may affect their businesses in the subsequent days. Most of these analyses can be performed by simply collecting readily available data and making simple calculations. Let us discuss some of these very basic metrics below.

1. **Basic Balance:** The basic balance of the economy is the sum of **current account deficit** and the Foreign Direct Investment (FDI) inflows. Current Account Deficit happens when the country's payments to the rest of the world for goods, services and income transfers exceed their receipts over a period. Ideally, this should be financed by FDI and other stable financial inflows. So, a negative basic balance indicates that current account defi-

current account deficit refers to excess payments over receipts for goods, services, and transfers—usually when exports are lower than imports.

cit is financed by borrowing or other unsustainable financial sources and therefore not good for the economy's health. A positive basic balance indicates a healthy external sector in the economy.

2. **Import Cover:** This is a measure of the number of months of imports that can be covered with foreign exchange reserves available with the RBI, and this should ideally be about 6–10 months for a fully open economy. This is alternately also known as current account risk. A low import cover usually indicates thin buffers against external shocks and indicates a weaker currency defense. This can also affect firm-level confidence among businesses because the currency and reserve pressure may be amplified if firms or banks begin to hoard foreign exchange.
3. **Capital Flight Risk:** The risk of sudden, large-scale outflow of domestic capital triggered by loss of confidence in the economy's policies, politics, banking system, or exchange rate is known as capital flight risk. This leads to weakening of the currency and can destabilize the economy. Usually, a good measure for capital flight risk is the ratio of foreign exchange reserves to foreign portfolio holdings. A minimum ratio of about 1/3 indicates good health for the economy, whereas a too low number can indicate that the country is susceptible to even modest outflows, and that can lead to macroeconomic volatility.

9-3 b Currency Valuation

When managers say a currency is "overvalued" or "undervalued," they're asking whether today's exchange rate deviates from an economically justified fundamental value. This fundamental value is essentially the level of currency implied by prices, productivity, and external balance conditions. The key question that managers are interested in answering in the wake of a currency crisis or unprecedented depreciation of the Indian rupee is the following: Will the rupee depreciate further or appreciate soon?

Box 9.2 Exchange Rates and Currency Valuations

Exchange rate is the price of one currency in terms of another. Quoted the usual Indian way from the perspective of Indian businesses, it will be INR per USD. Essentially, the exchange rate tells you how many rupees one US dollar costs.

- Rupee appreciation (against the $) means the rupee **buys more dollars**. So, numerically, the ₹/$ rate **falls**. Example: from **₹83/$** → **₹80/$** is an appreciation of the rupee from roughly (83–80)/83 ≈ 3.6 percent
- Rupee depreciation means the rupee **buys fewer dollars**. So, numerically the **₹/$** rate rises. Example. from **₹83/$** → **₹86/$** is a depreciation of about (86–83)/83≈3.6 percent.

To answer this question, managers usually will need to have an understanding of the principal fundamental value of the rupee. The theoretical prediction is that if the rupee overshoots its value, then it will subsequently be appreciated. On the other hand, if the rupee undershoots its value, then it will depreciate further or remain constant.

Managerial Insight: Suppose the fundamental value of the rupee is ₹84 per USD. The manager observes that the exchange rate reported on a given day is ₹87 per USD. The manager immediately notices that the rupee has overshot its predicted value and therefore can reasonably conclude that it will eventually appreciate soon and come down closer to the value of 84 per USD.

Dornbusch Overshooting Model and Fundamental Value

Economist Rudiger Dornbusch in 1976 proposed a sticky-price model, which suggests that the overshooting of the exchange rate happens due to stickiness of commodity prices but volatile currency exchange rates. Dornbusch notes a long-run fundamental value where the exchange rate settles with fully flexible prices but because good prices are sticky and take time to adjust, whereas financial markets can adjust faster in response to a monetary shock, there exist short-run dynamics leading to overshooting of the exchange rate. A good marker for the fundamental value or rather fundamental anchor is the **purchasing power parity** (PPP) exchange rate of the economy's currency. PPP gives baseline fair value for the exchange rate as the ratio of price levels and is often used to gauge trend misalignment.

purchasing power parity
is the idea that, in the long run, exchange rates adjust so that a given basket of goods costs the same across countries.

Quick**Quiz**

1. If Basic Balance is negative, which of the following is true?
   a. The country is financing its current account deficit only through FDI.
   b. The country has a current account surplus.
   c. The country finances some of its current account deficit through non-FDI inflows.
   d. All of the above
2. Focusing on inclusive growth shifts the goalposts of policymaking by:
   a. Switching to different forms of averages
   b. Switching from averages to percentiles
   c. Building sustainable supply chains
   d. None of the above
3. If the fundamental value of India's currency is ₹81 per USD, and the manger observes that the current value of the currency is ₹79 per USD, she will:
   a. Expect the currency to appreciate
   b. Expect the currency to depreciate
   c. Expect the fundamental value to fall
   d. Expect the fundamental value to rise

Answers are at the end of the chapter.

9-3 c Calculating the PPP Exchange Rate and Fundamental Value

It is possible to calculate the PPP exchange rates to get a reasonable approximation of the fundamental value of the exchange rate using the simple rule below:

$$\text{PPP Exchange Rate in Time } 't' = \text{Exchange Rate in 'base year'} \times \frac{\dfrac{(\text{CPI of India in } 't')}{(\text{CPI of India in 'base year'})}}{\dfrac{(\text{CPI of USA in } 't')}{(\text{CPI of USA in 'base year'})}}$$

Where the CPI indicates the Consumer Price Index of the relevant country. The base year can be a benchmark that allows the comparison of how price of the consumer basket has moved. The above rule tells us that the PPP fundamental anchor can be predicted by the manager if the data on exchange rates for a base year is available and the data on CPIs for the two countries in the current and the base year is known. Then, if the current rate overshoots this PPP exchange rate, the firm can predict that the currency may soon appreciate.

Example: Suppose the exchange rate in India in 2025 is ₹95/USD and CPI in India is 200 and that in USA is 150. Consider a base year of 2014 where the exchange rate was ₹63/USD, and the India CPI was 120 and the US CPI was 130. Let us predict what the PPP exchange rate would be in 2025 and whether the rate of 95 ₹/USD has overshot or undershot this predicted fundamental anchor value. Using the rule above:

$$\text{PPP Exchange Rate in Time } t' = 63 \times \frac{\frac{(200)}{(120)}}{\frac{(150)}{(130)}}$$

Therefore, the predicted PPP exchange rate is approximately ₹91/USD. So, the manager can predict that the current exchange rate of ₹95/USD has overshot the predicted value and therefore expect the currency to appreciate.

9-4 Conclusion

Recognizing the challenges and pitfalls of the economy along with the policy landscape are critical for understanding the realities of the business environment in which Indian firms operate. Indian economic development was founded on the basic premise of the twin policy objectives, viz, promote savings to increase investments and achieve higher efficiency through technological progress. This was based on Harrod–Domar Model of economic growth.

Following independence, the story of structural transformation of India has been that of a missing middle stage. Usually, most economies move from agriculture to industry and then to services, but India has seen a rapid growth in services, as agricultural sector shrunk, before recent policy focus has shifted towards industry. Businesses will therefore need to take into account that a lot of India's growth strategy in the coming decades would be focused on industrial sector incentives and industrial growth with relatively lesser focus on services.

The other aspect of focus in the coming years will be that on diversity and inclusivity in an attempt to reduce inequality and disparities in the economy. Firms will also need to embrace these changing priorities. Finally, the chapter touched upon basic metrics of trade and finance to enable managers to assess the health of the economy and forecast changes in exchange rate and the likelihood of ensuing currency crises.

Chapter in a Nutshell

- India's growth strategy was initially based on Harrod–Domar model of economic growth. Therefore, majority of the policies either focused on improving savings rate or encouraging technological progress, as Harrod–Domar predict that these are the fundamental ways to stimulate growth.
- India has seen rapid growth in services sector while the agricultural sector has declined. However, unlike most conventional economies, the industrial sector growth has been largely stagnant until recent policy focus shifts.
- Reducing inequality and promoting inclusivity remains a top priority for the policymakers in the country, and businesses also have to adapt to this dynamic business environment and institutional obligations, even if specific mandates are not present.
- Knowing the primary measures of external economic health is critical for managers in gauging the economic environment. The idea of a fundamental PPP exchange anchor of the currency and being able to calculate it can allow managers to predict appreciation or depreciation of currency.

Key Concepts

G-20 group, p. 181
harrod–domar model, p. 182
structural transformation, p. 183
affirmative action, p. 188
current account deficit, p. 188
purchasing power parity, p. 190

Questions for Review

1. Describe the basic functioning of the Harrod–Domar Model of growth. What are the two primary parameters that policymakers can target to achieve economic growth?
2. What is structural transformation, and describe how India's dynamic sectoral composition of GDP exhibits incomplete structural transformation?
3. Why should managers care about inclusive growth? What are the potential strategies they may adopt?
4. Define Basic Balance, Capital Flight Risk, and Import cover. How are these indicators of the economy's health?
5. Discuss the model of PP exchange rate of Dornbusch. How does it help managers to predict ensuing currency fluctuations?

Problems and Applications

1. Think about the discussion on structural change in the Indian and the global economy. Which of the following statements would most accurately summarize the crux of structural change in India?
   a. Unlike rest of the world and contrary to historical patterns, services sector has by-passed the industrial sector growth in India in substituting away from the dominance of the agricultural sector.
   b. Industrial and manufacturing sector growth has been much higher than services sector over the last few decades, leading to a dominant manufacturing sector, unlike the rest of the world.
   c. Agrarian growth has dominated growth in industrial or services sector in the Indian economy, unlike the rest of the world's emerging markets.
   d. Just like the other great growth stories of the world, India's manufacturing sector has overtaken the agricultural sector at the expense of services sector and our growth over decades has mostly been led by manufacturing.
2. Consider two countries in the world: Syldavia and Borduria. The currency of Syldavia is Syldavian Dollars (SD) and that of Borduria is the Bordurian Pound (BP).
   a. Suppose we are interested in the exchange rate of SD per BP. How do we express it?
   b. If Syldavia makes FDI worth 25 million SD into Borduria and Borduria has a basic balance of –50,000 (in terms of SD). How will you calculate the current account deficit/surplus of Borduria?
   c. Suppose the fundamental rate of the Bordurian Pound is 35 BP per SD and the current exchange rate is 40. What will Bordurian firms predict about the exchange rate?
3. Inclusivity gaps in India matter for business and economic environment.
   a. Mention what these gaps are, and why these gaps matter.
   b. What are firm level strategies to mitigate these gaps?
   c. What are government or state policies that can mitigate these gaps?
   d. Are the policies likely to differ based on the kind of gap, for example, do we expect gender and caste gaps to attract different policy responses?
4. India's structural transformation has seen a dramatic shift from agricultural sector to services sector.
   a. Discuss why India is an outlier compared to other economies.
   b. What are the direct consequences of such structural transformation in terms of growth and employment?
   c. What policies should businesses in India expect the government to adopt over the next decade in view of the state of India's current sectoral composition to GDP?
5. Consider the two countries as in Question 2 above: Syldavia and Borduria. Suppose the exchange rate is denoted as BP/SD. Consider that this rate was 42 in 2021, 44 in 2022, 49 in 2023, and 47 in 2024.

a. If the CPI in Borduria was 135 in 2021 and 210 in 2024 and that in Syldavia it was 120 and 130 respectively, calculate what the PPP exchange rate would be in 2024 using 2021 as a base year.
b. Consider that the CPI in 2022 was 140 and 115 in Borduria and Syldavia. How will your answer to (a) change if you used 2022 as the base year.
c. The corresponding CPIs in Borduria and Syldavia were 165 and 125, respectively, in 2023. Suppose the exchange rate in 2023 at Christmas appeared to be 55. How would Bordurian businesses predict the exchange rate to move? Use different base years to see how your response changes.

Quick**Quiz Answers**

1. **d** 2. **a** 3. **c** 4. **c** 5. **b** 6. **b**

externality
the uncompensated impact of a person's actions on the well-being of a bystander

The market failures examined here fall under a general category called **externalities**. An **externality** arises when someone engages in an action that influences a bystander's well-being and when no compensation is paid for that effect. If the impact on the bystander is adverse, it is a **negative externality**. If it is beneficial, it is a **positive externality**.

When externalities are present, society's interest in a market outcome extends beyond the well-being of buyers and sellers in the market and includes the well-being of bystanders. Because buyers and sellers do not take into account the external effects of their actions when deciding how much to demand or supply, the market equilibrium is not efficient. In other words, societal well-being is not maximized, and government policies can potentially correct the market failure.

The release of dioxin into the environment, for instance, is a negative externality—and a grave one. Without government intervention, the producers of paper may not consider the full cost of the pollution they create, and the consumers of paper may not consider the full cost of the pollution they contribute to through their purchases. The market will allow too much dioxin to be emitted unless the government intervenes with well-designed policies. And indeed, the Environmental Protection Agency monitors dioxin levels and regulates its release.

Externalities come in many forms, as do the policy responses that try to deal with them. Here are some examples:

- The exhaust from automobiles is a negative externality because it creates smog that other people breathe and contributes to global climate change. Because drivers may ignore this externality when deciding what cars to buy and how much to use them, they tend to pollute too much. The federal government addresses this problem by setting emission standards for cars. It also taxes gasoline, subsidizes mass transit, and builds bicycle paths to reduce the amount that people drive.
- Restored historic buildings confer a positive externality because people who see them enjoy their beauty and the sense of history they convey. But building owners, who do not capture the benefits experienced by passers-by, tend to tear down older buildings too quickly. Recognizing this problem, many local governments regulate the destruction of historic buildings and provide tax breaks to owners who restore them.
- Barking dogs create a negative externality when neighbors are annoyed by their noise. Dog owners don't bear the full burden of the noise and tend to take too few precautions to prevent it. Local governments address this problem by making it illegal to disturb the peace.
- Research into new technologies provides a positive externality because it creates knowledge that others can use. If individual inventors, firms, and universities cannot capture the benefits of their inventions, they may devote too few resources to research. The federal government addresses this problem partially through the patent system, which gives inventors exclusive use of their inventions for a limited period.
- During the peak of a pandemic, busy restaurants create a negative externality by providing an opportunity for the disease to spread. Restaurant owners may ignore the health impact of their businesses on society. The government can address the problem by requiring restaurants to temporarily switch to take-out only (and perhaps compensating the restaurant owners and workers).

In all these cases, people may fail to take into account the external effects of their behavior. The government responds by trying to influence their behavior to protect the interests of bystanders.

10-1 Externalities and Market Inefficiency

In this section, we use the tools of welfare economics to examine how externalities affect economic well-being. The analysis shows why externalities cause markets to allocate resources inefficiently. Later sections examine the ways private individuals and public policymakers can remedy this type of market failure.

10-1a Welfare Economics: A Recap

Let's first review the lessons of welfare economics from Chapter 7, using the market for steel as an example. Figure 1 shows the supply and demand curves in the steel market.

Chapter 7 showed that the supply and demand curves contain important information about costs and benefits. The demand curve reflects the value of steel to consumers, as measured by what they are willing to pay. At any quantity, the height of the demand curve shows the willingness to pay of the marginal buyer. In other words, it shows the value to the consumer of the last unit of steel bought. Similarly, the supply curve reflects the costs of producing steel. At any quantity, the height of the supply curve shows the cost to the marginal seller. In other words, it shows the cost to the producer of the last unit of steel sold.

The price adjusts to balance the supply and demand for steel. The quantity produced and consumed in the market equilibrium, shown as Q_{MARKET} in Figure 1, is efficient in the sense that it maximizes the sum of producer and consumer surplus. That is, the market allocates resources in a way that maximizes the total value to the consumers who buy and use steel minus the total costs to the producers who make and sell steel.

Figure 1

The Market for Steel

The demand curve reflects the value to buyers, and the supply curve reflects the costs of sellers. The equilibrium quantity, Q_{MARKET}, maximizes the total value to buyers minus the total costs of sellers. In the absence of externalities, the market equilibrium is efficient.

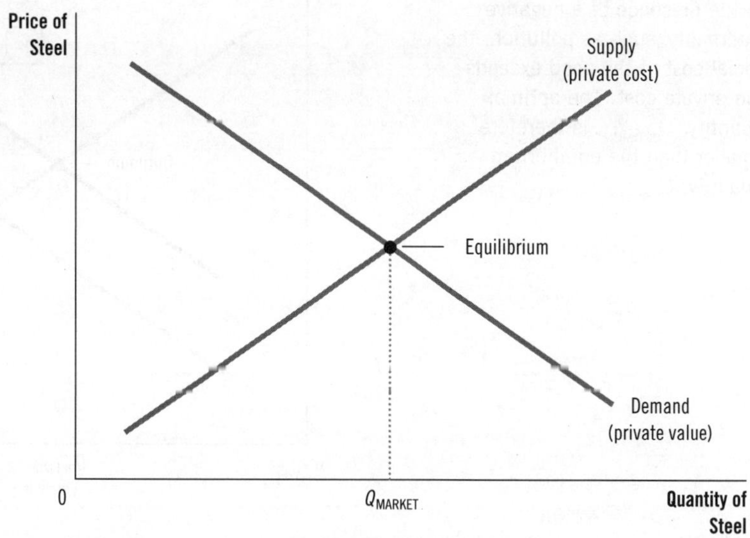

J.B. HANDELSMAN/THE NEW YORKER COLLECTION/THE CARTOON BANK

"All I can say is that if being a leading manufacturer means being a leading polluter, so be it."

10-1b Negative Externalities

Now suppose that steel factories emit pollution: For each unit of steel produced, a certain amount of smoke enters the atmosphere. Because these emissions create health and climate risks, they are a negative externality. How does this externality affect market efficiency?

Because of this externality, the cost to society of producing steel exceeds the cost to steel producers. For each unit of steel produced, the **social cost** equals the direct, private costs of the steel producers plus the costs to bystanders harmed by the emissions. Figure 2 shows the social cost of producing steel. The social-cost curve is above the supply curve because it takes into account the external costs imposed on society by steel production. The difference between these two curves reflects the cost of the pollution emitted.

What quantity of steel should be produced? Consider what a committee of benevolent social planners would do. The planners want to maximize the total surplus derived from the market—the value to consumers of steel minus the cost of producing it. They take a broad perspective, however, and understand that the cost of producing steel includes the external costs of pollution.

The planners would choose the production level at which the demand curve crosses the social-cost curve. This intersection determines the optimal amount of steel from the standpoint of society as a whole. Below this level of production, the value of the steel to consumers (measured by the height of the demand curve) exceeds the social cost of producing it (measured by the height of the social-cost curve). Above this level, the social cost of producing additional steel exceeds the value to consumers.

Note that the equilibrium quantity of steel, Q_{MARKET}, is larger than the socially optimal quantity, $Q_{OPTIMUM}$. This inefficiency occurs because the market equilibrium reflects only the private costs of production. In the market equilibrium, the

Figure 2

Pollution and the Social Optimum

In the presence of a negative externality, such as pollution, the social cost of the good exceeds the private cost. The optimal quantity, $Q_{OPTIMUM}$, is therefore smaller than the equilibrium quantity, Q_{MARKET}.

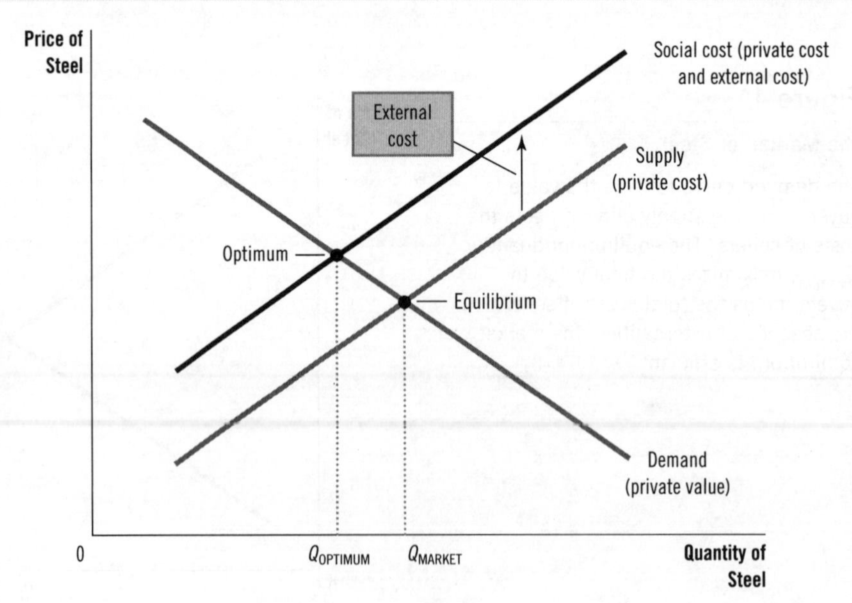

marginal consumer values steel at less than the social cost of producing it. That is, at Q_{MARKET}, the demand curve lies below the social-cost curve. Reducing steel production and consumption below the market equilibrium level raises total economic well-being.

How can the social planners achieve the optimal outcome? One way is to tax steel producers for each ton of steel sold. The tax would shift the supply curve upward by the size of the tax. If the tax accurately reflected the external cost of pollutants released into the atmosphere, the new supply curve would coincide with the social-cost curve. In the new market equilibrium, steel producers would produce the socially optimal quantity of steel.

Economists say that such a tax **internalizes the externality** because it gives buyers and sellers in the market an incentive to consider the external effects of their actions. Steel producers would, in essence, take the costs of pollution into account when deciding how much steel to supply because the tax would make them pay for these external costs. And, because the market price would reflect the tax on producers, consumers of steel would have an incentive to buy less. The policy is based on the idea that people respond to incentives. Later in this chapter, we discuss more fully how policymakers can deal with externalities.

internalizing the externality
altering incentives so that people take into account the external effects of their actions

10-1c Positive Externalities

Although some activities impose costs on third parties, others yield benefits. Consider education. To a large extent, the benefit of education is private. Put in strictly monetary terms, the consumers of education become more productive workers and reap much of the benefit in the form of higher wages. In addition, education helps people become more well-rounded by broadening their horizons. Beyond these private benefits, however, education also yields positive externalities. One is that a more educated population leads to more informed voters, which means better government for everyone. Another is that a more educated population tends to result in lower crime rates. A third is that a more educated population may encourage the development and dissemination of technological advances, leading to higher productivity and wages for everyone. Given these positive externalities, people may prefer to have neighbors who are well educated.

The analysis of positive externalities is similar to the analysis of negative externalities. As Figure 3 shows, the demand curve does not reflect the value to society of the good. Because the social value exceeds the private value, the social-value curve lies above the demand curve. The optimal quantity is found where the social-value curve and the supply curve intersect. The socially optimal quantity exceeds the quantity that the private market would reach on its own. In other words, without outside intervention, the market would yield too little education.

Once again, the government can correct the market failure by inducing market participants to internalize the externality. The appropriate policy to deal with positive externalities is the opposite of the policy for negative externalities. To move the market equilibrium closer to the social optimum, a positive externality requires a subsidy. In fact, that is the policy the government follows: Education is heavily subsidized through public schools, government scholarships, and tax breaks.

To summarize: **Negative externalities lead markets to produce a larger quantity than is socially desirable. Positive externalities lead markets to produce a smaller quantity than is socially desirable. To remedy the problem, the government can internalize the externality by taxing goods with negative externalities and subsidizing goods with positive externalities.**

Figure 3

Education and the Social Optimum

In the presence of a positive externality, the social value of the good exceeds the private value. The optimal quantity, $Q_{OPTIMUM}$, is therefore larger than the equilibrium quantity, Q_{MARKET}.

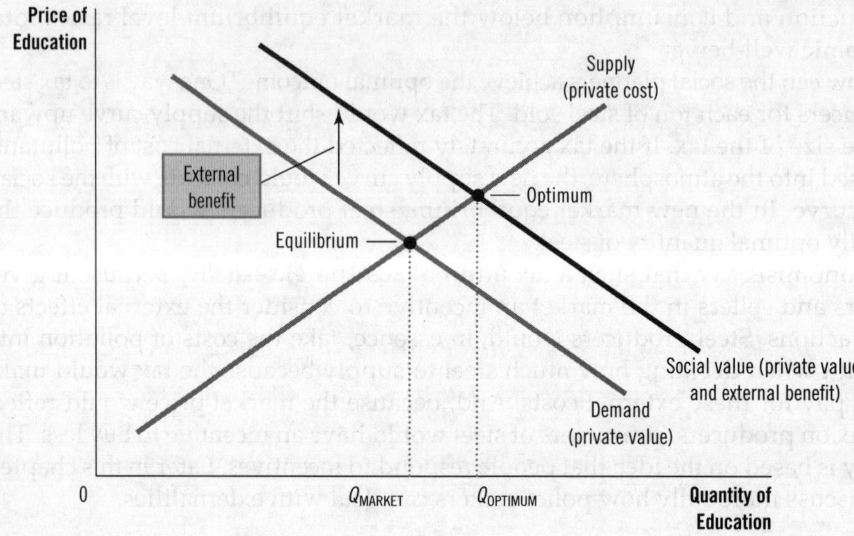

Quick**Quiz**

1. Which of the following is an example of a positive externality?
   a. Myra mows Dev's lawn and is paid ₹100 for the service.
   b. Myra's lawnmower emits smoke that Dev's neighbor Xavier has to breathe.
   c. Dev's newly cut lawn makes his neighborhood more attractive.
   d. Dev's neighbor Xavier offers to pay him if he keeps his lawn well groomed.

2. If the production of a good yields a negative externality, the social-cost curve lies ______ the supply curve, and the socially optimal quantity is ______ than the equilibrium quantity.
   a. above; greater
   b. above; less
   c. below; greater
   d. below; less

Answers are at the end of the chapter.

10-2 Public Policies toward Externalities

We have seen why externalities lead markets to allocate resources inefficiently but have mentioned only briefly how this inefficiency can be remedied. In practice, both public policymakers and private individuals respond to externalities in various ways. All of the remedies share the goal of moving the allocation of resources closer to the social optimum.

This section considers governmental solutions. As a general matter, the government can respond to externalities in one of two ways. **Command-and-control policies** regulate behavior directly. **Market-based policies** provide incentives so that private decision makers choose to solve the problem on their own. It will come as no surprise that economists tend to prefer market-based policies, though command-and-control policies are sometimes needed.

10-2a Command-and-Control Policies: Regulation

The government can remedy an externality by either requiring or forbidding certain behaviors. For example, it is a crime to dump poisonous chemicals into the water supply. In this case, the external costs to society far exceed the benefits to the polluter. The government therefore institutes a command-and-control policy that prohibits this act altogether.

In many cases of pollution, however, the situation is not this simple. Despite the stated goals of some environmentalists, it would be impossible to prohibit all polluting activity. For example, virtually all forms of transportation—even the horse—produce some undesirable by-products. But it would not make sense for the government to ban all transportation. Instead of trying to eradicate pollution entirely, society must weigh the costs and benefits to decide the kinds and quantities of pollution it will allow.

Environmental regulations can take many forms. These may dictate the maximum level of pollution that a factory may emit. Sometimes, it requires firms to adopt a particular technology to reduce emissions. In all cases, to design good rules, the government regulators need to know the details about specific industries and about the alternative technologies that they could adopt. This information may be difficult for government regulators to obtain. Profit-seeking industries have little reason (other than from a general sense of social responsibility) to share what they know. Rather, they often have an incentive to conceal the adverse health effects from their production and exaggerate the cost of moving toward cleaner technologies.

Ask the Experts — **Covid Vaccines**

"Given the positive externalities from vaccination, an effective Covid-19 vaccine should be mandatory for every US resident (except those with health exceptions, such as infants and people with compromised immunity) with the cost covered by the federal government."

What do economists say?

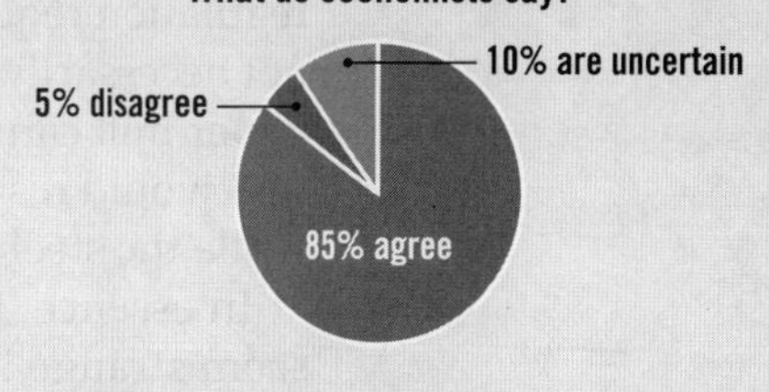

Source: IGM Economic Experts Panel, June 23, 2020.

10-2b Market-Based Policy 1: Corrective Taxes and Subsidies

Instead of regulating behavior in response to an externality, the government can use market-based policies to align private incentives with social efficiency. For instance, as we saw earlier, the government can internalize the externality by taxing activities with negative externalities and subsidizing activities with positive externalities. Taxes enacted to deal with the effects of negative externalities are called **corrective taxes**. They are also called **Pigovian taxes** after the economist Arthur Pigou (1877–1959), an early advocate of their use. An ideal corrective tax would equal the external cost from an activity with negative externalities, and an ideal corrective subsidy would equal the external benefit from an activity with positive externalities.

corrective tax
a tax designed to induce private decision makers to take into account the social costs that arise from a negative externality

Economists usually prefer corrective taxes to regulations as a way to deal with pollution because they can reduce pollution at a lower cost to society. To see why, consider an example.

Suppose that two factories—a paper mill and a steel mill—are each dumping 500 tons of "glop" into a river every year. Assume, further, that the glop from the two imaginary factories is identical, and that glop, while benign in small amounts, is dangerous in large quantities.

The regulator wants to reduce the amount emitted. It considers two solutions:

- Regulation: The regulator could tell each factory to reduce its pollution to 300 tons of glop per year.

CHRONICLE/ALAMY STOCK PHOTO

Arthur Pigou

- Corrective tax: The regulator could levy a tax on each factory of ₹50,000 for each ton of glop it emits.

The regulation would dictate a level of pollution, while the tax would give factory owners an incentive to reduce pollution. Which solution do you think is better?

In a case like this, most economists prefer the tax. To explain this preference, they would first point out that a tax is just as effective as regulation in reducing the overall level of many forms of pollution. The Regulator can achieve whatever level of pollution it wants by setting the tax at the appropriate level. The higher the tax, the larger the reduction in pollution. If the tax is high enough, the factories will close altogether, reducing pollution to zero.

Although regulation and corrective taxes are both capable of reducing many types of pollution, the tax accomplishes this goal more efficiently. That's because the regulation requires each factory to reduce pollution by the same amount, which is not necessarily the least expensive way to clean up the water. It is possible that the paper mill can reduce pollution at a lower cost than the steel mill. If so, the paper mill would respond to the tax by reducing pollution substantially to avoid the tax, while the steel mill would reduce pollution less and pay the tax.

In essence, the corrective tax places a price on the right to pollute. This may seem strange if you're not accustomed to the way economists think. But just as markets allocate goods to those buyers who value them most, a corrective tax allocates pollution rights to those factories that face the highest cost of reducing it. With this flexible tool, the Regulator can achieve any level of emission at the lowest total cost.

Economists also argue that corrective taxes are often better for the environment. Under the command-and-control policy of regulation, the factories have no reason to reduce emissions further once they reach the target of 300 tons of glop. By contrast, the tax gives the factories an incentive to develop cleaner technologies because a cleaner technology would reduce the amount of taxes they have to pay.

Case Study

Why Is Gasoline Taxed So Heavily?

In many nations, gasoline is among the most heavily taxed goods. The gas tax can be viewed as a corrective tax aimed at addressing three negative externalities associated with driving:

- **Pollution:** Car emissions cause smog, which increases the risk of heart and lung disease. In addition, the burning of fossil fuels such as gasoline is a primary cause of global climate change. The gas tax reduces these adverse effects by discouraging gas consumption.
- **Congestion:** Bumper-to-bumper traffic could be alleviated if there were fewer cars on the road. A gas tax keeps congestion down by encouraging people to take public transportation, ride bikes, carpool more often, and live closer to work.
- **Accidents:** When people buy large cars or sport utility vehicles, they may make themselves safer, but they also put their neighbors at risk. A person driving a smaller car is much more likely to be hurt if hit by a large car or a sport utility vehicle than if hit by another smaller car. The gas tax is an indirect way of making people pay when their large, gas-guzzling vehicles put others at risk. It induces them to take this risk into account when choosing what vehicle to buy.

Rather than causing deadweight losses like most taxes, the gas tax makes the economy work better. It means a clearer environment, less traffic congestion, and safer roads.

The tax revenue from a higher gasoline tax could be used to lower taxes that distort incentives and cause deadweight losses, such as income taxes. In addition, the government regulations that require automakers to produce more fuel-efficient cars would be unnecessary, as would government subsidies to electric cars, because car consumers would face the right incentives. A higher gas tax, however, has never been politically popular. ●

Delhi's Odd–Even Policy – Experimenting with Pollution Control

In India, government responses to negative externalities are increasingly supported by legal mandates and public demand. Notable examples include the environmental damage caused by brick kilns in the National Capital Region (NCR), groundwater exploitation by beverage manufacturers, and urban vehicular emissions but perhaps most importantly and most politically sensitive – crop residue burning across Northern India by farmers, especially in Haryana and Punjab.

These externalities have resulted in policy interventions such as mandated caps on emissions, fines, and outright bans on operations under specific conditions (e.g., ban on bursting firecrackers during Diwali).

One case of managerial relevance is the Odd-–Even traffic rule in Delhi, first implemented in 2016 during severe air pollution intensity. This rule mandated that cars with odd number license plates will be allowed on the streets on certain dates whereas those with even number license plates would be allowed on other days.

Although framed as a policy to reduce negative externalities from car missions, it can potentially create behavioral shifts in both consumers and businesses. For firms, especially in sectors like logistics, transport, and mobility services, such policies may require operational adaptations, re-scheduling, and even replanning or reorganizing their fleet size and fleet composition, e.g., increased reliance on electric vehicles or CNG.

10-2c Market-Based Policy 2: Tradable Pollution Permits

Returning to the paper mill and the steel mill, let's suppose that, despite the advice of its economists, the regulator adopts the regulation and requires each factory to reduce its pollution to 300 tons of glop per year. Then one day, after the regulation is in place and both mills have complied, the two firms go to the Regulator with a proposal. The steel mill wants to increase its emission of glop from 300 to 400 tons. The paper mill has agreed to reduce its emission from 300 to 200 tons if the steel mill pays it ₹5 million. The total emission of glop would remain at 600 tons. Should the Regulator allow the two factories to make this deal?

From the standpoint of economic efficiency, the answer is yes. The deal makes the owners of the two factories better off. After all, they are voluntarily agreeing to it. Moreover, the deal does not have any external effects because the total amount of pollution stays the same. Thus, social welfare is enhanced by allowing the paper mill to sell its pollution rights to the steel mill.

The same logic applies to any voluntary transfer of the right to pollute from one firm to another. When the Regulator allows firms to make such deals, in essence, it creates a new scarce resource: pollution permits. A market to trade these permits develops, and that market is governed by the forces of supply and demand. The invisible hand ensures that this new market allocates the right to pollute efficiently. That is, the permits will end up in the hands of those who value them most, as judged by their willingness to pay. A firm's willingness to pay for the right to pollute, in turn, will depend on its cost of reducing pollution: The more costly it is for a firm to cut back on pollution, the more it will be willing to pay for a permit.

An advantage of allowing a market for pollution permits is that the initial allocation of the permits among firms does not matter from the standpoint of economic efficiency. Those firms that can reduce pollution at a low cost will sell whatever permits they get, while firms that can reduce pollution only at a high cost will buy whatever permits they need. If there is a market for the permits, the final allocation will be efficient regardless of the initial allocation.

Pollution permits may seem very different from corrective taxes, but the two policies have much in common. In both cases, firms pay for their pollution. With corrective taxes, polluting firms must pay a tax to the government. With pollution permits, polluting firms must buy the permits. (Even firms that already own permits must pay to pollute, in the sense that they could have sold their permits on the open market, and, by foregoing that revenue, they incur an opportunity cost.) In the language of economics, both corrective taxes and pollution permits internalize the externality of pollution by making it costly for firms to pollute.

The similarity of the two policies can be seen by considering the market for pollution rights. Both panels in Figure 4 show the demand curve for the permission to pollute. This curve shows that the lower the price of polluting, the more firms will pollute. In panel (a), the Regulator uses a corrective tax to set a price for pollution. In this case, the supply curve for pollution rights is perfectly elastic (because firms can pollute as much as they want by paying the tax), and the demand curve determines the quantity of pollution. In panel (b), the Regulator sets a quantity of pollution by issuing permits. In this case, the supply curve for pollution rights is perfectly inelastic (because the quantity of pollution is fixed by the number of permits), and the demand curve determines the price. The Regulator can achieve any point on the demand curve either by setting a price with a corrective tax or by setting a quantity with pollution permits.

Figure 4

The Equivalence of Corrective Taxes and Pollution Permits

In panel (a), the Regulator sets a price on pollution by levying a corrective tax, and the demand curve determines the quantity of pollution. In panel (b), the Regulator limits the quantity of pollution by limiting the number of pollution permits, and the demand curve determines the price of pollution. The price and quantity of pollution are the same in the two cases.

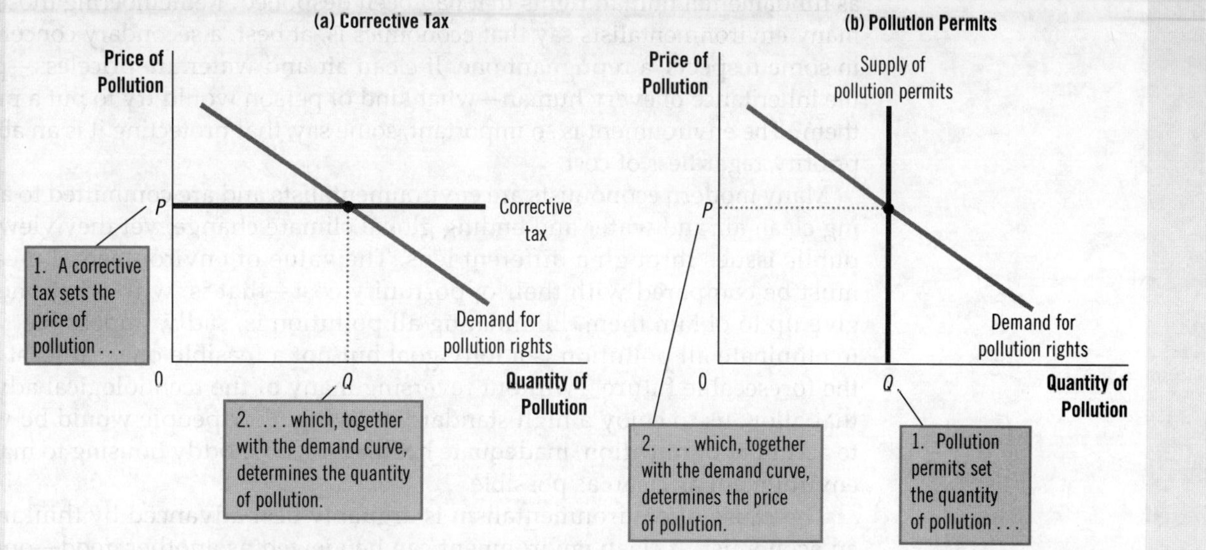

The choice between selling pollution permits and levying a corrective tax starts to matter, however, if the demand curve for pollution rights is uncertain. Suppose the Regulator wants no more than 600 tons of glop dumped into the river, but because the Regulator does not know the demand curve, it is not sure what size tax would hit that target. In this case, it can auction off 600 pollution permits. The auction price would, in effect, yield the corrective tax needed to achieve the Regulator's goal. On the other hand, suppose the Regulator knows the external cost of pollution is ₹50,000 per ton of glop but is uncertain how much glop factories would emit at that price. In this case, the Regulator can reach the efficient outcome by setting a corrective tax of ₹50,000 per ton and letting the market determine the quantity of pollution.

The idea of the government auctioning off the right to pollute may at first sound like a creature of some economist's imagination. And, in fact, that is how the idea began. But increasingly, the Regulator has used this system to control pollution. A notable success story has been the case of sulfur dioxide (SO_2), a leading cause of acid rain. In 1990, amendments to the Clean Air Act required power plants to reduce SO_2 emissions substantially. At the same time, the amendments set up a system that allowed plants to trade their SO_2 allowances. Initially, both industry representatives and environmentalists were skeptical of the proposal, but over time, the system reduced pollution with minimal disruption and at a low cost. Pollution permits, like corrective taxes, are now widely viewed as a cost-effective way to keep the environment clean.

- Jairam could eat more locally produced foods, which need less fuel to transport.
- Jairam could stop eating beef, as its production releases an immense amount of greenhouse gases.

By now, you get the idea. Every day, we all make lifestyle choices that affect how much carbon is emitted. These decisions are personal, but they have a global impact.

The main question for policymakers is how society can ensure that people make the right decisions, which take into account both the personal impact of their actions and the externalities. There are three approaches.

One approach is to appeal to individuals' sense of social responsibility. Some people may, in fact, reduce their carbon footprint to the optimal level out of concern for the planet. But expecting most people to act this way is unrealistic. Life is busy, people have their own priorities, and even knowing the global impact of one's own actions is a daunting task.

The second approach is to use government regulation to change the decisions that people make. An example is Corporate Average Fuel Economy, or CAFE, standards, which regulate car emissions in the United States.

But this regulatory approach is fraught with problems. One is that it creates tension between the products that consumers want to buy and the products that companies are allowed to sell. Robert A. Lutz, a former top auto executive, laments that CAFE standards are "a huge bureaucratic nightmare." He says, "CAFE is like trying to cure obesity by requiring clothing manufacturers to make smaller sizes."

A more important problem with such regulations is that they can influence only a few crucial decisions. The government can regulate the kind of car that Jairam finds at auto dealers, but it can't easily regulate how close Jairam lives to work or whether he carpools with his neighbor. Yet reducing carbon emissions at minimum cost requires a policy that encompasses all possible margins of adjustment.

Fortunately, a policy broader in scope is possible, which brings us to the third approach to dealing with climate externalities: putting a price on carbon emissions. This can be done either by taxing them or by creating a "cap-and-trade" system of tradable pollution permits. If sellers of gasoline, electricity, beef, and so on had to pay a fee for each emission of carbon implicit in their products, that fee would be built into their prices. When making everyday decisions, Jairam and other consumers would look at the prices they face and, in effect, take into account the global impact of their choices. A price on carbon would internalize the externality. It has worked effectively in Europe, though it hasn't caught on in the United States. In India, Bharat Stage (BS) norms regulate how much air pollution output is permissible from internal combustion and spark-ignition engine equipment. For instance, BS-6 for Indian vehicles was considered equivalent to Euro-6 norms of Europe.

Ask the Experts

Carbon Taxes

"The Brookings Institution recently described a U.S. carbon tax of ₹20 per ton, increasing at 4 percent per year, which would raise an estimated ₹150 billion per year in federal revenues over the next decade. Given the negative externalities created by carbon dioxide emissions, a federal carbon tax at this rate would involve fewer harmful net distortions to the U.S. economy than a tax increase that generated the same revenue by raising marginal tax rates on labor income across the board."

What do economists say?

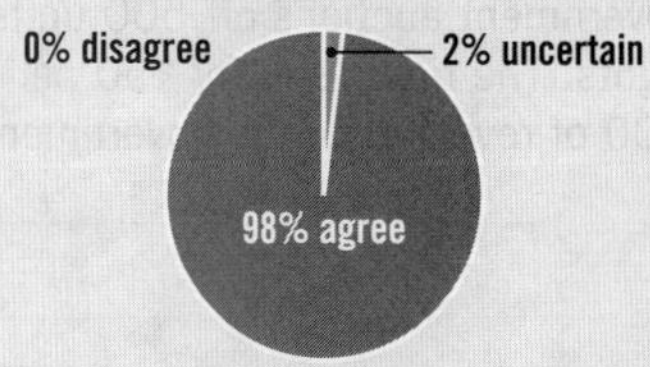

"A tax on the carbon content of fuels would be a less expensive way to reduce carbon dioxide emissions than would a collection of policies such as 'corporate average fuel economy' requirements for automobiles."

What do economists say?

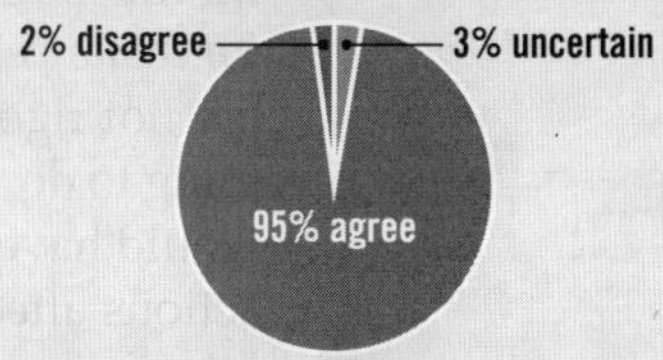

"Carbon taxes are a better way to implement climate policy than cap-and-trade."

What do economists say?

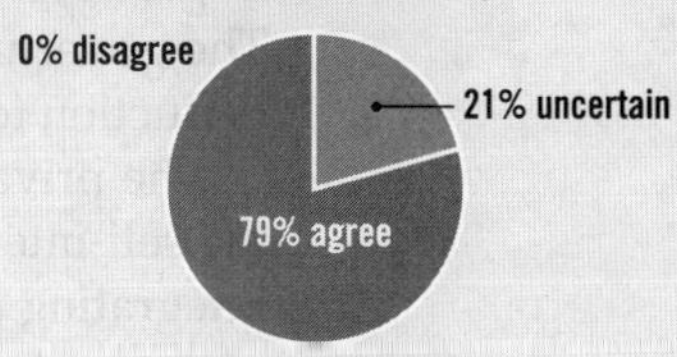

Source: IGM Economic Experts Panel, December 4, 2012, December 20, 2011, and November 13, 2018.

Quick**Quiz**

3. When the government levies a tax equal to the external cost associated with a good's production, it ________ the price paid by consumers and makes the market outcome ________ efficient.
   a. increases; more
   b. increases; less
   c. decreases; more
   d. decreases; less

4. Which of the following statements about corrective taxes is generally NOT true?
   a. They reduce consumer surplus.
   b. They raise government revenue.
   c. They reduce the quantity sold in a market.
   d. They cause deadweight losses.

5. The government auctions off 500 units of pollution rights. The rights sell for ₹50 per unit, raising ₹25,000 of revenue for the government. This policy is equivalent to a corrective tax of _____ per unit of pollution.
   a. ₹10
   b. ₹50
   c. ₹450
   d. ₹500

6. Command-and-control regulation may be better than a corrective tax if
   a. a corrective tax would have differential effects on different industries.
   b. some polluters can reduce emissions more cheaply than others.
   c. the negative externality is so large that the optimal quantity is zero.
   d. knowledge about the cost of pollution abatement is dispersed and hard to obtain.

Answers are at the end of the chapter.

10-3 Private Solutions to Externalities

Externalities tend to make market outcomes inefficient, but government action isn't the only remedy. Sometimes, people can find private solutions.

10-3a The Types of Private Solutions

Moral codes and social sanctions can solve the problem of externalities. Consider, for instance, why most people do not litter. There are laws against littering, but they are not rigorously enforced. Most people don't litter just because it is the wrong thing to do. The Golden Rule taught to many children says, "Do unto others as you would have them do unto you." This moral injunction tells us to consider how our actions affect other people. In the less poetic language of economics, it tells us to internalize externalities.

Another private solution involves charities. For example, the Sierra Club is a non-profit organization funded by private donors who seek to protect the environment. Colleges and universities receive gifts from alumni, corporations, and foundations in part because education has great benefits—positive externalities—for society. The government encourages these private solutions by allowing an income tax deduction for charitable donations.

The private market can often solve the problem of externalities by relying on the self-interest of the relevant parties. Sometimes, the solution takes the form of integrating different types of businesses. For example, consider an apple grower and a beekeeper who are located next to each other. Each business benefits the other, conveying a positive externality: By pollinating the flowers on the trees, the bees help the orchard produce apples, while the bees use the nectar from the apple trees to produce honey. But that doesn't mean that the two take these benefits into account. When the apple grower decides how many trees to plant and the beekeeper determines how many bees to keep, they neglect the positive externality. As a result, the apple grower plants too few trees, and the beekeeper keeps too few bees. These externalities could be internalized if the bee and apple businesses merged: Both activities would then take place within the same firm, which could choose the optimal number of trees and bees. Internalizing externalities is one reason that some firms are involved in multiple types of businesses.

Another private approach is for the apple grower and beekeeper to negotiate a contract, setting the right number of trees and bees and perhaps a payment from one party to the other. The contract can solve the inefficiency that normally arises from these externalities and make both parties better off.

10-3b The Coase Theorem

How effective is the private market in dealing with externalities? A famous result, called the **Coase theorem** after the economist Ronald Coase, suggests that it can be very effective in some circumstances. According to the Coase theorem, if private parties can bargain over the allocation of resources at no cost, then the private market will always solve the problem of externalities and allocate resources efficiently.

Coase theorem
the proposition that if private parties can bargain without cost over the allocation of resources, they can solve the problem of externalities on their own

To see how the Coase theorem works, consider an example. Suppose that Enakshi owns a dog named Toby. Toby barks and disturbs Hitesh, Enakshi's neighbor. Enakshi benefits greatly from Toby's companionship, but the dog confers a negative externality on Hitesh, who would prefer a sound sleep. Should Enakshi find Toby a new home, or should Hitesh suffer restless nights because of Toby's barking?

Consider first what outcome is socially efficient. An economist with society's interest at heart would compare the benefit that Enakshi gets from the dog with the cost that Hitesh bears from the barking. If the benefit exceeds the cost, it is efficient for Enakshi to keep the dog and for Hitesh to live with the barking. Yet if the cost exceeds the benefit, then Enakshi should get rid of the dog.

According to the Coase theorem, the private market will reach the efficient outcome on its own. How? Hitesh can offer to pay Enakshi to move Toby to a new home. Enakshi will accept the deal if the amount of money Hitesh offers is greater than her benefit of keeping the dog.

By bargaining over the price, Enakshi and Hitesh can always reach the efficient outcome. For instance, suppose that Enakshi gets a ₹1,000 benefit from the dog and Hitesh bears a ₹1,500 cost from the barking. In this case, Hitesh can offer Enakshi ₹1,200 to get rid of the dog, and Enakshi will accept. Both parties are better off than they were before, and the efficient outcome is reached.

It is possible, of course, that Hitesh would not be willing to offer any price that Enakshi would accept. For instance, suppose that Enakshi gets a ₹3,000 benefit from the dog and Hitesh bears a ₹1,500 cost from the barking. In this case, Enakshi would turn down any offer below ₹3,000, while Hitesh would not offer any amount above ₹1,500. Enakshi ends up keeping Toby. Given these costs and benefits, this outcome is efficient.

These examples so far assume that Enakshi has the legal right to keep a barking dog. In other words, Enakshi can keep Toby unless Hitesh pays her enough to induce her to give up the dog voluntarily. But how different would the outcome be if Hitesh had the legal right to peace and quiet?

According to the Coase theorem, the initial distribution of rights does not matter for the market's ability to reach the efficient outcome. For instance, suppose that Hitesh can legally compel Enakshi to get rid of the dog. Having this right works to Hitesh's advantage, but it probably won't change the outcome. In this case, Enakshi can offer to pay Hitesh to allow her to keep the dog. If the benefit of the dog to

Enakshi exceeds the cost of the barking to Hitesh, then Enakshi and Hitesh will strike a bargain in which Enakshi gets to keep her dog.

Although Enakshi and Hitesh can reach the efficient outcome regardless of how rights are initially distributed, the distribution of rights is not irrelevant: It determines the distribution of economic well-being. Whether Enakshi has the right to a barking dog or Hitesh the right to peace and quiet determines who pays whom in the final bargain. But in either case, the two parties can bargain with each other and solve the externality problem. Enakshi will end up keeping Toby only if her benefit exceeds Hitesh's cost.

To sum up: **The Coase theorem says that private economic actors can potentially solve the problem of externalities among themselves. Whatever the initial distribution of rights, the interested parties can reach a bargain in which everyone is better off and the outcome is efficient.**

10-3c Why Private Solutions Do Not Always Work

Despite the appealing logic of the Coase theorem, private individuals on their own often fail to resolve the problems caused by externalities. The Coase theorem applies only when the interested parties have no trouble reaching and enforcing an agreement. In the real world, however, bargaining does not always work, even when a mutually beneficial agreement is possible.

transaction costs the costs that parties incur during the process of agreeing to and following through on a bargain

Sometimes, the interested parties fail to solve an externality problem because of **transaction costs**, the costs that parties incur in the process of agreeing to and following through on a bargain. In our example, imagine that Enakshi and Hitesh speak different languages so, to reach an agreement, they need to hire a translator. If the benefit of solving the barking problem is less than the cost of the translator, Enakshi and Hitesh might choose to leave the problem unsolved. In more realistic examples, the transaction costs are the expenses not of translators but of lawyers required to draft and enforce contracts.

At other times, bargaining simply breaks down. The recurrence of wars and labor strikes shows that reaching an agreement can be difficult and that failing to reach one can be costly. The problem is often that each party tries to hold out for a better deal. For example, suppose that Enakshi gets a ₹1,000 benefit from having Toby, while Hitesh bears a ₹1,500 cost from the barking. Although it is efficient for Hitesh to pay Enakshi to find another home for the dog, there are many prices that could lead to this outcome. Enakshi might demand ₹1,400, and Hitesh might offer only ₹1,100. As they haggle over the price, the inefficient outcome with the barking dog persists.

Reaching an efficient bargain is especially difficult when the number of interested parties is large because coordinating everyone is costly. For example, consider a factory that pollutes the water of a nearby lake. The pollution confers a negative externality on the local fishermen. According to the Coase theorem, if the pollution is inefficient, then the factory and the fishermen could reach a bargain in which the fishermen pay the factory not to pollute. If there are many fishermen, however, trying to coordinate them all to bargain with the factory may be almost impossible. Combating global climate change is similar: There are far too many people and firms responsible for greenhouse gas emissions for them to be able to bargain together and come up with a worldwide solution.

When private bargaining does not work, governments can sometimes play a role. A government is an institution designed for collective action. In the example of the lake, the government can act on behalf of the fishermen, even when it is impractical for the fishermen to act for themselves.

10-4 Public Goods – A Positive Externality

When thinking about the ability of markets to efficiently allocate the economy's resources, it helps to classify goods more systematically. As we will see with some examples, two characteristics are most important:

- **Excludability:** If people can be prevented from using a good, it is excludable. If it is impossible to prevent people from using the good, it is not excludable.
- **Rivalry in consumption:** If one person's use of a unit of a good reduces another person's ability to use it, the good is rival in consumption. If one person's use does not diminish another person's use, the good is not rival in consumption.

excludability
the property of a good whereby a person can be prevented from using it

rivalry in consumption
the property of a good whereby one person's use diminishes other people's use

On a grid, these two characteristics define four categories, shown in Figure 5:

1. **Private goods** are both excludable and rival in consumption. An ice-cream cone, for instance, is excludable because it is possible to prevent someone from eating one—you just don't give it to her. It is also rival in consumption because if one person eats an ice-cream cone, another person cannot eat the same cone.

   Most goods in the economy are private goods like ice-cream cones: You don't get one unless you pay for it, and once you have it, you are the only person who benefits. When we analyzed supply and demand and the efficiency of markets in previous chapters, we implicitly assumed that goods were both excludable and rival in consumption.

2. **Public goods** are neither excludable nor rival in consumption. They aren't excludable because people cannot be prevented from using a public good, and they aren't rival because one person's use does not reduce another person's ability to use it.

   An example is a tornado siren in a small town. Once the siren sounds, it is impossible to prevent a person from hearing it, so it is not excludable. And when one person gets the benefit of the warning, that does not reduce the benefit to others, so the siren is not rival in consumption. Therefore, public goods can be considered as a special type of positive externalities.

private goods
goods that are both excludable and rival in consumption

Figure 5

Four Types of Goods

Goods can be grouped into four categories according to two characteristics: (1) A good is **excludable** if people can be prevented from using it. (2) A good is **rival in consumption** if one person's use of the good diminishes other people's use of it. This diagram gives examples of goods in each category.

Excludable?	Rival in consumption? Yes	Rival in consumption? No
Yes	Private Goods • Ice-cream cones • Clothing • Congested toll roads	Club Goods • Satellite TV • Fire protection • Uncongested toll roads
No	Common Resources • Fish in the ocean • The environment • Congested nontoll roads	Public Goods • Tornado siren • National defense • Uncongested nontoll roads

common resources
goods that are rival in consumption but not excludable

club goods
goods that are excludable but not rival in consumption

3. **Common resources** are rival in consumption but not excludable. Consider fish in the ocean. They are rival in consumption because when one person catches fish, fewer fish are left for the next person. Fishes are not excludable because it is hard to stop fishermen from taking fish out of a vast ocean.
4. **Club goods** are excludable but not rival in consumption. An example is satellite TV. If you don't pay your bill, the company can cut you off, making the good excludable. But your use of the satellite signal does not diminish anyone else's ability to use it, so the service is not rival in consumption.

Figure 1 separates goods into four distinct categories. That's helpful in thinking about these categories, but it is not completely realistic because the boundaries can be fuzzy. Whether goods are excludable or rival in consumption is often a matter of degree. Fish in an ocean may not be excludable because monitoring fishing every- where is so hard, but a large enough coast guard could make fish partly excludable, at least in some sections of the ocean. Similarly, although fish are generally rival in consumption, this would be less true if the number of fishermen were small relative to the number of fish. (Think of North America before the arrival of European settlers.) Despite this fuzziness, however, it is useful to group goods into these four categories. Because people cannot be prevented from using public goods or common resources, these goods are available to everyone free of charge. But when something of value has no price attached to it, externalities arise. For example, if a private individual were to provide a public good, such as a tornado siren, other people would be better off. They would receive a benefit without paying for it—a positive externality. Similarly, when one person uses a common resource like fish in the ocean, other people are worse off because there are fewer fish to catch, yet they are not compensated for their loss. This is an externality too, but a negative one. Because of these external effects, private decisions about consumption and production can lead to an inefficient allocation of resources unless the government policy steps in to fix the problem.

10-4a The Free-Rider Problem

The citizens of Smalltown, U.S.A., love fireworks on the Fourth of July. Each of the town's 500 residents places a $10 value on this experience for a total benefit of $5,000. The cost of putting on the display is $1,000. Because the $5,000 benefit exceeds the $1,000 cost, it is efficient for Smalltown residents to enjoy Fourth of July fireworks.

Would the private market produce this outcome? Probably not. Imagine that Zoe, a Smalltown entrepreneur, decided to put on a fireworks display. Zoe would have trouble selling tickets because potential customers would realize that they could see the fireworks without a ticket. Because fireworks are not excludable, it is easy to be a **free rider**—the term for a person who receives the benefit of a good without paying for it. If most people would choose to be free riders rather than ticket buyers, the market would fail to provide the efficient outcome.

free rider
a person who receives the benefit of a good but avoids paying for it

This market failure can be viewed as arising from an externality. If Zoe puts on the fireworks display, she confers an external benefit on those who see it without paying for it. When deciding whether to put on the display, however, Zoe does not take the external benefits into account. Zoe isn't a philanthropist. Even though the fireworks display is socially desirable, it is not profitable, so Zoe makes the privately rational but socially inefficient decision not to put on the display.

Although the private market fails to supply the fireworks display Smalltown residents want, the solution to Smalltown's problem is obvious: The local government can sponsor a Fourth of July celebration. The town council can raise everyone's taxes by ₹ 2 and hire Zoe to produce the fireworks. Everyone in Smalltown is better off by ₹ 8—the ₹ 10 at which residents value the fireworks minus the ₹2 tax bill. Zoe can help Smalltown reach the efficient outcome as a public employee even though she could not do so as a private entrepreneur.

This story of Smalltown's government-sponsored fireworks is simplified but realistic. In fact, many local governments in the United States pay for fireworks on the Fourth of July. More importantly, the story shows a general lesson: Because public goods are not excludable, the free-rider problem often prevents the private market from supplying them. The government, however, can remedy the problem. If the government decides that the total benefits of a public good exceed its costs, it can provide the public good, pay for it with tax revenue, and potentially make everyone better off.

10-4b Some Important Public Goods

There are many examples of public goods. Here are three of the most critical.

National Defense The defense of a country from foreign aggressors is a classic example of a public good. Once a country has paid for a military to defend it, it is impossible to prevent a person in the country from enjoying the benefit of this defense. And when one person enjoys the benefit of national defense, she does not reduce the benefit to anyone else. National defense is neither excludable nor rival in consumption.

Research and Development (R&D) R&D increases knowledge about many things. When evaluating the public policy toward research, it is important to distinguish general knowledge from specific technological knowledge, like the invention of a longer- lived battery, a smaller microchip, or a better digital music player. This kind of knowledge can be patented. The patent gives the inventor the exclusive right to the creation for a limited period. Anyone else who wants to use it must pay the inventor for the right to do so. In other words, the patent makes the inventor's work excludable.

By contrast, general knowledge is a public good. For example, a mathematician cannot patent a theorem. Once proven, the knowledge is not excludable: The theorem enters the collective pool of knowledge that anyone can use without charge. The theorem is also not rival in consumption: One person's use of the theorem does not prevent any other person from using it.

Profit-seeking firms spend a lot on R&D to develop products they can patent and sell, but most don't spend much on basic research. Their incentive, instead, is to free ride on the general knowledge created by others. As a result, in the absence of any public policy, society would devote too few resources to creating knowledge.

10-5 Common Resources

Common resources, like public goods, are not excludable: They are available free of charge to anyone who wants to use them. Common resources are, however, rival in consumption: One person's use of the common resource reduces other people's ability to use it. Thus, common resources give rise to a new problem: Once the good is provided, policymakers need to be concerned about how much it is used.

Tragedy of the Commons
a parable that illustrates why common resources are used more than is desirable from the standpoint of society as a whole

This problem is best understood from a classic parable called the **Tragedy of the Commons.**

10-5a The Tragedy of the Commons

Of the many economic activities that take place in a small medieval town, one of the most important is raising sheep. Many families own flocks of sheep and support themselves by selling wool, which is used to make clothing.

As our story begins, the sheep spend much of their time grazing on the land surrounding the town, called the Town Commons. No family owns the land. Instead, the town residents own it collectively, and all the residents are allowed to graze their sheep on it. Collective ownership works well because land is plentiful. As long as everyone can get all the good grazing land they want, the Town Commons is not rival in consumption, and allowing residents' sheep to graze for free causes no problems. Everyone is happy.

As the years pass, the population grows, and so does the number of sheep grazing on the Town Commons. With a growing number of sheep, the land starts to lose its ability to replenish itself. Eventually, the land is grazed so heavily that it becomes barren. With no grass left on the Town Commons, raising sheep is impossible, and the once prosperous wool industry disappears. Many families lose their source of livelihood.

What causes this tragedy? Why do the shepherds allow the sheep population to grow so large that it destroys the Town Commons? The reason is that social and private incentives differ. Avoiding the destruction of the grazing land depends on the collective action of the shepherds. If they acted together, they could reduce the sheep population to a size that the Town Commons can support. Yet no single family has an incentive to reduce the size of its own flock because each flock represents only a small part of the problem.

In essence, the Tragedy of the Commons arises because of an externality. When one family's flock grazes on the common land, it reduces the quality of the land available for other families. Because people neglect this negative externality when deciding how many sheep to own, the result is an excessive number of sheep.

If the tragedy had been foreseen, the town could have solved the problem in various ways. It could have regulated the number of sheep in each family's flock, internalized the externality by taxing sheep, or auctioned off a limited number of sheep-grazing permits. That is, the medieval town could have dealt with overgrazing in the way that modern society deals with pollution.

In the case of land, however, there is a simpler solution. The town can divide the land among the town families. Each family can enclose its parcel of land with a fence and then protect it from excessive grazing. In this way, the land becomes a private good rather than a common resource. This occurred in England during the 17th century in what is known as the enclosure movement.

The Tragedy of the Commons teaches a general lesson: A person who uses a common resource diminishes other people's ability to enjoy it. Because of this negative externality, common resources tend to be used excessively. But the government can solve the problem by regulating or taxing the undesirable behavior. Alternatively, the government can sometimes turn the common resource into a private good.

This lesson has been known for thousands of years. The ancient Greek philosopher Aristotle pointed out the problem: "What is common to many is taken least care of, for all men have greater regard for what is their own than for what they possess in common with others."

10-5b Some Important Common Resources

There are many examples of common resources, leading to various government policies to mitigate the problem of overuse.

Clean Air and Water We showed that unfettered markets do not adequately protect the environment. Pollution is a negative externality that can be remedied with regulations or corrective taxes. This market failure can be seen as a common-resource problem. Clean air and water are com- mon resources like open grazing land, and excessive pollution is like excessive grazing. Environmental degradation is a modern Tragedy of the Commons.

Congested Roads Roads can be either public goods or common resources. If a road is not congested, then one person's use does not affect anyone else. In this case, use is not rival in consumption, and the road is a public good. But in many urban areas, empty roads are an unattainable dream. If a road is congested, its use confers a negative externality. Whenever another vehicle drives on the road, it becomes more crowded, and others must drive more slowly. In this case, the road is a common resource.

One way for the government to address road congestion is to charge drivers a toll, which is, in essence, a corrective tax on the externality of congestion. Sometimes, as in the case of local roads, tolls are not a practical solution because the cost of collecting them is too high. But several major cities, including London and Stockholm, have found increasing tolls to be a very effective way to reduce congestion, and the idea is spreading.

Sometimes, congestion is a problem only at certain times of the day. If a bridge is heavily traveled only during rush hour, for instance, the congestion externality is largest then. The efficient solution is to charge higher tolls during rush hour, such as Electronic Road Pricing (ERP) Sytem in Singapore which makes it very difficult to get yourself caught up in a traffic jam. This would give drivers an incentive to alter their schedules, reducing traffic when congestion is greatest.

Fish, Whales, and Other Wildlife Many species are common resources. Fish and whales, for instance, have commercial value, and anyone can go to the ocean and catch whatever is available. Each person has little incentive to maintain the species for the next year. Just as excessive grazing can ruin the Town Commons, excessive fishing and whaling can destroy commercially valuable marine populations.

Oceans remain one of the least regulated common resources. Two problems prevent an easy solution. First, many countries have access to the oceans, so any solution would require international cooperation among countries that hold different values. Second, because the oceans are so vast, enforcing any agreement is difficult. As a result, fishing rights have been a frequent source of tension among normally friendly countries.

Within the United States, various laws aim to manage fish and other wildlife resources. The government charges for fishing and hunting licenses, and it restricts the lengths of the fishing and hunting seasons. Fishermen are often required to throw back small fish, and hunters are permitted to kill only a limited number of animals. All these laws reduce the use of a common resource and help maintain animal populations.

In the News

The Coase Theorem in Action

Whenever people come in close contact, externalities abound.

Don't Want Me to Recline My Airline Seat? You Can Pay Me

By Josh Barro

I fly a lot. When I fly, I recline. I don't feel guilty about it. And I'm going to keep doing it, unless you pay me to stop.

I bring this up because of a dispute you may have heard about: On Sunday, a United Airlines flight from Newark to Denver made an unscheduled stop in Chicago to discharge two passengers who had a dispute over seat reclining. According to The Associated Press, a man in a middle seat installed the Knee Defender, a ₹21.95 device that keeps a seat upright, on the seatback in front of him.

A flight attendant asked him to remove the device. He refused. The woman seated in front of him turned around and threw water at him. The pilot landed the plane and booted both passengers off the flight.

Obviously, it's improper to throw water at another passenger on a flight, even if he deserves it. But I've seen a distressing amount of sympathy for Mr. Knee Defender, who wasn't just instigating a fight but usurping his fellow passenger's property rights. When you buy an airline ticket, one of the things you're buying is the right to use your seat's reclining function. If this passenger so badly wanted the passenger in front of him not to recline, he should have paid her to give up that right.

I wrote an article to that effect in 2011, noting that airline seats are an excellent case study for the Coase Theorem. This is an economic theory holding that it doesn't matter very much who is initially given a property right; so long as you clearly define it and transaction costs are low, people will trade the right so that it ends up in the hands of whoever values it most. That is, I own the right to recline, and if my reclining bothers you, you can pay me to stop. We could (but don't) have an alternative system in which the passenger sitting behind

Quick**Quiz**

7. According to the Coase theorem,
   a. private actors can reach an agreement to solve the problem of externalities without the government.
   b. corrective subsidies are the best policy to solve the problem of positive externalities.
   c. negative externalities are a problem for society, but positive externalities are not.
   d. when two private actors amicably solve the problem of externalities, they shift the problem to a third party.
8. The Coase theorem does NOT apply if
   a. there is a significant externality between two parties.
   b. the court system vigorously enforces all contracts.
   c. transaction costs make negotiation difficult.
   d. both parties understand the externality fully.

Answers are at the end of the chapter.

10-6 Conclusion

The invisible hand is powerful but not omnipotent. A market's equilibrium maximizes the sum of producer and consumer surplus. When the buyers and sellers in the market are the only interested parties, this outcome is efficient from the standpoint of society. But when there are external effects, such as pollution, evaluating a market outcome requires accounting for the well-being of third parties. In this case, the invisible hand of the marketplace may fail to allocate resources efficiently.

Chapter in a Nutshell

- When a transaction between a buyer and seller directly affects a third party, the effect is called an externality. If an activity yields negative externalities, such as pollution, the socially optimal quantity in a market is less than the equilibrium quantity. If an activity yields positive externalities, such as technology spillovers, the socially optimal quantity is greater than the equilibrium quantity.
- Government can remedy the inefficiencies caused by externalities. Sometimes, it regulates behavior. Other times, it internalizes an externality using corrective taxes. Another policy is to issue permits. For example, the government could protect the environment by issuing a limited number of pollution permits. The result of this policy is similar to imposing corrective taxes on polluters.
- Those affected by externalities can sometimes solve the problem privately. For instance, when one business imposes an externality on another business, the two businesses can internalize the externality by merging. Alternatively, the interested parties can solve the problem by negotiating a contract. According to the Coase theorem, if people can bargain without cost, they can reach an agreement in which resources are allocated efficiently. In many cases, however, reaching a bargain among the many interested parties is difficult, so the Coase theorem does not apply.
- Goods differ in whether they are excludable and whether they are rival in consumption. A good is excludable if it is possible to prevent someone from using it. It is rival in consumption if one person's use of the good reduces others' ability to use the same unit of the good. Markets work best for private goods, which are both excludable and rival in consumption. Markets do not work as well for other types of goods.
- Public goods are neither excludable nor rival in consumption. Examples of public goods include fireworks displays, national defense, and the discovery of fundamental knowledge. Because people are not charged for their use of the public good, they have an incentive to free ride, making private provision of the good infeasible. Governments can improve the allocation of resources by providing public goods and determining the quantity of each good with cost–benefit analysis.
- Common resources are not excludable but are rival in consumption. Examples include common grazing land, clean air, and congested roads. Because people are not charged for their use of common resources, they tend to use them excessively. Governments can remedy this problem using various methods, such as regulations and corrective taxes, to limit the use of common resources.

Key Concepts

externality, p. 196
internalizing the externality, p. 199
corrective taxes, p. 201
coase theorem, p. 209
transaction costs, p. 210
excludability, p. 211
rivalry in consumption, p. 211
private goods, p. 211
public goods, p. 211
common resources, p. 212
club goods, p. 212
free rider, p. 212
tragedy of the Commons, p. 214

Questions for Review

1. Give an example of a negative externality and an example of a positive one.
2. Draw a supply-and-demand diagram to explain the effect of a negative externality that occurs because of a firm's production process.
3. How does the patent system help society solve an externality problem?
4. What are corrective taxes? Why do economists prefer them to regulations as a way of protecting the environment from pollution?
5. List some of the ways that the problems caused by externalities can be solved without government intervention.
6. Imagine that you are a nonsmoker sharing a room with a smoker. According to the Coase theorem, what

determines whether your roommate smokes in the room? Is this outcome efficient? How do you and your roommate reach this solution?

1. Explain what is meant by a good being "excludable." Explain what is meant by a good being "rival in consumption." Is a slice of pizza excludable? Is it rival in consumption?
2. Define and give an example of a public good. Can the private market provide this good on its own? Explain.
3. What is cost–benefit analysis of public goods? Why is it important? Why is it hard?
4. Define and give an example of a common resource. Without government intervention, will people use this good too much or too little? Why?

Problems and Applications

1. Consider two ways to protect your car from theft. The Club (a steering wheel lock) makes it difficult for a car thief to take your car. Lojack (a tracking system) makes it easier for the police to catch the car thief who has stolen it. Which of these methods confers a negative externality on other car owners? Which confers a positive externality? Do you think there are any policy implications of your analysis?
2. Consider the market for fire extinguishers.
   a. Why might fire extinguishers exhibit positive externalities?
   b. Draw a graph of the market for fire extinguishers, labeling the demand curve, the social-value curve, the supply curve, and the social-cost curve.
   c. Indicate the market equilibrium level of output and the efficient level of output. Give an intuitive explanation for why these quantities differ.
   d. If the external benefit is ₹10 per extinguisher, describe a government policy that would yield the efficient outcome.
3. Greater consumption of alcohol leads to more motor vehicle accidents and, thus, imposes costs on people who do not drink and drive.
   a. Illustrate the market for alcohol, labeling the demand curve, the social-value curve, the supply curve, the social-cost curve, the market equilibrium level of output, and the efficient level of output.
   b. On your graph, shade the area corresponding to the deadweight loss of the market equilibrium. (Hint: The deadweight loss occurs because some units of alcohol are consumed for which the social cost exceeds the social value.) Explain.
4. Some observers believe that the current levels of pollution in our society are too high.
   a. If society wishes to reduce overall pollution by a certain amount, why might different amounts of reduction at different firms be efficient?
   b. Command-and-control approaches often rely on uniform reductions among firms. Why are these approaches generally unable to target the firms that should undertake bigger reductions?
   c. Economists argue that appropriate corrective taxes or tradable pollution permits will result in efficient pollution reduction. How do these approaches target the firms that should undertake bigger reductions?
5. The many identical residents of Whoville love drinking Zlurp. Each resident has the following willingness to pay for the tasty refreshment:

First bottle	₹5
Second bottle	4
Third bottle	3
Fourth bottle	2
Fifth bottle	1
Further bottles	0

   a. The cost of producing Zlurp is ₹1.50, and the competitive suppliers sell it at this price. (The supply curve is horizontal.) How many bottles will each Whovillian consume? What is each person's consumer surplus?
   b. Producing Zlurp creates pollution. Each bottle has an external cost of ₹1. Taking this additional cost into account, what is total surplus per person in the allocation you described in part (a)?
   c. Cindy Lou Who, one of the residents of Whoville, decides on her own to reduce her consumption of Zlurp by one bottle. What happens to Cindy's welfare (her consumer surplus minus the cost of pollution she experiences)? How does Cindy's decision affect total surplus in Whoville?
   d. Mayor Grinch imposes a ₹1 tax on Zlurp. What is consumption per person now? Calculate consumer surplus, the external cost, government revenue, and total surplus per person.
   e. Based on your calculations, would you support the mayor's policy? Why or why not?
6. Bruno loves playing rock 'n' roll music at high volume. Placido loves opera and hates rock 'n' roll.

Unfortunately, they are next-door neighbors in an apartment building with paper-thin walls.

a. What is the externality here?
b. What command-and-control policy might the landlord impose? Could such a policy lead to an inefficient outcome?
c. Suppose the landlord lets the tenants do whatever they want. According to the Coase theorem, how might Bruno and Placido reach an efficient outcome on their own? What might prevent them from reaching an efficient outcome?

7. Figure 4 shows that for any given demand curve for the right to pollute, the government can achieve the same outcome either by setting a price with a corrective tax or by setting a quantity with pollution permits. Suppose there is a sharp improvement in the technology for controlling pollution.
   a. Using graphs similar to those in Figure 4, illustrate the effect of this development on the demand for pollution rights.
   b. What is the effect on the price and quantity of pollution under each regulatory system? Explain.

8. Suppose that the government decides to issue tradable permits for a certain form of pollution.
   a. Does it matter for economic efficiency whether the government distributes or auctions the permits? Why or why not?
   b. If the government chooses to distribute the permits, does the allocation of permits among firms matter for efficiency? Explain.

9. There are three industrial firms in Happy Valley.

Firm	Initial Pollution Level	Cost of Reducing Pollution by 1 Unit
A	30 units	₹20
B	40 units	₹30
C	20 units	₹10

The government wants to reduce pollution to 60 units, so it gives each firm 20 tradable pollution permits.

   a. Who sells permits, and how many do they sell? Who buys permits, and how many do they buy? Briefly explain why the sellers and buyers are each willing to do so. What is the total cost of pollution reduction in this situation?
   b. How much higher would the costs of pollution reduction be if the permits could not be traded?

10. Think about the goods and services provided by your local government.
    a. Using the categories in Figure 1, classify each of the following goods, explaining your choice:
       - police protection
       - snow plowing
       - education
       - rural roads
       - city streets
    b. Why do you think the government provides items that are not public goods?

11. Both public goods and common resources involve externalities.
    a. Are the externalities associated with public goods generally positive or negative? Is the free-market quantity of public goods generally greater or less than the socially efficient quantity? Cite examples in your answer.
    b. Are the externalities associated with common resources generally positive or negative? Is the free-market use of common resources generally greater or less than the socially efficient use? Cite examples in your answer.

12. Fredo loves watching *Downton Abbey* on his local public TV station, but he never sends any money to support the station during its fund-raising drives.
    a. What name do economists have for people like Fredo?
    b. How can the government solve the problem caused by people like Fredo?
    c. Can you think of ways the private market can solve this problem? How does the option of cable TV alter the situation?

13. Wireless high-speed Internet is provided for free in the airport of the city of Communityville.
    a. At first, only a few people use the service. What type of good is this and why?
    b. Eventually, as more people find out about the service and start using it, the speed of the connection begins to fall. Now what type of good is the wireless Internet service?
    c. What problem might result and why? What is one possible way to correct this problem?

14. Four roommates are planning to spend the weekend in their dorm room watching old movies, and they are debating how many to watch. Here is their willingness to pay for each film:

	Dwayne	Javier	Salman	Chris
First film	₹7	₹5	₹3	₹2
Second film	6	4	2	1
Third film	5	3	1	0
Fourth film	4	2	0	0
Fifth film	3	1	0	0

a. Within the dorm room, is the showing of a movie a public good? Why or why not?
b. If it costs $8 to stream a movie, how many movies should the roommates stream to maximize total surplus?
c. If they choose the optimal number from part (b) and then split the cost of streaming the movies equally, how much surplus does each person obtain from watching the movies?
d. Is there any way to split the cost to ensure that everyone benefits? What practical problems does this solution raise?
e. Suppose they agree in advance to choose the efficient number and to split the cost of the movies equally. When Dwayne is asked his willingness to pay, will he have an incentive to tell the truth? If so, why? If not, what will he be tempted to say?
f. What does this example teach you about the optimal provision of public goods?

15. Some economists argue that private firms will not undertake the efficient amount of basic scientific research.
    a. Explain why this might be so. In your answer, classify basic research in one of the categories shown in Figure 1.
    b. What sort of policy has the United States adopted in response to this problem?
    c. It is often argued that this policy increases the technological capability of American producers relative to that of foreign firms. Is this argument consistent with your classification of basic research in part (a)? (Hint: Can excludability apply to some potential beneficiaries of a public good and not others?)
16. Two towns, each with three residents, are deciding whether to put on a fireworks display to celebrate the New Year. Fireworks cost $360. In each town, some people enjoy fireworks more than others.
    a. In the town of Bayport, each of the residents values the public good as follows:

Frank	₹50
Joe	₹100
Callie	₹300

    Would fireworks pass a cost–benefit analysis? Explain.
    b. The mayor of Bayport proposes to decide by majority rule and, if the fireworks referendum passes, to split the cost equally among all residents. Who would vote in favor, and who would vote against? Would the vote yield the same answer as the cost–benefit analysis?
    b. In the town of River Heights, each of the residents values the public good as follows:

Nancy	₹20
Bess	₹140
Ned	₹160

    Would fireworks pass a cost–benefit analysis? Explain.
    c. The mayor of River Heights also proposes to decide by majority rule and, if the fireworks referendum passes, to split the cost equally among all residents. Who would vote in favor, and who would vote against? Would the vote yield the same answer as the cost–benefit analysis?
    d. What do you think these examples say about the optimal provision of public goods?
17. There is often litter along highways but rarely in people's yards. Provide an economic explanation for this fact.
18. Many transportation systems, such as the Washington, D.C., Metro (subway), charge higher fares during rush hours than during the rest of the day. Why might they do this?
19. High-income people are willing to pay more than lower-income people to avoid the risk of death. For example, they are more likely to pay for cutting-edge safety features on cars. Do you think cost–benefit analysts should take this fact into account when evaluating public projects? Consider, for instance, a rich town and a poor town, both of which are considering the installation of a traffic light. Should the rich town use a higher dollar value for a human life in making this decision? Why or why not?

Quick**Quiz Answers**

1. **c** 2. **b** 3. **a** 4. **d** 5. **b** 6. **c** 7. **a** 8. **c** 10. **a** 11. **b** 12. **b** 13. **b** 14. **d** 15. **d** 16. **c** 17. **d**

Chapter

11

The Economics of Healthcare

All of us would like to lead long, healthy lives. And given the choice, we would prefer to do so without having to endure the surgeon's scalpel, the nurse's needle, or the dentist's drill. Yet good health rarely comes so easily. Achieving a long, healthy life often requires the use of scarce resources, and that makes it, at least in part, an economic problem. Indian government's total health expenditure is around 4% of its GDP. Understanding the modern economy requires an appreciation of the special economics of healthcare.

This chapter begins by examining the economic forces that shape the healthcare system. The standard model of supply and demand, in which prices guide buyers and sellers to an efficient allocation of resources, explains how large parts of the world work, but the market for healthcare deviates from this benchmark in many ways. These deviations often call for government policies to ensure that healthcare resources are allocated efficiently and equitably. And in most nations, governments are deeply involved in healthcare markets. That involvement increased greatly in 2020 and 2021 when governments around the world needed to take emergency action to curb the fatal effects of the novel coronavirus pandemic.

SAUDILAB/SHUTTERSTOCK.COM; LESHATNOIR/E+/GETTY IMAGES

11-1 The Special Characteristics of the Market for Healthcare

The standard theory of how markets work is the model of supply and demand, which has several notable features:

1. The main interested parties are the buyers and sellers in the market.
2. Buyers are good judges of what they get from sellers.
3. Buyers pay sellers directly for the goods and services being exchanged.
4. Market prices are the primary mechanism for coordinating the decisions of market participants.
5. The invisible hand on its own leads to an efficient allocation of resources.

For many goods and services, this model offers a reasonably good description.

Yet none of the five features of the standard model reflects what occurs in the market for healthcare. The healthcare market has consumers (patients) and producers (doctors, nurses, etc.). But various factors complicate the analysis of their interactions. In particular:

1. Third parties—insurers, governments, and unwitting bystanders—often have an interest in healthcare outcomes.
2. Patients often don't know what they need and cannot evaluate the treatment they are getting.
3. Healthcare providers are often paid not by the patients but by private or government health insurance.
4. The rules established by these insurers, more than market prices, determine the allocation of resources.
5. In light of these issues, the invisible hand can't work its magic, so the allocation of resources can be highly inefficient.

Healthcare is not the only good or service in the economy that departs from the standard model of supply, demand, and the invisible hand. But healthcare may be the most important one that departs radically from this benchmark. Examining the special features of this market is a good starting point for understanding why the government plays a large role in the provision of healthcare and why health policy is often complex and vexing.

11-1a Externalities Galore

Chapter 10 showed that market outcomes may be inefficient when there are externalities. To recap: An **externality** arises when a person engages in an activity that influences the well-being of a bystander but neither pays nor receives compensation for that effect. If the impact on the bystander is adverse, it is a **negative externality**. If it is beneficial, it is a **positive externality**. In the presence of externalities, society's interest extends beyond the well-being of buyers and sellers in the market to include the well-being of bystanders who are affected indirectly. Because buyers and sellers neglect the external effects of their actions when deciding how much to demand or supply, the externality can render the unregulated market outcome inefficient.

This general conclusion is crucial for understanding healthcare, where externalities are rampant. These externalities can call for government action to remedy the market failure.

Take vaccines, for example. If Vicki vaccinates herself against a disease, she is less likely to catch it and become a carrier who infects other people. In the language of economics, Vicki's action conveys a positive externality. If getting a jab has some cost, either in money, time, discomfort, or risk of adverse side effects, too few people will do it because they may not fully take into account the positive externalities when weighing the costs and benefits. The government can remedy this problem by requiring vaccination or encouraging it through media campaigns and incentives. The government can also increase the supply of vaccines by subsidizing their development, manufacture, and distribution.

Another example of a healthcare externality concerns medical research. When a physician or scientist figures out a new way to treat an ailment, that information enters society's pool of medical knowledge. The benefit to other physicians and patients is a positive externality. Without government intervention, there will be too little research.

Government responds to this problem in many ways. Sometimes, it grants a researcher a patent, as is the case with new pharmaceutical drugs. The patent provides an incentive for research by allowing the researcher to profit from a temporary monopoly. The patent is said to internalize the externality. Yet this approach is not perfect because the monopoly price is higher than the marginal cost of production. As we will see later in the book, the high monopoly price reduces consumption of the patented treatment, leading to inefficiency as measured by the deadweight loss. Moreover, the high price may be particularly hard on patients with lower incomes.

Healthcare externalities sometimes point policymakers in conflicting directions. Again, consider vaccines. Because research into new vaccines conveys a positive externality, the government grants patent protection. But once a vaccine is devised, the high price charged by the patent holder slows its dissemination, undermining the positive externality from vaccination. One possible solution to this conflict, advocated by the Nobel Laureate economist Michael Kremer, is for the government to buy out the patent holder. This approach could put the innovation in the public domain, making it more widely available while still providing incentives for research.

Another way the government can deal with the positive externality from medical research is to subsidize research directly. This policy requires taxation to raise the necessary funds, and most taxation entails deadweight losses of its own. But if the externalities from the funded research exceed the cost of the research, including the deadweight losses, overall welfare can increase.

Case Study

Vaccine Hesitancy

The disease of measles illustrates the externalities central to health economics. Measles is highly contagious and dangerous, especially for children. Before a vaccine was developed in 1963, between 3 and 4 million people in the United States caught the disease every year. Tens of thousands required hospitalization, and many hundreds died.

Fortunately, immunization proved effective. By 2000, measles was largely eliminated as a health risk in the United States. During the subsequent decade, only about 60 cases were reported per year. The measles vaccine was one of the great success stories of modern medicine. In the language of economics, the research that created the vaccine had large positive externalities both in the United States and around the world.

The elimination of the disease, however, had some unintended consequences. In particular, it reduced the vigilance of some parents in ensuring that their children were vaccinated. Their decision to forgo vaccination was partly based on the belief—debunked among scientists but persistent among some segments of the public—that vaccines entail a significant risk of adverse side effects. Some claimed a religious basis for their decision not to vaccinate. Because of declining immunization, measles started to become more common again. There were 372 reported cases in 2018 and more than 1,000 in 2019.

Policymakers struggled with how to respond. In several states, lawmakers strengthened requirements that all children be vaccinated. Exemptions were allowed for valid medical reasons but not for religious or philosophical beliefs. Critics of these laws viewed them as a violation of personal liberty. Supporters viewed them as supporting the community's need to deal with the externalities inherent in infectious diseases.

A similar issue arose during the COVID-19 pandemic of 2020–2021. Soon after vaccines for this new virus were developed, they became widely and freely available. According to medical experts, eradicating the disease would require vaccinating most of the population. But because the vaccines were new, many people were hesitant. Some economists proposed paying people to get vaccinated—a Pigovian subsidy to internalize the externality and quicken the end of the pandemic. The proposal was not widely adopted at the national level, but some states and localities experimented with such incentives. In New York City, for example, those who got vaccinated were offered a voucher for a burger at Shake Shack. ●

11-1b The Difficulty of Monitoring Quality

In most markets, consumers know what they want, and after a transaction is completed, they can judge whether they are happy with what they got. Healthcare is a credence good. When you get sick, you may not know which treatment is best. You rely on the advice of a physician who has years of specialized training. And even with hindsight, you cannot reliably judge whether the treatment offered to you was the right one. Sometimes state-of-the-art medicine fails to improve a patient's health. And given the restorative power of the human body, the wrong treatment can sometimes appear to work.

The inability of healthcare consumers to monitor the quality of the product they are buying leads to government regulations. Most importantly, the government requires physicians, dentists, nurses, and other health professionals to have licenses to practice. These licenses are granted only after an individual attends an approved school and passes rigorous tests. Those caught practicing without a license can be imprisoned.

In addition to government regulation, the medical profession monitors itself by accrediting medical schools, promoting best practices, and establishing norms of professional behavior. A physician's advice is supposed to be based entirely on the patient's best interest, not the physician's personal gain. When patients accept this advice, they rely on a degree of trust, which may be fostered by long-term relationships between doctor and patient. But conflict-of-interest problems exist in healthcare as they do elsewhere in society, and this trust is sometimes breached.

While public and private regulations of healthcare have many benefits for patients, they also have some drawbacks. For example, some economists have argued that there are too many hurdles to opening new medical schools. They suggest that the medical profession acts like a monopoly: By restricting the number of doctors, it drives up doctors' salaries and consumers' healthcare costs. Other economists have argued that the regulators are too slow in approving new drugs. Some patients who might have benefited from experimental treatments are forced to go without them. The proper balance between protecting public safety and giving people the freedom to make their own healthcare decisions is a subject of ongoing debate.

11-1c The Insurance Market and Its Imperfections

Because people don't know when they are going to get sick or what kind of medical treatments they will need, spending on healthcare is unpredictable. This uncertainty, along with people's responses to it, helps to explain why we have the health institutions that we do.

The Value of Insurance Most people dislike uncertainty, which gives rise to insurance markets.

The way insurance generally works is that a person facing a risk pays a fee (called a **premium**) to an insurance company, which in return agrees to accept all or part of the risk. There are many types of insurance. Car insurance covers the risk that you get into an auto accident, fire insurance covers the risk that your house burns down, and health insurance covers the risk that you need expensive medical treatment.

Markets for insurance are useful in reducing risk, but two problems hamper their ability to do so fully and efficiently.

Moral Hazard The first problem that impedes the operation of insurance markets is **moral hazard**: When people have insurance to cover their spending on healthcare, they have less incentive to engage in behavior that will keep that spending to a reasonable level. For example, if patients don't have to pay for each visit to a doctor, some may go whenever they experience minor symptoms (a runny nose, an achy finger). Similarly, physicians may be more likely to order tests of dubious value when they know an insurance company is picking up the tab.

moral hazard
the tendency of a person who is imperfectly monitored to engage in dishonest or otherwise undesirable behavior

Adverse Selection The second problem that impedes the operation of insurance markets is **adverse selection**: If customers differ in relevant attributes (such as whether they have a chronic disease) and those differences are known to them but not to insurers, the mix of people who buy insurance may be especially expensive to insure. In particular, people with hidden conditions are more likely to buy health insurance than healthy people. As a result, for an insurance company to cover its costs, the price of health insurance must reflect the cost of a sicker-than-average person. That price may be high enough that some people with average health may forgo buying insurance. As people drop coverage, the insurance market fails to achieve its purpose of reducing the financial risk from illness.

adverse selection
the tendency for the mix of unobserved attributes to become undesirable from the standpoint of an uninformed party

Even worse, adverse selection can lead to a phenomenon called the **death spiral**. Suppose that insurance companies must charge everyone the same price. It might seem to make sense for a company to base the price of insurance on the health characteristics of the average person. But after it does so, the healthiest people may decide that insurance is not worth the cost and drop out of the insured pool. With a sicker-than-expected group of customers, the company has higher costs and must therefore raise the price of insurance. The price increase then induces the next healthiest group of people to drop insurance coverage, driving up the cost and price again. As this process continues, more people drop coverage, the insured pool gets less healthy, and the price keeps rising. In the end, the insurance market may disappear.

Ayushman Bharat and the Economics of Health Insurance in India

India's health insurance policy space has recently been restructured and upgraded with policies like Ayushman Bharat or the Pradhan Mantri Jan Arogya Yojana (PM-JAY). This program extends cashless coverage for hospitalisation to over 500 million economically vulnerable individuals, PM-JAY and is focused on removing constraints of access to health insurance against the backdrop of rising out of pocket expenditures in healthcare. Let us think about the implications of PM-JAY on adverse selection and moral hazard.

Since PM-JAY enrollment is automatic and eligibility-based, not purely demand-driven, one may argue that it helps mitigate the issue of adverse selection somewhat. Individuals do not self-select based on their health risks, but beneficiaries are pre-identified based on socio-economic criteria. This makes it structurally different from voluntary private insurance, where adverse selection is likely to be more pronounced.

On the other hand, patients face zero marginal cost at the point of service, and provider reimbursement is largely public and centralized, making misrepresentation and overbilling a real possibility. Consequently, it is not obvious whether it can address moral hazard but rather may end up accentuating it. This makes underwriting very important and supervisory guidelines are needed from the government.

Managerial Insight: If hospitals and facilities worry too much about the moral hazard and potential high underwriting leading to rejection rates, hospitals may optimally choose to deny patients with this insurance policy. This can potentially be problematic and therefore incentives need to be designed to avoid such pitfalls. Can you think of some managerial insight on how to address this problem?

11-1d Healthcare as a Right

Typically, when some people don't buy a good or service, the outcome is not a major problem for society. For example, suppose that admission to a water park becomes expensive and people with lower incomes choose other forms of entertainment. Some may lament that the water park is not enjoyed more widely, but few would argue this amounts to a great injustice.

Healthcare is different. When people get sick, it seems wrong to deny them treatment because they have low incomes. Healthcare, unlike admission to a water park, is widely viewed as a human right. This judgment goes beyond the traditional scope of economics, but the study of healthcare economics needs to take it into account.

In some ways, healthcare is like food: It is essential to survive. Government steps in when needed to ensure that everyone can get the essentials. For example, in the United States, resources for food are provided by the Supplemental Nutrition Assistance Program (SNAP), formerly known as the Food Stamp Program. There is, however, an important difference between food and healthcare. In recent decades, the price of food has risen more slowly than incomes, so affording an adequate diet has required a declining share of the typical household's budget. By contrast, because the cost of state-of-the-art healthcare has risen rapidly, affording it has required an increasing share of the typical household's budget.

The judgment that healthcare is a right, along with its rising cost, has led to a large role for the government. In many nations, such as Canada and England, the government runs the healthcare systems, financed mostly by taxes. These are sometimes called **single-payer** systems because one entity—the government's health service—pays all the bills.

In the United States, most people have private health insurance, often through their employers, but the government still has a large role. Medicare provides health insurance for those 65 and older, Medicaid provides health insurance for those with low incomes, the Veterans Health Administration offers healthcare to former members of the military, and the Affordable Care Act regulates the market for private health insurance and gives insurance subsidies to many households with lower incomes. Whether these programs can be improved and, if so, how, remains a topic of debate. But there is little doubt that, with healthcare often viewed as a human right, the government will continue to play a large role in the healthcare system.

In India, out-of-pocket expenditures on healthcare have been very high. However, as per latest estimates from the Economic Survey, the out-of-pocket component of health care expenditure has significantly gone down. As seen in Figure , government estimates suggest that the proportion of government spending on health care has significantly gone up whereas the out-of-pocket expenditure as a fraction of total health expenditure has significantly come down since the year 2016-17 in India, which coincides with the launch of the Ayushman Bharat program.

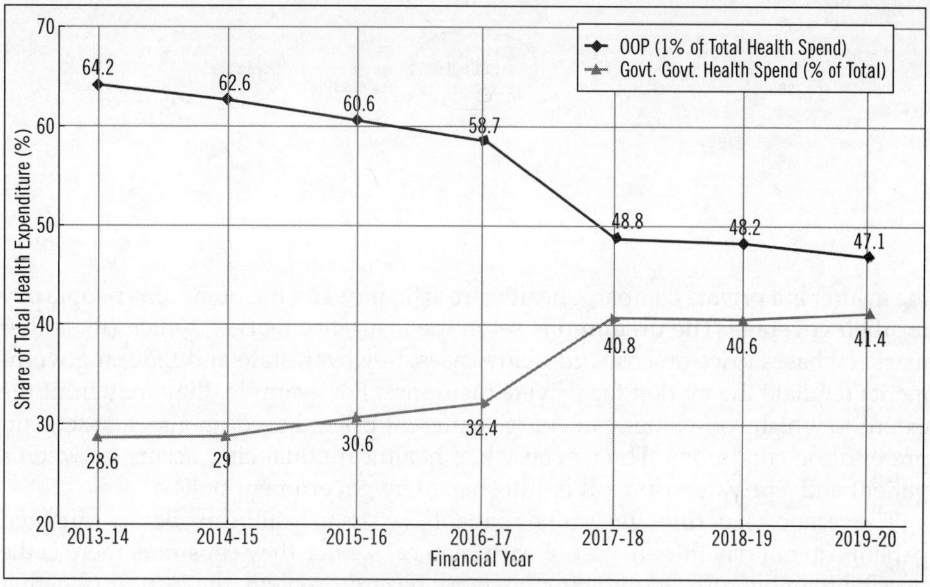

Share of Health Expenditures in India.

Source: Author recreation using Indian Economic Survey 2023—24 data for a similar graph which in turn is based on National Health Accounts 2019—20 of India from the Ministry of Health and Family Welfare.

11-1e The Rules Governing the Healthcare Marketplace

The importance of health insurance, whether provided by private companies or the government, requires that the market for healthcare work differently than most other markets in the economy. Most markets, such as the market for ice cream, look like panel (a) of Figure 1. They consist of buyers and sellers. Sellers offer a good or service at the market price. Buyers who want the item simply have to offer up the right amount of money to purchase it. Exchanges are made, and soon, the sellers are counting their profits, and the buyers are enjoying their ice-cream cones.

The market for healthcare looks more like panel (b) of Figure 1. Providers (the sellers of medical services) are not paid directly by patients (the buyers). Instead, patients pay money to insurers in the form of either a premium (if the insurer is a private company) or taxes (if the insurer is the government). The insurers use this money to compensate the providers, who in turn provide medical services to the patients.

This process requires three sets of rules to guide behavior. The first set determines the financing—that is, who pays for the insurance and how much they pay. If the insurer is the government, the payment for healthcare is part of the tax system. If

Figure 1

How an Insurer Changes a Market

In a typical market, shown in panel (a), sellers deliver a good or service to buyers, who pay sellers a market-determined price. In the healthcare market, shown in panel (b), providers deliver healthcare to patients, but providers are paid by insurers (either the government or private companies). This arrangement requires rules for financing, access, and payment.

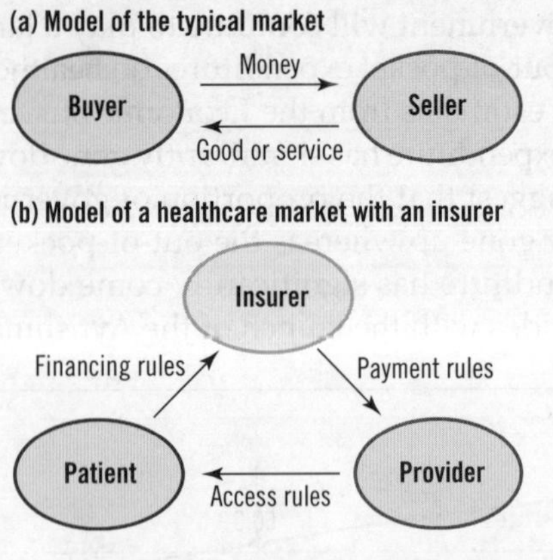

the insurer is a private company, healthcare is financed by the premiums people pay for their coverage. The premium is set in the insurance market, which (like other markets) bases price on costs. In many cases, however, state and federal governments regulate the market for private insurance. For example, they may limit the extent to which companies can charge different prices based on age, gender, and pre-existing conditions. Thus, even when healthcare financing occurs between a patient and a private insurer, it is still shaped by government policy.

The second set of rules determines patients' access to healthcare. Because insured patients do not pay the full cost of each medical service they consume, there is the possibility of overuse. To mitigate the moral hazard problem, the insurer (whether the government or a private company) tries to limit access to when it makes sense. To do so, the insurer establishes rules that ration the use of medical services based on estimated costs and benefits. For example, patients may be able to get a routine checkup no more than once a year, may have access only to certain doctors with whom the insurer has contractual arrangements, or may need a referral from a general practitioner before seeing a more expensive specialist. Such access rules can be annoying, but they are necessary because, once people have insurance to pick up the cost, market prices no longer give them accurate signals about how to allocate scarce resources.

The third set of rules determines the payments from insurers to providers. These rules establish what treatment and care an insurer will pay for and how much it will pay. Insurers may deem some treatments too expensive, too experimental, or insufficiently valuable to pay for them at all. In such cases, providers will often not offer patients the services. Sometimes, providers will offer the services only if the patient pays the full cost of the treatment (as is often the case with cosmetic procedures). The healthcare market then reverts from panel (b) in Figure 1 to the more typical market in panel (a).

The rules regarding financing, access, and payment together shape a healthcare system. For nations with government-run systems, these rules are set by public policy. For nations with more private insurance, such as the United States, these rules are often set by insurance companies as they compete for customers, subject to government regulations.

Quick**Quiz**

1. The market for healthcare differs from most other markets because
   a. consumers often don't know what they need.
   b. producers are paid by insurers rather than consumers.
   c. third parties have an interest in outcomes.
   d. All of the above
2. People buy health insurance to reduce
   a. moral hazard.
   b. adverse selection.
   c. uncertainty.
   d. externalities.
3. Health insurance has access rules for patients to reduce
   a. moral hazard.
   b. adverse selection.
   c. uncertainty.
   d. externalities.
4. If healthy people are less likely to buy health insurance, the market for health insurance experiences the problem of
   a. moral hazard.
   b. adverse selection.
   c. uncertainty.
   d. externalities.

Answers are at the end of the chapter.

Key Healthcare Facts from India

As per the report on health dynamics in India published by the Ministry of health and family welfare , India has a very dense network of health care facilities across the country as of March 2023. There are 714 district hospitals, 362 medical colleges, 6359 community health centres, 31,882 primary health centres with more than 1.6 lakh sub-centres. Overall, India's healthcare infrastructure follows a 3-tier system. The sub centres are the peripheral point of contact in rural areas and the primary health centre serving as the referral point for 6 sub-centres. The community health centres are 30-bedded hospitals serving 4 primary health care centres each. For urban healthcare, the National Urban Health Mission covers cities, towns and district headquarters. The urban health program is largely implemented with the help of urban local bodies. While there is a huge number of workers employed in the heath care sector of India, the shortfalls still remain across the board, ranging from doctors, para medical staff, lab technicians, pharmacists, radiologists etc.

India's fertility rates have gone down significantly. As per reports, the birth rates were around 5.7 per woman in the 1950s to under 2 births per woman in most states on average. The average birth rate is now about 16 births per 1000 population in urban India and just above 21 in rural India. The death rates are around 6 per 1000 population. Infant mortality rates have significantly come down in a span of a decade from 39 per 1000 live births to around 28 per 1000 live births with a much better number of 19 per 1000 in urban India.

Over past many years, healthcare has become much more accessible and affordable to Indian citizens. Health expenditure has largely moved towards primary healthcare and focus on providing basic access and reducing morbidities and mortality rates at low cost. As per Economic survey reports, the shares of primary and secondary care in private health expenditure has declined and that of government expenditure has significantly gone up. Social security health expenses and employer provided benefits and reimbursements have also increased. Maternal mortality rates have also substantially declined in India and much of that is attributable to better institutional facilities for delivery and childbirth.

11-1f Mental Health Focus in India

As per WHO estimates. 1 in 8 people live with some kind of mental health disorder. Anxiety and depression are the most commonly observed traits and India is no different. The National mental Health Survey of India (2015) shows that above 10% adults in India have reported mental health issues. Alarmingly, a survey of school students from India, as reported in the 2023-24 Economic Survey, also suggest increasing problems among adolescents and youth.

In the News

Lessons from the Pandemic of 2020

Reducing wasteful medical spending is a good goal, but it is not easy to achieve.

Why It's So Hard to Cut Waste in Health Care

By Amy Finkelstein

Cutting waste while preserving critically important treatment is the holy grail of health care policy. The coronavirus pandemic has shown why that goal has been so stubbornly difficult to achieve.

One of the pandemic's startling effects is that despite the overwhelming need for Covid-19 treatments and vaccinations, health care spending in the United States has declined sharply. That's because people have been reluctant or unable to get medical care that isn't connected to the coronavirus. My own calculations, based on government data, show that overall total care expenditures dropped 10 percent in the first nine months of 2020, compared with the same period a year earlier.

This indiscriminate reduction in spending closely resembles the unfortunate effects of an array of policies over the past half-century intended to reduce unnecessary medical care. These too cut essential and inessential care alike.

Consider what has happened during the pandemic. Essential health care visits have plummeted: Hospital admissions for severe heart attacks and strokes and visits for routine childhood vaccinations have fallen sharply. Those reductions could have grave consequences.

At the same time, some types of care that are often overused—and can produce unnecessary follow-up treatments, anxiety and spending—also declined in frequency during the pandemic. This includes radiological scans and routine cancer screenings. Indeed, a broad spectrum of medical care has declined at roughly comparable rates, as patients avoided in-person visits and medical providers cut availability.

In short, the pandemic has pushed two basic levers used in strategies to limit wasteful medical care. These strategies aim to decrease patient demand and to restrict the availability of treatment by health care providers. And they tend to have indiscriminate effects, reducing treatment that is critical, along with care that is not essential.

The economic importance of reducing wasteful spending is hard to overstate. The health care sector accounts for almost one-fifth of the U.S. economy, and one-quarter or more of this spending is wasted, a range of studies have shown. Excessive administrative costs, high prices and inappropriate medical care are the three major culprits in wasteful spending, driving insurance premiums and taxes without helping patients.

For decades, the driving principle behind reducing needless medical care has been that if patients or their providers have financial "skin in the game," they will make prudent decisions. To encourage patients to make good decisions, insurers make them pay some share of their medical costs. High-deductible health insurance plans, in which the patient herself pays the first thousand (or more) dollars of any medical spending for the year, are one increasingly common example.

The economic theory is simple: If something becomes more expensive, people will buy less of it. And the empirical evidence is overwhelming: When patients have to pay more, they use less medical care.

The problem is they use less of all types of care. Introducing a high-deductible plan, for example, reduces scans for nonspecific low back pain and antibiotics for respiratory infections, as intended. But high deductibles also tend to reduce use of mental health services and of prescription drugs for managing chronic diabetes and high cholesterol, which can have negative consequences.

My own research shows covering uninsured individuals with Medicaid is a similarly blunt instrument for encouraging people to get critically important care. Medicaid increased preventive care, which was intended, but also increased emergency room visits, which was

While several disorders are already covered under PM-JAY, India also is developing a comprehensive National mental health program. Many health facilities are being upgraded to what are being called "Ayushman Arogya Mandirs" dedicated to provide mental health services. Primary health workers are also being trained under the program to deliver quality services in this domain. Also, a large scale tele mental health program is being rolled out with tele counselling being provided to lakhs of callers and a thrust is on increasing the employment of workers in the mental healthcare sub sector. Several programs like Rashtriya Kishor Swasthya Karyakram and Ayushman Bharat School Health and Wellness program are being developed to help adolescents, young adults and children to become aware about emotional and mental well beingwell-being.

not. Even more targeted insurance that lowers only the price of specific and valuable care has modest effects at best, in encouraging the desired outcome.

Similarly, financial incentives that encourage physicians and hospitals to refrain from superfluous treatments may also jettison some indispensable care. Traditionally, these providers were reimbursed piece-rate, billing separately for each test and procedure, so that the more they did, the more they were paid.

To encourage only essential care, there has been a widespread shift to paying a fixed fee for a patient, regardless of what treatment is provided. A hospital might be paid ₹25,000 for a patient's knee replacement, for example, and then have to absorb all the associated costs, including the hospital stay, surgeon's fees and post-discharge rehabilitative care. Or a network of health care providers might be paid ₹10,000 a year for all of a patient's health care needs.

That way, the medical provider is on the hook for the costs of treatment. But such incentives are a double-edged sword: What encourages cost-consciousness can discourage optimal care.

Countries around the world are grappling with these issues. A recent study of health care in 10 countries—including several with single-payer systems—concluded that, to one degree or another, they all are rife with inefficient and unnecessary care.

One reason it is so hard to trim waste is that physicians and regulators have already eliminated so many demonstrably harmful or useless treatments. Patients are no longer offered patent medicines, routine bloodlettings or lobotomies.

PAT GREENHOUSE/BOSTON GLOBE/GETTY IMAGES

Amy Finkelstein

Reducing unnecessary administrative costs and curbing high prices is similarly difficult. Some red tape is purposeless, but not all of it is. Lowering prices can imperil the availability of valuable treatment. An adage about advertising applies to health care: Half of spending is wasted; we just don't know which half.

Low-value doesn't mean no-value-ever. That's presumably why Choosing Wisely, a campaign to reduce unnecessary care, identified a large number of tests and procedures that patients and physicians should "question" but not eliminate. We don't "question" whether it's wise to stick a finger in an electric socket. We warn that you shouldn't do it. But most medical procedures are different. They are a matter of judgment.

Ordering a computerized tomography, or C.T., scan for a patient the first time she complains of a nondescript headache is generally not a wise move. Neither is getting married after a first date. But occasionally that unnecessary scan catches a life-threatening problem before it's too late much as, once in a while, a whirlwind marriage leads to happily-ever-after. Unlikely isn't the same as never, which can make it hard for a well-intentioned physician or a hopeless romantic to resist.

That doesn't mean we should stop trying to cut waste. But a simple, miracle cure for excising most unnecessary medical care? Don't buy it, with or without insurance coverage. ■

Source: New York Times, January 24, 2021.

Questions to Discuss

1. If you faced a larger co-pay when you visited a physician, would it change how often you sought medical care? Why or why not?
2. Are you good at judging when you need medical care and when it is best to let your body heal on its own? Give some examples.
3. How much do you trust your physician in deciding what tests to order? Why?

Ms. Finkelstein is an economics professor at M.I.T.

11.1g Managerial Economics of Mental Health

If mental health leads to absenteeism from work or education, it will be strongly correlated with decreases in productivity. As a result, it will have large costs associated with it in terms of loss in efficiency and overall increased healthcare expenses. If wages are paid based on marginal products of the workers, with a loss in productivity the true potential is not realized and the returns on the wages and salaries paid by the firm are not as expected. Consequently, to recover these losses or to prevent these losses, firms have incentives to provide employee wellness programs or alternately provide support or insurance coverage for treatment of mental health disorders. Firms will have to make sure not to view these as additional costs but as potential hedges against future losses in nthe face of changing complexities in the world of mental health illnesses.

11-2 Conclusion: The Policy Debate over Healthcare

This chapter introduced some of the facts and economic insights useful for understanding the market for healthcare. Most of these ideas are widely accepted by the economists who study healthcare. Despite this consensus, there is an ongoing debate among policymakers worldwide about the government's role in the healthcare system.

While those on the political left disagree about many things, most agree that a large government role is essential in healthcare. They often say that private insurance companies are inefficient and tend to put profit ahead of people. Some would like the government to offer people a **public option** in the healthcare system—that is, a government-run insurance program that any person can buy into instead of purchasing private insurance. Others would like to move toward a **single-payer** system in which the government pays for healthcare for everyone out of tax revenue, as the US Medicare now does for those age 65 and older. They point to Canada as a worthwhile example. Centralized systems run by intelligent administrators, they say, are best able to reduce administrative inefficiency, eliminate wasteful treatment, bargain with providers for lower costs, and allocate healthcare resources most equitably to where they are most needed.

The political right is also diverse, but it is fair to say that many people there would like to reduce the government's role in the healthcare system, as in many other spheres. They acknowledge that the market for health insurance needs to be regulated but would like the regulation to be less heavy-handed than it is now. They say that the best healthcare will arise if private insurers and providers openly compete for consumers. They fear that a centralized, government-run system would limit individual freedom, excessively ration care, and stifle innovation. In their view, Canada is an example of what could go wrong: Waiting times for medical procedures there can be uncomfortably long, and those who can afford it sometimes choose not to wait and instead seek treatment in the United States.

The debate over health policy is part of the larger debate over income inequality and the role of government. As Chapter 1 pointed out, society often faces a trade-off between equality and efficiency, and that fact looms large when discussing the provision of healthcare. Those on the political left generally want to achieve universal health coverage by providing government insurance or by subsidizing private insurance for households with lower incomes. But paying for these policies requires increased taxes on households with higher incomes, and those taxes are likely to distort incentives and shrink the size of the economic pie. Those on the political right emphasize the distortionary effects of taxes and income redistribution. They advocate more limited government and lower taxes and say this approach will expand the economic pie. But smaller government and less revenue mean fewer public resources to help those who struggle to get the healthcare they need.

This debate raises hard and important questions, and this chapter does not offer easy answers. But this introduction to health economics should give you a starting point for thinking through the many issues.

Chapter in a Nutshell

- The market for healthcare differs from most other markets in several ways. First, there are pervasive externalities, such as those associated with vaccination and medical research. Second, because consumers cannot easily gauge the quality of what they are buying, private and public institutions intervene to ensure that treatment is appropriate. Third, healthcare is often judged to be a right, leading to a government role to make sure that everyone has access to it.
- Spending on healthcare can be large and unpredictable, but health insurance reduces the financial risk that people face from a costly event. The problems of moral hazard and adverse selection, however, hinder the effectiveness of the market for health insurance. When people have insurance, either from a private company or a government program, the insurer establishes rules regarding financing, access, and payment.
- For the last decade, infant and maternal mortality has significantly come down in India.
- Over years, healthcare spending has grown substantially as a percentage of national income. The infrastructure in India has significantly grown and become more dense.
- The percentage of healthcare spending paid out of pocket, rather than by insurance, has declined substantially over time. Some economists say that reliance on insurance is excessive, exacerbating moral hazard and driving up healthcare costs. Government spending on healthcare has significantly gone up as a proportion of total health expenditure.

Key Concepts

moral hazard, p. 227 adverse selection, p. 227

Questions for Review

1. Give two examples of externalities in the healthcare system.
2. Explain moral hazard and adverse selection in the market for health insurance.
3. Describe the three sets of rules that are necessary in a healthcare market with an insurer.

Problems and Applications

1. Consider how health insurance affects the quantity of healthcare services performed. Suppose that the typical medical procedure costs ₹100, yet a person with health insurance pays only ₹20 out of pocket. An insurance company pays the remaining ₹80. (The insurance company recoups the ₹80 through premiums, but the premium a person pays does not depend on how many procedures that person chooses to undertake.)
   a. Draw the demand curve in the market for medical care. (In your diagram, the horizontal axis should represent the number of medical procedures.) Show the quantity of procedures demanded if each procedure has a price of ₹100.
   b. On your diagram, show the quantity of procedures demanded if consumers pay only ₹20 per procedure. If the cost of each procedure to society is truly ₹100 and if individuals have health insurance as described above, will the number of procedures performed maximize total surplus? Explain.
   c. Economists often blame the health insurance system for excessive use of medical care. Given your analysis, why might the use of care be viewed as "excessive"?
   d. What sort of policies might prevent this excessive use?
2. The Live-Long-and-Prosper Health Insurance Company charges ₹5,000 annually for a family insurance policy. The company's president suggests that the company raise the annual price to ₹6,000 to increase its profits. If the firm follows this suggestion, what economic problem might arise? Would the firm's pool of customers tend to become more or less healthy

on average? Would the company's profits necessarily increase?

3. Consider an example of the death spiral. An economy consists of five types of people in equal numbers with different pre-existing health problems. Here are their expected healthcare costs for the coming year:
A ₹1,000
B ₹2,000
C ₹3,000
D ₹4,000
E ₹5,000
   a. If all five types of people buy health insurance, what will be the average cost of healthcare paid by insurance companies? The companies need to cover this average cost, plus other expenses (including a normal profit) of ₹700. Assuming the companies must charge all consumers the same price, what price will that be?
   b. While all consumers would like to be insured to reduce uncertainty, they value this feature at ₹1,000 and, therefore, will forgo insurance if its price exceeds their own expected healthcare costs by more than ₹1,000. Which consumers will buy insurance at the price calculated in part (a)?
   c. For the new insured pool identified in part (b), what is the average cost of healthcare? When insurance companies observe this new average cost, what price will they charge for insurance?
   d. When consumers see the new price in part (c), which consumers will buy insurance?
   e. For the new insured pool identified in part (d), what is the average cost of healthcare? When insurance companies observe this new average cost, what price will they charge for insurance?
   f. When consumers see the new price in part (e), which consumers will buy insurance?
   g. For the new insured pool identified in part (f), what is the average cost of healthcare? When insurance companies observe this new average cost, what price will they charge for insurance?
   h. When consumers see the new price in part (g), which consumers will buy insurance? Does this outcome now look like an equilibrium?
   i. The value of insurance to each person is the ₹1,000 from reduced uncertainty plus the expected cost of healthcare; the cost of providing it is the insurance premium, and the consumer surplus is the excess of value over the premium. How much consumer surplus is derived from the insurance market as described in part (h)?
   j. Now suppose the government mandates that everyone buy insurance, so we return to the situation in part (a). What surplus would each consumer get? What is total surplus in the market?
   k. If this society voted on the insurance mandate and everyone voted based on their self-interest, how would the vote turn out?
   l. To ensure that everyone obeys the mandate, how large would the penalty for failing to buy insurance need to be?

QuickQuiz Answers

1. d 2. c 3. a 4. b 5. b 6. a 7. c

Chapter

12

The Costs of Production

The economy includes thousands of firms that produce the goods and services you enjoy every day: Maruti Suzuki produces automobiles, Syska produces lightbulbs, and Kellog's produces breakfast cereals. Some firms, like these three, are large; they employ thousands of workers and have thousands of stockholders who share the firms' profits. Other firms, such as the local general store, barbershop, or café, are small; they employ only a few workers and are owned by a single person or family.

Previous chapters used the supply curve to summarize firms' production decisions. According to the law of supply, firms are willing to produce and sell a greater quantity of a good when its price is higher. This response leads to an upward-sloping supply curve. For many questions, the law of supply is all you need to know about firm behavior.

This chapter and the ones that follow examine firm behavior in more detail. This topic will give you a better understanding of the decisions behind the supply curve. It will also introduce you to a part of economics called **industrial organization**—the study of how firms' decisions about prices and quantities depend on the

SHIFT DRIVE/SHUTTERSTOCK.COM; IRDARK/E+/GETTY IMAGES

market conditions they face. The town in which you live, for instance, may have several pizzerias but only one cable television company. This raises a key question: How does the number of firms affect the prices in a market and the efficiency of the market outcome? The field of industrial organization addresses this question.

Before turning to these issues, it's important to understand the costs of production. All firms, from Indigo Airlines to your local cafeteria, incur costs while making the goods and services they sell. As the coming chapters show, a firm's costs are a key determinant of its production and pricing decisions. This chapter defines the variables that economists use to measure such costs and considers the relationships among these variables.

A word of warning: This topic is a bit technical. To be frank, you might even call it boring. Hang in there. This material provides the foundation for the fascinating topics that follow.

12-1 What Are Costs?

Enter Chitwan's Cookie Factory. Chitwan, the owner, bakes irresistible cookies. To do so, she buys flour, sugar, chocolate chips, and other cookie ingredients. She also buys mixers and ovens and hires workers to run this equipment for her. She then sells the cookies to grateful consumers. Some of the issues that Chitwan faces in her business apply to all firms.

12-1a Total Revenue, Total Cost, and Profit

To understand the decisions a firm makes, let's begin by asking what it is trying to do. Chitwan may have started her firm because of an altruistic desire to provide the world with cookies or simply out of love for the cookie business, but the truth, in her case, is that she started it to make money. Economists typically assume that the goal of a firm is to maximize profit, and they find that this assumption works well in most cases.

total revenue
the amount a firm receives for the sale of its output

total cost
the market value of the inputs a firm uses in production

profit
total revenue minus total cost

What is a firm's profit? The amount that it receives for the sale of its output (cookies) is **total revenue**. The amount that it pays to buy inputs (flour, sugar, workers, ovens, and so forth) is **total cost**. As the business owner, Chitwan gets to keep any revenue above her costs. That is, a firm's **profit** equals its total revenue minus its total cost:

Profit 5 Total revenue 2 Total cost.

Chitwan wants to make her profit as large as possible.

To see how a firm maximizes profit, the first step is to measure its total revenue and total cost. Total revenue is simple: It is the quantity of output the firm produces multiplied by the sales price. If Chitwan produces 10,000 cookies and sells them at ₹2 a cookie, her total revenue is ₹20,000. The measurement of a firm's total cost, however, is more subtle.

12-1b Why Opportunity Costs Matter

When measuring costs at Chitwan's Cookie Factory or any other firm, keep in mind one of the principles from Chapter 1: The cost of something is what you give up to get it. Recall that the **opportunity cost** of an item refers to all the things that must be forgone to acquire it. When economists speak of a firm's cost of production, they include all the opportunity costs of making its output of goods and services.

Some of these opportunity costs are obvious. When Chitwan pays ₹1,000 for flour, that ₹1,000 is an opportunity cost because Chitwan can no longer use that ₹1,000 to buy something else. Similarly, when Chitwan hires workers to make the cookies, their wages are part of the firm's costs. Because these opportunity costs require the firm to pay out some money, they are called **explicit costs**.

explicit costs
input costs that require an outlay of money by the firm

implicit costs
input costs that do not require an outlay of money by the firm

By contrast, some of a firm's opportunity costs, called **implicit costs**, do not require a cash outlay. These costs may not be immediately obvious, but they are nonetheless meaningful. Imagine that Chitwan is good with computers and could earn ₹100 per hour working as a programmer. For every hour that she works at her cookie factory, she gives up ₹100 in programming income, and this forgone income is also part of her costs. The total cost of Chitwan's business is the sum of her explicit and implicit costs.

Economists and accountants analyze businesses differently. Economists are interested in how firms make production and pricing decisions. Because these decisions are based on both explicit and implicit costs, economists include both when measuring a firm's costs. But accountants keep track of the money that flows into and out of firms, so they measure the explicit costs but usually ignore the implicit ones.

The difference between the methods of economists and accountants is easy to see at Chitwan's Cookie Factory. When Chitwan gives up the opportunity to earn money as a programmer, her accountant will not count this as a cost of her cookie business. Because no money flows out of the business to pay for this cost, it never appears on the accountant's financial statements. An economist, however, will count the forgone income as a cost because it will affect the decisions that Chitwan makes in her cookie business. For example, if Chitwan's wage as a copyeditor rises from ₹100 to ₹300 per hour, she might decide that running her cookie business is too costly. She might choose to shut down the factory so she can work as a programmer.

12-1c The Cost of Capital Is an Opportunity Cost

An implicit cost of almost every business is the opportunity cost of the money—economists call it financial capital—that has been invested in it. Suppose, for instance, that Chitwan used ₹300,000 of her savings to buy the cookie factory. If she had instead left this money in a savings account that paid an interest rate of 5 percent, she would have earned ₹15,000 per year. To own her cookie factory, therefore, Chitwan has given up ₹15,000 a year in interest income. This forgone ₹15,000 is one of the implicit opportunity costs of Chitwan's business.

The cost of capital is a prime case in which economists and accountants view businesses differently. An economist views the ₹15,000 in interest income that Chitwan gives up every year as an implicit cost. Chitwan's accountant, however, will not show this ₹15,000 as a cost because no money flows out of the business to pay for it.

To further explore the difference between the methods of economists and accountants, let's change the example slightly. Suppose that Chitwan did not have the entire ₹300,000 to buy the factory but instead, used ₹100,000 of her own savings and borrowed ₹200,000 from a bank at an interest rate of 5 percent. Chitwan's accountant, who only measures explicit costs, will now count the ₹10,000 interest paid on the bank loan every year as a cost because this money flows out of the firm. By contrast, according to an economist, the opportunity cost of owning the business is still ₹15,000. The opportunity cost equals the interest on the bank loan (an explicit cost of ₹10,000) plus the forgone interest on savings (an implicit cost of ₹5,000).

12-1d Economists and Accountants Measure Profit Differently

economic profit
total revenue minus total cost, including both explicit and implicit costs

Now let's return to the firm's objective: profit. Economists and accountants measure this differently, too. An economist measures a firm's **economic profit** as its total

Figure 1

Economists versus Accountants

Because economists include all opportunity costs when analyzing a firm, while accountants measure only explicit costs, economic profit is smaller than accounting profit.

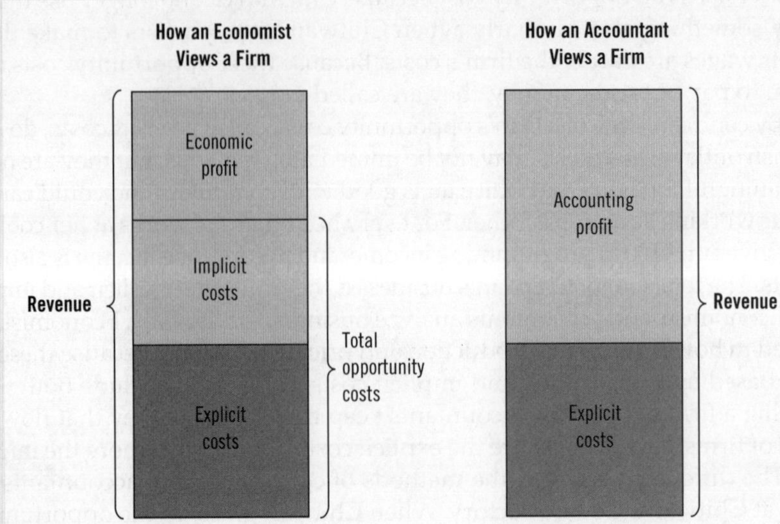

accounting profit
total revenue minus total explicit cost

revenue minus all its opportunity costs (explicit and implicit) of producing the goods and services sold. An accountant measures the firm's **accounting profit** as its total revenue minus only its explicit costs.

Figure 1 summarizes this difference. Notice that because the accountant ignores the implicit costs, accounting profit is larger than economic profit. For a business to be profitable from an economist's standpoint, total revenue must exceed all the opportunity costs, both explicit and implicit.

Economic profit is an important concept because it motivates the firms that supply goods and services. As we will see, a firm that makes positive economic profit will stay in business. It is covering all its opportunity costs and has some revenue left to reward the firm's owners. When a firm makes economic losses (that is, when economic profits are negative), it is failing to bring in enough revenue to cover all the costs of production. Unless conditions change, the owners will eventually close the business and exit the industry. To understand business decisions, keep an eye on economic profit.

Quick**Quiz**

1. Farmer McDonald gives banjo lessons for ₹20 per hour. One day, he spends 10 hours planting ₹100 worth of seeds on his farm. What total cost has he incurred?
   a. ₹100
   b. ₹200
   c. ₹300
   d. ₹400

2. Xavier opens a lemonade stand for two hours. He spends ₹10 for ingredients and sells ₹60 worth of lemonade. In the same two hours, he could have mowed his neighbor's lawn for ₹40. Xavier earns an accounting profit of ________ and an economic profit of ________.
   a. ₹50; ₹10
   b. ₹90; ₹50
   c. ₹10; ₹50
   d. ₹50; ₹90

Answers are at the end of the chapter.

12-2 Production and Costs

Firms incur costs when they buy inputs to produce the goods and services they plan to sell. This section examines the link between a firm's production process and its total cost. Once again, consider Chitwan's Cookie Factory.

The analysis that follows makes a simplifying assumption: The size of Chitwan's factory is fixed, and Chitwan can vary the quantity of cookies produced only by changing the number of workers she employs. This assumption is realistic in the short run but not in the long run. That is, Chitwan cannot build a larger factory overnight, but she could do so over the next year or two. This analysis, therefore, describes the production decisions that Chitwan faces in the short run. The relationship between costs and time horizon is examined more fully later in the chapter.

12-2a The Production Function

Table 1 shows how the quantity of cookies produced per hour at Chitwan's factory depends on the number of workers. As you can see in columns (1) and (2), if there are no workers in the factory, Chitwan produces no cookies. When there is 1 worker, she produces 50 cookies. When there are 2 workers, she produces 90 cookies and so on. Panel (a) of Figure 2 presents a graph of these two columns of numbers. The number of workers is on the horizontal axis, and the number of cookies produced is on the vertical axis. This relationship between the quantity of inputs (workers) and quantity of output (cookies) is called the **production function**.

production function the relationship between the quantity of inputs used to make a good and the quantity of output of that good

Table 1

A Production Function and Total Cost: Chitwan's Cookie Factory

(1) Number of Workers	(2) Output (quantity of cookies produced per hour)	(3) Marginal Product of Labor	(4) Cost of Factory	(5) Cost of Workers	(6) Total Cost of Inputs (cost of factory + cost of workers)
0	0		₹30	₹0	₹30
		50			
1	50		30	10	40
		40			
2	90		30	20	50
		30			
3	120		30	30	60
		20			
4	140		30	40	70
		10			
5	150		30	50	80
		5			
6	155		30	60	90

Figure 2

Chitwan's Production Function and Total-Cost Curve

The production function in panel (a) shows the relationship between the number of workers hired and the quantity of output produced. Here, the number of workers hired (on the horizontal axis) is from column (1) in Table 1, and the quantity of output (on the vertical axis) is from column (2). The production function gets flatter as the number of workers increases, reflecting diminishing marginal product. The total-cost curve in panel (b) shows the relationship between the quantity of output and total cost of production. Here, the quantity of output produced (on the horizontal axis) is from column (2) in Table 1, and the total cost (on the vertical axis) is from column (6). The total-cost curve gets steeper as the quantity of output increases because of diminishing marginal product.

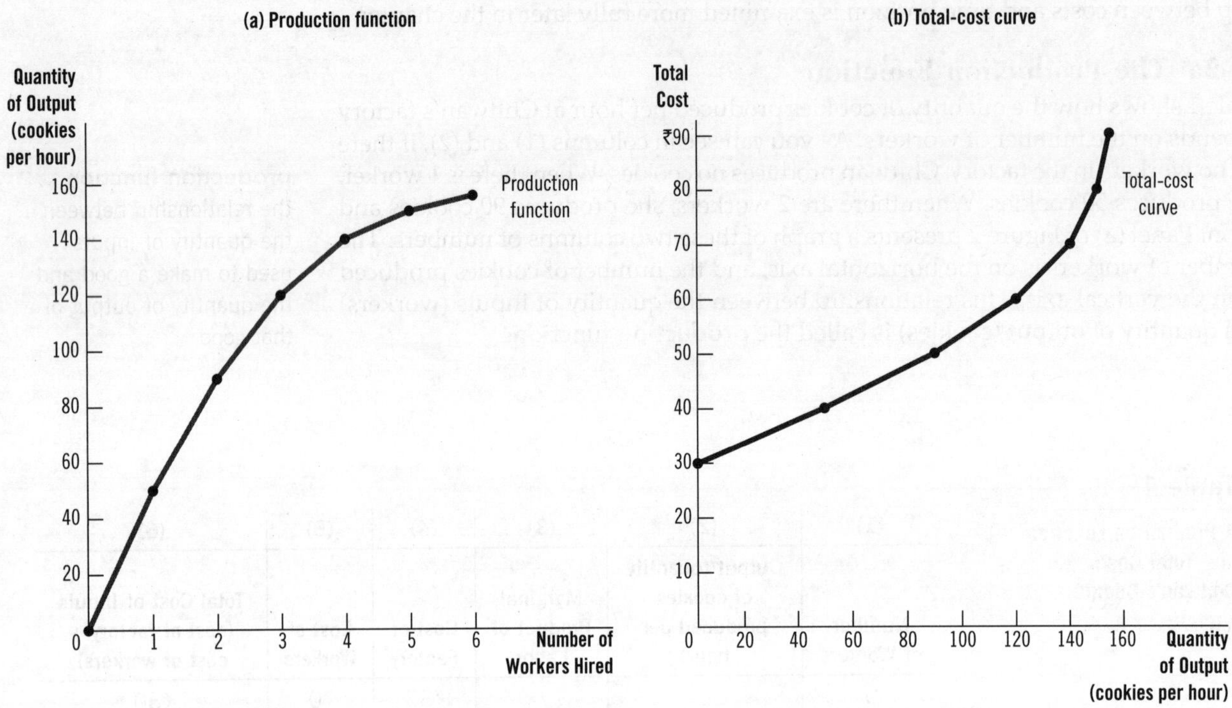

marginal product
the increase in output that arises from an additional unit of input

One of the principles in Chapter 1 is that rational people think at the margin. As future chapters show, this idea is the key to understanding the decisions a firm makes about how many workers to hire and how much output to produce. To take a step toward understanding these decisions, column (3) in the table gives the marginal product of a worker. The **marginal product** of any input in the production process is the change in the quantity of output obtained from one additional unit of that input. When the number of workers goes from 1 to 2, cookie production increases from 50 to 90, so the marginal product of the second worker is 40 cookies. When the number of workers goes from 2 to 3, cookie production increases from 90 to 120, so the marginal product of the third worker is 30 cookies. In the table, the marginal product is shown halfway between two rows because it represents the change in output as the number of workers increases from one level to another.

Notice that as the number of workers increases, the marginal product declines. The second worker has a marginal product of 40 cookies, the third has a marginal product of 30 cookies, and the fourth has a marginal product of 20 cookies. This property is called **diminishing marginal product**. At first, when there are only a few workers at the factory, they have easy access to the kitchen equipment. As Chitwan increases hiring, the workers must share equipment and deal with more crowded conditions. Eventually, the kitchen becomes so overcrowded that workers get in each other's way. Hence, as more workers are hired, each extra worker contributes fewer additional cookies to total production.

diminishing marginal product
the property whereby the marginal product of an input declines as the quantity of the input increases

Diminishing marginal product is apparent in Figure 2. The production function's slope ("rise over run") measures the change in Chitwan's output of cookies ("rise") for each additional input of labor ("run"). That is, the slope of the production function measures the marginal product. As the number of workers increases, the marginal product declines, and the production function becomes flatter.

12-2b From the Production Function to the Total-Cost Curve

Columns (4), (5), and (6) in Table 1 show Chitwan's cost of producing cookies. In this example, the cost of Chitwan's factory is ₹30 per hour, and the cost of hiring a worker is ₹10 per hour. If she hires 1 worker, her total cost is ₹40 per hour. If she hires 2, her total cost is ₹50 per hour, and so on. This information ties things together. The table shows how the number of workers hired determines the quantity of cookies produced and the total cost of production.

The goal of the next several chapters is to study firms' production and pricing decisions. For this purpose, the most important relationship in Table 1 is between quantity produced [in column (2)] and total cost [in column (6)]. Panel (b) of Figure 2 graphs these two columns of data with quantity produced on the horizontal axis and total cost on the vertical axis. This graph is called the **total-cost curve**.

Now compare the total-cost curve in panel (b) with the production function in panel (a). These two curves are opposite sides of the same coin. The total-cost curve grows steeper as the amount produced rises, while the production function becomes flatter as production rises. These changes in slope occur for the same reason. High production of cookies means that Chitwan's kitchen is crowded with workers. In this case, because of diminishing marginal product, each additional worker adds little to production. That's why the production function is relatively flat. But flip this logic around: When the kitchen is crowded, producing an additional cookie requires a lot more labor, which is costly. Therefore, when the quantity produced is large, the total-cost curve is relatively steep.

Quick**Quiz**

3. Farmer Kishen faces diminishing marginal product. If he plants no seeds on her farm, he gets no harvest. If he plants 1 bag of seeds, he gets 3 bushels of wheat. If he plants 2 bags, he gets 5 bushels. If he plants 3 bags, he gets
   a. 6 bushels.
   b. 7 bushels.
   c. 8 bushels.
   d. 9 bushels.

4. Diminishing marginal product explains why, as output increases,
   a. the production function and total-cost curve both get steeper.
   b. the production function and total-cost curve both get flatter.
   c. the production function gets steeper, and the total-cost curve gets flatter.
   d. the production function gets flatter, and the total-cost curve gets steeper.

Answers are at the end of the chapter.

12-3 The Many Measures of Cost

The analysis of Chitwan's Cookie Factory showed how a firm's total cost reflects its production function. From data on total cost, we can derive several related measures of cost that will be later useful in analyzing production and pricing decisions. Now, consider the example in Table 2, which presents cost data on Chitwan's neighbor—Charan's Coffee Shop.

Column (1) in the table shows the number of cups of coffee that Charan might produce, ranging from 0 to 10 cups per hour. Column (2) shows Charan's total cost of producing coffee. Figure 3 plots Charan's total-cost curve. The quantity of coffee [from column (1)] is on the horizontal axis, and total cost [from column (2)] is on the vertical axis. Charan's total-cost curve has a shape like Chitwan's. In particular,

Table 2

The Various Measures of Cost: Charan's Coffee Shop

(1) Output (cups of coffee per hour)	(2) Total Cost	(3) Fixed Cost	(4) Variable Cost	(5) Average Fixed Cost	(6) Average Variable Cost	(7) Average Total Cost	(8) Marginal Cost
0	₹3.00	₹3.00	₹0.00	—	—	—	
							₹0.30
1	3.30	3.00	0.30	₹3.00	₹0.30	₹3.30	
							0.50
2	3.80	3.00	0.80	1.50	0.40	1.90	
							0.70
3	4.50	3.00	1.50	1.00	0.50	1.50	
							0.90
4	5.40	3.00	2.40	0.75	0.60	1.35	
							1.10
5	6.50	3.00	3.50	0.60	0.70	1.30	
							1.30
6	7.80	3.00	4.80	0.50	0.80	1.30	
							1.50
7	9.30	3.00	6.30	0.43	0.90	1.33	
							1.70
8	11.00	3.00	8.00	0.38	1.00	1.38	
							1.90
9	12.90	3.00	9.90	0.33	1.10	1.43	
							2.10
10	15.00	3.00	12.00	0.30	1.20	1.50	

Figure 3

Charan's Total Cost Curve

Here, the quantity of output produced (on the horizontal axis) is from column (1) in Table 2, and the total cost (on the vertical axis) is from column (2). As in Figure 2, the total-cost curve gets steeper as the quantity of output increases, reflecting diminishing marginal product.

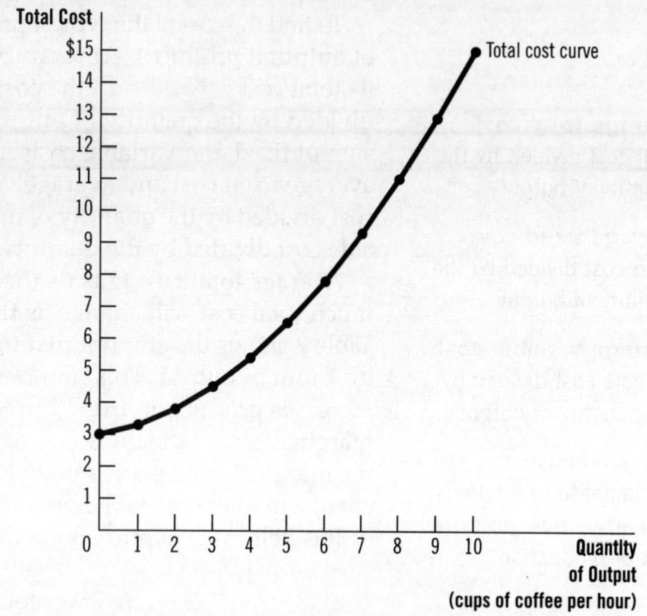

it becomes steeper as the quantity produced rises, which (as we have discussed) reflects diminishing marginal product.

12-3a Fixed and Variable Costs

Charan's total cost can be divided into two types. **Fixed costs** do not vary with the quantity of output produced. They are incurred even if the firm produces nothing at all. Charan's fixed costs include rent, which is the same regardless of how much coffee he produces. Similarly, if Charan needs to hire a full-time bookkeeper to pay bills, regardless of the quantity of coffee produced, the bookkeeper's salary is a fixed cost. The third column in Table 2 shows Charan's fixed cost, which in this example is ₹3.00.

fixed costs
costs that do not vary with the quantity of output produced

On the other hand, **variable costs** change as the firm alters the quantity of output produced. Charan's variable costs include the cost of coffee beans, milk, sugar, and paper cups: The more coffee Charan produces, the more of these items he needs to buy. Similarly, if Charan has to hire more workers to make more cups of coffee, the salaries of these workers are variable costs. Column (4) in the table shows Charan's variable cost. The variable cost is 0 if he produces nothing, ₹0.30 if he produces 1 cup of coffee, ₹0.80 if he produces 2 cups, and so on.

variable costs
costs that vary with the quantity of output produced

A firm's total cost is the sum of fixed and variable costs. In Table 2, total cost in column (2) equals fixed cost in column (3) plus variable cost in column (4).

12-3b Average and Marginal Cost

As the owner, Charan decides how much to produce. When making this decision, he will want to consider how the level of production affects his costs. Charan might ask his production supervisor the following two questions about the cost of producing coffee:

- How much does it cost to make the typical cup of coffee?
- How much does it cost to increase production of coffee by 1 cup?

These questions might seem to have the same answer, but they do not. Both answers are important for understanding how firms make production decisions.

To find the cost of the typical unit produced, divide the firm's costs by the quantity of output it produces. For example, if the firm produces 2 cups of coffee per hour, its total cost is ₹3.80, and the cost of the typical cup is ₹3.80/2, or ₹1.90. Total cost divided by the quantity of output is **average total cost**. Because total cost is the sum of fixed and variable costs, average total cost can be expressed as the sum of average fixed cost and average variable cost. **Average fixed cost** equals the fixed cost divided by the quantity of output, and **average variable cost** equals the variable cost divided by the quantity of output.

average total cost
total cost divided by the quantity of output

average fixed cost
fixed cost divided by the quantity of output

average variable cost
variable cost divided by the quantity of output

marginal cost
the increase in total cost that arises from an extra unit of production

Average total cost tells us the cost of the typical unit, but it does not say how much total cost will change as the firm alters its production level. Column (8) in Table 2 shows the amount that total cost rises when the firm increases production by 1 unit of output. This number is called **marginal cost**. For example, if Charan increases production from 2 to 3 cups, total cost rises from ₹3.80 to ₹4.50, so the marginal cost of the third cup of coffee is ₹4.50 minus ₹3.80, or ₹0.70. In the table, the marginal cost appears halfway between any two rows because it represents the change in total cost as the quantity of output increases from one level to another.

It is helpful to express these definitions mathematically:

$$\text{Average total cost} = \text{Total cost/Quantity}$$
$$ATC = TC/Q$$

and

$$\text{Marginal cost} = \text{Change in total cost/Change in quantity}$$
$$MC = \Delta TC/\Delta Q.$$

Here, Δ, the Greek letter delta, represents the change in a variable. These equations show how average total cost and marginal cost are derived from total cost. **Average total cost tells us the cost of a typical unit of output if total cost is divided evenly over all the units produced. Marginal cost tells us the increase in total cost that arises from producing an additional unit of output.** The next chapter explains why business managers like Charan need to keep in mind the concepts of average total cost and marginal cost when deciding how much of their product to supply to the market.

12-3c Cost Curves and Their Shapes

Just as graphs of supply and demand were useful when analyzing the behavior of markets, graphs of average and marginal cost will help when analyzing the behavior of firms. Figure 4 graphs Charan's costs using the data from Table 2. The horizontal axis measures the quantity the firm produces, and the vertical axis measures marginal and average costs. The graph shows four curves: average total cost (*ATC*), average fixed cost (*AFC*), average variable cost (*AVC*), and marginal cost (*MC*).

The cost curves shown here for Charan's Coffee Shop have some features that are common to the cost curves of many firms in the economy. Note three features in particular: the shape of the marginal-cost curve, the shape of the average-total-cost curve, and the relationship between marginal cost and average total cost.

Rising Marginal Cost Charan's marginal cost rises as the quantity of output produced increases. This upward slope reflects diminishing marginal product. When Charan produces a small quantity of coffee, he has few workers, and much of his

Figure 4

Charan's Average-Cost and Marginal-Cost Curves

This figure shows the average total cost (*ATC*), average fixed cost (*AFC*), average variable cost (*AVC*), and marginal cost (*MC*) for Charan's Coffee Shop. These curves are all obtained by graphing the data in Table 2. They show three common features: (1) Marginal cost rises with the quantity of output. (2) The average-total-cost curve is U-shaped. (3) The marginal-cost curve crosses the average-total-cost curve at the minimum of average total cost.

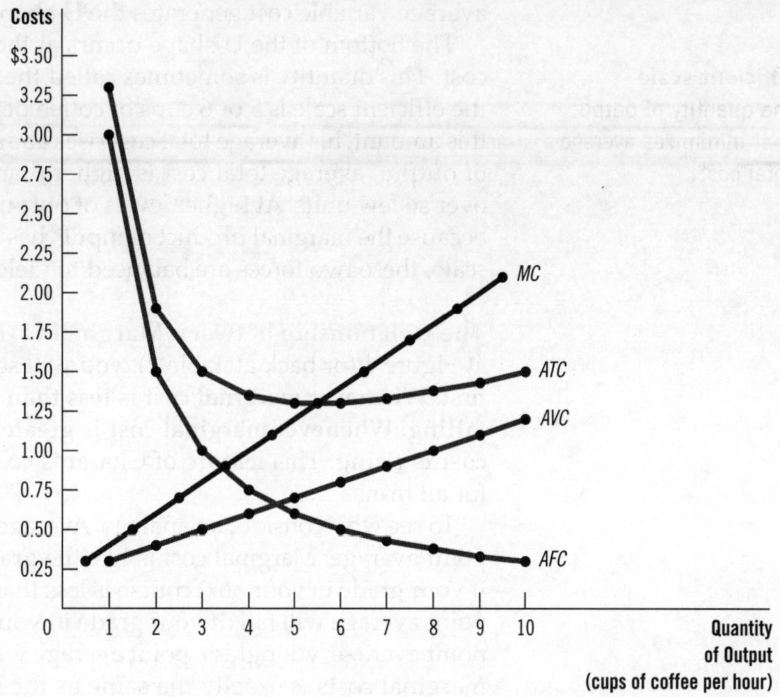

equipment isn't being used. Because he can easily put these idle resources to use, the marginal product of an extra worker is large, and the marginal cost of producing an extra cup of coffee is small. But when Charan produces a large quantity of coffee, his shop has a lot of workers, and his equipment is busy. If Charan produces more coffee by adding new workers, they will operate in crowded conditions and may need to wait to use the equipment. Therefore, when the quantity of coffee produced is already high, the marginal product of an extra worker is low, and the marginal cost of producing an extra cup of coffee is large.

U-Shaped Average Total Cost Charan's average-total-cost curve in Figure 4 is U-shaped: It first falls and then rises. To understand why it takes this shape, remember that average total cost is the sum of average fixed cost and average variable cost. Average fixed cost declines as output rises because the fixed cost is getting spread over a larger number of units. But average variable cost usually rises as output increases because of diminishing marginal product.

The U shape occurs because average total cost reflects the shapes of both average fixed cost and average variable cost. At very low levels of output, such as 1 or 2 cups per hour, average total cost is very high. Even though average variable cost is low, average fixed cost is high because the fixed cost is spread over only a few units. As output increases, the fixed cost is spread over more units. Average fixed cost declines rapidly at first and then more slowly. As a result, average total cost also declines until the firm's output reaches 5 cups of coffee per hour, when average total cost is ₹1.30 per cup. When the firm produces more than 6 cups per hour, however, the increase in average variable cost becomes the dominant force, and average total cost starts rising. The tug of war between average fixed cost and average variable cost generates the U-shape in average total cost.

efficient scale
the quantity of output that minimizes average total cost

The bottom of the U-shape occurs at the quantity that minimizes average total cost. This quantity is sometimes called the **efficient scale** of the firm. For Charan, the efficient scale is 5 or 6 cups of coffee per hour. If he produces more or less than this amount, his average total cost rises above the minimum of ₹1.30. At lower levels of output, average total cost is higher than ₹1.30 because the fixed cost is spread over so few units. At higher levels of output, average total cost is higher than ₹1.30 because the marginal product of inputs has diminished significantly. At the efficient scale, these two forces are balanced to yield the lowest average total cost.

The Relationship between Marginal Cost and Average Total Cost If you look at Figure 4 (or back at Table 2), you will see something that may be surprising at first. **Whenever marginal cost is less than average total cost, average total cost is falling. Whenever marginal cost is greater than average total cost, average total cost is rising.** This feature of Charan's cost curves is not a coincidence: It is true for all firms.

To see why, consider an analogy. Average total cost is like your cumulative grade point average. Marginal cost is like the grade you get in the next course you take. If your grade in your next course is less than your grade point average, your grade point average will fall. If your grade in your next course is higher than your grade point average, your grade point average will rise. The mathematics of average and marginal costs is exactly the same as the mathematics of average and marginal grades.

This relationship between average total cost and marginal cost has an important corollary: **The marginal-cost curve crosses the average-total-cost curve at its minimum.** Why? At low levels of output, marginal cost is below average total cost, so average total cost is falling. But after the two curves cross, marginal cost rises above average total cost. As a result, average total cost must start to rise at this level of output. That's why this point of intersection is the minimum of average total cost. As the next chapter shows, minimum average total cost plays a central role in the analysis of competitive firms.

12-3d Typical Cost Curves

In the examples so far, the firms have exhibited diminishing marginal product and rising marginal cost at all levels of output. This simplifying assumption was useful because it allowed us to focus on the features of cost curves that are most important in analyzing firm behavior. Yet actual firms are often more complex. In many businesses, marginal product does not start to fall immediately after the first worker is hired. Depending on the production process, the second or third worker might have a higher marginal product than the first because a team of workers can divide tasks and work more productively than one person. A firm with this pattern would have increasing marginal product for a while before diminishing marginal product set in.

Figure 5 shows the cost curves for such a firm, including average total cost (*ATC*), average fixed cost (*AFC*), average variable cost (*AVC*), and marginal cost (*MC*). At low levels of output, the firm experiences increasing marginal product, and the marginal-cost curve falls. Eventually, the firm starts to experience diminishing marginal product, and the marginal-cost curve starts to rise. This combination of increasing then diminishing marginal product also makes the average-variable-cost curve U-shaped.

Figure 5

Cost Curves for a Typical Firm

Many firms experience increasing marginal product before diminishing marginal product. As a result, they have cost curves shaped like those in this figure. Notice that marginal cost and average variable cost fall for a while before starting to rise.

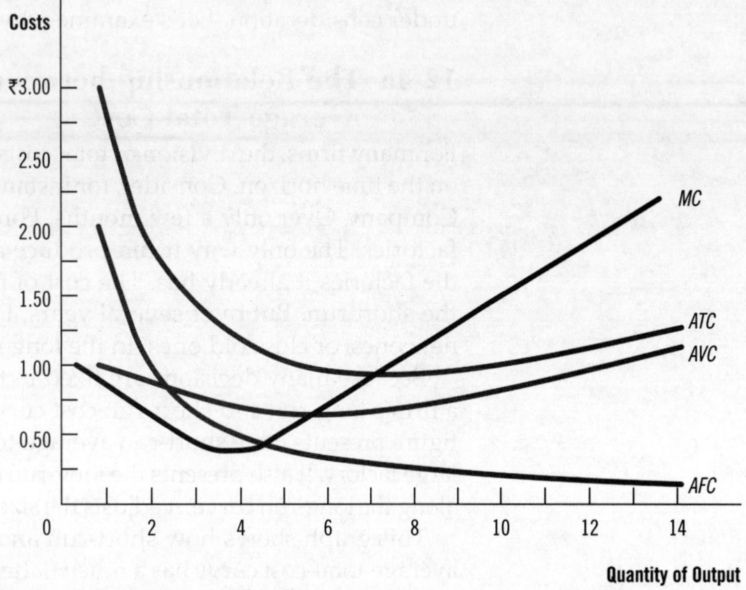

Despite these differences, the cost curves in Figure 5 and those in the previous example share three important properties:

- Marginal cost eventually rises with the quantity of output.
- The average-total-cost curve is U-shaped.
- The marginal-cost curve crosses the average-total-cost curve at the minimum of average total cost.

Quick**Quiz**

5. A firm is producing 1,000 units at a total cost of ₹5,000. When it increases production to 1,001 units, its total cost rises to ₹5,008. For this firm,
   a. marginal cost is ₹5, and average variable cost is ₹8.
   b. marginal cost is ₹8, and average variable cost is ₹5.
   c. marginal cost is ₹5, and average total cost is ₹8.
   d. marginal cost is ₹8, and average total cost is ₹5.

6. A firm is producing 20 units with an average total cost of ₹25 and a marginal cost of ₹15. If it increases production to 21 units, which of the following must occur?
   a. Marginal cost will decrease.
   b. Marginal cost will increase.
   c. Average total cost will decrease.
   d. Average total cost will increase.

7. The government imposes a ₹1,000 per year license fee on all pizza restaurants. As a result, which cost curves shift?
   a. average total cost and marginal cost
   b. average total cost and average fixed cost
   c. average variable cost and marginal cost
   d. average variable cost and average fixed cost

Answers are at the end of the chapter.

12-4 Costs in the Short Run and in the Long Run

Earlier in this chapter, we noted that a firm's costs might depend on the time horizon under consideration. Let's examine why this is the case.

12-4a The Relationship between Short-Run and Long-Run Average Total Cost

For many firms, the division of total costs between fixed and variable costs depends on the time horizon. Consider, for instance, a car manufacturer such as Ford Motor Company. Over only a few months, Ford cannot adjust the number or sizes of its factories. The only way it can produce additional cars is to hire more workers at the factories it already has. The cost of these factories is, therefore, a fixed cost in the short run. But over several years, Ford can expand its factories' sizes, build new ones, or close old ones. In the long run, its factories represent a variable cost.

Because many decisions are fixed in the short run but variable in the long run, a firm's long-run and short-run cost curves differ. Figure 6 shows an example. The figure presents three short-run average-total-cost curves—for a small, medium, and large factory. It also presents the long-run average-total-cost curve. As the firm moves along the long-run curve, it adjusts the size of the factory to the quantity of production.

This graph shows how short-run and long-run costs are related. The long-run average-total-cost curve has a much flatter U-shape than the short-run average-total-cost curve. In addition, all the short-run curves lie on or above the long-run curve. This is because firms have greater flexibility in the long run. In essence, in the long run, the firm gets to choose which short-run curve it wants. But in the short run, it has to use whatever short-run curve it already has, determined by decisions made in the past.

The figure shows how a change in production alters costs over different time horizons. When Ford wants to increase production from 1,000 to 1,200 cars per day, it has no choice in the short run but to hire more workers at its existing medium-sized

Figure 6

Average Total Cost in the Short and Long Runs

Because fixed costs are variable in the long run, the average-total-cost curve in the short run differs from the average-total-cost curve in the long run.

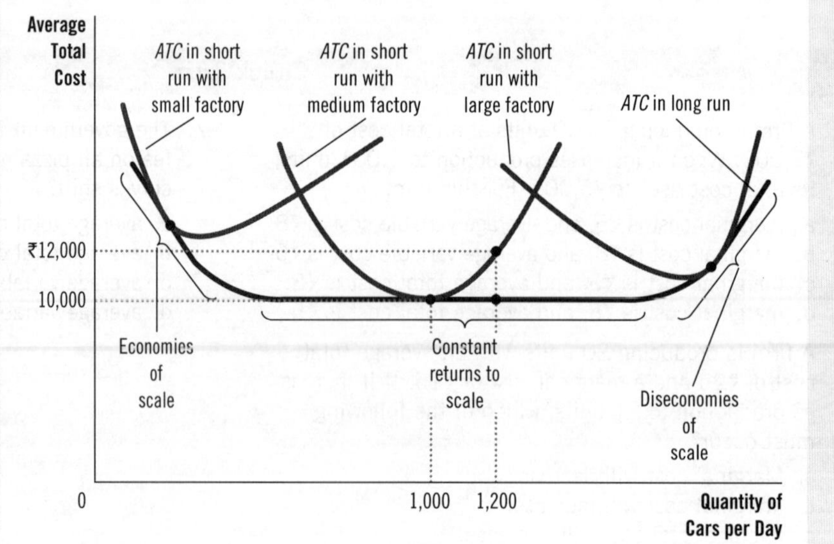

factory. Because of diminishing marginal product, average total cost rises from ₹10,000 to ₹12,000 per car. In the long run, however, Ford can expand both the size of the factory and its workforce, and average total cost returns to ₹10,000.

How long does it take a firm to get to the long run? It depends on the firm. A major manufacturer, such as a car company, may need a year or more to build a larger factory. But a person running a coffee shop can buy another coffee maker within a few days. There is no single answer to how long it takes a firm to adjust its production facilities.

12-4b Economies and Diseconomies of Scale

The shape of the long-run average-total-cost curve conveys important information about a firm's production processes. In particular, it tells us how costs vary with the scale—that is, the size—of a firm's operations. When long-run average total cost declines as output increases, there are said to be **economies of scale**. When the opposite occurs and long-run average total cost rises as output increases, there are **diseconomies of scale**. And when long-run average total cost does not vary with the level of output, there are **constant returns to scale**. In Figure 6, Ford has economies of scale at low levels of output, constant returns to scale at intermediate levels of output, and diseconomies of scale at high levels of output.

economies of scale
the property whereby long-run average total cost falls as the quantity of output increases

diseconomies of scale
the property whereby long-run average total cost rises as the quantity of output increases

constant returns to scale
the property whereby long-run average total cost stays the same as the quantity of output changes

What might cause economies or diseconomies of scale? Economies of scale often arise because higher production levels allow **specialization** among workers, which enables them to become better at specific tasks. For instance, if Ford hires a large number of workers and produces many cars, it can reduce costs using modern assembly-line production. Diseconomies of scale can arise because of **coordination problems** that often occur in large organizations. The more cars Ford produces, the more stretched the management team becomes, and the less effective the managers become at keeping costs down.

This analysis shows why long-run average-total-cost curves are often U-shaped. At low levels of production, the firm benefits from increased size because it can take

FYI Lessons from a Pin Factory

"Jack of all trades, master of none." This adage means that a person who tries to do everything ends up doing nothing very well, and it helps explain the shapes of cost curves. If a firm wants its workers to be as productive as possible, it should expect each worker to master a limited number of tasks. But this organization of work is possible only if a firm employs many workers and produces a large quantity of output.

In his book *The Wealth of Nations*, Adam Smith described a visit he made to a pin factory. Smith was impressed by the specialization among the workers and the resulting economies of scale. He wrote,

> One man draws out the wire, another straightens it, a third cuts it, a fourth points it, a fifth grinds it at the top for receiving the head; to make the head requires two or three distinct operations; to put it on is a peculiar business; to whiten it is another; it is even a trade by itself to put them into paper.

Smith reported that because of this specialization, the factory produced thousands of pins per worker every day. He conjectured that if the workers had chosen to work separately, rather than as a team of specialists, "they certainly could not each of them make twenty, perhaps not one pin a day." Because of specialization, a large pin factory could achieve higher output per worker and lower average cost per pin than a small factory.

The specialization that Smith observed in the pin factory is common in the modern economy. If you want to build a house, you could do all the work yourself. But most people these days turn to a builder, who in turn hires carpenters, plumbers, electricians, painters, and people in many other trades. These workers become better at particular jobs than if they were generalists. The use of specialization to achieve economies of scale is one reason modern societies are as prosperous as they are. ■

advantage of greater specialization, and coordination problems are not yet acute. At high levels of production, the benefits of specialization have already been realized, and coordination problems become more severe as the firm grows larger. As a result, long-run average total cost is falling at low levels of production because of increasing specialization and rising at high levels of production because of growing coordination problems.

Quick**Quiz**

8. If a higher level of production allows workers to specialize in particular tasks, a firm will likely exhibit ______ of scale and ______ average total cost.
   a. economies; falling
   b. economies; rising
   c. diseconomies; falling
   d. diseconomies; rising

9. If Boeing produces 9 jets per month, its long-run total cost is ₹9 million per month. If it produces 10 jets per month, its long-run total cost is ₹11 million per month. Boeing exhibits
   a. rising marginal cost.
   b. falling marginal cost.
   c. economies of scale.
   d. diseconomies of scale.

Answers are at the end of the chapter.

12-5 Conclusion

This chapter has developed tools to study how firms make production and pricing decisions. You should now understand what economists mean by the term **costs** and how costs vary with the quantity of output a firm produces. Table 3 summarizes some of the definitions we have encountered.

By themselves, a firm's cost curves do not tell us what decisions the firm will make. But they are a key component of that decision, as the next chapter shows.

Table 3

The Many Types of Cost: A Summary

Term	Definition	Mathematical Description
Explicit costs	Costs that require an outlay of money by the firm	
Implicit costs	Costs that do not require an outlay of money by the firm	
Fixed costs	Costs that do not vary with the quantity of output produced	FC
Variable costs	Costs that vary with the quantity of output produced	VC
Total cost	The market value of all the inputs that a firm uses in production	$TC = FC + VC$
Average fixed cost	Fixed cost divided by the quantity of output	$AFC = FC/Q$
Average variable cost	Variable cost divided by the quantity of output	$AVC = VC/Q$
Average total cost	Total cost divided by the quantity of output	$ATC = TC/Q$
Marginal cost	The increase in total cost that arises from an extra unit of production	$MC = \Delta TC/\Delta Q$

The Harappan Farm produces a quantity of milk, *Q*, and sells each unit at the market price, *P*. The farm's total revenue is $P \times Q$. For example, if a gallon of milk sells for ₹6 and the farm sells 1,000 gallons, its total revenue is ₹6,000.

Because the Harappan Farm is small compared with the world market for milk, it takes the price given by the market. This means that the price does not depend on how much milk the Harappan Farm produces and sells. If the Harappans double what they produce to 2,000 gallons, the price remains the same, and their total revenue doubles to ₹12,000. Total revenue is proportional to output.

Table 1 shows the revenue for the Harappan Family Dairy Farm. Columns (1) and (2) show the amount of output the farm produces and the price at which it sells its output. Column (3) is the farm's total revenue. The table assumes that the price of milk is ₹6 a gallon, so total revenue is ₹6 times the number of gallons.

Just as the concepts of average and marginal were useful in the preceding chapter when analyzing costs, they are also useful when discussing revenue. To see what these concepts reveal, consider two questions:

- How much revenue does the farm receive for the typical gallon of milk?
- How much additional revenue does the farm receive if it increases the production of milk by 1 gallon?

Columns (4) and (5) in Table 1 answer these questions.

Table 1

Total, Average, and Marginal Revenue for a Competitive Firm

(1) Quantity (*Q*)	(2) Price (*P*)	(3) Total Revenue ($TR = P \times Q$)	(4) Average Revenue ($AR = TR / Q$)	(5) Marginal Revenue ($MR = \Delta TR / \Delta Q$)
1 gallon	₹6	₹6	₹6	
				₹6
2	6	12	6	
				6
3	6	18	6	
				6
4	6	24	6	
				6
5	6	30	6	
				6
6	6	36	6	
				6
7	6	42	6	
				6
8	6	48	6	

average revenue total revenue divided by the quantity sold

Column (4) in the table shows **average revenue**, which is total revenue [from column (3)] divided by the amount of output [from column (1)]. Average revenue is what a firm receives for the typical unit sold. Table 1 shows that average revenue equals ₹6, the price of a gallon of milk. This illustrates a general lesson that applies to all firms, competitive or not. Average revenue is total revenue ($P \times Q$) divided by quantity (Q). **Therefore, for all types of firms, average revenue equals the price of the good.**

marginal revenue the change in total revenue from an additional unit sold

Column (5) shows **marginal revenue**, which is the change in total revenue from the sale of each additional unit of output. In Table 1, marginal revenue equals ₹6, the price of a gallon of milk. This illustrates a lesson that applies only to firms in competitive markets. Because total revenue is $P \times Q$ and P is fixed for a competitive firm, when Q rises by 1 unit, total revenue rises by P dollars. **Therefore, for competitive firms, marginal revenue equals the price of the good.**

Quick**Quiz**

1. A perfectly competitive firm
   a. chooses its price to maximize profits.
   b. sets its price to undercut other firms selling similar products.
   c. takes its price as given by market conditions.
   d. picks the price that yields the largest market share.

2. When a perfectly competitive firm increases the quantity it produces and sells by 10 percent, its marginal revenue _______ and its total revenue rises by _______.
   a. falls; less than 10 percent
   b. falls; exactly 10 percent
   c. stays the same; less than 10 percent
   d. stays the same; exactly 10 percent

Answers are at the end of the chapter.

13-2 Profit Maximization and the Competitive Firm's Supply Curve

The goal of a firm is to maximize profit, which equals total revenue minus total cost. The previous section discussed the competitive firm's revenue, and the previous chapter analyzed the firm's costs. Let's now consider how a competitive firm maximizes profit and how that decision determines its supply curve.

13-2a A Simple Example of Profit Maximization

Table 2 presents more information about the Harappan Family Dairy Farm. Column (1) in the table shows the number of gallons of milk the farm produces. Column (2) shows the farm's total revenue, which is ₹6 times the number of gallons. Column (3) shows the farm's total cost. Total cost includes fixed costs, which are ₹3 in this example, and variable costs, which depend on the quantity produced.

Column (4) shows the farm's profit, which is computed by subtracting total cost from total revenue. If the farm produces nothing, it has a loss of ₹3 (its fixed cost). If it produces 1 gallon, it has a profit of ₹1. If it produces 2 gallons, it has a profit of ₹4, and so on. The Harappan family wants to produce the quantity of milk that makes its profit as large as possible. In this example, the farm maximizes profit by producing either 4 or 5 gallons of milk for a profit of ₹7.

There is another way to look at Harappan Farm's decision: The Harappans can find the profit-maximizing quantity by comparing the marginal revenue and marginal cost of each unit produced. Columns (5) and (6) in Table 2 compute marginal

Table 2

Profit Maximization: A Numerical Example

(1) Quantity (*Q*)	(2) Total Revenue (*TR*)	(3) Total Cost (*TC*)	(4) Profit (*TR* − *TC*)	(5) Marginal Revenue (*MR* = Δ*TR* / Δ*Q*)	(6) Marginal Cost (*MC* = Δ*TC* / Δ*Q*)	(7) Change in Profit (*MR* − *MC*)
0 gallons	₹0	₹3	−₹3			
				₹6	₹2	₹4
1	6	5	1			
				6	3	3
2	12	8	4			
				6	4	2
3	18	12	6			
				6	5	1
4	24	17	7			
				6	6	0
5	30	23	7			
				6	7	−1
6	36	30	6			
				6	8	−2
7	42	38	4			
				6	9	−3
8	48	47	1			

revenue and marginal cost from the changes in total revenue and total cost, and column (7) shows the change in profit for each additional gallon produced. The first gallon of milk the farm produces has a marginal revenue of ₹6 and a marginal cost of ₹2, so producing that gallon increases profit by ₹4 (from −₹3 to ₹1). The second gallon produced has a marginal revenue of ₹6 and a marginal cost of ₹3, so that gallon increases profit by ₹3 (from ₹1 to ₹4). As long as marginal revenue exceeds marginal cost, increasing the quantity produced raises profit. Once the farm's output reaches 5 gallons of milk, however, the situation changes. The sixth gallon would have a marginal revenue of ₹6 and a marginal cost of ₹7, so producing it would reduce profit by ₹1 (from ₹7 to ₹6). As a result, the Harappans do not produce more than 5 gallons.

One of the learnings from in Chapter 1 is that rational people think at the margin. The Harappans can apply this principle. If marginal revenue is greater than marginal cost—as it is at 1, 2, and 3 gallons—they should increase the production of milk because it will put more money in their pockets (marginal revenue) than it takes out (marginal cost). If marginal revenue is less than marginal cost—as it is at 6, 7, and 8 gallons—the Harappans should decrease production. By thinking at the margin and making incremental adjustments to the level of production, the Harappans end up producing the profit-maximizing quantity.

13-2b The Marginal-Cost Curve and the Firm's Supply Decision

To extend this analysis, consider the cost curves in Figure 1. These cost curves exhibit the three features that, as the preceding chapter explained, are thought to describe most firms: The marginal-cost curve (*MC*) slopes upward, the average-total-cost curve (*ATC*) is U-shaped, and the marginal-cost curve crosses the average-total-cost curve at the minimum of average total cost. The figure also shows a horizontal line at the market price (*P*). The price line is horizontal because a competitive firm is a price taker: The price of the firm's output is the same regardless of how much it produces. Keep in mind that, for a competitive firm, the price equals both the firm's average revenue (*AR*) and its marginal revenue (*MR*).

We can use Figure 1 to find the quantity of output that maximizes profit. Imagine that the firm is producing at Q_1. At this level of output, the marginal-revenue curve is above the marginal-cost curve, indicating that marginal revenue is greater than marginal cost. This means that if the firm were to raise production by 1 unit, the additional revenue (MR_1) would exceed the additional cost (MC_1). Profit, which equals total revenue minus total cost, would increase. Hence, if marginal revenue is greater than marginal cost, as it is at Q_1, the firm can increase profit by increasing production.

A similar argument applies when output is at Q_2. In this case, the marginal-cost curve is above the marginal-revenue curve, showing that marginal cost is greater than

Figure 1

Profit Maximization for a Competitive Firm

This figure shows the marginal-cost curve (*MC*), the average-total-cost curve (*ATC*), and the average-variable-cost curve (*AVC*). It also shows the market price (*P*), which for a competitive firm equals both marginal revenue (*MR*) and average revenue (*AR*). At the quantity Q_1, marginal revenue MR_1 exceeds marginal cost MC_1, so raising production increases profit. At the quantity Q_2, marginal cost MC_2 is above marginal revenue MR_2, so reducing production increases profit. The profit-maximizing quantity, Q_{MAX}, is found where the horizontal line representing the price intersects the marginal-cost curve.

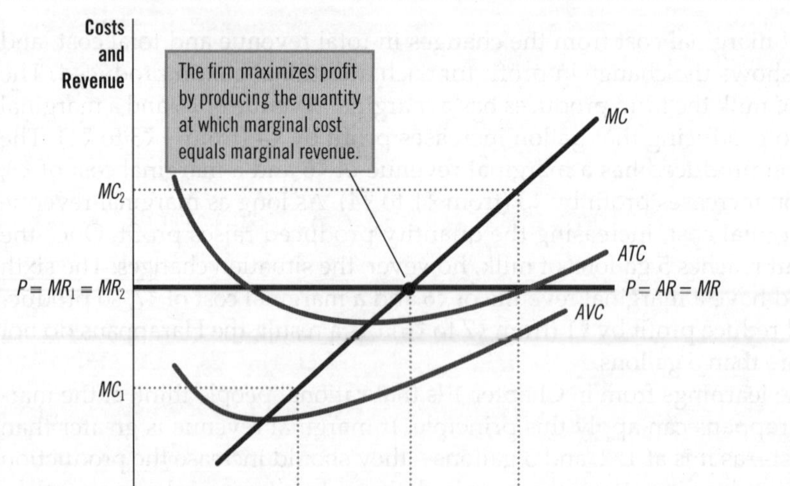

marginal revenue. If the firm were to reduce production by 1 unit, the costs saved (MC_2) would exceed the revenue lost (MR_2). Therefore, if marginal cost is greater than marginal revenue, as it is at Q_2, the firm can increase profit by reducing production.

Where do these marginal adjustments to production end? Regardless of whether the firm begins with production at a low level (such as Q_1) or at a high level (such as Q_2), it will eventually adjust production until the quantity produced reaches the profit-maximizing quantity, Q_{MAX}. This analysis yields three rules for profit maximization:

- If marginal revenue exceeds marginal cost, the firm should increase its output.
- If marginal cost exceeds marginal revenue, the firm should decrease its output.
- At the profit-maximizing level of output, marginal revenue equals marginal cost.

These rules are the key to rational decision making by any profit-maximizing firm. They apply not only to competitive firms but, as the next chapter shows, to other types of firms as well.

We can now see how the competitive firm decides what quantity of its good to supply to the market. Because a competitive firm is a price taker, its marginal revenue equals the market price. For any price, the competitive firm's profit-maximizing quantity of output is found by looking at the intersection of the price with the marginal-cost curve. In Figure 1, that quantity is Q_{MAX}.

Suppose that the price prevailing in this market rises, perhaps because of an increase in market demand. Figure 2 shows how a competitive firm responds to the price increase. When the price is P_1, the firm produces quantity Q_1, the quantity that equates marginal cost to the price. When the price rises to P_2, the firm finds that marginal revenue is higher than marginal cost at the previous level of output, so it increases production. The new profit-maximizing quantity is Q_2, at which marginal cost equals the new, higher price. **Because the firm's marginal-cost curve**

Figure 2

Marginal Cost as the Competitive Firm's Supply Curve

An increase in the price from P_1 to P_2 leads to an increase in the firm's profit-maximizing quantity from Q_1 to Q_2. Because the marginal-cost curve shows the quantity supplied at any price, it is the firm's supply curve.

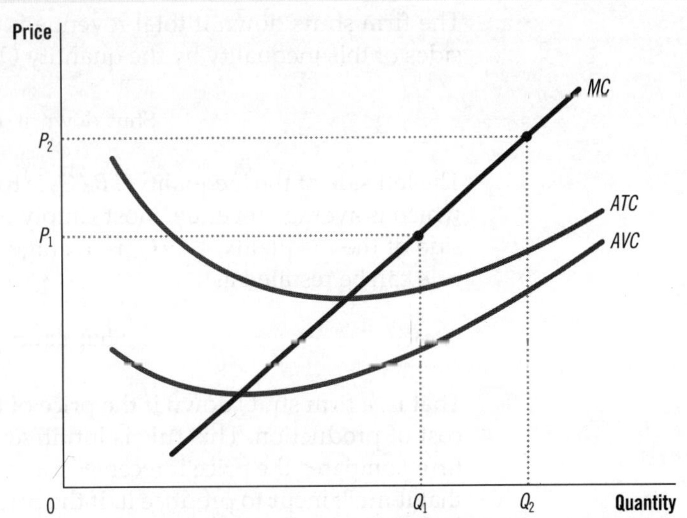

QuickQuiz

3. A competitive firm maximizes profit by choosing the quantity at which
   a. average total cost is at its minimum.
   b. marginal cost equals the price.
   c. average total cost equals the price.
   d. marginal cost equals average total cost.
4. A competitive firm's short-run supply curve is its _______ cost curve above its _______ cost curve.
   a. average-total-; marginal-
   b. average-variable-; marginal-
   c. marginal-; average-total-
   d. marginal-; average-variable-
5. If a profit-maximizing competitive firm is producing a quantity at which marginal cost is between average variable cost and average total cost, it will
   a. keep producing in the short run but exit the market in the long run.
   b. shut down in the short run but return to production in the long run.
   c. shut down in the short run and exit the market in the long run.
   d. keep producing both in the short run and in the long run.

Answers are at the end of the chapter.

13-3 The Supply Curve in a Competitive Market

The supply curves for entire markets are built on the supply decisions of individual firms. There are two cases to consider: (1) markets with a fixed number of firms and (2) markets in which firms can enter and exit. Both cases are important, for each applies to a specific time horizon. Over short periods, entry and exit are often difficult, making it reasonable to assume a fixed number of firms. But over long stretches, entry and exit become easier, and so the number of firms can adjust to changing market conditions.

13-3a The Short Run: Market Supply with a Fixed Number of Firms

Imagine a market with 1,000 identical firms. Each firm acts according to our standard model: For any price, it supplies the quantity of output at which its marginal cost equals the price. Panel (a) of Figure 6 shows this. As long as price exceeds average variable cost, each firm's marginal-cost curve is its supply curve. The quantity of output supplied to the market equals the sum of the quantities supplied by each of the 1,000 firms. The market supply curve is derived by horizontally adding the supply curves of all the firms. As panel (b) of Figure 6 shows, the quantity supplied to the market is 1,000 times the quantity supplied by each of these identical firms.

13-3b The Long Run: Market Supply with Entry and Exit

Now consider what happens when firms can enter and exit the market. Let's suppose that everyone has access to the same production technology and access to the same markets to buy the inputs for production. As a result, all current and potential firms have the same cost curves.

Decisions about entry and exit in a market of this type depend on the incentives facing the owners of existing firms and the entrepreneurs who could start new firms. If firms already in the market are profitable, new firms will enter. This entry will expand the number of firms, increase the quantity of the good supplied, and drive down prices and profits. Conversely, if firms in the market are making losses, some existing firms will exit. Their exit will reduce the number of firms, decrease the quantity of the good supplied, and drive up prices and profits. **At the end of**

Figure 6

Short-Run Market Supply

In the short run, the number of firms in the market is fixed. As a result, the market supply curve, shown in panel (b), reflects the sum of individual firms' marginal-cost curves, shown in panel (a). Here, in a market of 1,000 identical firms, the quantity of output supplied to the market is 1,000 times the quantity supplied by each firm.

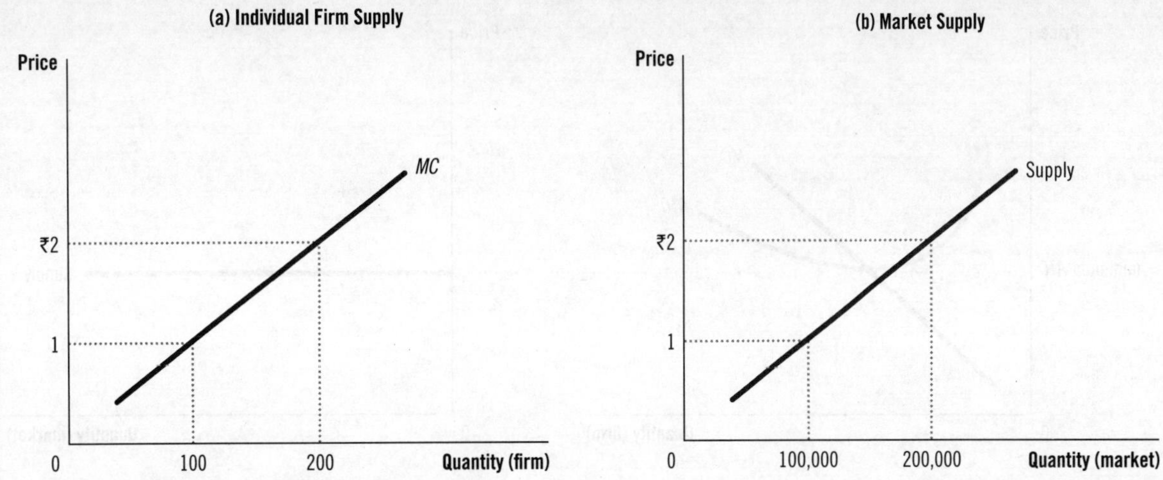

this process of entry and exit, firms that remain in the market must be making zero economic profit. That conclusion may seem strange but have no fear: It will be explained shortly.

Recall that we can write a firm's profit as

$$\text{Profit} = (P - ATC) \times Q.$$

This equation shows that an operating firm has zero profit if and only if the price of the good equals the average total cost of production. If price is above average total cost, profit is positive, which encourages new firms to enter. If price is less than average total cost, profit is negative, which encourages some firms to exit. **The process of entry and exit ends only when price and average total cost are driven to equality.**

This line of reasoning leads to a surprising implication. We noted earlier in the chapter that competitive firms maximize profits by choosing a quantity at which price equals marginal cost. We just noted that free entry and exit force price to equal average total cost. But if price is to equal both marginal cost and average total cost, these two measures of cost must equal each other. Marginal cost and average total cost are equal, however, only when the firm is operating at the minimum of average total cost. Recall from the preceding chapter that economists use the term **efficient scale** to describe the level of production with the lowest average total cost. **Therefore, in the long-run equilibrium of a competitive market with free entry and exit, firms operate at their efficient scale.**

Figure 7

Long-Run Market Supply

In the long run, firms will enter or exit the market until profit is driven to zero. As a result, price equals the minimum of average total cost, as shown in panel (a). The number of firms adjusts to ensure that all demand is satisfied at this price. The long-run market supply curve is horizontal at this price, as shown in panel (b).

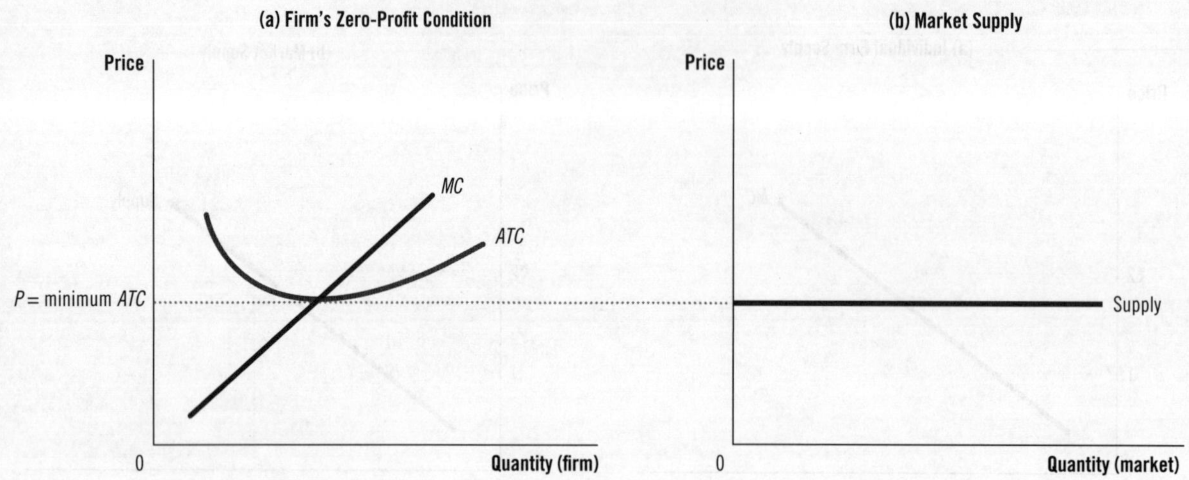

Panel (a) of Figure 7 shows a firm in such a long-run equilibrium. In this figure, price *P* equals marginal cost *MC*, so the firm is maximizing profit. Price also equals average total cost *ATC*, so profit is zero. New firms have no incentive to enter the market, and existing firms have no incentive to leave the market.

From this analysis of firm behavior, we can determine the long-run supply curve for the market. In a market with free entry and exit, there is only one price consistent with zero profit—the minimum of average total cost. As a result, the long-run market supply curve must be horizontal at this price, as illustrated by the perfectly elastic supply curve in panel (b) of Figure 7. Any price above this level would generate profits, leading to entry and an increase in the total quantity supplied. Any price below this level would generate losses, leading to exit and a decrease in the total quantity supplied. Eventually, the number of firms in the market adjusts so that price equals the minimum of average total cost, and there are enough firms to satisfy all the demand at this price.

13-3c Why Do Competitive Firms Stay in Business If They Make Zero Profit?

"We're a nonprofit organization—we don't intend to be, but we are!"

At first, it might seem odd that competitive firms earn zero profit in the long run. After all, people start businesses to make money. If entry eventually drives profit to zero, there might seem to be little reason to stay in business.

To understand the zero-profit condition more fully, recall that profit equals total revenue minus total cost and that total cost includes all the opportunity costs of the firm. In particular, total cost includes the time and money that the firm owners devote to the business. What is crucial is that in the zero-profit equilibrium, the firm's revenue must compensate the owners for these opportunity costs.

Consider an example. Suppose that, to start a farm, a farmer had to invest ₹10 lakhs, which otherwise could have earned ₹40,000 a year in interest in a bank account. In addition, the farmer had to give up another job that would have paid ₹60,000 a year. Then the opportunity cost of farming includes both the forgone interest and the forgone wages—a total of ₹100,000. Even if the farm's profit is driven to zero, its revenue compensates the farmer for these opportunity costs.

Recall that accountants and economists measure costs differently. As the previous chapter noted, accountants keep track of explicit costs but not implicit ones. They measure costs that require an outflow of money but ignore the opportunity costs for which no money leaves the firm. As a result, in the zero-profit equilibrium, economic profit is zero, but accounting profit is positive. The farmer's accountant, for instance, would conclude that the farm earned a profit of ₹100,000, which is why the farmer stays in business.

13-3d A Shift in Demand in the Short Run and Long Run

Now let's turn to how markets respond to changes in demand. Because firms can enter and exit in the long run but not in the short run, the response of a market to a change in demand depends on the time horizon. To see this, let's trace the effects of a shift in demand over time.

Suppose the market for milk begins in a long-run equilibrium. Firms are earning zero profit, so price equals the minimum of average total cost. Panel (a) of Figure 8 shows this situation. The long-run equilibrium is point A, the quantity sold in the market is Q_1, and the price is P_1.

Now suppose scientists discover that milk has miraculous health benefits, causing a surge in demand. That is, the quantity of milk demanded at every price increases, and the demand curve for milk shifts outward from D_1 to D_2, as in panel (b). The short-run equilibrium moves from point A to point B; the quantity rises from Q_1 to Q_2, and the price rises from P_1 to P_2. All the firms in the market respond to the higher price by producing more milk. Because each firm's supply curve reflects its marginal-cost curve, how much each firm increases production depends on the marginal-cost curve. In the new short-run equilibrium, the price of milk exceeds average total cost, so the firms are making positive profit.

Over time, this profit encourages new firms to enter. For example, some farmers supplying other products may switch to producing milk. As the number of suppliers grows, the quantity supplied at every price increases, the short-run supply curve shifts to the right from S_1 to S_2, as in panel (c), and this shift causes the price to fall. Eventually, the price is driven back down to the minimum of average total cost, profits are zero, and firms stop entering. The market reaches a new long-run equilibrium, point C. The price of milk has returned to P_1, but the quantity produced has risen to Q_3. Each firm is again producing at its efficient scale, but because more firms are in the dairy business, the quantity of milk produced and sold is higher.

13-3e Why the Long-Run Supply Curve Might Slope Upward

We have seen that entry and exit can cause the long-run market supply curve to be perfectly elastic. In essence, there are many potential entrants, each of which faces the same costs. As a result, the long-run market supply curve is horizontal at the minimum of average total cost. When demand increases, the long-run result is an increase in the number of firms and in the total quantity supplied, without any change in the price.

There are, however, two reasons that the long-run market supply curve might slope upward. The first is that some resources used in production may be available only

Figure 8

An Increase in Demand in the Short Run and Long Run

Panel (a) shows a market in a long-run equilibrium at point A. In this equilibrium, each firm makes zero profit, and the price equals the minimum average total cost. Panel (b) shows what happens in the short run when demand rises from D_1 to D_2. The equilibrium goes from point A to point B, price rises from P_1 to P_2, and the quantity sold in the market rises from Q_1 to Q_2. Because price now exceeds average total cost, each firm now makes a profit, which, over time, encourages new firms to enter the market. Panel (c) shows how this entry shifts the short-run supply curve to the right from S_1 to S_2. In the new long-run equilibrium, point C, price has returned to P_1, but the quantity sold has increased to Q_3. Profits are again zero, and price is back to the minimum of average total cost, but the market has more firms to satisfy the greater demand.

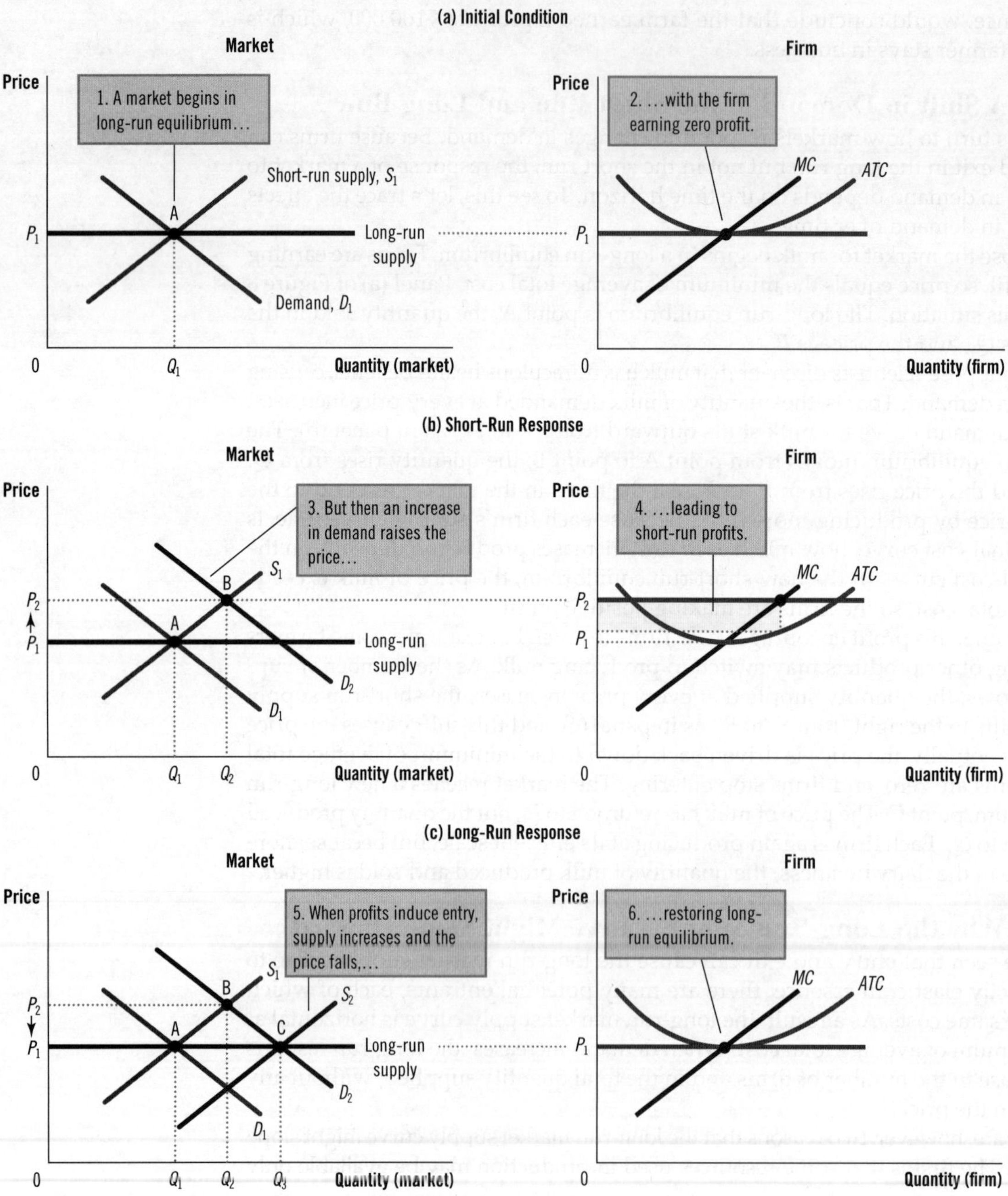

Chapter in a Nutshell

- A firm's goal is to maximize profit, which equals total revenue minus total cost.
- When analyzing a firm's behavior, it is important to include all the opportunity costs of production. Some opportunity costs, such as the wages a firm pays its workers, are explicit. Others, like the wages the firm owner forgoes by not taking another job, are implicit. While accounting profit considers only explicit costs, economic profit accounts for both explicit and implicit costs.
- A firm's costs reflect its production process. A typical firm's production function gets flatter as the quantity of an input increases, displaying the property of diminishing marginal product. As a result, the total-cost curve gets steeper as the quantity produced rises.
- A firm's total cost can be separated into fixed costs and variable costs. Fixed costs remain constant when the firm alters the quantity of output produced. Variable costs change when the firm alters the quantity of output produced.
- From a firm's total cost, two related measures of cost are derived. Average total cost is total cost divided by the quantity of output. Marginal cost is the amount by which total cost rises if output increases by 1 unit.
- When analyzing firm behavior, it is often useful to graph average total cost and marginal cost. For a typical firm, marginal cost rises with the quantity of output. Average total cost first falls as output increases and then rises as output increases further. The marginal-cost curve always crosses the average-total-cost curve at the minimum of average total cost.
- A firm's costs often depend on the time horizon considered. In particular, many costs are fixed in the short run but variable in the long run. As a result, when the firm changes its level of production, average total cost may rise more in the short run than in the long run.

Key Concepts

total revenue, p. 238
total cost, p. 238
profit, p. 238
explicit costs, p. 239
implicit costs, p. 239
economic profit, p. 239
accounting profit, p. 240
production function, p. 241
marginal product, p. 242
diminishing marginal product, p. 243
fixed costs, p. 245
variable costs, p. 245
average total cost, p. 246
average fixed cost, p. 246
average variable cost, p. 246
marginal cost, p. 246
efficient scale, p. 248
economies of scale, p. 251
diseconomies of scale, p. 251
constant returns to scale, p. 251

Questions for Review

1. What is the relationship between a firm's total revenue, total cost, and profit?
2. Give an example of an opportunity cost that an accountant would not count as a cost. Why would the accountant ignore this cost?
3. What is marginal product, and what is meant by diminishing marginal product?
4. Draw a production function that exhibits diminishing marginal product of labor. Draw the associated total-cost curve. (In both cases, be sure to label the axes.) Explain the shapes of the two curves you have drawn.
5. Define **total cost, average total cost,** and **marginal cost**. How are they related?
6. Draw the marginal-cost and average-total-cost curves for a typical firm. Explain why the curves have the shapes they do and why they intersect where they do.
7. How and why does a firm's average-total-cost curve in the short run differ from its average-total-cost curve in the long run?
8. Define **economies of scale** and explain why they might arise. Define **diseconomies of scale** and explain why they might arise.

Problems and Applications

1. This chapter discusses many types of costs: opportunity cost, total cost, fixed cost, variable cost, average total cost, and marginal cost. Fill in the type of cost that best completes each sentence:
   a. What you give up in taking some action is called the ______.
   b. ______ is falling when marginal cost is below it and rising when marginal cost is above it.
   c. A cost that does not depend on the quantity produced is a(n) ______.
   d. In the ice-cream industry in the short run, ______ includes the cost of cream and sugar but not the cost of the factory.
   e. Profits equal total revenue minus ______.
   f. The cost of producing an extra unit of output is the ______.

2. Buffy is thinking about opening an amulet store. She estimates that it would cost ₹350,000 per year to rent the location and buy the merchandise. In addition, she would have to quit her ₹80,000 per year job as a vampire hunter.
   a. Define **opportunity cost.**
   b. What is Buffy's opportunity cost of running the store for a year?
   c. Buffy thinks she can sell ₹400,000 worth of amulets in a year. What would her accountant consider the store's profit?
   d. Should Buffy open the store? Explain.
   e. How much revenue would the store need to generate for Buffy to earn positive economic profit?

3. A commercial fisherman notices the following relationship between hours spent fishing and the quantity of fish caught:

Hours	Quantity of Fish (in pounds)
0 hours	0 lb.
1	10
2	18
3	24
4	28
5	30

   a. What is the marginal product of each hour spent fishing?
   b. Use these data to graph the fisherman's production function. Explain its shape.
   c. The fisherman has a fixed cost of ₹10 (his pole). The opportunity cost of his time is ₹5 per hour. Graph the fisherman's total-cost curve. Explain its shape.

4. Nimbus, Inc. makes brooms and sells them door-to-door. Here is the relationship between the number of workers and Nimbus's output during a given day:

Workers	Output	Marginal Product	Total Cost	Average Total Cost	Marginal Cost
0	0		___	___	
		___			___
1	20		___	___	
		___			___
2	50		___	___	
		___			___
3	90		___	___	
		___			___
4	120		___	___	
		___			___
5	140		___	___	
		___			___
6	150		___	___	
		___			___
7	155		___	___	

   a. Fill in the column of marginal products. What pattern do you see? How might you explain it?
   b. A worker costs ₹100 a day, and the firm has fixed costs of ₹200. Use this information to fill in the column for total cost.
   c. Fill in the column for average total cost. (Recall that $ATC = TC/Q$.) What pattern do you see?
   d. Now fill in the column for marginal cost. (Recall that $MC = \Delta TC/\Delta Q$.) What pattern do you see?
   e. Compare the column for marginal product with the column for marginal cost. Explain the relationship.
   f. Compare the column for average total cost with the column for marginal cost. Explain the relationship.

5. You are the chief financial officer for a firm that sells gaming consoles. Your firm has the following average-total-cost schedule:

Quantity	Average Total Cost
600 consoles	₹300
601	301

Your current level of production is 600 consoles, all of which have been sold. Someone calls, desperate to buy one of your consoles. The caller offers you ₹550 for it. Should you accept the offer? Why or why not?

6. Consider the following cost information for a pizzeria:

Quantity	Total Cost	Variable Cost
0 dozen pizzas	₹300	₹0
1	350	50
2	390	90
3	420	120
4	450	150
5	490	190
6	540	240

   a. What is the pizzeria's fixed cost?
   b. Construct a table in which you calculate the marginal cost per dozen pizzas using the information on total cost. Also, calculate the marginal cost per dozen pizzas using the information on variable cost. What is the relationship between these sets of numbers? Explain.

7. Your cousin Vinnie owns a painting company with fixed costs of ₹200 and the following schedule for variable costs:

Quantity of Houses Painted per Month	1	2	3	4	5	6	7
Variable Costs	₹10	₹20	₹40	₹80	₹160	₹320	₹640

   Calculate average fixed cost, average variable cost, and average total cost for each quantity. What is the efficient scale of the painting company?

8. The city government is considering two tax proposals:
   - A lump-sum tax of ₹300 on each producer of hamburgers
   - A tax of ₹1 per burger, paid by producers of hamburgers

   a. Which of the following curves—average fixed cost, average variable cost, average total cost, and marginal cost—would shift as a result of the lump-sum tax? Why? Show this in a graph. Label the graph as precisely as possible.
   b. Which of these same four curves would shift as a result of the per-burger tax? Why? Show this in a new graph. Label the graph as precisely as possible.

9. Jane's Juice Bar has the following cost schedules:

Quantity	Variable Cost	Total Cost
0 vats of juice	₹0	₹30
1	10	40
2	25	55
3	45	75
4	70	100
5	100	130
6	135	165

   a. Calculate average variable cost, average total cost, and marginal cost for each quantity.
   b. Graph all three curves. What is the relationship between the marginal-cost curve and the average-total-cost curve? Between the marginal-cost curve and the average-variable-cost curve? Explain.

10. Consider the following table of long-run total costs for three different firms:

Quantity	1	2	3	4	5	6	7
Firm A	₹60	₹70	₹80	₹90	₹100	₹110	₹120
Firm B	11	24	39	56	75	96	119
Firm C	21	34	49	66	85	106	129

   Does each of these firms experience economies of scale or diseconomies of scale?

Quick**Quiz** Answers

1. **c** 2. **a** 3. **a** 4. **d** 5. **d** 6. **c** 7. **b** 8. **a** 9. **d**

Chapter

13

Firms in Competitive Markets

If a local kirana store raised its price for multigrain Atta by 20 percent and others didn't, its customers would quickly start buying Atta elsewhere. By contrast, if mineral water suppliers raised the price of water by 20 percent, they wouldn't lose much business. People might buy more purifiers and install water filters and, in suburban areas, may choose to boil water or purify at home, but they would be hard-pressed to find another source of water. The difference between the Atta market and the water market is that most consumers have alternate choices for Atta but not for water, in this example. This difference in market structure shapes the pricing and production decisions of the firms that operate in these markets.

This chapter examines the behavior of competitive firms, such as a local kirana store. Recall that a market is competitive if each buyer and seller is small compared with the size of the market and, therefore, has little ability to influence market prices. By contrast, a firm that can influence the market price of the good it sells, such as the only supplier of mineral water, is said to have **market power**. The next chapter takes up that topic.

AZMANJAKA/E+/GETTY IMAGES; CARLOS FLORES/EYEEM/GETTY IMAGES

Competitive firms are the natural place to begin the study of firm behavior for two reasons. First, because competitive firms have negligible influence on market prices, they are simpler to understand than those with market power. Second, because competitive markets allocate resources efficiently, they provide a benchmark for comparison with other market structures.

The analysis of competitive firms in this chapter helps explain the decisions behind market supply curves. Not surprisingly, the supply curve in a market is closely linked to firms' costs of production. Less obvious is which among the different types of cost—fixed, variable, average, and marginal—are most relevant for its supply decisions. As we will see, all of these cost measures play important and interrelated roles in supply decisions.

13-1 What Is a Competitive Market?

Our goal in this chapter is to examine how firms make production decisions in competitive markets. Let's begin by reviewing what a competitive market is.

13-1a The Meaning of Competition

competitive market
a market with many buyers and sellers trading identical products so that each buyer and seller is a price taker

A **competitive market**, sometimes called a **perfectly competitive market**, has two characteristics:

- The market has many buyers and many sellers.
- The goods offered by the various sellers are largely the same.

Under these conditions, the actions of any single buyer or seller have a negligible impact on the market price. Each buyer and seller takes the market price as given.

Consider the market for milk. No single consumer can influence the price of milk because each buys a small amount relative to the size of the market. Similarly, each dairy farmer has limited control over the price because many other farmers offer milk that is essentially identical. Because sellers can sell all they want at the going price, none of them has any reason to charge less, and if one of them charges more, buyers will go elsewhere. Buyers and sellers in competitive markets must accept the price the market determines and are said to be **price takers**.

In addition to the previous two conditions for competition, a third condition is sometimes said to characterize perfectly competitive markets:

- Firms can freely enter or exit the market.

If, for instance, anyone can start a new dairy farm and any existing dairy farmer can leave the business, then the dairy industry satisfies this condition. Much of the analysis of competitive firms does not require the assumption of free entry and exit because firms can be price takers without it. Yet, as we will see, free entry and exit is a powerful force that shapes the long-run equilibrium in competitive markets.

13-1b The Revenue of a Competitive Firm

The standard model of competitive markets assumes that firms aim to maximize profit (total revenue minus total cost). To see how they do this, let's start by considering the revenue of a typical competitive firm: the Harappan Family Dairy Farm.

determines the quantity of the good the firm is willing to supply at any price, the marginal-cost curve is also the competitive firm's supply curve.

There are, however, some caveats to this conclusion, which we examine next.

13-2c The Firm's Short-Run Decision to Shut Down

So far, we have been analyzing the question of how much a competitive firm will produce. In some circumstances, however, the firm will decide to shut down and not produce anything at all.

It's important to distinguish between a firm's temporary shutdown and its permanent exit from the market. A **shutdown** refers to a short-run decision not to produce anything during a specific period because of current market conditions. **Exit** refers to a long-run decision to leave the market. The short-run and long-run decisions differ because most firms cannot avoid their fixed costs in the short run but can do so in the long run. That is, a firm that shuts down temporarily still must pay its fixed costs, while a firm that exits the market doesn't pay any costs at all, fixed or variable.

For example, consider production decisions at a farm. The cost of the land is a fixed cost. If the farm owners decide not to produce any crops one season, the land lies fallow, and they cannot recover this cost. When making the short-run decision of whether to shut down for a season, the fixed cost of land is said to be a **sunk cost**. By contrast, if the farm owners decide to leave farming altogether, they can sell the land. When making the long-run decision of whether to exit the market, the cost of land is not sunk. (Sunk costs will come up again shortly.)

What determines a firm's shutdown decision? If the firm shuts down, it loses all revenue from the sale of its product. At the same time, it saves the variable costs of making the product (but must still pay the fixed costs). **Therefore, the firm shuts down if the revenue that it would earn from producing is less than its variable costs of production.**

A bit of mathematics can make this shutdown rule more useful. If *TR* stands for total revenue and *VC* stands for variable cost, then the firm's decision can be written as

$$\text{Shut down if } TR < VC.$$

The firm shuts down if total revenue is less than variable cost. By dividing both sides of this inequality by the quantity Q, we can write it as

$$\text{Shut down if } TR/Q < VC/Q.$$

The left side of the inequality, TR/Q, is total revenue $P \times Q$ divided by quantity Q, which is average revenue, most simply expressed as the good's price, P. The right side of the inequality, VC/Q, is average variable cost, AVC. The firm's shutdown rule can be restated as

$$\text{Shut down if } P < AVC.$$

That is, a firm shuts down if the price of the good is less than the average variable cost of production. This rule is intuitive: When deciding whether to produce, the firm compares the price it receives for the typical unit to the average variable cost that it must incur to produce it. If the price doesn't cover the average variable cost, the firm is better off stopping production altogether. The firm still loses money

Figure 3

The Competitive Firm's Short-Run Supply Curve

In the short run, the competitive firm's supply curve is the portion of its marginal-cost curve (*MC*) that lies above its average-variable-cost curve (*AVC*). If the price falls below average variable cost, the firm is better off shutting down temporarily.

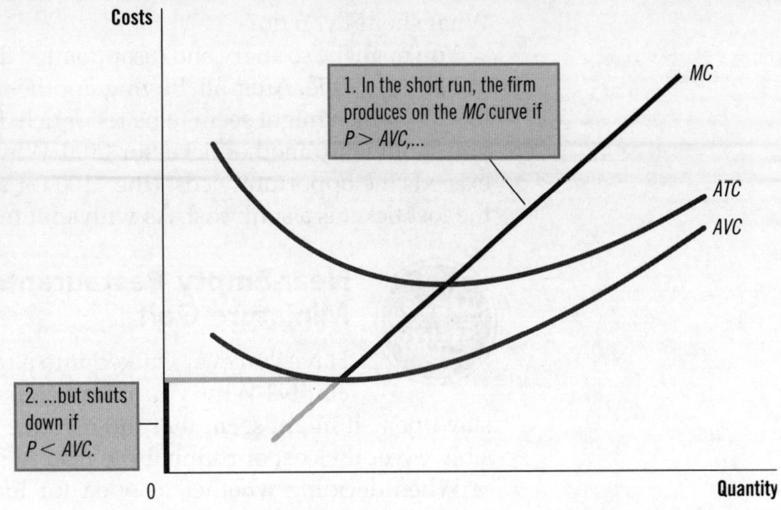

(because it incurs fixed costs), but it would lose even more money by staying open. The firm can reopen in the future if conditions change so that price exceeds average variable cost.

We now have a full description of a competitive firm's profit-maximizing strategy. If the firm produces anything, it produces the quantity at which marginal cost equals the good's price, which the firm takes as given. Yet if the price is less than average variable cost at that quantity, the firm is better off shutting down temporarily and not producing anything. Figure 3 illustrates these results. **The competitive firm's short-run supply curve is the portion of its marginal-cost curve that lies above the average-variable-cost curve.**

13-2d Spilt Milk and Other Sunk Costs

At some point in your life, you may have been told, "Don't cry over spilt milk," or "Let bygones be bygones." These adages were not written by economists, but they could have been. They express an important truth about rational decision making. A **sunk cost** is a cost that has already been committed and cannot be recovered. Because nothing can be done about sunk costs, it's rational to ignore them when making many decisions in life, including those regarding business strategy.

sunk cost
a cost that has already been committed and cannot be recovered

Our analysis of the firm's shutdown decision is an example of the irrelevance of sunk costs. We assume that the firm can't recover its fixed costs by temporarily stopping production. That is, regardless of the quantity of output supplied (even if it is zero), the firm still must pay its fixed costs. In the short run, the fixed costs are sunk, and the firm should ignore them when deciding how much to produce. The firm's short-run supply curve is the part of the marginal-cost curve that lies above average variable cost. Because the fixed costs are sunk, their size doesn't matter for this supply decision.

The irrelevance of sunk costs is worth remembering in your personal life. Imagine, for instance, that you want to see a new movie. You're willing to pay ₹150 to see it, and a ticket only costs ₹100, so you decide to go. Before entering the theater, however, you lose the ticket. The theater management doesn't believe that you lost it. What should you do?

You might be so angry and disappointed that you're inclined to go home and forget about the movie. After all, buying another ticket now would bring your total cost to ₹200, which might seem to be too much. But that would be a mistake. Rationally, you should buy another ticket for ₹100. Why? The benefit of seeing the movie (₹150) exceeds the opportunity cost (the ₹100 for the second ticket). The ₹10 you paid for the lost ticket is a sunk cost. As with spilt milk, there is no point in crying about it.

Case Study

Near-Empty Restaurants and Off-Season Miniature Golf

Have you ever walked into a restaurant for lunch and found it almost empty? Why, you might ask, does such a restaurant even bother to stay open? It might seem that the revenue from so few customers could not possibly cover the cost of running the restaurant.

When deciding whether to open for lunch, a restaurant owner must keep in mind the distinction between fixed and variable costs. Many of a restaurant's costs—the rent, kitchen equipment, tables, plates, silverware, and so on—are fixed. Shutting down during lunch would not reduce these costs, which are sunk in the short run. When the owner is deciding whether to serve lunch, only the variable costs—the price of the additional food and the wages of the extra staff—are relevant. The owner shuts down the restaurant at lunchtime only if the revenue from the few lunchtime customers would fail to cover the variable costs.

An operator of a miniature golf course in a summer resort community faces a similar decision. Because revenue varies substantially from season to season, the firm must decide what date to open and what date to close. Once again, the fixed

ADRIAN SHERRATT/ALAMY STOCK PHOTO

Staying open can be profitable, even with many tables empty.

costs—the costs of buying the land and building the course—are irrelevant to this short-run decision. The miniature golf course should open for business only during those times of the year when its revenue exceeds its variable costs. ●

13-2e The Firm's Long-Run Decision to Exit or Enter a Market

A firm's long-run decision to leave a market is similar to its shutdown decision. If it exits, it will again lose all revenue from the sale of its product, but now it will save not only its variable costs of production but also its fixed costs. **The firm exits the market if the revenue it would get from producing is less than its total cost of production.**

We can again make this rule more useful by writing it mathematically. If *TR* stands for total revenue and *TC* stands for total cost, then the firm's exit rule can be written as

$$\text{Exit if } TR < TC.$$

The firm exits if total revenue is less than total cost. By dividing both sides of this inequality by quantity *Q*, we can write it as

$$\text{Exit if } TR/Q < TC/Q.$$

This can be simplified by noting that *TR*/*Q* is average revenue, which equals the price *P*, and that *TC*/*Q* is average total cost, *ATC*. The firm's exit rule is

$$\text{Exit if } P < ATC.$$

That is, a firm exits if the price of its good is less than the average total cost of production.

A parallel analysis applies to entrepreneurs who could establish new firms. They have an incentive to enter the market if doing so would be profitable, which occurs if the price exceeds average total cost. The entry rule is

$$\text{Enter if } P > ATC.$$

The rule for entry is exactly the opposite of the rule for exit.

We can now describe a competitive firm's long-run profit-maximizing strategy. If it produces anything, it chooses the quantity at which marginal cost equals the price of the good. Yet if the price is less than the average total cost at that quantity, the firm decides to exit (or not enter) the market. Figure 4 illustrates these results. **The competitive firm's long-run supply curve is the portion of its marginal-cost curve that lies above the average-total-cost curve.**

13-2f Measuring Profit in Our Graph for the Competitive Firm

As we study exit and entry, it is useful to analyze the firm's profit in more detail. Recall that profit equals total revenue (*TR*) minus total cost (*TC*):

$$\text{Profit} = TR - TC.$$

We can rewrite this definition by multiplying and dividing the right side by *Q*:

$$\text{Profit} = (TR/Q - TC/Q) \times Q.$$

Note that *TR*/*Q* is average revenue, which is the price, *P*, and *TC*/*Q* is average total cost, *ATC*. Therefore,

Figure 4

The Competitive Firm's Long-Run Supply Curve

In the long run, the competitive firm's supply curve is the portion of its marginal-cost curve (*MC*) that lies above its average-total-cost curve (*ATC*). If the price falls below average total cost, the firm is better off exiting the market.

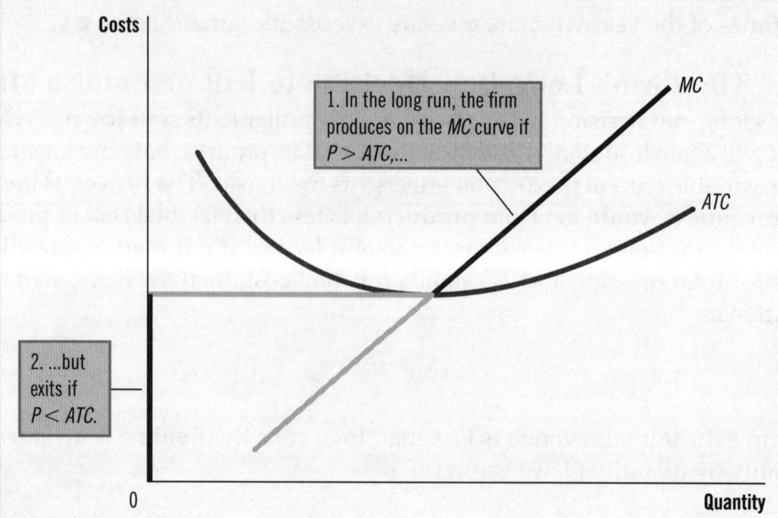

$$\text{Profit} = (P - ATC) \times Q.$$

This way of expressing the firm's profit allows us to measure profit on our graphs.

Panel (a) of Figure 5 shows a firm earning positive profit. As we have already discussed, the firm maximizes profit by producing the quantity at which price equals marginal cost. Now look at the shaded rectangle. The height of the rectangle

Figure 5

Profit as the Area between Price and Average Total Cost

The area of the shaded box between price and average total cost represents the firm's profit. The height of this box is price minus average total cost ($P - ATC$), and the width of the box is the quantity of output (Q). In panel (a), price is greater than average total cost, so the firm has positive profit. In panel (b), price is less than average total cost, so the firm incurs a loss.

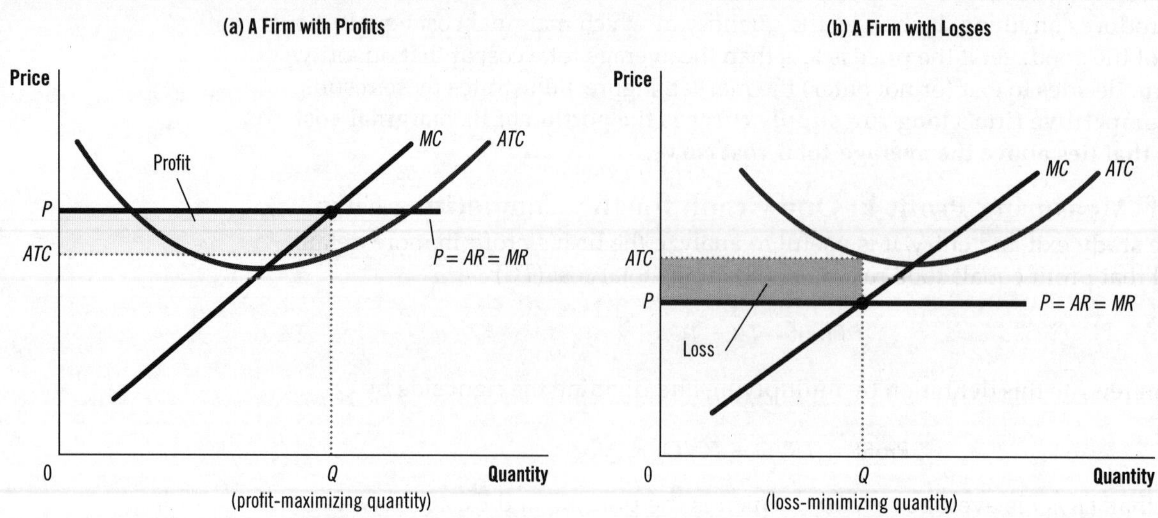

is $P - ATC$, the difference between price and average total cost. The width of the rectangle is Q, the quantity produced. Therefore, the area of the rectangle is $(P - ATC) \times Q$, which is the firm's profit.

Similarly, panel (b) of this figure shows a firm with losses (negative profit). In this case, maximizing profit means minimizing losses, a task accomplished once again by producing the quantity at which price equals marginal cost. Now consider the shaded rectangle. The height of the rectangle is $ATC - P$, and the width is Q. The area is $(ATC - P) \times Q$, which is the firm's loss. Because a firm in this situation is not making enough revenue on each unit to cover its average total cost, it would exit the market in the long run.

13-2g A Brief Recap

We can sum up our analysis of the competitive firm with a dialogue between two business partners. Firhad and Ridhima have just bought a granite quarry, which produces material for kitchen countertops. Because they compete with many other quarries, they take the price of granite as given by market conditions. Ridhima, an economics major, is explaining to Firhad how they should make supply decisions.

Firhad: How much output should we produce to maximize profit?
Ridhima: If we produce anything, we should pick the level of output at which $P = MC$.
Firhad: Will we make a profit?
Ridhima: We will if, at that level of output, $P > ATC$. If $P < ATC$, we will make a loss.
Firhad: What should we do if that output makes a profit?
Ridhima: Be happy and stay in business.
Firhad: And if that output makes a loss?
Ridhima: Plan on exiting in the long run.
Firhad: In that case, should we keep operating in the short run?
Ridhima: We should if $P > AVC$. Staying open minimizes our losses.
Firhad: What if $P < AVC$?
Ridhima: Then we should shut down as quickly as possible and plan our exit.
Firhad: So our long-run supply curve is the *MC* curve above the *ATC* curve, and our short-run supply curve is the *MC* curve above the *AVC* curve.
Ridhima: Yes, Firhad, that's the plan. Table 3 summarizes everything you need to know. (Theirs is carved in granite.)

Table 3
Profit-Maximizing Rules for a Competitive Firm

1. Find Q at which $P = MC$.
2. If $P < AVC$, shut down immediately and remain out of business.
3. If $AVC < P < ATC$, operate in the short run but exit in the long run.
4. If $ATC < P$, stay in business and enjoy your profits!

in limited quantities. Consider the market for farm products. Anyone can buy land and start a farm, but the quantity of land is limited. As more people become farmers, they bid up the price of farmland, increasing the costs of all farmers in the market. An increase in demand for farm products can't increase the quantity supplied without also inducing a rise in farmers' costs, which means a rise in price. The result is a long-run market supply curve that slopes upward, even with free entry into farming.

A second reason for an upward-sloping long-run supply curve is that firms may have different costs. Take the market for painters. Anyone can enter it, but not everyone has the same costs. People differ in how fast they work, and they differ in the alternative uses of their time. For any price, those with lower costs are more likely to enter than those with higher costs. To increase the quantity of painting services supplied, additional entrants must be induced to enter the market. Because these new entrants have higher costs, the price must rise to make entry profitable for them. As a result, the long-run market supply curve for painting services slopes upward even with free entry into the market.

Notice that when firms have different costs, some firms earn profit even in the long run. In this case, the market price reflects the average total cost of the **marginal firm**—the firm that would exit if the price were any lower. This firm earns zero profit, but firms with lower costs earn positive profit. Entry does not eliminate this profit because would-be entrants have higher costs than firms already in the market. Higher-cost firms will enter only if the price rises, making the market profitable for them.

For these two reasons, a higher price may be necessary to induce a larger quantity supplied, in which case the long-run supply curve is upward-sloping rather than horizontal. Nonetheless, the basic lesson about entry and exit remains true. **Because firms can enter and exit more easily in the long run than in the short run, the long-run supply curve is typically more elastic than the short-run supply curve.**

Quick**Quiz**

6. In the long-run equilibrium of a competitive market with identical firms, what are the relationships among price P, marginal cost MC, and average total cost ATC?
   a. $P > MC$ and $P > ATC$.
   b. $P > MC$ and $P = ATC$.
   c. $P = MC$ and $P > ATC$.
   d. $P = MC$ and $P = ATC$.

7. In the short-run equilibrium of a competitive market with identical firms, if new firms are getting ready to enter, what are the relationships among price P, marginal cost MC, and average total cost ATC?
   a. $P > MC$ and $P > ATC$.
   b. $P > MC$ and $P = ATC$.
   c. $P = MC$ and $P > ATC$.
   d. $P = MC$ and $P = ATC$.

8. Suppose momo kiosks in Chinatown, Kolkata are a perfectly competitive market in long-run equilibrium. One day, the Kolkata Municipal Corporation starts imposing a ₹100 per month tax on each kiosk. How does this policy affect the number of momos consumed in the short run and the long run?
   a. down in the short run, no change in the long run
   b. up in the short run, no change in the long run
   c. no change in the short run, down in the long run
   d. no change in the short run, up in the long run

Answers are at the end of the chapter.

13-4 Conclusion: Behind the Supply Curve

We have been discussing the behavior of profit-maximizing firms that supply goods in perfectly competitive markets. You may recall from Chapter 1 that one of the **Ten Principles of Economics** is that rational people think at the margin. This chapter has applied this idea to the competitive firm. Marginal analysis has given us a

The Price of Cauliflower in Winter – Perfect Competition? Close Enough!

If you ever have the opportunity to walk into the Azadpur Subzi Mandi, which is probably one of the largest wholesale markets for fruits and vegetables, on a winter morning, you will probably come across heaps of cauliflowers stacked in large bamboo baskets with dozens of vendors line up selling what appears to be the exact same product. Whether you're a hotel buyer, a local grocer, or a household consumer, you will find that nearly all vendors are quoting the same price, such as Rs. 20 per kilogram on a given morning. This setup closely resembles the textbook model of a perfectly competitive market. Each seller is a small player in a large market, offering a homogeneous product, which is the cauliflower in this case. This market also has free entry and exit. No individual seller has the power to set prices. Each seller is so negligible relative to the size of the market, that no single seller can influence the market price. Instead, prices are determined by the broader forces of market supply and demand. Therefore, these cauliflower vendors in Azadpur mandi are all price takers. This implies that they must accept the prevailing mandi rate. Suppose one seller attempts to charge ₹Rs. 2 more than the prevailing rate, she risks losing the buyer to any of the dozens of neighboring sellers offering the same product. This is the critical feature of a perfectly competitive market.

Having said this, it is important to realize that truly perfectly competitive markets are rare. A way to think about this is that there are two extreme forms of competition in the spectrum. One end of this is perfectly competitive market, i.e., max possible competition. This is a situation like above where there cannot be any more competition (in prices , for our example). The opposite extreme will be monopoly, which is having zero competition. There we will have only one seller. This is the topic of the next chapter. Most market forms are somewhere in between and managerial economists care mostly about these forms. However, learning the extremes makes it easier to appreciate what happens when we move from a less (more) to a more (less) competitive environment. In other words, as the industry gets more competitive, the managers can predict that the firms will now mimic behavior and responses closer to that of perfect competition whereas if competition declines, firms will predict having more and more market power and pricing ability.

theory of the supply curve in a competitive market and a deeper understanding of market outcomes.

We have learned that when you buy a good from a firm in a competitive market, the price you pay is close to the cost of producing it. In particular, if firms are competitive and profit-maximizing, the price of a good equals the marginal cost of making that good. And if firms can freely enter and exit the market, the price also equals the lowest possible average total cost of production.

We have assumed throughout this chapter that firms are price takers, but many of the tools developed here are also useful for studying firms in less competitive markets. The next chapter examines the behavior of firms with market power. Marginal analysis will again be useful, but it will have very different implications for a firm's production decisions and for the nature of market outcomes.

Chapter in a Nutshell

- Because a competitive firm is a price taker, its revenue is proportional to the amount of output it produces. The price of the good equals both the firm's average revenue and its marginal revenue.
- To maximize profit, a firm chooses a quantity of output such that marginal revenue equals marginal cost. Because marginal revenue for a competitive firm equals the market price, the firm chooses the quantity at which price equals marginal cost. Thus, the firm's marginal-cost curve is its supply curve.
- In the short run, when fixed costs are sunk, the firm will shut down temporarily if the price of the good is less than average variable cost. In the long run, when the firm can recover both fixed and variable costs, it will exit if the price is less than average total cost.
- In a market with free entry and exit, economic profit is driven to zero in the long run. In this long-run equilibrium, all firms produce at the efficient scale, price equals the minimum of average total cost, and

the number of firms adjusts to satisfy the quantity demanded at this price.

- Changes in demand have different effects over different time horizons. In the short run, an increase in demand raises prices and leads to profits, and a decrease in demand lowers prices and leads to losses. But if firms can freely enter and exit the market, then, in the long run, the number of firms adjusts to drive the market back to the zero-profit equilibrium.

Key Concepts

competitive market, p. 258
average revenue, p. 260
marginal revenue, p. 260
sunk cost, p. 265

Questions for Review

1. What are the main characteristics of a competitive market?
2. Explain the difference between a firm's revenue and its profit. Which do firms maximize?
3. Draw the cost curves for a typical firm. Explain how a competitive firm chooses the level of output that maximizes profit. At that level of output, show on your graph the firm's total revenue and total cost.
4. Under what conditions will a firm shut down temporarily? Explain.
5. Under what conditions will a firm exit a market? Explain.
6. Does a competitive firm's price equal its marginal cost in the short run, in the long run, or both? Explain.
7. Does a competitive firm's price equal the minimum of its average total cost in the short run, in the long run, or both? Explain.
8. Are market supply curves typically more elastic in the short run or in the long run? Explain.

Problems and Applications

1. Many small boats are made of fiberglass and a resin derived from crude oil. Suppose that the price of oil rises.
   a. Using diagrams, show what happens to the cost curves of an individual boat-making firm and to the market supply curve.
   b. What happens to the profits of boat makers in the short run? What happens to the number of boat makers in the long run?
2. Leah's lawn-mowing service is a profit-maximizing competitive firm. Leah mows lawns for ₹27 each. Her total cost each day is ₹280, of which ₹30 is a fixed cost. She mows 10 lawns a day. What can you say about Leah's short-run decision regarding shutdown and her long-run decision regarding exit?
3. Consider total cost and total revenue given in the following table:

Quantity	0	1	2	3	4	5	6	7
Total cost	₹8	9	10	11	13	19	27	37
Total revenue	₹0	8	16	24	32	40	48	56

   a. Calculate profit for each quantity. How much should the firm produce to maximize profit?
   b. Calculate marginal revenue and marginal cost for each quantity. Graph them. (Hint: Put the points between whole numbers. For example, the marginal cost between 2 and 3 should be graphed at 2½.) At what quantity do these curves cross? How does this relate to your answer to part (a)?
   c. Can you tell whether this firm is in a competitive industry? If so, can you tell whether the industry is in a long-run equilibrium?
4. Ball Bearings, Inc., faces costs of production as follows:

Quantity (cases)	Total Fixed Cost	Total Variable Cost
0	₹100	₹0
1	100	50
2	100	70
3	100	90
4	100	140

Quantity (cases)	Total Fixed Cost	Total Variable Cost
5	100	200
6	100	360

a. Calculate the company's average fixed cost, average variable cost, average total cost, and marginal cost at each level of production.
b. The price of a case of ball bearings is ₹50. Seeing that the company can't make a profit, the chief executive officer (CEO) decides to shut down operations. What is the firm's profit or loss? Is shutting down a wise decision? Explain.
c. Vaguely remembering an introductory economics course, the chief financial officer tells the CEO it is better to produce 1 case of ball bearings because marginal revenue equals marginal cost at that quantity. What is the firm's profit or loss at that level of production? Is producing 1 case the best decision? Explain.

5. Suppose the book-printing industry is competitive and begins in a long-run equilibrium.
   a. Draw a diagram showing the average total cost, marginal cost, marginal revenue, and supply curve of the typical firm in the industry.
   b. Hi-Tech Printing Company invents a new process that sharply reduces the cost of printing books. What happens to Hi-Tech's profits and to the price of books in the short run when Hi-Tech's patent prevents other firms from using the new technology?
   c. What happens in the long run when the patent expires and other firms are free to use the technology?
6. A firm in a competitive market receives ₹500 in total revenue and has marginal revenue of ₹10. What is the average revenue, and how many units were sold?
7. A profit-maximizing firm in a competitive market is currently producing 100 units of output. It has average revenue of ₹10, average total cost of ₹8, and fixed costs of ₹200.
   a. What is its profit?
   b. What is its marginal cost?
   c. What is its average variable cost?
   d. Is the efficient scale of the firm more than, less than, or exactly 100 units?
8. The market for fertilizer is perfectly competitive. Firms in the market are producing output but are currently incurring economic losses.
   a. How does the price of fertilizer compare to the average total cost, the average variable cost, and the marginal cost of producing fertilizer?
   b. Draw two graphs, side by side, illustrating the present situation for the typical firm and for the market.
   c. Assuming there is no change in either demand or the firms' cost curves, explain what will happen in the long run to the price of fertilizer, marginal cost, average total cost, the quantity supplied by each firm, and the total quantity supplied to the market.
9. The market for apple pies in the city of Ectenia is competitive and has the following demand schedule:

Price	Quantity Demanded
₹1	1,200 pies
2	1,100
3	1,000
4	900
5	800
6	700
7	600
8	500
9	400
10	300
11	200
12	100
13	0

Each producer in the market has fixed costs of ₹9 and the following marginal cost schedule:

Quantity	Marginal Cost
1 pie	₹2
2	4
3	6
4	8
5	10
6	12

a. Compute each producer's total cost and average total cost for each quantity from 1 to 6 pies.
b. The price of a pie is now ₹11. How many pies are sold? How many pies does each producer make? How many producers are there? How much profit does each producer earn?

c. Is the situation described in part (b) a long-run equilibrium? Why or why not?
d. Suppose that in the long run, there is free entry and exit. How much profit does each producer earn in the long-run equilibrium? What is the market price? How many pies does each producer make? How many pies are sold in the market? How many pie producers are operating?

10. An industry currently has 100 firms, each of which has fixed costs of ₹16 and average variable cost as follows:

Quantity	Average Variable Cost
1	₹1
2	2
3	3
4	4
5	5
6	6

a. Compute a firm's marginal cost and average total cost for each quantity from 1 to 6.
b. The equilibrium price is currently ₹10. How much does each firm produce? What is the total quantity supplied in the market?
c. In the long run, firms can enter and exit the market, and all entrants have the same costs as above. As this market makes the transition to its long-run equilibrium, will the price rise or fall? Will the quantity demanded rise or fall? Will the quantity supplied by each firm rise or fall? Explain your answers.
d. Graph the long-run supply curve for this market with specific numbers on the axes as relevant.

11. Suppose that each firm in a competitive industry has the following costs:

Total cost: $TC = 50 + \frac{1}{2} q^2$

Marginal cost: $MC = q$

where q is an individual firm's quantity produced. The market demand curve for this product is:

Demand: $Q^D = 120 - P$

where P is the price and Q is the total quantity of the good. Currently, there are 9 firms in the market.

a. What is each firm's fixed cost? What is its variable cost? Give the equation for average total cost.
b. Graph the average-total-cost curve and the marginal-cost curve for q from 5 to 15. At what quantity is the average-total-cost curve at its minimum? What is marginal cost and average total cost at that quantity?
c. Give the equation for each firm's supply curve.
d. Give the equation for the market supply curve for the short run in which the number of firms is fixed.
e. What is the equilibrium price and quantity for this market in the short run?
f. In this equilibrium, how much does each firm produce? Calculate each firm's profit or loss. Do firms have an incentive to enter or exit?
g. In the long run, with free entry and exit, what is the equilibrium price and quantity in this market?
h. In this long-run equilibrium, how much does each firm produce? How many firms are in the market?

Quick**Quiz** Answers

1. **c** 2. **d** 3. **b** 4. **d** 5. **a** 6. **d** 7. **c** 8. **c**

Total cost: $TC = [illegible]$

Marginal cost: $MC = [illegible]$

Demand: $Q^D = [illegible] - [illegible]P$

1. [illegible] 2. d 3. b 4. a 5. [illegible] 6. d 7. [illegible]

Chapter

14 Monopoly

In the 1990s, if you owned a personal computer, it most likely used some version of Windows, the operating system sold by the Microsoft Corporation, and even today, Windows computers remain popular. When Microsoft originally designed Windows, it applied for and received a copyright from the government. The copyright gives Microsoft the exclusive right to make and sell copies of the Windows operating system. Someone who wants to buy a copy has little choice but to fork over the roughly $100 that Microsoft charges for its product. These days, other operating systems are available, but they are often very different. Microsoft is said to have a **monopoly** in the market for Windows.

Microsoft's business decisions aren't well described by the model of firm behavior developed in the previous chapter. That chapter analyzed competitive markets, in which many firms offer largely identical products, so each firm has little influence over the price it receives. By contrast, because a monopoly has no close competitors, it has the power to influence the market price of its product. While a competitive firm is a **price taker**, a monopoly firm is a **price maker**.

ROMAN SAMBORSKYI/SHUTTERSTOCK.COM; ARNO VAN ENGELAND/EYEEM/GETTY IMAGES

This chapter examines the implications of this market power. We will see that market power alters the relationship between the costs a firm incurs producing a good and the price at which it sells that good. So far, we have seen that a competitive firm takes the price of its output as given by the market and then chooses the quantity it will supply so that price equals marginal cost. A monopoly is different. It charges a price that exceeds marginal cost. Sure enough, this practice is evident in the case of Microsoft's Windows. The marginal cost of Windows—the extra cost that Microsoft incurs when a customer downloads one more copy—is trivial. The market price of Windows is many times its marginal cost.

It is not surprising that monopolies charge high prices for their products. Customers of a monopoly might seem to have little choice but to pay whatever the monopoly charges. But if so, why doesn't Microsoft charge ₹1,000 for a copy of Windows? Or ₹10,000? The reason is that if the price were that high, fewer people would buy it. People would buy fewer computers, switch to other operating systems, or make illegal copies. A monopoly can control the price of what it sells, but because a high price reduces the quantity demanded, the monopoly's profits are not unlimited.

In examining how monopolies make production and pricing decisions, this chapter considers the implications of monopoly for society as a whole. Monopolies, like competitive firms, aim to maximize profit, but the pursuit of this goal has very different ramifications. In a competitive market, self-interested consumers and producers reach an equilibrium that promotes general economic well-being, as if guided by an invisible hand. But because monopolies are unchecked by competition, the outcome in a monopolized market is often not in the best interest of society.

One of the other lessons from Chapter 1 is that governments can sometimes improve market outcomes. This chapter sheds more light on this principle by examining the inefficiencies that monopolies cause and discussing how government policymakers can respond to these problems. The U.S. government keeps a close eye on Microsoft's business decisions, for example. In 1994, the government blocked Microsoft from acquiring Intuit, a leading seller of personal finance software, on the grounds that a merger between the two firms would concentrate too much market power. Similarly, in 1998, the U.S. Department of Justice objected when Microsoft started integrating its Internet Explorer browser into its Windows operating system, claiming that this practice would extend the firm's market power into new areas. In recent years, regulators in the United States and abroad have shifted their focus to firms with growing market power, such as Apple, Google, and Amazon, but they continue to monitor Microsoft's compliance with antitrust laws.

14-1 Why Monopolies Arise

monopoly
a firm that is the sole seller of a product without close substitutes

A firm is a **monopoly** if it is the sole seller of a product that doesn't have close substitutes. The fundamental cause of monopoly is **barriers to entry**: A monopoly remains the only seller in its market because other firms can't enter and compete with it. Barriers to entry, in turn, have three main sources:

- **Monopoly resources:** A single firm owns a key resource required for production.
- **Government regulation:** The government gives a single firm the exclusive right to produce a good or service.
- **The production process:** A single firm can produce output at a lower cost than a larger number of firms can.

Here's more on these barriers to entry.

14-1a Monopoly Resources

The simplest way for a monopoly to arise is for a single firm to own a key resource. Consider the market for water in a small town. If dozens of residents have working wells, the model of competitive markets in the preceding chapter describes sellers' behavior. Competition among suppliers drives the price of a gallon of water to equal the marginal cost of pumping an extra gallon. But if there is only one well in town and it is impossible to get water from anywhere else, then the owner of the well has a monopoly. Not surprisingly, the monopolist has much greater market power than any single firm in a competitive market. For a necessity like water, the monopolist can command quite a high price, even if the marginal cost of pumping an extra gallon is low.

A classic example of market power arising from the ownership of a key resource is DeBeers, the diamond company. Founded in South Africa in 1888 by Cecil Rhodes, an English businessman (and benefactor of the Rhodes scholarship), DeBeers has at times controlled up to 80 percent of the production from the world's diamond mines. Because its market share is less than 100 percent, DeBeers is not exactly a monopoly, but the company has nonetheless exerted substantial influence over the market price of diamonds.

Although exclusive ownership of a key resource can create a monopoly, this is relatively rare in practice. Economies are large, and resources are owned by many people. The natural scope of many markets is worldwide because goods are often traded internationally. There are few examples of firms that own resources for which there are no close substitutes.

DAVE CARPENTER/CARTOONSTOCK.COM

"Rather than a monopoly, we like to consider ourselves 'the only game in town.'"

14-1b Government-Created Monopolies

In many cases, monopolies arise when the government gives one person or firm the exclusive right to sell a good or service. Sometimes, a would-be monopolist receives the right out of sheer political clout. Kings once granted exclusive business licenses to their friends and allies. Autocrats continue to do so. Sometimes, the government grants a monopoly because doing so is in the public interest.

Patent and copyright laws are two important examples of how a government can create a monopoly. When a pharmaceutical company discovers a new drug, it can apply to the government for a patent. If the government deems the drug to be original, it approves the patent, which grants the company the exclusive right to manufacture and sell the drug for 20 years. Similarly, after finishing a book, a novelist can copyright it. The copyright is a government guarantee that no one can sell the work without the author's permission. Writers who can barely support themselves may not think of themselves as monopolists. But this only goes to show that being the sole seller of a product does not guarantee a large number of buyers.

The effects of patent and copyright laws are easy to see. Because these laws give one producer a monopoly, they lead to higher prices and higher profits than would occur under competition. But the laws also encourage some desirable behavior. By allowing drug companies to be monopolists in the drugs they discover, the patent laws encourage their research. By allowing authors to be monopolists in the sale of their books, the copyright laws encourage them to write more and better books.

The laws governing patents and copyrights have both benefits and costs. The benefits are the increased incentives for creative activity. They are offset, to some extent, by the costs of monopoly pricing, which we examine later in this chapter.

14-1c Natural Monopolies

natural monopoly
a type of monopoly that arises because a single firm can supply a good or service to an entire market at a lower cost than could two or more firms

An industry is a **natural monopoly** when a single firm can supply a market with a good or service at a lower cost than two or more firms could. This happens when there are economies of scale over the relevant range of output. Figure 1 shows the average total costs of a firm with economies of scale. In this case, a single firm can produce any amount of output at the lowest cost. That is, for any given amount of output, a larger number of firms leads to less output per firm and higher average total cost. Two classic examples of Natural monopolies in our country would be the Indian Railways and the state-run electricity boards for distribution of power supply.

The distribution of tap water is also an example of a natural monopoly. To provide water to town residents, a firm must build a network of pipes. If two or more firms were to compete, each would have to incur the fixed cost of building a network. The average total cost is lowest if a single firm provides water to the entire market.

Other examples of natural monopolies appeared in Chapter 11, which noted that **club goods** are excludable but not rival in consumption. An example is a bridge used so rarely that it is never congested. The bridge is excludable because a toll collector can prevent someone from using it. The bridge is not rival in consumption because one person's use of the bridge does not hinder others' use of it. There is a large fixed cost of building the bridge but a negligible marginal cost of additional users, so the average total cost (the total cost divided by the number of trips) declines as the number of trips rises, making the bridge a natural monopoly.

When a firm is a natural monopoly, it is less concerned about new entrants eroding its monopoly power. Normally, a firm has trouble maintaining a monopoly position without government protection or ownership of a key resource. The monopolist's profit attracts entrants into the market, and these entrants make the market more competitive. By contrast, entering a market in which another firm has a natural monopoly is unattractive. Would-be entrants know that they cannot achieve the same low costs that the monopolist enjoys because, after entry, each firm would have a smaller piece of the market.

In some cases, the size of the market determines whether an industry is a natural monopoly. Again, consider a bridge across a river. When the population is small, the bridge may be a natural monopoly. A single bridge can meet the entire demand

Figure 1

Economies of Scale as a Cause of Monopoly

When a firm's average-total-cost curve continually declines, the firm has what is called a natural monopoly. In this case, when production is divided among more firms, each firm produces less, and average total cost rises. As a result, a single firm can produce any given amount at the lowest cost.

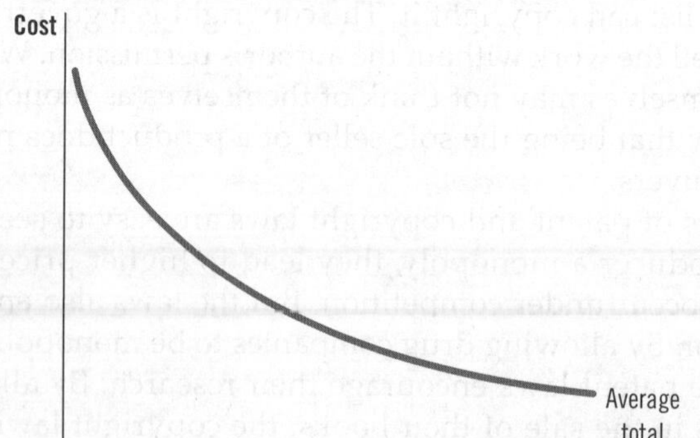

for trips across the river at the lowest cost. Yet as the population grows and the bridge becomes congested, meeting demand may require multiple bridges. As the market expands, the natural monopoly can evolve into a more competitive market.

QuickQuiz

1. Some government grants of monopoly power may be desirable if they
   a. curtail the adverse effects of cut-throat competition.
   b. make industries more profitable.
   c. provide incentives for invention and artistic creation.
   d. save consumers from having to choose among alternative suppliers.

2. A firm is a natural monopoly if it exhibits ________ as its output increases.
   a. increasing total revenue
   b. increasing marginal cost
   c. decreasing marginal revenue
   d. decreasing average total cost

Answers are at the end of the chapter.

14-2 How Monopolies Make Production and Pricing Decisions?

Having seen how monopolies arise, let's consider how a monopoly firm decides how much to produce and what price to charge. The analysis of monopoly behavior in this section is the starting point for evaluating whether monopolies are desirable and what policies a government might pursue in monopoly markets.

14-2a Monopoly versus Competition

The key difference between a competitive firm and a monopoly is the monopoly's ability to influence the price of its output. A competitive firm is small relative to the market in which it operates and, therefore, has no power to influence the price of its output. It takes the price as given by market conditions. By contrast, because a monopoly is the sole producer in its market, it can alter the price of its good by adjusting the quantity it supplies.

One way to view this difference between a competitive firm and a monopoly is to consider the demand curve that each faces. In the analysis of competitive firms in the preceding chapter, we drew the market price as a horizontal line. Because a competitive firm can sell as much or as little as it wants at this price, the competitive firm faces a horizontal demand curve, as in panel (a) of Figure 2. In effect, because the competitive firm sells a product with many perfect substitutes (the products of all the other firms in its market), the demand curve for any one firm is perfectly elastic.

By contrast, because a monopoly is the sole producer in its market, its demand curve is simply the market demand curve, which slopes downward, as in panel (b) of Figure 2. If the monopolist raises the price of its good, consumers buy less of it. Put another way, if the monopolist reduces the quantity of output it produces and sells, the price of its output increases.

The market demand curve provides a constraint on a monopoly's ability to profit from its market power. A monopolist would prefer to charge a high price and sell a large quantity at that high price. But its demand curve makes that outcome impossible. The market demand curve describes the combinations of price and quantity

Figure 2

Demand Curves for Competitive and Monopoly Firms

As a price taker, a competitive firm faces a horizontal demand curve, as in panel (a). It can sell all it wants at the going price. But a monopoly is the sole producer in its market, so it faces the downward-sloping market demand curve, as in panel (b). If it wants to sell more output, it has to accept a lower price.

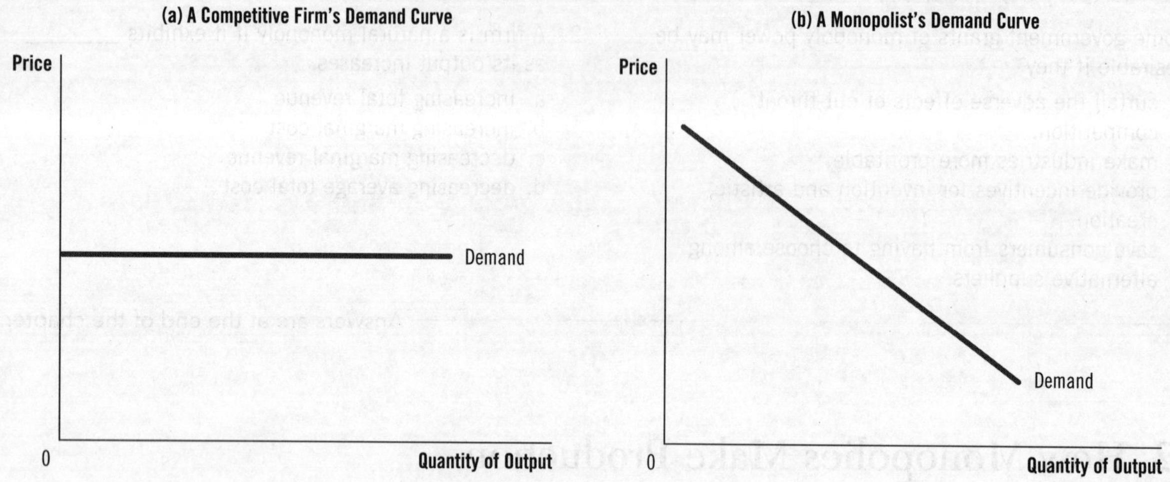

available to a monopoly firm. By adjusting the quantity produced (or equivalently, the price charged), the monopolist can choose any point on the demand curve, but it can't choose a point above the demand curve.

What price and quantity of output will the monopolist choose? As with competitive firms, we assume that the monopolist's goal is to maximize profit. Because the firm's profit is total revenue minus total costs, our next task in explaining monopoly behavior is to examine a monopolist's revenue.

14-2b A Monopoly's Revenue

Consider a town with a single water producer. Table 1 shows how the monopoly's revenue might depend on the amount of water produced.

Columns (1) and (2) show the monopolist's demand schedule. If the monopolist produces 1 gallon of water, it can sell that gallon for ₹10. If it produces 2 gallons, it must lower the price to ₹9 to sell both gallons. If it produces 3 gallons, it must lower the price to ₹8. And so on. If you graphed these two columns of numbers, you would get a typical downward-sloping demand curve.

Column (3) of the table presents the monopolist's **total revenue**. It equals the quantity sold [from column (1)] times the price [from column (2)]. Column (4) computes the firm's **average revenue,** the amount the firm receives per unit sold. Average revenue is calculated by taking the number for total revenue in column (3) and dividing it by the quantity of output in column (1). As the previous chapter explained, average revenue always equals the price of the good. This is true for monopolists as well as for competitive firms.

Column (5) of Table 1 computes the firm's **marginal revenue**, the amount of revenue that the firm receives for each additional unit of output. Marginal revenue

Table 1

A Monopoly's Total, Average, and Marginal Revenue

(1) Quantity of Water (*Q*)	(2) Price (*P*)	(3) Total Revenue ($TR = P \times Q$)	(4) Average Revenue ($AR = TR/Q$)	(5) Marginal Revenue ($MR = \Delta TR/\Delta Q$)
0 gallons	₹11	₹0	—	
				₹10
1	10	10	₹10	
				8
2	9	18	9	
				6
3	8	24	8	
				4
4	7	28	7	
				2
5	6	30	6	
				0
6	5	30	5	
				−2
7	4	28	4	
				−4
8	3	24	3	

is calculated by taking the change in total revenue when output increases by 1 unit. For example, when the firm increases production from 3 to 4 gallons of water, the total revenue it receives increases from ₹24 to ₹28. Marginal revenue from the sale of the fourth gallon is ₹28 minus ₹24, or ₹4.

Table 1 shows an important result in the basic model of monopoly behavior: **A monopolist's marginal revenue is less than the price of its good.** For example, if the firm raises the production of water from 3 to 4 gallons, it increases total revenue by only ₹4, even though it sells each gallon for ₹7. For a monopoly, marginal revenue is lower than price because a monopoly faces a downward-sloping demand curve. To increase the amount sold, a monopoly firm must lower the price it charges to all customers. To sell the fourth gallon of water, the monopolist must earn ₹1 less revenue for each of the first 3 gallons. This ₹3 loss accounts for the difference between the price of the fourth gallon (₹7) and the marginal revenue of that fourth gallon (₹4).

Marginal revenue for monopolies is very different from marginal revenue for competitive firms. When a monopoly increases the amount it sells, there are two effects on total revenue ($P \times Q$):

- **The output effect:** More output is sold, so Q is higher, which increases total revenue.
- **The price effect:** The price falls, so P is lower, which decreases total revenue.

Because a competitive firm can sell all it wants at the market price, there is no price effect. When it increases production by 1 unit, it receives the market price for that unit, and it does not receive any less for the units it was already selling. That is, because the competitive firm is a price taker, its marginal revenue equals the price of its good. By contrast, when a monopoly increases production by 1 unit, it must reduce the price it charges for every unit it sells, and this price cut reduces revenue from the units it was already selling. As a result, a monopoly's marginal revenue is less than its price.

Figure 3 graphs the demand curve and the marginal-revenue curve for a monopoly. (Because the monopoly's price equals its average revenue, the demand curve is also the average-revenue curve.) These two curves always start at the same point on the vertical axis because the marginal revenue of the first unit sold equals the price of the good. But for the reason just discussed, the monopolist's marginal revenue on all units after the first is less than the price. That's why a monopoly's marginal-revenue curve lies below its demand curve.

You can see in Figure 3 (as well as in Table 1) that marginal revenue can even become negative. That happens when the price effect on revenue outweighs the output effect. In this case, an additional unit of output causes the price to fall by enough that the firm, despite selling more units, receives less revenue.

14-2c Profit Maximization

Now that we have considered the revenue of a monopoly firm, we are ready to examine how such a firm maximizes profit. Here, we apply the logic of marginal analysis to the monopolist's decision about how much to produce.

Figure 4 graphs the demand curve, the marginal-revenue curve, and the cost curves for a monopoly firm. These should all seem familiar: The demand and

Figure 3

Demand and Marginal-Revenue Curves for a Monopoly

The demand curve shows how the quantity sold affects the price. The marginal-revenue curve shows how the firm's revenue changes when the quantity increases by 1 unit. Because the price on **all** units sold must fall if the monopoly increases production, marginal revenue is less than the price.

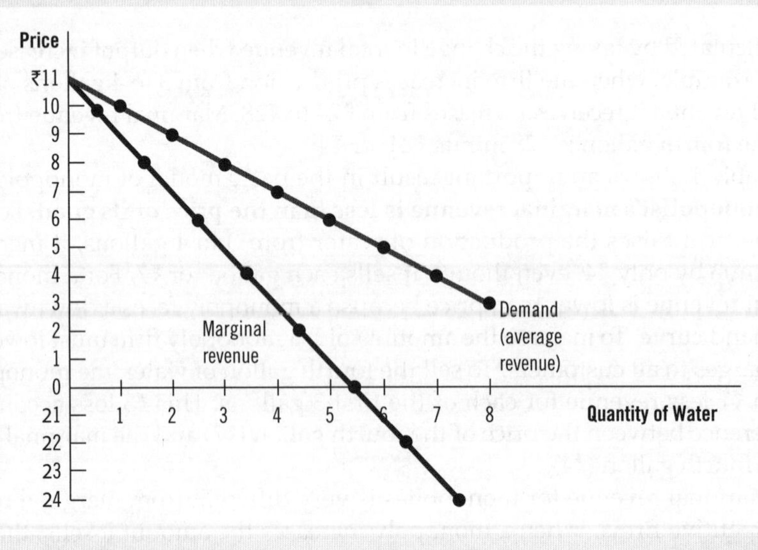

Figure 4

Profit Maximization for a Monopoly

A monopoly maximizes profit by choosing the quantity at which marginal revenue equals marginal cost (point A). It then uses the demand curve to find the price that will induce consumers to buy that quantity (point B).

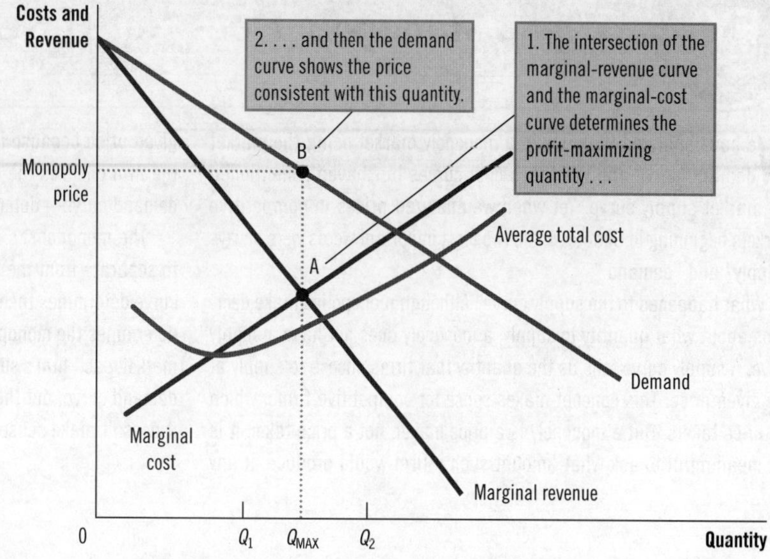

marginal-revenue curves are like those in Figure 3, and the cost curves are like those encountered in the last two chapters. These curves contain all the information we need to determine the level of output that a profit-maximizing monopolist will choose.

Suppose that the firm is producing at a low level of output, such as Q_1. In this case, marginal revenue exceeds marginal cost. If the firm were to increase production by 1 unit, the additional revenue would more than cover the additional costs, and profit would rise. In other words, when marginal revenue exceeds marginal cost, the firm should increase output.

Similar reasoning applies at a high level of output, such as Q_2. In this case, marginal cost exceeds marginal revenue. If the firm were to reduce production by 1 unit, the costs saved would be greater than the revenue lost, increasing profit. Thus, when marginal cost exceeds marginal revenue, the firm should reduce output.

In the end, the firm adjusts production until it reaches Q_{MAX}, the quantity at which marginal revenue equals marginal cost. **The monopolist's profit-maximizing quantity of output is determined by the intersection of the marginal-revenue curve and the marginal-cost curve.** In Figure 4, this intersection occurs at point A.

How does the monopoly find the profit-maximizing price for its product? The demand curve gives the answer. It relates the amount that customers are willing to pay to the quantity sold. After the monopoly finds the profit maximizing quantity (at which $MR = MC$), it looks to the demand curve to find the highest price it can charge at that quantity. In Figure 4, the profit-maximizing price is found at point B.

Now compare the outcomes for a competitive firm and a monopoly. They are alike in one way: To maximize profit, both firms choose the quantity of output at which marginal revenue equals marginal cost. Yet there is an important difference:

FYI Why a Monopoly Does Not Have a Supply Curve

We have analyzed the price in a monopoly market using the market demand curve and the firm's cost curves but haven't mentioned the market supply curve. Yet when we analyzed prices in competitive markets beginning in Chapter 4, the two most important words were always "supply" and "demand."

What happened to the supply curve? Although monopolies make decisions about what quantity to supply, a monopoly does not have a supply curve. A supply curve tells us the quantity that firms choose to supply at any given price. This concept makes sense for competitive firms, which are price takers. But a monopoly is a price maker, not a price taker. It is not meaningful to ask what amount such a firm would produce at any given price because it does not take the price as given. Instead, when the firm chooses the quantity to supply, that decision—along with the demand curve—determines the price.

The monopolist's decision about how much to supply is impossible to separate from the demand curve it faces. The shape of the demand curve determines the shape of the marginal-revenue curve, which in turn determines the monopolist's profit-maximizing quantity. In a competitive market, each firm's supply decisions can be analyzed without knowing the demand curve, but the same is not true in a monopoly market. Therefore, it doesn't make sense to talk about a monopoly's supply curve. ■

At the profit-maximizing quantity, the price equals marginal revenue for a competitive firm but exceeds marginal revenue for a monopoly. That is:

For a competitive firm: $P = MR = MC$.
For a monopoly firm: $P > MR = MC$.

This highlights a key difference between competition and monopoly: **In competitive markets, price equals marginal cost. In monopolized markets, price exceeds marginal cost.** As we will see in a moment, this result is crucial to understanding the social cost of monopoly.

14-2d A Monopoly's Profit

How much profit does a monopoly make? To see a monopoly firm's profit in a graph, recall that profit equals total revenue (*TR*) minus total costs (*TC*):

$$\text{Profit} = TR - TC.$$

We can rewrite this as:

$$\text{Profit} = (TR/Q - TC/Q) \times Q.$$

TR/Q is average revenue, which equals the price, P, and TC/Q is average total cost, ATC. Therefore:

$$\text{Profit} = (P - ATC) \times Q.$$

This equation for profit (which also holds for competitive firms) allows us to measure the monopolist's profit in our graph.

Consider the shaded box in Figure 5. The height of the box (the segment BC) is price minus average total cost, $P - ATC$, which is the profit on the typical unit sold. The width of the box (the segment DC) is the quantity sold, Q_{MAX}. The area of this box is the monopoly's total profit.

Table 2 summarizes how a monopoly maximizes profit.

Figure 5

The Monopolist's Profit

The area of the box BCDE equals the profit of the monopoly firm. The height of the box (BC) is price minus average total cost, which equals profit per unit sold. The width of the box (DC) is the number of units sold.

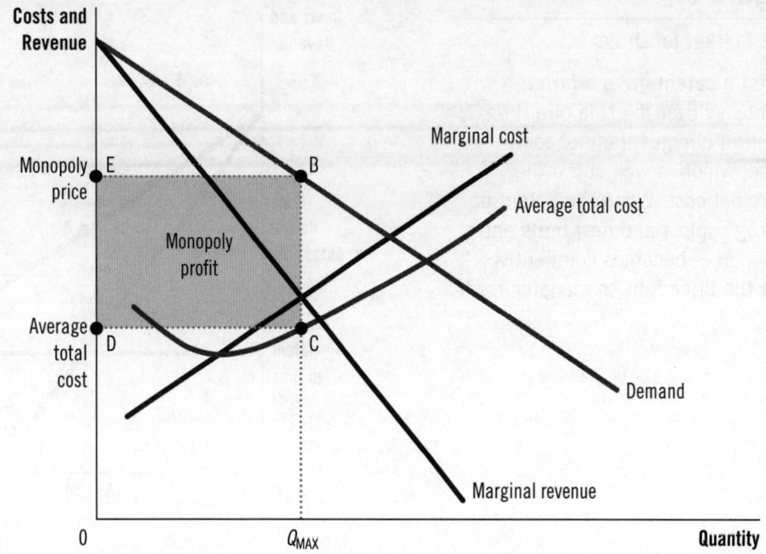

Table 2

Profit-Maximizing Rules for a Monopoly Firm

1. Derive the *MR* curve from the demand curve.
2. Find *Q* at which *MR* = *MC*.
3. On the demand curve, find *P* at which consumers will buy *Q*.
4. If *P* > *ATC*, the monopoly earns a profit.

Case Study

Monopoly Drugs versus Generic Drugs

According to our analysis, prices are determined differently in monopolized and competitive markets. A natural place to test this theory is the market for pharmaceutical drugs, which takes on both market structures. When a firm discovers a drug, patent laws give it a monopoly on the sale of that drug. But when the patent expires, any company can make and sell the drug. At that point, the market becomes competitive rather than monopolistic.

What does theory predict will happen to the price of a drug when the patent expires? Consider Figure 6, which shows the market for a typical drug. The marginal cost of producing the drug is assumed to be constant here. (This is roughly true for many drugs.) During the life of the patent, the monopoly maximizes profit by producing the quantity at which marginal revenue equals marginal cost and charging a price well above marginal cost. But when the patent expires, the profit from making the drug encourages new firms to enter the market. With competition, the price should fall to equal marginal cost.

Figure 6

The Market for Drugs

When a patent gives a firm a monopoly over the sale of a drug, the firm charges the monopoly price, which is well above the marginal cost. When the patent on a drug expires and new firms enter, the market becomes competitive, and the price falls to marginal cost.

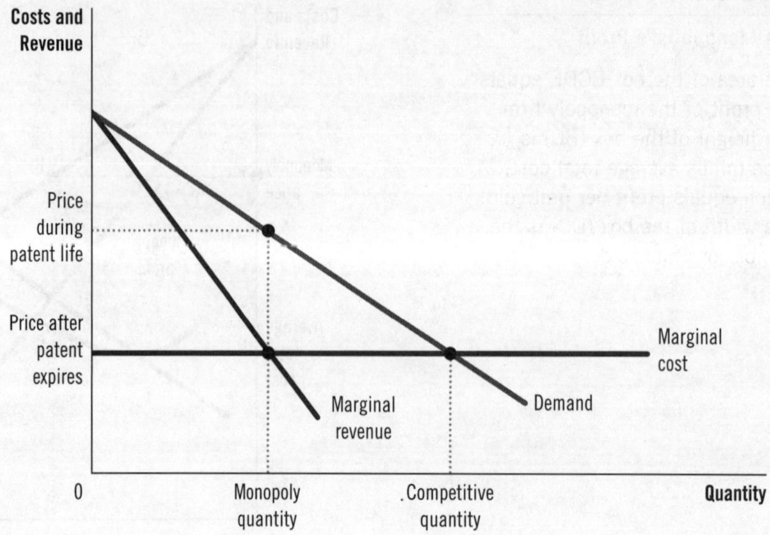

Experience supports the theory. When the patent on a drug expires, other companies quickly enter and begin selling generics that are chemically identical to the former monopolist's brand-name product. Just as theory predicts, the competitively produced generic drugs are priced well below the price that the monopolist was charging.

The expiration of a patent, however, does not cause the monopolist to lose all its market power. Some consumers remain loyal to the brand-name drug, perhaps out of fear that the new generic drugs are not the same as the drug they have been using for years. As a result, the former monopolist can charge a higher price than its new competitors.

For example, the drug fluoxetine, an antidepressant taken by millions of Americans, was originally sold under the brand name Prozac. Since the patent expired in 2001, consumers have had a choice between the original drug and generic versions. Prozac today sells for much more than generic fluoxetine. This price differential persists because some consumers doubt that the two pills are perfect substitutes. ●

Quick Quiz

3. For a profit-maximizing monopoly that charges a single price, what is the relationship between price *P*, marginal revenue *MR*, and marginal cost *MC*?
   a. $P = MR$ and $MR = MC$.
   b. $P > MR$ and $MR = MC$.
   c. $P = MR$ and $MR > MC$.
   d. $P > MR$ and $MR > MC$.

4. If a monopoly's fixed costs increase, its price will _____, and its profit will _____.
   a. increase; decrease
   b. decrease; increase
   c. increase; stay the same
   d. stay the same; decrease

Answers are at the end of the chapter.

14-3 The Welfare Cost of Monopolies

Is monopoly a good way to organize a market? Unlike a competitive firm, a monopoly charges a price above marginal cost. For consumers, this high price makes monopoly undesirable. But for the owners of the firm, the high price generates more profit and makes monopoly extremely attractive. Is it possible that the benefits to the firm's owners exceed the costs imposed on consumers, making monopoly desirable from the standpoint of society as a whole?

We can answer this question using the tools of welfare economics. Recall that total surplus measures the economic well-being of buyers and sellers in a market. Total surplus is the sum of consumer surplus and producer surplus. Consumer surplus is consumers' willingness to pay for a good minus the amount they actually pay for it. Producer surplus is the amount producers receive for a good minus their costs of producing it. In this case, there is a single producer—the monopolist.

You can probably guess the result of this analysis. Previously, we concluded that the equilibrium of supply and demand in a competitive market is not only a natural outcome but also a desirable one. The invisible hand of the market leads to an allocation of resources that makes total surplus as large as it can be. Because a monopoly leads to an allocation of resources different from that in a competitive market, the outcome must, in some way, fail to maximize total economic well-being. Let's see why this is the case.

14-3a The Deadweight Loss

Consider what the monopoly firm would do if it were run by a committee of benevolent social planners. The planners care not only about the firm owners' profit but also about the benefits received by consumers. The planners want to maximize total surplus, which equals producer surplus (profit) plus consumer surplus. Recall that total surplus equals the value of the good to consumers minus the costs of making the good incurred by the monopoly producer.

Figure 7 analyzes how the planners would choose the monopoly's level of output. The demand curve reflects the value of the good to consumers, as measured by their willingness to pay for it. The marginal-cost curve reflects the costs of the monopolist. **The socially efficient quantity is found where the demand curve and the marginal-cost curve intersect.** Below this quantity, the value of an extra unit to consumers exceeds the cost of providing it, so increasing output would raise total surplus. Above this quantity, the cost of producing an extra unit exceeds the value of that unit to consumers, so decreasing output would raise total surplus. At the optimal quantity, the value of an extra unit to consumers exactly equals the marginal cost of production.

If the social planners were running the monopoly, the firm could achieve this efficient outcome by charging the price found at the intersection of the demand and marginal-cost curves. Like a competitive firm and unlike a profit-maximizing monopoly, a social planner would charge a price equal to marginal cost. Because this price would give consumers an accurate signal about the cost of producing the good, consumers would buy the efficient quantity.

We can evaluate the welfare effects of monopoly by comparing the output that the monopolist chooses with the output that a social planner would choose. As we have seen, the monopolist chooses to produce and sell the quantity of output at which the marginal-revenue and marginal-cost curves intersect; the social planner would choose the quantity at which the demand and marginal-cost curves intersect.

Figure 7

The Efficient Level of Output

Social planners maximize total surplus in the market by choosing the level of output where the demand curve and marginal-cost curve intersect. Below this level, the value of the good to the marginal buyer (as reflected in the demand curve) exceeds the marginal cost of making the good. Above this level, the value to the marginal buyer is less than marginal cost.

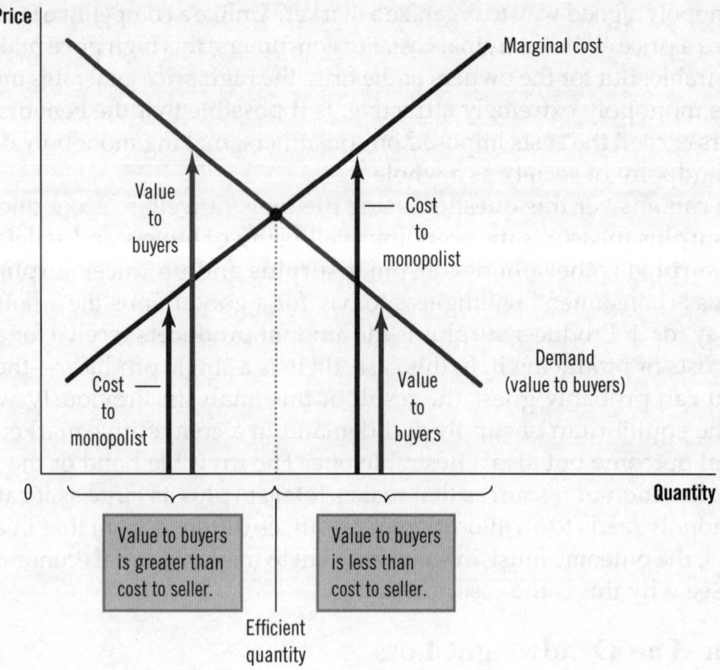

Figure 8 shows the comparison. **The monopolist produces less than the socially efficient quantity of output.**

We can also view the inefficiency of monopoly in terms of the monopolist's price. Because the market demand curve describes a negative relationship between the price and quantity of the good, producing a quantity that is inefficiently low is equivalent to charging a price that is inefficiently high. When a monopolist charges a price above marginal cost, some potential consumers value the good at more than its marginal cost but less than the monopolist's price. These consumers don't buy the good. Because the value they place on the good exceeds the firm's cost of providing it to them, this result is inefficient. Monopoly pricing prevents some mutually beneficial trades from taking place.

The inefficiency of monopoly can be measured with a deadweight loss triangle, as illustrated in Figure 8. Because the demand curve reflects the value to consumers and the marginal-cost curve reflects the costs to the monopoly producer, the area of the deadweight loss triangle between the demand curve and the marginal-cost curve equals the total surplus lost because of monopoly pricing. It represents the reduction in economic well-being that results from the monopoly's use of its market power.

The deadweight loss caused by a monopoly is similar to the deadweight loss caused by a tax. In a sense, a monopolist is like a private tax collector. As we showed before, a tax on a good puts a wedge between consumers' willingness to pay (as reflected by the demand curve) and producers' costs (as reflected by the supply curve). Because a monopoly exerts its market power by charging a price above marginal cost, it creates a similar wedge. In both cases, the wedge causes the quantity sold to fall short of the social optimum. The difference between the two cases is

Figure 8

The Inefficiency of Monopoly

Because a monopoly charges a price above marginal cost, not all consumers who value the good at more than its cost buy it. That means that the quantity produced and sold by a monopoly is below the socially efficient level. The deadweight loss is represented by the area of the triangle between the demand curve (which reflects the value of the good to consumers) and the marginal-cost curve (which reflects the costs of the monopoly producer).

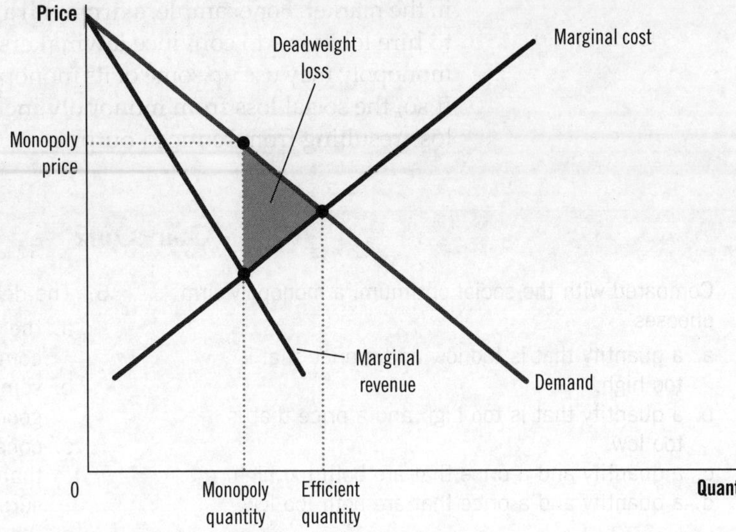

that a tax generates revenue for the government, while a monopoly price generates profit for the firm.

14-3b The Monopoly's Profit: A Social Cost?

It is tempting to decry monopolies for "profiteering" at the public's expense. To be sure, a monopoly earns a profit by virtue of its market power. But according to the economic analysis of monopoly, the firm's profit is not in itself necessarily a problem for society.

Welfare in a monopolized market, as in all markets, includes the welfare of both consumers and producers. When a consumer pays an extra dollar to a producer because of a monopoly price, the consumer is worse off by a dollar, and the producer is better off by the same amount. Because total surplus equals the sum of consumer and producer surplus, this transfer from consumers to the owners of the monopoly does not affect the market's total surplus. In other words, the monopoly profit itself represents not a reduction in the size of the economic pie but merely a bigger slice for producers and a smaller one for consumers. Unless consumers are for some reason more deserving than producers—a normative judgment about equity that goes beyond the realm of economic efficiency—the monopoly profit is not a social problem.

The problem, instead, is that the monopoly firm produces and sells a quantity of output below the level that maximizes total surplus. The deadweight loss measures how much the economic pie shrinks as a result. This inefficiency is connected to the monopoly's high price: Consumers buy fewer units when the firm raises its price above marginal cost. But remember that the profit earned on the units that continue to be sold is not the problem. The problem stems from the inefficiently low quantity of output. Put differently, if the high monopoly price did not discourage some consumers from buying the good, it would raise producer surplus by exactly the amount it reduced consumer surplus, leaving total surplus the same as that achieved by the social planners.

There is, however, a possible exception to this conclusion. Suppose that a monopoly has to incur additional costs to maintain its position as the sole producer in the market. For example, a firm with a government-created monopoly might need to hire lobbyists to convince lawmakers to continue its monopoly. In this case, the monopoly may use up some of its monopoly profits paying for these additional costs. If so, the social loss from monopoly includes both these costs and the deadweight loss resulting from reduced output.

QuickQuiz

5. Compared with the social optimum, a monopoly firm chooses
   a. a quantity that is too low and a price that is too high.
   b. a quantity that is too high and a price that is too low.
   c. a quantity and a price that are both too high.
   d. a quantity and a price that are both too low.

6. The deadweight loss from monopoly arises because
   a. the monopoly makes higher profits than a competitive firm would.
   b. some potential consumers who forgo buying the good value it more than its marginal cost.
   c. consumers who buy the good have to pay more than marginal cost, reducing their consumer surplus.
   d. the monopoly chooses a quantity that fails to equate price and average revenue.

Answers are at the end of the chapter.

14-4 Price Discrimination

price discrimination the business practice of selling the same good at different prices to different customers

So far, we have been assuming that the monopoly firm charges the same price to all customers. Yet in many cases, firms sell the same good to different customers for different prices, even though the costs of producing the good for the two customers are the same. This practice is called **price discrimination**. (Marketing experts sometimes call it **price customization**, perhaps because the word "discrimination" sounds negative. This book uses the standard name.)

Before discussing the behavior of a price-discriminating monopolist, we should note that price discrimination is not possible in a competitive market, where many firms are selling the same good at the market price. No firm is willing to charge a lower price to any customer because it can sell all it wants at the market price. And if any firm tried to charge a higher price to a customer, that customer would buy from another firm. For a firm to price discriminate, it must have some market power.

14-4a A Parable about Pricing

To understand why a monopolist would price discriminate, consider an example. Imagine that you are the president of Readalot Publishing Company. Your best-selling children's book author has just written a new graphic cartoon novel. To keep things simple, assume that you pay the author a flat ₹20 lakhs for exclusive rights to the book and that the cost of printing the book is zero. Readalot's profit, therefore, is the revenue from selling the book minus the ₹20 lakhs it pays the author. Given these assumptions, how would you, as Readalot's president, decide the book's price?

Your first step is to estimate the demand for the book. Readalot's marketing department tells you that the book will attract two types of readers: 100,000 die-hard fans who are willing to pay as much as ₹30 and 400,000 less enthusiastic readers who will pay no more than ₹5.

If Readalot charges everyone the same price, what price maximizes profit? There are two natural prices to consider: ₹30 is the most Readalot can charge and attract the 100,000 die-hard fans, and ₹5 is the highest price that will attract the entire market of 500,000 potential readers. Solving this problem is a matter of simple arithmetic. At ₹30, Readalot sells 100,000 copies, has revenue of ₹3 million, and makes ₹10 lakhs in profit. At ₹5, it sells 500,000 copies, has revenue of ₹25 lakhs, and makes ₹500,000. The profit-maximizing strategy is to charge ₹30 and say goodbye to the 400,000 less enthusiastic readers.

Readalot's decision causes a deadweight loss. There are 400,000 readers willing to pay ₹5 for the book, and the marginal cost of providing it to them is zero. Society loses ₹20 lakhs of total surplus when Readalot charges the higher price. This deadweight loss is the inefficiency that arises whenever a monopolist charges a price above marginal cost.

Now suppose that Readalot's marketing department makes a discovery: The Deccan Plateau separates these two groups of readers. The die-hard fans live in Southern India, the less hard-core readers live in the Northern plains, and readers in one part of India can't easily buy books in the other, because Readalot only sells through physical stores.

Eureka! Readalot quickly changes its marketing strategy. It charges the 100,000 South Indian readers ₹30 for the book, while asking only ₹5 of the 400,000 North Indian readers. Now, revenue is ₹3 million in Southern India and ₹20 lakhs in Northern India, for a total of ₹50 lakhs. Profit is ₹30 lakhs, a lot more than the ₹10 lakhs the company could earn by charging the same ₹30 price to all customers. As Readalot's president, you embrace this strategy of price discrimination.

The story of Readalot Publishing is entirely hypothetical, but it describes the business practice of many companies. Consider the prices of hardcover books, e-books, and paperbacks. When a publisher has a new novel, it initially releases an expensive hardcover edition and an e-book, usually at a lower price. For readers who prefer print but won't pay the high price of a hardcover, it later releases a cheaper paperback edition. The price differences among these various editions far exceed the differences in marginal production costs. The publisher is price discriminating by selling the hardcover to die-hard fans, the e-book to those who prefer the lower cost and don't mind reading on a tablet, and the paperback to price-sensitive print readers, thereby maximizing its profit.

14-4b The Moral of the Story

Like any parable, the story of Readalot Publishing is stylized, yet it contains some important truths. This parable teaches three lessons about price discrimination.

The first is that price discrimination is a rational strategy for a profit-maximizing monopolist. By charging different prices to different customers, a monopolist can increase its profit. In essence, a price-discriminating monopolist charges prices closer to each customer's willingness to pay than is possible with a single price.

The second lesson is that for price discrimination to work, the seller must be able to separate customers according to their willingness to pay. In the Readalot story, customers were separated geographically. But monopolists can use other differences, such as age or income, to distinguish among customers.

A corollary to this second lesson is that certain market forces can prevent firms from price discriminating. One such force is **arbitrage**, the process of buying a good in one market at a low price and selling it in another market at a higher price to profit from the price difference. Suppose that in our example, Hyderabad bookstores could buy the book in Lucknow and resell it to Telangana and Andhra Pradesh

-based children. This arbitrage would prevent Readalot from price discriminating because no Hyderabad reader would buy the book at the higher price.

The third lesson may be the most surprising: Price discrimination can raise welfare as measured by total surplus. Recall that a deadweight loss arises when Readalot charges a single ₹30 price because the 400,000 less enthusiastic readers don't get the book, even though they value it at more than its marginal cost of production. But when Read a lot price discriminates, all readers buy the book, and the outcome is efficient. Thus, price discrimination can eliminate the inefficiency inherent in monopoly pricing.

Note that in this example, the increase in welfare from price discrimination shows up as higher producer surplus rather than higher consumer surplus. Consumers are no better off for having bought the book: The price they pay exactly equals the value they place on the book, so they receive no consumer surplus. The entire increase in total surplus from price discrimination accrues to Readalot Publishing in the form of higher profit.

14-4c The Analytics of Price Discrimination

Let's consider a bit more formally how price discrimination affects welfare. We begin by assuming that the monopolist can price discriminate perfectly. **Perfect price discrimination** describes a situation in which the monopolist knows exactly each customer's willingness to pay and can charge each customer a different price. In this case, the monopolist charges customers exactly their willingness to pay, and the monopolist gets the entire surplus in every transaction.

Figure 9 shows producer and consumer surplus with and without price discrimination. To keep things simple, this figure is drawn assuming constant unit costs—that is, marginal cost and average total cost are constant and equal. Without price discrimination, the firm charges a single price above marginal cost, as in

Figure 9

Welfare with and without Price Discrimination

Panel (a) shows a monopoly that charges the same price to all customers. Total surplus in this market equals the sum of profit (producer surplus) and consumer surplus. Panel (b) shows a monopoly that can price discriminate perfectly. Because consumer surplus equals zero, total surplus now equals the firm's profit. Comparing these two panels, you can see that perfect price discrimination raises profit, raises total surplus, and lowers consumer surplus.

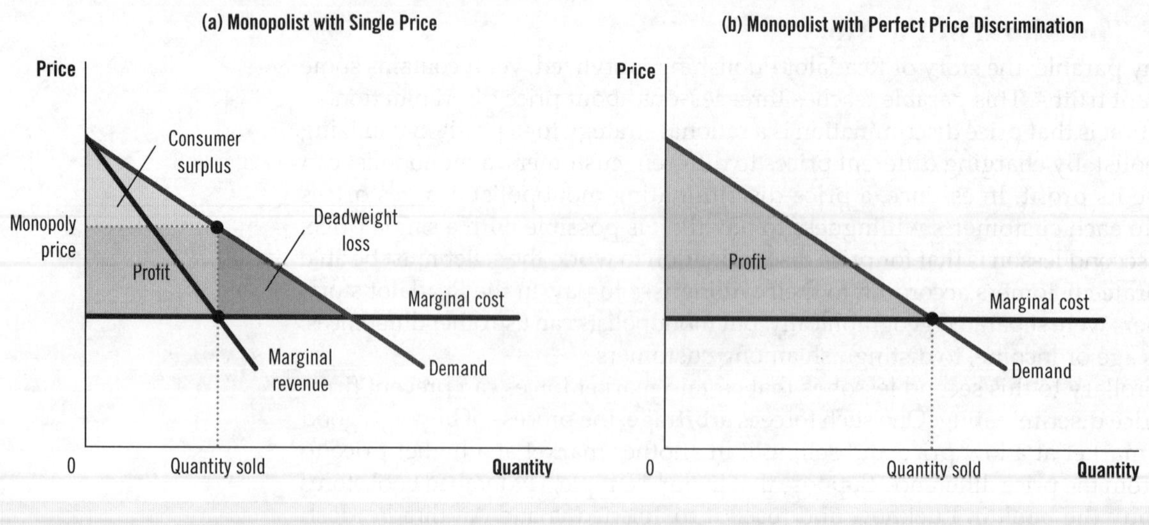

panel (a). Because some potential customers who value the good at more than marginal cost do not buy it at this high price, the monopoly causes a deadweight loss. Yet when a firm can price discriminate perfectly, as in panel (b), all customers who value the good at more than marginal cost buy it and are charged their willingness to pay. Every mutually beneficial trade takes place, no deadweight loss occurs, and the entire surplus derived from the market goes to the monopoly producer in the form of profit.

In reality, of course, price discrimination is not perfect. Customers do not walk into stores with signs displaying their willingness to pay. Instead, firms price discriminate by dividing customers into groups: young versus old, weekday versus weekend shoppers, Americans versus Australians, print versus e-book readers, and so on. Unlike those in the parable of Readalot Publishing, customers within each group differ in their willingness to pay for the product, making perfect price discrimination impossible.

How does this imperfect price discrimination affect welfare as measured by total surplus? The analysis of these pricing schemes is complicated, and it turns out that there is no general answer to this question. Compared with the single-price monopoly outcome, imperfect price discrimination can raise, lower, or leave unchanged the total surplus in a market. The only certain conclusion is that price discrimination raises the monopoly's profit; otherwise, the firm would choose to charge all customers the same price.

14-4d Examples of Price Discrimination

Firms in the economy use various business strategies to charge different prices to different customers. Here are some examples.

Movie Tickets Many movie theaters charge a lower price for children and people over 65 than for other patrons. This is hard to explain in a competitive market where price equals marginal cost because the marginal cost of providing a seat is the same for anyone of any age. Yet the differential pricing is easily explained if movie theaters have some local monopoly power and if children and older people have a lower willingness to pay for a ticket. In this case, movie theaters increase their profit by price discriminating.

Airline Prices Seats on airplanes are sold at many different prices. Most airlines charge a lower price for a round-trip ticket between two cities if the traveler stays over a Saturday night. At first, this seems odd. Why should it matter to the airline whether a passenger stays over a Saturday night? The reason is that this rule provides a way to separate business and leisure travelers. Passengers on business trips have a high willingness to pay and, most likely, do not want to stay over a Saturday night because business meetings are rarely held during weekends. But passengers on vacation or visiting friends and family have a lower willingness to pay and are more likely to want to spend the weekend at their destinations. For airlines, charging lower prices to passengers who stay over a Saturday night is successful price discrimination.

LUCY HAMILTON

"Would it bother you to hear how little I paid for this flight?"

Discount Opportunities Many companies offer discount coupons online and in newspapers and magazines. And some vendors offer online savings on special days that occur so frequently that they aren't really very special. To get a discount, a buyer simply has to clip a coupon or buy on the right day. Why do companies bother? Why don't they just cut the price of the product in the first place?

The answer is that these strategies allow companies to price discriminate. Companies know that not all customers are willing to spend time clipping coupons or navigating online bargains. Moreover, the willingness to seek bargains is related to customers' willingness to pay for the good. Rich and busy executives are unlikely to spend their time doing so, and they are probably willing to pay a higher price for many goods. The unemployed are more likely to hunt for cheaper deals and have a lower willingness to pay. By charging a lower price only to those customers willing to spend the time to seek discounts, firms can successfully price discriminate.

Financial Aid Many colleges and universities give financial aid based on family income. One can view this policy as a type of price discrimination. Students from wealthy families have greater financial resources and, therefore, a higher willingness to pay than students from lower-income families. By charging high tuition and selectively offering financial aid, schools in effect charge prices to customers based on the value they place on going to that school. This behavior is like that of any price-discriminating monopolist.

Quantity Discounts So far in these examples of price discrimination, the monopolist charges different prices to different customers. Sometimes, however, monopolists price discriminate by charging different prices to the same customer for different units that the customer buys. For example, many firms offer lower prices to customers who buy large quantities. A bakery might charge ₹0.50 for each donut but ₹5 for a dozen. This is a form of price discrimination because customers pay a higher price for the first unit they buy than for the twelfth. Quantity discounts are often a successful way to price discriminate because customers' willingness to pay for an additional unit declines as they buy more units.

Quick**Quiz**

7. Price discrimination by a monopolist refers to charging different prices based on
   a. the consumer's willingness to pay.
   b. the consumer's racial or ethnic group.
   c. the cost of producing the good for a particular consumer.
   d. whether the consumer is likely to become a repeat buyer.

8. When a monopolist switches from charging a single price to practicing perfect price discrimination, it reduces
   a. the quantity produced.
   b. the firm's profit.
   c. consumer surplus.
   d. total surplus.

Answers are at the end of the chapter.

14-5 Public Policy toward Monopolies

Unlike competitive markets, monopolies fail to allocate resources efficiently. They produce less than the socially desirable quantity of output and charge prices above marginal cost. Government policymakers can deal with the problem of monopoly in several ways:

- By trying to make monopolized industries more competitive
- By regulating the behavior of the monopolies
- By turning some private monopolies into public enterprises
- By doing nothing at all

14-5a Increasing Competition with Antitrust Laws

If Coca-Cola and PepsiCo wanted to merge, the federal government would scrutinize the deal before it went into effect. The lawyers and economists in the Department of Justice might well decide that a merger between these two large soft-drink companies would make the U.S. soft-drink market substantially less competitive and, as a result, would reduce the well-being of the country as a whole. If so, the Department of Justice would challenge the merger in court, and, if the judge agreed, the two companies would not be allowed to merge. Traditionally, the courts are especially wary of **horizontal mergers**, those between two firms in the same market, like Coca-Cola and PepsiCo. They are less likely to block **vertical mergers**, those between firms at different stages of the production process, such as a merger between a tire company and an auto company. In other words, if a company wants to merge with a competitor, it will face closer scrutiny than if it wants to merge with one of its suppliers or one of its customers.

SCIENCECARTOONSPLUS.COM

"But if we do merge with Amalgamated, we'll have enough resources to fight the antitrust violation caused by the merger."

The government derives this power over private industry from **antitrust laws**, statutes aimed at curbing monopoly power. In the United States, the first and most important of these laws was the Sherman Antitrust Act, passed in 1890 to reduce the market power of "trusts," the dominant monopolies of that era. The Clayton Antitrust Act, passed in 1914, strengthened the government's powers and authorized private lawsuits. As the U.S. Supreme Court put it, the antitrust laws are "a comprehensive charter of economic liberty aimed at preserving free and unfettered competition as the rule of trade."

The antitrust laws give the government tools to promote competition. They allow the government to prevent mergers and, at times, to break up large companies. The antitrust laws also prevent companies from colluding to reduce competition.

Stopping mergers and breaking up companies can have costs as well as benefits. Sometimes, companies combine to lower costs through more efficient joint production. These advantages are called **synergies**. For example, many U.S. banks have merged in recent years to reduce administrative expenses. The airline industry has also experienced consolidation. If antitrust laws are to raise social welfare, the government must be able to determine which mergers are desirable and which are not. That is, it must measure and compare the social benefit from synergies with the social costs of reduced competition. It is open to debate whether the government can perform the necessary cost–benefit analysis with sufficient accuracy. In the end, the application of antitrust laws is often controversial, even among the experts.

14-5b Regulation

Another way the government deals with the problem of monopoly is by regulating monopolists' behavior. This solution is common for natural monopolies, such as water and electric companies, whose prices are often regulated by the government.

What price should the government set for a natural monopoly? This question is not as easy as it might at first appear. One might conclude that the price should equal the monopolist's marginal cost. If price equals marginal cost, customers will buy the quantity of the monopolist's output that maximizes total surplus, and the allocation of resources will be efficient.

Yet two practical problems arise with marginal-cost pricing as a regulatory system. The first arises from the logic of cost curves. By definition, natural monopolies have declining average total cost. As we discussed in a previous chapter, when average total cost is declining, marginal cost is less than average total cost. This situation is

Ask the Experts: Mergers and Competition

"If regulators had not approved mergers in the past decade between major networked airlines, travelers would be better off today."

What do economists say?

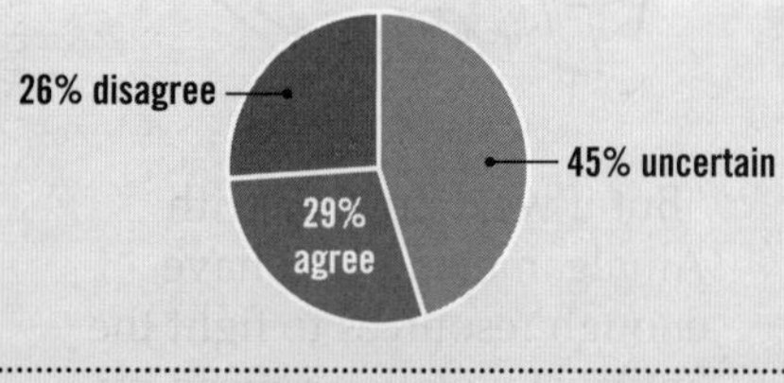

"Americans pay too much for broadband, cable television, and telecommunications services, in part because of a lack of adequate competition."

What do economists say?

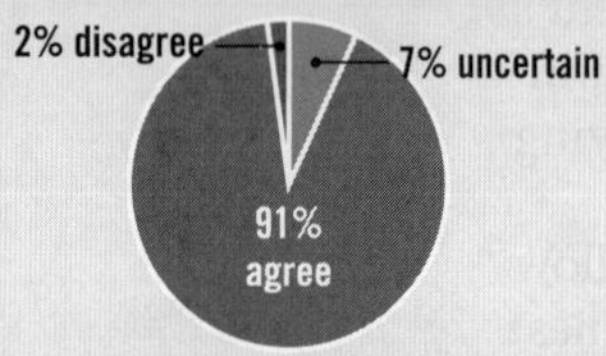

Source: IGM Economic Experts Panel, August 28, 2013, July 20, 2021.

illustrated in Figure 10, which shows a firm with a large fixed cost and then a constant marginal cost thereafter. If regulators were to set price equal to marginal cost, that price would be less than the firm's average total cost, and the firm would lose money. Instead of charging such a low price, the monopoly firm would just exit the industry.

Regulators can respond to this problem in various ways, none of which is perfect. One way is to subsidize the monopolist. In essence, the government picks up the losses inherent in marginal-cost pricing. Yet to finance the subsidy, the government needs to raise money through taxation, which itself generates deadweight losses. Alternatively, the regulators can allow the monopolist to charge a price higher than marginal cost. If the regulated price equals average total cost, the monopolist earns exactly zero economic profit. Yet average-cost pricing leads to deadweight losses because the monopolist's price no longer reflects the marginal cost of producing the good. In essence, average-cost pricing is like a tax on the good the monopolist is selling.

The second problem with marginal-cost pricing as a regulatory system (and with average-cost pricing as well) is that it gives the monopolist no incentive to reduce costs. Each firm in a competitive market tries to reduce its costs because lower costs mean higher profits. But if a regulated monopolist knows that regulators will reduce prices whenever costs fall, the monopolist won't benefit from lower costs. In practice, regulators deal with this problem by allowing monopolists to keep some of the benefits from lower costs in the form of higher profit, a practice that requires some departure from marginal-cost pricing.

Figure 10

Marginal-Cost Pricing for a Natural Monopoly

Because a natural monopoly has declining average total cost, marginal cost is less than average total cost. Therefore, if regulators require a natural monopoly to charge a price equal to marginal cost, the price will be below average total cost, and the monopoly will lose money.

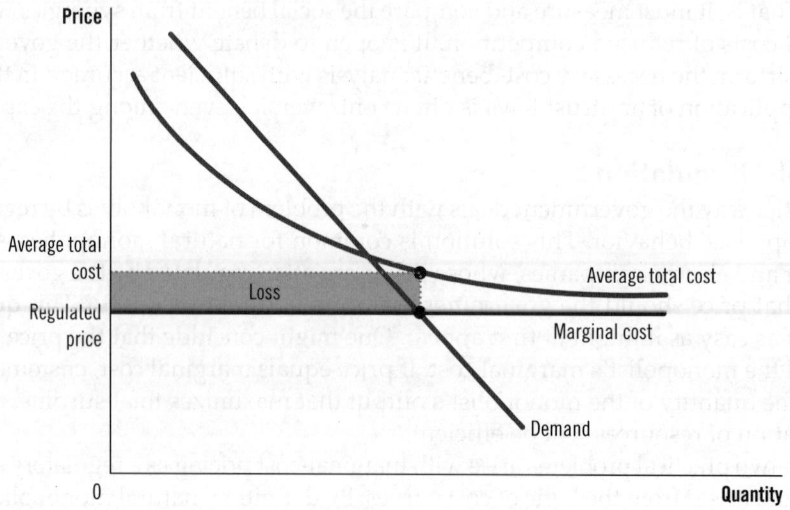

14-5c Public Ownership

The third policy for dealing with monopoly is public ownership. That is, rather than regulating a natural monopoly run by a private firm, a government unit can run the monopoly itself. This solution is common in European countries, where the government owns and operates utilities such as telephone, water, and electric companies. It's fairly common in the United States, too. The government runs the Postal Service, which is often considered to be a natural monopoly. And there are many publicly owned water and power utilities throughout the country.

While public ownership of natural monopolies often has popular support, many economists prefer private to public ownership. The key issue is how the ownership affects the costs of production. Private owners have an incentive to minimize costs as long as they reap part of the benefit in the form of higher profit. If the managers do a bad job of keeping costs down, the firm's owners will fire them. But if public employees do a bad job, the losers are the customers and taxpayers, whose only recourse is the political system. Public employees may become a special-interest group and seek to bend the political system to their advantage. Put simply, as a way of ensuring that firms are efficiently run, the voting booth is less reliable than the profit motive.

14-5d Above All, Do No Harm

Each of the foregoing policies aimed at reducing the problem of monopoly has drawbacks. As a result, some economists argue that the government should be careful not to make matters worse when dealing with monopoly pricing. Here is the assessment of George Stigler, who won the Nobel Prize for his work in industrial organization.

> A famous theorem in economics states that a competitive enterprise economy will produce the largest possible income from a given stock of resources. No real economy meets the exact conditions of the theorem, and all real economies will fall short of the ideal economy—a difference called "market failure." In my view, however, the degree of "market failure" for the American economy is much smaller than the "political failure" arising from the imperfections of economic policies found in real political systems.

As this quotation suggests, the political world is sometimes even less perfect than a highly imperfect market. An institute at the University of Chicago named after Stigler continues to analyze the uneasy relationship between the power of monopolies and the political system. The best solution isn't always clear. In some, though not all, cases, it may be wiser to do nothing.

QuickQuiz

9. Antitrust regulators are likely to prohibit two firms from merging if
   a. there are many other firms in the industry.
   b. there are sizable synergies to the combination.
   c. the combined firm will have a large share of the market.
   d. the combined firm will undercut competitors with lower prices.

10. If regulators impose marginal-cost pricing on a natural monopoly, a possible problem is that
    a. consumers will buy more of the good than is efficient.
    b. consumers will buy less of the good than is efficient.
    c. the firm will lose money and exit the market.
    d. the firm will make excessive profits.

Answers are at the end of the chapter.

14-6 Conclusion: The Prevalence of Monopolies

This chapter has discussed the behavior of firms that have control over the prices they charge. We have seen that such firms behave very differently from the competitive firms studied in the previous chapter. Table 3 summarizes some of the key similarities and differences between competitive and monopoly markets.

An important finding for public policy is that a monopolist produces less than the efficient quantity and charges a price above marginal cost. As a result, a monopoly

India's Big 5 firms and Market Power

There has been considerable debate off late, mostly arising from research findings and policy commentary on whether the big 5 conglomerates of India should be broken down. While on the one hand, some commentators argue that having such large conglomerates results in economies of scale and drives the economy more towards efficiency. Other economists have pointed out that the big 5 firms have been growing at the expense of others and their market shares and turnovers are highly correlated with industry adjusted markup prices, which in the long run can lead to inflation in the economy. This is exactly related to the idea of markup pricing of a monopolist who can charge a price higher than the marginal cost and this likely leads to higher overall prices in the market. Consequently, one may view big industrial conglomerates as "price makers" in the Indian economy.

Ref: https://economictimes.indiatimes.com/news/india/break-up-indias-biggest-firms-says-former-rbi-deputy-governor-viral-acharya/articleshow/99104787.cms?from=mdr

Also see: https://www.brookings.edu/wp-content/uploads/2023/02/BPEA_Spring2023_EM-Panel_Acharya_unembargoed_updated.pdf

Table 3

Competition versus Monopoly: A Summary Comparison

	Competition	Monopoly
Similarities		
Goal of firms	Maximize profits	Maximize profits
Rule for maximizing	$MR = MC$	$MR = MC$
Can earn economic profits in the short run?	Yes	Yes
Differences		
Number of firms	Many	One
Marginal revenue	$MR = P$	$MR < P$
Price	$P = MC$	$P > MC$
Produces welfare-maximizing level of output?	Yes	No
Entry in the long run?	Yes	No
Can earn economic profits in the long run?	No	Yes
Price discrimination possible?	No	Yes

causes deadweight losses. Price discrimination can sometimes mitigate these inefficiencies. But other times, they call for policymakers to take an active role.

How prevalent are the problems of monopoly?

In one sense, monopolies are common. Most firms have some control over the prices they charge. They are not forced to charge the market price for their goods because their goods are not exactly the same as those offered by other firms. A Tesla is not the same as an electric Mustang. Ben and Jerry's ice cream is not the same as Breyer's. Each of these goods has a downward-sloping demand curve, which gives the producer some degree of monopoly power.

Yet firms with substantial monopoly power are rare. Few goods are truly unique. Most have substitutes that, even if not exactly the same, are similar. Ben and Jerry can raise the price of their ice cream a little without losing all their sales, but if they raise it a lot, sales will fall substantially as their customers switch to other brands.

In the end, monopoly power is a matter of degree. It is true that many firms have some monopoly power. Still, for most firms, their monopoly power is limited. In many situations, we will not go far wrong assuming that firms operate in competitive markets, even if that is not precisely the case.

Chapter in a Nutshell

- A monopoly is the sole seller in its market. A monopoly arises when a single firm owns a key resource, when the government gives a firm the exclusive right to produce a good, or when a single firm can supply the entire market at a lower cost than many firms could.
- Because a monopoly is the sole producer in its market, it faces a downward-sloping demand curve for its product. When a monopoly increases production by 1 unit, it causes the price of its good to fall, which reduces the amount of revenue earned on all units produced. As a result, a monopoly's marginal revenue is always less than the price of its good.
- Like a competitive firm, a monopoly maximizes profit by producing the quantity at which marginal revenue equals marginal cost. The monopoly then sets the price at which consumers demand that quantity. Unlike a competitive firm, a monopoly's price exceeds its marginal revenue, so its price exceeds marginal cost.
- A monopolist's profit-maximizing output is below the level that maximizes the sum of consumer and producer surplus. That is, when the monopoly charges a price above marginal cost, some consumers who value the good more than its cost of production don't buy it. As a result, monopoly leads to deadweight losses similar to those that arise from taxes.
- A monopolist can often increase profits by charging different prices for the same good based on a buyer's willingness to pay. This practice of price discrimination can raise economic welfare by getting the good to some consumers who would otherwise not buy it. In the extreme case of perfect price discrimination, the deadweight loss of monopoly is eliminated, and the entire surplus in the market goes to the monopoly producer. More generally, when price discrimination is imperfect, it can either raise or lower welfare compared with the outcome from a single monopoly price.
- Policymakers can respond to the inefficiency of monopoly behavior in several ways. They can use the antitrust laws to try to make the industry more competitive. They can regulate the prices that the monopoly charges. They can turn the monopolist into a government-run enterprise. Or, if the market failure is deemed small compared with the inevitable imperfections of policies, they can do nothing at all.

Key Concepts

monopoly, p. 282 natural monopoly, p. 284 price discrimination, p. 296

Questions for Review

1. Give an example of a government-created monopoly. Is creating this monopoly necessarily bad public policy? Explain.
2. Define **natural monopoly**. What does the size of a market have to do with whether an industry is a natural monopoly?
3. Why is a monopolist's marginal revenue less than the price of its good? Can marginal revenue ever be negative? Explain.
4. Draw the demand, marginal-revenue, average-total-cost, and marginal-cost curves for a monopolist. Show the profit-maximizing output, the profit-maximizing price, and the amount of profit.
5. In your diagram from the previous question, show the output that maximizes total surplus. Show the deadweight loss from the monopoly. Explain your answer.
6. Give two examples of price discrimination. In each case, explain why the monopolist chooses to follow this business strategy.
7. What gives the government the power to regulate mergers between firms? From the perspective of society's welfare, give one reason that a merger might be good and one reason that a merger might be bad.
8. Describe the two problems that arise when regulators tell a natural monopoly that it must set a price equal to marginal cost.

Problems and Applications

1. A publisher faces the following demand schedule for the next novel from one of its popular authors:

Price	Quantity Demanded
₹100	0 novels
90	100,000
80	200,000
70	300,000
60	400,000
50	500,000
40	600,000
30	700,000
20	800,000
10	900,000
0	1,000,000

The author is paid ₹2 million to write the book, and the marginal cost of publishing the book is a constant ₹10 per book.

a. Compute total revenue, total cost, and profit at each quantity. What quantity would a profit-maximizing publisher choose? What price would it charge?
b. Compute marginal revenue. (Recall that $MR = \Delta TR/\Delta Q$.) How does marginal revenue compare with the price? Explain.
c. Graph the marginal-revenue, marginal-cost, and demand curves. At what quantity do the marginal-revenue and marginal-cost curves cross? What does this signify?
d. In your graph, shade in the deadweight loss. Explain in words what this means.
e. If the author were paid ₹3 million instead of ₹2 million to write the book, how would this affect the publisher's decision regarding what price to charge? Explain.
f. Suppose the publisher was not profit-maximizing but was instead concerned with maximizing economic efficiency. What price would it charge for the book? How much profit would it make at this price?

2. A small town is served by many competing supermarkets, which have the same constant marginal costs.
   a. Using a diagram of the market for groceries, show the consumer surplus, producer surplus, and total surplus.
   b. Now suppose that the independent supermarkets combine into one chain. Using a new diagram, show the new consumer surplus, producer surplus, and total surplus. Relative to the competitive market, what is the transfer from consumers to producers? What is the deadweight loss?

3. Taylor Swift has just finished recording her latest album. Her recording company determines that the demand for the CD is as follows:

Price	Number of CDs
₹24	10,000
22	20,000
20	30,000
18	40,000
16	50,000
14	60,000

The company can produce the CD with no fixed cost and a variable cost of ₹5 per CD.

a. Find total revenue for quantity equal to 10,000, 20,000, and so on. What is the marginal revenue for each 10,000 increase in the quantity sold?

b. What quantity of CDs would maximize profit? What would the price be? What would the profit be?

c. If you were Swift's agent, what recording fee would you advise her to demand from the recording company? Why?

4. A company is considering building a bridge across a river. The bridge would cost ₹2 million to build and nothing to maintain. The following table shows the company's anticipated demand over the lifetime of the bridge:

Price per Crossing	Number of Crossings, in Thousands
₹8	0
7	100
6	200
5	300
4	400
3	500
2	600
1	700
0	800

a. If the company were to build the bridge, what would be its profit-maximizing price? Would that level of output be efficient? Why or why not?

b. If the company is interested in maximizing profit, should it build the bridge? What would be its profit or loss?

c. If the government were to build the bridge, what price should it charge?

d. Should the government build the bridge? Explain.

5. Consider the relationship between monopoly pricing and price elasticity of demand.

a. Explain why a monopolist will never produce a quantity at which the demand curve is inelastic. (Hint: If demand is inelastic and the firm raises its price, what happens to total revenue and total costs?)

b. Draw a diagram for a monopolist, precisely labeling the portion of the demand curve that is inelastic. (Hint: The answer is related to the marginal-revenue curve.)

c. On your diagram, show the quantity and price that maximize total revenue.

6. You live in a town with 300 adults and 200 children, and you are thinking about putting on a play to entertain your neighbors and make some money. A play has a fixed cost of ₹2,000, but selling an extra ticket has zero marginal cost. Here are the demand schedules for your two types of customer:

Price	Adults	Children
₹10	0	0
9	100	0
8	200	0
7	300	0
6	300	0
5	300	100
4	300	200
3	300	200
2	300	200
1	300	200
0	300	200

a. To maximize profit, what price would you charge for an adult ticket? For a child's ticket? How much profit do you make?

b. The city council passes a law prohibiting you from charging different prices to different customers. What price do you set for a ticket now? How much profit do you make?

c. Who is worse off because of the law prohibiting price discrimination? Who is better off? (If you can, quantify the changes in welfare.)

d. If the fixed cost of the play were ₹2,500 rather than ₹2,000, how would your answers to parts (a), (b), and (c) change?

7. The residents of the town of Ectenia all love economics, and the mayor proposes building an economics museum. The museum has a fixed cost of ₹2,400,000 and no variable costs. There are 100,000 town residents, and each has the same demand for museum visits: $Q^D = 10 - P$, where P is the price of admission.

a. Graph the museum's average-total-cost curve and its marginal-cost curve. What kind of market would describe the museum?
b. The mayor proposes financing the museum with a lump-sum tax of ₹24 and then opening the museum to the public for free. How many times would each person visit? Calculate the benefit each person would get from the museum, measured as consumer surplus minus the new tax.
c. The mayor's anti-tax opponent says the museum should finance itself by charging an admission fee. What is the lowest price the museum can charge without incurring losses? (Hint: Find the number of visits and museum profits for prices of ₹2, ₹3, ₹4, and ₹5.)
d. For the break-even price you found in part (c), calculate each resident's consumer surplus. Compared with the mayor's plan, who is better off with this admission fee, and who is worse off? Explain.
e. What real-world considerations absent in the problem above might justify an admission fee?

8. Henry Potter owns the only well in Hogwarts town that produces clean drinking water. He faces the following demand, marginal-revenue, and marginal-cost curves:

Demand: P 5 70 2 Q

Marginal Revenue: MR 5 70 2 2Q

Marginal Cost: MC 5 10 1 Q

a. Graph these three curves. If Mr. Potter maximizes profit, what quantity does he produce? What price does he charge? Show these results on your graph.
b. Mayor George Bailey, concerned about water consumers, is considering a price ceiling 10 percent below the monopoly price derived in part (a). What quantity would be demanded at this new price? Would the profit-maximizing Mr. Potter produce that amount? Explain. (Hint: Think about marginal cost.)
c. George's Wizard Uncle Billy says that a price ceiling is a bad idea because price ceilings cause shortages. Is he right in this case? What size shortage would the price ceiling create? Explain.
d. George's muggle friend Clarence, who is even more concerned about consumers, suggests a price ceiling 50 percent below the monopoly price. What quantity would be demanded at this price? How much would Mr. Potter produce? In this case, is Uncle Billy right? What size shortage would the price ceiling create?

9. Only one firm produces and sells soccer balls in the country of Wiknam, and as the story begins, international trade in soccer balls is prohibited. The following equations describe the monopolist's demand, marginal revenue, total cost, and marginal cost:

Demand: P 5 10 2 Q

Marginal Revenue: MR 5 10 2 2Q

Total Cost: TC 5 3 1 Q 1 0.5Q^2

Marginal Cost: MC 5 1 1 Q

where Q is quantity and P is the price measured in Wiknamian dollars.

a. How many soccer balls does the monopolist produce? At what price are they sold? What is the monopolist's profit?
b. One day, the King of Wiknam decrees that henceforth there will be free trade—either imports or exports—of soccer balls at the world price of ₹6. The firm is now a price taker in a competitive market. What happens to domestic production of soccer balls? To domestic consumption? Does Wiknam export or import soccer balls?
c. In our analysis of international trade in Chapter 9, a country becomes an exporter when the price without trade is below the world price and an importer when the price without trade is above the world price. Does that conclusion hold in your answers to parts (a) and (b)? Explain.
d. Suppose that the world price was not ₹6 but, instead, happened to be exactly the same as the domestic price without trade as determined in part (a). Would allowing trade have changed anything in the Wiknamian economy? Explain. How does the result here compare with the analysis in Chapter 9?

10. Based on market research, a company obtains the following information about the demand and production costs of its new product:

Demand: $P = 1{,}000 - 10Q$

Total Revenue: $TR = 1{,}000Q - 10Q^2$

Marginal Revenue: $MR = 1{,}000 - 20Q$

Marginal Cost: $MC = 100 + 10Q$

where Q indicates the number of units sold and P is the price in dollars.

a. Find the price and quantity that maximize the company's profit.
b. Find the price and quantity that would maximize social welfare.
c. Calculate the deadweight loss from monopoly.
d. Suppose, in addition to the costs above, the product's inventor has to be paid. The company is considering four options:
   i. a flat fee of 2,000 dollars.
   ii. 50 percent of the profits.
   iii. 150 dollars per unit sold.
   iv. 50 percent of the revenue.

For each option, calculate the profit-maximizing price and quantity. Which, if any, of these compensation schemes would alter the deadweight loss from monopoly? Explain.

11. Larry, Curly, and Moe run the only saloon in town. Larry wants to sell as many drinks as possible without losing money. Curly wants the saloon to bring in as much revenue as possible. Moe wants to make the largest possible profit. Using a single diagram of the saloon's demand curve and its cost curves, show the price and quantity combinations favored by each of the three partners. Explain. (Hint: Only one of these partners will want to set marginal revenue equal to marginal cost.)

12. Many schemes for price discrimination involve some cost. For example, discount coupons take up the time and resources of both the buyer and the seller. This question considers the implications of costly price discrimination. To keep things simple, let's assume that our monopolist's production costs are simply proportional to output so that average total cost and marginal cost are constant and equal to each other.
    a. Draw the cost, demand, and marginal-revenue curves for the monopolist. Show the price the monopolist would charge without price discrimination.
    b. In your diagram, mark the area equal to the monopolist's profit and call it *X*. Mark the area equal to consumer surplus and call it *Y*. Mark the area equal to the deadweight loss and call it *Z*.
    c. Now suppose that the monopolist can perfectly price discriminate. What is the monopolist's profit? (Give your answer in terms of *X*, *Y*, and *Z*.)
    d. What is the change in the monopolist's profit from price discrimination? What is the change in total surplus from price discrimination? Which change is larger? Explain. (Give your answer in terms of *X*, *Y*, and *Z*.)
    e. Now suppose that there is some cost associated with price discrimination. To model this cost, let's assume that the monopolist has to pay a fixed cost, *C*, to price discriminate. How would a monopolist make the decision whether to pay this fixed cost? (Give your answer in terms of *X*, *Y*, *Z*, and *C*.)
    f. How would a social planner who cares about total surplus decide whether the monopolist should price discriminate? (Give your answer in terms of *X*, *Y*, *Z*, and *C*.)
    g. Compare your answers to parts (e) and (f). How does the monopolist's incentive to price discriminate differ from the social planner's? Is it possible that the monopolist will price discriminate even though doing so is not socially desirable?

Quick**Quiz** Answers

1. **c** 2. **d** 3. **b** 4. **d** 5. **a** 6. **b** 7. **a** 8. **c** 9. **c** 10. **c**

Chapter 15

Monopolistic Competition

You walk into a bookstore to buy a book to read. On the store's shelves, you find a James Patterson thriller, a Maya Angelou memoir, a Ron Chernow history, a Stephenie Meyer paranormal romance, and many other choices. When you pick out a book and buy it, what kind of market are you participating in?

On the one hand, the market for books seems competitive. As you browse, hundreds of authors and publishers vie for your attention. And because anyone can enter the industry by writing and publishing a book, the business is not very profitable. For every highly paid writer, there are dozens of struggling ones.

On the other hand, the market for books also seems monopolistic. Because each title is unique, publishers have some latitude in pricing. Sellers in this market are price makers rather than price takers, and the price of books greatly exceeds the marginal cost of producing them. The list price of a typical hardcover novel, for instance, is about ₹300, but the cost of printing one additional copy is less than ₹100. The price of e-books is often around ₹150, while the marginal cost of permitting one extra download is zero.

GAUDILAB/SHUTTERSTOCK.COM; LECHATNOIR/E+/GETTY IMAGES

The market for books fits neither the competitive nor the monopoly model. Instead, it is best described by the model of **monopolistic competition**, the subject of this chapter. The term "monopolistic competition" might at first seem to be an oxymoron, like "jumbo shrimp." But as we will see, monopolistically competitive industries are monopolistic in some ways and competitive in others. The model describes not only the publishing industry but also the market for many other goods and services.

15-1 Between Monopoly and Perfect Competition

The previous two chapters analyzed markets with many competitive firms and markets with a single monopoly firm. Chapter 13 showed that the price in a perfectly competitive market always equals the marginal cost of production. In addition, in the long run, entry and exit drive economic profit to zero, so the price also equals average total cost. The last chapter examined how a monopoly firm can use its market power to keep price above marginal cost, leading to a positive economic profit for the firm and a deadweight loss for society. Perfect competition and monopoly are two extreme forms of market structure. Perfect competition describes a market with many firms offering essentially identical products; monopoly describes a market with only one firm.

Although the cases of perfect competition and monopoly illustrate important ideas about how markets work, most markets in the real world include elements of both these cases and are not completely described by either of them. The typical firm faces competition, but the competition is not so rigorous that it makes the firm a price taker like the firms in Chapter 13. The typical firm also has some degree of market power, but not so much that the firm can be described exactly by the monopoly model in Chapter 14. In other words, many industries fall somewhere between the polar cases of perfect competition and monopoly. Economists call this situation **imperfect competition**.

oligopoly
a market structure in which only a few sellers offer similar or identical products

One type of imperfectly competitive market is an **oligopoly**, a market with only a few sellers, each offering a product similar or identical to those of other sellers in the market. Economists often measure a market's domination by a small number of firms with a statistic called the **concentration ratio**, which is the percentage of total output in the market supplied by the four largest firms. In the India economy, most industries have a four-firm concentration ratio under 50 percent, but in some industries, the biggest firms are more dominant. Industries with four-firm concentration ratios of 90 percent or more include airlines, telecom, video game consoles, and quick commerce services. These industries are best described as oligopolies. As the next chapter discusses, the small number of firms in oligopolies makes strategic interactions among them crucial to how these markets work. When deciding how much to produce and what price to charge, each firm in an oligopoly is concerned not only with what its competitors are doing but also with how its competitors would react to what it might do.

monopolistic competition
a market structure in which many firms sell products that are similar but not identical

A second type of imperfectly competitive market is called **monopolistic competition**, a market structure in which many firms sell similar but not identical products. In such a market, each firm has a monopoly over its product, but many other firms make similar products that compete for the same customers.

To be more precise, monopolistic competition describes a market with the following attributes:

- **Many sellers:** Numerous firms are competing for the same group of customers.
- **Product differentiation:** Each firm offers a product that is at least slightly different from those of other firms. Rather than being a price taker, each firm faces a downward-sloping demand curve.
- **Free entry and exit:** Firms can enter or exit the market without restriction. The number of firms in the market adjusts until economic profits are driven to zero.

A moment's thought reveals a long list of markets with these attributes: books, video games, restaurants, piano lessons, cookies, clothing, and so on.

Monopolistic competition, like oligopoly, is a market structure that lies between the extreme cases of perfect competition and monopoly. But oligopoly and monopolistic competition are quite different. Oligopoly departs from the perfectly competitive ideal of Chapter 13 because the market has only a few sellers. The small number of sellers makes rigorous competition less likely and strategic interactions among them vitally important. By contrast, a monopolistically competitive market has many sellers, each of which is small compared with the market. It departs from the perfectly competitive ideal because each seller offers a somewhat different product.

Figure 1 summarizes the four types of market structure. The first question to ask about any market is how many firms there are. If there is only one firm, the market is a monopoly. If there are only a few, it is an oligopoly. If there are many firms, we need to ask another question: Do they sell identical or differentiated products? If their products are identical, the market is perfectly competitive. But if their products are differentiated, the market is monopolistically competitive.

Figure 1

The Four Types of Market Structure

Economists who study industrial organization divide markets into four types: monopoly, oligopoly, monopolistic competition, and perfect competition.

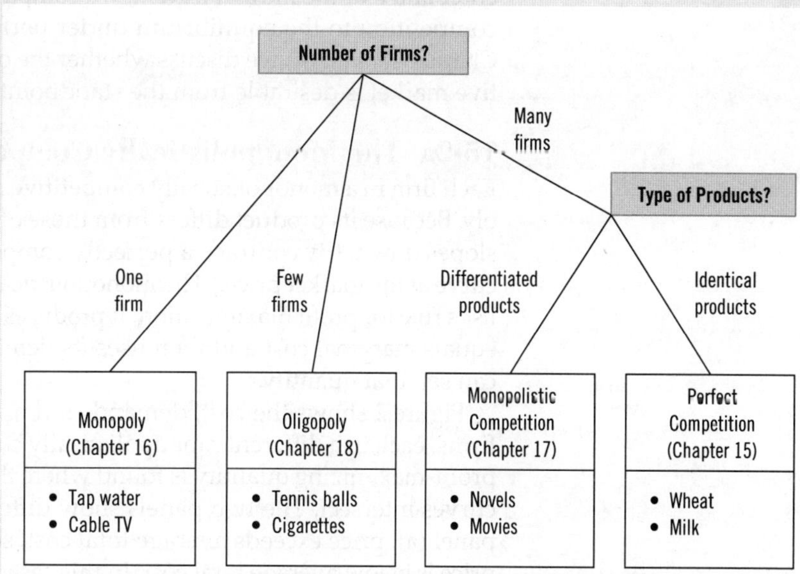

Because reality is never as clear-cut as theory, you may sometimes find it hard to decide what structure best describes a particular market. There is, for instance, no magic number that separates "few" from "many" when counting the number of firms. (Do the approximately dozen companies that sell cars in India make the market an oligopoly, or is it more competitive? The answer is open to debate.) Similarly, there is no sure way to determine when products are differentiated and when they are largely identical. (Are different brands of milk really the same? Again, the answer is debatable.) When analyzing actual markets, economists must keep in mind the lessons learned from studying all types of market structures and then apply each lesson as they deem appropriate.

Having defined the various market structures, let's continue our analysis of each of them. This chapter examines monopolistic competition, and the next examines oligopoly.

Quick**Quiz**

1. Which of the following conditions does NOT describe a firm in a monopolistically competitive market?
   a. It sells a product different from its competitors.
   b. It takes its price as given by market conditions.
   c. It maximizes profit both in the short run and in the long run.
   d. It has the freedom to enter or exit in the long run.

2. Which of the following markets best fits the definition of monopolistic competition?
   a. wheat
   b. tap water
   c. crude oil
   d. haircuts

Answers are at the end of the chapter.

15-2 Competition with Differentiated Products

To understand monopolistically competitive markets, we first consider the decisions facing an individual firm. We then examine what happens in the long run as firms enter and exit the industry. Next, we compare the equilibrium under monopolistic competition to the equilibrium under perfect competition that we examined in Chapter 13. Finally, we discuss whether the outcome in a monopolistically competitive market is desirable from the standpoint of society as a whole.

15-2a The Monopolistically Competitive Firm in the Short Run

Each firm in a monopolistically competitive market is, in many ways, like a monopoly. Because its product differs from those offered by other firms, its demand curve slopes down. (By contrast, a perfectly competitive firm faces a horizontal demand curve at the market price.) The monopolistically competitive firm follows a monopolist's rule for profit maximization: It produces the quantity at which marginal revenue equals marginal cost and then uses its demand curve to find the price at which it can sell that quantity.

Figure 2 shows the cost, demand, and marginal-revenue curves for two typical firms, each in a different monopolistically competitive industry. In both panels, the profit-maximizing quantity is found where the marginal-revenue and marginal-cost curves intersect. The two panels show different outcomes for the firm's profit. In panel (a), price exceeds average total cost, so the firm makes a profit. In panel (b), price is below average total cost. In this case, the firm cannot make a positive profit, so the best it can do is to minimize its losses.

All this should seem familiar. A monopolistically competitive firm chooses its quantity and price just as a monopoly does. In the short run, these two market structures are similar.

Figure 2

Monopolistic Competitors in the Short Run

Monopolistic competitors, like monopolists, maximize profit by producing the quantity at which marginal revenue equals marginal cost. The firm in panel (a) makes a profit because, at this quantity, price is greater than average total cost. The firm in panel (b) makes losses because, at this quantity, price is less than average total cost.

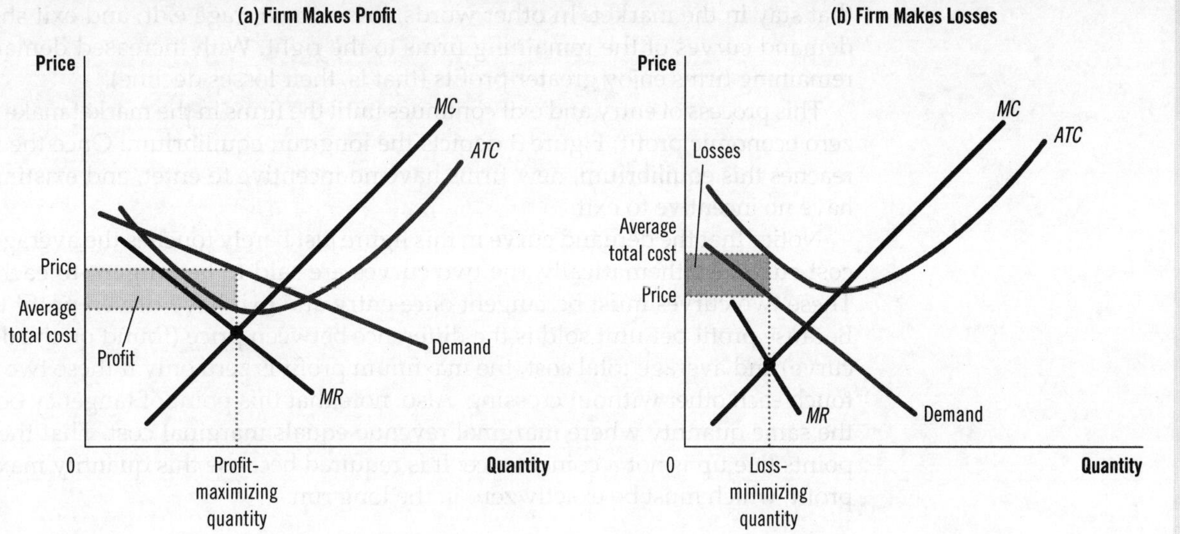

SCIENCECARTOONSPLUS.COM

"GIVEN THE DOWNWARD SLOPE OF OUR DEMAND CURVE, AND THE EASE WITH WHICH OTHER FIRMS CAN ENTER THE INDUSTRY, WE CAN STRENGTHEN OUR PROFIT POSITION ONLY BY EQUATING MARGINAL COST AND MARGINAL REVENUE. ORDER MORE JELLY BEANS."

15-2b The Long-Run Equilibrium

The situations depicted in Figure 2 do not last long. When firms are making profits, as in panel (a), new firms have an incentive to enter the market. This entry increases the number of products from which customers can choose and, therefore, reduces the demand faced by each firm already in the market. In other words, profit encourages entry, and entry shifts the demand curves of the incumbent firms to the left. As the demand for incumbent firms' products falls, these firms experience declining profits.

Conversely, when firms are making losses, as in panel (b), firms in the market have an incentive to exit. As firms exit, customers have fewer products from which to choose. This decrease in the number of firms expands the demand faced by those that stay in the market. In other words, losses encourage exit, and exit shifts the demand curves of the remaining firms to the right. With increased demand, the remaining firms enjoy greater profits (that is, their losses decline).

This process of entry and exit continues until the firms in the market make exactly zero economic profit. Figure 3 depicts the long-run equilibrium. Once the market reaches this equilibrium, new firms have no incentive to enter, and existing firms have no incentive to exit.

Notice that the demand curve in this figure just barely touches the average-total-cost curve. Mathematically, the two curves are said to be **tangent** to each other. These two curves must be tangent once entry and exit have driven profit to zero. Because profit per unit sold is the difference between price (found on the demand curve) and average total cost, the maximum profit is zero only if these two curves touch each other without crossing. Also, note that this point of tangency occurs at the same quantity where marginal revenue equals marginal cost. That these two points line up is not a coincidence: It is required because this quantity maximizes profit, which must be exactly zero in the long run.

Figure 3

A Monopolistic Competitor in the Long Run

In a monopolistically competitive market, if firms are making profits, new ones enter, causing the demand curves for the incumbent firms to shift to the left. Similarly, if firms are making losses, some of the firms in the market exit, causing the demand curves of the remaining firms to shift to the right. Because of these shifts in demand, monopolistically competitive firms eventually find themselves in the long-run equilibrium shown here. In this long-run equilibrium, price equals average total cost, and each firm earns zero profit.

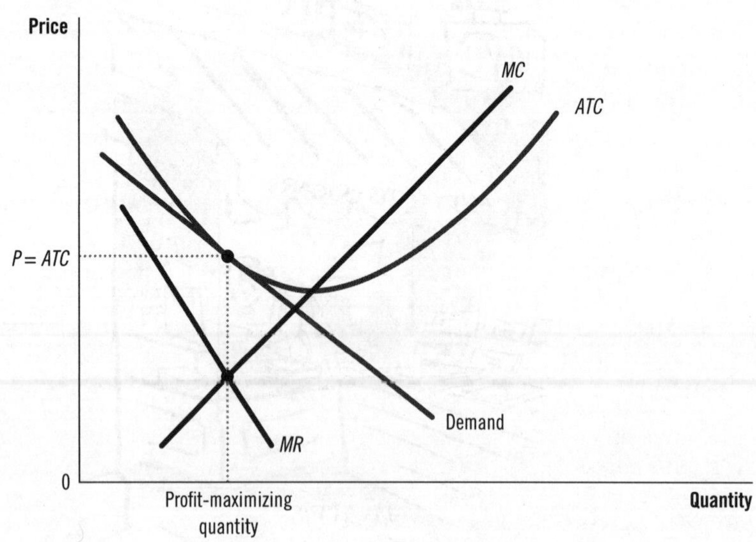

To sum up, two characteristics describe the long-run equilibrium in a monopolistically competitive market:

- As in a monopoly market, price exceeds marginal cost ($P > MC$). This occurs because profit maximization requires marginal revenue to equal marginal cost ($MR = MC$) and because the downward-sloping demand curve makes marginal revenue less than the price ($MR < P$).
- As in a perfectly competitive market, price equals average total cost ($P = ATC$). This arises because free entry and exit drive economic profit to zero in the long run.

The second characteristic shows how monopolistic competition differs from monopoly. Because a monopoly is the sole seller of a product without close substitutes, it can earn positive economic profit, even in the long run. By contrast, because monopolistically competitive markets have free entry, the economic profit of a firm in this type of market is driven to zero in the long run.

15-2c Monopolistic versus Perfect Competition

Figure 4 compares the long-run equilibria under monopolistic competition and perfect competition. (Chapter 15 discussed the equilibrium with perfect competition.) There are two noteworthy differences: excess capacity and the markup.

Figure 4

Monopolistic versus Perfect Competition

Panel (a) shows the long-run equilibrium in a monopolistically competitive market, and panel (b) shows the long-run equilibrium in a perfectly competitive market. Two differences are notable. (1) The perfectly competitive firm produces at the efficient scale, where average total cost is minimized. By contrast, the monopolistically competitive firm produces at less than the efficient scale. (2) Price equals marginal cost under perfect competition, but price is above marginal cost under monopolistic competition.

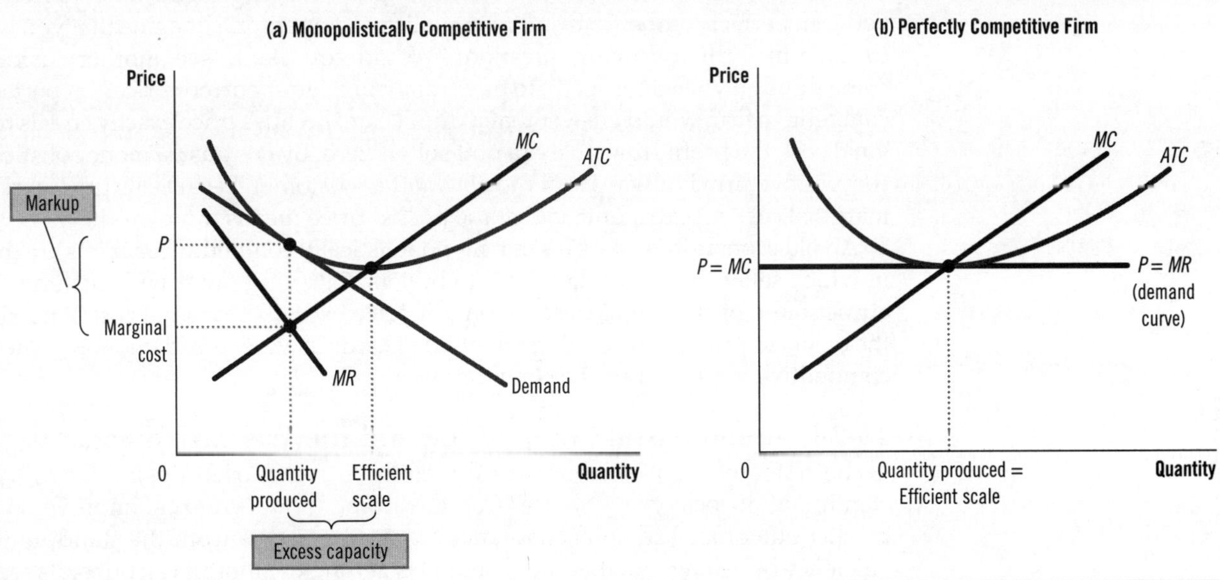

Excess Capacity As we have just seen, the process of entry and exit drives each firm in a monopolistically competitive market to a point of tangency between its demand and average-total-cost curves. Panel (a) of Figure 4 shows that the quantity of output at this point is smaller than the quantity that minimizes average total cost. Under monopolistic competition, firms produce on the downward-sloping portion of their average-total-cost curves. In this way, monopolistic competition contrasts starkly with perfect competition. As panel (b) of Figure 4 shows, free entry in competitive markets drives firms to produce at the minimum of average total cost.

The quantity that minimizes average total cost is called the **efficient scale** of the firm. In the long run, perfectly competitive firms produce at the efficient scale, while monopolistically competitive firms produce below this level. Firms are said to have **excess capacity** under monopolistic competition. In other words, a monopolistically competitive firm, unlike a perfectly competitive firm, could increase the quantity it produces and lower the average total cost of production. The firm forgoes this opportunity because, to sell the additional output, it would need to cut its price for all the units it produces. It is more profitable for a monopolistic competitor to continue operating with excess capacity.

Markup over Marginal Cost A second difference between perfect competition and monopolistic competition is the relationship between price and marginal cost. For a perfectly competitive firm, such as the one in panel (b) of Figure 4, price equals marginal cost. For a monopolistically competitive firm, such as the one in panel (a), price exceeds marginal cost because the firm always has some market power.

How is this markup over marginal cost consistent with free entry and zero profit? The zero-profit condition ensures only that price equals average total cost. It does **not** ensure that price equals marginal cost. Indeed, in the long-run equilibrium, monopolistically competitive firms operate on the declining portion of their average-total-cost curves, so marginal cost is below average total cost. For price to equal average total cost, price must be above marginal cost.

This relationship between price and marginal cost highlights a key difference between perfect competitors and monopolistic competitors. Imagine that you were to ask a firm the following question: "Would you like to see another customer come through your door ready to buy from you at your current price?" A perfectly competitive firm would answer that it didn't care. Because price exactly equals marginal cost, the profit from an extra unit sold is zero. By contrast, a monopolistically competitive firm is always eager to get another customer. Because its price exceeds marginal cost, an extra unit sold at the posted price means more profit.

An old economist's joke says that monopolistically competitive markets are those in which sellers send holiday cards to buyers. Currying favor with customers to attract more of them makes sense only if price exceeds marginal cost. And since the business practice of sending out holiday cards is widespread, monopolistically competitive markets must be commonplace.

15-2d Monopolistic Competition and the Welfare of Society

Is the outcome in a monopolistically competitive market desirable from the standpoint of society as a whole? Can government policymakers improve on the market outcome? Previous chapters evaluated markets from the standpoint of efficiency by asking whether the economy is getting the most it can out of its scarce resources. We learned that perfectly competitive markets achieve efficient outcomes (unless there are externalities), while monopoly markets entail deadweight losses.

Monopolistically competitive markets are more complex than either of these polar cases, so evaluating welfare in these markets is a more subtle exercise.

One source of inefficiency in monopolistically competitive markets is the markup of price over marginal cost. Because of the markup, some consumers who value the good at more than the marginal cost of production (but less than the price) will be deterred from buying it. A monopolistically competitive market has the normal deadweight loss of monopoly pricing.

This outcome is undesirable compared with the efficient quantity that arises when price equals marginal cost, but policymakers can't easily fix the problem. To enforce marginal-cost pricing, they would need to regulate all firms that produce differentiated products. Because such products are so common, the administrative burden of such regulation would be overwhelming.

Regulating monopolistic competitors would also entail all the problems of regulating natural monopolies. In particular, because monopolistic competitors are already making zero profits, requiring them to lower their prices to equal marginal cost would cause them to incur losses. To keep these firms in business, the government would need to help them cover these losses. Rather than financing these subsidies with higher taxes, which would entail their own deadweight losses, policymakers may decide it is better to live with the inefficiency of monopolistic pricing.

Another source of inefficiency under monopolistic competition is that the number of firms in the market may not be ideal. That is, there may be too much or too little entry. Think of the externalities associated with entry. Whenever a new firm considers entering the market with a new product, it takes into account only the profit it would make. Yet its entry would also have two effects that are external to the firm:

- **The product-variety externality:** Because consumers benefit from the introduction of a new product, the entry of a new firm confers a positive externality on consumers.
- **The business-stealing externality:** Because other firms lose customers and profits when faced with a new competitor, the entry of a new firm imposes a negative externality on existing firms.

Thus, in a monopolistically competitive market, the entry of new firms entails both positive and negative externalities. Depending on which is larger, a monopolistically competitive market could have too few or too many products.

Both externalities are closely related to the conditions for monopolistic competition. The product-variety externality arises because new firms under monopolistic competition offer products that differ from those of the existing firms. The greater range of choices increases consumer surplus. The business-stealing externality arises because monopolistically competitive firms post a price above marginal cost and, therefore, are eager to sell additional units. Conversely, because perfectly competitive firms produce identical goods and charge a price equal to marginal cost, neither of these externalities exists under perfect competition.

In the end, we can conclude only that monopolistically competitive markets do not have all the desirable welfare properties of perfectly competitive markets. That is, the invisible hand does not ensure that total surplus is maximized under monopolistic competition. Yet because the inefficiencies are subtle, hard to measure, and hard to fix, public policy cannot easily improve the market outcome.

Quick Quiz

3. A monopolistically competitive firm will increase its production if
   a. marginal revenue is greater than marginal cost.
   b. marginal revenue is greater than average total cost.
   c. price is greater than marginal cost.
   d. price is greater than average total cost.
4. New firms will enter a monopolistically competitive market if
   a. marginal revenue is greater than marginal cost.
   b. marginal revenue is greater than average total cost.
   c. price is greater than marginal cost.
   d. price is greater than average total cost.
5. What is true of a monopolistically competitive market in long-run equilibrium?
   a. Price is greater than marginal cost.
   b. Price is equal to marginal revenue.
   c. Firms make positive economic profits.
   d. Firms produce at the minimum of average total cost.

Answers are at the end of the chapter.

15-3 Advertising

In the modern world, it is nearly impossible to go through a typical day without being bombarded with advertising. Whether you are surfing the Internet, watching television, or driving down the highway, some firm will try to convince you to buy its product. Such behavior is a natural feature of monopolistic competition (as well as some oligopolistic industries). When firms sell differentiated products and charge prices above marginal cost, each firm has an incentive to advertise to attract more buyers to its particular product.

The amount of advertising varies substantially across products. Firms that sell differentiated consumer goods, such as over-the-counter drugs, perfumes, soft drinks, razor blades, breakfast cereals, and dog food, typically spend between 10 and 20 percent of their revenue on advertising. Firms that sell industrial products, such as drill presses and communications satellites, typically spend very little on advertising. And those that sell homogeneous products, such as wheat, salt, sugar, and crude oil, often spend nothing at all.

For the overall economy, about 2 percent of total firm revenue is spent on advertising. This spending takes many forms, including ads on websites, social media, television, radio, and billboards and in newspapers, magazines, and direct mail.

15-3a The Debate over Advertising

Is society wasting the resources it devotes to advertising? Or does advertising serve a valuable purpose? Assessing the social value of advertising is difficult and often generates heated arguments among economists. Let's consider both sides of the debate.

The Critique of Advertising Critics argue that firms advertise to manipulate people's tastes. Much advertising is psychological rather than informational. Consider, for example, the typical television commercial for some brand of soft drink. The commercial most likely does not tell the viewer about the product's price or quality. Instead, it might show a group of happy and beautiful people at a party on a beach on a sunny day. In their hands are cans of the soft drink. The goal of the commercial is to convey a subconscious (if not subtle) message: "You too can have many friends and be happy and beautiful, if you drink our product." Critics of advertising argue that such a commercial creates a desire that otherwise might not exist.

Critics also argue that advertising impedes competition. Advertising often tries to convince consumers that products are more different than they truly are. By increasing the perception of product differentiation and fostering brand loyalty, advertising makes buyers less concerned with price differences among similar goods, making the demand for the brand being advertised less elastic. When a firm faces a less elastic demand curve, it can increase its profits by charging a larger markup over marginal cost.

The Defense of Advertising Defenders of advertising argue that firms use advertising to inform customers. Advertising often conveys the prices of the goods offered for sale, the existence of new products, and the ways in which they can be purchased. This information allows customers to make better choices about what to buy, contributing to the efficient allocation of resources.

Defenders also argue that advertising fosters competition. Because advertising may make customers more aware of the available products, customers can more easily take advantage of price differences, thereby reducing the market power of each firm. In addition, advertising allows new firms to enter more easily because it gives them a way to inform and attract customers.

Over time, the view that advertising can make markets more competitive has gained adherents. One important example is the regulation of advertising for lawyers, doctors, and pharmacists. In the past, these groups succeeded in getting state governments to prohibit advertising in their fields on the grounds that it was "unprofessional." In recent years, however, the courts have concluded that the primary effect of these restrictions was to curtail competition. They have, therefore, overturned many of the laws that prohibit advertising in these fields.

Case Study

How Advertising Affects Prices

What effect does advertising have on prices? On the one hand, it might make consumers view products as being more different from each other than they otherwise would. If so, it would make markets less competitive and firms' demand curves less elastic, allowing firms to charge higher prices. On the other hand, advertising might make it easier for consumers to find the firms with the best prices. In this case, it would make markets more competitive and firms' demand curves more elastic, which would lead to lower prices.

In an article published in *The Journal of Law and Economics* in 1972, the economist Lee Benham tested these two hypotheses. In the United States during the 1960s, state governments had vastly different rules about advertising by optometrists. Some states allowed advertising for eyeglasses and eye examinations, but many prohibited it. For example, a Florida law justified the advertising ban as "in the interest of public health, safety, and welfare." Optometrists endorsed these restrictions.

Benham used the differences in state laws as a natural experiment to test the two views of advertising. The results were striking. In states that prohibited advertising, the average price paid for a pair of eyeglasses was \$33, or ₹288 in 2021 dollars. In states that did not restrict advertising, the average price was \$26, or ₹227 in 2021 dollars. Advertising reduced average prices by more than 20 percent.

A similar natural experiment occurred in 1996 when the U.S. Supreme Court struck down a Rhode Island law that banned advertising the prices of liquor products. A study by Jeffrey Milyo and Joel Waldfogel, published in the *American Economic Review* in 1999, examined liquor prices in Rhode Island after the legal change, compared with liquor prices in the neighboring state of Massachusetts, where there was no change. According to this research, stores in Rhode Island that started advertising cut their prices substantially, often by more than 20 percent, but only on those products that they or their rivals advertised. In addition, after these stores began advertising, they attracted a larger share of customers.

The bottom line: In many markets, advertising fosters competition and leads to lower prices for consumers. ●

15-3b Advertising as a Signal of Quality

Advertising often contains little apparent information about the product being advertised. Consider a firm introducing a new breakfast cereal. It might saturate the airwaves with advertisements showing some actor eating the cereal and exclaiming how wonderful it tastes. How much information does that provide?

According to one theory, the answer is more than you might think. Even advertising that appears to contain little hard information may tell consumers something about product quality. The willingness of the firm to spend a large amount of money on advertising can itself be a **signal** to consumers about the quality of the product being offered.

In general, advertising is profitable if the brand has a good product that consumers will buy repeatedly. Only then the firm that owns the brand chooses to advertise.

Now consider the behavior of consumers. We begin by asserting that consumers are inclined to try a new brand that they see advertised. But is this behavior rational? Should a consumer try a new brand just because the seller has chosen to advertise it?

U6PIX/MEG/NEWSCOM

Is it rational for consumers to be impressed that George Clooney endorses this product?

In fact, it may be completely rational for consumers to try new products that they see advertised. In this story, consumers decide to try Safolla's new millet meal because Safolla advertises. Safolla chooses to advertise because it knows that its cereal is quite good, while BadMillets chooses not to advertise because it knows that its cereal is not good at all. By its willingness to spend on advertising, Safolla signals to consumers the quality of its cereal. Each consumer thinks, quite sensibly, "If the Safolla company is willing to spend so much money advertising this new cereal, it must be really good."

What is striking about this theory of advertising is that the content of the advertisement is irrelevant. Safolla signals the quality of its product by its willingness to spend money on advertising. What the advertisements say is not as important as the fact that consumers know the ads are expensive. By contrast, cheap advertising cannot be effective at signaling quality to consumers. Because both good and bad cereals would now be advertised if cheap, consumers could not infer the quality of a new cereal from the fact that it is advertised. Over time, consumers would learn to ignore such cheap advertising.

This theory can explain why firms pay famous actors large sums of money to make advertisements that, on the surface, appear to convey no information at all. The information is not in the ad's content but simply in its existence and expense.

15-3c Brand Names

Many markets have two types of firms: those that sell products with widely recognized brand names and those that sell generic substitutes. For example, Bayer aspirin competes with generic aspirin. Coke and Pepsi compete with less familiar colas. Firms with brand names usually spend more on advertising and charge more for their products. Just as there is debate about the economics of advertising, there is debate about the economics of brand names.

Critics argue that brand names cause consumers to perceive differences that do not really exist. In many cases, the generic is almost indistinguishable from the brand-name good. Consumers' willingness to pay more for the brand-name good, these critics assert, is a form of irrationality fostered by advertising. The economist Edward Chamberlin, one of the early developers of the theory of monopolistic competition, concluded from this argument that brand names were bad for the economy. He proposed that the government discourage their use by refusing to enforce the trademarks that companies use to identify their products.

More recently, economists have defended brand names as a way for consumers to ensure that the goods they buy are of high quality. There are two related arguments. First, brand names provide consumers with **information** about quality when quality cannot be easily judged in advance of purchase. Second, brand names give firms an **incentive** to maintain high quality because firms have a financial stake in maintaining their brands' reputations.

To see how these arguments work in practice, consider a famous brand name: McDonald's. Imagine that you are driving through an unfamiliar town and want to stop for lunch. You see a McDonald's and a local restaurant next to it. Which do you choose? The local restaurant may offer better food at lower prices, but you don't really know. By contrast, McDonald's offers a consistent product across many cities and countries. Its brand name is useful to you as a way of judging the quality of what you are about to buy.

The McDonald's brand name also ensures that the company has an incentive to maintain quality. For example, if some customers were to become ill from spoiled food sold at a McDonald's, the news would be disastrous for the company. McDonald's would lose much of the valuable reputation that it has built up with years of expensive advertising. As a result, it would lose sales and profit

not only in the outlet that sold the bad food but also in many other McDonald's outlets throughout the country. By contrast, if some customers were to become ill from bad food at a local restaurant, that restaurant might have to close, but the lost profits would be much smaller. McDonald's has a greater incentive to ensure that its food is safe.

The debate over brand names thus centers on the question of whether consumers are rational in preferring brand-name products. Critics argue that brand names are the result of an irrational consumer response to advertising. Defenders argue that consumers have good reason to pay more for brand-name products because they can be more confident in these products' quality.

QuickQuiz

6. If advertising makes consumers more loyal to particular brands, it could _______ the elasticity of demand and _______ the markup of price over marginal cost.
   a. increase; increase
   b. increase; decrease
   c. decrease; increase
   d. decrease; decrease
7. If advertising makes consumers more aware of alternative products, it could _______ the elasticity of demand and _______ the markup of price over marginal cost.
   a. increase; increase
   b. increase; decrease
   c. decrease; increase
   d. decrease; decrease
8. Advertising can be a signal of quality
   a. if advertising is freely available to all firms.
   b. if the benefit of attracting customers is greater for firms with better products.
   c. only if consumers are irrationally attracted to the products they see advertised.
   d. only if the content of the ads contains credible information about the products.

Answers are at the end of the chapter.

15-4 Conclusion

Monopolistic competition is true to its name: It is a hybrid of monopoly and competition. Like a monopoly, each monopolistic competitor faces a downward-sloping demand curve and charges a price above marginal cost. As in a perfectly competitive market, there are many firms, and entry and exit drive the profit of each monopolistic competitor toward zero in the long run. Table 1 summarizes these lessons.

Because monopolistically competitive firms produce differentiated products, each advertises to attract customers to its own brand. To some extent, advertising manipulates consumers' tastes, promotes irrational brand loyalty, and impedes competition. Often, however, it informs consumers, establishes brand names of reliable quality, and fosters competition.

The theory of monopolistic competition describes many markets in the economy. It is somewhat disappointing, therefore, that the theory does not yield simple and compelling advice for public policy. From the standpoint of economic theorists, the allocation of resources in monopolistically competitive markets is not perfect. Yet from the standpoint of practical policymakers, there may be little that can be done to improve it.

Table 1

Monopolistic Competition: Between Perfect Competition and Monopoly

	Market Structure		
	Perfect Competition	**Monopolistic Competition**	**Monopoly**
Features that all three market structures share			
Goal of firms	Maximize profits	Maximize profits	Maximize profits
Rule for maximizing	$MR = MC$	$MR = MC$	$MR = MC$
Can earn economic profits in the short run?	Yes	Yes	Yes
Features that monopolistic competition shares with monopoly			
Price taker?	Yes	No	No
Price	$P = MC$	$P > MC$	$P > MC$
Produces welfare-maximizing level of output?	Yes	No	No
Features that monopolistic competition shares with perfect competition			
Number of firms	Many	Many	One
Entry in the long run?	Yes	Yes	No
Can earn economic profits in the long run?	No	No	Yes

Chapter in a Nutshell

- A monopolistically competitive market is characterized by three attributes: many firms, differentiated products, and free entry and exit.
- The long-run equilibrium in a monopolistically competitive market differs from that in a perfectly competitive market in two ways. First, in a monopolistically competitive market, each firm has excess capacity. That is, it chooses a quantity that puts it on the downward-sloping portion of the average-total-cost curve. Second, each firm charges a price above marginal cost.
- Monopolistic competition does not have all the desirable properties of perfect competition. There is the standard deadweight loss of monopoly caused by the markup of price over marginal cost. In addition, the number of firms (and thus the number of product varieties) can be too large or too small. In practice, the ability of policymakers to correct these inefficiencies is limited.
- The product differentiation inherent in monopolistic competition leads to the use of advertising and brand names. Critics of advertising and brand names argue that firms use them to manipulate consumers' tastes and reduce competition. Defenders of advertising and brand names argue that firms use them to inform consumers and compete more vigorously on price and product quality.

Key Concepts

oligopoly, p. 312

monopolistic competition, p. 312

Questions for Review

1. Describe the three attributes of monopolistic competition. How is monopolistic competition like monopoly? How is it like perfect competition?
2. Draw a diagram depicting a firm that is making a profit in a monopolistically competitive market. Now show what happens to this firm as new firms enter the industry.
3. Draw a diagram of the long-run equilibrium in a monopolistically competitive market. How is price related to average total cost? How is price related to marginal cost?
4. Does a monopolistic competitor produce too much or too little output compared with the most efficient level? What practical considerations make it difficult for policymakers to solve this problem?
5. How might advertising reduce economic well-being? How might advertising increase economic well-being?
6. How might advertising with no apparent informational content still inform consumers?
7. Explain two benefits that might arise from the existence of brand names.

Problems and Applications

1. Among monopoly, oligopoly, monopolistic competition, and perfect competition, how would you classify the markets for each of the following drinks?
   a. tap water
   b. bottled water
   c. cola
   d. beer
2. Classify the following markets as perfectly competitive, monopolistic, or monopolistically competitive, and explain your answers.
   a. wooden no. 2 pencils
   b. copper
   c. local electricity service
   d. peanut butter
   e. lipstick
3. For each of the following characteristics, say whether it describes a perfectly competitive firm, a monopolistically competitive firm, both, or neither.
   a. sells a product differentiated from that of its competitors
   b. has marginal revenue less than price
   c. earns economic profit in the long run
   d. produces at the minimum of average total cost in the long run
   e. equates marginal revenue and marginal cost
   f. charges a price above marginal cost
4. For each of the following characteristics, say whether it describes a monopoly firm, a monopolistically competitive firm, both, or neither.
   a. faces a downward-sloping demand curve
   b. has marginal revenue less than price
   c. faces the entry of new firms selling similar products
   d. earns economic profit in the long run
   e. equates marginal revenue and marginal cost
   f. produces the socially efficient quantity of output
5. You are hired as a consultant to a monopolistically competitive firm, which reports the following information about its price, marginal cost, and average total cost. Can the firm possibly be maximizing profit? If not, what should it do to increase profit? If the firm is maximizing profit, is the market in a long-run equilibrium? If not, what will happen to restore long-run equilibrium?
   a. $P < MC, P > ATC$
   b. $P > MC, P < ATC$
   c. $P = MC, P > ATC$
   d. $P > MC, P = ATC$
6. Sparkle is one of the many firms in the market for toothpaste, which is in a long-run, monopolistically competitive equilibrium.
   a. Draw a diagram showing Sparkle's demand curve, marginal-revenue curve, average-total-cost curve, and marginal-cost curve. Label Sparkle's profit-maximizing output and price

16-2 Nash Equilibrium and Managerial Decision-Making

Let us begin by focusing on a basic "game" called the **prisoners' dilemma,** which teaches a general lesson on why cooperation is difficult in strategic interdependence situations and presents an elementary example of a simultaneous move game of complete information.

prisoners' dilemma particular "game" between two captured prisoners that illustrates why cooperation is difficult to maintain even when it is mutually beneficial

16-2 a The Prisoners' Dilemma

The prisoners' dilemma is a story about two criminals who have been captured by the police. Call them Bonnie and Clyde. The police have enough evidence to convict them of the minor crime of carrying an unregistered gun, so each would spend a year in jail. The police also suspect that these criminals committed a bank robbery but lack evidence to convict them for it. The police question Bonnie and Clyde in separate rooms and offer each of them the following deal:

"Right now, we can lock you up for 1 year. But if you confess to the bank robbery and implicate your partner, we'll give you immunity, and you can go free. Your partner will get 20 years in jail. If you both confess, we won't need your testimony, and we can avoid the cost of a trial, so you'll each get a sentence of 8 years."

If Bonnie and Clyde, heartless bank robbers that they are, care only about their own individual sentences, what would you expect them to do? Figure 1 shows the **payoff matrix** for their choices. Each prisoner has two strategies: confess or remain silent. The sentence each prisoner gets depends on the strategy he or she chooses, and the strategy chosen by his or her partner in crime.

Figure 1

The Prisoners' Dilemma

In this game between two criminals suspected of committing a major crime, the sentence that each receives depends both on his or her decision whether to confess or remain silent and on the decision

		Bonnie's Decision	
		Confess	Remain Silent
Clyde's Decision	Confess	Bonnie goes free / Clyde gets 8 years	Bonnie gets 20 years / Clyde goes free
	Remain Silent	Bonnie goes free / Clyde gets 20 years	Bonnie gets 1 year / Clyde gets 1 year

Consider first Bonnie's decision. She reasons as follows: "We had a fabulous time robbing banks together, but now I don't know what Clyde is going to do. If he remains silent, my best strategy is to confess because then I'll go free rather than spending a year in jail. If he confesses, I should still confess because then I'll spend just 8 years in jail rather than 20. So, whatever Clyde does, I'm better off confessing."

dominant strategy strategy that is best for a player in a game, regardless of the strategies chosen by the other players

In the language of game theory, a strategy is called a **dominant strategy** if it is the best one for a player to follow regardless of the strategies pursued by other players. In this case, confessing is a dominant strategy for Bonnie. She spends less time in jail if she confesses, regardless of whether Clyde confesses or remains silent. Now, consider Clyde's decision. He faces the same choices as Bonnie, and he reasons the same way. Regardless of what Bonnie does, Clyde can reduce his jail time by confessing. In other words, confessing is also a dominant strategy for Clyde.

Nash equilibrium a situation in which economic actors interacting with one another each choose their best strategy, given the strategies that all the other actors have chosen

In the end, both Bonnie and Clyde confess, and they each spend 8 years in jail. This outcome is a **Nash equilibrium** Each chooses the best strategy available, given the strategy the other is following. Yet, from their standpoint, the outcome is terrible. If they had **both** remained silent, both would have been better off, spending only 1 year in jail on gun charge. Because they pursue their own interests, the two prisoners together reach an outcome that is worse for each of them.

You might have thought that Bonnie and Clyde would have planned this situation. But even if they had, they would still run into problems. Imagine that, before the police captured them, the two criminals had sworn undying love and agreed never to confess. Clearly, this pact would make them both better off **if** they both lived up to it because each would spend only 1 year in jail. They could then ride off into a glorious sunset. But would Bonnie and Clyde remain silent simply because they had agreed they would? Once they are being questioned separately, the logic of self-interest takes over and leads them to confess. Cooperation between the prisoners is difficult to maintain because cooperation is individually irrational. So is love, but it's easier to maintain when you're not facing a prison sentence.

However, not all games will have a dominant strategy for players. In these cases, a more general concept to use is that of the best **response**. The best response is the strategy that yields the highest payoff given what others do. In the above example, confessing is Bonnie's best response, given Clyde's strategy of playing "Confess." Similarly, Bonnie's best response to Clyde's strategy of "Confess" is again Confess. In this case, since Bonnie has the same best response for all of Clyde's strategies, or in other words, Confess is the best response regardless of what Clyde does, it is also a dominant strategy. So, the best response is a necessary condition for having a dominant strategy. A Nash equilibrium is a profile of strategies, one for each player, such that each strategy is the best response to the others' strategies. At a Nash equilibrium, no player wants to deviate unilaterally. While the prisoner's dilemma Nash equilibrium is also a **dominant strategy equilibrium**, since all players play their dominant strategies, not all Nash equilibria will be dominant strategy equilibria. However, all dominant strategy equilibria, are by design, Nash Equilibria.

Dominant strategy equilibrium a situation in which economic actors interacting with one another play their dominant strategies.

Box 16.1 Dominant Strategies in Managerial Decisions

Example: Pricing Rivalry between Pizza Delight and Desi Pizzas
Two popular local pizza chains–Pizza Delight and Desi Pizzas–are deciding whether to offer a Buy-One-Get-One (BOGO) promotion or stick to their regular price menu for the upcoming cricket season. Each store's weekly profit (in INR thousand) depends on its own decision and the rival's choice.

Dominant-Strategy Matrix for Pizza Promotions
(Payoffs in INR thousand for Pizza Delight, Desi Pizzas)

	Desi Pizzas: Regular Price	Desi Pizzas: BOGO
Pizza Delight: Regular Price	(90, 90)	(60, 110)
Pizza Delight: BOGO	(110, 60)	(70, 70)

No matter what Desi Pizzas does, Pizza Delight earns more by choosing BOGO: If Desi Pizzas keeps Regular Price, 110 > 90. If Desi Pizzas also runs BOGO, 70 > 60. The same logic applies to Desi Pizzas. Thus, "Run BOGO Promotion" is a dominant strategy for both firms. The dominant strategy equilibrium is (BOGO, BOGO), yielding (70, 70).

Although both would earn higher profits (INR 90 thousand each) if neither is discounted, competitive incentives push them toward mutual discounting. This presents a managerial analogue of a Prisoners' Dilemma.

Managerial Insight
When dominant strategies lead to collectively inferior outcomes, the remedy lies not in goodwill but in strategic design, such as product differentiation, staggered promotions, or loyalty schemes, that alter payoffs and reduce incentives for direct competition by positioning your rival product as an imperfect substitute for your product.

This example reinforces a central lesson from the Prisoners' Dilemma. When firms possess dominant strategies, the rational play can yield inefficient outcomes. In such cases, cooperation fails not because managers are irrational, but because the equilibrium logic itself drives mutually detrimental behavior. Recognizing these patterns helps managers design credible coordination mechanisms, such as long-term contracts, brand differentiation, or staggered market entry, that shift the game toward more efficient outcomes.

16-2b Games without Dominant Strategies

As discussed above, not every game allows a simple prediction based on dominant strategies. These games will not have a dominant strategy equilibrium but will still, under certain conditions, have at least one Nash equilibrium. In many real interactions, a player's best choice depends on what others do. For these games, we arrive at a Nash equilibrium prediction by studying each player's decision as the best response to the other's.

The Classic Battle of the Sexes

Two friends, Asha and Ravi, are deciding how to spend their evening in EconIsland, where their mobile networks are not activated with international roaming. As a result, they cannot communicate with each other, and the Government of EconIsland does not allow WhatsApp or messenger chats. Therefore, they must make their decisions without communicating. This presents a case of a simultaneous move game. However, they both know the following information. Asha prefers going to a music concert, while Ravi prefers watching cricket. Both, however, would rather be together than alone. We can represent their payoff matrix as follows:

	Ravi: Concert	Ravi: Cricket
Asha: Concert	(2, 1)	(0, 0)
Asha: Cricket	(0, 0)	(1, 2)

Consider Asha's strategies and think about Ravi's best responses. If Asha were to choose "Concert," then Ravi's best response is "Concert", given that 1 > 0. If Asha were to choose "Cricket," then Ravi's best response is to choose "Cricket," given that a payoff of 2 > 0. Notice that Ravi does not have a dominant strategy here. His best responses flip depending on the contingency in which he must act.

Similarly, for Ravi's strategies, Asha's best responses are to mimic what Ravi does. So, both (Concert, Concert) and (Cricket, Cricket) are Nash equilibria because each player is making the best response to the other's actions. However, neither player has a dominant strategy and hence there does not exist a dominant strategy equilibrium here. Asha's best choice depends on Ravi's, and vice versa. This game illustrates a **managerial insight**: Coordination problems often have multiple equilibria, and the challenge lies in selecting the focal point, which is the equilibrium that both players believe the other will choose.

Box 16.2 Coordination and Focal Points in Business

Consider the previous example of two rival pizza chains, Pizza Delight and Desi Pizzas, who now must decide which online delivery platform to prioritize for their Holi marketing campaign. Both would benefit if they appeared on the same platform, since customers can choose between alternatives easily rather than having to switch apps, but each prefers a different one due to prior partnerships.

	Pizza Delight: Zomato	Pizza Delight: Swiggy
Desi Pizzas: Zomato	(3, 2)	(0, 0)
Desi Pizzas: Swiggy	(0, 0)	(2, 3)

Here, there are two Nash equilibria where both coordinate on Zomato or both coordinate on Swiggy. Yet neither firm has a dominant strategy. Desi Pizzas' best action depends on what Pizza Delight chooses, and vice versa. The equilibrium that occurs may depend on brand reputation, customer expectations, or prior coordination. Remember that Nash equilibrium essentially tells us what are the situations from which no player can unilaterally deviate and benefit, all else equal, but not about "how" the equilibrium is attained. That is where the managerial discretion and effectiveness come into play when game theory is applied in the business world.

Managerial Insight: Coordination games like this are common in business. Firms often converge on one equilibrium because of focal points that are predefined such as market conventions, early commitments, or informal communication. In this case, if Pizza Delight already has a large Zomato following, Desi Pizzas might rationally align there even if it slightly prefers Swiggy.

16-2c Mixed Strategies

In some strategic situations, there is no pure-strategy Nash equilibrium. This means that no single set of deterministic choices exists from which no player wants to deviate. Consider a classic example, commonly known as the game of **Matching Pennies**. Two players simultaneously show a coin–Head or Tail. Player A wins if both matches, whereas Player B wins if they differ. The payoff matrix for this game can be drawn out as below.

	Player B: Head	Player B: Tail
Player A: Head	(+1, −1)	(−1, +1)
Player A: Tail	(−1, +1)	(+1, −1)

Let us think of the best responses here. If A plays Head, B's best response is to play Tails. If A plays Tails, B's best response is to play Head. Clearly, there is no dominant strategy for B. Similarly, if B plays Heads, which is her best response to A playing Tails, A's best response, however, is to play Heads because A wins if both matches. Consequently, these strategies cannot lead to a Nash equilibrium prediction. Therefore, players may deliberately randomize across available actions, assigning probabilities to each possible move. This approach is called a **mixed strategy**.

Mixed strategy
a single strategy that is a combination of multiple strategies randomly chosen based on a probability distribution.

Why Randomize?

Randomization prevents predictability. If a rival can perfectly anticipate your move, they can exploit it. By mixing strategies using randomization, a player can keep opponents indifferent among their own possible actions. In equilibrium, each player's randomization makes the other's expected payoff equal across their available choices.

Solving for Mixed Strategy Equilibrium

To solve for mixed strategy equilibrium, let us first conceptualize the problem at hand. Essentially, players are looking for best responses to the other's strategies. A best response is defined as a situation where the payoff from one strategy exceeds the payoff from the other for a given player and for a given strategy of the other player. This is a **pure strategy** case because we assume that for a given strategy of the other player, we play one single strategy for sure or with probability 1.

However, if for a given strategy of the other player, we randomize between two of our strategies, this will be the case **for mixed strategy**. For instance, in the game above, suppose player A thinks of the following mixed strategy: "I will play Heads with probability p and Tails with probability $(1 - p)$" and similarly player B's mixed strategy is to play Heads with probability q and Tails with probability $(1 - q)$.

	Player B: Head with probability q	**Player B: Tail with probability (1 – q)**
Player A: Head with probability p	(+1, −1)	(−1, +1)
Player A: Tail with probability (1 – p)	(−1, +1)	(+1, −1)

Indifference Condition This condition implies that a player will only randomize if and only if she is indifferent between playing the two strategies. Consider that Player A decides to play the mixed strategy as described above and depicted in the matrix. Then what is Player B's best response? If player B chooses Heads, she gets: −1 with prob p and 1 with prob $(1 - p)$. So, her expected payoff by choosing Head is $[p(-1) + (1 - p)\,1]$. Similarly, her expected payoff by choosing Tails is $[p \times 1 + (1 - p) \times (-1)]$. Now, if either of these expressions is larger in value, then player B should surely choose that option as a best response to the mixed strategy played by player A. So only if these two expected payoffs are identical, player B's best response will be to play a mixed strategy with probabilities q and $(1 - q)$.

So, we set these two expressions equal:

$$[\,p \times (-1) + (1 - p) \times 1] = [\,p \times 1 + (1 - p) \,.\, (-1)]$$

This is the indifference condition. If we solve for p, we get the value $p = 0.5$
Similarly, we can derive an indifference condition for player A as follows:

$$[q \times 1 + (1 - q) \times (-1)\,] = (q \times (-1) + (1 - q) \times 1]$$

Solving this gives us the value of $q = 0.5$. Therefore, the unique mixed-strategy Nash equilibrium occurs when both randomize equally. In other words, each plays Head or Tail with 50% probability. Neither can improve by deviating, because each keeps the other indifferent. It is possible to think of all strategies as mixed strategies, where pure strategies are nothing but a degenerate special case where $p = 1$ and $(1 - p) = 0$ for a given strategy profile.

Consider a situation where airlines such as IndiGo and SpiceJet face a dilemma in announcing fare sales. If both run discounts in the same week, margins collapse. If one moves first, it gains temporary advantage but risks retaliation with the other. Since each airline's best response depends on the other's timing, there is no pure-strategy equilibrium. Hence, airlines often randomize the timing of fare sales within a period such as a quarter. These are sometimes announced on a Tuesday, sometimes on a Friday, to make rivals indifferent and reduce predictability.

Similarly, consumer goods giants such as HUL and P&G compete for prime television slots during major events (such as the IPL or the World Cup). If both target the same break, ads lose visibility. If one shifts, viewership shifts too. Since neither time dominates the other, both firms mix across different ad slots, choosing probabilistic schedules that balance reach and clutter.

Managerial Insights Randomization helps avoid being pre-empted and undercutting of prices. In terms of business strategy, maintaining the unpredictability can provide advantages and deter exploitation by rivals. In advertising, rival campaigns and counter messaging strategies can be blunted by using algorithmic mixed strategies and randomizing on time and content of ads.

Quick**Quiz**

1. Which of the following statements is false?
   a. All dominant strategy equilibria are Nash equilibria.
   b. Nash equilibria involve best responses.
   c. Dominant strategies are best responses.
   d. All Nash equilibria are dominant strategy equilibria.
2. The prisoners' dilemma is a two-person game illustrating that
   a. the cooperative outcome could be worse for both people than the Nash equilibrium.
   b. even if the cooperative outcome is better than the Nash equilibrium for one person, it might be worse for the other.
   c. even if cooperation is better than the Nash equilibrium, each person might have an incentive not to cooperate.
   d. rational, self-interested individuals will naturally avoid the Nash equilibrium because it is worse for both of them.
3. Two people facing the prisoners' dilemma may cooperate if they
   a. recognize that the Nash equilibrium is worse for both people than the cooperative equilibrium.
   b. play the game repeatedly and expect noncooperation to be met with future retaliation.
   c. each chooses their dominant strategy.
   d. each realizes that the strategy they choose is not known to the other until the outcome is realized.
4. A pure strategy is a special type of mixed strategy where a given degenerate strategy is played _________.
   a. With probability 1
   b. With probability >0 but <1
   c. With probability 1/2
   d. Never

Answers are at the end of the chapter.

16-3 Sequential Games and Subgame Perfection

Not all strategic choices are simultaneous. In sequential settings, later movers observe some of the earlier moves. The earlier game play, in technical terms, is known as the **history of the game**. We model these with extensive form representations, or using decision trees, and solve by invoking the idea of **backwards induction**. The payoff matrix form of representing games is often known as the normal form representation, whereas decision tree-type representations are known as extensive forms.

In many markets, actions unfold over time. One firm moves first; others observe their actions (fully or partly) and then respond with their own actions. Such settings are sequential games. We solve them by backward induction: start at the last decision, pick the payoff-maximizing action there, roll one step back, and repeat. The resulting prediction is a **Subgame Perfect Nash Equilibrium (SPNE)**—a set of strategies that form a Nash equilibrium in every subgame.

Subgame Perfect Nash Equilibrium a strategy profile in a sequential move game that constitutes a Nash equilibrium in every subgame

A **subgame** is any portion of a sequential (extensive form) game that can be analyzed as a complete game on its own. Formally, a subgame begins with a single decision node that is independent and includes all its future decision nodes and payoffs. Additionally, the subgame has no incomplete information about prior moves in the history of the game. In simpler terms, a subgame is a self-contained mini game within the larger sequence of play. Essentially, it starts from a particular point and proceeding to the end, with all players aware of the history up to that point.

16-3a Subgame Perfect Nash Equilibrium Solution Concept

Consider our earlier example about Ravi and Asha deciding whether to meet at the Cricket or the Concert. However, instead of simultaneously choosing, let us now consider that Asha moves first; Ravi observes Asha's action and then moves second. This game can be depicted in extensive form as follows:

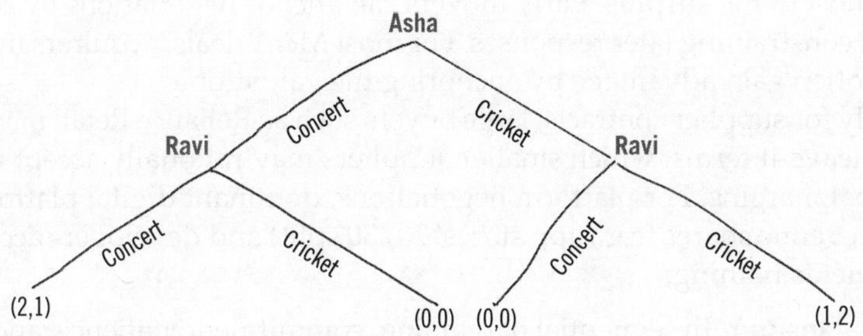

The above indicates that Asha moves first and chooses between Concert and Cricket. Ravi has two potential contingencies in which he must act. These are his two decision nodes. Essentially, going by the definition of **strategy** discussed earlier, every strategy of Ravi must specify an action for every decision node. Therefore, one valid strategy for Ravi would be (Concert, Concert), which would indicate that he would choose Concert at both nodes. Similarly, Ravi has four strategies in all: the other three being (Concert, Cricket), (Cricket, Concert), and (Cricket, Cricket).

To solve the game, let us consider the subgame where Ravi moves after Asha chooses cricket. In this subgame, the choice of Ravi is between Concert that yields 0 and Cricket that yields 2. So, we can collapse these two branches and conclude that, if the game reaches this node, Ravi will choose cricket. Consider the first node, where Asha chooses concert. Here, Ravi compares a payoff of 1 by choosing concert and 0 by choosing cricket, and, therefore, if the game reaches this node, Ravi will choose Concert. Now, we have solved the second stage of the game, and using backwards induction can now analyze Asha's actions. Asha knows that if she chooses Concert, Ravi will choose Concert, and so she will get 2. She compares this to choosing Cricket. If she chooses this option, we already solved that Ravi will also choose Cricket, and so Asha will get 1. Since 2>1, Asha will obviously choose Concert at the start. So, Asha's SPNE strategy is Concert, and Ravi's SPNE strategy is (Concert, Cricket). This leads to an SPNE outcome of both ending up at the Concert.

Chapter

17 Oligopoly

If you play tennis, you have probably used balls from one of a handful of brands: Wilson, Dunlop, or Babolat. These few companies supply most of the tennis balls sold in India. Together, they determine the quantity of tennis balls produced and, given the market demand curve, the price at which tennis balls are sold.

The market for tennis balls is an example of an **oligopoly**. The essence of an oligopolistic market is that there are only a few sellers, so the actions of any one of them can have a large impact on the profits of all the others. This chapter examines how this interdependence shapes the firms' behavior and what problems it raises for public policy.

oligopoly
a market structure in which only a few sellers offer similar or identical products

The analysis of oligopoly follows from the discussion of **game theory**, the study of how people behave in strategic situations. Oligopoly markets, depending on the type, are direct applications of either simultaneous games or sequential games discussed in Chapter 16.

Game theory isn't necessary for analyzing competitive or monopoly markets. In a market that is either perfectly or monopolistically competitive, each firm is so small compared

ELACKCAT/E+/GETTY IMAGES; GOWTHSTOCK/SHUTTERSTOCK.COM

with the overall market that strategic interactions are insignificant. And for a monopoly, there are no other firms to worry about. But game theory is important for understanding oligopolies and may be applied whenever a small number of players interact with one another. It helps explain the strategies that people choose, whether they are playing tennis or selling tennis balls.

17-1 Markets with Only a Few Sellers

An oligopolistic market has only a small group of sellers and is characterized by the tension between cooperation and self-interest. Oligopolists can make the most profit if they cooperate and together act like one big monopolist—producing a small quantity of output and charging a price well above marginal cost. Yet because each oligopolist cares only about its own profit, powerful incentives pull them apart, making it hard to maintain the cooperative outcome.

17-1a A Duopoly Example

Consider the simplest type of oligopoly, one with only two members, called a **duopoly**. Oligopolies with three or more members face the same problems as duopolies, so little is lost by starting with the simpler case.

Imagine a town in which only two residents, Jack and Jill, own wells that produce water safe for drinking. Each Saturday, Jack and Jill decide how many gallons of water to pump, bring the water to town, and sell it for whatever price the market will bear. To keep things simple, suppose that they can pump as much as they want without cost. That is, the marginal cost of water is zero.

Table 1 shows the town's demand schedule for water. The first column shows the total quantity demanded, and the second shows the price. If the well owners sell a total of 10 gallons of water, water goes for ₹110 a gallon. If they sell a total of 20 gallons, the price falls to ₹100 a gallon. And so on. If you graphed these two columns of numbers, you would get a standard downward-sloping demand curve.

The last column in Table 1 shows total revenue from the sale of water. It equals the quantity sold times the price. Because there is no cost to pumping water, the total revenue of the two producers equals their total profit.

Now consider how the organization of the town's water industry affects the price of water and the quantity sold.

17-1b Competition, Monopolies, and Cartels

Before examining the price and quantity of water that results from the Jack and Jill duopoly, let's consider the outcomes that would result if the water market were either perfectly competitive or monopolistic. These polar cases are natural benchmarks.

If the market for water were perfectly competitive, the production decisions of each firm would drive price to equal marginal cost. Because here the marginal cost of pumping additional water is zero, the equilibrium price of water under perfect competition would be zero as well. The equilibrium quantity would then be 120 gallons. The price of water would reflect the cost of producing it, and the efficient quantity of water would be produced and consumed.

Table 1

The Demand Schedule for Water

Quantity	Price	Total Revenue (and total profit)
0 gallons	₹120	₹0
10	110	1,100
20	100	2,000
30	90	2,700
40	80	3,200
50	70	3,500
60	60	3,600
70	50	3,500
80	40	3,200
90	30	2,700
100	20	2,000
110	10	1,100
120	0	0

Now consider how a monopoly would behave. Table 1 shows that total profit is maximized at a quantity of 60 gallons and a price of ₹60 a gallon. A profit-maximizing monopolist, therefore, would produce this quantity and charge this price. As is standard for monopolies, price would exceed marginal cost. The result would be inefficient because the quantity of water produced and consumed would fall short of the socially efficient level of 120 gallons.

What outcome would the duopolists achieve? One possibility is that Jack and Jill get together and agree on the quantity of water to produce and the price to charge for it. Such an agreement among firms over production and price is called **collusion**, and the group of firms acting in unison is called a **cartel**. Once a cartel is formed, the market is in effect served by a monopoly, and the analysis from Chapter 16 applies. That is, if Jack and Jill collude, they will agree on the monopoly outcome because it maximizes their total profit. Together, they produce a total of 60 gallons, which sell at a price of ₹60 a gallon. Price exceeds marginal cost, and the outcome is socially inefficient.

collusion
an agreement among firms in a market about quantities to produce or prices to charge

cartel
a group of firms acting in unison

A cartel must agree not only on total production but also on the amount produced by each member. Each wants a larger share of the market because that means more individual profit. In this case, Jack and Jill must agree on how to split the production of 60 gallons. If they agree to split the market equally, each produces 30 gallons, the price is ₹60 a gallon, and each earns a profit of ₹1,800.

17-1c The Equilibrium for an Oligopoly

Oligopolists would like to form cartels and earn monopoly profits, but that is often impossible. Squabbling among cartel members over how to divide the profit can make agreement among members difficult. In addition, antitrust laws prohibit explicit agreements among oligopolists. Even talking about pricing and production restrictions with competitors can be a criminal offense. Let's consider, therefore, what happens if Jack and Jill decide separately how much water to produce.

One might expect Jack and Jill to reach the monopoly outcome on their own because this outcome maximizes their joint profit. In the absence of a binding agreement, however, the monopoly outcome is unlikely. To see why, imagine that Jack expects Jill to produce only 30 gallons (half the monopoly quantity). Jack would reason as follows:

"I could produce 30 gallons as well. Together, we'd sell 60 gallons of water at ₹60 a gallon. My profit would be ₹1,800 (30 gallons × ₹60 a gallon). But why settle for that? I could produce 40 gallons. Then together, we'd sell 70 gallons of water at ₹50 a gallon. My profit would be ₹2,000 (40 gallons × ₹50 a gallon). Total profit in the market would fall, but who cares? My profit would rise because I'd have more of the market."

That's logical, as far as it goes. But there's a catch: Jill might well think the same way. Then she would bring 40 gallons to the market, too. Total sales would be 80 gallons, the price would fall to ₹40, and total profits would be ₹3,200. Jack and Jill would each earn only ₹1,600. By pursuing their individual self-interest when deciding how much to produce, the duopolists produce a total quantity greater than the monopoly quantity, charge a price lower than the monopoly price, and earn total profit less than the monopoly profit.

The logic of self-interest increases the duopoly's output above the monopoly level, but it does not push the duopolists all the way to the competitive allocation. Consider what happens when Jack and Jill each produce 40 gallons. The price is ₹40, and they each make a profit of ₹1,600. Jack ponders the situation further, but his self-interested logic leads to a different conclusion:

"Right now, my profit is ₹1,600. Suppose I increase production to 50 gallons. In this case, a total of 90 gallons would be sold, and the price would be ₹30 a gallon. Then, my profit would be only ₹1,500. Hmmm. Rather than increasing production and driving down the price, I am better off keeping my production at 40 gallons."

Jill, on her own, reaches the same conclusion.

The outcome in which Jack and Jill each produce 40 gallons looks like some sort of equilibrium. In fact, this outcome is essentially a Nash equilibrium, which we learnt in the context of Game Theory in the previous chapter. (It is named after the Nobel Prize–winning mathematician and economic theorist John Nash, whose life was portrayed in the book and movie *A Beautiful Mind*.) As we learnt, a **Nash equilibrium** is a situation in which economic actors interacting with one another each choose their best strategy given the strategies that the others have chosen. In this case, once Jill is producing 40 gallons, the best strategy for Jack is also to produce 40 gallons. Similarly, once Jack is producing 40 gallons, the best strategy for Jill is also to produce 40 gallons. At this Nash equilibrium, neither Jack nor Jill has an incentive to make a different decision.

This example shows the tension between cooperation and self-interest that is the essence of oligopolies. Oligopolists would be better off cooperating to attain the monopoly outcome. Yet because they each pursue their own self-interest, they fail to do so. Each oligopolist is tempted to raise production and capture a larger share of the market. As each tries to do this, total production rises, the price falls, and total profit falls.

Yet self-interest does not drive the market all the way to the competitive outcome. Like monopolists, oligopolists know that producing more reduces the price they will receive, which in turn affects profits. So they stop short of following the competitive firm's rule of producing up to the point where price equals marginal cost.

In summary, when firms in an oligopoly individually choose production to maximize profit, they produce a quantity greater than the level produced by a monopoly and less than the level produced under perfect competition. The oligopoly price is less than the monopoly price but greater than the competitive price (which equals marginal cost).

17-1d How the Size of an Oligopoly Affects the Market Outcome

We can use the insights from studying duopoly to discuss how the size of an oligopoly affects the market outcome. Suppose, for instance, that Jude and Jade suddenly discover water sources on their properties and join Jack and Jill in the water oligopoly. The demand schedule in Table 1 remains the same, but more producers are available to satisfy this demand. How does an increase from two to four sellers affect the price and quantity of water in the town?

If the sellers formed a cartel, they would again try to maximize total profit by producing the monopoly quantity and charging the monopoly price. Just as with only two sellers, the cartel members would need to agree on individual production levels and find a way to enforce the agreement. As the cartel grows larger, however, this outcome is less likely. If you have ever been a member of a team or a club, you might have noticed that working harmoniously becomes more difficult as the size of the group increases. In addition, evading the antitrust laws may be harder with a larger group of conspirators.

If the oligopolists do not form a cartel, they must each decide on their own how much water to produce. To see how the increase in the number of sellers affects the outcome, consider the decision facing each seller. At any time, each well owner has the option to raise production by one gallon. In making this decision, the well owner weighs two effects:

- **The output effect:** Because price exceeds marginal cost, selling one more gallon of water at the going price increases profit.
- **The price effect:** Because raising production increases the total quantity sold, the price of water declines, as does the profit on all the other gallons sold.

If the output effect outweighs the price effect, the well owner increases production. If the price effect outweighs the output effect, the owner does not raise production. (In this case, it is profitable to reduce production.) Each oligopolist increases production until these two marginal effects exactly balance, taking the other firms' production as given.

Now consider how the number of firms in the industry affects the marginal analysis of each oligopolist. The more firms there are, the smaller each firm's market share is. As a firm's market share shrinks, the less the firm is concerned about its own impact on the market price. That is, as the oligopoly grows, the magnitude of the price effect falls.

When the oligopoly grows very large, the price effect disappears altogether. In this extreme case, the production decision of an individual firm no longer affects the market price. Each firm takes the market price as given when deciding how much to produce and, therefore, increases production as long as price exceeds marginal cost. In other words, a large oligopoly is essentially a group of competitive firms.

In summary, as the number of sellers in an oligopoly grows, an oligopolistic market increasingly resembles a competitive market. The price approaches marginal cost, and the quantity produced approaches the socially efficient level.

This analysis of oligopoly offers a new perspective on international trade. Imagine that Toyota and Honda are the only automakers in Japan, Volkswagen and BMW are the only ones in Germany, Maruti and Tata Motors in India, and Ford and General Motors are the only ones in the United States. If these countries prohibited international trade in autos, each would have an oligopoly with only two members, and the market price and quantity would likely depart substantially from the competitive ideal. With international trade, however, a world market arises, and the oligopoly in this example has six members. Allowing free trade increases the number of producers from which each consumer can choose, and the greater competition keeps prices closer to marginal cost. Thus, the theory of oligopoly provides another reason, in addition to the theory of comparative advantage discussed in Chapter 3, why countries can benefit from free trade.

Ask the Experts

Market Share and Market Power

"If a small number of firms have a large combined market share in a properly defined market, it is strong evidence that those firms have substantial market power."

What do economists say?

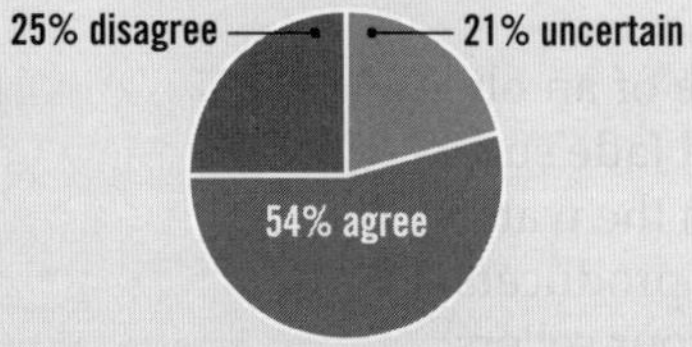

Source: IGM Economic Experts Panel, September 25, 2018.

Quick**Quiz**

1. The key feature of an oligopolistic market is that
   a. each firm sells a product different from other firms.
   b. a single firm chooses a point on the market demand curve.
   c. each firm takes the market price as given.
   d. a small number of firms are acting strategically.

2. If an oligopolistic industry organizes itself as a cooperative cartel, it will produce a quantity of output ________ the competitive level and ________ the monopoly level.
   a. less than; more than
   b. more than; less than
   c. less than; equal to
   d. equal to; more than

3. If an oligopoly does not cooperate and each firm chooses its own quantity, the industry will produce a quantity of output ________ the competitive level and ________ the monopoly level.
   a. less than; more than
   b. more than; less than
   c. less than; equal to
   d. equal to; more than

4. As the number of firms in an oligopoly grows, the industry approaches a level of output ________ the competitive level and ________ the monopoly level.
   a. less than; more than
   b. more than; less than
   c. less than; equal to
   d. equal to; more than

Answers are at the end of the chapter.

17-2 The Economics of Cooperation

Oligopolists would like to reach the monopoly outcome but may find it hard to cooperate. This situation is not unusual: Often in life, people fail to cooperate with one another even when cooperation would make them all better off. An oligopoly is just one example.

if firms in an oligopoly compete rather than cooperate. Let's consider how policymakers can foster competition.

17-3a Restraint of Trade and the Antitrust Laws

The common law can inhibit cooperation among oligopolists. Normally, freedom of contract is an essential part of a market economy. Businesses and households use contracts to arrange mutually advantageous trades, and they rely on the court system to enforce contracts. Yet, for many centuries, judges in England and the United States have deemed agreements among competitors to reduce quantities and raise prices to be contrary to the public good. They have, therefore, refused to enforce such agreements.

The Sherman Antitrust Act of 1890 codified and reinforced this policy in the United States:

> Every contract, combination in the form of trust or otherwise, or conspiracy, in restraint of trade or commerce among the several States, or with foreign nations, is declared to be illegal . . . Every person who shall monopolize, or attempt to monopolize, or combine or conspire with any person or persons to monopolize any part of the trade or commerce among the several States, or with foreign nations, shall be deemed guilty of a misdemeanor, and on conviction thereof, shall be punished by fine not exceeding fifty thousand dollars, or by imprisonment not exceeding one year, or by both said punishments, in the discretion of the court.

The Sherman Act elevated agreements among oligopolists from unenforceable contracts to criminal conspiracies.

The Clayton Act of 1914 further strengthened the antitrust laws. According to this statute, plaintiffs who could prove that they were damaged by an illegal arrangement to restrain trade could sue and recover three times the damages sustained. The purpose of this unusual rule of triple damages is to encourage private lawsuits against conspiring oligopolists.

Today, the U.S. Justice Department and private parties have the authority to bring legal suits to enforce the antitrust laws. As Chapter 16 discussed, these laws are used to prevent mergers that would give a firm excessive market power. These laws are also used to prevent oligopolists from acting together in ways that would make their markets less competitive.

Case Study

An Illegal Phone Call

Firms in oligopolies have a strong incentive to collude to reduce production, raise prices, and increase profits. The great 18th-century economist Adam Smith was well aware of this potential market failure. In *The Wealth of Nations*, he wrote, "People of the same trade seldom meet together, but the conversation ends in a conspiracy against the public, or in some diversion to raise prices."

For a modern example of Smith's observation, consider this phone conversation between two airline executives in the early 1980s. The call was reported in the *New York Times* on February 24, 1983. Robert Crandall was president of American Airlines, and Howard Putnam was president of Braniff Airways, a major airline at the time. Here's an excerpt:

Crandall: I think it's dumb as hell . . . to sit here and pound the @#₹% out of each other and neither one of us making a #₹%& dime.

Putnam: Do you have a suggestion for me?
Crandall: Yes, I have a suggestion for you. Raise your ₹%*& fares 20 percent. I'll raise mine the next morning.
Putnam: Robert, we . . .
Crandall: You'll make more money, and I will, too.
Putnam: We can't talk about pricing!
Crandall: Oh @#₹%, Howard. We can talk about any &*#@ thing we want to talk about.

Putnam was right: The Sherman Antitrust Act prohibits competing executives from even talking about fixing prices. When Putnam gave a recording of this conversation to the Justice Department, the Justice Department filed suit against Crandall.

Two years later, Crandall and the Justice Department reached a settlement in which Crandall agreed to restrictions on his business activities, including his contacts with officials at other airlines. The Justice Department said that the terms of the settlement would "protect competition in the airline industry, by preventing American and Crandall from any further attempts to monopolize passenger airline service on any route through discussions with competitors about the prices of airline services." ●

17-3b Controversies over Antitrust Policy

What kinds of behavior the antitrust laws should prohibit is often controversial. Most commentators agree that price-fixing agreements among competing firms should be illegal. Yet the antitrust laws have been used to condemn some business practices whose effects are less obvious. Here are three examples.

Resale Price Maintenance One example of a controversial business practice is **resale price maintenance**. Imagine that Dhamaka Electronics sells smartphones to retail stores for ₹400. If Dhamaka requires the retailers to charge customers ₹500, it is said to engage in resale price maintenance. Any retailer that charged less than ₹500 would violate its contract with Dhamaka.

At first, resale price maintenance might seem anticompetitive. Like an agreement among cartel members, it prevents the retailers from competing on price. For this reason, the courts have sometimes viewed resale price maintenance as an antitrust violation.

Yet some economists defend the practice. First, they deny that it is aimed at reducing competition. If Dhamaka Electronics wanted to exert its market power, it would raise the wholesale price rather than control the resale price. What's more, Dhamaka has no reason to discourage competition among its retailers. Because a cartel of retailers sells less than a group of competitive retailers, Dhamaka would be worse off if its retailers were a cartel.

Second, resale price maintenance may have a legitimate goal. Dhamaka may want its retailers to provide customers with a pleasant showroom and a knowledgeable sales force. Yet, without resale price maintenance, some customers would take advantage of one store's service to learn about the smartphone's special features and then buy the item at a discount retailer that does not provide this service. Good customer service can be viewed as a public good among the retailers that sell Dhamaka products. As Chapter 11 discussed, when one person provides a public good, others can use it without paying for it. In this case, discounters would free ride on the service provided by other retailers, leading to less service than is desirable. Resale price maintenance is one way for Dhamaka to solve this free-rider problem.

The example of resale price maintenance illustrates an important principle: **Business practices that appear to reduce competition sometimes have legitimate purposes.** This principle makes the application of the antitrust laws all the more difficult. Those in charge of enforcing these laws must determine what kinds of behavior impede competition and reduce economic well-being. Often that job is not easy.

Predatory Pricing Firms with market power typically use it to raise prices above the competitive level. But should policymakers ever be concerned that firms with market power might charge prices that are too low? This question is at the heart of a second debate over antitrust policy.

Imagine that a large airline, call it Coyote Air, has a monopoly on some route. Then, Roadrunner Express enters and takes 20 percent of the market, leaving Coyote with 80 percent. In response to this competition, Coyote starts slashing its fares. Some antitrust analysts argue that Coyote's move could be anticompetitive: The price cuts may be intended to drive Roadrunner out of the market so Coyote can recapture its monopoly and raise prices again. Such behavior is called **predatory pricing**.

Although predatory pricing is a common claim in antitrust suits, some economists say that predatory pricing is rarely, if ever, a profitable business strategy. Why? For a price war to drive out a rival, prices must be below cost. Yet if Coyote starts selling cheap tickets at a loss, it had better be ready to fly more planes because low fares will attract more customers. Roadrunner, meanwhile, can respond to Coyote's predatory move by cutting back on flights. As a result, Coyote ends up bearing more than 80 percent of the losses, putting Roadrunner in a good position to survive the price war. As in the old Roadrunner–Coyote cartoons, the predator suffers more than the prey.

Economists debate whether predatory pricing should concern antitrust policymakers. When, if ever, is predatory pricing a profitable strategy? Are the courts capable of distinguishing between competitive and predatory price cuts? These are hard questions.

Bundling A third example of a controversial business practice is **bundling**. Suppose that Makemoney Movies produces two new films—*Superheroes* and *Hamlet*. If Makemoney offers theaters the two films together at a single price, rather than separately, the studio is said to be bundling its two products.

When the practice of bundling movies was challenged, the Supreme Court banned it. The court reasoned as follows: Imagine that *Superheroes* is a blockbuster and *Hamlet* is an unprofitable art film. The studio could use the high demand for *Superheroes* to force theaters to buy *Hamlet*. Bundling, the court concluded, could be a mechanism for a firm to expand its market power.

In 1963, the economist George Stigler offered a rebuttal to this argument. Imagine that theaters are willing to pay

Ask the Experts: Antitrust in the Digital Economy

"Google's dominance of the market for internet search arose mainly from a combination of economies of scale and a quality algorithm."

What do economists say?

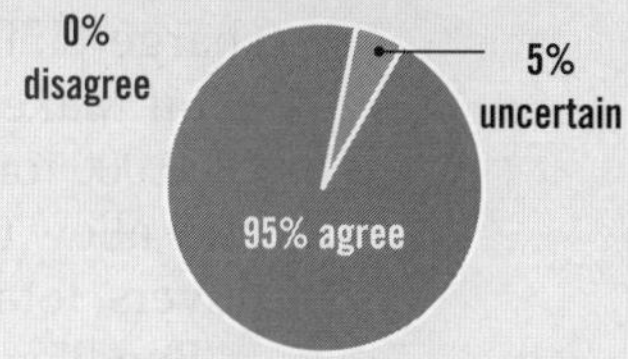

"In light of Google's dominance, its current operating practices could have a substantial negative effect on social welfare in the long run."

What do economists say?

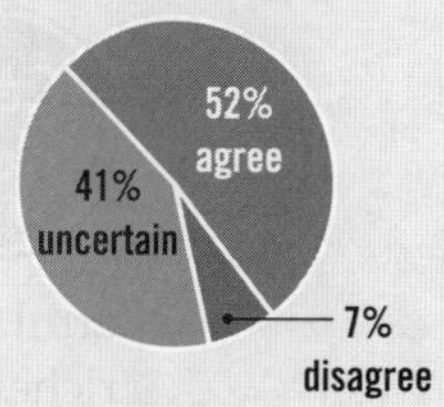

"The nature of the market dominance of technology giants in the digital economy warrants either the imposition of some kind of regulation or a fundamental change in antitrust policy."

What do economists say?

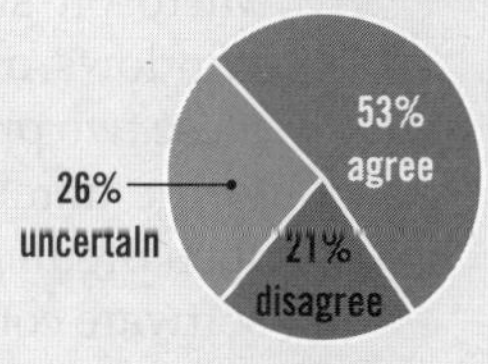

"Requiring Facebook to divest WhatsApp and Instagram is likely to make society better off."

What do economists say?

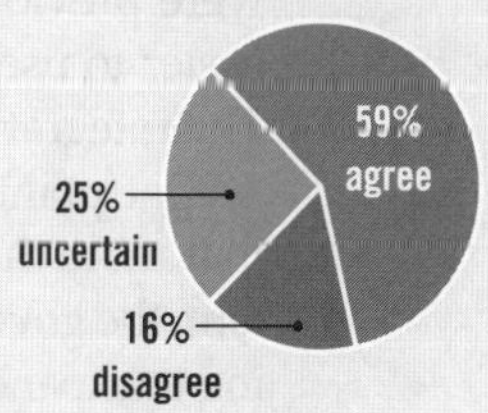

Source: IGM Economic Experts Panel, November 3, 2020, December 22, 2020.

₹200,000 for *Superheroes* and nothing for *Hamlet*. Then the most that a theater would pay for the two movies together is ₹200,000—the same as it would pay for *Superheroes* by itself. Forcing the theater to accept a worthless movie as part of the deal does not increase its willingness to pay. Makemoney cannot increase its market power simply by bundling the two movies together.

Stigler suggested another explanation for why bundling exists: It is a form of price discrimination. Suppose there are two theaters. City Theater is willing to pay ₹150,000 for *Superheroes* and ₹50,000 for *Hamlet*. Country Theater is just the opposite: It is willing to pay ₹50,000 for *Superheroes* and ₹150,000 for *Hamlet*. If Makemoney charges separate prices for the two films, its best strategy is to charge ₹150,000 for each film, and each theater chooses to show only one film. Yet if Makemoney offers the two movies as a bundle, it can charge each theater ₹200,000 for the movies. If different theaters value the films differently, bundling may allow the studio to increase profit by charging a combined price closer to the buyers' total willingness to pay.

Bundling remains a controversial business practice. The Supreme Court's argument that bundling allows a firm to extend its market power to other goods may not be well founded, at least in its simplest form. Yet economists have proposed more elaborate theories for how bundling can impede competition. Given the current state of economic knowledge, debate continues whether bundling is generally adverse for society.

Case Study

The Microsoft Case

A particularly important and controversial antitrust case was the U.S. government's suit against the Microsoft Corporation, filed in 1998. The case did not lack drama. It pitted one of the world's most powerful regulatory agencies (the U.S. Justice Department) against one of the world's richest men (Bill Gates). Testifying for the government was a prominent economist (MIT professor Franklin Fisher). Testifying for Microsoft was another prominent economist (MIT professor Richard Schmalensee, a former student of Franklin Fisher). At stake was the future of one of the world's most valuable companies (Microsoft) in one of the economy's fastest-growing industries (software).

Bundling was a central issue in the Microsoft case—in particular, whether Microsoft should be allowed to integrate its Internet Explorer browser into its Windows operating system. The government said that Microsoft was bundling these two products together to extend its power in the market for operating systems to the unrelated market of Internet browsers. Allowing Microsoft to incorporate such products into its operating system, the government argued, would deter other software companies from entering the market and offering new products.

Microsoft said that putting new features into old products is a natural part of technological progress. By the 1990s, cars included CD players and air conditioners, which were once sold separately, and cameras came with built-in flashes. The same was true with operating systems. Over time, Microsoft added many features to Windows that were previously stand-alone products. This has made computers more reliable and easier to use because consumers could be confident that the pieces worked together. The integration of Internet technology, Microsoft argued, was the natural next step.

One point of disagreement concerned the extent of Microsoft's market power. Noting that more than 80 percent of new personal computers used a Microsoft operating system, the government argued that the company was effectively a monopoly and was trying to expand its influence into new markets. Microsoft replied that the software market was always changing and that Microsoft's Windows was constantly being challenged by competitors, such as the Apple Mac and Linux operating systems. It also argued that the low price it charged for Windows—about $50 then, or only 3 percent of the price of a typical computer—was evidence that its market power was severely limited.

Like many large antitrust suits, the Microsoft case became a legal morass. In November 1999, after a long trial, Judge Penfield Jackson ruled that Microsoft had great monopoly power and that it had illegally abused that power. In June 2000, after hearings on possible remedies, he ordered that Microsoft be broken up into two companies—one that sold the operating system and one that sold applications software. A year later, an appeals court overturned Jackson's breakup order and handed the case to a new judge. In September 2001, the Justice Department announced that it no longer sought a breakup of the company and wanted to settle the case quickly.

AP IMAGES/LAURA RAUCH

"Me? A monopolist? Now just wait a minute . . ."

The two sides reached a settlement in November 2002. Microsoft accepted some restrictions on its business practices, and the government accepted that a browser would remain part of the Windows operating system. But the settlement did not end Microsoft's antitrust troubles. In subsequent years, the company contended with several private antitrust suits, as well as suits brought by the European Union alleging a variety of anticompetitive behaviors.

Technological development has relegated the dispute over the once-mighty Explorer browser to the level of a historical footnote. In June 2021, Microsoft said it was retiring Explorer, which had lost most of its market share, replacing it with a new browser called Edge. Some analysts credited the Justice Department's settlement with Microsoft as a crucial step that allowed browsers like Google Chrome and Apple Safari to grow and ultimately supplant Explorer. ●

17-4 Sequential Games as Oligopolies

So far, we have studied how firms behave when they choose simultaneously. But in many real markets, firms move sequentially, i.e., one firm makes its decision first, and the other follows after observing that move.

This introduces strategic timing and the possibility of a first-mover advantage. This sequential structure transforms an oligopoly from a simple simultaneous game into a sequential move game driven by dynamic mechanisms and making ideas of commitment and foresight relevant in the managerial decision-making process. By moving first, the leader firm can influence the follower's behavior and capture a larger share of industry profit. The follower firm, in turn, best responds given the leader's action. This setting mirrors several real business situations where a market-share leader sets production targets or prices before competitors, who then have to adapt rather than compete head-on.

Just like any dynamic game, such as the battle of the sexes, consider an oligopoly with 2 firms, such that firm A moves first and chooses an output q1. Observing, q1, firm B makes a move and chooses q2. How do we solve this game? It's straightforward: use Backwards Induction. Firm A will know that firm B will choose q2 based on q1. So firm A can compute firm B's best response fuction such that q2 is a function of q1. In other words, for every possible q1, firm A will know what q2 the B will choose. Accordingly, therefore, firm A will choose a q1 which maximizes its own profits by taking this into account. Notice, because firm B moves second, it cannot credibly threaten the firm A and firm A therefore has a first-mover advantage. Imagine a leader follower game in the Indian banking industry. Suppose the SBI moves first and revises its FD interest rates. The followers may then adjust their strategies observing SBI's promotions.

In the News

Amazon in the Crosshairs

The Washington, D.C., attorney general takes aim at the giant online retailer.

A New Antitrust Case Cuts to the Core of Amazon's Identity

By Gilad Edelman

"I founded Amazon 26 years ago with the long-term mission of making it Earth's most customer-centric company," Jeff Bezos testified before the House Antitrust Subcommittee last summer. "Not every business takes this customer-first approach, but we do, and it's our greatest strength."

Bezos' obsession with customer satisfaction is at the center of Amazon's self-mythology. Every move the company makes, in this account, is designed with only one goal in mind: making the customer happy. If Amazon has become an economic juggernaut, the king of ecommerce, that's not because of any unfair practices or sharp elbows; it's simply because customers love it so much.

The antitrust lawsuit filed against Amazon on Tuesday directly challenges that narrative. The suit, brought by Karl Racine, the Washington, DC, attorney general, focuses on Amazon's use of a so-called most-favored-nation clause in its contracts with third-party sellers, who account for most of the sales volume on Amazon. A most-favored-nation clause requires sellers not to offer their products at a lower price on any other website, even their own. According to the lawsuit, this harms consumers by artificially inflating prices across the entire internet, while preventing other ecommerce sites from competing against Amazon on price. "I filed this antitrust lawsuit to put an end to Amazon's ability to control prices across the online retail market," Racine said in a press conference announcing the case.

For a long time, Amazon openly did what DC is alleging; its "price parity provision" explicitly restricted third-party sellers from offering lower prices on other sites. It stopped in Europe in 2013, after competition authorities in the UK and Germany began investigating it. In the US, however, the provision lasted longer, until Senator Richard Blumenthal wrote a letter to antitrust agencies in 2018 suggesting Amazon was violating antitrust law. A few months later, in early 2019, Amazon dropped price parity.

But that wasn't the end of the story. The DC lawsuit alleges that Amazon simply substituted a new policy that uses different language to accomplish the same result as the old rule. Amazon's Marketplace Fair Pricing Policy informs third-party sellers that they can be punished or suspended for a variety of offenses, including "setting a price on a product or service that is significantly higher than recent prices offered on or off Amazon." This rule can protect consumers when used to prevent price-gouging for scarce products, as happened with face masks in the early days of the pandemic. But it can also be used to **inflate** prices for items that sellers would prefer to offer more cheaply. The key phrase is "off Amazon." In other words, Amazon reserves the right to cut off sellers if they list their products more cheaply on another website—just as it did under the old price parity provision. According to the final report filed by the House Antitrust Subcommittee last year, based on testimony from third-party sellers, the new policy "has the same effect of blocking sellers from offering lower prices to consumers on other retail sites."

The main form that this price discipline takes, according to sellers who have spoken out against Amazon either publicly or in anonymous testimony, is through manipulating access to the Buy Box—those Add to Cart and Buy Now buttons at the top right of an Amazon product listing. When you go to buy something, there are often many sellers trying to make the sale. Only one can "win the Buy Box," meaning they're the one who gets the sale when you click one of those buttons. Because most customers don't scroll down to see what other sellers are offering the product, winning the Buy Box is crucial for anyone trying to make a living by selling on Amazon . . .

Jason Boyce, a longtime Amazon seller turned consultant, explained to me how this works. He

QuickQuiz

7. The antitrust laws aim to
   a. facilitate cooperation among firms in oligopolistic industries.
   b. encourage mergers to take advantage of economies of scale.
   c. discourage firms from moving production facilities overseas.
   d. prevent firms from acting in ways that reduce competition.

8. Antitrust enforcement is controversial mainly because
   a. cooperative domestic firms are best equipped to deal with international competitors.
   b. some business practices that seem anticompetitive may have legitimate purposes.
   c. excessive competition can drive some firms out of business, causing job losses.
   d. vigorous enforcement can reduce business profitability, lowering shareholder value.

Answers are at the end of the chapter.

and his partners were excited when the last third-party seller contract they signed with Amazon, to sell sporting goods on the site, didn't include the price parity provision. "We thought, 'This is great! We can offer discounts on Walmart, and Sears, and wherever else,'" he said. But then something odd happened. Boyce (who spoke with House investigators as part of the antitrust inquiry) noticed that once his company lowered prices on other sites, sales on Amazon started tanking. "We went to the listing, and the Add to Cart button was gone, the Buy Now button was gone. Instead, there was a gray box labeled 'See All Buying Options.' You could still buy the product, but it was an extra click. Now, an extra click on Amazon is an eternity—they're all about immediate gratification." Moreover, his company's ad spending plummeted, which he realized was because Amazon doesn't show users ads for products without a Buy Box. "So what did we do? We went back and raised our prices everywhere else, and within 24 hours everything came back. Traffic improved, clicks improved, and sales came back." . . .

Boyce's experience illustrates something important about most-favored-nation clauses: On their own, they aren't illegal. The problem comes when they're used by a company with a dominant share of the market. If a store wants to feature a certain brand on its shelves in exchange for an agreement not to sell more cheaply at a rival chain, the brand can decide whether the deal is worth it. But in the case of Amazon, according to sellers like Boyce, there is no real choice. The DC attorney general's lawsuit points out that Amazon accounts for somewhere between 50 and 70 percent of the US online retail market, and it notes that "a staggering 74 percent [of consumers] go directly to Amazon when they are ready to buy a specific product." It accuses Amazon of using its price policy to maintain that monopoly power by preventing rival platforms from using lower prices to eat into its market share.

In a statement emailed to reporters, Amazon did not exactly deny that it punishes sellers who offer lower prices elsewhere. Rather, it suggested that this is ultimately good for the consumer. "The DC attorney general has it exactly backward—sellers set their own prices for the products they offer in our store," the company said. "Amazon takes pride in the fact that we offer low prices across the broadest selection, and like any store we reserve the right not to highlight offers to customers that are not priced competitively. The relief the AG seeks would force Amazon to feature higher prices to customers, oddly going against core objectives of antitrust law."

But this logic relies on a very idiosyncratic definition of "priced competitively." When someone goes to Amazon to buy something, they want the site to show them the best deal available **on Amazon**. If Jenny's Bike Supply has the best deal on Amazon for chain locks, then it's the best deal, regardless of whether Jenny is also selling the locks for an even better price on eBay. If Amazon makes it harder to buy the lock from Jenny in this scenario, the only thing it accomplishes is forcing customers to settle for the second-best deal. And, of course, it will probably succeed in forcing Jenny to raise prices on eBay. What it won't do is result in **lower** prices on Amazon.

All of which makes the DC lawsuit a narrower and potentially more winnable case than some of the other antitrust litigation that has been brought against tech companies. ■

RVLSOFT/SHUTTERSTOCK.COM

Questions to Discuss

1. Have you ever bought anything from Amazon? If so, do you think you got a good price and good service?
2. Do you think Amazon should be barred from favoring sellers that offer Amazon customers their lowest prices? Why or why not?

Source: Wired, May 25, 2021.

17-5 Conclusion

Oligopolies would like to act like monopolies, but self-interest drives them toward competition. Where oligopolies end up on this spectrum depends on the number of firms in the oligopoly and the extent to which the firms cooperate. The story of the prisoners' dilemma shows why oligopolies can fail to maintain cooperation, even when cooperation is in their best interest.

Policymakers regulate the behavior of oligopolists through the antitrust laws. The proper scope of these laws is the subject of ongoing debate. There is little doubt that price fixing among competing firms reduces economic welfare and is an appropriate target for regulators, but some business practices that appear to reduce competition may have legitimate, if subtle, purposes. As a result, policymakers need to be careful when they use the substantial powers of the antitrust laws to place limits on firm behavior.

b. What is Sparkle's profit? Explain.
c. On your diagram, show the consumer surplus derived from the purchase of Sparkle toothpaste. Also, show the deadweight loss relative to the efficient outcome.
d. If the government forced Sparkle to produce the efficient level of output, what would happen to the firm? What would happen to Sparkle's customers?

7. Consider a monopolistically competitive market with N firms. Each firm's business opportunities are described by the following equations:

$$\text{Demand: } Q = 100/N - P.$$

$$\text{Marginal Revenue: } MR = 100/N - 2Q.$$

$$\text{Total Cost: } TC = 50 + Q^2.$$

$$\text{Marginal Cost: } MC = 2Q.$$

   a. How does N, the number of firms in the market, affect each firm's demand curve? Why?
   b. How many units does each firm produce? (The answers to this and the next two questions depend on N.)
   c. What price does each firm charge?
   d. How much profit does each firm make?
   e. In the long run, how many firms will exist in this market?

8. The market for peanut butter in Nutville is monopolistically competitive and in long-run equilibrium. One day, consumer advocate Jif Skippy discovers that all brands of peanut butter in Nutville are identical. Thereafter, the market becomes perfectly competitive and again reaches its long-run equilibrium. Using an appropriate diagram, explain whether each of the following variables increases, decreases, or stays the same for a typical firm in the market.
   a. price
   b. quantity
   c. average total cost
   d. marginal cost
   e. profit

9. For each of the following pairs of firms, explain which one would be more likely to engage in advertising.
   a. a family-owned farm or a family-owned restaurant
   b. a manufacturer of forklifts or a manufacturer of cars
   c. a company that invented a very comfortable razor or a company that invented a less comfortable razor

10. Sleek Sneakers Co. is one of many firms in the market for shoes.
   a. Assume that Sleek is currently earning short-run economic profit. On a correctly labeled diagram, show Sleek's profit-maximizing output and price as well as the area representing profit.
   b. What happens to Sleek's price, output, and profit in the long run? Explain this change in words, and show it on a new diagram.
   c. Suppose that over time, consumers become more focused on stylistic differences among shoe brands. How would this change in attitudes affect each firm's price elasticity of demand? In the long run, how will this change in demand affect Sleek's price, output, and profit?
   d. At the profit-maximizing price you identified in part (c), is Sleek's demand curve elastic or inelastic? Explain.

Quick**Quiz Answers**

1. **b** 2. **d** 3. **a** 4. **d** 5. **a** 6. **c** 7. **b** 8. **b**

Chapter

16

Game Theory and Business Application

In this chapter, we will be introduced to the field of **game theory**, the study of how people behave in strategic situations. By "strategic," we mean a situation in which people, when choosing a course of action, must anticipate how others might respond to their choice. Strategic thinking is crucial not only in chess, checkers, and tic-tac-toe but also in many business decisions. Because some markets have only a few firms, each firm must be strategic when making supply decisions. The firms are keenly aware that each firm's profit depends not only on how much it produces but also on how much each of the others produce.

game theory
the study of how people behave in strategic situations

Game theory isn't necessary for analyzing competitive or monopoly markets. In a market that is either perfectly or monopolistically competitive, each firm is so small compared with the overall market that strategic interactions are insignificant. And for a monopoly, there are no other firms to worry about. But game theory is important for understanding oligopolies, which we will study in the next chapter, and may be applied whenever a small number of players interact with one another. It helps explain the strategies that people choose whether they are playing tennis or selling tennis balls.

AZMANJAKA/E+/GETTY IMAGES, CARLOS FLORES/EYEEM/GETTY IMAGES

16-1 When Decisions Are Interdependent

In many markets, a manager's best choice depends on how their rivals or other agents, such as regulators or consumers, will respond. Game theory equips managers to analyze such strategic interdependence. When mobile operators consider tariff cuts, when airlines time fare sales, when FMCG firms choose their ad intensities, or when Smart Bazaar outlets announce Diwali discounts, each decision's payoff hinges on the likely reactions of others.

This chapter introduces the basic tools of game theory with an emphasis on managerial applications. We will define the core elements of a game and then explain the equilibrium and solution concepts for solving games.

We will study two types of games, namely, simultaneous moves and sequential moves. We will then apply these ideas to oligopolies where firms compete on quantity (Cournot) and price (Bertrand). Game Theory is also useful to study coordination problems, bargaining, and repeated interactions.

16-1a The Elements of a Game

A game has four essential elements:

1. **Players** These are the main decision makers of any game. You should think about different games and players therein. For instance, firms, managers, platforms, regulators can all be players in various games. In a price war game between Indigo and Akasa Air, these aviation companies are the players.
2. **Strategies** A complete and contingent plan of actions that specifies what a player will do in every situation that can potentially arise will be known as strategies. Think of this as a situation before the game commences. Consider a penalty shootout in a football match. The kick-taker and the goalkeeper are the players. The goalkeeper may have several actions, such as dive left, dive right, stay put, etc. However, a strategy must define an action for every possible contingency in which the player has to act. Let's say there are three such contingencies, depending on the kick-taker's strategies. The kick-taker may kick left, right, or center. Then one strategy for the goalkeeper would be "I dive left if he kicks right, I dive right if he kicks left, I stay put if he kicks center." Another strategy would be "I dive left no matter what" and so on. As you observe, a single strategy specifies one action for every possibility. And this set of actions constitutes a single strategy for a player. Strategies may involve randomization (mixed strategies). In this example, this would mean, I dive left with probability ½ and so on.
3. **Payoffs** These indicate what players essentially care about (often profits), possibly including nonpecuniary considerations (market share, risk, reputation). Managers, as players in a game, will aim to maximize payoffs.
4. **Information** What players know when choosing their actions will be defined as information. This may include things such as whether moves are simultaneous or sequential, or whether payoffs are known and actions are observed. Many applications assume complete information about the structure of the game, though not about the actions chosen in the moment. In this chapter, we will only focus on simultaneous and sequential games of complete information.

A standard assumption in Game Theory is that players are all rational and that rationality is **common knowledge**. Common knowledge means that each player is rational, knows others are rational, knows others know she is rational, and so on.

However, a characteristic of SPNE is that it rules out noncredible threats (actions a player would never actually carry out once the relevant node is reached). For instance, a strategy such as (Cricket, Cricket) would involve a potential threat from Ravi that he would choose Cricket, no matter what. But, since Ravi moves second, we can rule out, using backward induction, any predicted equilibrium of that form. Notice, in the simultaneous version, there was a Nash equilibrium that involved Noth going to the Cricket. Making the game sequential, with Asha having a first mover advantage, eliminates that possibility. Similarly, if Ravi were to have a first mover advantage, then the SPNE outcome would be both ending up at the Cricket game.

16-3b Bargaining and Managerial Applications

Consider the following scenario. Two firms—Alpha Technologies (Acquirer) and Beta Systems (Target)—are negotiating a merger. Alpha wants to buy Beta. If talks fail, both remain independent. The negotiation unfolds sequentially. Alpha makes an initial offer; Beta either accepts or rejects. If Beta rejects, there is no deal. The player making the first credible offer (Alpha) can use backwards induction to offer enough to make Beta better off compared to its payoff if it rejects. In doing so, Alpha captures most of the surplus. Early movers can anchor negotiations by setting the frame and constraining later responses. For most M&A deals, acquirers making the first offer often gain advantage by anchoring the valuation.

Similarly for supplier contracts, large buyers such as Reliance Retail may propose take-it-or-leave-it terms, which smaller suppliers may rationally accept maintaining minimal margins. For platform negotiations, dominant digital platforms offer standard revenue shares (e.g., app stores' 70/30 split) and developers accept, since rejecting yields nothing.

Managerial Insight In sequential bargaining, commitment, patience, and credible fallback, options determine who gets the surplus. First-mover advantage is real but only if the follower's rejection threat is not credible. In practice, managers may want to increase bargaining payoffs by improving outside options. These may include alternative suppliers, parallel channels, and reducing delay costs by funding runway, inventory buffers, etc.

16-3c Repeated Games

In the real world, many of the games are not simply one shot but repeated for multiple periods. In that case, a simultaneous game that is repeated can be considered as a sequential game. However, the logic of backwards induction suggests that if a **repeated game** ends after finite periods, then in the last period, we should replicate the standard Nash equilibrium, just as in the one-shot case. So, knowing this, in period $n - 1$, the Nash should be played, and so on. Essentially, a finitely repeated game should, therefore, theoretically have the Nash equilibrium played in every period.

However, if a game is infinitely repeated, which implies that there is always a positive probability estimated by the players that the game might be played again in future, then we may have certain strategies that can ensure that a cooperative outcome can be played. For instance, a **trigger strategy**, which suggests that players agree to cooperate as long as the others cooperate but start defecting as soon as one cheats, can sustain longer term cooperation, provided the players estimate that the likelihood of the game being repeated is high enough.

Quick**Quiz**

5. Which of the following is not a feature of a subgame?
   a. It starts at a given node and includes all subsequent games.
   b. It begins where the history of the game is not known.
   c. It includes multiple branches originating at a node till the end of the game.
   d. It is a mini game that is wholly contained.
6. In an infinitely repeated game cooperation is ________ if the ________.
   a. Not sustainable, game has a possibility of continuing
   b. Sustainable, game is unlikely to continue
   c. Sustainable, probability that the game continues is sufficiently high
   d. Not sustainable, probability that the game continues is sufficiently high

Answers are at the end of the chapter.

16-4 Conclusion

The tools of game theory allow managers to analyze decision-making when outcomes depend not only on their own actions but also on those of others. Across different strategic settings, we can have simultaneous or sequential move interactions. Each framework highlights a distinct managerial challenge and corresponding way of thinking.

It is important to mention here that the timing is not really what defines the decision-making approach. For instance, even if the game is not truly simultaneous, as long as one player is making a choice without knowing what the other is choosing, it is equivalent to a simultaneous game. The simultaneity matters in the context of decision metrics, not really the time of the decision.

Chapter in a Nutshell

- Strategic interdependence implies that managers often operate in environments where outcomes depend on rivals' actions. Game theory provides tools to analyze these interactions systematically.
- Simultaneous games use the Nash equilibrium to predict outcomes where each firm's choice is the best response to others.
- Sequential games rely on Subgame Perfect Nash Equilibrium (SPNE) and backward induction-based approaches. Here, the methods rely on emphasizing credibility, commitment, and the advantages of moving first or second.
- In repeated games, cooperation can emerge through trust, trigger strategies, and reputation, turning short-term rivalry into long-term discipline and stability.

Key Concepts

game theory, p. 329
nash equilibrium, p. 330
prisoners' dilemma, p. 331
dominant strategy, p. 332
dominant strategy equilibrium, p. 332
mixed strategy, p. 335
subgame perfect Nash equilibrium, p. 337

Questions for Review

1. Define the four components of a game. Give one business example for each component.
2. What is Nash equilibrium? How is it different from dominant strategy equilibrium?
3. When do mixed strategies arise? Provide a real-world context in which purposeful randomness pays.
4. Explain backward induction and SPNE with a brief entry deterrence example. What makes a threat credible?
5. Under what conditions can repeated interaction sustain cooperative outcomes? When will it fail?

Problems and Applications

1. Consider trade relations between the United States and Mexico. Assume that the leaders of the two countries believe the payoffs to alternative trade policies are as follows:

Mexico's Decision \ United States's Decision	Low Tariffs	High Tariffs
Low Tariffs	U.S. gains ₹25 billion; Mexico gains ₹25 billion	U.S. gains ₹30 billion; Mexico gains ₹10 billion
High Tariffs	U.S. gains ₹10 billion; Mexico gains ₹30 billion	U.S. gains ₹20 billion; Mexico gains ₹20 billion

   a. What is the dominant strategy for the United States? For Mexico? Explain.
   b. Define **Nash equilibrium**. What is the Nash equilibrium for trade policy?
   c. In 1993, the U.S. Congress ratified the North American Free Trade Agreement, in which the United States and Mexico agreed to reduce trade barriers simultaneously. Do the perceived payoffs shown here justify this approach to trade policy? Explain.
   d. Based on your understanding of the gains from trade (discussed in Chapters 3 and 9), do you think that these payoffs actually reflect a nation's welfare under the four possible outcomes?

2. Synergy and Dynaco are the only two firms in a specific high-tech industry. They face the following payoff matrix as they determine the size of their research budget:

Dynaco's Decision \ Synergy's Decision	Large Budget	Small Budget
Large Budget	Synergy gains ₹20 million; Dynaco gains ₹30 million	Synergy gains zero; Dynaco gains ₹70 million
Small Budget	Synergy gains ₹30 million; Dynaco gains zero	Synergy gains ₹40 million; Dynaco gains ₹50 million

   a. Does Synergy have a dominant strategy? Explain.
   b. Does Dynaco have a dominant strategy? Explain.
   c. Is there a Nash equilibrium for this scenario? Explain. (Hint: Look closely at the definition of Nash equilibrium.)

3. You and a classmate are assigned a project on which you will receive one combined grade. You each want to receive a good grade, but you also want to avoid hard work. In particular, here is the situation:
   - If both of you work hard, you both get an A, which gives each of you 40 units of happiness.
   - If only one of you works hard, you both get a B, which gives each of you 30 units of happiness.
   - If neither of you works hard, you both get a D, which gives each of you 10 units of happiness.
   - Working hard costs 25 units of happiness.

   a. Fill in the following payoff matrix:

Classmate's Decision \ Your Decision	Work	Shirk
Work	You: ; Classmate:	You: ; Classmate:
Shirk	You: ; Classmate:	You: ; Classmate:

   b. What is the likely outcome? Explain your answer.
   c. If you get this classmate as your partner on a series of projects throughout the year rather than only once, how might that change the outcome you predicted in part (b)?
   d. Another classmate cares more about good grades: She gets 50 units of happiness for a B and 80 units of happiness for an A. If this classmate were your partner (but your preferences remained the same), how would your answers to parts (a) and (b) change? Which of the two classmates would you prefer as a partner? Would she also want you as a partner?

4. A case study in the chapter describes a phone conversation between the presidents of American Airlines and Braniff Airways. Let's use game theory to analyze the interaction between the two companies. Suppose that each company can charge either a high price for tickets or a low price. If one company charges $300, it earns low profit if the other company also charges $300 and high profit if the other company charges $600. On the other hand, if the company charges $600, it earns very low profit if the other company charges $300 and medium profit if the other company also charges $600.
   a. Draw the payoff matrix for this game.
   b. What is the Nash equilibrium in this game? Explain.

c. Is there an outcome that would be better than the Nash equilibrium for both airlines? How could it be achieved? Who would lose if it were achieved?

5. Two athletes of equal ability are competing for a prize of $10,000. Each is deciding whether to take a dangerous performance-enhancing drug. If one athlete takes the drug and the other does not, the one who takes the drug wins the prize. If both or neither take the drug, they tie and split the prize. Taking the drug imposes health risks that are equivalent to a loss of X dollars.
   a. Draw a 2×2 payoff matrix describing the decisions the athletes face.
   b. For what X is taking the drug the Nash equilibrium?
   c. Does making the drug safer (that is, lowering X) make the athletes better or worse off? Explain.

6. Little Kona is a small coffee company that is considering entering a market dominated by Big Brew. Each company's profit depends on whether Little Kona enters and whether Big Brew sets a high price or a low price:

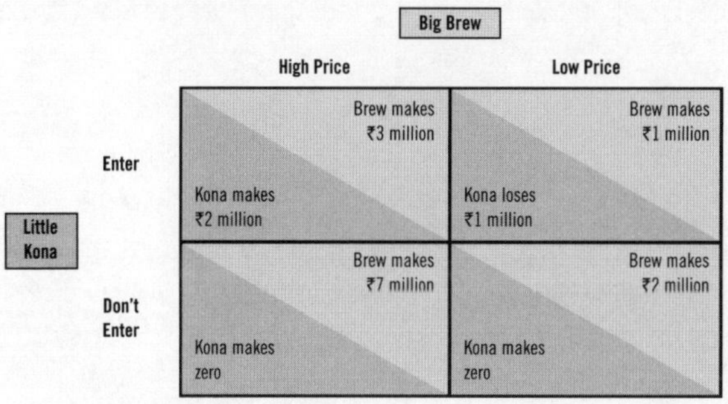

   a. Does either player in this game have a dominant strategy?
   b. Does your answer to part (a) help you figure out what the other player should do? What is the Nash equilibrium? Is there only one?
   c. Big Brew threatens Little Kona by saying, "If you enter, we're going to set a low price, so you had better stay out." Do you think Little Kona should believe the threat? Why or why not?
   d. If the two firms could collude and agree on how to split the total profits, what outcome would they pick?

7. Look at Question 1 above for the interaction between US and Mexico.
   a. Suppose now US moves first. Draw the extensive form of this game.
   b. What is the new equilibrium? Which solution concept did you use?
   c. Does the US have a first mover advantage?
   d. What happens is Mexico moves first? Can US still leverage some advantage? Explain why or why not, and how.

8. Three players, Maria, and Rubia, have found 500 gold coins from outside the fort of SonaGarh. They wish to share it among themselves.
   a. Suppose Maria makes an offer. Rubia can either accept or reject the offer. If she accepts, the proposal goes through. If she does not, then the entire bounty is returned to Sona Garh museum. How much will Maria offer? Will Rubia accept the offer?
   b. What happens if we change the game as follows. If Rubia rejects, she gets to make a counter offer. However, the bounty gets reduced to 90. Now Maria can either accept or reject. If Maria rejects, the bounty is returned, if she accepts, it goes through. Knowing this, how much should Maria offer in the first round?
   c. Suppose instead Rubia has left before the discovery of the bounty. Now Maria has to decide how much to leave behind for Rubia. Whatever she decides goes through since Rubia has no say any longer. How much should Maria offer?

This section looks more closely at the problems that arise when cooperation is desirable but difficult. This requires an understanding of game theory. We focus on the **prisoners' dilemma**, introduced in Chapter 16, which teaches a general lesson that applies to any group trying to maintain cooperation among its members.

prisoners' dilemma
a particular "game" between two captured prisoners that illustrates why cooperation is difficult to maintain even when it is mutually beneficial

17-2a Oligopolies as a Prisoners' Dilemma

What does the prisoners' dilemma have to do with markets and imperfect competition? It turns out that the decisions oligopolists face in trying to reach the monopoly outcome are similar to those that Bonnie and Clyde faced in the prisoners' dilemma.

Consider again the choices facing Jack and Jill. After prolonged negotiation, the two water suppliers agree to keep production at 30 gallons. That way, the price will be high, and together, they will earn the maximum profit. After they agree on production levels, however, each of them must decide whether to honor this agreement or to ignore it and produce at a higher level. Figure 2 shows how the profits of the two producers depend on the strategies they choose.

Jack might reason as follows: "I could keep production at 30 gallons as we agreed, or I could raise my production and sell 40 gallons. If Jill lives up to the agreement and keeps her production at 30 gallons, then my profit is ₹2,000 if I sell 40 gallons and ₹1,800 if I sell 30 gallons. In this case, I am better off with the higher production level. If Jill fails to live up to the agreement and produces 40 gallons, then I earn ₹1,600 by selling 40 gallons and ₹1,500 by selling 30 gallons. Again, I am better off with higher production. So, whatever Jill chooses to do, I am better off reneging on our agreement and producing at the higher level."

Producing 40 gallons is a dominant strategy for Jack. Of course, Jill reasons in the same way, and so both produce at the higher level of 40 gallons. The result is the inferior outcome (from Jack and Jill's standpoint) with low profits for each of the two producers.

This example shows why oligopolies have trouble maintaining monopoly profits. The monopoly outcome is jointly rational, but each oligopolist has an incentive to cheat. Just as self-interest drives the suspects in the prisoners' dilemma to confess, self-interest makes it hard for the oligopolists to maintain the cooperative outcome with low production, high prices, and monopoly profits.

Figure 2

Jack and Jill's Oligopoly Game

In this game between Jack and Jill, the profit that each earns from selling water depends on both the quantity he or she chooses to sell and the quantity the other chooses to sell.

Jill's Decision \ Jack's Decision	High Production: 40 Gallons	Low Production: 30 Gallons
High Production: 40 Gallons	Jack gets ₹1,600 profit; Jill gets ₹1,600 profit	Jack gets $1,500 profit; Jill gets ₹2,000 profit
Low Production: 30 Gallons	Jack gets ₹2,000 profit; Jill gets ₹1,500 profit	Jack gets ₹1,800 profit; Jill gets ₹1,800 profit

Case Study: OPEC and the World Oil Market

The story about the town's market for water is fictional, but if we change water to crude oil and Jack and Jill to Saudi Arabia and Iraq, the story is close to reality. Much of the world's oil is produced by a few countries, mostly in the Middle East. These countries together make up an oligopoly. Their decisions about how much oil to pump are much the same as Jack and Jill's decisions about how much water to pump.

In 1960, the countries that produce much of the world's oil formed a cartel called the Organization of Petroleum Exporting Countries (OPEC). It includes Saudi Arabia, Iraq, Iran, United Arab Emirates, Kuwait, Venezuela, and several other nations. In 2016, ten other oil-producing nations, led by Russia, joined forces with OPEC, and the cartel is now known as OPEC Plus. Together, OPEC Plus countries control most of the world's oil reserves. The cartel tries to raise the price of its product through a coordinated reduction in quantity produced. To do so, it sets production targets for each of the member countries.

The problem that OPEC Plus faces is much the same as the problem that Jack and Jill face in our story. The countries in the cartel would like to maintain a high price for oil. But each member is tempted to increase its production to get a larger share of the total profit. OPEC Plus members frequently agree to reduce production but then cheat on their agreements.

OPEC was quite successful at maintaining cooperation and high prices in the period from 1973 to 1985. The price of crude oil rose from ₹3 a barrel in 1972 to ₹11 in 1974 and then to ₹35 in 1981. But in the mid-1980s, member countries began arguing about production levels, and OPEC became ineffective at maintaining cooperation. By 1986, the price of crude oil had fallen back to ₹13 a barrel.

In recent years, the members of OPEC have continued to meet regularly and to confer with allies in the larger oil bloc, but they have been less successful at reaching and enforcing agreements. Changes in technology, such as the development of fracking, have expanded oil supply around the world and reduced OPEC's market power. As a result, fluctuations in oil prices have been driven more by the natural forces of supply and demand than by the cartel's artificial restrictions on production. ●

Common Resources We have earlier noted that people tend to overuse common resources. One can view this problem as an example of cooperation as in an oligopoly.

Imagine that two oil companies— Hindustan Oil and Indian Petroleum—own adjacent oil fields. Under the fields is a common pool of oil worth ₹120 million. Drilling a well to recover the oil costs ₹10 million. If each company drills one well, each will get half of the oil and earn a ₹50 million profit (₹60 million in revenue minus ₹10 million in costs).

Because the pool of oil is a common resource, the companies will not use it efficiently. Suppose that either company could drill a second well. If one company has two of the three wells, that company gets two-thirds of the oil, which yields a profit of ₹60 million. The other company gets one-third of the oil for a profit of ₹30 million. Yet if each company drills a second well, the two companies again split the oil. In this case, each bears the cost of a second well and earns a profit of only ₹40 million.

Figure 3 shows the game. Drilling two wells is a dominant strategy for each company. Once again, the self-interest of the two players leads them to an inferior outcome.

17-2d The Prisoners' Dilemma and the Welfare of Society

The prisoners' dilemma shows that cooperation can be difficult to maintain, even when it would make both players in the game better off. This lack of cooperation

Figure 3

A Common-Resources Game

When firms pump oil from a common pool, each firm's profit depends on both the number of wells it drills and the number of wells drilled by the other firm.

		Hindustan Oil: Drill Two Wells	Hindustan Oil: Drill One Well
Indian Petroleum	Drill Two Wells	Hindustan Oil gets ₹40 million profit; Indian Petroleum gets ₹40 million profit	Hindustan Oil gets ₹30 million profit; Indian Petroleum gets ₹60 million profit
	Drill One Well	Hindustan Oil gets ₹60 million profit; Indian Petroleum gets ₹30 million profit	Hindustan Oil gets ₹50 million profit; Indian Petroleum gets ₹50 million profit

is a problem for those directly involved. But is it a problem from the standpoint of society as a whole? The answer depends on the circumstances.

In some cases, the noncooperative equilibrium is bad for society as well as the players. In the arms race depicted in Figure 3, both the United States and the Soviet Union end up at risk (and so does everyone else on the planet). In the common-resources game in Figure 4, the extra wells dug by Indian Petroleum and Hindustan Oil are pure waste. In these cases, society would be better off if the two players could reach the cooperative outcome.

By contrast, in the case of oligopolists trying to maintain monopoly profits, a lack of cooperation is desirable from the standpoint of society. The monopoly outcome is good for the oligopolists but bad for consumers. As Chapter 7 showed, the competitive outcome is best for society because it maximizes total surplus. When oligopolists fail to cooperate, the quantity they produce is closer to this optimal level. Put differently, the invisible hand guides markets to allocate resources efficiently only when markets are competitive, and markets are competitive only when firms in the market fail to cooperate with one another.

Similarly, consider the case of the police questioning two suspects. Lack of cooperation between the suspects is desirable for society because it allows the police to convict more criminals. The prisoners' dilemma is a dilemma for the prisoners, but it can be a boon to everyone else.

17-2e Why People Sometimes Cooperate?

The prisoners' dilemma shows that cooperation is difficult. But is it impossible? Not all prisoners, when questioned by the police, turn in their partners. Cartels sometimes manage to maintain collusive arrangements, despite the incentive for members to defect. Very often, players can solve the prisoners' dilemma because they play the game not once but many times.

To see why cooperation is easier to enforce in repeated games, let's return to our duopolists, Jack and Jill, whose choices were given in Figure 2. They would like to achieve the monopoly outcome in which each produces 30 gallons. Yet if Jack and Jill are to play this game only once, neither has any incentive to live up to an agreement to do so. Self-interest drives each of them to renege and choose the dominant strategy of 40 gallons.

Now suppose that Jack and Jill know that they will play the same game every week. When making their initial agreement to keep production low, they can specify what happens if one party reneges. They might agree, for instance, that once one of them produces 40 gallons, both will produce 40 gallons forever after. This penalty is easy to enforce because if one party produces at the high level, the other has every reason to do the same.

The threat of this penalty may be all that is needed to maintain cooperation. Each person knows that defecting would raise his or her profit from ₹1,800 to ₹2,000. But this benefit would last for only one week. Thereafter, profit would fall to ₹1,600 and stay there. As long as the players care enough about future profits, they will forgo the one-time gain from defection. In a game of repeated prisoners' dilemma, like an ongoing arms race, the two players may well be able to reach the cooperative outcome.

Case Study

The Prisoners' Dilemma Tournament

Imagine that you are playing the prisoners' dilemma with a person being questioned in a separate room and that you are to play with this other person many times. Your score at the end of the game is the total number of years you will spend in jail, a total you'd like to make as small as possible. What strategy would you play? Would you begin by confessing or remaining silent? How would the other player's actions in one round affect your choices in subsequent rounds?

This has now become a complicated game. To encourage cooperation, each player will want to impose some penalty when the player in the other room does not cooperate. Yet the strategy described earlier for Jack and Jill's water cartel—defect forever as soon as the other player defects—is not in the least forgiving. If the game is going to be repeated many times, a strategy that allows players to return to the cooperative outcome after a period of noncooperation may be preferable.

To see what strategies work best, the political scientist Robert Axelrod held a contest. People entered by submitting computer programs designed to play a game of repeated prisoners' dilemma. Each program was then paired with each of the others as in a round-robin tournament. The goal was to receive the fewest total years in jail.

The winning program turned out to be a simple strategy called **tit-for-tat**. According to tit-for-tat, a player should start by cooperating and then do whatever the other player did last time. A tit-for-tat player cooperates until the other player defects and then defects until the other player cooperates again. This strategy starts out friendly, penalizes unfriendly players, and forgives them if warranted. To Axelrod's surprise, this simple strategy did better than the more complex strategies that people had sent in.

The tit-for-tat strategy has a long history. It is essentially "an eye for an eye, a tooth for a tooth." The prisoners' dilemma tournament suggests that this classic strategy may be a good rule of thumb for playing some of the games of life. ●

17-3 Public Policy toward Oligopolies

One of the learnings in Chapter 1 is that governments can sometimes improve market outcomes. This principle applies to oligopolistic markets, where cooperation leads to production that is too low and prices that are too high from the standpoint of society as a whole. The allocation of resources will be closer to the social optimum

Chapter in a Nutshell

- Oligopolists maximize their total profits by forming a cartel and acting like a monopolist. Yet, if oligopolists make decisions about production levels individually, the result is a greater quantity and a lower price than under the monopoly outcome. The larger the number of firms in the oligopoly, the closer the quantity and price will be to the levels that would prevail under perfect competition.
- The prisoners' dilemma shows that self-interest can prevent people from maintaining cooperation, even when cooperation is in their mutual interest. The logic of the prisoners' dilemma applies to many situations, including arms races, common-resource problems, and oligopolies.
- Policymakers use the antitrust laws to prevent oligopolies from engaging in behavior that reduces competition. The application of these laws can be controversial because some behavior that can appear to reduce competition may have legitimate business purposes.

Key Concepts

oligopoly, p. 343
game theory, p. 343
collusion, p. 345
cartel, p. 345
nash equilibrium, p. 346
prisoners' dilemma, p. 349

Questions for Review

1. If a group of sellers could form a cartel, what quantity and price would they try to set?
2. Compare the quantity and price of an oligopoly with that of a monopoly.
3. Compare the quantity and price of an oligopoly with that of a perfectly competitive market.
4. How does the number of firms in an oligopoly affect the outcome in the market?
5. What is the prisoners' dilemma, and what does it have to do with oligopoly?
6. Give two examples other than oligopoly that can be explained by the logic of the prisoners' dilemma.
7. What kinds of behavior do the antitrust laws prohibit?

Problems and Applications

1. A large share of the world supply of diamonds comes from Russia and South Africa. Suppose that the marginal cost of mining diamonds is constant at ₹1,000 per diamond and the demand for diamonds is described by the following schedule:

Price	Quantity
₹8,000	5,000 diamonds
7,000	6,000
6,000	7,000
5,000	8,000
4,000	9,000
3,000	10,000
2,000	11,000
1,000	12,000

   a. If there were many suppliers of diamonds, what would the price and quantity be?
   b. If there were only one supplier of diamonds, what would the price and quantity be?
   c. If Russia and South Africa formed a cartel, what would the price and quantity be? If the countries split the market evenly, what would South Africa's production and profit be? What would happen to South Africa's profit if it increased its production by 1,000 while Russia stuck to the cartel agreement?
   d. Use your answers to part (c) to explain why cartel agreements are often not successful.

2. Some years ago, the *New York Times* reported that "the inability of OPEC to agree last week to cut production has sent the oil market into turmoil . . .

[leading to] the lowest price for domestic crude oil since June 1990."

a. Why were the members of OPEC trying to agree to cut production?

b. Why do you suppose OPEC was unable to agree on cutting production? Why did the oil market go into "turmoil" as a result?

c. The newspaper also noted OPEC's view "that producing nations outside the organization, like Norway and Britain, should do their share and cut production." What does the phrase "do their share" suggest about OPEC's desired relationship with Norway and Britain?

3. This chapter discusses companies that are oligopolists in the markets for the goods they sell. Many of the same ideas apply to companies that are oligopolists in the markets for the inputs they buy.

a. If sellers who are oligopolists try to increase the price of goods they sell, what is the goal of buyers who are oligopolists?

b. Major league baseball team owners have an oligopoly in the market for baseball players. What is the owners' goal regarding players' salaries? Why is this goal difficult to achieve?

c. Baseball players went on strike in 1994 because they would not accept the salary cap that the owners wanted to impose. If the owners were already colluding over salaries, why did they feel the need for a salary cap?

4. Consider trade relations between the United States and Mexico. Assume that the leaders of the two countries believe the payoffs to alternative trade policies are as follows:

Mexico's Decision \ United States's Decision	Low Tariffs	High Tariffs
Low Tariffs	U.S. gains ₹25 billion; Mexico gains ₹25 billion	U.S. gains ₹30 billion; Mexico gains ₹10 billion
High Tariffs	U.S. gains ₹10 billion; Mexico gains ₹30 billion	U.S. gains ₹20 billion; Mexico gains ₹20 billion

a. What is the dominant strategy for the United States? For Mexico? Explain.

b. Define **Nash equilibrium**. What is the Nash equilibrium for trade policy?

c. In 1993, the U.S. Congress ratified the North American Free Trade Agreement, in which the United States and Mexico agreed to reduce trade barriers simultaneously. Do the perceived payoffs shown here justify this approach to trade policy? Explain.

d. Based on your understanding of the gains from trade (discussed in Chapters 3 and 9), do you think that these payoffs actually reflect a nation's welfare under the four possible outcomes?

5. Synergy and Dynaco are the only two firms in a specific high-tech industry. They face the following payoff matrix as they determine the size of their research budget:

Dynaco's Decision \ Synergy's Decision	Large Budget	Small Budget
Large Budget	Synergy gains ₹20 million; Dynaco gains ₹30 million	Synergy gains zero; Dynaco gains ₹70 million
Small Budget	Synergy gains ₹30 million; Dynaco gains zero	Synergy gains ₹40 million; Dynaco gains ₹50 million

a. Does Synergy have a dominant strategy? Explain.

b. Does Dynaco have a dominant strategy? Explain.

c. Is there a Nash equilibrium for this scenario? Explain. (Hint: Look closely at the definition of Nash equilibrium.)

6. You and a classmate are assigned a project on which you will receive one combined grade. You each want to receive a good grade, but you also want to avoid hard work. In particular, here is the situation:

- If both of you work hard, you both get an A, which gives each of you 40 units of happiness.
- If only one of you works hard, you both get a B, which gives each of you 30 units of happiness.
- If neither of you works hard, you both get a D, which gives each of you 10 units of happiness.
- Working hard costs 25 units of happiness.

a. Fill in the following payoff matrix:

Classmate's Decision \ Your Decision	Work	Shirk
Work	You: ; Classmate:	You: ; Classmate:
Shirk	You: ; Classmate:	You: ; Classmate:

b. What is the likely outcome? Explain your answer.

c. If you get this classmate as your partner on a series of projects throughout the year rather than only once, how might that change the outcome you predicted in part (b)?

d. Another classmate cares more about good grades: She gets 50 units of happiness for a B and 80 units of happiness for an A. If this classmate were your partner (but your preferences remained the same), how would your answers to parts (a) and (b) change? Which of the two classmates would you prefer as a partner? Would she also want you as a partner?

7. A case study in the chapter describes a phone conversation between the presidents of American Airlines and Braniff Airways. Let's use game theory to analyze the interaction between the two companies. Suppose that each company can charge either a high price for tickets or a low price. If one company charges ₹300, it earns low profit if the other company also charges ₹300 and high profit if the other company charges ₹600. On the other hand, if the company charges ₹600, it earns very low profit if the other company charges ₹300 and medium profit if the other company also charges ₹600.
   a. Draw the payoff matrix for this game.
   b. What is the Nash equilibrium in this game? Explain.
   c. Is there an outcome that would be better than the Nash equilibrium for both airlines? How could it be achieved? Who would lose if it were achieved?

8. Two athletes of equal ability are competing for a prize of ₹10,000. Each is deciding whether to take a dangerous performance-enhancing drug. If one athlete takes the drug and the other does not, the one who takes the drug wins the prize. If both or neither take the drug, they tie and split the prize. Taking the drug imposes health risks that are equivalent to a loss of *X* dollars.
   a. Draw a 2×2 payoff matrix describing the decisions the athletes face.
   b. For what *X* is taking the drug the Nash equilibrium?
   c. Does making the drug safer (that is, lowering *X*) make the athletes better or worse off? Explain.

9. Little Kona is a small coffee company that is considering entering a market dominated by Big Brew. Each company's profit depends on whether Little Kona enters and whether Big Brew sets a high price or a low price:

Little Kona \ Big Brew	High Price	Low Price
Enter	Brew makes ₹3 million; Kona makes ₹2 million	Brew makes ₹1 million; Kona loses ₹1 million
Don't Enter	Brew makes ₹7 million; Kona makes zero	Brew makes ₹2 million; Kona makes zero

   a. Does either player in this game have a dominant strategy?
   b. Does your answer to part (a) help you figure out what the other player should do? What is the Nash equilibrium? Is there only one?
   c. Big Brew threatens Little Kona by saying, "If you enter, we're going to set a low price, so you had better stay out." Do you think Little Kona should believe the threat? Why or why not?
   d. If the two firms could collude and agree on how to split the total profits, what outcome would they pick?

10. Two automobile manufacturers, Indicar and Autonova, compete in quantities. Indicar moves first and chooses its production level; Autonova observes and then decides how much to produce.
    a. Draw a diagram showing Indicar's and Autonova's best response functions.
    b. Using backward induction, identify the equilibrium output levels for both firms. Compare total output, price, and profits with the simultaneous-move case.
    c. Explain in words how commitment gives the leader a first-mover advantage.

11. In the Indian telecom industry, Jio often announces new tariff plans before Airtel and Vi.
    a. Discuss why Jio's early announcement can be viewed as a sequential-move strategy rather than simultaneous competition.
    b. Under what conditions does Jio's first move give it a leadership advantage?
    c. Suppose the same firms interact repeatedly every quarter. How might repeated interaction change the outcome compared with the one-time game?

Quick**Quiz Answers**

1. **d** 2. **c** 3. **a** 4. **d** 5. **c** 6. **b** 7. **d** 8. **b**

Chapter

18

The Markets for the Factors of Production

When you finish school, your income will be determined largely by what kind of job you take. If you work as a computer programmer, you are likely to earn more than if you work as a petrol pump attendant. This fact is puzzling. No law requires that computer programmers be paid more than petrol pump attendants. No ethical principle says that programmers are more deserving. What, then, determines which job pays the higher wage?

Your income is a small piece of a larger economic picture. In 2023, the total income of all Indian residents, a statistic called **national income**, was about ₹250 lakh crores. People earned this income in various ways. Workers earned the bulk of it in the form of wages and fringe benefits. The rest went to landowners and to the owners of **capital**—the economy's stock of equipment and structures—in the form of rent, profit, and interest. What determines how much goes to workers? To landowners? To the owners of capital? Why do some workers earn higher wages than others, some landowners higher rental income than others, and some capital owners greater profit than others? Why, in particular, do computer programmers earn more than petrol pump attendants?

SHIFT DRIVE/SHUTTERSTOCK.COM; FRDARK/E+/GETTY IMAGES

The answers to these questions, like most in economics, hinge on supply and demand. The supply and demand for labor, land, and capital determine the prices paid to workers, landowners, and capital owners. To understand why some people earn more than others, we need to look more deeply at the markets for the services they provide. We take up that task in this and the next two chapters.

factors of production the inputs used to produce goods and services

This chapter presents the basic theory of factor markets. As you may recall from Chapter 2, the **factors of production** are the inputs used to produce goods and services. Labor, land, and capital are the three most important factors of production. When a computer firm produces software, it uses programmers' time (labor), the physical space where its offices are located (land), and an office building and computer equipment (capital). When a petrol pump sells petrol or diesel, it uses attendants' time (labor), the station's physical space (land), and gas tanks and the actual pumps (capital).

Factor markets differ from the markets for goods and services analyzed in previous chapters in one important way: The demand for a factor of production is a **derived demand**. That is, a firm's demand for a factor of production is derived from its decision to supply a good in another market. For example, the demand for programmers is linked to the supply of software, and the demand for petrol pump attendants is linked to the supply of gasoline.

This chapter analyzes factor demand by considering how competitive, profit-maximizing firms decide how much of a factor to buy. The analysis begins by examining the demand for labor. Labor is the most important factor of production, as reflected by the fact that workers receive most of national income. Later in the chapter, the analysis is extended to the other factors of production.

The theory of factor markets developed in this chapter takes a large step toward explaining how the income of an economy is distributed among workers, landowners, and owners of capital.

18-1 The Demand for Labor

The forces of supply and demand govern most markets in the economy, and the labor market is no exception. This is illustrated in Figure 1. In panel (a), the supply and demand for apples determine the price of apples. In panel (b), the supply and demand for apple pickers determine the price, or wage, of apple pickers.

As we have noted, labor demand is a derived demand. Rather than being final goods ready to be consumed, most labor services are inputs into the production of other goods. To understand labor demand, we focus on the firms that hire the labor and use it to produce goods for sale. The link between the supply of goods and the demand for labor to produce them is crucial in determining equilibrium wages.

18-1a The Competitive, Profit-Maximizing Firm

Consider how an apple producer decides what quantity of labor to demand. The firm owns an orchard and each week decides how many apple pickers to hire to harvest its crop. After the firm hires its workers, they pick the apples. The firm sells the apples, pays the workers, and keeps what's left as profit.

The theory developed in this chapter is based on two assumptions about the firm. First, the firm is **competitive** both in the market for apples (where it is a seller) and in the market for apple pickers (where it is a buyer). A competitive firm is a price taker. Because many firms sell apples and hire apple pickers, a single firm has little

Figure 1

The Versatility of Supply and Demand

The basic tools of supply and demand apply to goods and to labor services. Panel (a) shows how the supply and demand for apples determine the price of apples. Panel (b) shows how the supply and demand for apple pickers determine the wage of apple pickers.

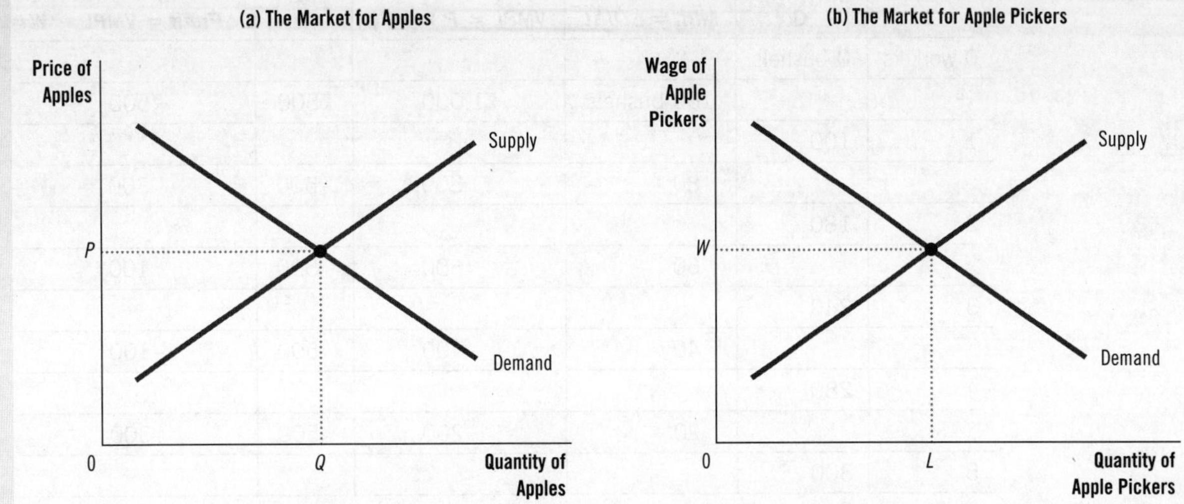

influence over the price it gets for apples or the wage it pays apple pickers. The firm takes the price and wage as given by market conditions. It only has to decide how many apples to sell and how many workers to hire.

Second, the firm is **profit-maximizing.** It does not care about the number of workers it employs or the number of apples it produces, except insofar as they affect profit, which equals the total revenue from the sale of apples minus the total cost of producing them. The firm's supply of apples and its demand for workers are derived from its primary goal of maximizing profit.

18-1b The Production Function and the Marginal Product of Labor

To make its hiring decision, a firm considers how the size of its workforce affects its output. For the apple producer, the question is how the number of apple pickers affects the quantity of apples it can harvest and sell. Table 1 gives a numerical example. Column (1) shows the number of workers. Column (2) shows the quantity of apples the workers harvest each week.

These two columns of numbers describe the firm's ability to produce apples. Recall that economists use the term **production function** to describe the relationship between the quantity of the inputs used in production and the quantity of output from production. Here the "input" is the apple pickers, and the "output" is the apples. The other inputs—the trees themselves, the land, the firm's trucks and tractors, and so on—are held fixed for now. This firm's production function shows that if the firm hires 1 worker, that worker will pick 100 bushels of apples per week. If the firm hires 2 workers, the 2 workers together will pick 180 bushels per week. And so on.

production function
the relationship between the quantity of inputs used to make a good and the quantity of output of that good

Table 1

How the Competitive Firm Decides How Much Labor to Hire

(1) Labor L	(2) Output Q	(3) Marginal Product of Labor $MPL = \Delta Q/\Delta L$	(4) Value of the Marginal Product of Labor $VMPL = P \times MPL$	(5) Wage W	(6) Marginal Profit $\Delta Profit = VMPL - W$
0 workers	0 bushels				
		100 bushels	₹1,000	₹500	₹500
1	100				
		80	800	500	300
2	180				
		60	600	500	100
3	240				
		40	400	500	–100
4	280				
		20	200	500	–300
5	300				

Figure 2 graphs the data on labor and output presented in Table 1. The number of workers is on the horizontal axis, and the amount of output is on the vertical axis. This figure illustrates the production function.

Figure 2

The Production Function

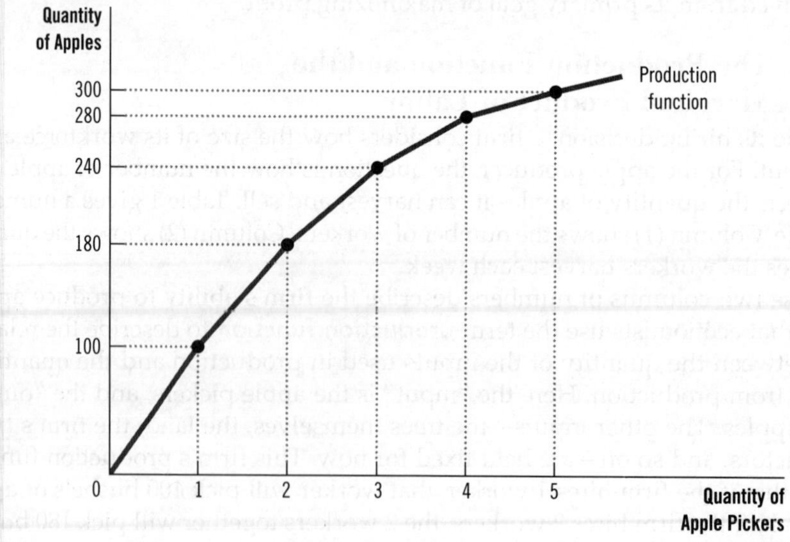

The production function shows how an input into production (apple pickers) influences the output from production (apples). As the quantity of the input increases, the production function gets flatter, reflecting the property of diminishing marginal product.

For now, let's put aside the possibility of backward-sloping labor supply. That is, we assume that the substitution effect dominates, so the labor-supply curve slopes upward.

18-2b What Causes the Labor-Supply Curve to Shift?

The labor-supply curve shifts whenever people change the amount they want to work at a given wage. Consider some of the events that might cause such a shift.

Changes in Preferences In 1950, 34 percent of women were employed at paid jobs or looking for work. By 2020, that number had risen to 56 percent. One of the many explanations for this development is changing preferences or attitudes toward work. In 1950, women routinely stayed at home and raised their children. Today, the typical family size is smaller, and more mothers choose to work. One result is an increase in the supply of labor.

Changes in Alternative Opportunities The supply of labor in any one labor market depends on the opportunities available in other labor markets. If the wage earned by pear pickers suddenly rises, some apple pickers may choose to switch occupations, causing the supply of labor in the market for apple pickers to fall.

Immigration The movement of workers from region to region or country to country is an important source of shifts in labor supply. When migrant workers come north for the autumn harvest, the supply of labor increases in apple orchards, but it declines in orange-processing plants in the south. When immigrants come to the United States, the supply of labor increases in the United States and falls in the immigrants' home countries. Much of the policy debate about immigration centers on its effect on labor supply and equilibrium wages. Similar logic applies for within state migration in India. For instance, if people from West Bengal migrate to work in Karnataka, then labor supply in Karnataka will increase and that in West Bengal will decrease.

Quick**Quiz**

4. Who has a greater opportunity cost of leisure—janitors or surgeons?
   a. janitors because their wages are lower
   b. surgeons because their wages are higher
   c. whoever has the greater income effect
   d. whoever has the greater substitution effect

5. A person works more hours at a higher wage if the substitution effect
   a. equals zero.
   b. equals the income effect.
   c. is smaller than the income effect.
   d. is larger than the income effect.

6. Which of the following events will shift the labor supply curve to the right?
   a. More dads leave the workforce to spend time raising children.
   b. Great new video games are introduced, enhancing the value of leisure.
   c. Relaxed immigration laws allow more workers to come in from abroad.
   d. Government benefits for the retired are increased.

Answers are at the end of the chapter.

18-3 Equilibrium in the Labor Market

So far, we have established two facts about how wages are determined in competitive labor markets:

- The wage adjusts to balance the supply and demand for labor.
- The wage equals the value of the marginal product of labor.

At first, it might seem surprising that the wage can do both things at once. In fact, there is no real puzzle here, but understanding why is an important step toward understanding wage determination.

Figure 4 shows the labor market in equilibrium. The wage and the quantity of labor have adjusted to balance supply and demand. When the market is in this equilibrium, each firm has bought as much labor as it finds profitable at the equilibrium wage. That is, each firm has followed the rule for profit maximization: It has hired workers until the value of the marginal product equals the wage. Hence, the wage must equal the value of the marginal product of labor once it has brought supply and demand into equilibrium.

This brings us to an important lesson: **Any event that changes the supply or demand for labor must change the equilibrium wage and the value of the marginal product by the same amount because these must always be equal.** To see how this works, let's consider some events that shift these curves.

18-3a Shifts in Labor Supply

Suppose that immigration increases the number of workers willing to pick apples. As Figure 5 shows, the supply of labor shifts to the right from S_1 to S_2. At the initial wage W_1, the quantity of labor supplied now exceeds the quantity demanded. This surplus of labor puts downward pressure on the wage of apple pickers, and the fall in the wage from W_1 to W_2 makes it profitable for firms to hire more workers. As the number of workers employed in each apple orchard rises, the marginal product of a worker falls, and so does the value of the marginal product. In the new equilibrium, both the wage and the value of the marginal product of labor are lower than they were before the influx of new workers.

An episode from Israel, studied by the economist Joshua Angrist, illustrates how a shift in labor supply can alter the equilibrium in a labor market. During most of the 1980s, many thousands of Palestinians regularly commuted from their homes in the Israeli-occupied West Bank and Gaza Strip to jobs in Israel, primarily in the construction and agriculture industries. In 1988, however, political unrest in these occupied areas induced the Israeli government to take steps that, as a by-product, reduced this supply of workers. Curfews were imposed, work permits were checked more thoroughly, and a ban on overnight stays of Palestinians in Israel was enforced more rigorously. The economic impact of these steps was exactly as theory predicts: The number of Palestinians with jobs in Israel fell by half, while those who

Ask the Experts

Immigration

"The average U.S. citizen would be better off if a larger number of highly educated foreign workers were legally allowed to immigrate to the U.S. each year."

What do economists say?

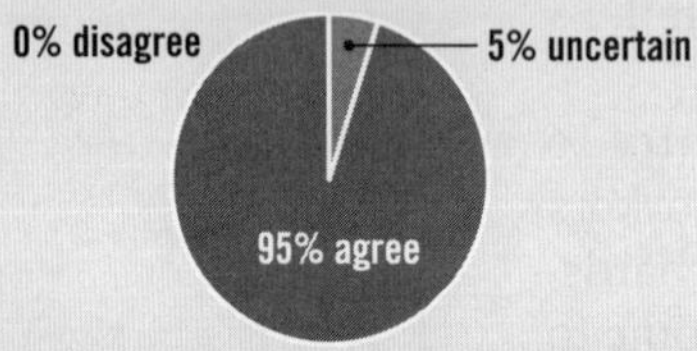

"The average U.S. citizen would be better off if a larger number of low-skilled foreign workers were legally allowed to enter the U.S. each year."

What do economists say?

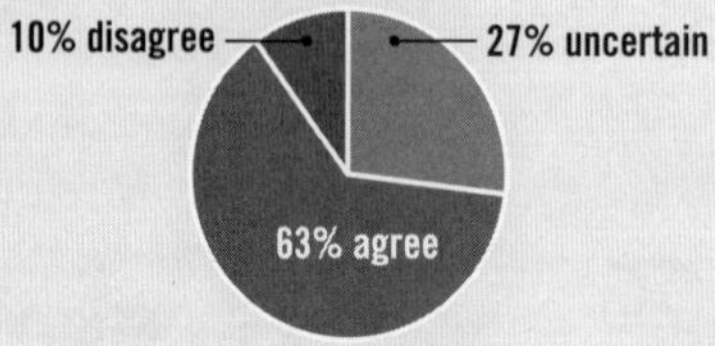

"Unless they were compensated by others, many low-skilled American workers would be substantially worse off if a larger number of low-skilled foreign workers were legally allowed to enter the U.S. each year."

What do economists say?

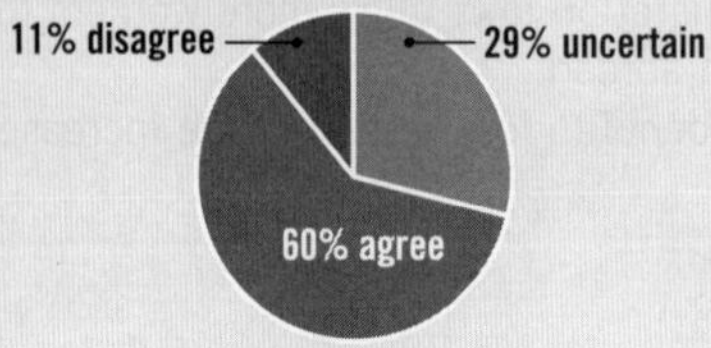

Source: IGM Economic Experts Panel, February 12, 2013, December 10, 2013.

Figure 4

Equilibrium in a Labor Market

Like all prices, the price of labor (the wage) depends on supply and demand. Because the demand curve reflects the value of the marginal product of labor, in equilibrium, workers receive the value of their marginal contribution to the production of goods and services.

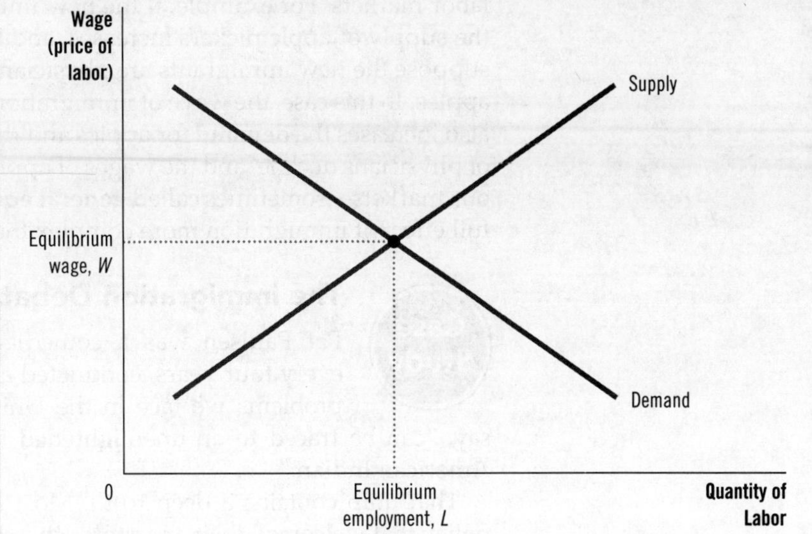

Figure 5

A Shift in Labor Supply

When labor supply increases from S_1 to S_2, perhaps because of an immigration wave of new workers, the equilibrium wage falls from W_1 to W_2. At this lower wage, firms hire more labor, so employment rises from L_1 to L_2. The change in the wage reflects a change in the value of the marginal product of labor: With more workers, the added output from an extra worker is smaller.

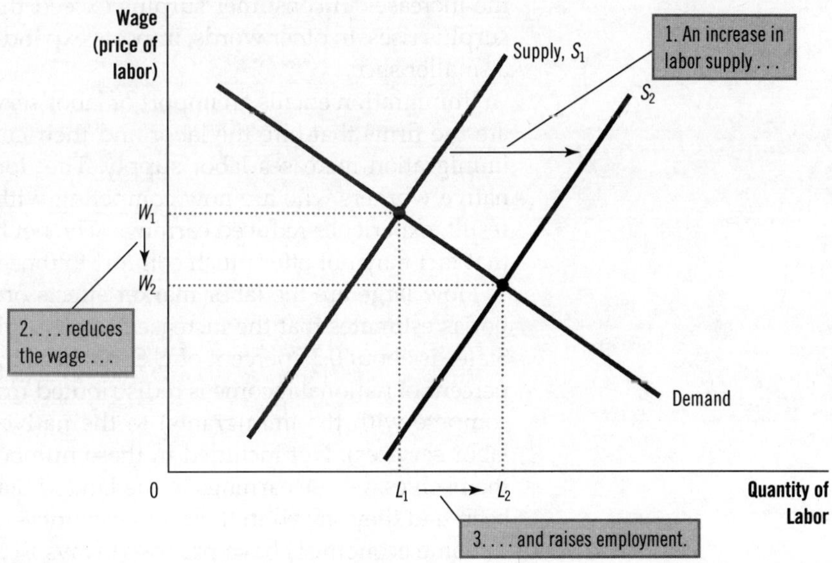

continued to work in Israel enjoyed wage increases of about 50 percent. With a reduced number of Palestinian workers in Israel, the value of the marginal product of the remaining workers was much higher.

When considering the economics of immigration, keep in mind that the economy consists not of a single labor market but of a variety of labor markets for different kinds of workers. A wave of immigration may lower wages in those labor markets in which the new immigrants seek work, but it could have the opposite effect in other labor markets. For example, if the new immigrants look for jobs as apple pickers, the supply of apple pickers increases, and the wage of apple pickers declines. But suppose the new immigrants are physicians who use some of their income to buy apples. In this case, the wave of immigration increases the **supply** of physicians but also increases the **demand** for apples and thus apple pickers. As a result, the wages of physicians decline, and the wages of apple pickers rise. The linkages among various markets—sometimes called **general equilibrium effects**—make analyzing the full effect of immigration more complex than it first appears.

Case Study

The Immigration Debate

Pat Paulsen was a comedian from the 1960s to the 1990s who, every four years, conducted a faux campaign for president. "All the problems we face in the United States today," Mr. Paulsen would say, "can be traced to an unenlightened immigration policy on the part of the American Indian."

That quip contains a deep truth. Most Americans today are beneficiaries of a policy that welcomed their ancestors when they arrived at the border. But that does not stop immigration from being a divisive political issue. One reason for this divisiveness is immigration's economic impact.

The welfare effects of immigration can be seen through the lens of international trade. Recall that when a nation allows a good to be imported, the price falls. Consumers of the good are better off, and domestic producers are worse off. But the increases in consumer surplus exceed the losses in producer surplus, so total surplus rises. In other words, imports expand the economic pie but leave some with a smaller slice.

Immigration entails an import of labor services. The consumers of these services are the firms that hire the labor and their customers, both of which benefit when immigration increases labor supply. The domestic producers in this case are the native workers who are now competing with new workers from abroad and, as a result, experience reduced earnings. The net benefit to the economy is positive, but that fact may not offer much comfort to those with depressed incomes.

How large are the labor market effects of immigration? The economist George Borjas estimates that the increased total surplus from immigration into the United States is about 0.25 percent of U.S. national income annually. In addition, about 2.5 percent of national income is redistributed from the native losers (the workers who compete with the immigrants) to the native winners (those who consume these labor services). Not included in these numbers are the benefits to the immigrants themselves, whose earnings in the United States far exceed what they would have been had they stayed in their home countries.

Some economists have proposed ways to distribute the gains from immigration more equitably. For example, immigrants could be subject to a special tax levied on either them or their employers. The revenue could be used to reduce the tax burden on native workers. If native workers shared more of the benefits from immigration, they might be more likely to welcome it.

The debate over immigration is not just about economics, however. It also has a powerful, emotional element that concerns cultural and national identity. But most Americans would do well to remember how lucky they are that the American Indian did not pursue the enlightened immigration policy suggested by Mr. Paulsen. ●

Figure 6

A Shift in Labor Demand

When labor demand increases from D_1 to D_2, perhaps because of an increase in the price of the firm's output, the equilibrium wage rises from W_1 to W_2, and employment rises from L_1 to L_2. The change in the wage reflects a change in the value of the marginal product of labor: With a higher output price, the added output from an extra worker is more valuable.

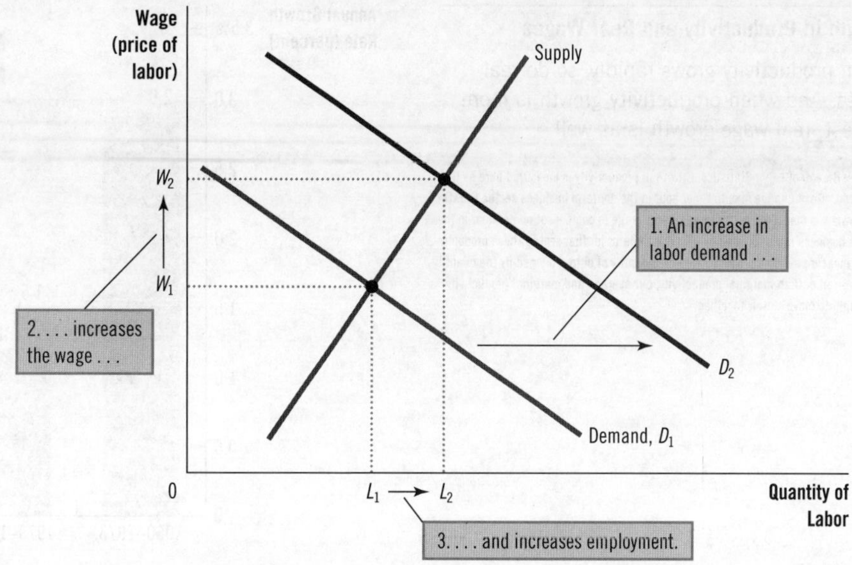

18-3b Shifts in Labor Demand

Now suppose that an increase in the popularity of apples causes their price to rise. This price increase does not change the marginal product of labor for any given number of workers, but it does raise the **value** of the marginal product. With a higher price for apples, hiring more apple pickers is now profitable. As Figure 6 shows, when the demand for labor shifts to the right from D_1 to D_2, the equilibrium wage rises from W_1 to W_2, and equilibrium employment rises from L_1 to L_2. Once again, the wage and the value of the marginal product of labor move together.

This analysis shows that prosperity for firms in an industry is often linked to prosperity for workers in that industry. When the price of apples rises, apple producers make a greater profit, and apple pickers earn higher wages. When the price of apples falls, apple producers earn a smaller profit, and apple pickers earn lower wages. This lesson is well known to workers in industries with highly volatile prices. Workers in oil fields, for instance, know from experience that their earnings are closely linked to the world price of crude oil.

From these examples, you should now have a good understanding of how wages are set in competitive labor markets. Labor supply and labor demand together determine the equilibrium wage, and shifts in the supply or demand curve for labor cause the equilibrium wage to change. At the same time, profit maximization by the firms that demand labor ensures that the equilibrium wage always equals the value of the marginal product of labor.

Case Study

Productivity and Wages in the US Economy

Our analysis of labor demand shows that wages equal productivity as measured by the value of the marginal product of labor. Put simply, highly productive workers tend to be highly paid, and less productive workers typically earn less.

Figure 7

Growth in Productivity and Real Wages

When productivity grows rapidly, so do real wages. And when productivity growth is more modest, real wage growth is as well.

Source: Bureau of Labor Statistics. Growth in productivity is measured here as the annualized rate of change in output per hour in the nonfarm business sector. Growth in real wages is measured as the annualized change in compensation per hour in the nonfarm business sector divided by the price deflator for that sector. These productivity data measure average productivity—the quantity of output divided by the quantity of labor—rather than marginal productivity, but average and marginal productivity are thought to move closely together.

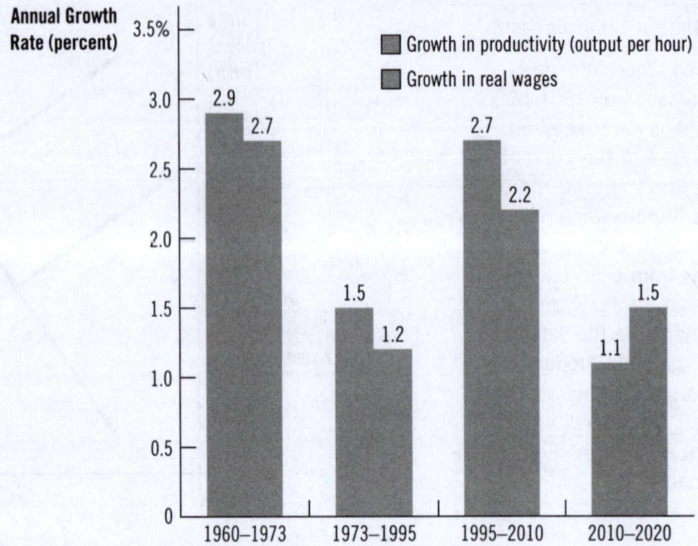

This lesson is key to understanding why workers today are generally better off than workers in previous generations. From 1960 to 2020, economy-wide productivity as measured by output per hour of work grew about 2.0 percent per year. Real wages (that is, wages adjusted for inflation) grew at 1.9 percent per year—almost the same rate. This change in wages may be too small to notice year to year, but it compounds over many years. With a growth rate of 2 percent per year, productivity and real wages double about every 35 years.

The link between productivity and real wages appears again when we examine various historical periods with different productivity experiences, as shown in Figure 7. When productivity grows rapidly, real wages rise quickly. When productivity grows slowly, the increase in real wages is more modest. The most recent period, 2010 to 2020, exhibited low growth in both productivity and real wages.

The bottom line: Both theory and history confirm the close connection between productivity and real wages. ●

Quick**Quiz**

7. A technological advance that increases the marginal product of labor shifts the labor-_______ curve to the _______.
   a. demand; left
   b. demand; right
   c. supply; left
   d. supply; right

8. Around 1973, the U.S. economy experienced a significant _______ in productivity growth, coupled with a _______ in the growth of real wages.
   a. pickup; pickup
   b. pickup; slowdown
   c. slowdown; pickup
   d. slowdown; slowdown

Answers are at the end of the chapter.

18-4 The Other Factors of Production: Land and Capital

We have seen how firms decide how much labor to hire and how these decisions affect workers' wages. As firms hire workers, they also decide about other inputs to production. For example, our apple-producing firm might have to choose the size of its orchard and the number of ladders for apple pickers. Think of the firm's factors of production as falling into three categories: labor, land, and capital.

The meanings of the terms **labor** and **land** are clear, but the definition of **capital** is tricky. Economists use the term **capital** to refer to the stock of equipment and structures used for production. That is, capital represents the accumulation of goods produced in the past that are being used in the present to produce new goods and services. For our apple firm, the capital stock includes the ladders used to climb the trees, the trucks used to transport the apples, the buildings used to store the apples, and even the apple trees themselves.

capital
the equipment and structures used to produce goods and services

18-4a Equilibrium in the Markets for Land and Capital

What determines how much the owners of land and capital earn for their contribution to production? Before answering this question, we need to distinguish between two prices: the purchase price and the rental price. The **purchase price** of land or capital is the price paid to own it indefinitely. The **rental price** is the price paid to use that factor for a limited period. Keep this distinction in mind because, as we will see, these prices are determined by somewhat different economic forces.

Here's the key insight: The theory of factor demand that we developed for the labor market also applies to the markets for land and capital. Because the wage is the rental price of labor, much of what we have learned about wage determination is relevant to the rental prices of land and capital. As Figure 8 illustrates, the rental

Figure 8

The Markets for Land and Capital

Supply and demand determine the compensation paid to the owners of land, as shown in panel (a), and the compensation paid to the owners of capital, as shown in panel (b). The demand for each factor, in turn, depends on the value of its marginal product.

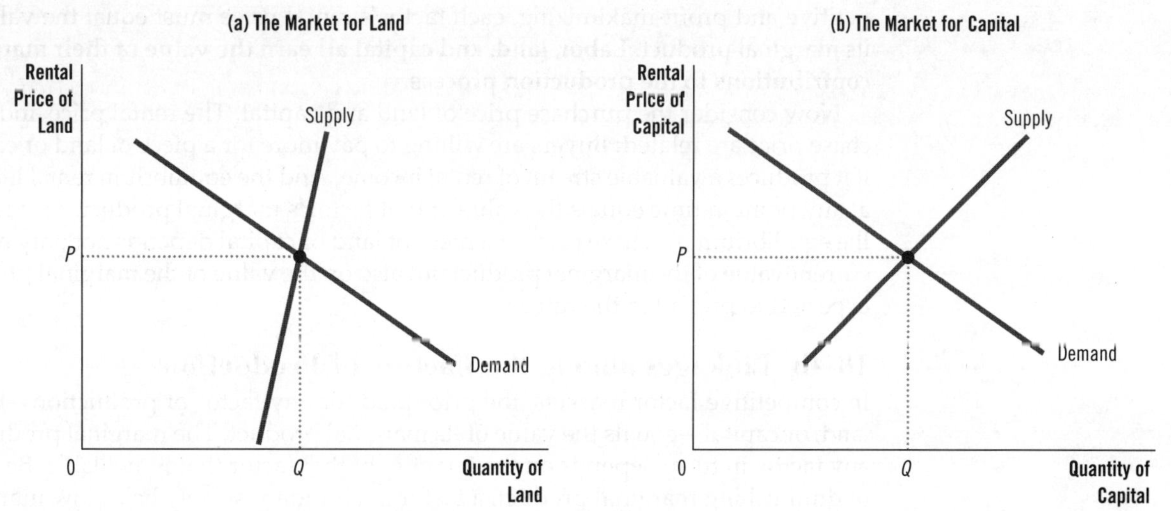

a. In what kind of market structure does the firm sell its output? How can you tell?
b. In what kind of market structure does the firm rent robots? How can you tell?
c. Calculate the marginal product and the value of the marginal product of each additional robot.
d. How many robots should the firm rent? Explain.

5. The nation of Ectenia has 20 competitive apple orchards, all of which sell apples at the world price of ₹2 per apple. The following equations describe the production function and the marginal product of labor in each orchard:

$$Q = 100L - L^2$$

$$MPL = 100 - 2L$$

where Q is the number of apples produced in a day, L is the number of workers, and MPL is the marginal product of labor.
   a. What is each orchard's labor demand as a function of the daily wage W? What is the market's labor demand?
   b. Ectenia has 200 workers who supply their labor inelastically. Solve for the wage W. How many workers does each orchard hire? How much profit does each orchard owner make?
   c. Calculate what happens to the income of workers and orchard owners if the world price doubles to ₹4 per apple.
   d. Now suppose that the price is back at ₹2 per apple, but a hurricane destroys half the orchards. Calculate how the hurricane affects the income of each worker and of each remaining orchard owner. What happens to the income of Ectenia as a whole?

6. Your enterprising uncle opens a sandwich shop that employs 7 people. The employees are paid ₹12 per hour, and a sandwich sells for ₹6. If your uncle is maximizing his profit, what is the value of the marginal product of the last worker he hired? What is that worker's marginal product?

7. Leadbelly Co. sells pencils in a perfectly competitive product market and hires workers in a perfectly competitive labor market. Assume that the market wage rate for workers is ₹150 per day.
   a. What rule should Leadbelly follow to hire the profit-maximizing amount of labor?
   b. At the profit-maximizing level of output, the marginal product of the last worker hired is 30 boxes of pencils per day. Calculate the price of a box of pencils.
   c. Draw a diagram of the labor market for pencil workers (as in Figure 4 of this chapter) next to a diagram of the labor supply and demand for Leadbelly Co. (as in Figure 3). Label the equilibrium wage and quantity of labor for both the market and the firm. How are these diagrams related?
   d. Suppose some pencil workers switch to jobs in the growing computer industry. On the side-by-side diagrams from part (c), show how this change affects the equilibrium wage and quantity of labor both for the pencil market and for Leadbelly. How does this change affect the marginal product of labor at Leadbelly?

8. Sometimes, laws require firms to give workers certain fringe benefits, such as health insurance or paid parental leave. Let's consider the effects of such a policy on the labor market.
   a. Suppose that a law requires firms to give each worker ₹3 of fringe benefits for every hour that the worker is employed by the firm. How does this law affect the marginal profit that a firm earns from each worker at a given cash wage? How does the law affect the demand curve for labor? Draw your answer on a graph with the cash wage on the vertical axis.
   b. If there is no change in labor supply, how would this law affect employment and wages?
   c. Why might the labor-supply curve shift in response to this law? Would this shift in labor supply raise or lower the impact of the law on wages and employment?
   d. As discussed in Chapter 6, minimum-wage laws keep the wages of some workers, particularly the unskilled and inexperienced, above the equilibrium level. What effect would a fringe-benefit mandate have for these workers?

9. Some economists believe that our economy as a whole can be modeled with the following production function, called the **Cobb–Douglas production function:**

$$Y = AK^{1/3}L^{2/3},$$

where Y is the amount of output, K is the amount of capital, L is the amount of labor, and A is a parameter that measures the state of technology. For this production function, the marginal product of labor is

$$MPL = (2/3)\ A(K/L)^{1/3}.$$

Suppose that the price of output P is 2, A is 3, K is 1,000,000, and L is 1,000. The labor market is competitive, so labor is paid the value of its marginal product.

a. Calculate the amount of output produced Y and the dollar value of output PY.
b. Calculate the wage W and the real wage W/P. (Note: The wage is labor compensation measured in dollars, whereas the real wage is labor compensation measured in units of output.)
c. Calculate the labor share (the fraction of the value of output that is paid to labor), which is $(WL)/(PY)$.
d. Calculate what happens to output Y, the wage W, the real wage W/P, and the labor share $(WL)/(PY)$ in each of the following scenarios:
   i. Inflation increases P from 2 to 3.
   ii. Technological progress increases A from 3 to 9.
   iii. Capital accumulation increases K from 1,000,000 to 8,000,000.
   iv. A plague decreases L from 1,000 to 125.
e. Despite many changes in the economy over time, the labor share has been relatively stable. Is this observation consistent with the Cobb–Douglas production function? Explain.

Quick**Quiz Answers**

1. **c** 2. **b** 3. **a** 4. **b** 5. **d** 6. **c** 7. **b** 8. **d** 9. **b** 10. **d**

Chapter

19

Wages, Inequality and Diversity in Indian Businesses

Consider the vast income differences in the Indian labor market. A delivery executive on an app-based platform might earn about ₹2.5 lakh annually whereas a government school-teacher in a metro city might take home ₹7–8 lakhs. A specialist doctor in a private hospital may earn well over ₹50 lakh, while a CEO at a top Indian conglomerate can take home ₹25–30 crore or even more. Meanwhile, celebrity performers, such as cricket stars or Bollywood actors, may command ₹100 crore per film or endorsement cycle or every season of cricket. These gaps are not just cooked up numbers but they reflect enormous differences in living standards, opportunity, and influence.

What explains these disparities in earnings? The standard economic approach, introduced earlier in the chapter on labor markets, begins with the theory of supply and demand for labor. Firms demand labor based on its marginal productivity. In competitive markets, workers are paid the value of their marginal contribution to production. This neoclassical framework offers a powerful explanation for many observed patterns.

Yet, this is only the starting point. In India's complex labor market, factors such as education, social capital, access to networks, caste and gender-based discrimination, informal employment arrangements, and regional disparities also play significant roles. For instance, even if two workers are equally productive, differences in formal credentials or social identity may result in unequal pay.

By applying these ideas to real-world Indian labor markets this chapter aims to equip future managers with a more nuanced view of compensation, talent acquisition, and fairness.

AZMANJAKA/E+/GETTY IMAGES; CARLOS FLORES/EYEEM/GETTY IMAGES

19-1 What Determines Wages?

Let's first consider how the characteristics of jobs and workers affect labor supply, labor demand, and equilibrium wages.

19-1a Compensating Differentials

When a worker is deciding whether to take a job, the wage is only one of many factors to consider. Some jobs are easy, fun, and safe. Others are hard, boring, and even dangerous. The more a job appeals to people, the more people are willing to do it at a given wage. In other words, the supply of labor is greater for easy, fun, and safe jobs than for hard, boring, and dangerous ones. As a result, other things being equal, appealing jobs will tend to have lower equilibrium wages than less appealing ones.

DANA FRADON/CARTOON COLLECTIONS

"On the one hand, I know I could make more money if I left public service for the private sector, but, on the other hand, I couldn't chop off heads."

Imagine you are looking for a summer job in a beach community. Two jobs are available: beach-badge checker and garbage collector. The beach-badge checkers take leisurely strolls near the water during the day and ensure that the tourists have bought the required permits. The garbage collectors wake up before dawn and drive dirty, noisy trucks around town to pick up garbage. Which job would you want? If the wages were the same, most people would prefer the job on the beach. To induce people to become garbage collectors, the town must offer higher wages to garbage collectors than to beach-badge checkers.

Economists use the term **compensating differential** to refer to a wage difference that arises from nonmonetary characteristics of different jobs. Compensating differentials are common. Here are some examples:

compensating differential
a difference in wages that arises to offset the nonmonetary characteristics of different jobs

- Roofers are paid more than other workers with similar levels of education. Their higher wage compensates them for the nasty smell of tar and the constant risk of accidents.
- Workers on night shifts are paid more than similar workers on day shifts. The higher wage compensates them for having to work at night and sleep during the day, a lifestyle that most people find undesirable.
- Professors are paid less than lawyers and doctors, who have similar amounts of education. The higher wages of lawyers and doctors compensate them for missing the intellectual and personal satisfaction that professors' jobs offer. (Indeed, teaching economics is so much fun that it is surprising economics professors are paid anything at all!)

19-1b Human Capital

As the previous chapter discussed, an economy's stock of equipment and structures is called **capital**. The capital stock includes the farmer's tractor, the manufacturer's factory, and the teacher's chalkboard. The essence of capital is that it is a factor of production that itself has been produced.

Another type of capital, though less tangible than physical capital, is just as important to the economy's production: It is **human capital**, the accumulation of investments in people. The most important type of human capital is education. Like all forms of capital, education represents an expenditure of resources to raise future productivity. But this investment is tied to a specific person, and this linkage makes it human capital.

human capital
the accumulation of investments in people, such as education and on-the-job training

Workers with more human capital earn more, on average, than those with less. College graduates, for example, earn almost twice as much as those who are only high-school pass-outs. This large difference has been documented around the world. The gap tends to be even larger in less developed countries, where educated workers are in scarce supply.

From the perspective of supply and demand, it is easy to see why education raises wages. Firms—the demanders of labor—pay more for highly educated workers because these workers have higher marginal products. Workers—the suppliers of labor—bear the cost of education because they expect a reward for doing so. The difference in wages between highly educated workers and less educated workers may be considered a compensating differential for the cost of acquiring human capital.

Case Study

The Increasing Value of Skills

"The rich get richer, and the poor get poorer." Like many adages, this one is not always true, but it has been recently in many nations. Numerous studies have documented that the earnings gap between workers with high skills and workers with low skills has increased substantially over the past several decades.

Table 1 presents US data on the average earnings of college graduates and of high school graduates without any additional education. These data show the increase in the financial reward from education. In 1974, a man with a college degree earned 42 percent more on average than a man without one; by 2019, this figure had risen to 85 percent. Among women, the earnings gap between those with and without college degrees rose from 35 percent in 1974 to 78 percent in 2019. The incentive to stay in school today is large by historical standards.

Why has the gap in earnings between skilled and unskilled workers widened? Economists have proposed two hypotheses, both of which suggest that the demand for skilled labor has risen relative to the demand for unskilled labor. The shift in demand has led to a corresponding change in the wages of both groups, increasing inequality.

The first hypothesis focuses on international trade. Over the past half century, the amount of trade with other countries has markedly increased. As a percentage

Table 1

Average Annual Earnings by Educational Attainment

College graduates have always earned more than workers who did not attend college, but the gap has grown larger over the past few decades.

	1974	2019
Men		
High school, no college	$56,855	$52,677
College graduates	$80,973	$97,554
Percent extra for college grads	+42%	+85%
Women		
High school, no college	$32,675	$39,669
College graduates	$44,200	$70,657
Percent extra for college grads	+35%	+78%

Note: Earnings data are adjusted for inflation and are expressed in 2019 dollars. Data apply to full-time, year-round workers age 18 and over. Data for college graduates exclude workers with additional schooling beyond college, such as a master's degree or Ph.D.

Source: U.S. Census Bureau, Tables P-32 and P-35, and author's calculations.

Ask the Experts

Inequality and Skills

"One of the leading reasons for rising U.S. income inequality over the past three decades is that technological change has affected workers with some skill sets differently than others."

What do economists say?

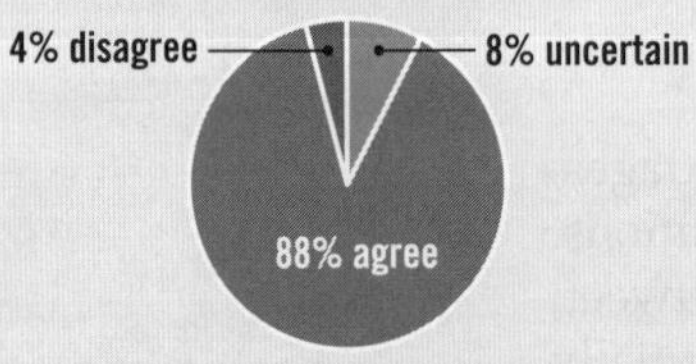

Source: IGM Economic Experts Panel, January 24, 2012.

of total U.S. production of goods and services, imports have risen from 5 percent in 1970 to 13 percent in 2020, and exports have risen from 6 percent in 1970 to 10 percent in 2020. Because unskilled labor is plentiful and cheap in many countries, the United States tends to import goods produced with unskilled labor and export those produced with skilled labor. This means that when international trade expands, domestic demand rises for skilled labor and falls for unskilled labor.

The second hypothesis emphasizes technological change. Consider computers. For keeping business records, many companies have replaced filing cabinets with computer databases, reducing the demand for filing clerks and increasing the demand for programmers and data analysts. Similarly, industrial robots have replaced the unskilled factory workers whose tasks can be automated, but they require skilled engineers to produce and maintain them. Economists call this shift in demand **skill-biased technological change**.

Economists debate the importance of trade, technology, and other forces on the distribution of wages. There is likely no single reason for the growing earnings gap between skilled and unskilled workers. The next chapter discusses income inequality in more detail. ●

19-1c Ability, Effort, and Chance

Why do Indian Premier League (IPL) cricket players earn more than those in the Tamil Nadu Premier League (TNPL) or other state leagues? Certainly, the higher wage is not a compensating differential: Playing in the majors is hardly less pleasant than playing in the minors. Nor is human capital the key: The IPL teams do not require more schooling or years of experience, though some training certainly helps. For the most part, players in the IPL earn more simply because they have greater ability.

Ability is important in all occupations. Because of heredity and upbringing, people differ in personal attributes. Some people are strong, others weak. Some people are smart, others dull. Some people are affable, others awkward. These and many other characteristics affect workers' productivity and, therefore, their wages.

Closely related to ability is effort. Some people work harder than others, and this extra effort makes them more productive, which usually leads to higher earnings. Sometimes, firms reward hard work directly by paying people based on what they produce. Salespeople, for instance, are often paid a percentage of the sales they make. At other times, hard work is rewarded less directly in the form of a higher annual salary or a bonus.

But chance also plays a role in determining wages. Consider those who attended trade school to learn how to repair televisions with vacuum tubes and then found this skill made obsolete by the invention of solid-state electronics. They ended up earning a low wage compared with others with similar years of training. Or imagine what might happen to the future earnings of truck drivers if self-driving trucks are perfected. The decline in income experienced by these workers is due to random technological change.

Chance also arises from accidents of birth. If you are born to a family with a high income and deep education, that good fortune gives you an advantage in life. If you are born into extreme poverty, with a severe disability, or in a neighborhood without good role models, that's also a matter of chance.

instance, to create memory in a hard drive. In economics, hysteresis is typically associated with damage after shocks, though there can be positive transformations too, such as the development of vaccine technologies and work-from-home options.

For many years, economists have looked for evidence of hysteresis in labor markets. In Europe in the 1970s and 1980s, economists Olivier Blanchard and Lawrence Summers noticed that unemployment tended to increase during economic downturns, as expected, but didn't fully return to previous levels when the economy revived. The rubber band, in other words, didn't regain its shape.

In a 1986 paper, "Hysteresis in Unemployment," the professors surmised that this was because of structural problems in these markets. Unions tended to fight hard to keep their workers from losing jobs but did little to help them after they were released, making it hard for them to be re-employed. Labor protections encoded in the law had the same effect: Firms were reluctant to rehire after downturns because it was so hard to let go of people in a recession. "Shocks that we thought should be temporary had long-lasting effects," Mr. Blanchard said in a recent interview.

Three decades later, Mr. Blanchard went back and looked at the problem of hysteresis in labor markets after the 2007–09 financial crisis. Millions of Americans were experiencing long spells of unemployment. In 2010, nearly half of unemployed workers were without a job for at least six months, an astonishingly high number. In the half-century before the crisis, just one of every eight unemployed workers, on average, went without work for that long.

Mr. Blanchard and other economists worried about the lasting damage to people who sat on the sidelines of the job market and saw their skills deteriorate. Some stopped looking for work; others found income on federal disability rolls. As the expansion marched on, however, some were drawn back into the labor market. Mr. Blanchard, to his surprise, found evidence of hysteresis less compelling than he had expected.

In the current economic crisis, policy makers in Washington are eager to drive the jobless rate down as fast as possible to reverse a new upsurge in long-term unemployment. It's one reason why Treasury Secretary Janet Yellen—a labor economist—has called for Congress to "go big" on a relief package.

Hysteresis may be acting on whole industries this time, Mr. Blanchard said. Air travel, commercial real estate and bricks-and-mortar retailing, for example, might never be the same.

Like Mr. Hanushek and Ms. Raymond, Mr. Blanchard is most worried about the long-run effects of the Covid crisis on children and their future as workers. "I would do everything I can to allow children to go safely back to school in person," he said. Ms. Raymond said that it might be time to start thinking about sending children to summer school to make up for lost time. At the very least, she said, it is time for educators to start thinking about how to fix schooling once the pandemic ends. ■

Questions to Discuss

1. Did you lose educational opportunities during the Covid pandemic? If so, do you think you subsequently caught up to where you otherwise would have been?
2. How do you think educational systems can best compensate for lost opportunities due to the pandemic?

Source: The Wall Street Journal, February 27, 2021.

times, they act more like monopolists, pricing their labor above the competitive level. Studies suggest that union workers earn about 10 to 20 percent more than similar, nonunion workers.

efficiency wages above-equilibrium wages paid by firms to increase worker productivity

A third reason for above-equilibrium wages is based on the theory of **efficiency wages**. This theory holds that high wages increase worker productivity by reducing turnover, motivating greater effort, and enticing superior candidates to apply for jobs. If these effects are strong enough, firms may find it profitable to pay wages above the equilibrium level.

Above-equilibrium wages, whether caused by minimum-wage laws, unions, or efficiency wages, have similar effects on the labor market. In each case, setting a wage above the equilibrium level increases the quantity of labor supplied and reduces the quantity of labor demanded. That creates a surplus of labor, or unemployment. The study of unemployment is usually considered a topic within macroeconomics, which is beyond the scope of this chapter. But these issues can be important when analyzing earnings. Most earnings differences can be understood while assuming that wages balance supply and demand, but above-equilibrium wages play a role in some cases.

Quick**Quiz**

1. Tanmay leaves his job as a high school math teacher and returns to school to study the latest developments in computer programming, after which he takes a higher-paying job at a software firm. This is an example of
   a. a compensating differential.
   b. human capital.
   c. monopsony.
   d. efficiency wages.
2. Marshall and Lillee work at a local department store. Marshall, who greets customers as they arrive, is paid less than Lillee, who cleans the store. This is an example of
   a. a compensating differential.
   b. monopsony.
   c. signaling.
   d. efficiency wages.
3. Baidyanath runs a small manufacturing company. He pays his employees about twice as much as other firms, even though he could pay less and still recruit all the workers he needs. He believes that higher wages make his workers more loyal and hard-working. This is an example of
   a. monopsony.
   b. human capital.
   c. signaling.
   d. efficiency wages.
4. A business consulting firm hires Rituparna because she was a math major in college. Her new job does not require any of the mathematics she learned, but the firm's managers believe that anyone who can graduate with a math degree must be very smart. This is an example of
   a. a compensating differential.
   b. human capital.
   c. signaling.
   d. monopsony.

Answers are at the end of the chapter.

19-2 The Economics of Discrimination

discrimination
the offering of different opportunities to similar individuals who differ only by race, ethnicity, gender, age, religion, sexual orientation, or other personal characteristics

Another source of differences in wages is discrimination. **Discrimination** occurs when people are offered or denied opportunities based on race, ethnicity, gender, age, religion, sexual orientation, or other personal characteristics. Discrimination in the workplace reflects broader prejudices in society. Economists study the problem to attain a better understanding of its magnitude and sources.

19-2a Measuring Labor-Market Discrimination

How much does discrimination in labor markets affect the earnings of different groups of workers? This question is important, but answering it precisely is not easy.

There is no doubt that different groups of workers earn substantially different wages, as Table 2 shows. In 2019, the median Black man in the United States was paid 24 percent less than the median White man, and the median Black woman was paid

Table 2

Median Annual Earnings by Race and Sex

	White	Black	Percent by Which Earnings Are Lower for Black Workers
Men	$60,017	$45,644	24%
Women	$48,845	$41,098	16%
Percent by Which Earnings Are Lower for Women Workers	19%	10%	

Note: Earnings data are for the year 2019 and apply to full-time, year-round workers aged 14 and over. Individuals who report more than one race are excluded from these data.

Source: U.S. Census Bureau, Table P-38, and author's calculations.

16 percent less than the median White woman. The median White woman was paid 19 percent less than the median White man, and the median Black woman was paid 10 percent less than the median Black man. Taken at face value, these differentials look like incontrovertible evidence that employers discriminate against Black people and women.

Yet there is a potential problem with this inference. Even in a labor market free of discrimination, different people have different wages. People differ in the amount of human capital they have and in the kinds of work they are able and willing to do. The wage differences in an economy are, to some extent, attributable to the determinants of equilibrium wages discussed in the preceding section. Simply observing differences in wages among broad groups—White and Black people, men and women—does not prove that employers discriminate.

Consider the role of human capital. In 2019, among those aged 25 and older, 36 percent of White Americans had a bachelor's degree, compared with 26 percent of Black Americans. These educational differences explain some of the wage gap. And public schools in predominantly Black areas have historically been of lower quality—as measured by expenditure, class size, and so on—than public schools in predominantly White areas. If we could measure the quality as well as the quantity of education, the differences in human capital would likely appear even larger.

Human capital acquired in the form of job experience also helps explain wage differences. Women are more likely to interrupt their careers to raise children. Among the population aged 25 to 44 (when many people have children at home), 24 percent of women are out of the labor force, compared with 10 percent of men. As a result, female workers, especially at older ages, tend to have less job experience than male workers.

Compensating differentials are another source of wage differences. Men and women do not always choose the same type of work. For example, women are more likely to be administrative assistants, and men are more likely to be truck drivers. The relative wages of administrative assistants and truck drivers depend in part on the working conditions of each job. Because these nonmonetary aspects are hard to measure, it is difficult to gauge the practical importance of compensating differentials in explaining observed wage differences.

In the end, the study of wage differences among groups does not establish any clear conclusion about the prevalence of discrimination in U.S. labor markets. Most economists believe that some degree of discrimination is at work, but it's hard to say precisely how much. The only certain conclusion is a negative one: Because the differences in average wages among groups in part reflect differences in human capital and job characteristics, they do not by themselves measure the extent of labor-market discrimination.

Differences in human capital among groups of workers may, however, reflect a kind of discrimination. The less rigorous curriculums historically offered to female students, for instance, can be considered a discriminatory practice. Similarly, the inferior schools historically available to Black students may be traced to prejudice on the part of city councils and school boards. But this kind of discrimination occurs before workers enter the labor market. In this case, the disease is political, even if the symptom is economic.

Case Study

Is Emily More Employable Than Lakisha?

Although gauging discrimination from labor-market outcomes is hard, compelling evidence for the existence of such discrimination comes from a creative field experiment. The economists Marianne Bertrand and Sendhil Mullainathan answered more than 1,300 help-wanted ads run in Boston and Chicago newspapers by sending in nearly 5,000 fake résumés. Half of the résumés had names that were common in the African American community, such as Lakisha Washington or Jamal Jones. The other half had names that were more common among the White population, such as Emily Walsh and Greg Baker. Otherwise, the résumés were similar. The results of this experiment appeared in the *American Economic Review* in September 2004.

The researchers found large differences in how employers responded to the two groups of résumés. Job applicants with White names received about 50 percent more calls from employers than those with African American names. The study found that this discrimination occurred for all types of employers, including those who claimed to be an "Equal Opportunity Employer" in their help-wanted ads. The researchers concluded that "racial discrimination is still a prominent feature of the labor market."

More recently, the economist Philip Oreopoulos has examined Canadian labor markets by sending out some fake résumés with English names and others with Indian, Pakistani, Chinese, and Greek names. Published in the *American Economic Journal: Economic Policy* in November 2011, the study again found significant evidence of discrimination. English-sounding names received 39 percent more callbacks from employers. The differences were similar across the four ethnic groups. And the results were much the same if the fictional applicant had an English-sounding first name and a Chinese last name (such as James Liu or Amy Wang). When company recruiters were later asked about these findings, they tried to justify their behavior by saying that it is based on concern about language skills. Yet the discrimination occurred even when the applicant had a Canadian education and Canadian job experience, and there was no relationship between the advantage given to English names and the degree of language skills necessary for the type of job.

"What's in a name?" Shakespeare wrote in *Romeo and Juliet*. Like the Montagues and Capulets, many employers fail to look beyond the names of the people they are evaluating. ●

19-2b Discrimination by Employers: Evidence from Indian Labor Markets

Let's now turn from measurement to the economic forces that lie behind discrimination in Indian labor markets. If one group in society receives a lower wage than another, even after controlling for human capital and job characteristics, who is to blame?

The answer may seem obvious: employers. They make the hiring decisions that determine labor demand and wages. If some groups of workers earn less than they should, then employers seem to be the natural culprits. The same holds true if similarly qualified individuals are disproportionately hired based on other characteristics, such as caste, gender, or similar demographics.

Just like the Emily–Lakisha case study above, in the Indian context, similar experiments have been conducted. It does turn out that a Mr Sharma is more employable than a Mr Yadav? Why? Apparently, the names potentially reveal castes. Paul Attewell and Sukhadeo Thorat in their Economic and Political Weekly (EPW) article of Oct 2007, show that in Indian labor markets, strong evidence of discrimination exists even in the first stage of the hiring process. They apply to jobs in response to job advertisements with fictitious CVs having names randomized to reflect Hindu upper- caste, Dalit, and Muslim. They find evidence that Hindu upper caste names receive significantly higher number of callbacks relative to Dalits or Muslims. Similar work using such correspondence studies have been conducted to uncover gender discrimination as well as evidence of motherhood penalties in labor markets for women.

Case Study

Segregated Streetcars and the Profit Motive

In the early 20th century, streetcars in many southern cities were segregated by race. White passengers sat in the front of the streetcars, and Black passengers sat in the back. The firms that ran the streetcars enforced this practice, but historical research shows that they didn't start it.

In a 1986 article in the *Journal of Economic History*, the economic historian Jennifer Roback found that the segregation of races on streetcars resulted from laws that required segregation. Before these laws existed, racial discrimination in seating was rare. It was far more common to segregate smokers and nonsmokers.

In fact, the firms that ran the streetcars often opposed the laws requiring racial segregation. Providing separate seating for different races raised the firms' costs and reduced their profits. One railroad company manager complained to the city council that, under the segregation laws, "the company has to haul around a good deal of empty space."

Here is how Roback describes the situation in one southern city:

> The railroad company did not initiate the segregation policy and was not at all eager to abide by it. State legislation, public agitation, and a threat to arrest the president of the railroad were all required to induce them to separate the races on their cars. . . . There is no indication that the management was motivated by belief in civil rights or racial equality. The evidence indicates their primary motives were economic; separation was costly. . . . Officials of the company may or may not have disliked blacks, but they were not willing to forgo the profits necessary to indulge such prejudice.

The story of southern streetcars illustrates a general lesson: Usually, business owners are most interested in making profits, not in discriminating against a particular group. When firms engage in discriminatory practices, the source of the discrimination often lies not with the firms themselves but elsewhere. In this case, the streetcar companies segregated White and Black people because discriminatory laws, which the companies opposed, required them to do so. ●

19-2c Discrimination by Customers and Governments

The profit motive acts to eliminate discriminatory wage differentials, but its corrective abilities only go so far. Two limiting factors are customer preferences and government policies.

To see how customer preferences for discrimination can affect wages, consider again the imaginary economy with blondes and brunettes. Suppose that restaurant owners discriminate against blondes when hiring waiters, so blonde waiters earn less than brunette waiters. In this case, an enterprising restaurant can open with blonde waiters and charge lower prices. If customers care only about the price and quality of meals, the discriminatory firms will be driven out of business, and the wage differential will disappear.

But imagine that customers prefer being served by brunettes. If this discriminatory preference is strong, the entry of blonde restaurants will not eliminate the wage differential. That is, if customers have discriminatory preferences, a competitive market may maintain a discriminatory wage differential. An economy with such discrimination would contain two types of restaurants. Blonde restaurants would have lower costs and charge lower prices. Brunette restaurants would have higher costs and charge higher prices. Customers who did not care about the hair color of their waiters would be attracted to the lower prices at the blonde restaurants. Bigoted customers would go to the brunette restaurants and would pay for their discriminatory preference in the form of higher prices.

Another way for discrimination to persist in competitive markets is for the government to require it. If, for instance, the government passed a law stating that blondes could wash dishes but not work as waiters, a wage differential could persist in a competitive market. The segregated streetcars in the previous case study are one example of government-mandated discrimination. Similarly, before South Africa abandoned the formal policy of racial segregation called apartheid in 1990, Black people were prohibited from working in some jobs. When discriminatory governments pass such laws, they suppress the equalizing force of competitive markets.

To sum up: **Competitive markets contain a natural remedy for employer discrimination. The entry of firms that care only about profit tends to eliminate discriminatory wage differentials. These differentials persist in competitive markets when customers are willing to pay to maintain the discriminatory practice or when the government mandates it.**

Case Study

Discrimination in Sports

Measuring discrimination is often difficult. To determine whether a group of workers is discriminated against, a researcher must correct for differences in the productivity between that group and others in the economy. Yet in most firms, it is difficult to measure a worker's contribution to the production of goods and services.

Sports are something of an exception. Professional sports teams revel in objective measures of productivity. In basketball, for instance, statistics on players' averages for scoring, assists, and rebounds are compiled instantaneously and pored over by voracious fans. For economists, this extensive documentation amounts to a bonanza.

Studies of sports teams suggest that racial discrimination has, in fact, been common and that much of the blame lies with customers. One study, published in the *Journal of Labor Economics* in 1988, examined the salaries of basketball players and found that Black players earned 20 percent less than White players of comparable ability. The study also found that attendance at basketball games was larger for teams with a greater proportion of White players. One interpretation of these facts is that, at least at the time of the study, customer discrimination made Black players less profitable than White players for team owners. In the presence of such customer discrimination, a discriminatory wage gap can persist, even if team owners care only about profit.

A similar situation once existed for baseball players. A study using data from the late 1960s showed that Black players earned less than comparable White players. Moreover, fewer fans attended games pitched by Black pitchers than games pitched by White pitchers, even though Black pitchers had better records than White pitchers. Studies of more recent salaries in baseball, however, have found no evidence of discriminatory wage differentials.

Another study, published in the *Quarterly Journal of Economics* in 1990, examined the market prices of old baseball cards. This study found similar evidence of discrimination. The cards of Black hitters sold for 10 percent less than the cards of comparable White hitters, and the cards of Black pitchers sold for 13 percent less than the cards of comparable White pitchers. These results suggest customer discrimination among baseball fans. ●

19-2d Statistical Discrimination

Beyond animosity toward particular groups, there is another possible cause of discrimination, called **statistical discrimination**. This theory assumes that employers have imperfect information about possible employees. If some relevant but unobservable employee characteristic happens to be correlated with an otherwise irrelevant but observable characteristic, employers may rely on the observable characteristic when making hiring decisions.

statistical discrimination discrimination that arises because an irrelevant but observable personal characteristic is correlated with a relevant but unobservable attribute

Suppose that employers care about punctuality but don't know whether a job applicant is likely to be punctual once hired. And suppose that employers have found that 10 percent of workers with blue eyes are chronically late, compared with only 5 percent of workers with brown eyes. Because of this correlation, employers might prefer hiring brown-eyed workers, even if they do not otherwise care about eye color. Blue-eyed people as a group would suffer from discrimination, even though 90 percent of them are punctual. The discrimination is "statistical" in the sense that each blue-eyed person is being stereotyped by the average behavior of the group.

This example is silly (punctuality is not really related to eye color). But the same phenomenon arises in real cases.

Some employers, for instance, prefer not to hire workers with criminal records. The simplest way to avoid doing so is to ask job applicants whether they have criminal records, and many employers do. Some states, however, have passed "ban the box" laws that prohibit employers from asking. (The "box" refers to the place on the job application that a person would check to signal a clean record.) The goal of these laws is to help ex-offenders find jobs and reenter society.

Despite the noble intent of these laws, one unintended consequence is that they foster statistical discrimination. Statistics show that Black men are more likely to have served time in prison than White men. Some employers who are aware of this but are prohibited from asking about criminal records may avoid hiring Black men. As a result, Black men without a criminal past would suffer from discrimination because of their group's average characteristics. Some studies have compared states with and without "ban the box" policies and have found that these laws significantly reduce employment for young Black men without college degrees. These results suggest that policymakers should look for ways to help ex-offenders that do not inadvertently increase statistical discrimination.

Box 19.1: Diversity and Inclusion in Indian Businesses

Indian businesses are increasingly recognizing the strategic importance of diversity and inclusivity within organizations. These can turn out to be major markers for business perception and employer retention, as well as talent acquisition. Major firms like Tata Consultancy Services (TCS), Wipro, and Godrej have rolled out formal initiatives, aiming to improve representation across gender, caste, religion, as well as disability categories. Many firms are actually committed to increasing the share of women in leadership following recent industry data from a 2024 KPMG report on women in corporate leadership, which notes that representation of women in senior management roles in India remains disproportionately low despite increasing female workforce participation. Some studies estimate that women hold under 20% of senior leadership roles in India as of 2024.

The challenge, however, extends beyond gender. Representation of Dalit, Adivasi, and other marginalized caste groups in private sector white-collar employment remains more acutely limited. Caste-based DEI initiatives in Indian companies are coming up, but even as gender representational diversity in corporate boardrooms is becoming a topic for discussion, caste representation on these boards, are discussed sparingly. In this context, while India Inc is embracing the language of inclusion following the west, the true and meaningful progress will depend on robust and sustained institutional commitment, alongwith managerial accountability that goes beyond tokenism.

One of the implied learnings from in Chapter 1 is that rational people think at the margin. This idea is the key to understanding how firms decide how much labor to hire. To take a step toward this decision, column (3) in Table 1 shows the **marginal product of labor**, the additional output produced by an additional unit of labor. When the firm increases the number of workers from 1 to 2, for example, the quantity of apples produced rises from 100 to 180 bushels. Therefore, the marginal product of the second worker is 80 bushels.

marginal product of labor
the increase in the amount of output from an additional unit of labor

Notice that as the number of workers increases, the marginal product of labor declines. That is, the production process exhibits **diminishing marginal product.** At first, when only a few workers are hired, they can pick the low-hanging fruit. As the number of workers increases, additional workers must climb higher up the ladders to find apples to pick. So as more workers are hired, each additional one contributes less to production. For this reason, the production function in Figure 2 becomes flatter as the number of workers rises.

diminishing marginal product
the property whereby the marginal product of an input declines as the quantity of the input increases

18-1c The Value of the Marginal Product and the Demand for Labor

Our profit-maximizing firm is concerned not about the apples themselves but rather about the money it can make by producing and selling them. As a result, when deciding how many workers to hire to pick apples, the firm considers how much profit each worker will bring in. Because profit is total revenue minus total cost, the profit from an additional worker is the worker's contribution to revenue minus the worker's wage.

To find the worker's contribution to revenue, we must convert the marginal product of labor (which is measured in bushels of apples) into the **value** of the marginal product (which is measured in dollars). We do this using the price of apples. If a bushel of apples sells for ₹10 and an additional worker produces 80 bushels of apples, then the worker produces ₹800 of revenue.

The **value of the marginal product** of any input is the marginal product of that input multiplied by the market price of the output. Column (4) in Table 1 shows the value of the marginal product of labor, assuming the price of apples is ₹10 per bushel. Because the market price is constant for a competitive firm while the marginal product declines with more workers, the value of the marginal product diminishes as the number of workers rises. Economists sometimes call this column of numbers the firm's **marginal revenue product**: It is the extra revenue the firm gets from hiring an additional unit of a factor of production.

value of the marginal product
the marginal product of an input times the price of the output

Now consider how many workers the firm will hire. Suppose that the market wage for apple pickers is ₹500 per week. In this case, as Table 1 shows, hiring the first worker is profitable: The first worker yields ₹1,000 in revenue and ₹500 in profit. Similarly, the second worker yields ₹800 in additional revenue and ₹300 in profit. The third yields ₹600 in additional revenue and ₹100 in profit. After the third worker, however, hiring workers is unprofitable. The fourth worker would generate only ₹400 of additional revenue. Because the worker's wage is ₹500, hiring the fourth worker would mean a ₹100 reduction in profit. The rational decision is clear: The firm hires 3 workers.

Figure 3 graphs the value of the marginal product. This curve slopes downward because the marginal product of labor diminishes as the number of workers rises. The figure also includes a horizontal line at the market wage. To maximize profit, the firm hires workers up to the point where these two curves cross. Below this level of employment, the value of the marginal product exceeds the wage, so hiring

Figure 3

The Value of the Marginal Product of Labor

This figure shows how the value of the marginal product (the marginal product times the price of the output) depends on the number of workers. The curve slopes downward because of diminishing marginal product. For a competitive, profit-maximizing firm, this value-of-marginal-product curve is also the firm's labor-demand curve.

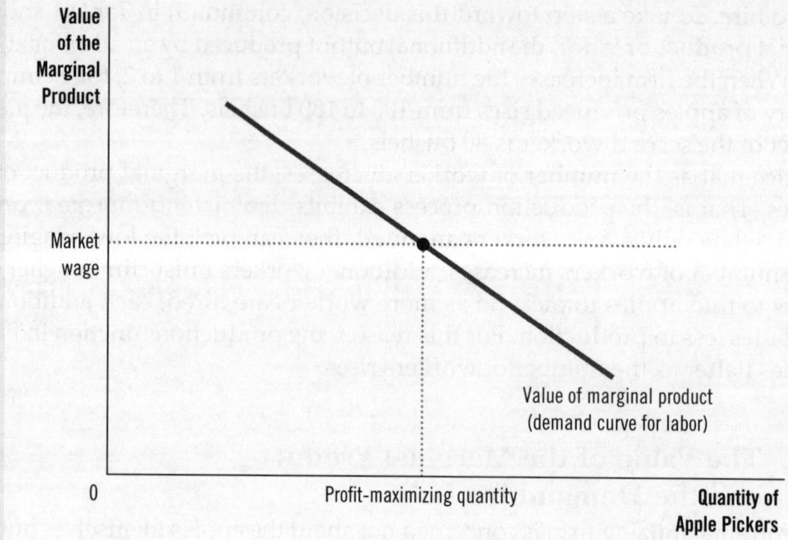

another worker increases profit. Above this level of employment, the value of the marginal product is less than the wage, so the marginal worker is unprofitable. **A competitive, profit-maximizing firm hires workers up to the point at which the value of the marginal product of labor equals the wage.**

Based on the profit-maximizing hiring strategy for a competitive firm, we can offer a theory of labor demand. Recall that a firm's labor-demand curve tells us the quantity of labor that a firm decides to hire at any given wage. Figure 3 shows that the firm makes that decision by choosing the quantity of labor at which the value of the marginal product equals the wage. **As a result, the value-of-marginal-product curve is the labor-demand curve for a competitive, profit-maximizing firm.**

18-1d What Causes the Labor-Demand Curve to Shift?

The labor-demand curve reflects the value of the marginal product of labor. With this insight in mind, consider a few of the things that might cause the labor-demand curve to shift.

The Output Price The value of the marginal product is marginal product times the price of the firm's output. When the output price changes, the value of the marginal product changes, and the labor-demand curve shifts. An increase in the price of apples, for instance, raises the value of the marginal product of each worker who picks apples and, therefore, increases labor demand from the firms that supply apples. Conversely, a decrease in the price of apples reduces the value of the marginal product and decreases labor demand.

Technological Change Between 1960 and 2020, the output a typical U.S. worker produced in an hour rose by 236 percent. Why? The most important reason is

FYI Input Demand and Output Supply: Two Sides of the Same Coin

Chapter 15 discussed how a competitive, profit-maximizing firm decides how much of its output to sell: It chooses the quantity of output at which the price of the good equals the marginal cost of production. We have just seen how such a firm decides how much labor to hire: It chooses the quantity of labor at which the wage equals the value of the marginal product. Because the production function links the quantity of inputs to the quantity of output, the firm's decision about input demand and its decision about output supply are two sides of the same coin.

To see this relationship more fully, consider how the marginal product of labor (*MPL*) and marginal cost (*MC*) are related. Suppose an additional worker costs ₹500 and has a marginal product of 50 bushels of apples. In this case, producing 50 more bushels costs the firm ₹500, so the marginal cost of a bushel is ₹500/50, or ₹10. More generally, if *W* is the wage, and an extra unit of labor produces *MPL* units of output, then the marginal cost of a unit of output is $MC = W/MPL$.

This analysis shows that diminishing marginal product is closely related to increasing marginal cost. When the apple orchard grows crowded with workers, each additional worker adds less to the production of apples (*MPL* falls). Similarly, when the apple firm is producing a large quantity of apples, the orchard is already crowded with workers, so it is more costly to produce an additional bushel of apples (*MC* rises).

Now consider our criterion for profit maximization. We determined that a profit-maximizing firm chooses the quantity of labor at which the value of the marginal product ($P \times MPL$) equals the wage (*W*). We can write this mathematically as:

$$P \times MPL = W.$$

Dividing both sides of this equation by *MPL* yields:

$$P = W/MPL.$$

We just noted that *W/MPL* equals marginal cost, *MC*. Therefore, we can substitute to obtain:

$$P = MC.$$

This equation states that the price of the firm's output equals the marginal cost of producing a unit of output. **When a competitive firm hires labor up to the point at which the value of the marginal product equals the wage, it also produces up to the point at which the price equals marginal cost.** The analysis of labor demand in this chapter is just another way of looking at the production decision discussed in Chapter 15. ■

technological progress: Scientists and engineers figured out new and better ways of doing things. This has profound implications for the labor market. Advances in technology usually raise the marginal product of labor, increasing the demand for labor and shifting the labor-demand curve to the right.

But technological change can also reduce labor demand. The invention of a cheap industrial robot, for instance, could reduce the marginal product of labor, shifting the labor-demand curve to the left. Economists call this a **labor-saving** technological change. History suggests, however, that most technological progress is instead **labor-augmenting**. For example, a carpenter with a nail gun is more productive than a carpenter with only a hammer. Labor-augmenting technological advances explain persistently rising employment in the face of rising wages: Even though wages (adjusted for inflation) increased by 201 percent from 1960 to 2020, firms roughly doubled the amount of labor they employed.

The Supply of Other Factors The quantity of one factor of production that is available can affect the marginal product of other factors. The productivity of apple pickers depends, for instance, on the availability of ladders. If the supply of ladders declines, the marginal product of apple pickers will decline as well, reducing the demand for apple pickers. We consider the linkage among the factors of production more fully later in the chapter.

QuickQuiz

1. Approximately what percentage of U.S. national income is paid to workers rather than to owners of capital and land?
   a. 25 percent
   b. 45 percent
   c. 65 percent
   d. 85 percent
2. If firms are competitive and profit-maximizing, the demand curve for labor is determined by
   a. the opportunity cost of workers' time.
   b. the value of the marginal product of labor.
   c. the value of the marginal product of capital.
   d. the ratio of the marginal product of labor to the marginal product of capital.
3. A bakery operating in competitive markets sells its output for ₹20 per cake and pays workers ₹10 per hour. To maximize profit, it should hire workers until the marginal product of labor is
   a. 1/2 cake per hour.
   b. 2 cakes per hour.
   c. 10 cakes per hour.
   d. 15 cakes per hour.

Answers are at the end of the chapter.

18-2 The Supply of Labor

Having analyzed labor demand, let's turn to the other side of the market and consider labor supply. Here we informally discuss the decisions that lie behind the labor-supply curve.

18-2a The Trade-Off between Work and Leisure

Probably no trade-off in a person's life is more important than the trade-off between work and leisure. The more hours you spend working, the fewer hours you have to enjoy dinner with friends, browse social media, or pursue your favorite hobby. The trade-off between labor and leisure lies behind the labor-supply curve.

What do you give up to get an hour of leisure? You give up an hour of work, which in turn means an hour of wages. If your wage is ₹20 per hour, the opportunity cost of an hour of leisure is ₹20. And when you get a raise to ₹25 per hour, the opportunity cost of leisure increases.

PETER C. VEY/ THE NEW YORKER COLLECTION/THE CARTOON BANK

"I really didn't enjoy working five days a week, fifty weeks a year for forty years, but I needed the money."

The labor-supply curve reflects how workers' decisions about the labor-leisure trade-off respond to a change in that opportunity cost. An upward-sloping labor-supply curve means that an increase in the wage induces workers to increase the quantity of labor they supply. Because time is limited, more work means less leisure. That is, workers respond to the increase in the opportunity cost of leisure by taking less of it.

It is worth noting that the labor-supply curve need not be upward-sloping. Imagine you got that raise from ₹20 to ₹25 per hour. The opportunity cost of leisure is now greater, but you are also richer than you were before. You might decide that, with your extra wealth, you can now afford to enjoy more leisure. That is, at the higher wage, you might choose to work fewer hours. If so, your labor-supply curve would slope backward in terms of conflicting effects on your labor-supply decision, called the **income effect** and **substitution effect**. The income effect reflects the response of hours worked due to a change in a person's level of economic well-being, while the substitution effect reflects the response of hours worked due to a change in the opportunity cost of leisure.

FYI What Is Capital Income?

Labor income is easy to understand: It's the paycheck that workers get from their employers. The income earned by capital is less obvious.

Our analysis implicitly assumed that households own the economy's stock of capital—ladders, drill presses, warehouses, and so on—and rent it to the firms that use it. Capital income, in this case, is the rent that households receive for the use of their capital. This assumption simplified our analysis of how capital owners are compensated, but it is not entirely realistic. In fact, firms usually own the capital they use and receive the earnings from this capital.

These earnings from capital are eventually paid to households in various ways. Some of the earnings are paid as interest to households that have lent money to firms. Bondholders and bank depositors are two examples. When you receive interest on your bank account, that income is part of the economy's capital income.

In addition, some of the earnings from capital are paid to households as dividends. Dividends are payments by a firm to its stockholders. A stockholder (or shareholder) is a person who has bought a share in the firm's ownership and, therefore, is entitled to a portion of its profits.

A firm does not have to pay out all its earnings to households in the form of interest and dividends. Instead, it can keep some of its earnings within the firm. Retained earnings can be used to add to the firm's cash position or to buy additional capital. Unlike dividends, retained earnings do not yield a direct cash payment to the firm's stockholders, but the stockholders benefit from them nonetheless. Because retained earnings increase the firm's assets, they tend to increase the value of the firm's stock.

These institutional details are important, but they do not alter our conclusion about the income earned by the owners of capital. Capital is paid according to the value of its marginal product, regardless of whether this income is transmitted to households in the form of interest or dividends or whether it is kept within firms as retained earnings. ■

price of land, shown in panel (a), and the rental price of capital, shown in panel (b), are determined by supply and demand. What's more, the demands for land and capital are determined just like the demand for labor. That is, when the apple-producing firm decides how much land and how many ladders to rent, it follows the same logic as it does when deciding how many workers to hire. For both land and capital, the firm increases the quantity rented until the value of the factor's marginal product equals the factor's price. The demand curve for each factor reflects that factor's marginal productivity.

This theory can now explain how much income goes to labor, landowners, and the owners of capital. As long as the firms using the factors of production are competitive and profit-maximizing, each factor's rental price must equal the value of its marginal product. **Labor, land, and capital all earn the value of their marginal contributions to the production process.**

Now consider the purchase price of land and capital. The rental price and purchase price are related: Buyers are willing to pay more for a piece of land or capital if it produces a valuable stream of rental income. And the equilibrium rental income at any point in time equals the value of that factor's marginal product. As a result, the equilibrium purchase price of a piece of land or capital depends not only on the current value of the marginal product but also on the value of the marginal product expected to prevail in the future.

18-4b Linkages among the Factors of Production

In competitive factor markets, the price paid for any factor of production—labor, land, or capital—equals the value of its marginal product. The marginal product of any factor, in turn, depends on the quantity of that factor that is available. Because of diminishing marginal product, a factor in abundant supply has a low marginal product and a low price, and a factor in scarce supply has a high marginal product and a high price. When the supply of a factor falls, its equilibrium price rises.

But when the supply of any factor changes, the effects are not limited to the market for that factor. In most situations, factors of production are used together in a way that makes the productivity of each factor depend on the quantities of the other factors available for use in the production process. As a result, when some event changes the supply of any one factor of production, it will typically affect not only the earnings of that factor but also the earnings of all the other factors as well.

For example, suppose a cyclone destroys many of the ladders that workers use to pick apples. (To keep things simple, imagine that the storm miraculously leaves the orchards intact.) What happens to the earnings of the various factors of production? Most obviously, when the supply of ladders falls, the equilibrium rental price of ladders rises. Those owners lucky enough to have avoided damage to their ladders now earn a higher return when they rent them out to the firms that produce apples.

Yet the effects of this event do not stop at the ladder market. Because there are fewer ladders, the workers who pick apples can't perform their jobs as efficiently. In other words, the marginal product of labor declines. The reduction in the supply of ladders reduces the demand for the labor of apple pickers, and this shift in demand causes the equilibrium wage to fall.

This story shows a general lesson: **An event that changes the supply of any factor of production can alter the earnings of all the factors.** The change in earnings of any factor can be found by analyzing the impact of the event on the value of the marginal product of that factor.

BETTMANN/GETTY IMAGES

Workers who survived the plague were lucky in more ways than one.

The Economics of the Black Death

Case Study

In 14th-century Europe, the bubonic plague wiped out about one-third of the population within a few years—a vastly more calamitous event than even the tragic Covid pandemic of 2020 and 2021, which killed less than 1 percent of the population. This event, called the **Black Death**, provides a grisly natural experiment to test the theory of factor markets that we have just developed. Consider the effects of the Black Death on those who were lucky enough to survive. What do you think happened to the wages earned by workers and the rents earned by landowners?

To answer this question, let's examine the effects of a reduced population on the marginal product of labor and the marginal product of land. With a smaller supply of workers, the marginal product of labor rises. This is diminishing marginal product working in reverse. We would, therefore, expect the Black Death to raise wages.

Because land and labor are used together in production, a smaller supply of workers also affects the market for land, the other major factor of production in medieval Europe. With fewer workers available to farm the land, an additional unit of land produced less additional output. This decline in the marginal product of land would be expected to reduce rents.

Both theoretical predictions conform with the historical evidence. Wages approximately doubled during this period, and rents declined 50 percent or more. For survivors, the Black Death led to economic prosperity for the peasant classes and reduced incomes for the landed classes. ●

Quick**Quiz**

9. A bakery operating in competitive markets sells its output for ₹20 per cake and rents ovens at ₹30 per hour. To maximize profit, it should rent ovens until the marginal product of an oven is
   a. 2/3 cake per hour.
   b. 3/2 cakes per hour.
   c. 10 cakes per hour.
   d. 25 cakes per hour.

10. A storm destroys several factories, reducing the stock of capital. What effect does this event have on factor markets?
    a. Wages and the rental price of capital both rise.
    b. Wages and the rental price of capital both fall.
    c. Wages rise, and the rental price of capital falls.
    d. Wages fall, and the rental price of capital rises.

Answers are at the end of the chapter.

18-5 Conclusion

This chapter has explained how labor, land, and capital are compensated for the roles they play in the production process. The theory developed here is called the **neoclassical theory of distribution**. According to the neoclassical theory, the amount paid to each factor of production depends on the supply and demand for that factor. The demand, in turn, depends on that factor's marginal productivity. In equilibrium, each factor of production earns the value of its marginal contribution to the production of goods and services.

The neoclassical theory of distribution is widely accepted. Most economists begin with it when trying to explain how the economy's income is distributed among the economy's various members. The next two chapters consider the distribution of income in more detail. The neoclassical theory provides the framework for that discussion.

Even at this point, you can use the theory to answer the question that began this chapter: Why are computer programmers paid more than petrol pump attendants? It is because programmers can produce a good of greater market value than can petrol pump attendants. People are willing to pay dearly for a good video game, but they are willing to pay little to have their gas pumped and windshield washed. The wages of these workers reflect the market prices of the goods they produce. If people suddenly got tired of using computers and decided to spend more time driving, the prices of these goods would change and so would the equilibrium wages of these workers.

Chapter in a Nutshell

- The economy's income is distributed in the markets for the factors of production. The three most important factors are labor, land, and capital.
- The demand for factors, such as labor, is a derived demand that comes from firms that use the factors to produce goods and services. Competitive, profit-maximizing firms hire each factor up to the point at which the value of the factor's marginal product equals its price.
- The supply of labor arises from individuals' trade-off between work and leisure. An upward-sloping labor supply curve means that people respond to an increase in the wage by working more hours and enjoying less leisure.
- In competitive factor markets, the price paid to each factor adjusts to balance supply and demand. Because factor demand reflects the value of the factor's marginal product, in equilibrium, each factor is compensated according to its marginal contribution to the production of goods and services.
- Because factors of production are used together, the marginal product of any one factor depends on the available quantities of all factors. A change in the supply of one factor alters the equilibrium earnings of all of them.

Key Concepts

factors of production, p. 364
production function, p. 365
marginal product of labor, p. 367
diminishing marginal product, p. 367
value of the marginal product, p. 367
capital, p. 377

Questions for Review

1. Explain how a firm's production function is related to its marginal product of labor, how a firm's marginal product of labor is related to the value of its marginal product, and how a firm's value of marginal product is related to its demand for labor.
2. Give two examples of events that could shift the demand for labor, and explain why they do so.
3. Give two examples of events that could shift the supply of labor, and explain why they do so.
4. Explain how the wage can adjust to balance the supply and demand for labor while simultaneously equaling the value of the marginal product of labor.
5. If the population of Assam suddenly grew because of a large wave of immigration, what would happen to wages in Assam? What would happen to the rents earned by the owners of land and capital in Assam?

Problems and Applications

1. Suppose that the president of Powerful Nation proposes a new law aimed at reducing healthcare costs: All citizens are required to eat one apple daily.
   a. How would this apple-a-day law affect the demand and equilibrium price of apples?
   b. How would the law affect the marginal product and the value of the marginal product of apple pickers?
   c. How would the law affect the demand and equilibrium wage for apple pickers?
2. Show the effect of each of the following events on the market for labor in the computer manufacturing industry.
   a. The Ministry of Education buys personal computers for all Indian college students.
   b. More college students major in engineering and computer science.
   c. Computer firms build new manufacturing plants.
3. Suppose that labor is the only input used by a perfectly competitive firm. The firm's production function is as follows:

Days of Labor	Units of Output
0 days	0 units
1	7
2	13
3	19
4	25
5	28
6	29
7	29

   a. Calculate the marginal product of each additional worker.
   b. Each unit of output sells for ₹10. Calculate the value of the marginal product of each worker.
   c. Compute the demand schedule showing the number of workers hired for all wages from zero to ₹100 a day.
   d. Graph the firm's labor-demand curve.
   e. What happens to this demand curve if the price of output rises from ₹10 to ₹12 per unit?
4. Smiling Cow Dairy can sell all the milk it wants for ₹4 a gallon, and it can rent all the robots it wants to milk the cows at a capital rental price of ₹100 a day. It faces the following production schedule:

Number of Robots	Total Product
0	0 gallons
1	50
2	85
3	115
4	140
5	150
6	155

How important are ability, effort, and chance in determining wages? These factors are hard to measure, but indirect evidence suggests that they are very important. When labor economists study wages, they relate a worker's wage to those variables that can be measured, such as years of schooling, years of experience, age, and job characteristics. All these measured variables affect a worker's wage as theory predicts, but they account for less than half of the variation in wages in the economy. Because so much of the variation in wages is left unexplained, omitted variables—including ability, effort, and chance—must be important.

Case Study

The Benefits of Beauty

People differ in many ways, one of which is physical attractiveness. The actor Gal Gadot, for instance, is a beautiful woman—indeed, she was once a beauty pageant winner. Her good looks help attract large audiences to her movies, and the large audiences mean a large income for Ms. Gadot. In 2020, she reportedly earned more than $30 million.

Physical attractiveness is obviously useful for an actor, but how widespread are the economic benefits of beauty? The labor economists Daniel Hamermesh and Jeff Biddle addressed this question in a study published in the December 1994 issue of the *American Economic Review*. Hamermesh and Biddle examined data from surveys of people in the United States and Canada. The interviewers who conducted the surveys were asked to rate each respondent's physical appearance. Hamermesh and Biddle then examined how much the wages of the respondents could be explained by the standard determinants—education, experience, and so on—and how much they depended on physical appearance.

They found that beauty pays. People deemed more attractive than average earn 5 percent more than people of average looks, and people of average looks earn 5 to 10 percent more than people considered less attractive than average. Similar results were found for men and women.

What explains these wage differences? There are several possible interpretations of the beauty premium.

One is that good looks are a type of innate ability determining productivity and wages. Some people are born with the physical attributes of a movie star; others are not. Good looks are useful in any public-facing job—not just acting, but also modeling, sales, and waiting on tables. In this case, attractive workers are more valuable to the firm, and its willingness to pay a beauty premium reflects its customers' preferences.

DFREE/SHUTTERSTOCK.COM

Good looks pay.

A second interpretation is that reported beauty is an indirect measure of other types of ability. How attractive a person appears depends on more than just heredity. It also depends on dress, hairstyle, personal demeanor, and other attributes that a person can control. Perhaps a person who successfully projects an attractive image in a survey interview is more likely to be a talented person who succeeds at other tasks as well.

A third interpretation is that the beauty premium is a type of discrimination, a topic to which we will return. ●

19-1d An Alternative View of Education: Signaling

Recall that the human-capital view of education holds that schooling makes workers more productive. Some economists have proposed another theory, which says that firms use educational attainment as a way of sorting between high-ability and low-ability workers. According to this view, when people earn a college degree, they don't become more productive, but they do **signal** their high productivity to prospective employers. Because it is easier for high-ability people to earn a college degree than it is for low-ability people, more high-ability people get degrees. That makes it rational for firms to interpret a college degree as a signal of ability.

The signaling theory of education is similar to the signaling theory of advertising discussed in earlier chapters. In the case of advertising, the advertisements themselves contain no real information, but firms signal the quality of their products to consumers by their willingness to spend money on advertising. In the signaling theory of education, schooling has no real productivity benefit, but workers signal their innate productivity to employers by their willingness to spend years at school. In both cases, an action is being taken not for its intrinsic benefit but because the willingness to take that action conveys private information to someone observing it.

Both the human-capital theory and the signaling theory can explain why more educated workers tend to earn more than less educated ones. According to the human-capital view, education makes workers more productive; according to the signaling view, education is correlated with ability. But the two views have radically different predictions for policies that aim to increase educational attainment. According to the human-capital view, increasing educational levels for all workers would raise all workers' productivity and wages. According to the signaling view, education does not enhance productivity, so raising all workers' educational levels would not affect wages.

Most likely, the truth lies somewhere between these two extremes. The benefits of education are probably a combination of the productivity-enhancing effects of human capital and the productivity-revealing effects of signaling. The relative size of these two effects is an open question.

19-1e The Superstar Phenomenon

Although most actors earn little and often take jobs as waiters to support themselves, Scarlett Johansson earns millions of dollars for each film she makes. Similarly, while most people who play tennis do it as a hobby, Daniil Medvedev earns millions on the pro tour. Johansson and Medvedev are superstars in their fields, and their great public appeal is reflected in astronomical incomes.

Why do Johansson and Medvedev earn so much? It is not surprising that incomes differ within occupations. Good carpenters earn more than mediocre carpenters, and good plumbers earn more than mediocre plumbers. People vary in talent and effort, and these differences lead to differences in income. Yet the best carpenters and plumbers do not earn the fortunes that are common among the best actors and athletes. What explains the difference?

To understand the tremendous incomes of Johansson and Medvedev, consider the special features of the markets in which they sell their services. Superstars arise in markets with two characteristics:

- Every customer in the market wants to enjoy the services supplied by the best producers.
- The services are produced with a technology that makes it possible for the best producers to supply every customer at low cost.

If Scarlett Johansson is one of the best actors around, then everyone will want to see her next movie; seeing twice as many movies by an actor half as appealing is not a good substitute. Moreover, it is **possible** for everyone to enjoy a performance by Scarlett Johansson. Because it is easy to make multiple copies of a film, Johansson can provide her acting services to millions of people simultaneously. Similarly, because tennis matches are broadcast on television, millions of fans can enjoy the extraordinary skills of Daniil Medvedev.

This logic shows why there are no superstar carpenters and plumbers. Other things being equal, everyone prefers to hire the best plumber, but a plumber, unlike a movie actor, can only work for a limited number of customers. Although the best plumber can command a somewhat higher wage than the average plumber, the average plumber can still earn a good living.

19-1f Below-Equilibrium Wages: Monopsony

Most often, economists analyze labor markets using the tools of supply and demand. The market is assumed to be competitive with many buyers and many sellers, each of whom has a negligible effect on the wage. Yet that assumption doesn't always apply.

Imagine that the labor market in a small town is dominated by a single, large employer. That employer can exert a large influence on the going wage, substantially changing the outcome in the labor market. A market in which there is a single buyer is called a **monopsony**.

monopsony
a market that has only one buyer

A monopsony (a market with one buyer) is like a monopoly (a market with one seller). Recall that a monopoly produces less of the good than a competitive firm would; by reducing the quantity offered for sale, the monopoly moves along the product's demand curve, increasing the price and its profit. Similarly, a monopsony in a labor market hires fewer workers than a competitive firm would; by reducing the number of jobs available, the monopsony moves along the labor supply curve, reducing the wage it pays and increasing its profit. Both monopolists and monopsonists reduce economic activity in a market below the socially optimal level. In both cases, the existence of market power distorts the outcome and causes deadweight losses. Workers employed by monopsonies earn less than they would under competition.

This book does not present the formal model of monopsony because true monopsonies are rare. In most labor markets, workers have many possible employers, and firms compete with one another to attract workers. In such cases, the model of supply and demand is the best one to use.

Yet the concept of monopsony, developed by the economist Joan Robinson in the 1930s, is important in some cases. In 2021, the Supreme Court of the United States (SCOTUS) declared that the NCAA has functioned as a monopsony, depriving college athletes of the compensation they would earn in a more competitive market. Around the same time, the Biden administration placed a spotlight on monopsonies in an executive order, seeking to reduce the power of big tech companies and increase workers' bargaining power. A growing problem, according to many economists, is the frequent use of employment contracts with non-compete clauses, which bar employees from leaving to work for a competitor. While these agreements protect employers' trade secrets, they also curb competition in the labor market, keeping wages below their equilibrium level.

Monopsonies in a pure form are not common, but the tendency toward monopsony still bedevils some parts of the modern economy. The effects of monopsony power may help explain some workers' wages.

Ask the Experts **Competition in Labor Markets**

"The use of non-compete clauses in U.S. employment contracts reduces workers' mobility and wages by more than is justified by the protection of employers' intellectual property and trade secrets."

What do economists say?

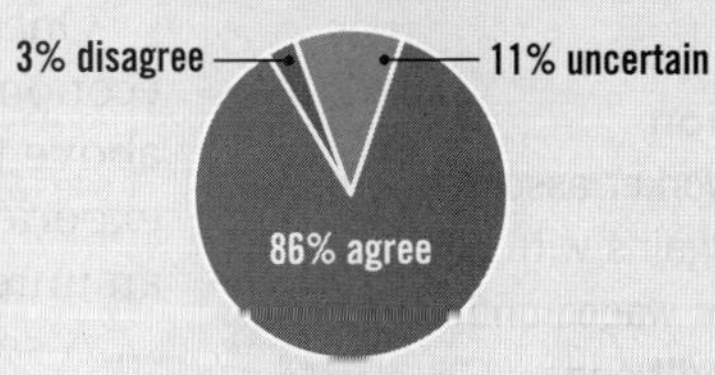

Source: IGM Economic Experts Panel, August 3, 2021.

In the News: The Aftereffects of the Covid Pandemic

Some economists worry that students who fell behind because of Covid restrictions may never catch up in their skills, job prospects, and income.

The Long-Term Economic Costs of Lost Schooling

By Jon Hilsenrath

Imagine for a moment two objects in your hands. One is a piece of paper and the other a rubber band. If you squeeze your hands together hard and let go, the paper will remain crumpled, but the rubber band will return to its original shape.

Economists tend to think of the economy as the rubber band. After a shock, they expect it to go back to normal. When it doesn't, like the crumpled paper, they call the effect "hysteresis"—lasting changes caused by some large perturbation. The Covid-19 pandemic is a classic example. What permanent damage to the economy will it leave behind?

The first place to look is in classrooms, say Eric Hanushek and Margaret Raymond, economists and education researchers at Stanford University. Lost study time for children during the pandemic has the potential to do lasting harm not just to their own long-term prospects but to American prosperity in general, say the married couple.

Ms. Raymond studied 18 states and Washington, D.C. and concluded that, on average, children lost 116 days of reading time during the early stages of the pandemic last year and 215 days of math work—instruction that will be hard to regain and could leave a whole generation of children struggling to keep up in their studies and testing. If your child misses out on learning fractions now, how will she perform in algebra later?

And the shock has been distributed unevenly. Children in rural areas and areas with large Black and Hispanic populations were hit the hardest. Among the states suffering the most are South Carolina and Illinois, according to Ms. Raymond's study.

Economic output is a function of innovation, the skills that workers bring to their jobs and the machines that they use to create goods and services. Innovation and skills are shaped by education. Over the next century, the skill shock of 2020 will produce $25 trillion to $30 trillion of lost economic output in today's dollars, Mr. Hanushek estimates, and the lifetime household incomes of the affected students will be 6% to 9% lower.

He came to this conclusion in part by examining the experience of German students. In 1966 and 1967, the German government temporarily shortened the school year in a rejiggering of the school calendar. Longitudinal studies, he says, show that this lost class time reduced the incomes of that cohort of students by 5% over their lifetimes. Today's students "are going to feel the long-term effects of Covid even when they are back in school," Mr. Hanushek says.

Economists borrowed the term hysteresis from the physics of magnetism. If you apply a large enough magnetic force to a metal object, the polarity of the object can be permanently transformed. It's the mechanism used, for

19-1g Above-Equilibrium Wages: Minimum-Wage Laws, Unions, and Efficiency Wages

While workers employed by a monopsony have wages below the level that would prevail in a competitive market equilibrium, other workers are paid above that level. Above-equilibrium wages can arise for three reasons.

One reason is minimum-wage laws, as Chapter 6 discussed. Most workers in the economy are not affected by these laws because their equilibrium wages are well above the legal minimum. But for some workers, especially the least skilled and experienced, minimum-wage laws raise wages above the level they would earn in an unregulated labor market.

union
a worker association that bargains with employers over wages and working conditions

strike
a collective refusal to work organized as a form of protest

A second reason that wages might rise above their equilibrium level is the market power of labor unions. A **union** is a worker association that bargains with employers over wages and working conditions. Unions often raise wages above the level that would prevail in their absence, perhaps because they can organize workers to withhold their labor by calling a **strike**. Sometimes, unions act as a countervailing power to offset the monopsonistic behavior of employers; other

Quick**Quiz**

5. Among full-time U.S. workers, White women earn about _______ percent less than White men, and Black men earn about _______ percent less than White men.
   a. 5; 20
   b. 5; 40
   c. 20; 20
   d. 20; 40

6. It is difficult to measure to what extent discrimination affects labor market outcomes because
   a. data on wages are crucial but not readily available.
   b. firms misreport the wages they pay to hide discriminatory practices.
   c. workers differ in their attributes and the types of jobs they have.
   d. the same minimum-wage law applies to workers in all groups.

7. The forces of competition in markets with free entry and exit tend to eliminate wage differentials that arise from discrimination by
   a. employers.
   b. customers.
   c. government.
   d. all of the above.

Answers are at the end of the chapter.

19-3 Conclusion

In competitive markets, workers earn a wage equal to the value of their marginal contribution to the production of goods and services. But many things affect the value of the marginal product. Firms tend to pay more for workers who are talented, diligent, experienced, and educated because these workers are more productive. Firms are likely to pay less to those workers against whom customers discriminate because these workers contribute less to revenue.

The theory of the labor market developed in the last two chapters explains why some workers earn higher wages than other workers. The theory does not say that the resulting distribution of income is necessarily equal, fair, or desirable in any way. The next chapter takes up that topic.

Chapter in a Nutshell

- Workers earn different wages for many reasons. One is that wage differentials play a role in compensating workers for job attributes. Other things being equal, workers in hard, unpleasant jobs are paid more than workers in easy, pleasant jobs.
- Workers with more human capital are paid more than workers with less. The return to accumulating human capital is high and has increased over the past several decades.
- Years of education, experience, and job characteristics affect earnings in the way that theory predicts, but many differences in earnings cannot be explained by things that economists can easily measure. The unexplained variation in earnings is largely attributable to ability, effort, and chance.
- Some economists have suggested that more educated workers earn higher wages not because education raises productivity but because it signals to employers that these workers have high levels of ability. If this signaling theory is correct, then increasing the educational attainment of all workers would not raise the overall level of wages.
- Wages are sometimes kept away from the level that balances supply and demand. An explanation for below-equilibrium wages is the monopsony power of some employers. Three explanations for above-equilibrium wages are minimum-wage laws, unions, and efficiency wages.
- Some differences in earnings are attributable to discrimination based on race, gender, or other factors. Measuring the amount of discrimination is difficult because one must correct for differences in human capital and job characteristics.
- Competitive markets tend to limit discriminatory wage differences. If one group of workers earns less than another for reasons unrelated to productivity,

then nondiscriminatory firms will be more profitable than discriminatory ones. Profit-seeking behavior can, therefore, reduce discriminatory wage gaps. Still, discrimination persists in competitive markets if customers are willing to pay more to discriminatory firms or if the government enacts laws that require firms to discriminate.

- Discrimination can also occur for statistical reasons. If employers have imperfect information about employees, they may discriminate against all members of a group whose average characteristics the employers find undesirable.

Key Concepts

compensating differential, p. 386
human capital, p. 386
monopsony, p. 391
union, p. 392
strike, p. 392
efficiency wages, p. 393
discrimination, p. 394
statistical discrimination, p. 399

Questions for Review

1. Why are roofers paid more than other workers with similar amounts of education?
2. In what sense is education a type of capital?
3. How might education raise a worker's wage without raising the worker's productivity?
4. What conditions lead to highly compensated superstars? Would you expect to see superstars in dentistry? In music? Explain.
5. Give three reasons a worker's wage might be above the level that balances supply and demand.
6. What difficulties arise in deciding whether a group of workers has a lower wage because of discrimination?
7. Explain how the forces of economic competition affect racial discrimination.
8. Give an example of how discrimination might persist in a competitive market.

Problems and Applications

1. College students sometimes work as summer interns for private firms or the government. Some of these positions pay little or nothing.
   a. What is the opportunity cost of taking such a job?
   b. Explain why students are willing to take these jobs.
   c. If you were to compare the earnings later in life of workers who had worked as interns and those who had taken summer jobs that paid more, what would you expect to find?
2. A minimum-wage law distorts the market for low-wage labor. To reduce this distortion, some economists advocate a two-tiered minimum-wage system, with a regular minimum wage for adult workers and a lower, "subminimum" wage for teenage workers. Give two reasons a single minimum wage might distort the labor market for teenage workers more than it would the market for adult workers.
3. A basic finding of labor economics is that workers who have more experience in the labor force are paid more than workers who have less experience (holding constant the amount of formal education). Why might this be so? Some studies have also found that experience at the same job has an extra positive influence on wages. Explain why this might occur.
4. At some colleges and universities, economics professors receive higher salaries than professors in some other fields.
   a. Why might this be true?
   b. Some other colleges and universities have a policy of paying equal salaries to professors in all fields. At some of these schools, economics professors have lighter teaching loads than professors in some other fields. What role do the differences in teaching loads play?
5. Imagine that someone offered you a choice: You could spend four years studying at the world's best

university, but you would have to forever keep your attendance there a secret. Or you could be awarded an official degree from the world's best university, but you couldn't actually attend. Which choice do you think would enhance your future earnings more? What does your answer say about the debate over signaling versus human capital in the role of education?

6. When recording devices were first invented more than 100 years ago, musicians could suddenly supply their music to large audiences at low cost. How do you suppose this development affected the income of the best musicians? How do you suppose it affected the income of average musicians?

7. A current debate in education is whether teachers should be paid on a standard pay scale based solely upon their years of training and teaching experience or whether part of their salary should be based upon their performance (called "merit pay").
   a. Why might merit pay be desirable?
   b. Who might be opposed to a system of merit pay?
   c. What is a potential challenge of merit pay?
   d. A related issue: Why might a school district decide to pay teachers significantly more than the salaries offered by surrounding districts?

8. When Alan Greenspan (an economist who would later chair the Federal Reserve) ran a consulting firm in the 1960s, he primarily hired female economists. He once told the *New York Times*, "I always valued men and women equally, and I found that because others did not, good women economists were cheaper than men." Is Greenspan's behavior profit-maximizing? Is it admirable or despicable? If more employers were like Greenspan, what would happen to the wage differential between men and women? Why might other economic consulting firms at the time not have followed Greenspan's business strategy?

Quick**Quiz Answers**

1. b 2. a 3. d 4. c 5. c 6. c 7. a

Chapter

20

Poverty and Human Capital Development

The great British Prime Minister Winston Churchill once said, "The inherent vice of capitalism is the unequal sharing of blessings. The inherent virtue of socialism is the equal sharing of miseries." In 1945, when he made those remarks, Churchill was both a famous critic of socialism and an eloquent celebrant of the British Empire and the economic system that helped fuel it. His observation underscores two facts. First, thanks to Adam Smith's invisible hand, nations that use market mechanisms to allocate resources usually achieve greater prosperity than those that do not. Second, prosperity in market economies is not shared equally. Incomes can differ greatly between the top and bottom of the economic ladder.

The previous two chapters analyzed why people's incomes differ so much. Incomes arise from payments to the factors of production—labor, land, and capital. When markets are competitive, factor prices adjust to balance supply and demand. In equilibrium, the factors of production are paid the value of their marginal product.

ROMAN SAMBORSKYI/SHUTTERSTOCK.COM; ARNO VAN ENGELAND/EYEEM/GETTY IMAGES

Labor supply and demand depend on ability, effort, human capital, compensating differentials, discrimination, and so on. For the most part, these things determine how much workers earn. But sometimes, because of minimum-wage laws, unions, efficiency wages, and monopsony power, the payments to labor depart from their competitive equilibrium levels. All these diverse forces influence whether a person ends up rich, poor, or somewhere in between.

The distribution of income raises fundamental questions about the economy and public policy. This chapter addresses the topic in three steps. First, we consider how inequality is measured and how great it is in our economy and around the world. Second, we examine different views about the role that government should play in altering the income distribution. Third, we discuss public policies aimed at helping those members of society most in need.

20-1 Measuring Inequality

20-1a Income Inequality

BOB MANKOFF/CARTOON COLLECTIONS

Imagine that you lined up all the families in the economy according to annual incomes. Then you divided them into five equal groups, called **quintiles**. Table 1 shows the income ranges for each quintile in 2019 and for the top 5 percent (a subset of the highest quintile). You can use this table to find where your family lies in the income distribution.

For studying the income distribution, economists find it useful to calculate the share of total income that each quintile received. Table 2 shows that information in selected years. In 2019, the lowest quintile earned 3.9 percent of all income, and the highest quintile earned 49.5 percent. Even though all the quintiles include the same number of families, the highest quintile had almost 13 times as much income as the lowest quintile.

The last column shows the income share of the richest families. In 2019, the top 5 percent of families earned 21.9 percent of all income, which was greater than the total income of the bottom 40 percent.

Table 1

The Distribution of Family Income in the United States: 2019

Source: U.S. Bureau of the Census, Historical Income Tables, Table F-1.

Group	Annual Family Income
Lowest Quintile	$40,000 and below
Second Quintile	$40,001–$69,000
Middle Quintile	$69,001–$105,038
Fourth Quintile	$105,039–$164,930
Highest Quintile	$164,931 and above
Top 5 percent	$304,153 and above

Table 2

Income Inequality in the United States

This table shows the percentage of total before-tax income received by families in each fifth of the income distribution and by families in the top 5 percent.

Source: U.S. Bureau of the Census, Historical Income Tables, Table F-2.

Year	Lowest Quintile	Second Quintile	Middle Quintile	Fourth Quintile	Highest Quintile	Top 5%
2019	3.9%	9.2%	14.8%	22.5%	49.5%	21.9%
2010	3.8	9.4	15.4	23.5	47.9	20.0
2000	4.3	9.8	15.4	22.7	47.7	21.1
1990	4.6	10.8	16.6	23.8	44.3	17.4
1980	5.3	11.6	17.6	24.4	41.1	14.6
1970	5.4	12.2	17.6	23.8	40.9	15.6
1960	4.8	12.2	17.8	24.0	41.3	15.9
1950	4.5	12.0	17.4	23.4	42.7	17.3
1935	4.1	9.2	14.1	20.9	51.7	26.5

Table 2 also shows the distribution of income in various years beginning in 1935. At first glance, the distribution appears stable. Over many decades, the lowest quintile has earned about 4 to 5 percent of income, while the highest quintile has earned about 40 to 50 percent of income. Closer inspection reveals some trends in the degree of inequality. From 1935 to 1970, the distribution gradually became more equal. The share of the lowest quintile rose from 4.1 to 5.4 percent, and the share of the highest quintile fell from 51.7 to 40.9 percent. In more recent years, this trend has reversed itself. From 1970 to 2019, the share of the lowest quintile fell from 5.4 to 3.9 percent, and the share of the highest quintile rose from 40.9 to 49.5 percent.

Increased trade with low-wage countries (such as China) and skill-biased technological changes (such as robots) have tended to decrease the demand for unskilled labor and increase the demand for skilled labor. These shifts in demand have reduced the wages of unskilled workers relative to those of skilled workers, and the change in relative wages has increased inequality in family incomes.

20-1b Inequality around the World

How does inequality in the developed countries, such as United States compare with that in other countries, developed as well as developing economies? This question is interesting, but answering it is problematic. Some countries don't have reliable data, and those that do collect it in different ways. Some measure individual incomes, others measure family incomes, and still others measure expenditure as a crude approximation of income. We can never be sure whether an observed difference in inequality reflects a true difference in the economies or merely a difference in the way data are collected.

With this warning in mind, consider Figure 1, which compares inequality in two dozen major countries. The inequality measure used here is the **quintile ratio**, which is the income of the highest quintile divided by the income of the lowest quintile. The most equality is found in Pakistan and Sweden, where the highest quintile receives about 4.5 times as much income as the lowest quintile (though that relative equality occurs at a low level of average income in Pakistan and a high level

FYI Incomes of the Super-Rich

Tables 1 and 2 present some information about the affluent—the top 20 percent and the top 5 percent of the income distribution. But what about the very rich, such as the top 1 percent? Or the very, very rich, such as the top 0.01 percent?

Standard data derived from the Current Population Survey are less reliable about the extremes of the income distribution. One problem is sample size. If the government surveys 60,000 households, it will get only 600 households in the top 1 percent and only 6 households in the top 0.01 percent. Another problem is that participation in the survey is voluntary. When approached by government data collectors, the rich may be more likely to say, "no thanks."

To study the super-rich, economists turn to income tax returns. Because everyone is subject to income taxes, the sample sizes are large, and non-participation is not an option. Yet tax return data, while better in some ways, are worse in others. The tax code is designed to raise revenue, not to collect consistent data over time. As lawmakers revise the tax code, the incentives for people to receive and report income in any particular form can change. (For example, business income is especially important for the super-rich. How this income is reported depends on whether the business is organized as a partnership or a corporation, and business owners can change that.) Nonetheless, the tax data may be the best lens to see into the lives of the super-rich.

Two economists who have studied the U.S. tax data to gauge inequality are Thomas Piketty and Emmanuel Saez. Here are some of their findings:

- To be in the top 1 percent of the income distribution in 2018, a taxpayer had to have an income above $441,970. This group's share of total income increased from 7.8 percent in 1970 to 18.3 percent in 2018.
- To be in the top 0.1 percent of the income distribution in 2018, a taxpayer had to have an income above $1,753,300. This group's share of total income increased from 1.9 percent in 1970 to 7.9 percent in 2018.
- To be in the top 0.01 percent of the income distribution in 2018, a taxpayer had to have an income above $7,879,500. This group's share of total income increased from 0.5 percent in 1970 to 3.4 percent in 2018.

The bottom line: The increase in inequality over the past half century documented in Table 2 appears to be highly concentrated among the super-rich. ■

of average income in Sweden). The least equality is found in South Africa, where the top group receives 28 times as much income as the bottom group. All countries have significant disparities between rich and poor, but the degree of inequality varies substantially.

The United States has more inequality than most countries and much more than other economically advanced countries, such as Germany, France, and Japan. But it has a more equal income distribution than some developing countries, such as South Africa, Venezuela, and Brazil. The United States has about the same degree of inequality as China, the world's most populous nation, which claims to practice "socialism with Chinese characteristics" but has, in recent years, increasingly embraced market forces.

poverty rate
the percentage of the population whose family income falls below an absolute level called the poverty line

poverty line
an absolute level of income set by the federal government for each family size below which a family is deemed to be in poverty

20-1c The Poverty Rate

A commonly cited gauge of the distribution of income is the **poverty rate**, which is the percentage of the population whose family income falls below an absolute level called the **poverty line**. The poverty line is set by the federal government at roughly three times the cost of providing an adequate diet. This line depends on family size and adjusts every year to account for price changes.

Consider the data for 2019. In that year, the median family in the United States had an income of $86,011, and the poverty line for a family with two adults and two children was $25,926. The poverty rate was 10.5 percent. In other words, 10.5

Figure 1

Inequality around the World

This figure shows the ratio of the income of the highest quintile to the income of the lowest quintile. Among these nations, Sweden and Pakistan have the most equal income distribution, while South Africa and Venezuela have the least equal.

Source: Human Development Report 2018 Statistical Update.

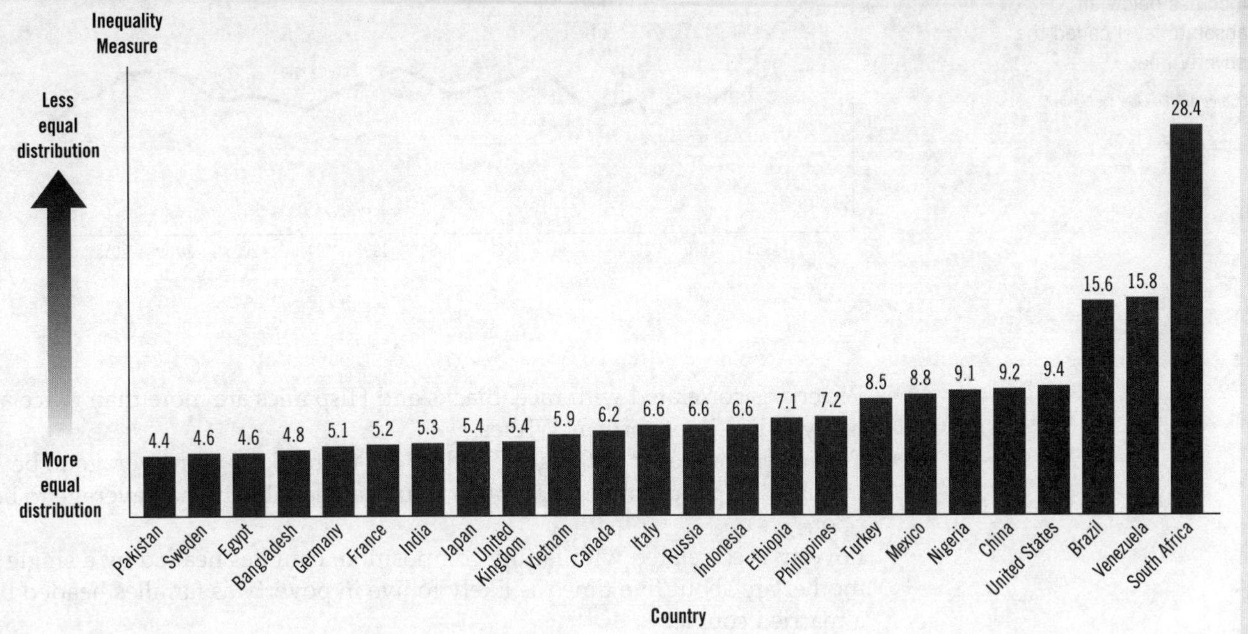

percent of the U.S. population were living below the poverty line for their family size.

Figure 2 shows the poverty rate since 1959, when the official data begin. You can see that the poverty rate fell from 22.4 percent in 1959 to 11.1 percent in 1973. This decline came as average income (adjusted for inflation) rose more than 50 percent. Because the poverty line is an absolute rather than a relative standard, more families tend to be pushed above the poverty line as economic growth pushes the entire income distribution upward. As President John F. Kennedy once put it, "a rising tide lifts all boats."

Since the early 1970s, however, the economy's rising tide has left smaller boats behind. Despite continued growth in average income, the poverty rate has not substantially changed since 1973. This lack of progress in reducing poverty in recent decades is closely related to the increasing inequality shown in Table 2. While economic growth has raised the income of the typical family, the increase in inequality has prevented the poorest families from sharing in this greater prosperity.

Poverty affects all groups within the population but not with equal frequency. Table 3 shows the poverty rates for several groups, and it reveals three striking facts:

Figure 2

The Poverty Rate

The poverty rate measures the percentage of the population with incomes below an absolute level called the poverty line.

Source: U.S. Bureau of the Census.

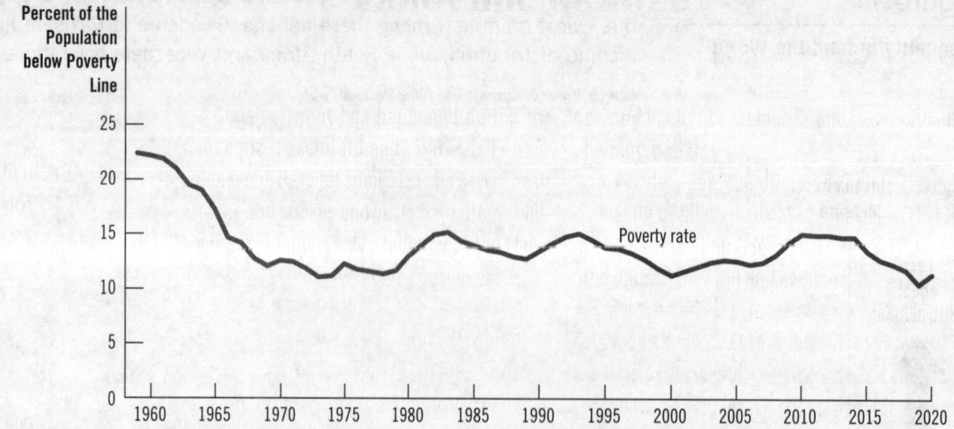

- Poverty is correlated with race. Blacks and Hispanics are more than twice as likely to live in poverty as Whites.
- Poverty is correlated with age. Children are more likely than average to be members of poor families, and older adults are less likely than average to be poor.
- Poverty is correlated with family composition. Families headed by a single mother are about five times as likely to live in poverty as families headed by a married couple.

These correlations have described American society for many years, and they show which people are most likely to be poor. These effects also work together: Children in Black and Hispanic female-headed households have especially high rates of poverty.

Table 3

Who Lives in Poverty?

This table shows that the poverty rate varies greatly among different groups within the population.

Source: U.S. Bureau of the Census. Data are for 2019.

Group	Poverty Rate
All persons	10.5%
White, not Hispanic	7.3
Black	18.8
Hispanic	15.7
Asian	7.3
Children (under age 18)	14.4
Older adults (over age 64)	8.9
Married-couple families	4.6
Female household, no spouse present	24.3

20-1d Poverty in India

Data on the income distribution and poverty rate give some idea about the degree of inequality in American society, but their interpretation is not always straightforward. The data are based on annual family incomes. What most people care about, however, is not their incomes in a single year but their ability to maintain a good standard of living. For several reasons, data on the income distribution and the poverty rate give an incomplete picture of inequality in living standards.

India's trajectory of poverty and development presents both remarkable advancements and enduring challenges. Over the past three decades, economic liberalization and structural reforms have led to a gradual reduction in absolute poverty, lifting large numbers of the population above the poverty threshold. According to World Bank estimates and National Sample Surveys, India has halved its poverty rate since the early 2000s. Nevertheless, multidimensional poverty, encompassing the composite lack of access to education, healthcare, meaningful employment, continues to pose a concern, particularly in rural regions.

Consequently, development strategies have transcended income-centric metrics to encompass broader indicators such as the Human Development Index (HDI), sanitation access, nutrition, and women's empowerment. Government initiatives such as Mahatma Gandhi National Rural Employment Guarantee Act (MGNREGA), Prime Minister's Rural Empowerment Scheme (PM-KISAN), Ayushman Bharat, and rural electrification drives have attempted to address the issue of deprivation through direct transfers and last mile delivery of public services and benefits. However, managerial challenges persist in implementation, targeting, and avoidance of leakage.

For businesses, comprehending poverty and development extends beyond a mere social concern, serving as a strategic factor that influences market size, consumer segmentation, labor availability, and corporate social responsibility (CSR) priorities. As India aspires to attain a ₹5 trillion economy, targeted by 2027, inclusive development remains both a policy imperative and a managerial opportunity.

Human Capital Development, Skills, and the Firm: An Indian Perspective

While traditional economic frameworks treat poverty alleviation as the domain of governments and NGOs, we can think of increasing strategic relevance of anti-poverty programs for businesses. For this, the Indian business context is particularly relevant. For example, India's large and diverse labor force represents both a development challenge and a business opportunity. Firms operating in India must understand how public initiatives such as targeted welfare schemes, skill-building programs, and rural employment guarantees have the potential to shape the talent pool and have direct implications for labor costs, and long-run productivity.

One such flagship initiative is the **Pradhan Mantri Kaushal Vikas Yojana (PMKVY)**–, a central government scheme aimed at skill certification and placement of youth across diverse sectors. By equipping first-time job seekers with basic technical and soft skills, PMKVY aimed to enhance the employability of workers, thereby potentially reducing the onboarding costs for firms. This program, along with initiatives, such as apprenticeship programs, or state -specific schemes, such as Tamil Nadu's Naal Mudhalvan, can help to create a broader base of semi-skilled labor for industries. For managers, these translate into wider recruitment pools and lower on-the-job training costs.

Having said that, firms, in general, are increasingly investing in the upskilling of their workers and executives as is evident from sponsored training programs for lower hierarchy staff to more senior -level corporate programs for managers such as executive education or management development programs (MDPs) from leading business schools and institutions. Many of these programs are offered in partnership with educational institutions to upgrade internal capabilities without losing talent to attrition. These investments not only address skill gaps but also improve employee retention, succession planning, and alignment with firm strategy.

Moreover, Corporate Social Responsibility (CSR) mandates in India (applicable to firms exceeding specified profit and turnover thresholds) have encouraged many companies to align their CSR spending with skilling and education. Case studies of firms such as **Infosys Foundation, Godrej Good & Green, and Tata STRIVE** show how skilling initiatives can deliver both reputational capital and operational benefits.

Ultimately, tackling poverty through skill- building is not just a moral imperative but also a managerial one. Firms that recognize the interlinkages between human capital, productivity, and inclusion will be better positioned in a future where both market and regulatory environments increasingly value inclusive growth.

Taxes and In-Kind Transfers Standard measures of the income distribution and poverty rate are based on families' **pre-tax** incomes. They don't account for the greater taxes that high-income households typically pay and the tax credits that low-income households often receive.

Another problem with the data on the income distribution and the official poverty rate is that they are based on **monetary** incomes. Yet various government programs provide low-income households with nonmonetary items, such as free food, housing vouchers, and medical services. Transfers in the form of goods and services rather than cash are called **in-kind transfers**. The alternate Poverty Measures take account of some of these in-kind transfers, but standard measures of inequality and poverty usually do not.

in-kind transfers
transfers given in the form of goods and services rather than cash

The Economic Life Cycle Incomes vary predictably over most people's lives. Young adults, especially those in school, often have low incomes. Incomes tend to rise as people gain maturity and experience in the workforce, peak at around age 50, and then fall sharply around age 65 when many people retire. This typical pattern of income variation is called the **life cycle**.

life cycle
the regular pattern of income variation over a person's life

Because people can borrow and save to smooth out life cycle changes in income, their standard of living in any year need not depend only on that year's income. The young often borrow, perhaps to go to school or buy a house, and then repay these loans later as their incomes rise. People tend to have their highest saving rates when they are middle-aged. These savings can be drawn down in retirement, so the standard of living of older adults need not decline as much as their earnings.

Most data sets lump together the incomes of college students, people in their prime working years, and retirees. Because of the common life cycle pattern, some of the inequality in annual income does not represent true inequality in living standards.

Transitory versus Permanent Income Incomes vary over people's lives not only because of predictable life cycle variation but also because of random and transitory forces. One year, a classic American winter frost kills off the Florida orange crop, and Florida orange growers see their incomes fall temporarily. At the same time, the Florida frost drives up the price of oranges, and California orange growers see their incomes temporarily rise. The next year, the reverse might happen. Or a pandemic may reduce the income of restaurant workers but increase the revenue of home-delivery pizza businesses. When public health is restored, the pattern shifts.

Just as people can borrow and save to smooth out life cycle variations in income, they can also borrow and save to smooth out transitory variations in income. To the extent that a family saves in good years and borrows (or depletes its savings) in bad ones, transitory changes in income need not affect its standard of living. A family's ability to buy goods and services would then depend on its **permanent income**, which is its normal, or average, income over several years.

permanent income
a person's normal income

To gauge inequality of living standards, the distribution of permanent income may be more relevant than the distribution of annual income. Because permanent income is less affected by transitory events, it is more equally distributed than current income.

20-1e Economic Mobility

People sometimes speak of "the rich" and "the poor" as if these groups consisted of the same families year after year. But this is not the case. Economic mobility, the movement of people among income classes, is significant in the U.S. economy. Movements up the income ladder can be due to good luck or hard work, and movements down can be due to bad luck or laziness. Some of this mobility reflects transitory variations in income, while some reflects more persistent changes in income.

Because family income changes over time, temporary poverty is more common than the poverty rate suggests, but persistent poverty is less common. In a typical 10-year period, about one in four families falls below the poverty line in at least one year. Yet fewer than 3 percent of families are poor for eight or more years. Because it is likely that the temporarily poor and the persistently poor face different problems, policies that aim to combat poverty often try to distinguish between these groups.

Another way to gauge mobility is with the persistence of economic success from generation to generation. According to studies of this topic, having an above-average income tends to carry over from parents to children, but the persistence is far from perfect, indicating substantial mobility among income classes. If a father earns 20 percent above his generation's average income, his son will most likely earn 8 percent above his generation's average income. The correlation between the income of a grandfather and the income of his grandson is small.

Studies have documented that the degree of intergenerational mobility varies from country to country and that mobility is negatively correlated with inequality. Nations with greater inequality than the United States, such as Brazil, tend to have lower mobility. Nations with lower inequality than even the United States, such as India, tend to have greater mobility. Whether these international differences mainly reflect disparities in populations, policies, institutions, culture, or other factors isn't clear.

Case Study

A Lifetime Perspective on Income Inequality

For the reasons we have discussed, the standard data on the income distribution can give a misleading picture about how much inequality there is. In a 2021 study titled "U.S. Inequality and Fiscal Progressivity," the economists Alan Auerbach, Laurence Kotlikoff, and Darryl Koehler tried to correct for these problems. Rather than lumping all ages together—college students, full-time workers, and retirees—they examined inequality within specific cohorts, such as those aged 40 to 49. In addition, they looked not at a single year's income but at the total resources people have available to spend over their remaining years of life, which includes wealth, current income, and expected future income. And they accounted for taxes and transfer payments attributable to federal, state, and local government policies, including in-kind transfers.

Here are their estimates of the distribution of lifetime resources for those aged 40 to 49:

- Lowest quintile: 6.6 percent
- Second quintile: 9.8 percent
- Middle quintile: 14.0 percent
- Fourth quintile: 19.7 percent
- Highest quintile: 49.8 percent
- Top 5 percent: 24.4 percent
- Top 1 percent: 11.8 percent

Comparing these results with those in Table 2, you will see a large difference for the lowest quintile. The standard data show that the lowest quintile gets about 4 percent of annual income, but these new data say that the lowest quintile gets 6.6 percent of lifetime resources. At the other end of the distribution, while the data from income tax returns (discussed in the preceding FYI box) say that the top 1 percent gets 18.3 percent of annual income, this research finds that the top 1 percent gets 11.8 percent of lifetime resources.

Recall that one measure of inequality is the quintile ratio, the ratio of the income of the highest 20 percent to that of the lowest 20 percent. This measure is about 12.5

QuickQuiz

1. In the United States today, the poorest fifth of the population earns about ____ percent of all pre-tax annual income, while the richest fifth earns about ____ percent.
   a. 2; 70
   b. 4; 50
   c. 6; 35
   d. 8; 25

2. When comparing income inequality across nations, one finds that the United States is
   a. the most equal nation in the world.
   b. more equal than most nations but not the most equal.
   c. less equal than most nations but not the least equal.
   d. the least equal nation in the world.

3. Because consumption is largely determined by _______ income, consumption is _______ equally distributed than current income.
   a. permanent; more
   b. permanent; less
   c. transitory; more
   d. transitory; less

Answers are at the end of the chapter.

in the data on pre-tax annual income in Table 2 but only 7.5 in the data on lifetime resources.

This research also quantifies how public policy—including both taxes and transfers—affects the distribution of lifetime resources. The highest quintile pays an average tax rate over their lifetimes of 31 percent, and the top 1 percent pays an average tax rate of 35 percent. The middle class, defined here as the middle quintile of lifetime resources, pays an average tax rate of 19 percent. But because of the earne ms, those in the lowest quintile face an average tax rate of **negative** 44 percent. The negative sign means that people in the lowest quintile receive more in government transfer payments than they pay in taxes.

The bottom line: The United States has substantial inequality, but not as much as conventional measures indicate. ●

20-2 Policies to Reduce Poverty

As we have just seen, political philosophers hold various views about income redistribution. Political debate reflects a similar disagreement. Nonetheless, most people believe that, at the very least, society should try to help those most in need and that the government needs to step in when private charity fails. According to a popular metaphor, society should provide a "safety net" to prevent any citizen from falling too far.

Poverty is a challenging problem. Families with low incomes are more likely than the overall population to experience homelessness, drug dependence, health problems, teenage pregnancy, illiteracy, unemployment, and low educational attainment. Members of these families are more likely both to commit crimes and to be victims of crimes. It is sometimes hard to distinguish the causes of poverty from the effects, but there is no doubt that poverty is associated with serious economic and social ills.

Suppose that you were a policymaker in the government and your goal was to reduce the number of people living in poverty. What would you do? Here we examine some of the policy options. Each helps some people escape poverty, but none are perfect, and deciding on the best combination is not easy. We begin by some policies in the US.

20-2a Minimum-Wage Laws

Laws setting a minimum wage that employers can pay workers are a perennial source of debate. Advocates view the minimum wage as a way of helping the working poor without any cost to the government. Critics view it as hurting those it is intended to help.

The minimum wage is easily understood using the tools of supply and demand, as discussed earlier. For workers with low levels of skill and experience, a high minimum wage forces the wage above the level that balances supply and demand. That raises the cost of labor to firms and reduces the quantity of labor that those firms demand. The result is higher unemployment among those groups of workers affected by the minimum wage. Those workers who remain employed benefit from a higher wage, but those who might have been employed at a lower wage are worse off.

The magnitude of these effects depends crucially on the elasticity of labor demand. Advocates of a high minimum wage argue that the demand for unskilled labor is relatively inelastic, so a high minimum wage depresses employment only slightly. Critics argue that labor demand is more elastic, especially in the long run when firms can adjust employment and production more fully. They also note that because many minimum-wage workers are teenagers from middle-class families, a high minimum wage is not well-targeted as a policy for helping the poor.

20-2b Welfare

welfare
government programs that supplement the incomes of the needy

One way for the government to raise the living standards of the poor is to supplement their incomes. The primary way the government does this is through the welfare system. **Welfare** is a broad and imprecise term that encompasses a variety of programs. Temporary Assistance for Needy Families (TANF) assists families with children and no adult able to support the family. Supplemental Security Income (SSI) helps people who have low incomes because of sickness or disability. For both programs, people cannot qualify for assistance simply by having limited financial resources. They must also establish some additional "need," such as having small children or a disability.

A common criticism of public assistance programs is that they create perverse incentives for those who might qualify. For example, it is said that these programs encourage families to break up (because many families qualify for financial assistance only if the father is absent) and encourage women to give birth out of wedlock (because many poor single women qualify for assistance only if they have children). Because poor single mothers are such a large part of the poverty problem, these policies are said to exacerbate the very problems they are supposed to cure. Such arguments led to an overhaul of the welfare system in 1996 with a law that limited the amount of time recipients could stay on welfare. That change in policy remains controversial.

Those who rebut these arguments and support more generous welfare point out that being a poor single mother on welfare is a difficult existence at best, and they do not believe that many people would choose such a life if it were not thrust upon them. Moreover, trends do not support the view that the decline of the two-parent family is connected to public assistance programs. The reduction in public assistance benefits in 1996 did not lead to a decline in the percentage of children living with only one parent.

20-2c Negative Income Tax

When the government collects taxes, it affects the distribution of income. This is clear in the case of a progressive income tax: Families with higher incomes pay a larger percentage of their income in taxes than do families with lower incomes. As Chapter 13 discussed, tax progressivity is a policy tool aimed at achieving vertical equity.

negative income tax
a tax system that collects revenue from high-income households and gives subsidies to low-income households

Many economists have advocated helping low-income households with a **negative income tax**. According to this policy, a progressive income tax would include not just rising average tax rates but also subsidies for families at the bottom of the income distribution. In other words, these families would "pay" a "negative tax."

For example, suppose the government used the following formula to compute a family's tax liability:

$$\text{Taxes owed} = (\tfrac{1}{3} \text{ of income}) - ₹15{,}000$$

In this case, a family that earned ₹180,000 would pay ₹45,000 in taxes, and a family that earned ₹90,000 would pay ₹15,000 in taxes. A family that earned ₹45,000 would owe nothing. And a family that earned ₹15,000 would "owe" –₹10,000. In other words, the government would send this family a check for ₹10,000.

A negative income tax provides what is sometimes called a **universal basic income**. In this example, a family that earns nothing on its own would receive ₹15,000 from the government. This way, no family would have an after-tax income below ₹15,000. Such a system can be viewed as a proportional tax of one-third of income, along with a grant to all families of ₹15,000.

Under a negative income tax, the only qualification required to receive government assistance is a low income. Depending on one's point of view, this feature can be either an advantage or a disadvantage. On the one hand, a negative income tax would establish a minimum standard of living for everyone, regardless of circumstance. On the other hand, a negative income tax would subsidize not only the unfortunate but also those who simply don't want to work and are, in some people's eyes, undeserving of public support.

Some actual tax provisions work much like a negative income tax. One is the Earned Income Tax Credit (EITC). This credit allows poor working families to receive income tax refunds greater than the taxes they paid during the year. Because the EITC applies only to the working poor, it does not discourage recipients from working as other antipoverty programs may. For the same reason, however, it also does not help alleviate poverty due to unemployment, sickness, or other inability to work.

Another tax provision that works like a negative income tax is the child tax credit. In 2021, this credit was increased so families were eligible to receive ₹3,600 for every child under age 6 and ₹3,000 for every child ages 6 to 17. Though the expanded child tax credit was passed as part of a pandemic relief bill and was scheduled to be temporary, President Biden proposed making it permanent as a policy to reduce childhood poverty.

20-2d In-Kind Transfers

Another way to help low-income households is to provide them directly with some of the goods and services they need to raise their living standards. For example, charities provide the poor with food, clothing, shelter, and toys at Christmas. And the government gives poor families food through the Supplemental Nutrition Assistance Program, or SNAP. This program, which replaced a similar one called food stamps, gives families a plastic card, like a debit card, that can be used to buy food at stores. The government also provides healthcare to many people with low income through a program called Medicaid.

Is it better to help the poor with these in-kind transfers or with cash payments? There is no clear answer.

Advocates of in-kind transfers say that such transfers are more reliable at helping those who are struggling. Among the poorest members of society, alcohol and drug addiction are more common than in society as a whole. By providing food, shelter, and healthcare directly, society can be more confident that it is not supporting such addictions but instead providing what the recipients truly need.

Advocates of cash payments say that in-kind transfers are inefficient and disrespectful. The government does not know what goods and services low-income households need most. Many of the poor are ordinary people down on their luck. Despite their misfortune, they are in the best position to decide how to raise their own living standards. Rather than giving people in-kind transfers of goods and services they may not want, it may be better to give them cash and allow them to buy what they think they need most.

20-2e Antipoverty Programs and Work Incentives

Policies aimed at combating poverty can sometimes have the unintended effect of discouraging people from escaping poverty on their own. For example, suppose that people need an income of ₹25,000 to maintain a minimally decent standard of living, and the government, out of concern for the less fortunate, guarantees everyone that income. Whatever a person earns, the government makes up the difference between that income and ₹25,000. What effect would you expect this policy to have?

The incentive effects of this policy are obvious: Anyone who would make less than ₹25,000 by working has little incentive to find and keep a job. For every dollar a person would earn, the government would reduce the income supplement by a dollar. In effect, the government taxes 100 percent of additional earnings. An effective marginal tax rate of 100 percent is a policy with a large deadweight loss.

This antipoverty program is hypothetical, but it is not entirely unrealistic. Welfare, Medicaid, SNAP, and the EITC are all programs aimed at helping those living in poverty, and they are all tied to income. As people's incomes increase, they become ineligible for these programs. When all these programs are taken together, effective marginal tax rates can be very high, sometimes even exceeding 100 percent, so low-income households are worse off when they earn more. By trying to help the less fortunate, the government discourages people from working. According to critics of antipoverty programs, these programs alter work attitudes and create a "culture of poverty."

The problem of disincentives might seem to have an easy solution: Reduce benefits to recipients more gradually as their incomes rise. For example, if people lose 30 cents of benefits for every dollar they earn, they face an effective marginal tax rate of 30 percent. This effective tax reduces work effort to some extent, but it does not eliminate the incentive to work completely.

The drawback of this solution is that it greatly increases the cost of programs to combat poverty. If benefits are phased out gradually as a person's income rises, then

In the News: Poverty during the Pandemic

During the Covid-19 pandemic, U.S. policymakers offered a safety net that, by historical standards, was very generous.

Temporary Pandemic Safety Net Drives Poverty to a Record Low

By Jason DeParle

Washington—The huge increase in government aid prompted by the coronavirus pandemic will cut poverty nearly in half this year from prepandemic levels and push the share of Americans in poverty to the lowest level on record, according to the most comprehensive analysis yet of a vast but temporary expansion of the safety net.

The number of poor Americans is expected to fall by nearly 20 million from 2018 levels, a decline of almost 45 percent. The country has never cut poverty so much in such a short period of time, and the development is especially notable since it defies economic headwinds—the economy has nearly seven million fewer jobs than it did before the pandemic.

The extraordinary reduction in poverty has come at extraordinary cost, with annual spending on major programs projected to rise fourfold to more than ₹1 trillion. Yet without further expensive new measures, millions of families may find the escape from poverty brief. The three programs that cut poverty most—stimulus checks, increased food stamps and expanded unemployment insurance—have ended or are scheduled to soon revert to their prepandemic size.

While poverty has fallen most among children, its retreat is remarkably broad: It has dropped among Americans who are white, Black, Latino and Asian, and among Americans of every age group and residents of every state.

"These are really large reductions in poverty—the largest short-term reductions we've seen," said Laura Wheaton of the Urban Institute, who produced the estimate with her colleagues Linda Giannarelli and Ilham Dehry. The institute's simulation model is widely used by government agencies. The New York Times requested the analysis, which expanded on an earlier projection.

The finding—that poverty plunged amid hard times at huge fiscal costs—comes at a moment of sharp debate about the future of the safety net.

The Biden administration has started making monthly payments to most families with children through an expansion of the child tax credit. Democrats want to make the yearlong effort permanent, which would reduce child poverty on a continuing basis by giving their families an income guarantee.

Progressives said the new numbers vindicated their contention that poverty levels reflected political choices and government programs could reduce economic need.

"Wow—these are stunning findings," said Bob Greenstein, a longtime proponent of safety net programs who is now at the Brookings Institution. "The policy response since the start of the pandemic goes beyond anything we've ever done, and the antipoverty effect dwarfs what most of us thought was possible."

Conservatives say that pandemic-era spending is unsustainable and would harm those just above the income threshold will also be eligible for substantial benefits. The more gradual the phase-out, the more people are eligible, and the more the program costs. Policymakers face a trade-off between burdening the poor with high effective marginal tax rates and burdening taxpayers with costly programs to reduce poverty.

There are other ways to reduce the work disincentive of antipoverty programs. One is to require any person collecting benefits to be employed or accept a government-provided job—a system sometimes called **workfare**. But this approach raises the question of whether the government is the best institution to serve as the employer of last resort. Another possibility is to provide benefits for only a limited period. This route was taken in the 1996 welfare reform bill, which imposed a five-year lifetime limit on benefits for welfare recipients. When President Clinton signed the bill, he said that welfare should be "a second chance, not a way of life." Yet cutting people off from benefits isn't a solution to poverty if they lack the skills needed to land well-paying jobs. That's why these issues are still with us, despite decades of efforts to solve them.

the poor in the long run, arguing that unconditional aid discourages work and marriage. The child tax credit offers families up to ₹300 per child a month whether or not parents have jobs, which critics call a return to failed welfare policies.

"There's no doubt that by shoveling trillions of dollars to the poor, you can reduce poverty," said Robert Rector of the Heritage Foundation. "But that's not efficient and it's not good for the poor because it produces social marginalization. You want policies that encourage work and marriage, not undermine it."

Poverty rates had reached new lows before the pandemic, Mr. Rector added, under policies meant to discourage welfare and promote work.

To understand how large the recent aid expansion has been, consider the experience of Kathryn Goodwin, a single mother of five in St. Charles, Mo., who managed a group of trailer parks before the pandemic eliminated her ₹33,000 job.

Without the pandemic-era expansions—passed in three rounds under both the Trump and Biden administrations Ms. Goodwin's job loss would have caused her income to plunge to about ₹29,000 (in jobless benefits, food stamps and other aid), leaving her officially poor.

Instead, her income rose above its prepandemic level, though she has not worked for a year. She received about ₹25,000 in unemployment benefits (about three times what she would have received before the pandemic) and ₹12,000 in stimulus checks. With increased food stamp benefits and other help, her income grew to ₹67,000—almost 30 percent more than when she had a job.

"Without that help, I literally don't know how I would have survived," she said. "We would have been homeless."

Still, Ms. Goodwin, 29, has mixed feelings about large payments with no stipulations.

"In my case, yes, it was very beneficial," she said. But she said that other people she knew bought big TVs and her former boyfriend bought drugs. "All this free money enabled him to be a worse addict than he already was," she said. "Why should taxpayers pay for that?"

The Urban Institute's projections show poverty falling to 7.7 percent this year from 13.9 percent in 2018. That decline, 45 percent, is nearly three times the previous three-year record, according to historical estimates by researchers at Columbia University. The projected drop in child poverty, to 5.6 from 14.2 percent, amounts to a decline of 61 percent. That exceeds the previous 50 years combined, the Columbia figures show....

Jessica Moore of St. Louis said the expanded aid helped her make a fresh start.

A single mother of three, Ms. Moore, 24, lost work as a banquet server at the pandemic's start but received enough in unemployment insurance and stimulus checks to buy a car and enroll in community college. She is studying to become an emergency medical technician, which promises to raise her earnings 50 percent.

"When you lose your job, you don't expect benefits that are more than you were making," she said. "It was a pure blessing." ■

Questions to Discuss

1. Do you think the unusual circumstances of the Covid pandemic called for a more generous safety net than is available in normal times? Why or why not?
2. Do you think the experiences described in the article argue for a more expansive safety net in normal times? Why or why not?

Source: New York Times, July 29, 2021.

Let us now look at some policies for India.

Employment Guarantee: The Case of MGNREGA

One of India's flagship anti-poverty programs is the Mahatma Gandhi National Rural Employment Guarantee Act (MGNREGA). It guaranteed 100 days of unskilled manual work to every rural household willing to do such work, and is a demand-based policy, which appeared particularly useful during the Covid Pandemic. The policy aims to help the rural poor particularly during a bad crop and adverse agricultural seasons along with uplifting and creating local infrastructure. Empirical research in development economics has shown that MGNREGA has helped reduce involuntary migration, improved rural wages, and improved the relative bargaining power for informal workers in the labor market.

From a managerial perspective, MGNREGA can influence firm decisions indirectly. By increasing the reservation wage in rural areas, the program may alter labor availability and wages for agribusinesses or rural contractors. Managers must anticipate seasonal spikes in labor cost or adapt through mechanization and location choices. Moreover, it provides a disincentive to work for more formal employers and therefore distorts the labor market equilibrium potentially. Proponents of a market-based solution would likely be irked as such policies are pursued in the long run.

Kasturba Gandhi Balika Vidyalaya (KGBV) - Building Human Capital and Bridging Gender Gaps

The KGBV scheme, launched in 2004, aims to provide residential schooling for girls from disadvantaged groups (SC/ST/OBC/minority/BPL) in educationally backward blocks, offering free boarding, lodging, uniforms, study materials, and schooling to ensure upper primary (and increasingly secondary) education for girls. Research on impact evaluations of the KGBV program has shown that the program has not only led to improvements in educational outcomes for girls but also has had indirect effects on health outcomes. Overall, the supply side measure has achieved its envisaged objectives, viz., bridging gender gaps in human capital accumulation. For managers and firms, this expands the future labor pool with potentially better educated female workers, enabling more inclusive recruitment, workforce diversification, and better planning around gender and social equity in human resources.

Kisan Credit Card Scheme (KCC) – Access and Expansion of Credit to Farming Households

The KCC scheme provides credit cards for farmers to enable them to obtain unsecured loans at subvented interest rates from scheduled commercial banks, including the nationalized banks in India. Research has shown that KCC has led to an expansion of credit option and led to higher yields and crop production. Although, in terms of actual usage of credit cards by farmers, the impact appears low. This suggests, KCCs could have effectively increased the risk tolerance of farmers, which helped them to make more productive investments, once they had access to these on-demand loans with ATM withdrawal facilities and other modern banking infrastructure.

Quick**Quiz**

7. A negative income tax is a policy under which
   a. all people with low income get government transfers.
   b. the government raises tax revenue without distorting incentives.
   c. everyone pays less than under a conventional income tax.
   d. some taxpayers are on the wrong side of the Laffer curve.

8. If the benefits from an antipoverty program are phased out as an individual's income increases, the program will
   a. encourage greater work effort from the poor.
   b. lead to an excess supply of labor among unskilled workers.
   c. cost the government more than a program that benefits everyone.
   d. increase the effective marginal tax rate that the poor face.

Answers are at the end of the chapter.

20-4 Conclusion

People have long reflected on the distribution of income in society. Plato, the ancient Greek philosopher, said that in an ideal society, the highest income would be no more than four times the lowest. Measuring inequality is difficult, but it is clear that most nations around the world, especially the United States, have much more inequality than Plato recommended.

It is known that governments can sometimes improve market outcomes. This principle is important when considering the distribution of income. Even when the allocation of resources reached by the invisible hand is efficient, it is usually far from equal, and it is not necessarily fair. Yet there is no broad consensus about what fairness means or how much the government should redistribute income. Lawmakers often debate the progressivity of the tax code and the generosity of the social safety net. Economics alone cannot settle the disagreement.

We have learnt that people face trade-offs and that people respond to incentives. These principles are intertwined in discussions of economic inequality. When the government enacts policies to partly equalize incomes, it may distort incentives, alter behavior, and make the allocation of resources less efficient. As a result, policymakers face a trade-off between equality and efficiency. The more equally they slice the economic pie, the smaller it may become. This doesn't mean that policymakers should necessarily refrain from income redistribution. But it does suggest that they approach redistributive policies aware of their potential costs.

Chapter in a Nutshell

- Data on the distribution of income show a wide disparity in U.S. society. The richest fifth of families earns more than twelve times as much as the poorest fifth.
- Because in-kind transfers, tax credits, the economic life cycle, transitory income, and economic mobility are so important for understanding variation in living standards, it is hard to gauge the degree of inequality in society using data on the distribution of income in a single year. When these other factors are considered, they tend to suggest that economic well-being is more equally distributed than annual income.
- Political philosophers differ in their views about the role of government in altering the distribution of income. Utilitarians (such as John Stuart Mill) would choose the distribution of income that maximizes the sum of utility of everyone in society. Liberal contractarians (such as John Rawls) would determine the distribution of income as if we were behind a "veil of igno-

rance" that prevented us from knowing our stations in life. Libertarians (such as Robert Nozick) would have the government enforce individual rights to ensure a fair process but then would not be concerned about inequality in the resulting distribution of income.

- Various policies aim to help people with low income—minimum-wage laws, welfare, negative income taxes, and in-kind transfers. While these policies help alleviate poverty, they can have unintended side effects. Because financial assistance declines as income rises, the poor often face very high effective marginal tax rates, which discourage them from escaping poverty on their own.

Key Concepts

poverty rate, p. 406
poverty line, p. 406
in-kind transfers, p. 410
life cycle, p. 410
permanent income, p. 411
welfare, p. 414
negative income tax, p. 414

Questions for Review

1. Does the richest fifth of the U.S. population earn closer to three, six, or twelve times the income of the poorest fifth?
2. What has happened to the income share of the richest fifth of the U.S. population over the past 50 years?
3. What groups in the U.S. population are most likely to live in poverty?
4. When gauging the amount of inequality, why do transitory and life cycle variations in income cause difficulties?
5. What are the pros and cons of in-kind (rather than cash) transfers to low-income households?
6. Describe how antipoverty programs can discourage people from working. How might you reduce this disincentive? What are the disadvantages of your proposed policy?
7. Describe some policy efforts in India undertaken for gender equality in employment and human capital.

Problems and Applications

1. Table 3 shows that the percentage of children in families with income below the poverty line far exceeds the percentage of the elderly in such families. How might the allocation of government money across different social programs contribute to this phenomenon?
2. This chapter discusses the importance of economic mobility.
   a. What policies might the government pursue to increase economic mobility from year to year within a generation?
   b. What policies might the government pursue to increase economic mobility from generation to generation?
   c. Do you think we should reduce spending on current welfare programs to increase spending on programs that enhance economic mobility? What are some of the advantages and disadvantages of doing so?
3. Consider two communities. In one community, ten families have incomes of ₹100,000 each, and ten families have incomes of ₹20,000 each. In the other community, ten families have incomes of ₹250,000 each, and ten families have incomes of ₹25,000 each.
   a. In which community is the distribution of income more unequal? In which community is the problem of poverty likely to be worse?
   b. Which distribution of income would Rawls prefer? Explain.
   c. Which distribution of income do you prefer? Explain.
   d. Why might someone have the opposite preference?
4. Suppose there are two possible income distributions in a society of ten people. In the first distribution,

nine people have incomes of $60,000, and one person has an income of $20,000. In the second distribution, all ten people have incomes of $50,000.

a. If the society had the first income distribution, what would be the utilitarian argument for redistributing income?
b. Which income distribution would Rawls consider more equitable? Explain.
c. Which income distribution would Nozick consider more equitable? Explain.

5. The poverty rate would be substantially lower if the market value of in-kind transfers were added to family income. The largest in-kind transfer is Medicaid, the government health program for those with low incomes. Let's say the program costs ₹10,000 per recipient family.
   a. If the government gave each recipient family a ₹10,000 check instead of enrolling them in the Medicaid program, do you think that most of these families would spend that money to purchase health insurance? Why? (Recall that the poverty level for a family of four is about ₹25,000.)
   b. How does your answer to part (a) affect your view about whether we should determine the poverty rate by valuing in-kind transfers at the price the government pays for them? Explain.
   c. How does your answer to part (a) affect your view about whether we should provide assistance to low-income families in the form of cash transfers or in-kind transfers? Explain.

6. Consider two of the income security programs in the United States: Temporary Assistance for Needy Families (TANF) and the Earned Income Tax Credit (EITC).
   a. When a woman with children and very low income earns an extra dollar, she receives less in TANF benefits. What do you think is the effect of this feature of TANF on the labor supply of low-income women? Explain.
   b. The EITC provides greater benefits as low-income workers earn more income (up to a point). What do you think is the effect of this program on the labor supply of low-income individuals? Explain.
   c. What are the disadvantages of eliminating TANF and allocating the savings to the EITC?

Quick**Quiz** Answers

1. c 2. a 3. d 4. c 5. a 6. d

Chapter

21

The Theory of Consumer Choice

When you walk into a big store or click on an online shopping site, you are confronted with thousands of goods you might buy. Many things may appeal to you, but because your financial resources are limited, you probably can't buy all of them. So you look at the prices and buy a selection of items that, given your resources, best suits your needs and desires.

This chapter develops a theory that describes how people make these decisions. So far, this book has summarized consumer behavior with the demand curve. As we have seen, the demand curve reflects consumers' willingness to pay for a good. When the price of the good rises, consumers are willing to pay for fewer units, so the quantity demanded falls. We now look more closely at the decisions that lie behind the demand curve. The theory of consumer choice presented here provides a deeper understanding of demand, just as the theory of the competitive firm provides a deeper understanding of supply.

GAUDILAB/SHUTTERSTOCK.COM; LEC-IATNOIR/E+/GETTY IMAGES

One of the recurring principles we have learnt is that people face trade-offs. This principle is the essence of the theory of consumer choice. When consumers buy more of one good, they can afford less of other goods they want. When they spend more time enjoying leisure and less time working, they earn less and consume less. When they spend more of their income now, they reduce their saving and have less to spend in the future. The theory of consumer choice examines how people facing these trade-offs make decisions and how they respond to changes in their environment.

The theory is useful in analyzing a wide range of issues. After developing the basic framework, we ask:

- Do all demand curves slope downward?
- How do wages affect labor supply?
- How do interest rates affect household saving?

These questions might seem unrelated, but the theory of consumer choice can help answer each of them.

21-1 The Budget Constraint: What a Consumer Can Afford

Other things being equal, most people would like to consume more—to drive nicer cars, wear trendier clothes, eat at better restaurants, or take grander vacations. People consume less than they desire because their spending is **constrained**, or limited, by their income. Our study of consumer choice begins with this constraint.

21-1a Representing Consumption Opportunities in a Graph

Consider Prakriti, a medieval age consumer who buys only two goods in the ancient town of Sonanagar: pizza and Pepsi. In the real world, people buy hundreds of different kinds of goods, and a diet of only pizza and Pepsi would not be healthy by any means in Sonanagar, or for that in the modern world. But assuming only two goods simplifies the model without altering the basic insights about consumer choice.

Prakriti's income is ₹1,000 per month, and because she is insatiable, she spends all of it on pizza and Pepsi. The price of a pizza is ₹10, and the price of a liter of Pepsi is ₹2. Her income and these market prices constrain her spending.

The table in Figure 1 shows some of the combinations of pizza and Pepsi that Prakriti can buy. The first row shows that if she spends all her income on pizza, she can eat 100 pizzas during the month, but she would not be able to buy any Pepsi at all. The second row shows another possible consumption bundle: 90 pizzas and 50 liters of Pepsi. And so on. Each consumption bundle in the table costs exactly ₹1,000.

The graph in Figure 1 illustrates the consumption bundles that Prakriti can choose. The vertical axis measures the number of liters of Pepsi, and the horizontal axis measures the number of pizzas. Three points are marked on this figure. At point A, Prakriti buys no Pepsi and consumes 100 pizzas. At point B, she buys no pizza and consumes 500 liters of Pepsi. At point C, she buys 50 pizzas and 250 liters of Pepsi. Point C, which is exactly at the middle of the line from A to B, is the point at which Prakriti spends an equal amount (₹500) on the two goods. These are only three of the many combinations of pizza and Pepsi that she can choose. All the points on the line from A to B are possible. This line, called the **budget constraint**, shows the consumption bundles that a consumer can afford. In this case, it shows the trade-off between pizza and Pepsi that Prakriti faces.

budget constraint the limit on the consumption bundles that a consumer can afford

Figure 1

The Consumer's Budget Constraint

The budget constraint shows the bundles of goods that the consumer can buy with a given income. Here, she buys bundles of pizza and Pepsi. The table and graph show what the consumer can afford if her income is ₹1,000, the price of pizza is ₹10, and the price of Pepsi is ₹2.

Number of Pizzas	Liters of Pepsi	Spending on Pizza	Spending on Pepsi	Total Spending
100	0	₹1,000	₹ 0	₹1,000
90	50	900	100	1,000
80	100	800	200	1,000
70	150	700	300	1,000
60	200	600	400	1,000
50	250	500	500	1,000
40	300	400	600	1,000
30	350	300	700	1,000
20	400	200	800	1,000
10	450	100	900	1,000
0	500	0	1,000	1,000

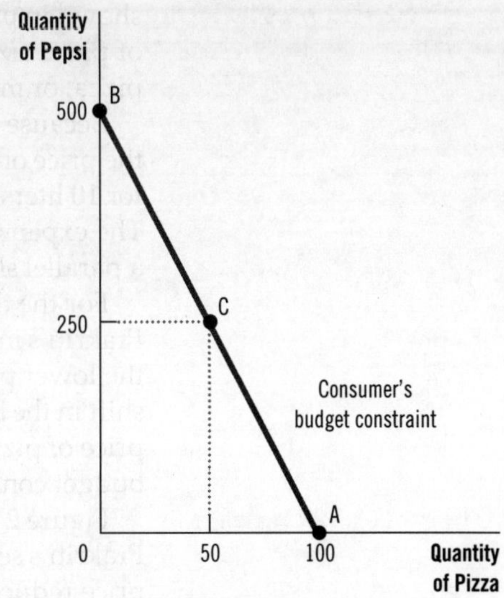

The slope of the budget constraint measures the rate at which the consumer can trade one good for the other. Recall that the slope between two points is calculated as the change in the vertical distance divided by the change in the horizontal distance ("rise over run"). From point A to point B, the vertical distance is 500 liters, and the horizontal distance is 100 pizzas, so the slope is 5 liters per pizza. (Actually, because the budget constraint slopes downward, the slope is a negative number. But for our purposes, we can ignore the minus sign.)

Notice that the slope of the budget constraint equals the **relative price** of the two goods—the price of one good compared with the price of the other. A pizza costs five times as much as a liter of Pepsi, so the opportunity cost of a pizza is 5 liters of Pepsi. The budget constraint's slope of 5 reflects the trade-off the market is offering Prakriti: 1 pizza for 5 liters of Pepsi.

21-1b Shifts in the Budget Constraint

The budget constraint shows the opportunities available to Prakriti. It is drawn given her income and the prices of the two goods. If her income or the prices change, the budget constraint shifts. Consider three examples of how such a shift might occur.

Suppose first that Prakriti's income increases from ₹1,000 to ₹2,000 while prices remain the same. With higher income, she can afford more of both goods. The increase in income shifts the budget constraint outward, as in panel (a) of Figure 2. Because the relative price of the two goods has not changed, the slope of the new budget constraint is the same as the slope of the initial budget constraint. That is, an increase in income leads to a parallel shift in the budget constraint.

Now suppose that the price of Pepsi falls from ₹2 to ₹1 while Prakriti's income remains at ₹1,000 and the price of pizza remains at ₹10. If she spends her entire income on pizza, the price of Pepsi is irrelevant. In this case, she can still buy only 100 pizzas, so the point on the horizontal axis representing 100 pizzas and 0 liters of Pepsi stays the same. But as long as she is buying some Pepsi, the lower price of Pepsi expands her set of opportunities. The budget constraint shifts outward, as shown in panel (b) of Figure 2. The lower price allows her to buy the same amount of pizza as before and more Pepsi, the same amount of Pepsi as before and more pizza, or more of both goods.

Because the slope reflects the relative price of pizza and Pepsi, it changes when the price of Pepsi falls. With the lower price of Pepsi, Prakriti can now trade a pizza for 10 liters of Pepsi rather than 5. As a result, the new budget constraint is steeper. The expansion in her opportunities is represented by a rotational shift rather than a parallel shift.

For the third example, suppose that the price of pizza falls from ₹10 to ₹5 while Prakriti's income remains at ₹1,000 and the price of Pepsi remains at ₹2. Once again, the lower price expands her set of opportunities and leads to a rotational outward shift in the budget constraint, as shown in panel (c) of Figure 2. Now, with the lower price of pizza, Prakriti can trade a pizza for 2.5 liters of Pepsi rather than 5, and the budget constraint becomes flatter.

Figure 2 shows what happens when a higher income or a lower price expands Prakriti's set of opportunities. The opposite occurs when a lower income or a higher price reduces her opportunities. The pictures look much the same as Figure 2, but

Figure 2

Shifts in the Consumer's Budget Constraint

In panel (a), an increase in the consumer's income shifts the budget constraint outward. The slope remains the same because the relative price of pizza and Pepsi has not changed. In panel (b), a decrease in the price of Pepsi shifts the budget constraint outward, while in panel (c), a decrease in the price of pizza shifts the budget constraint outward. In these two cases, the slope changes because the relative price of pizza and Pepsi has changed.

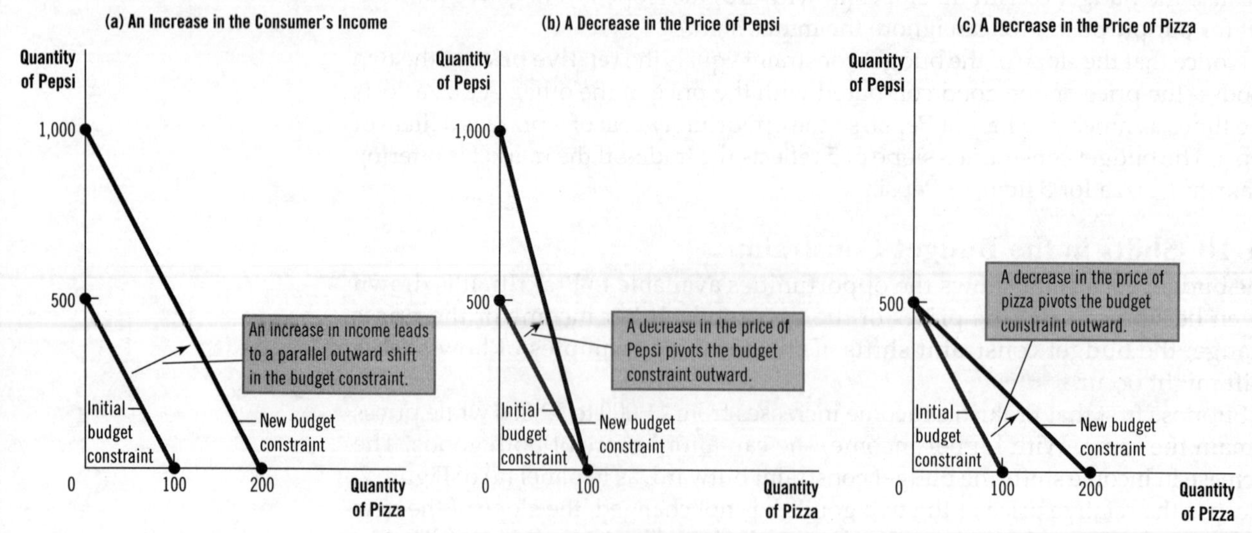

with the direction of the arrows reversed. And when more than one change occurs at the same time, we can analyze the overall impact by graphing and comparing the initial and final budget constraints.

Quick**Quiz**

1. Vyas buys hamburgers for ₹10 and kala khatta for ₹2. He has income of ₹100. His budget constraint will shift inward if
   a. the price of hamburgers rises to ₹12.
   b. the price of kala khatta falls to ₹1.
   c. his income rises to ₹150.
   d. the price of hamburgers, the price of kala khatta, and his income all rise by 50 percent.
2. Mandodari also buys hamburgers for ₹10 and kala khatta for ₹2. She has income of ₹200. Her budget constraint will
   a. the price of hamburgers falls to ₹5, the price of kala khatta falls to ₹1, and her income falls to ₹100.
   b. the price of hamburgers rises to ₹20, the price of kala khatta rises to ₹4, and her income remains the same.
   c. the price of hamburgers falls to ₹8, the price of kala khatta falls to ₹1, and her income rises to ₹240.
   d. the price of hamburgers rises to ₹20, the price of kala khatta rises to ₹4, and her income rises to ₹500.

Answers are at the end of the chapter.

21-2 Preferences: What a Consumer Wants

The goal of this chapter is to understand how consumers make choices. The budget constraint is one piece of the analysis: It shows the combinations of goods that consumers can afford given their income and the prices of the goods. Their choices, however, depend not only on their budget constraint but also on their preferences.

21-2a Representing Preferences with Indifference Curves

Prakriti's preferences allow her to choose among different bundles of pizza and Pepsi. If you offer her two different bundles, she chooses the one that best suits her tastes. If the two bundles suit her tastes equally well, we say that Prakriti is **indifferent** between the two bundles.

Just as we have represented Prakriti's budget constraint graphically, we can also represent her preferences graphically. We do this with indifference curves. An **indifference curve** shows the various bundles of consumption that make a consumer equally happy. In this case, the indifference curves show the combinations of pizza and Pepsi with which Prakriti is equally satisfied.

indifference curve a curve that shows consumption bundles that give the consumer the same level of satisfaction

Figure 3 shows two of Prakriti's many indifference curves. We can see that she is indifferent among combinations A, B, and C because they are all on the same curve. So if her consumption of pizza decreases, say, from point A to point B, her consumption of Pepsi must increase to keep her equally happy. If her consumption of pizza decreases again, from point B to point C, the amount of Pepsi consumed must increase yet again.

marginal rate of substitution the rate at which a consumer is willing to trade one good for another

The slope at any point on an indifference curve equals the rate at which Prakriti is willing to substitute one good for the other. (The slope is negative, but we can ignore the minus sign.) This rate is called the **marginal rate of substitution** (*MRS*). In this case, it measures how much additional Pepsi Prakriti requires to be compensated for a one-unit reduction in pizza consumption.

Figure 3

The Consumer's Preferences

The consumer's preferences are represented with indifference curves, which show the combinations of pizza and Pepsi that make the consumer equally satisfied. Because the consumer prefers more of a good, points on a higher indifference curve (I_2) are preferred to points on a lower indifference curve (I_1). The marginal rate of substitution (*MRS*) shows the rate at which the consumer is willing to trade Pepsi for pizza. It measures the quantity of Pepsi the consumer must receive in exchange for 1 pizza.

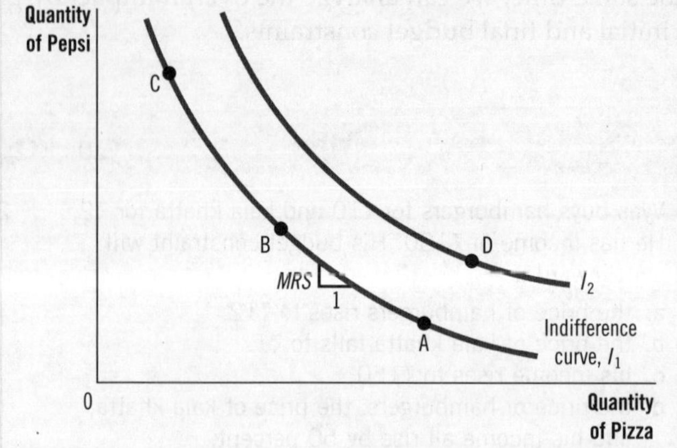

Because the indifference curves are not straight lines, the marginal rate of substitution is not the same at all points on a given indifference curve. The rate at which Prakriti is willing to trade one good for the other depends on the quantities of the goods she is already consuming. In other words, the rate at which she is willing to trade pizza for Pepsi depends on whether she is hungrier or thirstier, and her hunger and thirst, in turn, depend on her current consumption of pizza and Pepsi.

Prakriti is equally happy at all points on a given indifference curve, but she prefers some indifference curves to others. Because she prefers more consumption to less, higher indifference curves are preferred to lower ones. In Figure 3, any point on curve I_2 is preferred to any point on curve I_1.

Prakriti's set of indifference curves gives a complete ranking of her preferences. That is, we can use the indifference curves to rank any two bundles of goods. For example, the indifference curves tell us that Prakriti prefers the bundle at point D to the bundle at point A because point D is on a higher indifference curve than point A. (That may be obvious, however, because point D offers more of both goods.) The indifference curves also tell us that Prakriti prefers the bundle at point D to the bundle at point C because point D is on a higher indifference curve. Even though point D has less Pepsi than point C, it has more than enough extra pizza to make her prefer it. By seeing which point is on the higher indifference curve, we can use the set of indifference curves to rank any combinations of pizza and Pepsi.

21-2b Four Properties of Indifference Curves

Because indifference curves represent a consumer's preferences, their properties reflect those preferences. Here are four properties that describe most indifference curves:

- **Property 1: Higher indifference curves are preferred to lower ones.** People usually prefer to consume more rather than less. This preference for greater quantities is reflected in the indifference curves. As Figure 3 shows, higher indifference curves represent larger quantities of goods

Figure 4

The Impossibility of Intersecting Indifference Curves

This situation can never happen. According to these indifference curves, the consumer would be equally satisfied at points A, B, and C, even though point C has more of both goods than point A.

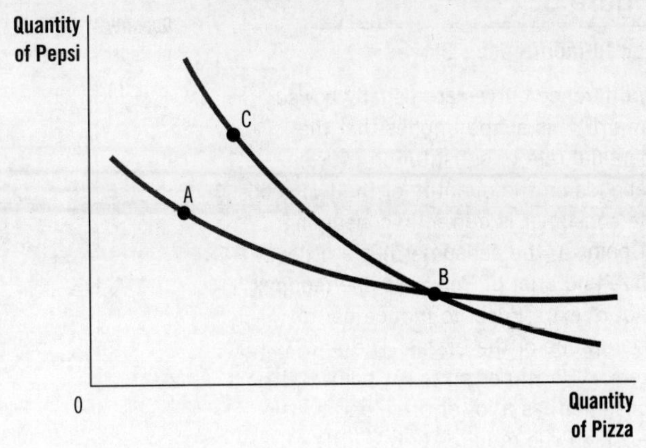

than lower indifference curves. Thus, a consumer prefers being on higher indifference curves.

- **Property 2: Indifference curves slope downward.** The slope of an indifference curve reflects the rate at which a consumer is willing to substitute one good for the other. In most cases, the consumer likes both goods, so if the quantity of one good decreases, the quantity of the other good must increase for the consumer to be equally happy. For this reason, most indifference curves slope downward.
- **Property 3: Indifference curves do not cross.** To see why this is true, suppose that two indifference curves did cross, as in Figure 4. Then, because point A is on the same indifference curve as point B, the two points would make the consumer equally happy. In addition, because point B is on the same indifference curve as point C, these two points would make the consumer equally happy. But this means that points A and C would also make the consumer equally happy, even though point C has more of both goods. This contradicts our assumption that the consumer always prefers more of both goods to less. Thus, indifference curves cannot cross.
- **Property 4: Indifference curves are bowed inward.** The slope of an indifference curve is the marginal rate of substitution—the rate at which the consumer will trade one good for the other. The marginal rate of substitution (*MRS*) usually depends on the amount of each good being consumed. Because people are more willing to trade away goods that they have in abundance and are less willing to trade away goods of which they have little, the indifference curves are bowed inward toward the graph's origin. As an example, consider Figure 5. At point A, Prakriti has a lot of Pepsi and only a little pizza, so she is hungry but not thirsty. To give up 1 pizza, she would have to receive 6 liters of Pepsi: The *MRS* is 6 liters of Pepsi per pizza. By contrast, at point B, Prakriti has a little Pepsi and a lot of pizza, so she is thirsty but not hungry. At this point, she would be willing to give up 1 pizza to get 1 liter of Pepsi: The *MRS*

Figure 5

Bowed Indifference Curves

Indifference curves are usually bowed inward. This shape implies that the marginal rate of substitution (*MRS*) depends on the quantity of the two goods the consumer is currently consuming. At point A, the consumer has a little pizza and a lot of Pepsi, so she requires a lot of extra Pepsi to induce her to give up one of the pizzas: The *MRS* is 6 liters of Pepsi per pizza. At point B, the consumer has a lot of pizza and a little Pepsi, so she requires only a little extra Pepsi to induce her to give up one of the pizzas: The *MRS* is 1 liter of Pepsi per pizza.

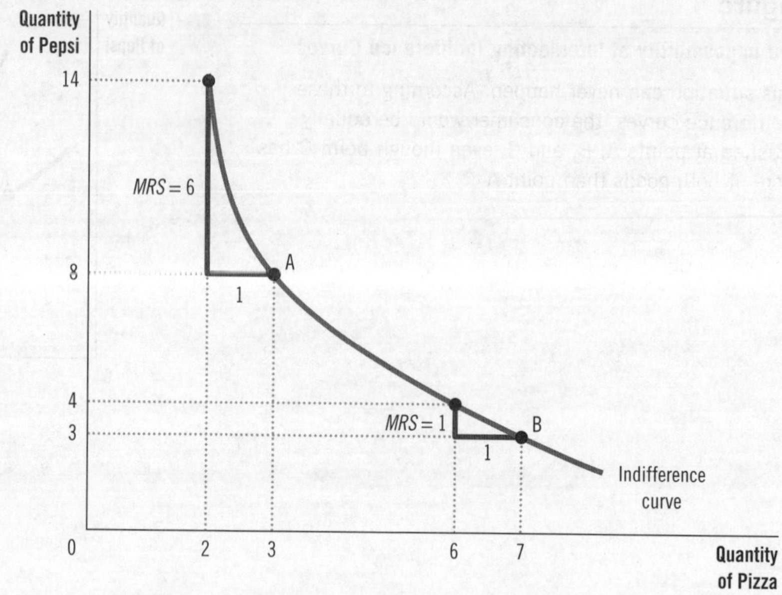

is 1 liter of Pepsi per pizza. Thus, the bowed shape of the indifference curve reflects Prakriti's greater willingness to give up something that she already has in abundance.

21-2c Two Extreme Examples of Indifference Curves

The shape of an indifference curve reveals a consumer's willingness to trade one good for the other. When the goods are easy to substitute for each other, the indifference curves are less bowed; when the goods are hard to substitute, the indifference curves are very bowed. To see why, consider two extreme cases.

Perfect Substitutes Suppose that someone offered you bundles of U.S. nickels and U.S. dimes. How would you rank the different bundles?

One possibility is that you would care only about the total monetary value of each bundle. If so, you would always be willing to trade 2 nickels for 1 dime. Your marginal rate of substitution between nickels and dimes would be a fixed number: $MRS = 2$, regardless of the number of nickels and dimes in the bundle.

We can represent these preferences for nickels and dimes with the indifference curves in panel (a) of Figure 6. Because the marginal rate of substitution is constant, the indifference curves are straight lines. In the case of straight indifference curves, the two goods are said to be **perfect substitutes.**

perfect substitutes two goods with straight-line indifference curves

Perfect Complements Suppose now that someone offered you bundles of shoes. Some of the shoes fit your left foot, others your right foot. How would you rank these different bundles?

In this case, you might care only about how many pairs of shoes you have. Single shoes aren't much good. So you would judge a bundle based on the number of

Figure 6

Perfect Substitutes and Perfect Complements

When two goods are perfectly substitutable, such as nickels and dimes, the indifference curves are straight lines, as shown in panel (a). When two goods are perfectly complementary, such as left shoes and right shoes, the indifference curves are right angles, as shown in panel (b).

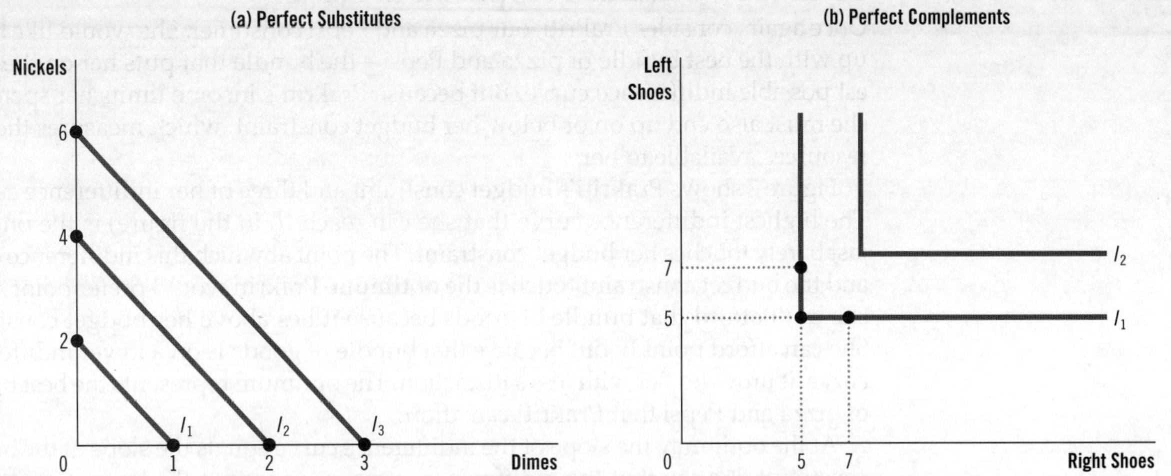

pairs you could assemble from it. A bundle of 5 left shoes and 7 right shoes yields only 5 pairs.

The indifference curves in panel (b) of Figure 6 represent these preferences. A bundle with 5 left shoes and 7 right shoes is just as good as a bundle with 7 left shoes and 5 right shoes. And these are equivalent to a bundle with 5 of each. The indifference curves are right angles. In the case of right-angle indifference curves, the two goods are said to be **perfect complements.**

perfect complements
two goods with right-angle indifference curves

In the real world, most goods are neither perfect substitutes (like nickels and dimes) nor perfect complements (like right and left shoes). Perfect substitutes and perfect complements are extreme cases. They are introduced here not because they are common but because they illustrate how indifference curves reflect a consumer's preferences. For most goods, the indifference curves are bowed inward, but not so bowed that they become right angles.

Quick**Quiz**

3. At two points on an indifference curve,
   a. the consumer has the same income.
   b. the consumer has the same marginal rate of substitution.
   c. the bundles of goods cost the consumer the same amount.
   d. the bundles of goods yield the consumer the same satisfaction.

4. At any point on an indifference curve, the slope of the curve measures the consumer's
   a. income.
   b. willingness to trade one good for the other.
   c. perception of the two goods as substitutes or complements.
   d. elasticity of demand.

Answers are at the end of the chapter.

21-3 Optimization: What a Consumer Chooses

We now have the building blocks of the theory of consumer choice: the budget constraint (which shows what consumers can afford) and preferences (which show what they want). Let's put them together to see what consumers choose.

21-3a The Consumer's Optimal Choices

Once again, consider Prakriti, our pizza and Pepsi consumer. She would like to end up with the best bundle of pizza and Pepsi—the bundle that puts her on the highest possible indifference curve. But because Prakriti's income limits her spending, she must also end up on or below her budget constraint, which measures the total resources available to her.

Figure 7 shows Prakriti's budget constraint and three of her indifference curves. The highest indifference curve that she can reach (I_2 in the figure) is the one that just barely touches her budget constraint. The point at which this indifference curve and the budget constraint touch is the **optimum**. Prakriti would prefer point A, but she can't afford that bundle of goods because it lies above her budget constraint. She can afford point B, but because that bundle of goods is on a lower indifference curve, it provides her with less satisfaction. The optimum represents the best bundle of pizza and Pepsi that Prakriti can afford.

At the optimum, the slope of the indifference curve equals the slope of the budget constraint. We say that the indifference curve is **tangent** to the budget constraint. The slope of the indifference curve is the marginal rate of substitution between pizza and Pepsi, and the slope of the budget constraint is the relative price of pizza and Pepsi. This leads to an important conclusion: **The consumer chooses the quantities of the two goods so the marginal rate of substitution equals the relative price.**

Chapter 7 discussed how market prices reflect the marginal value that consumers place on goods. This analysis of consumer choice shows the same result in another way. In making her consumption choices, Prakriti takes the relative price of the two goods as given and then chooses an optimum bundle of goods at which her marginal rate of substitution equals this relative price. The relative price is the rate at which the **market** is willing to trade one good for the other, while the marginal

Figure 7

The Consumer's Optimum

The consumer chooses the point on her budget constraint that lies on the highest indifference curve. Here, the highest indifference curve the consumer can reach is I_2. The consumer prefers point A, which lies on indifference curve I_3, but she can't afford this bundle of pizza and Pepsi. By contrast, point B is affordable, but because it lies on a lower indifference curve, she doesn't prefer it. At the optimum, the marginal rate of substitution equals the relative price of the two goods.

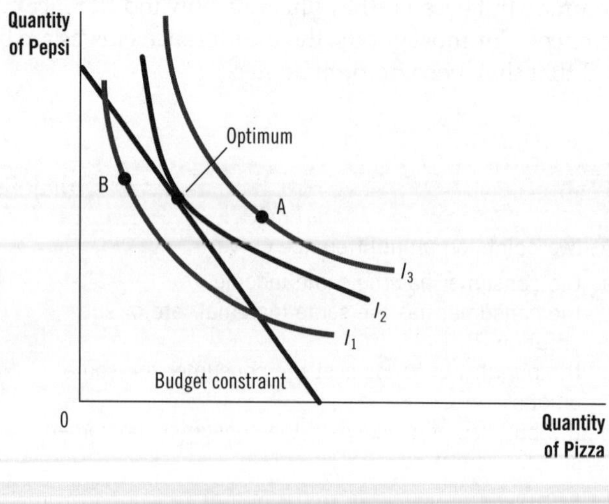

FYI

Utility: An Alternative Way to Describe Preferences and Optimization

We have used indifference curves to represent consumer preferences. Another common way to represent preferences is with the concept of **utility**. Utility is an abstract measure of the satisfaction or happiness that a consumer receives from a bundle of goods. Economists say that a consumer prefers one bundle of goods to another if it provides more utility than the other.

Indifference curves and utility are closely related. Because the consumer prefers points on higher indifference curves, bundles of goods on higher indifference curves provide higher utility. Because the consumer is equally happy with all points on the same indifference curve, all these bundles provide the same utility. You can think of an indifference curve as an "equal-utility" curve.

The **marginal utility** of any good is the increase in utility that the consumer gets from an additional unit of it. Most goods are assumed to exhibit **diminishing marginal utility**: The more of the good the consumer already has, the lower the marginal utility provided by an extra unit of that good.

The marginal rate of substitution between two goods depends on their marginal utilities. For example, if the marginal utility of good X is twice the marginal utility of good Y, then a person would need 2 units of Y to compensate for losing 1 unit of X, and the *MRS* equals 2. More generally, the marginal rate of substitution (and the slope of the indifference curve) equals the marginal utility of one good divided by the marginal utility of the other good.

Utility analysis provides another way to describe consumer optimization. Recall that, at the consumer's optimum, the marginal rate of substitution equals the ratio of prices. That is,

$$MRS = P_X/P_Y.$$

Because the marginal rate of substitution equals the ratio of marginal utilities, we can write this condition for optimization as

$$MU_X/MU_Y = P_X/P_Y.$$

Now rearrange this expression so it becomes

$$MU_X/P_X = MU_Y/P_Y.$$

This equation has a simple interpretation: At the optimum, the marginal utility per dollar spent on good X equals the marginal utility per dollar spent on good Y. If this equality did not hold, the consumer could increase her utility by spending less on the good that provided lower marginal utility per dollar and more on the good that provided higher marginal utility per dollar.

When economists discuss consumer choice, they sometimes express the theory using different words. One economist might say that the consumer's goal is to maximize utility. Another economist might say that the consumer's goal is to be on the highest possible indifference curve. The first economist would conclude that at the consumer's optimum, the marginal utility per dollar is the same for all goods, while the second would describe the optimum as the point at which the indifference curve is tangent to the budget constraint. These are two ways of saying the same thing. ■

rate of substitution is the rate at which the **consumer** is willing to trade one good for the other. At the optimum, Prakriti's valuation of the two goods (as measured by the marginal rate of substitution) equals the market's valuation (as measured by the relative price). Put another way, when consumers optimize, the relative prices of goods in the marketplace reflect the relative value that consumers place on them.

21-3b How Changes in Income Affect the Consumer's Choices

Let's now examine how Prakriti's consumption decision responds to changes in her income. To be specific, suppose her income increases. As we have seen, an increase in income leads to a parallel outward shift in the budget constraint, as in Figure 8. Because the relative price of the two goods has not changed, the slope of the new budget constraint is the same as the slope of the initial budget constraint.

The expanded budget constraint allows Prakriti to reach a higher indifference curve, reflecting a more desirable bundle of pizza and Pepsi. Given the shift in the budget constraint and Prakriti's preferences, her optimum moves from the point labeled "initial optimum" to the point labeled "new optimum."

In Figure 8, Prakriti chooses to consume more Pepsi **and** more pizza. The logic of the model does not require increased consumption of both goods in response to increased income, but this situation is the most common. As Chapter 4 discussed, if consumers want more of a good when their incomes rise, economists call it a

Figure 8

An Increase in Income

When the consumer's income rises, the budget constraint shifts outward. If both goods are normal goods, the consumer responds to the increase in income by buying more of both of them. Here, the consumer buys more pizza and more Pepsi.

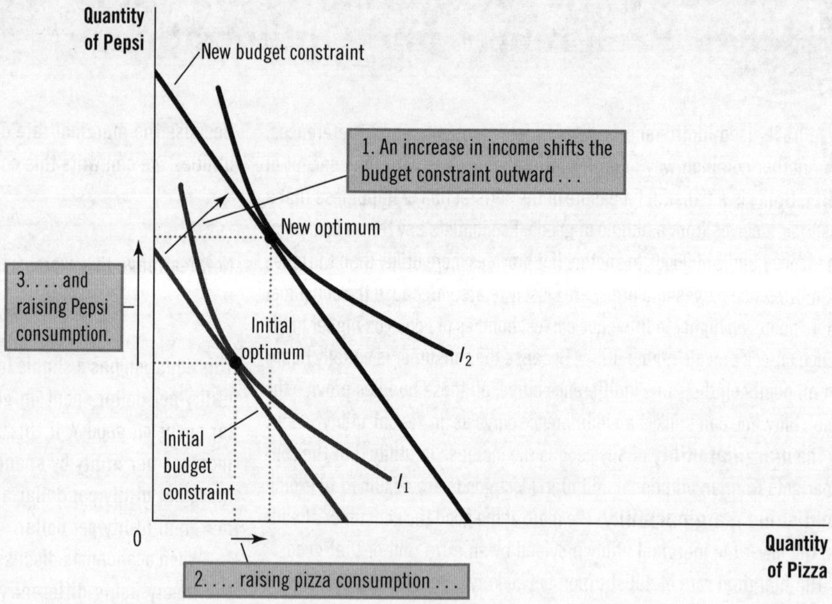

normal good
a good for which an increase in income raises the quantity demanded

inferior good
a good for which an increase in income reduces the quantity demanded

normal good. The indifference curves in Figure 8 are drawn assuming that both pizza and Pepsi are normal goods.

Figure 9 shows an example in which an increase in income induces Prakriti to buy more pizza but less Pepsi. If consumers buy less of a good when their incomes rise, economists call it an **inferior good**. Figure 9 is drawn assuming that pizza is a normal good and Pepsi is an inferior good.

Figure 9

An Inferior Good

A good is inferior if the consumer buys less of it when her income rises. Here, Pepsi is an inferior good: When the consumer's income increases and the budget constraint shifts outward, the consumer buys more pizza but less Pepsi.

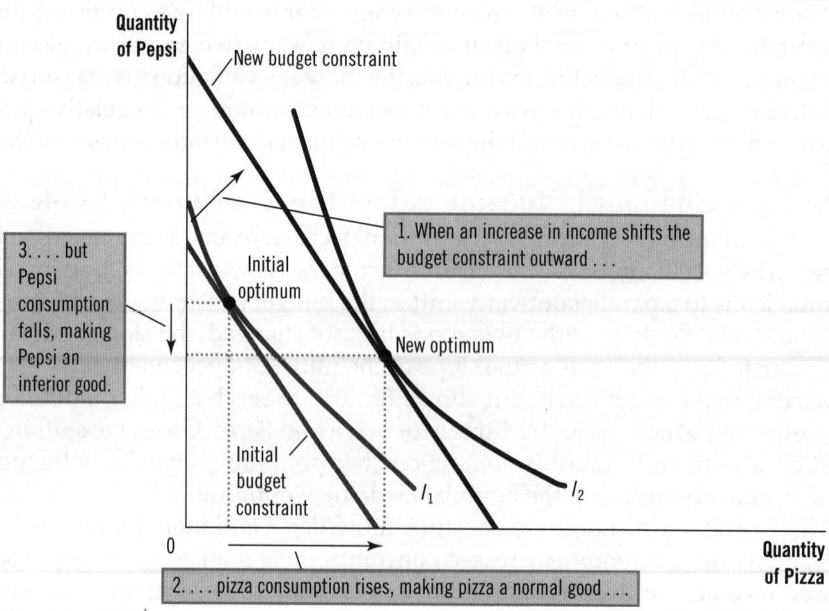

Although most goods in the world are normal goods, some are inferior goods. An example is bus rides. As income increases, consumers are more likely to own cars or use Uber and less likely to ride the bus. Bus rides, therefore, are an inferior good.

21-3c How Changes in Prices Affect the Consumer's Choices

Let's now use this model of consumer choice to consider how a change in the price of one of the goods alters Prakriti's choices.

Suppose that the price of Pepsi falls. As noted earlier, a fall in the price of either good shifts the budget constraint outward and, by changing the relative price of the two goods, changes the slope of the budget constraint as well. Figure 10 shows how the fall in the price of Pepsi rotates the budget constraint and changes the optimum.

How such a change in the budget constraint alters the quantities of the two goods purchased depends on Prakriti's preferences. For the indifference curves in this figure, she buys more Pepsi and less pizza. But it takes only a little creativity to draw indifference curves with other outcomes. A consumer could plausibly respond to the lower price of Pepsi by buying more of both goods.

income effect
the change in consumption that results when a price change moves the consumer to a higher or lower indifference curve

substitution effect
the change in consumption that results when a price change moves the consumer along a given indifference curve to a point with a new marginal rate of substitution

21-3d Income and Substitution Effects

The impact of a change in the price of a good on the quantities purchased can be decomposed into two effects: an **income effect** and a **substitution effect**. When consumers respond to a price change, both effects are at work.

To see what these effects are, consider how Prakriti might respond when she learns that the price of Pepsi has fallen. Two thoughts may occur to her:

- "Great news! Now that Pepsi is cheaper, my income has greater purchasing power. I am, in effect, richer than I was. Because I am richer, I can buy both more pizza and more Pepsi." (This is the income effect.)

Figure 10

A Change in Price

When the price of Pepsi falls, the consumer's budget constraint shifts outward and changes slope. The consumer moves from the initial optimum to the new optimum, which changes her purchases of both pizza and Pepsi. In this case, the quantity of Pepsi consumed rises, and the quantity of pizza consumed falls.

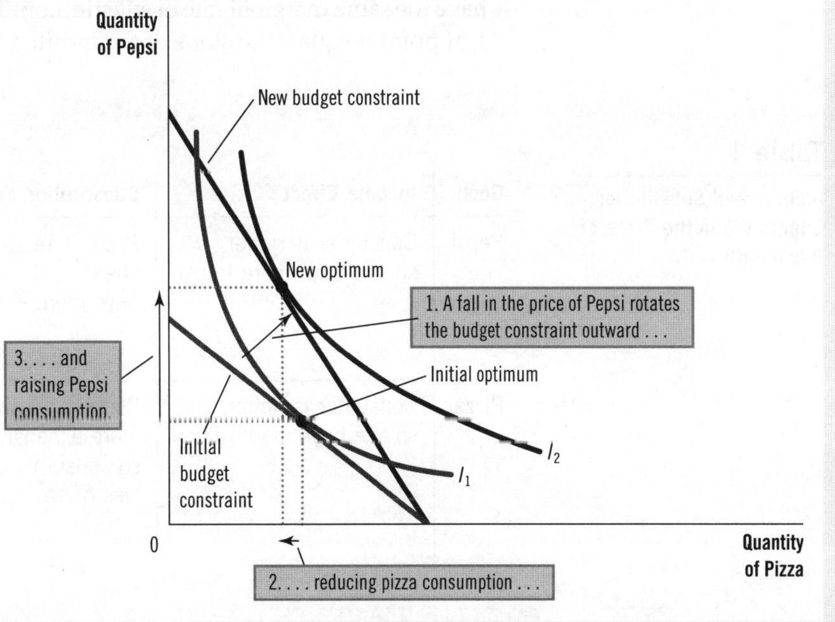

- "With the lower price of Pepsi, I get more liters of Pepsi for every pizza that I give up. Because pizza is now relatively more expensive, I should buy less pizza and more Pepsi." (This is the substitution effect.)

Both statements make sense. The decrease in the price of Pepsi makes Prakriti better off. If pizza and Pepsi are both normal goods, she will want to spread this increase in her purchasing power over both goods. This income effect tends to make her buy more pizza and more Pepsi. Yet at the same time, the opportunity cost of pizza (in terms of forgone Pepsi) has risen, and the opportunity cost of Pepsi (in terms of forgone pizza) has fallen. This substitution effect tends to make Prakriti choose less pizza and more Pepsi.

Now consider the result of these two effects occurring at the same time. Prakriti certainly buys more Pepsi because the income and substitution effects both act to increase the consumption of Pepsi. But for pizza, the income and substitution effects push in opposite directions. As a result, it is not clear whether Prakriti buys more pizza or less. The outcome could go either way, depending on the sizes of the income and substitution effects. Table 1 summarizes these conclusions.

The income and substitution effects can be interpreted using indifference curves. **The income effect is the change in consumption that results from the movement to a new indifference curve. The substitution effect is the change in consumption that results from moving to a new point on the same indifference curve with a different marginal rate of substitution.**

Figure 11 shows how to decompose the change in Prakriti's decision into the income effect and the substitution effect. When the price of Pepsi falls, she moves from the initial optimum, point A, to the new optimum, point C. We can imagine this change as occurring in two steps. First, Prakriti moves **along** the initial indifference curve, I_1, from point A to point B. She is equally happy at these two points, but at point B, the marginal rate of substitution reflects the new relative price. (The dashed line through point B is parallel to the new budget constraint and reflects the new relative price.) Next, Prakriti **shifts** to the higher indifference curve, I_2, by moving from point B to point C. Even though point B and point C are on different indifference curves, they have the same marginal rate of substitution. That is, the slope of the indifference curve I_1 at point B equals the slope of the indifference curve I_2 at point C.

Table 1

Income and Substitution Effects When the Price of Pepsi Falls

Good	Income Effect	Substitution Effect	Total Effect
Pepsi	Consumer is richer, so she buys more Pepsi.	Pepsi is relatively cheaper, so consumer buys more Pepsi.	Income and substitution effects act in the same direction, so consumer buys more Pepsi.
Pizza	Consumer is richer, so she buys more pizza.	Pizza is relatively more expensive, so consumer buys less pizza.	Income and substitution effects act in opposite directions, so the total effect on pizza consumption is ambiguous.

Figure 11

Income and Substitution Effects

The effect of a change in price can be broken down into an income effect and a substitution effect. The substitution effect—the movement along an indifference curve to a point with a different marginal rate of substitution—is the change from point A to point B along indifference curve I_1. The income effect—the shift to a higher indifference curve—is the change from point B on indifference curve I_1 to point C on indifference curve I_2.

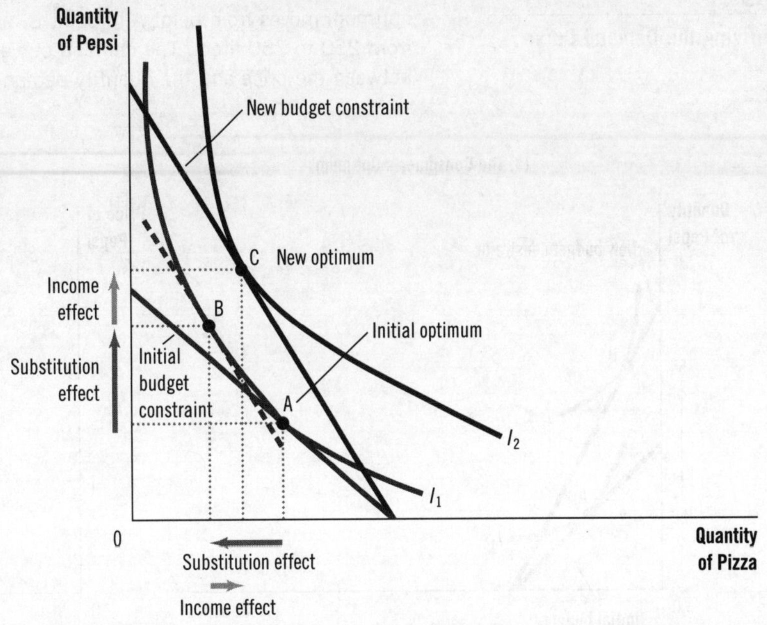

Prakriti never actually chooses point B, but this hypothetical point is useful to clarify the two effects that determine her decision. The change from point A to point B represents a pure change in the marginal rate of substitution without any change in Prakriti's welfare. And the change from point B to point C represents a pure change in welfare without any change in the marginal rate of substitution. The movement from A to B shows the substitution effect, and the movement from B to C shows the income effect.

21-3e Deriving the Demand Curve

A consumer's demand curve for any good shows the quantity demanded at any price. In essence, it summarizes the optimal decisions that arise from the consumer's budget constraint and preferences.

For example, Figure 12 considers Prakriti's demand for Pepsi. Panel (a) shows that when the price of a liter falls from ₹2 to ₹1, her budget constraint shifts outward. Because of both income and substitution effects, she increases her purchases of Pepsi from 250 to 750 liters. Panel (b) shows the demand curve that results from these decisions. In this way, the theory of consumer choice provides the theoretical foundation for an individual's demand curve.

It may be comforting to know that the demand curve arises naturally from the theory of consumer choice, but this exercise by itself does not justify developing the theory. There is no need for a rigorous analytic framework just to establish that people respond to price changes. The theory of consumer choice is, however, useful in studying various decisions that people make as they go about their lives, as we see in the next section.

Figure 12

Deriving the Demand Curve

Panel (a) shows that when the price of Pepsi falls from ₹2 to ₹1, the consumer's optimum moves from point A to point B, and the quantity of Pepsi consumed rises from 250 to 750 liters. The demand curve in panel (b) reflects this relationship between the price and the quantity demanded.

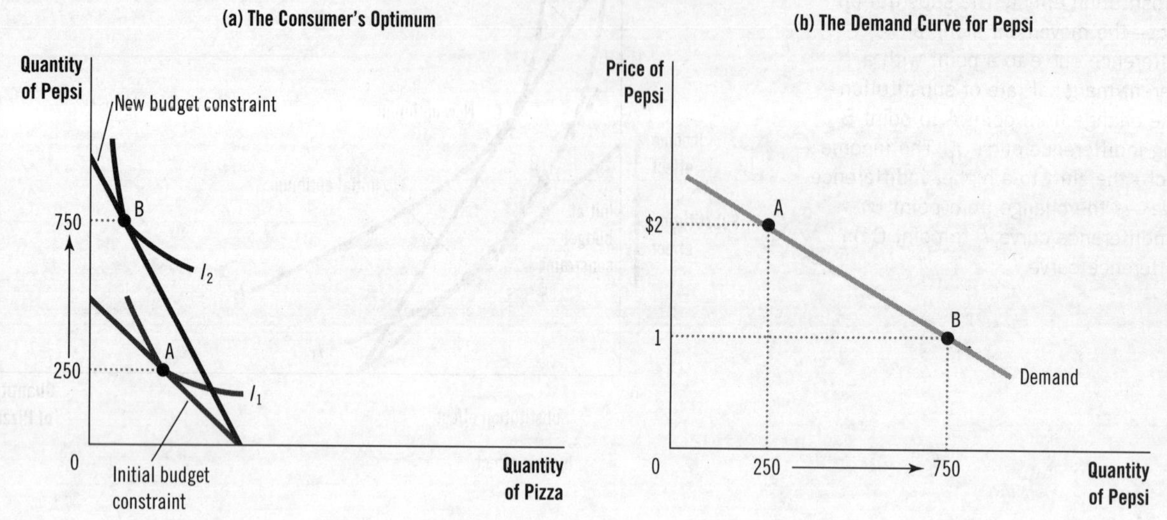

Quick**Quiz**

5. Bart and Lisa are both optimizing consumers in the markets for shirts and hats, where they pay ₹100 for a shirt and ₹50 for a hat. Bart buys 8 shirts and 4 hats, while Lisa buys 6 shirts and 12 hats. From this information, we can infer that Bart's marginal rate of substitution is _____ hats per shirt, while Lisa's is _____ hats per shirt.
   a. 2; 1
   b. 2; 2
   c. 4; 1
   d. 4; 2

6. Maggie buys peanut butter and jelly, both of which are normal goods. When the price of peanut butter rises, the income effect induces Maggie to buy _______ peanut butter and _______ jelly.
   a. more; more
   b. more; less
   c. less; more
   d. less; less

7. Ned buys wine and bread. When the price of wine rises, the substitution effect induces Ned to buy _______ wine and _______ bread.
   a. more; more
   b. more; less
   c. less; more
   d. less; less

Answers are at the end of the chapter.

21-4 Three Applications

Now that we have developed the basic theory of consumer choice, let's use it to shed light on three questions about how the economy works.

21-4a Do All Demand Curves Slope Downward?

Normally, when the price of a good rises, people buy less of it. This typical behavior, called the **law of demand**, is reflected in the downward slope of the demand curve.

As a matter of economic theory, however, demand curves can sometimes slope upward. In other words, consumers can sometimes violate the law of demand and buy **more** of a good when the price rises. To see how this can happen, consider Figure 13. In this example, Kanad the consumer buys two goods: meat and potatoes. Initially, his budget constraint is the line from point A to point B, and the optimum is point C. When the price of potatoes rises, his budget constraint shifts inward and is now the line from point A to point D. His optimum moves to point E. An increase in the price of potatoes leads Kanad to buy more potatoes.

Why does Kanad respond in this strange way? In this example, meat is a normal good, but potatoes are a strongly inferior good. That is, potatoes are a good that Kanad buys a lot less of when his income rises and a lot more of when his income falls. In Figure 13, the increase in the price of potatoes makes Kanad poorer in the sense that he moves to a lower indifference curve. Because he is poorer, the income effect makes him want to buy less meat (the normal good) and more potatoes (the inferior good). At the same time, because potatoes have become more expensive relative to meat, the substitution effect makes Kanad want to buy more meat and fewer potatoes. Note that the income and substitution effects push in opposite directions. If the income effect is larger than the substitution effect, as it is in this example, Kanad responds to the higher price of potatoes by buying less meat and more potatoes.

Economists use the term **Giffen good** to describe a good that violates the law of demand. The term is named for the economist Robert Giffen (1837–1910), who first noted this possibility. In this example, potatoes are a Giffen good. Giffen goods are inferior goods for which the income effect dominates the substitution effect. They therefore have demand curves that slope upward.

Giffen good
a good for which an increase in the price raises the quantity demanded

Figure 13

A Giffen Good

In this example, when the price of potatoes rises, the consumer's optimum shifts from point C to point E. In this case, the consumer responds to the higher price of potatoes by buying less meat and more potatoes.

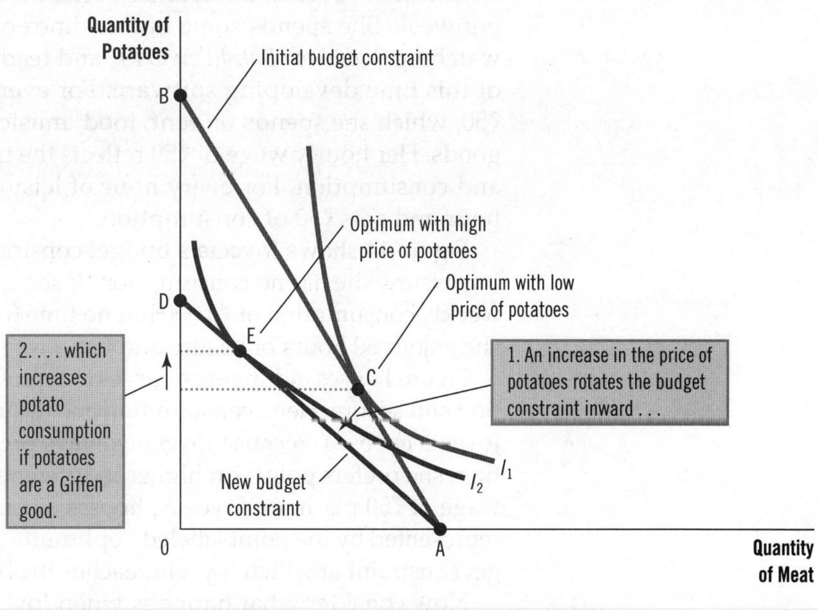

Case Study

The Search for Giffen Goods

Have any actual Giffen goods ever been observed? Some historians suggest that potatoes were a Giffen good during the Irish potato famine of the 19th century. Potatoes were such a large part of people's diet that when the price of potatoes rose, the change had a large income effect. People responded to their reduced living standard by cutting back on the luxury of meat and buying more of the staple food of potatoes. Thus, it is sometimes argued that a higher price of potatoes actually raised the quantity of potatoes demanded.

A study by Robert Jensen and Nolan Miller, published in the *American Economic Review* in 2008, produced more concrete evidence for the existence of Giffen goods. These two economists conducted a field experiment for five months in the Chinese province of Hunan. They gave randomly selected households vouchers that subsidized the purchase of rice, a staple in local diets, and used surveys to measure how the consumption of rice responded to changes in the price. They found strong evidence that many poor households exhibited Giffen behavior. Lowering the price of rice with the subsidy voucher caused these households to reduce their rice consumption, and removing the subsidy had the opposite effect. Jensen and Miller wrote, "To the best of our knowledge, this is the first rigorous empirical evidence of Giffen behavior."

Thus, the theory of consumer choice allows demand curves to slope upward, and sometimes that strange phenomenon actually occurs. As a result, the law of demand introduced earlier is not completely reliable. It is safe to say, however, that Giffen goods are rare. ●

21-4b How Do Wages Affect Labor Supply?

The theory of consumer choice can be used to analyze not only how people allocate their income but also how they allocate their time. Most people spend some of their time on leisurely pursuits and some of it working so they can afford to buy goods and services to consume. The essence of the time-allocation problem is the trade-off between leisure and consumption.

Consider Joyeeta, a freelance software designer. She is awake for 100 hours per week. She spends some of this time enjoying leisure—playing *Lego Friends*, watching *Byomkesh Bakshi on OTT*, and reading this textbook. She spends the rest of this time developing software. For every hour she works coding, she earns ₹50, which she spends on rent, food, music downloads, and other consumption goods. Her hourly wage of ₹50 reflects the trade-off Joyeeta faces between leisure and consumption. For every hour of leisure she gives up, she works one more hour and gets ₹50 of consumption.

Figure 14 shows Joyeeta's budget constraint. If she spends all 100 hours enjoying leisure, she has no consumption. If she spends all 100 hours working, she has a weekly consumption of ₹5,000 but no time for leisure. If she works a 40-hour week, she enjoys 60 hours of leisure and has a weekly consumption of ₹2,000.

Figure 14 uses indifference curves to represent Joyeeta's preferences for consumption and leisure. Here, consumption and leisure are the two "goods" between which Joyeeta chooses. Because Joyeeta always prefers more leisure and more consumption, she prefers points on higher indifference curves to points on lower ones. At a wage of ₹50 per hour, Joyeeta chooses a combination of consumption and leisure represented by the point labeled "optimum." The optimum is the point on the budget constraint at which Joyeeta reaches the highest possible indifference curve, I_2.

Now consider what happens when Joyeeta's wage increases from ₹50 to ₹60 per hour. Figure 15 illustrates two possible outcomes. In both cases, the budget

Figure 14

The Work-Leisure Decision

This figure shows Joyeeta's budget constraint for deciding how much to work, her indifference curves for consumption and leisure, and her optimum.

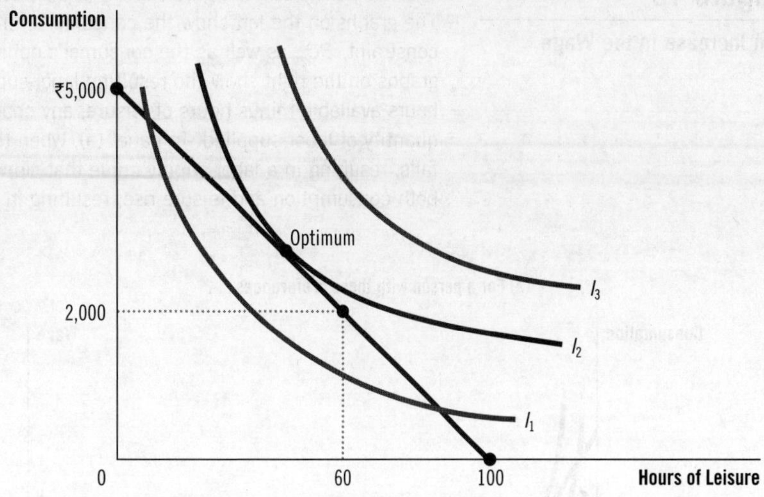

constraint, shown in the left graphs, shifts outward from BC_1 to BC_2. In the process, each budget constraint becomes steeper, reflecting the change in relative price: At the higher wage, Joyeeta earns more consumption for every hour of leisure that she gives up.

Joyeeta's preferences, as represented by her indifference curves, determine how her choice regarding consumption and leisure responds to the higher wage. In both panels, consumption rises. Yet the responses of leisure to the wage change are different in the two cases. In panel (a), Joyeeta responds to the higher wage by enjoying less leisure. In panel (b), Joyeeta responds by enjoying more leisure.

Joyeeta's decision between leisure and consumption determines her supply of labor because the more leisure she enjoys, the less time she has left to work. In each panel of Figure 15, the right graph shows the labor-supply curve implied by Joyeeta's decision. In panel (a), a higher wage induces Joyeeta to enjoy less leisure and work more, so the labor-supply curve slopes upward. In panel (b), a higher wage induces Joyeeta to enjoy more leisure and work less, so the labor-supply curve slopes "backward."

At first, the backward-sloping labor-supply curve is puzzling. Why would a person respond to a higher wage by working less? The answer comes from considering the income and substitution effects of a higher wage.

Consider first the substitution effect. When Joyeeta's wage rises, leisure becomes more expensive relative to consumption, encouraging Joyeeta to substitute away from leisure and toward consumption. In other words, the substitution effect induces Joyeeta to work more in response to higher wages and tends to make the labor-supply curve slope upward.

Now consider the income effect. When Joyeeta's wage rises, she moves to a higher indifference curve, so she is better off than before. As long as consumption and leisure are both normal goods, Joyeeta will want to use her increased well-being to enjoy both higher consumption and more leisure. In other words, the income effect induces her to work less and thus tends to make the labor-supply curve slope backward.

Figure 15

An Increase in the Wage

The two panels of this figure show how a person might respond to an increase in the wage. The graphs on the left show the consumer's initial budget constraint, BC_1, and new budget constraint, BC_2, as well as the consumer's optimal choices over consumption and leisure. The graphs on the right show the resulting labor-supply curve. Because hours worked equal the total hours available minus hours of leisure, any change in leisure implies an opposite change in the quantity of labor supplied. In panel (a), when the wage rises, consumption rises, and leisure falls, resulting in a labor-supply curve that slopes upward. In panel (b), when the wage rises, both consumption and leisure rise, resulting in a labor-supply curve that slopes backward.

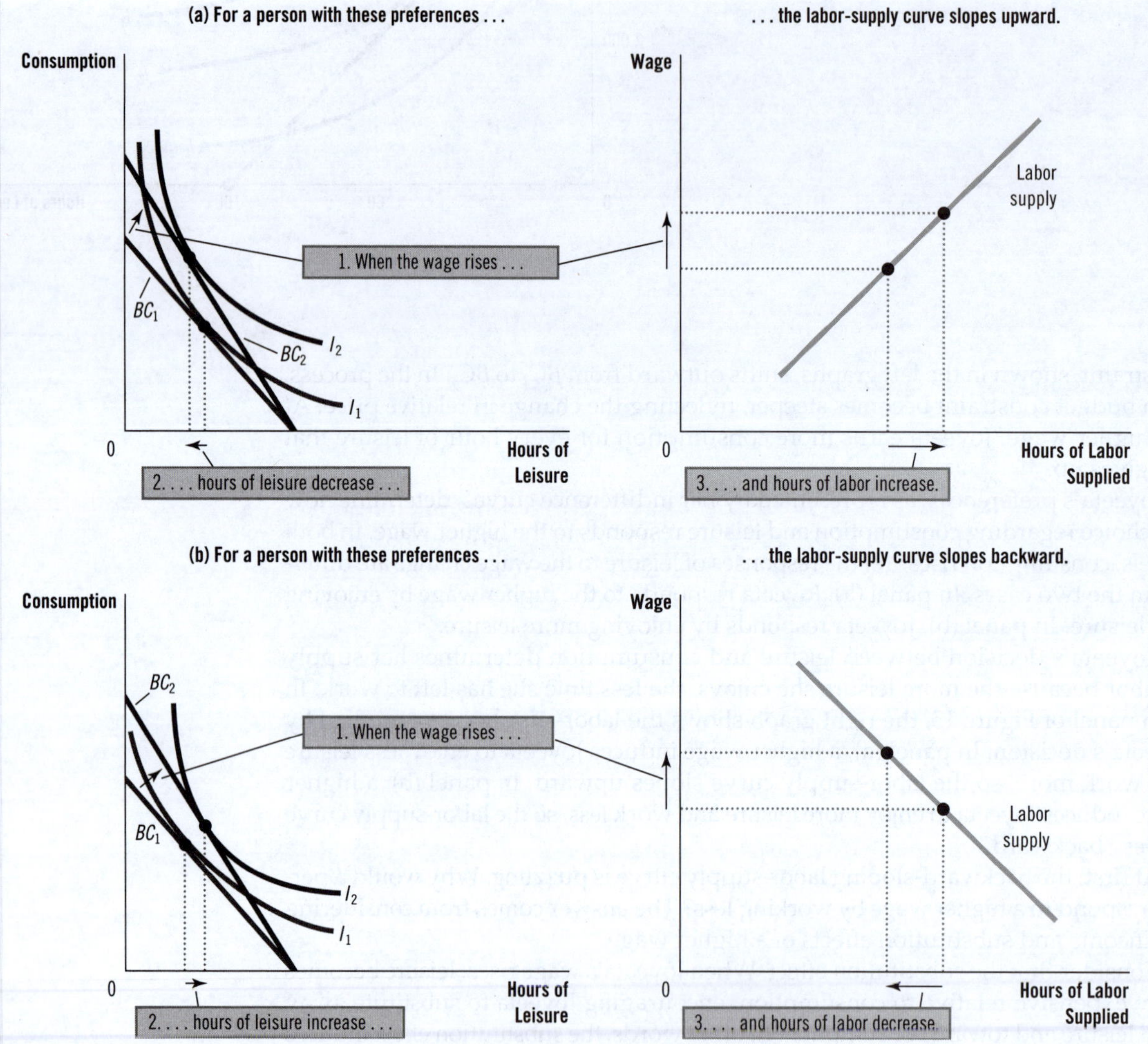

In the end, economic theory does not give a clear prediction about whether an increase in the wage induces Joyeeta to work more or less. If the substitution effect exceeds the income effect, she works more. If the income effect exceeds the substitution effect, she works less. The labor-supply curve, therefore, could be either upward- or backward-sloping.

Figure 16

A Backward-Bending Labor-Supply Curve

Here, the labor-supply curve slopes upward at low wages because the substitution effect dominates the income effect. But as the wage rises, the income effect starts to dominate the substitution effect, and the labor-supply curve bends backward.

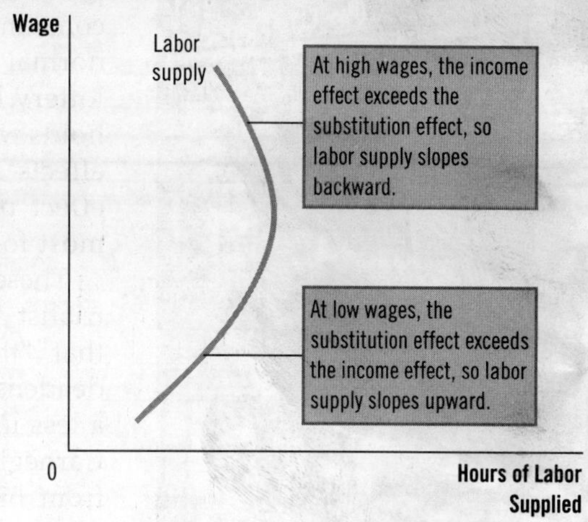

Moreover, the slope of the labor-supply curve need not be the same at all wages. For example, depending on a person's preferences, it is possible for the substitution effect to dominate the income effect at low wages and the income effect to dominate the substitution effect at high wages. In this case, as in Figure 16, the labor-supply curve starts off upward-sloping but then bends backward as the wage increases.

Case Study

Income Effects on Labor Supply: Historical Trends, Lottery Winners, and the Carnegie Conjecture

The idea of a backward-sloping labor-supply curve is not a mere theoretical curiosity. Evidence indicates that the labor-supply curve, considered over long periods, does indeed slope backward. A hundred years ago, many people worked six days a week. Today, five-day workweeks are the norm. While the length of the workweek has been falling, the wage of the typical worker (adjusted for inflation) has been rising.

Here is how economists explain this historical pattern: Over time, advances in technology increase workers' productivity and the demand for labor. This increase in labor demand raises equilibrium wages. As wages rise, so does the reward for working. Yet rather than responding to this increased incentive by working more, most workers take advantage of their greater prosperity by increasing leisure. In other words, the income effect of higher wages dominates the substitution effect.

Further evidence for a strong income effect on labor supply comes from a very different kind of data: winners of lotteries. Winners of large lottery prizes see large increases in their incomes and, as a result, large outward shifts in their budget constraints. Because the winners' wages have not changed, however, the **slopes** of their budget constraints remain the same. There is, therefore, no substitution effect. By comparing lottery winners with those who played the lottery but lost, researchers can isolate the income effect on labor supply.

A 2021 study by four University of Chicago economists did exactly that and found some striking results. For every dollar that people win, their total after-tax labor earnings decline by 40 cents. In other words, 40 percent of

DAVID EDSAM/ALAMY STOCK PHOTO

"No more 9 to 5 for me."

winnings are used to increase leisure (or perhaps to switch to a more pleasant, lower-paying job), while 60 percent are spent to increase consumption of goods and services. For example, for those near the normal retirement age, lottery winners are much more likely than lottery losers to retire early. The researchers also report that households with higher income before winning the lottery exhibited larger effects on leisure and smaller effects on consumption. The income effect on labor supply appears substantial, especially among the most fortunate.

These findings would not have surprised the 19th-century industrialist Andrew Carnegie. In his book *The Gospel of Wealth*, he warned that "the parent who leaves his son enormous wealth generally deadens the talents and energies of the son and tempts him to lead a less useful and less worthy life than he otherwise would." That is, Carnegie viewed the income effect on labor supply to be large and, from his paternalistic perspective, regrettable. That may be partly why, during his life and at his death, Carnegie gave much of his vast fortune to charity. ●

21-4c How Do Interest Rates Affect Household Saving?

An important decision that every person faces is how much income to consume today and how much to save for the future. We can use the theory of consumer choice to analyze this decision. In doing so, we examine how the amount that people save depends on the interest rate their savings will earn.

Consider the decision facing Ramvilas, a worker planning for retirement. To keep things simple, divide Ramvilas's life into two periods. In the first, Ramvilas is young and working. In the second, he is old and retired. When young, Ramvilas earns ₹100,000. He divides this income between current consumption and saving. When he is old, Ramvilas consumes what he has saved, including the interest that his savings have earned.

We can view "consumption when young" and "consumption when old" as the two goods that Ramvilas must choose between. The interest rate determines the relative price of these two goods. Suppose the interest rate is 10 percent. Then for every dollar that Ramvilas saves when young, he can consume ₹1.10 when old.

Figure 17 shows Ramvilas's budget constraint. If he saves nothing, he consumes ₹100,000 when young and nothing when old. If he saves everything, he consumes nothing when young and ₹110,000 when old. The budget constraint shows these and all the intermediate possibilities.

Figure 17 uses indifference curves to represent Ramvilas's preferences for consumption in the two periods. Because he prefers more consumption in both periods of his life, he prefers points on higher indifference curves to points on lower ones. Given his preferences, Ramvilas chooses the optimal combination of consumption in the two periods, which is the point on the budget constraint that is on the highest possible indifference curve. At this optimum, Ramvilas consumes ₹50,000 when young and ₹55,000 when old.

Now consider what happens when the interest rate increases from 10 percent to 20 percent. Figure 18 shows two possible outcomes. In both cases, the budget constraint shifts outward and becomes steeper. At the new, higher interest rate, Ramvilas gets more consumption when old for every dollar of consumption that he gives up when young

Figure 17

The Consumption-Saving Decision

This figure shows the budget constraint for a person deciding how much to consume in the two periods of his life, the indifference curves representing his preferences, and the optimum.

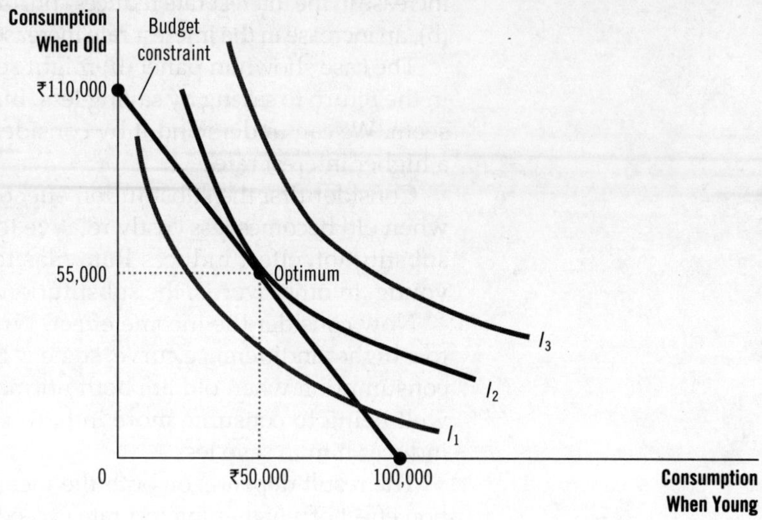

Figure 18

An Increase in the Interest Rate

In both panels, an increase in the interest rate shifts the budget constraint outward. In panel (a), consumption when young falls, and consumption when old rises. The result is an increase in saving when young. In panel (b), consumption in both periods rises. The result is a decrease in saving when young.

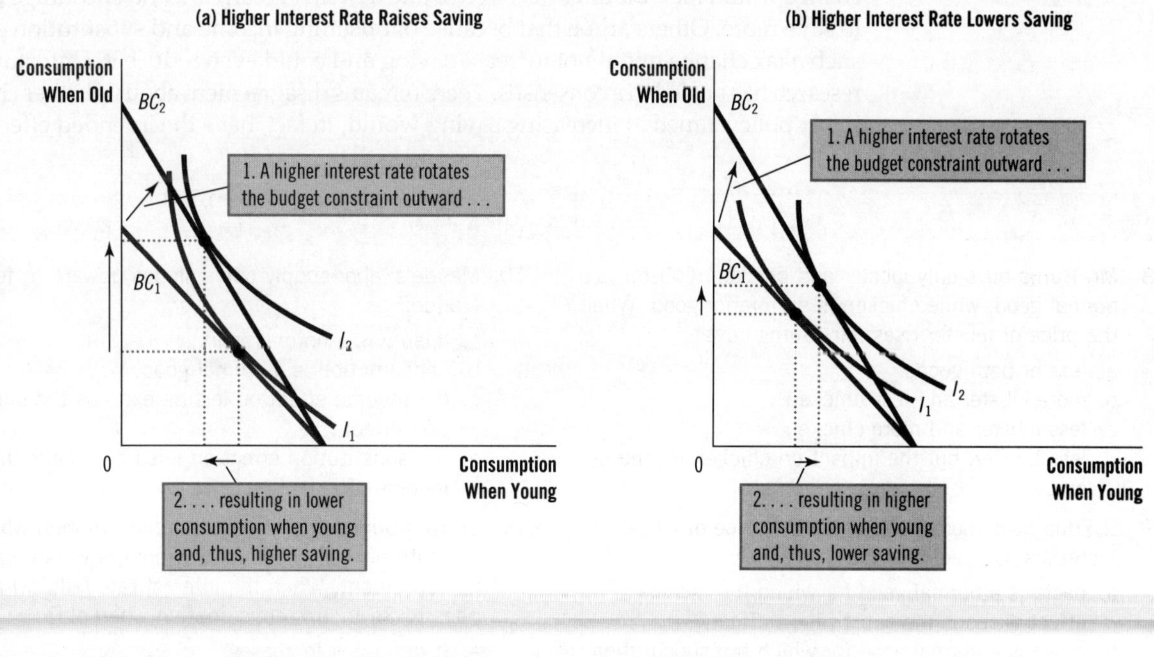

The two panels show the results given different preferences by Ramvilas. In both cases, consumption when old rises. Yet consumption when young responds differently in the two cases. In panel (a), Ramvilas responds to the higher interest rate by consuming less when young. In panel (b), Ramvilas responds by consuming more when young.

Ramvilas's saving is his income minus his consumption when young. In panel (a), an increase in the interest rate reduces consumption when young, so saving rises. In panel (b), an increase in the interest rate increases consumption when young, so saving falls.

The case shown in panel (b) might seem odd: Ramvilas responds to an increase in the return to saving by saving less. But this behavior is not as peculiar as it might seem. We can understand it by considering the income and substitution effects of a higher interest rate.

Consider first the substitution effect. When the interest rate rises, consumption when old becomes less costly relative to consumption when young. Therefore, the substitution effect induces Ramvilas to consume more when old and less when young. In other words, the substitution effect induces Ramvilas to save more.

Now consider the income effect. When the interest rate rises, Ramvilas moves to a higher indifference curve, so he is better off. If consumption when young and consumption when old are both normal goods, he will want to use his increased well-being to consume more in both periods. In other words, the income effect induces him to save less.

The result depends on both the income and substitution effects. If the substitution effect of a higher interest rate exceeds the income effect, Ramvilas saves more. If the income effect exceeds the substitution effect, Ramvilas saves less. The theory of consumer choice says that an increase in the interest rate could either encourage or discourage saving.

This ambiguous result is interesting from the standpoint of economic theory, but it is disappointing from the standpoint of economic policy. An important issue in tax policy hinges, in part, on how saving responds to interest rates. Some economists advocate reducing the taxation of interest and other capital income, arguing that such a policy change would raise the after-tax interest rate that savers can earn and encourage people to save more. Others argue that because of offsetting income and substitution effects, such a tax change might not increase saving and could even reduce it. Unfortunately, research has not led to a consensus. There remains disagreement about whether changes in tax policy aimed at increasing saving would, in fact, have the intended effect.

Quick**Quiz**

8. Mr. Burns buys only lobster and chicken. Lobster is a normal good, while chicken is an inferior good. When the price of lobster rises, Mr. Burns buys
   a. less of both goods.
   b. more lobster and less chicken.
   c. less lobster and more chicken.
   d. less lobster, but the impact on chicken is ambiguous.
9. If Edna buys more pasta when the price of pasta increases, we can infer that for Edna,
   a. pasta is a normal good for which the income effect exceeds the substitution effect.
   b. pasta is a normal good for which the substitution effect exceeds the income effect.
   c. pasta is an inferior good for which the income effect exceeds the substitution effect.
   d. pasta is an inferior good for which the substitution effect exceeds the income effect.
10. Maude's labor-supply curve slopes upward if, for Maude,
    a. leisure is a normal good.
    b. consumption is a normal good.
    c. the income effect on leisure exceeds the substitution effect.
    d. the substitution effect on leisure exceeds the income effect.
11. Consumption when young and consumption when old are both normal goods for Seymour, a worker saving for retirement. When the interest rate falls, what happens to Seymour's consumption when old?
    a. It definitely increases.
    b. It definitely decreases.
    c. It increases only if the substitution effect exceeds the income effect.
    d. It decreases only if the substitution effect exceeds the income effect.

Answers are at the end of the chapter.

21-5 Conclusion: Do People Really Think This Way?

The theory of consumer choice describes how people make decisions. As we have seen, it applies to many questions. It can explain how people choose between pizza and Pepsi, work and leisure, consumption and saving, and so on.

Now that we understand the theory, let's step back and consider whether it is credible. You might be tempted to look upon the theory of consumer choice with some skepticism. After all, you are a consumer. You decide what to buy every time you walk into a store. And you know that you do not make your purchasing decisions by writing down budget constraints and mapping out indifference curves. Doesn't this knowledge about your own decision making refute the theory?

No, it doesn't. The theory of consumer choice does not try to present a literal account of how people make decisions. It is a model. As Chapter 2 discussed, models are not supposed to be completely realistic.

The theory of consumer choice should be viewed as a metaphor for how consumers make decisions. No consumer (except an occasional economist) goes through the explicit optimization envisioned in the theory. Yet consumers know that their choices are constrained by their financial resources. And given those constraints, they do the best they can to achieve the highest level of satisfaction. The theory of consumer choice describes this intuitive process in a way that permits formal economic analysis.

Just as the proof of the pudding is in the eating, the test of a theory is in its applications. The last section of this chapter applied the theory of consumer choice to three practical issues. If you take more advanced courses in economics, you will see that this theory provides the framework for much additional analysis.

Chapter in a Nutshell

- A consumer's budget constraint shows the possible bundles of different goods she can buy given her income and the prices of the goods. The slope of the budget constraint equals the relative price of the goods.
- The consumer's indifference curves represent her preferences. An indifference curve shows the various bundles of goods that make the consumer equally happy. Points on higher indifference curves are preferred to points on lower indifference curves. The slope of an indifference curve at any point is the consumer's marginal rate of substitution—the rate at which the consumer is willing to trade one good for the other.
- The consumer optimizes by choosing the point on her budget constraint that lies on the highest indifference curve. At this point, the slope of the indifference curve (the marginal rate of substitution between the goods) equals the slope of the budget constraint (the relative price of the goods), and the consumer's valuation of the two goods (measured by the marginal rate of substitution) equals the market's valuation (measured by the relative price).
- When the price of a good falls, the impact on the consumer's choices can be broken down into an income effect and a substitution effect. The income effect is the change in consumption that arises because a lower price makes the consumer better off. The substitution effect is the change in consumption that arises because a price change encourages greater consumption of the good that has become relatively cheaper. The income effect is reflected in the movement from a lower to a higher indifference curve, while the substitution effect is reflected by a movement along an indifference curve to a point with a different slope.
- The theory of consumer choice can be applied in many situations. It explains why demand curves sometimes slope upward, why higher wages can either increase or decrease the quantity of labor supplied, and why higher interest rates can either increase or decrease saving.

Key Concepts

budget constraint, p. 424
indifference curve, p. 427
marginal rate of substitution, p. 427
perfect substitutes, p. 430
perfect complements, p. 431
normal good, p. 434
inferior good, p. 434
income effect, p. 435
substitution effect, p. 435
giffen good, p. 439

Questions for Review

1. Hari has income of ₹6,000. Wine costs ₹6 per glass, and cheese costs ₹12 per pound. Draw Hari's budget constraint with wine on the vertical axis. What is the slope of this budget constraint?
2. Hari has typical indifference curves for wine and cheese. Draw them and explain their four properties.
3. Pick a point on an indifference curve for wine and cheese, and show the marginal rate of substitution. What does the marginal rate of substitution tell us?
4. Show Hari's budget constraint and indifference curves for wine and cheese, along with his optimal consumption choice. If the price of wine is ₹6 per glass and the price of cheese is ₹12 per pound, what is the marginal rate of substitution at this optimum?
5. Hari gets a raise, so his income increases from ₹6,000 to ₹8,000. Show what happens if both wine and cheese are normal goods. Next, show what happens if cheese is an inferior good.
6. The price of cheese rises from ₹12 to ₹20 per pound, while the price of wine remains ₹6 per glass. Assuming Hari has a constant income of ₹6,000, show what happens to the consumption of wine and cheese. Decompose the change into income and substitution effects.
7. Can an increase in the price of cheese possibly induce Hari to buy more cheese? Explain.

Problems and Applications

1. Maya divides her income between coffee and croissants (both of which are normal goods). An early frost in Brazil causes a large increase in the price of coffee in the United States.
   a. Show the effect of the frost on Maya's budget constraint.
   b. Show the effect of the frost on Maya's optimal consumption bundle, assuming that the substitution effect outweighs the income effect for croissants.
   c. Show the effect of the frost on Maya's optimal consumption bundle, assuming that the income effect outweighs the substitution effect for croissants.
2. Compare the following two pairs of goods:
   - Coke and Pepsi
   - Skis and ski bindings

   a. In which case are the two goods complements? In which case are they substitutes?
   b. In which case do you expect the indifference curves to be fairly straight? In which case do you expect the indifference curves to be very bowed?
   c. In which case will the consumer respond more to a change in the relative price of the two goods?
3. You consume only soda and pizza. One day, the price of soda goes up, the price of pizza goes down, and you are just as happy as you were before the price changes.
   a. Illustrate this situation on a graph.
   b. How does your consumption of the two goods change? How does your response depend on income and substitution effects?
   c. Can you afford the bundle of soda and pizza you consumed before the price changes?
4. Raj consumes only cheese and crackers.
   a. Could cheese and crackers both be inferior goods for Raj? Explain.
   b. Suppose that cheese is a normal good for Raj and crackers are an inferior good. If the price of cheese falls, what happens to Raj's consumption

of crackers? What happens to his consumption of cheese? Explain.

5. Darius buys only milk and cookies.
   a. In year 1, Darius earns ₹100, milk costs ₹2 per quart, and cookies cost ₹4 per dozen. Draw Darius's budget constraint.
   b. Now suppose that all prices increase by 10 percent in year 2 and that Darius's salary increases by 10 percent as well. Draw Darius's new budget constraint. How would Darius's optimal bundle of milk and cookies in year 2 compare with his optimal bundle in year 1?

6. State whether each of the following statements is true or false. Explain your answers.
   a. "All Giffen goods are inferior goods."
   b. "All inferior goods are Giffen goods."

7. Priya, a college student, has two options for meals: eating at the dining hall for ₹6 per meal, or eating a cup of Ramen soup for ₹1.50 per meal. Her weekly food budget is ₹60.
   a. Draw the budget constraint showing the trade-off between dining-hall meals and cups of soup. Assuming that Priya spends equal amounts on both goods, draw an indifference curve showing the optimum choice. Label the optimum as point A.
   b. Suppose the price of a cup of soup rises to ₹2. Using your diagram from part (a), show the consequences of this change in price. Assume that Priya now spends only 30 percent of her income on dining-hall meals. Label the new optimum as point B.
   c. What happened to the quantity of soup consumed because of this price change? What does this result say about the income and substitution effects? Explain.
   d. Use points A and B to draw Priya's demand curve for cups of soup. What is this type of good called?

8. Consider your decision about how many hours to work.
   a. Draw your budget constraint, assuming that you pay no taxes on your income. On the same diagram, draw another budget constraint, assuming that you pay a 15 percent income tax.
   b. Show how the tax might lead you to work more hours, fewer hours, or the same number of hours. Explain.

9. Anya is awake for 100 hours per week. Using one diagram, show Anya's budget constraints if she earns ₹12 per hour, ₹16 per hour, and ₹20 per hour. Now draw indifference curves such that Anya's labor-supply curve is upward-sloping when the wage is between ₹12 and ₹16 per hour and backward-sloping when the wage is between ₹16 and ₹20 per hour.

10. Draw the indifference curve for someone deciding how to allocate time between work and leisure. Suppose the wage increases. Is it possible that the person's consumption would fall? Is this plausible? Discuss. (Hint: Think about income and substitution effects.)

11. The economist George Stigler once wrote that, according to consumer theory, "if consumers do not buy less of a commodity when their incomes rise, they will surely buy less when the price of the commodity rises." Explain this statement using the concepts of income and substitution effects.

12. Five consumers have the following marginal utility of apples and pears:

	Marginal Utility of Apples	Marginal Utility of Pears
Claire	6	12
Phil	6	6
Haley	6	3
Alex	3	6
Luke	3	12

The price of an apple is ₹1, and the price of a pear is ₹2. Which, if any, of these consumers are optimizing their choices of fruit? For those who are not, how should they change their spending?

QuickQuiz Answers

1. a 2. d 3. d 4. b 5. b 6. d 7. c 8. c 9. c 10. d 11. b

Chapter

22

Frontiers of Managerial Economics

Economics is a study of the choices that people make and the interactions among people as they go about their lives. As the preceding chapters demonstrate, the field has many facets. Yet the facets we have already seen do not make up a finished jewel, perfect and unchanging. Economists are always looking for new areas to study, new phenomena to explain, and new ways to see the world. This final chapter on microeconomics discusses three topics at the discipline's frontier to show how economists are trying to expand their understanding of human behavior and society.

The first topic is the economics of **asymmetric information**. In many situations, some people are better informed than others, and the imbalance in knowledge affects the choices they make and how they deal with one another. Thinking about this asymmetry sheds light on many aspects of the world, from the market for used cars to the custom of gift giving.

The second topic in this chapter is **political economy**, a term that once encompassed the entire field of economics but now refers to interdisciplinary work at the boundary of political science and

economics. Throughout this book, we have seen many examples in which markets fail to deliver desirable outcomes, and government policy can potentially improve matters. But "potentially" is a necessary qualifier: Whether this potential is realized depends on political institutions. The field of political economy uses the tools of economics to study how government works and, in doing so, provides a deeper understanding of economic policy.

The third topic in this chapter is **behavioral economics**. This field brings insights from psychology into the study of economic issues. It questions whether people are entirely rational, at least in the conventional sense, and it offers a view of human behavior that is more subtle and complex, and perhaps more realistic, than the one found in standard economic theory.

This chapter covers a lot of ground. To do so, it does not offer full helpings of these three topics but, instead, gives a taste of each. One goal of this chapter is to show where economists are heading in their efforts to expand knowledge. Another is to whet your appetite for more courses in economics and allied fields.

22-1 Asymmetric Information

"I know something you don't know." This common elementary-school taunt conveys a truth about how people sometimes interact with one another. Often in life, one person knows more about what is going on than another. When that difference in knowledge is relevant to an interaction, it is called **information asymmetry**.

Examples abound. Workers know more than their employers about how much effort they put into their jobs. Sellers of used cars know more than buyers about whether the cars offered for sale are in good condition. The first is an example of a **hidden action**, while the second is an example of a **hidden characteristic**. In each case, the uninformed party (the employer, the car buyer) would like to know the relevant information, but the informed party (the worker, the car seller) may have an incentive to conceal it.

Because asymmetric information is so common, economists have devoted much effort to studying its effects. Here are some insights this study has revealed.

22-1a Hidden Actions: Principals, Agents, and Moral Hazard

moral hazard
the tendency of a person who is imperfectly monitored to engage in dishonest or otherwise undesirable behavior

agent
a person who performs an act for another person, called the principal

principal
a person for whom another person, called the agent, performs some act

Moral hazard is a problem that arises when one person, called the **agent**, performs a task on behalf of another person, called the **principal**. If the principal cannot perfectly monitor the agent's behavior, the agent may act in a way that serves the agent's self-interest but is undesirable for the principal. Economists adopted the somewhat odd phrase **moral hazard** from the insurance industry: It refers to the risk, or "hazard," of inappropriate or otherwise "immoral" behavior by the agent. In such a situation, the principal tries various ways to encourage the agent to act more responsibly.

The employment relationship is a classic example. The employer is the principal, and the worker is the agent. The moral-hazard problem is the temptation of imperfectly monitored workers to shirk their responsibilities. Employers can respond to this problem in various ways:

- **Better monitoring.** Employers may plant hidden video cameras to record workers' behavior. The employers' aim is to catch irresponsible actions that might occur when supervisors are absent.
- **High wages.** According to **efficiency-wage theories**, some employers may choose to pay their workers a wage above the level that balances supply and

demand in the labor market. Workers who earn above-equilibrium wages—and are treated well in other ways—are less likely to violate their employers' trust.

- **Delayed payment.** Firms can delay part of workers' compensation, so a worker who is caught shirking and fired suffers a larger penalty. One example of delayed compensation is the year-end bonus. Similarly, a firm may pay its workers more later in their lives. The wage increases that workers usually get as they age may reflect not just the benefits of experience but also a response to moral hazard.

Employers can use any combination of these mechanisms to reduce moral hazard.

There are many examples of moral hazard beyond the workplace. A homeowner with fire insurance might buy too few fire extinguishers because the homeowner bears the cost of the extinguisher while the insurance company receives much of the benefit. A family may live near a river with a high risk of flooding because the

FYI Corporate Management

Corporations dominate the modern economy. In some ways, corporations are like other firms: They buy inputs in markets for the factors of production, sell their output in markets for goods and services, and typically aim to maximize profit for their owners. But large corporations raise some issues that do not arise in, say, small family-owned businesses.

From a legal standpoint, a corporation is an organization that is granted a charter recognizing it as a separate legal entity with its own rights and responsibilities distinct from those of its owners and employees. An important protection that corporations have is limited liability: The owners of the corporation can lose their entire investment in the business, but not more than that. They are not personally liable for any losses the corporation suffers.

Limited liability is related to another important feature of corporations: the separation of ownership and control. One group of people, the shareholders, own the corporation and share in its profits. Another group of people, the managers, are employed by the corporation to make decisions about how to deploy its resources. This arrangement requires limited liability because shareholders would be reluctant to invest in a business and let managers control it if the shareholders could incur unbounded losses.

The separation of ownership and control creates a principal-agent problem, with the shareholders as the principals and the managers as the agents. The chief executive officer and other managers are charged with the task of running the company for the shareholders. That makes sense because the managers are in the best position to know the available business opportunities. But the situation is fraught with moral hazard. While the shareholders typically want the managers to maximize profits, the managers may have goals of their own, such as taking life easy, having a plush office and a private jet, throwing lavish parties, or presiding over a large business empire.

The corporation's board of directors is responsible for hiring and firing the top management. The board monitors the managers' performance and sets their compensation packages. These packages often include incentives aimed at aligning the interests of shareholders with the interests of management. Managers might be given performance-based bonuses or stock options, which increase in value if the company performs well.

Note that the directors are themselves agents of the shareholders. The existence of a board overseeing management only shifts the principal-agent problem. The issue then becomes how to ensure that the board of directors fulfills its own legal obligation of acting in the best interest of the shareholders. If the directors become too friendly with management, they may not provide the required oversight.

The principal-agent problem inherent in corporations flares up periodically. It became big news around 2005. The top managers of several prominent companies, including Enron, Tyco, and WorldCom, were found to be engaging in activities that enriched themselves at the expense of their shareholders. In these cases, the actions were so extreme that they were criminal, and the corporate managers were not just fired but also sent to prison. Some shareholders sued the directors for failing to monitor management sufficiently.

Criminal activity by corporate managers is rare, but in some ways, it is only the tip of the iceberg. Whenever ownership and control are separated, as they are in most large corporations, there is an inevitable tension between the interests of shareholders and the interests of management, and the problem of moral hazard can impede businesses from operating as efficiently as they could. ■

family enjoys the scenic views, while the government bears the cost of disaster relief after a flood. Regulations aim to address the problem: An insurance company may require homeowners to buy fire extinguishers, and the government may prohibit building homes on land with a high risk of flooding. But the insurance company does not have perfect information about how cautious homeowners are, and the government does not have perfect information about the risks that families undertake when choosing where to live, so the problem of moral hazard persists.

22-1b Hidden Characteristics: Adverse Selection and the Lemons Problem

adverse selection
the tendency for the mix of unobserved attributes to become undesirable from the standpoint of an uninformed party

Adverse selection is a problem that arises when one party in a transaction knows more about the attributes of the item being exchanged than the other. For example, the seller of a good might know more about it than the buyer, so the buyer runs the risk of being sold something of low quality. The "selection" of goods sold may be "adverse" from the buyer's standpoint.

The classic example of adverse selection is the market for used cars. Sellers know their vehicles' defects while buyers often do not. Because the owners of the worst cars are more likely to sell them than the owners of the best cars, buyers worry about getting a "lemon," and many people avoid buying used cars entirely. This lemons problem can explain why a used car only a few weeks old sells for thousands of dollars less than a new car of the same type. A buyer of the used car might surmise that the seller is getting rid of the car quickly because the seller knows something the buyer does not.

The labor market provides a second example of adverse selection. According to one efficiency-wage theory, workers know their own abilities better than the firms that hire them do. If a firm reduces the wage it pays, the more talented workers are more likely to quit, knowing they will be able to find other jobs. Conversely, a firm may choose to pay an above-equilibrium wage to attract better workers.

A third example of adverse selection occurs in insurance markets, as Chapter 12 discussed. Buyers of health insurance know more about their own problems than insurance companies do. If people with greater hidden health problems are more likely to buy health insurance than other people, the price of health insurance will reflect the costs of a sicker-than-average person. That may discourage healthier people from buying insurance, which only makes health insurance even more expensive.

When markets suffer from adverse selection, the invisible hand does not necessarily work its magic by ensuring that the gains from trade are fully realized. In the used car market, owners of good cars may keep them rather than sell them at the low price that skeptical buyers are willing to pay. In the labor market, wages may be stuck above the level that balances supply and demand, resulting in unemployment. In insurance markets, some potential buyers may remain uninsured because the policies they are offered fail to reflect their true characteristics.

22-1c Signaling to Convey Private Information

Markets respond to problems of asymmetric information in many ways. One is **signaling**, which refers to actions taken by an informed party for the purpose of revealing private information.

signaling
an action taken by an informed party to reveal private information to an uninformed party

Signaling has turned up in previous chapters. We earlier discussed that firms may spend money on advertising to signal to potential customers that they have high-quality products. We also considered that students may earn college degrees to signal to potential employers that they are high-ability individuals, rather than to increase their productivity. These two examples of signaling (advertising, education) may seem very different, but below the surface, they are much the same: In both cases, the informed party (the firm, the student) uses the signal to convince the uninformed party (the customer, the employer) that the informed party is offering something of high quality.

What does it take for an action to be an effective signal? First, it must be costly. If a signal were free, everyone would use it, and it would convey no information. For the same reason, there is another requirement: The signal must be less costly, or more beneficial, to the person with the higher-quality product. Otherwise, everyone would have the same incentive to use the signal, and the signal would reveal nothing.

Consider again our two examples. In the advertising case, a firm with a good product reaps a larger benefit from advertising because customers who try the product once are more likely to become repeat customers. Thus, it is rational for the firm with a good product to pay for the cost of the signal (advertising), and it is rational for the customer to view the signal as informative about the product's quality. In the education case, a talented person can finish school more easily than a less talented one. Thus, it is rational for the talented person to pay for the cost of the signal (education), and it is rational for the employer to view the signal as informative about the person's talent.

The world is replete with instances of signaling. Magazine ads sometimes include the phrase "as seen on TV." Why stress this fact? One possibility is that the firm is trying to convey its willingness to pay for an expensive signal (an ad on television) in the hope that you will infer that its product is of high quality. For the same reason, graduates of elite schools are always sure to put that fact on their résumés.

Case Study

Gifts as Signals

A man is debating what to give his girlfriend for her birthday. "I know," he says to himself, "I'll give her cash. After all, I don't know her preferences as well as she does, and with cash, she can buy anything she wants." But when he hands her the money, she is offended. Convinced he doesn't really love her, she breaks off the relationship.

What's the economics behind this story?

In some ways, gift giving is a strange custom. As the man in our story suggests, people typically know their own tastes better than others do, so we might expect everyone to prefer cash to in-kind transfers. If your employer chose some merchandise and substituted it for your paycheck, you would likely object to this means of payment. But your reaction is very different when someone who (you hope) loves you does something similar.

One interpretation of gift giving is that it reflects asymmetric information and signaling. The man in our story has private information that the girlfriend would like to know: Does he really love her? He says he does, but should she believe him? Talk is cheap.

Choosing a good gift for her can be a signal of his love. Certainly, the act of picking out a good gift, rather than giving cash, has the right characteristics to be a signal. It is costly (it takes time), and its cost depends on private information (how much he loves her). If he really loves her, choosing a good gift is easy because he is

"Now we'll see how much he loves me."

thinking about her all the time. If he doesn't love her, finding the right gift is more difficult. Thus, giving a gift that suits his girlfriend is one way for him to convey the private information of his love for her. Giving cash shows that he isn't even bothering to try.

The signaling theory of gift giving is consistent with another observation: People care most about the custom when the strength of affection is most in question. Giving cash to a girlfriend or boyfriend is usually a bad move. But when college students receive a check from their parents, they are less often offended. The parents' love is less likely to be in doubt, so the recipient probably won't interpret the cash gift as a signal of insufficient affection. ●

22-1d Screening to Uncover Private Information

When an informed party takes actions to reveal private information, the phenomenon is called signaling. When an uninformed party takes actions to induce the informed party to reveal private information, the phenomenon is called **screening**.

screening
an action taken by an uninformed party to induce an informed party to reveal information

Some screening is common sense. People buying used cars often ask that the car be checked by an auto mechanic before the sale. If sellers refuse this request, they reveal their private information that the car is not in good shape. Buyers may then decide to offer a lower price or to look for another car.

Other examples of screening are more subtle. For example, consider a firm that sells car insurance. It would like to charge a lower premium to safe drivers than to risky ones. But how can it tell them apart? Drivers may know better than the insurance companies whether they are safe or risky, but the risky ones won't admit it. A driver's history is one piece of information (which insurance companies use), but because of the randomness of many car accidents, history is an imperfect indicator of future risk.

The insurance company might be able to sort out the two kinds of drivers by offering a menu of insurance policies that would induce the drivers to separate themselves. One policy would have a high premium and cover the full cost of any accidents that occur. Another policy would have low premiums but would have, say, a ₹2,000 deductible. (That is, the driver would be responsible for the first ₹2,000 of damage, and the insurance company would cover the remaining risk.) The deductible is more of a burden for risky drivers because they are more likely to have an accident. With a large enough deductible, the low-premium policy with a deductible would attract the safe drivers, while the high-premium policy without a deductible would attract the risky drivers. Faced with these two policies, the two kinds of drivers would reveal their private information by choosing different policies.

22-1e Asymmetric Information and Public Policy

We have examined two kinds of asymmetric information: moral hazard and adverse selection. And we have seen how individuals may respond to the problem with signaling or screening. Now let's consider what the study of asymmetric information suggests about the proper scope of public policy.

The tension between market success and market failure is central to microeconomics. Chapter 7 showed that the equilibrium of supply and demand in competitive markets is efficient in the sense that it maximizes the total surplus that society can obtain in a market. Adam Smith's invisible hand seemed to reign supreme.

The study of asymmetric information provides a new reason to be wary of markets. When some people know more than others, the market may fail to put resources to their best use. People with high-quality used cars may have trouble selling them for a good price because buyers are afraid of getting a lemon. People with few health problems may have trouble getting reasonably priced health insurance because insurance companies lump them together with those who have significant health problems.

Asymmetric information may justify government action in some cases, but three facts complicate the issue. First, the market can sometimes deal with information asymmetries on its own using a combination of signaling and screening. Second, the government rarely has more information than the private parties. Even if the market's allocation of resources is not ideal, it may be the best that can be achieved. That is, when there are information asymmetries, policymakers may find it hard to improve upon the market's admittedly imperfect outcome. Third, the government is itself an imperfect institution, as we discuss in the next section.

Quick**Quiz**

1. Because Eva has a family history of significant medical problems, she buys health insurance, while her friend Jerry, who has a healthier family, goes without. This is an example of
   a. moral hazard.
   b. adverse selection.
   c. signaling.
   d. screening.
2. Garvit has a life insurance policy that pays his family ₹1 million if he dies. As a result, he does not hesitate to enjoy his favorite hobby of bungee jumping. This is an example of
   a. moral hazard.
   b. adverse selection.
   c. signaling.
   d. screening.
3. Before selling anyone a life insurance policy, the Kramer Insurance Company requires that applicants undergo a medical examination. Those with significant preexisting medical problems are charged more. This is an example of
   a. moral hazard.
   b. adverse selection.
   c. signaling.
   d. screening.
4. Dr. Funnybones displays her medical degree in her office waiting room, hoping patients will be impressed that she attended a prestigious medical school. This is an example of
   a. moral hazard.
   b. adverse selection.
   c. signaling.
   d. screening.

Answers are at the end of the chapter.

22-2 Political Economy

When the market's outcome is deemed to be either inefficient or inequitable, the government may be able to improve the situation. Yet before embracing an active government, we need to consider one more fact: The government is also an imperfect institution. The field of **political economy** (sometimes called **public choice** or **social choice**) uses the methods of economics to study how government works.

political economy
the study of government using the analytic methods of economics

22-2a The Condorcet Voting Paradox

Democratic principles undergird the complex governmental institutions in the United States and in many other countries. Perhaps the most fundamental among these principles is majority rule. It seems straightforward enough. But majority rule can be more problematic than it seems.

Consider a town deciding where to build a new park. The town council decides to let the voters choose. How will this work? If there are only two options, the answer is simple: The majority gets its way. But what if the new park could be placed in many possible locations? In this case, as the 18th-century French political theorist Marquis de Condorcet noted, democracy might have trouble figuring out which option to pick.

Suppose there are three candidate locations, A, B, and C, and three voter types with the preferences shown in Table 1. The town council wants to aggregate these individual preferences into preferences for the town as a whole. How should it do it?

At first, the council might try pairwise voting. If it asks voters to choose first between B and C, voter types 1 and 2 will vote for B, giving B the majority. If it then asks voters to choose between A and B, voter types 1 and 3 will vote for A, giving A the majority. Observing that A beats B and that B beats C, the council might conclude that A is the voters' clear choice.

But wait: Suppose the town council then asks voters to choose between A and C. In this case, voter types 2 and 3 vote for C, giving C the majority. Under pairwise majority voting, A beats B, B beats C, and C beats A. Normally, we expect preferences to exhibit a property called **transitivity**: If A is preferred to B, and B is preferred to C, then we would expect A to be preferred to C. The **Condorcet paradox** is that democratic outcomes do not always obey this property. Pairwise voting might produce transitive preferences in some cases, but it cannot be counted on to do so.

Condorcet paradox
the failure of majority rule to produce transitive preferences for society

One implication of the Condorcet paradox is that the order in which things are voted on can affect the result. If the voters choose first between A and B and then compare the winner with C, the town ends up with C. But if the voters choose first between B and C and then compare the winner with A, the town ends up with A. And if the voters choose first between A and C and then compare the winner with B, the town ends up with B.

The Condorcet paradox teaches two lessons. The narrow lesson is that when there are more than two options, setting the agenda (that is, deciding the order in which items are voted on) can have a powerful influence over the outcome of a democratic election. The broad lesson is that majority voting by itself does not always tell us what outcome a society really wants.

Table 1

The Condorcet Paradox

If voters have these preferences over candidates A, B, and C, then in pairwise majority voting, A beats B, B beats C, and C beats A.

	Voter Type		
	Type 1	Type 2	Type 3
Percent of electorate	35	45	20
First choice	A	B	C
Second choice	B	C	A
Third choice	C	A	B

22-2b Arrow's Impossibility Theorem

Since political theorists first noticed the Condorcet paradox, they have spent much energy studying voting systems. Sometimes they propose new ones.

As an alternative to pairwise majority voting, the town council could ask each voter to rank the candidates. For each voter, we could give 1 point for last place, 2 points for second to last, 3 points for third to last, and so on. The candidate with the most total points wins. This voting method is called a **Borda count** after Jean-Charles de Borda, the 18th-century French mathematician and political theorist who devised it. It is often used in polls that rank sports teams. With the preferences in Table 1, you will find that B is the winner.

Another possible system is called **ranked-choice voting**, which many cities use to elect officials. Again, the voters rank all the candidates. Each vote is first assigned to that voter's first choice. The candidate with the fewest votes is then eliminated, and those votes are reallocated to the voters' second choice. And so on. Candidates are successively eliminated until one of them has a majority. With the preferences in Table 1, C is eliminated in the first round, the type 3 votes are reallocated from C to A, and A is the winner.

Is there a perfect voting system? The economist Kenneth Arrow addressed this question in his 1951 book *Social Choice and Individual Values*. Arrow started by defining what an ideal voting system would be. He assumed that individuals have preferences over the possible outcomes: A, B, C, and so on. He then assumed that society wants a voting system to choose among these outcomes that satisfies several properties:

- **Unanimity:** If everyone prefers A to B, then A beats B.
- **Transitivity:** If A beats B, and B beats C, then A beats C.
- **Independence of irrelevant alternatives:** The ranking between any two outcomes A and B does not depend on whether some third outcome C is also available.
- **No dictators:** There is no person who always gets to pick the outcome, regardless of everyone else's preferences.

These all seem desirable and compatible. Yet Arrow proved, mathematically and incontrovertibly, that **no voting system can satisfy all these properties**. This result is called **Arrow's impossibility theorem**.

Arrow's impossibility theorem
a mathematical result showing that, under certain assumed conditions, there is no method for aggregating individual preferences into a valid set of social preferences

The mathematics needed to prove Arrow's theorem is beyond the scope of this book, but for a sense of why the theorem is true, consider some examples. We have already seen the problem with the pairwise majority rule: The Condorcet paradox shows that it fails to produce a ranking of outcomes that always satisfies transitivity.

As another example, the Borda count fails to satisfy the independence of irrelevant alternatives. Recall that, using the preferences in Table 1, B wins with a Borda count. But suppose that C is no longer available. You will find that if the Borda count method is applied only to A and B, then A wins. Eliminating C changes the ranking between A and B because the Borda count depends on the number of points that A and B receive, and the number of points each receives depends on whether the irrelevant alternative, C, is in the running.

Ranked-choice voting also fails to satisfy the independence of irrelevant alternatives. Recall that, using the preferences in Table 1, ranked-choice voting produces A as the winner. But if B disappears as an alternative, the winner becomes C. This change occurs because when B drops out, more voters have C as their first choice, so rather than being eliminated, it wins a majority in the first round.

To be sure, the three systems discussed so far—pairwise majority voting, Borda counts, and ranked-choice voting—do not do justice to the rich and complex set of rules and institutions that make up actual democracies. But Arrow's impossibility theorem is a general result: It applies not just to these three simple systems but to any way a society might aggregate individual preferences to choose an outcome. Arrow's impossibility theorem doesn't say that we should abandon democracy as a form of government. But it does say that any democracy, no matter how well designed, must be flawed as a mechanism for social choice.

22-2c The Median Voter Is King

Despite Arrow's theorem, voting is how most societies choose leaders and public policies, often by majority rule. The next step in studying government is to examine how governments run by majority rule work. That is, in a democratic society, who determines what policy is chosen? In some cases, the theory of democratic government yields a surprisingly simple answer.

Imagine that society is deciding how much money to spend on a public good, such as the army or the national parks. Each voter has an optimal budget in mind, and voters always prefer outcomes closer to their optimum to outcomes farther away. We can line up voters from those who prefer the smallest budget to those who prefer the largest. Figure 1 is an example. Here, there are 100 voters, and the budget size varies from zero to ₹20 billion. Given these preferences, what outcome would a democracy produce?

median voter theorem
a mathematical result showing that if voters are choosing a point along a line and they all want the point closest to their own optimum, then majority rule will pick the optimum of the median voter

According to a result called the **median voter theorem**, majority rule produces the outcome preferred by the **median voter**, the person exactly in the middle of the distribution. In this example, if you take the line of voters ordered by their optimal budgets and count 50 voters from either end of the line, you will find that the median voter wants a budget of ₹10 billion. By contrast, the average preferred outcome (calculated by adding the preferred outcomes and dividing by the number

Figure 1

The Median Voter Theorem: An Example

This bar chart shows how 100 voters' optimal budgets are distributed over five options, ranging from zero to ₹20 billion. If society makes its choice by majority rule, the median voter, who here prefers ₹10 billion, determines the outcome.

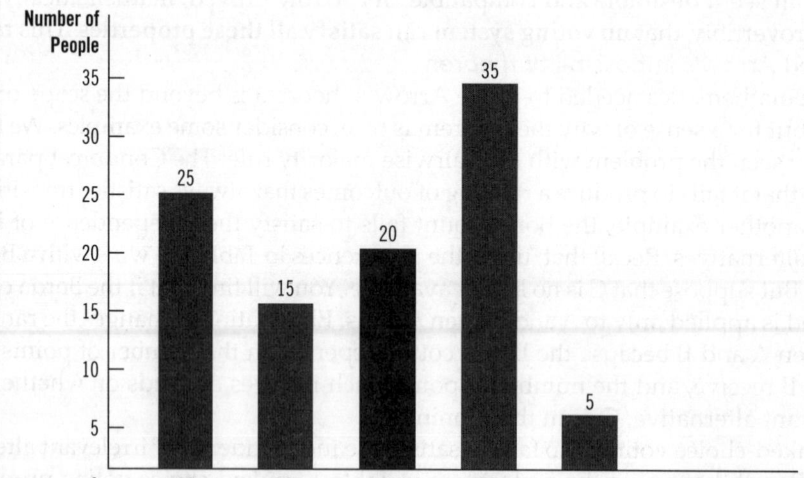

of voters) is ₹9 billion, and the modal outcome (the one preferred by the greatest number of voters) is ₹15 billion.

The median voter rules because her preferred outcome beats any other proposal in a two-way race. In this example, more than half the voters want ₹10 billion or more, and more than half want ₹10 billion or less. If someone proposes, say, ₹8 billion instead of ₹10 billion, everyone who prefers ₹10 billion or more will vote with the median voter. Similarly, if someone proposes ₹12 billion instead of ₹10 billion, everyone who wants ₹10 billion or less will vote with the median voter. In either case, the median voter has more than half the voters on her side.

What about the Condorcet voting paradox? When the voters are picking a point along a line and each voter aims to be close to her own optimum, the Condorcet paradox cannot arise. The median voter's preferred outcome beats all challengers.

One implication of the median voter theorem is that if two rational political parties are each trying to win an election, they will both move their positions toward the one favored by the median voter. Suppose, for example, that the Democratic Party advocates a budget of ₹15 billion, while the Republican Party advocates a budget of ₹10 billion. The Democratic position is more popular in the sense that ₹15 billion has more proponents than any other single choice. Nonetheless, the Republicans get more than 50 percent of the vote: They will attract the 20 voters who want ₹10 billion, the 15 voters who want ₹5 billion, and the 25 voters who want zero. If the Democrats want to win, they will move their platform toward the median voter. This theory can explain why the parties in a two-party system are often similar: They have good reason to move toward the median voter.

Another implication of the median voter theorem is that minority views are not given much weight. Imagine that 40 percent of the population want a lot of money spent on the national parks, and 60 percent want nothing spent. In this case, the median voter's preference is zero, regardless of the intensity of the minority's view. Rather than reaching a compromise that takes everyone's preferences into account, majority rule looks only to the person in the exact middle of the distribution. That is part of the logic of democracy.

22-2d Politicians Are People Too

When economists study consumer behavior, they assume that consumers buy the bundle of goods and services that gives them the greatest level of satisfaction. When economists study firm behavior, they assume that firms produce the quantity of goods and services that yields the greatest profit. What should they assume about the objectives of people involved in politics?

It would be comforting to assume that political leaders always look out for the well-being of society, that they aim for an optimal combination of efficiency and equality. Comforting, perhaps, but not realistic. Self-interest is as powerful a motive for political actors as it is for consumers and firm owners. Some politicians, motivated by a desire for reelection, are willing to sacrifice the national interest to solidify their base of voters. Others are motivated by simple greed. If you have any doubt, look at the world's poorest nations, where rampant corruption is often an impediment to economic development. Graft among political leaders is less common in advanced nations, but scandals still occur from time to time, and those scandals reveal only the corrupt leaders who were caught.

This book is not the place to develop a full-blown theory of political behavior. But when thinking about economic policy, remember that it is made not by a benevolent king (or even by benevolent economists) but by real people

CHRIS WILDT/CARTOONSTOCK LTD

"Isn't that the real genius of democracy? . . . The VOTERS are ultimately to blame."

with all-too-human desires. Sometimes they are motivated to further the national interest, but sometimes they are moved by their own political and financial ambitions. Don't be surprised when economic policy fails to resemble the ideals derived in economics textbooks.

QuickQuiz

5. The Condorcet paradox illustrates Arrow's impossibility theorem by showing that pairwise majority voting
   a. is inconsistent with the principle of unanimity.
   b. leads to social preferences that are not transitive.
   c. violates the independence of irrelevant alternatives.
   d. makes one person, in effect, a dictator.
6. Garima is about to win reelection as class president against her challenger Billie. But then Rozana enters the race as well, pulling votes from Garima and allowing Bilal to prevail. The school's voting system
   a. is inconsistent with the principle of unanimity.
   b. leads to social preferences that are not transitive.
   c. violates the independence of irrelevant alternatives.
   d. makes one person, in effect, a dictator.
7. Two political candidates are vying for town mayor, and the key issue is how much to spend on the Diwali festivities. Among the 100 voters, 40 want to spend ₹30,000, 30 want to spend ₹10,000, and 30 want to spend nothing at all. What is the winning position on this issue?
   a. ₹10,000
   b. ₹15,000
   c. ₹20,000
   d. ₹30,000

Answers are at the end of the chapter.

22-3 Behavioral Economics

Economics studies human behavior, but it is not the only field that makes that claim. The social science of psychology also sheds light on the choices that people make in their lives. The fields of economics and psychology are largely independent of one another, in part because they address different questions. But recently, a field called **behavioral economics** has emerged in which economists use psychological insights to better understand the decisions that people make.

behavioral economics the subfield of economics that integrates the insights of psychology

22-3a People Aren't Always Rational

Economic theory is populated by a particular species of organism, sometimes called **Homo economicus**. Members of this species are always rational. As firm owners, they maximize profits. As consumers, they maximize utility (or equivalently, pick the point on the highest indifference curve). Given the constraints they face, they rationally weigh all the costs and benefits and always choose the best possible course of action.

Real people, however, are **Homo sapiens**. Although in many ways they resemble the rational, calculating people assumed in economic theory, they are more complex. They can be forgetful, impulsive, confused, emotional, and shortsighted. These characteristics are a central focus of psychologists but, until recently, have often been neglected by economists.

Herbert Simon, one of the first social scientists to work at the boundary of economics and psychology, suggested that humans should be viewed not as rational maximizers but as what he called **satisficers**. Instead of always choosing the best course of action, they make decisions that are good enough. Similarly, other economists have suggested that humans are only "near rational" or that they exhibit "bounded rationality."

Studies of human decision making have found that people often make the following systematic mistakes:

- **People are overconfident.** Researchers have demonstrated that people frequently believe they know more than they do. Imagine, for example, that you were asked a series of numerical questions, such as how many African countries are in the United Nations, what the height of the tallest mountain in North America is, how many gold medals China won in the last Olympics, and so on. For each question, instead of being asked for a single estimate, you were asked to give a 90 percent **confidence interval**—a range that you were 90 percent confident the true number falls within. When psychologists run experiments like this, they find that most people give ranges that are too small: The true number falls within their intervals far less than 90 percent of the time. In other words, most people are too sure of their own abilities.
- **People give too much weight to a small number of vivid observations.** Imagine that you are thinking about buying a car of a particular brand. To learn about its reliability, you read *Consumer Reports*, which has systematically surveyed 1,000 owners of the car. Then you run into a friend who owns one, and she tells you that her car is a lemon. How do you treat your friend's observation? If you think rationally, you will realize that she has only increased your sample size from 1,000 to 1,001, providing little new information. But because your friend's story is vivid—simply because it comes from your friend—you may be tempted to give it more weight in your decision making than you should. This phenomenon has been called **undue salience**.
- **People are reluctant to change their minds.** People tend to interpret evidence to confirm beliefs they already hold. In one study, subjects were asked to read and evaluate a research report on whether capital punishment deters crime. After reading the report, those who initially favored the death penalty said they were more certain of their view, and those who initially opposed the death penalty also said they were more certain of their view. The two groups interpreted the same evidence in exactly opposite ways. This behavior is called **confirmation bias**.

Think about decisions you have made in your own life. Have you exhibited any of these traits?

Deviations from rationality are important for understanding some economic phenomena. An intriguing example arises in the study of 401(k) plans, the tax-advantaged retirement savings accounts that many firms offer their workers. In some firms, workers can choose to participate in the plan by filling out a simple form. In others, workers are automatically enrolled and can opt out of the plan by filling out a simple form. Many more people participate in the second case than in the first. If they were perfectly rational maximizers, they would choose the optimal amount of retirement saving, regardless of the default offered by their employer. In fact, employees' behavior appears to exhibit substantial inertia. Understanding their behavior seems easier once we abandon the model of rational humans.

Why, you might ask, is economics built on the rationality assumption when psychology and common sense cast doubt on it? One answer is that the assumption, even if not exactly true, may be close enough that it yields workable models of behavior. For example, when we compared competitive and monopoly firms, the assumption that firms rationally maximize profit yielded many important and valid insights. Incorporating deviations from rationality into the story might have added a bit of realism, but it would have also muddied the waters and made those insights harder to find. Recall from Chapter 2 that economic models are meant not to replicate reality but to show the essence of the problem at hand.

Another reason economists often assume rationality may be that economists are themselves not rational maximizers. Like most people, they are overconfident and reluctant to change their minds. Their choice among alternative theories of human behavior may exhibit excessive inertia. Moreover, economists may be content with a theory that is not perfect but is good enough. The model of rational humans may be the theory of choice for a satisficing social scientist.

22-3b People Care about Fairness

Another insight about human behavior is best illustrated by an experiment called the **ultimatum game**. It works like this: Two volunteers (who are strangers to each other) are told that they are going to play a game and could win a total of ₹100. The game begins with a coin toss, which is used to assign the volunteers to two roles: proposer and responder. The proposer must suggest a division of the ₹100 prize between the two players. After the proposer makes the offer, the responder decides whether to accept or reject it. If the responder accepts it, both players are paid accordingly. If the responder rejects the offer, neither player gets anything. In either case, the game then ends.

Before proceeding, think about what you would do. If you were the proposer, what division of the ₹100 would you offer? If you were the responder, what offers would you accept?

Conventional economic theory assumes that people in this situation are rational wealth maximizers. This assumption leads to a simple prediction: The proposer will offer to take ₹99 and to give the responder ₹1, and the responder will accept the offer. After all, once the offer is made, the responder is better off accepting it: ₹1 is better than nothing. And because the proposer knows that accepting the offer is in the responder's interest, the proposer has no reason to offer more than ₹1. In the language of game theory (discussed in Chapter 18), the 99–1 split is the Nash equilibrium.

Yet when experimental economists ask real people to play the ultimatum game, the results differ from this prediction. People in the responder's role usually reject offers of only ₹1 or a similarly small amount. Anticipating this, people in the proposer's role usually offer the responders much more than ₹1. Some people offer a 50–50 split, but it is more common for proposers to offer the responders an amount such as ₹30 or ₹40, keeping the larger share for themselves. In these cases, the responders usually accept the proposal.

What's going on here? One interpretation is that people are driven in part by some innate sense of fairness. A 99–1 split seems so wildly unfair to many people that they reject it, even to their own financial detriment. By contrast, a 70–30 split is still unfair, but it is not so bad that it induces people to abandon their normal self-interest.

Throughout our study of household and firm behavior, the innate sense of fairness has not played any role. But the results of the ultimatum game suggest that perhaps it should. Some economists have suggested that the perceived fairness of what a firm pays its workers should also enter the picture. When a firm has an especially good year, workers (like the responder) may expect to be paid a fair share of the prize, even if the conventional market equilibrium does not dictate it. The firm (like the proposer) might well decide to give workers more than the equilibrium wage for fear that the workers might otherwise try to punish the firm with reduced effort, strikes, or even vandalism.

22-3c People Are Inconsistent over Time

Imagine a task that you find dreary. It might be doing your laundry, shoveling snow off your driveway, or filling out your income tax forms. Now consider the following questions:

1. Would you prefer (A) to spend 50 minutes doing the task right now or (B) to spend 60 minutes doing the task tomorrow?
2. Would you prefer (A) to spend 50 minutes doing the task in 90 days or (B) to spend 60 minutes doing the task in 91 days?

When asked questions like these, many people choose B for question 1 and A for question 2. When looking ahead to the future (as in question 2), they minimize the amount of time spent on the dreary task. But faced with the prospect of doing the task immediately (as in question 1), they choose to put it off.

In some ways, this behavior is not surprising: Everyone procrastinates sometimes. But from the standpoint of conventional rationality, it is puzzling. Suppose that in response to question 2, people choose to spend 50 minutes in 90 days. Then, when the 90th day arrives and they are about to start the dreary task, we allow them to change their mind. In effect, they then face question 1, so they opt to put off the task until the next day. But why should the mere passage of time affect the choices they make?

Often in life, people make plans for themselves but then fail to follow through. Smokers promise themselves they will quit, but within a few hours of smoking their last cigarette, they crave another one and renege on their commitment. People trying to lose weight promise themselves they will stop eating dessert, but when the waiter brings the dessert cart, the diet goes out the window. In both cases, the desire for instant gratification overwhelms the rational plans set in the past.

Some economists believe that the consumption–saving decision is an important instance in which people exhibit this inconsistency over time. For many people, spending provides a type of instant gratification. Saving, like passing up the cigarette or the dessert, requires a sacrifice in the present for a reward in the distant future. And just as many smokers wish they could quit and many people wish they ate less, many consumers wish they saved more of their income. According to one survey, 76 percent of Americans said they were not saving enough for retirement.

An implication of this inconsistency over time is that people might be better off if they found ways to commit their future selves to following through on their plans. Smokers trying to quit may throw away their cigarettes, and people on a diet may put locks on their refrigerators. What can people who save too little do? Find some way to lock up their money before they spend it. Some retirement accounts, such as 401(k) plans, allow people to do something much like that. Workers can agree to have some money taken out

Ask the Experts — **Behavioral Economics**

"Insights from psychology about individual behavior—examples of which include limited rationality, low self-control, or a taste for fairness—predict several important types of observed market outcomes that fully-rational economic models do not."

What do economists say?

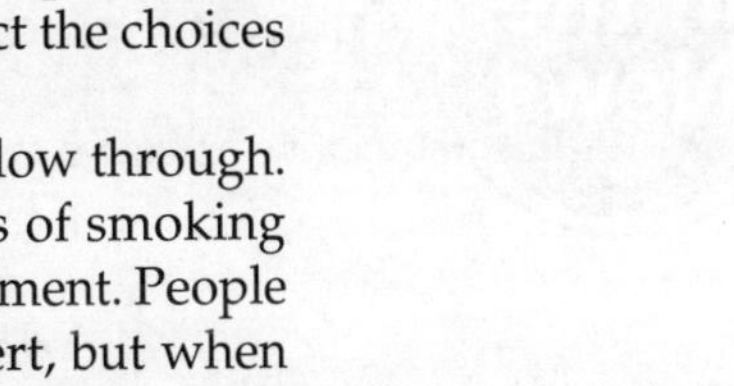

Source: IGM Economic Experts Panel, October 19, 2017.

of their paychecks before they ever see it. The money is deposited in a retirement account, and if it is withdrawn before a certain age, there is a financial penalty. Perhaps that is one reason these retirement accounts are so popular: They protect people from their own desires for instant gratification.

Quick**Quiz**

8. One documented deviation from rationality is that many people
   a. tend to be excessively confident in their own abilities.
   b. change their mind too quickly when they get new information.
   c. give too much weight to outcomes that will occur far in the future.
   d. make decisions by equating marginal benefits and marginal costs.

9. The experiment called the ultimatum game illustrates that people
   a. play the Nash equilibrium in strategic situations.
   b. are motivated by the desire for instant gratification.
   c. care about fairness, even to their own detriment.
   d. make decisions that are inconsistent over time.

Answers are at the end of the chapter.

In the News: Faults in Risk Assessment

Even after being fully vaccinated, many people remained fearful of Covid-19. Why is that, and what does it say about people's ability to assess risk?

Irrational Covid Fears

By David Leonhardt

Guido Calabresi, a federal judge and Yale law professor, invented a little fable that he has been telling law students for more than three decades.

He tells the students to imagine a god coming forth to offer society a wondrous invention that would improve everyday life in almost every way. It would allow people to spend more time with friends and family, see new places and do jobs they otherwise could not do. But it would also come with a high cost. In exchange for bestowing this invention on society, the god would choose 1,000 young men and women and strike them dead.

Calabresi then asks: Would you take the deal? Almost invariably, the students say no. The professor then delivers the fable's lesson: "What's the difference between this and the automobile?"

In truth, automobiles kill many more than 1,000 young Americans each year; the total U.S. death toll hovers at about 40,000 annually. We accept this toll, almost unthinkingly, because vehicle crashes have always been part of our lives. We can't fathom a world without them.

It's a classic example of human irrationality about risk. We often underestimate large, chronic dangers, like car crashes or chemical pollution, and fixate on tiny but salient risks, like plane crashes or shark attacks.

One way for a risk to become salient is for it to be new. That's a core idea behind Calabresi's fable. He asks students to consider whether they would accept the cost of vehicle travel if it did not already exist. That they say no underscores the very different ways we treat new risks and enduring ones.

I have been thinking about the fable recently because of Covid-19. Covid certainly presents a salient risk: It's a global pandemic that has upended daily life for more than a year. It has changed how we live, where we work, even what we wear on our faces. Covid feels ubiquitous.

Fortunately, it is also curable. The vaccines have nearly eliminated death, hospitalization and other serious Covid illness among people who have received shots. The vaccines have also radically reduced the chances that people contract even a mild version of Covid or can pass it on to others.

Yet many vaccinated people continue to obsess over the risks from Covid—because they are so new and salient.

To take just one example, major media outlets trumpeted new government data last week showing that 5,800 fully vaccinated Americans had contracted Covid. That may sound like a big number, but it indicates that a vaccinated person's chances of getting Covid are about one in 11,000. The chances of getting a version

22-4 Conclusion

This chapter took you on a trip to the frontier of microeconomics. You may have noticed that we sketched out ideas rather than fully developing them. One reason is that you might study these topics in more detail in advanced courses. Another is that these topics remain active areas of research and are still being fleshed out.

To see how these topics fit into the broader picture, recall the **Principles of Managerial Economics** from Chapter 1. One principle states that markets are usually a good way to organize economic activity. Another says that governments can sometimes improve market outcomes. As you study economics, you can more fully appreciate these principles as well as the caveats that come with them. The study of asymmetric information may make you more wary of market outcomes. The study of political economy may make you more wary of government solutions. And the study of behavioral economics may make you wary of any institution that relies on human decision making, including both the market and the government.

If these topics have a common theme, it is that life is messy. Information is imperfect, government is imperfect, and people are imperfect. Of course, you knew this long before you started studying economics. But economists need to understand these imperfections as precisely as they can if they are to explain, and perhaps improve, the world around them.

any worse than a common cold are even more remote.

But they are not zero. And they will not be zero anytime in the foreseeable future. Victory over Covid will not involve its elimination. Victory will instead mean turning it into the sort of danger that plane crashes or shark attacks present—too small to be worth reordering our lives.

That is what the vaccines do. If you're vaccinated, Covid presents a minuscule risk to you, and you present a minuscule Covid risk to anyone else. A car trip is a bigger threat, to you and others. About 100 Americans are likely to die in car crashes today. The new federal data suggests that either zero or one vaccinated person will die today from Covid....

Coming to grips with the comforting realities of post-vaccination life is going to take some time for most of us. It's only natural that so many vaccinated people continue to harbor irrational fears. Yet slowly recognizing that irrationality will be a vital part of overcoming Covid.

"We're not going to get to a place of zero risk," Jennifer Nuzzo, a Johns Hopkins epidemiologist, told me during a virtual Times event last week. "I don't think that's the right metric for feeling like things are normal."

After Nuzzo made that point, Dr. Ashish Jha of Brown University told us about his own struggle to return to normal. He has been fully vaccinated for almost two months, he said, and only recently decided to meet a vaccinated friend for a drink, unmasked. "It was hard—psychologically hard—for me," Jha said.

"There are going to be some challenges to re-acclimating and re-entering," he added. "But we've got to do it."

And how did it feel in the end, I asked, to get together with his friend?

"It was awesome," Jha said. ■

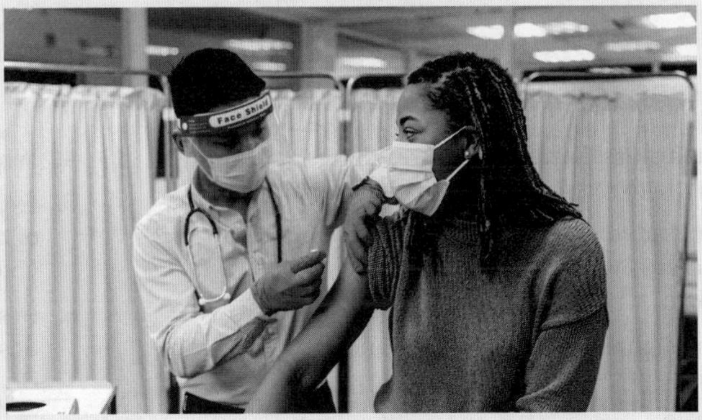

FLY VIEW PRODUCTIONS/E+/GETTY IMAGES

Questions to Discuss

1. How do you think you would have answered the question in Calabresi's parable? Do you think your answer is rational?
2. If you were vaccinated for Covid-19, how did the vaccination change your attitudes and behavior? Do you think your response was fully rational?

Source: New York Times, April 19, 2021.

Chapter in a Nutshell

- In many transactions, information is asymmetric. When there are hidden actions, principals may be concerned that agents suffer from the problem of moral hazard. When there are hidden characteristics, buyers may be concerned about the problem of adverse selection among the sellers. Private markets sometimes deal with asymmetric information with signaling and screening.
- Although government policy can sometimes improve market outcomes, governments are themselves imperfect institutions. The Condorcet paradox shows that majority rule fails to produce transitive preferences for society, and Arrow's impossibility theorem shows that no voting system can be perfect. In many situations, democratic institutions will produce the outcome desired by the median voter, regardless of the preferences of the rest of the electorate. Moreover, the individuals who set government policy may be motivated by self-interest rather than the national interest.
- The study of psychology and economics reveals that human decision making is more complex than is assumed in conventional economic theory. People are not always rational, they care about the fairness of economic outcomes (even to their own detriment), and they can be inconsistent over time.

Key Concepts

moral hazard, p. 452
agent, p. 452
principal, p. 452
adverse selection, p. 454
signaling, p. 454
screening, p. 456
political economy, p. 457
condorcet paradox, p. 458
arrow's impossibility theorem, p. 459
median voter theorem, p. 460
behavioral economics, p. 462

Questions for Review

1. What is moral hazard? List three things an employer might do to reduce the severity of this problem.
2. What is adverse selection? Give an example of a market in which adverse selection might be a problem.
3. Define **signaling** and **screening** and give an example of each.
4. What unusual property of voting did Condorcet notice?
5. Explain why majority rule respects the preferences of the median voter rather than those of the average voter.
6. Describe the ultimatum game. What outcome from this game does conventional economic theory predict? Do experiments confirm this prediction? Explain.

Problems and Applications

1. Each of the following situations involves moral hazard. In each case, identify the principal and the agent and explain why there is asymmetric information. How does the action described reduce the problem of moral hazard?
   a. Landlords require tenants to pay security deposits.
   b. Firms compensate top executives with options to buy company stock at a given price in the future.
   c. Car insurance companies offer discounts to customers who install antitheft devices in their cars.
2. A case study in this chapter describes how a boyfriend can signal his love to a girlfriend by giving an appropriate gift. Do you think saying "I love you" can also serve as a signal? Why or why not?
3. The Affordable Care Act signed into law by President Obama in 2010 included the following two provisions:
   i. Insurance companies must offer health insurance to everyone who applies and charge them the same price regardless of a person's preexisting health condition.
   ii. Everyone must buy health insurance or pay a penalty for not doing so.
   a. Which of these policies taken on its own makes the problem of adverse selection worse? Explain.
   b. Why do you think the policy you identified in part (a) was included in the law?
   c. Why do you think the other policy was included in the law?

4. Ken walks into an ice-cream parlor.

   Waiter: "We have vanilla and chocolate today."
   Ken: "I'll take vanilla."
   Waiter: "I almost forgot. We also have strawberry."
   Ken: "In that case, I'll take chocolate."

   What standard property of decision making is Ken violating? (Hint: Reread the section on Arrow's impossibility theorem.)

5. Three friends are choosing a restaurant for dinner. Here are their preferences:

	Rachel	Ross	Joey
First choice	Italian	Italian	Chinese
Second choice	Chinese	Chinese	Mexican
Third choice	Mexican	Mexican	French
Fourth choice	French	French	Italian

   a. If the three friends use a Borda count to make their decision, where do they go to eat?
   b. On their way to their chosen restaurant, they see that the Mexican and French restaurants are closed, so they use a Borda count again to decide between the remaining two restaurants. Where do they decide to go now?
   c. How do your answers to parts (a) and (b) relate to Arrow's impossibility theorem?

6. Three friends are choosing a TV show to watch. Here are their preferences:

	Chandler	Phoebe	Monica
First choice	*NCIS*	*Ted Lasso*	*Survivor*
Second choice	*Ted Lasso*	*Survivor*	*NCIS*
Third choice	*Survivor*	*NCIS*	*Ted Lasso*

   a. If the three friends try using a Borda count to make their choice, what would happen?
   b. Monica suggests a vote by majority rule. She proposes that they first choose between *NCIS* and *Ted Lasso*, and they then choose between the winner of the first vote and *Survivor*. If they all vote their preferences honestly, what outcome would occur?
   c. Should Chandler agree to Monica's suggestion? What voting system would he prefer?
   d. Phoebe and Monica convince Chandler to go along with Monica's proposal. In round one, Chandler dishonestly says he prefers *Ted Lasso* to *NCIS*. Why might he do this?

7. Five roommates are planning to spend the weekend in their apartment watching movies, and they are debating how many movies to watch. The table below shows each roommate's willingness to pay for each of the movies:

	Ava	Ridley	Spike	Chloe	Quentin
First film	₹14	₹10	₹8	₹4	₹2
Second film	12	8	4	2	0
Third film	10	6	2	0	0
Fourth film	6	2	0	0	0
Fifth film	2	0	0	0	0

   A movie on their streaming service costs ₹15, which the roommates split equally, so each pays ₹3 per movie.

   a. What is the efficient number of movies to watch (that is, the number that maximizes total surplus)?
   b. For each roommate, what is the preferred number of movies to watch?
   c. What is the preference of the median roommate?
   d. If the roommates held a vote on the efficient outcome versus the median voter's preference, how would each person vote? Which outcome would get a majority?
   e. If one of the roommates proposed a different number of movies, could the proposal beat the winning outcome from part (d) in a vote?
   f. Can majority rule be counted on to reach efficient outcomes in the provision of public goods?

8. Two ice-cream stands are deciding where to set up along a one-mile beach. The people are uniformly located along the beach, and each person sitting on the beach buys exactly one ice-cream cone per day from the nearest stand. Each ice-cream seller wants the maximum number of customers. Where along the beach will the two stands locate? Of which result in this chapter does this outcome remind you?

9. The government is considering two ways to help low-income families: giving them cash or giving them free meals at soup kitchens.
   a. Give an argument, based on the standard theory of the rational consumer, for giving cash.
   b. Give an argument, based on asymmetric information, for why free meals at soup kitchens may be better than cash handouts.
   c. Give an argument, based on behavioral economics, for why free meals at soup kitchens may be better than cash handouts.

Quick**Quiz** Answers

1. b 2. a 3. d 4. c 5. b 6. c 7. a 8. a 9. c

Chapter

23

Uncertainty and Risk Preferences

In chapter 21, we learnt about how people make decisions, given limited resources. We developed the theory of consumer choice and utility functions and discussed how optimal consumption is arrived at subject to budget constraints. This chapter takes us one step further to understanding choices under **uncertainty**. Essentially, we learn about how individuals make decisions where there is risk involved.

uncertainty
a state of incomplete knowledge in which future outcomes and their probabilities are unknown or not well defined.

Imagine buying an item that is fragile. There is a chance that the good is damaged when it is delivered to you and therefore you get lesser utility from it. Similarly, buying a used car is also a risky decision because there is a probability that the car may be of poor quality. These are examples of consumer decisions under risk. Managers routinely make decisions under uncertainty, and therefore it is important to understand the role of risk and the appetite for risk and how it can affect managerial decision-making. This chapter provides a fundamental understanding of these concepts.

FZMANJAKA/E+/GETTY IMAGES, CARLOS FLORES/EYEEM/GETTY IMAGES

23-1 Decision-Making under Uncertainty

Managers are making decisions under uncertainty all the time. In fact, only very rarely are managerial decisions of consequence made under zero uncertainty or sure environments. For instance, prices move, policies change, competitors react, monsoons fail, and exchange rates jump. All of these can indicate varying degrees of uncertainty in the business decision-making environment.

The motivation to study decision-making under uncertainty is rather straightforward in the Indian context. Firms price amid currency swings and commodity price fluctuations. They have to plan CapEx (Capital Expenditure) under strict regulatory and market demand uncertainties and plan their supply chain logistics under weather risks. A manufacturer of consumer durables must choose between raising prices now or waiting for GST credit to clear; an exporter must decide forward coverage as the current account and global rates shift; a food processor plans procurement under monsoon variance and MSP policy uncertainty. These are the types of decisions that come from the purview of decision-making under uncertainty, and the concepts we study in this chapter should give us a clearer understanding of how to navigate through uncertainty and risky decision-making environments.

23-1 a The Major Goals

This chapter has the following major goals that we wish to achieve:

1. Understand how uncertainty affects people's decisions and what parallels can we draw for managerial decision-making. The objective is to understand how managers' decision-making can be impacted by the mere presence of uncertainty and under more intensified uncertainty.
2. Understand why people generally dislike risk. This will allow us to draw up theories of "preferences" for risk. In Chapter 21, we learnt about consumer preferences for goods and services. In the same vein, we will study individuals' preferences for risk and, in doing so, extrapolate to managerial economics contexts to understand how risk appetite of firms can be natively created. Under varying risk preferences, how do managers and firms alter their business strategies because the preference for risk will eventually determine how the choice will be made under uncertainty.
3. Understand how managers can reduce or avoid risk. In general, if there is a natural disaster for risk, people would like to avoid taking risks and in risky environments may want to reduce risk or mitigate the ill effects of risk to the extent possible. We will learn about the concepts that discuss this and analyze its implications for managerial decisions.

lottery
an exhaustive list of various possibilities of an event with their associated probabilities for each possibility such that the sum of these probabilities is equal to 1.

probability
a numerical measure from 0 to 1 of how likely an event is to occur where 0 implies an impossible outcome and 1 implies sure outcome or certain outcome.

23-1 b Risky Outcomes as Lotteries

When a decision has more than one possible outcome, each with some chance of happening, we can think of it as a **lottery**. Think of a lottery as a tidy list of "what could happen" and "how likely each outcome is." Therefore, a lottery is a set of outcomes, each with a probability assigned to it, such that the probabilities add up to 1, if expressed in fractions, or 100% if expressed in percentages.

For example, a manager invests in a project and expects a rate of interest (ROI) of ₹2 lakhs with a 40% chance and an ROI of ₹10 lakhs with 60% chance. This is a lottery that describes all possibilities and their associated **probabilities** such that the probabilities add up to 100%.

Essentially, the term lottery can be used to describe any event for which the outcome is uncertain. So, the choice under uncertainty and risky decision-making

Box 23.1 Refresher on Probability Theory

Let 'i' denote a possible outcome among n total possible events, where i can take the values 1, 2, 3, ...n.

Suppose Pri denotes the probability that event i occurs.

Given the characterization of probability, this must mean that Pri lies between 0 and 1 for all possible values of 'i'.

Also, Pr1 + Pr2 + Pr3 +....... + Prn = 1. This means that all the probabilities should add up to 1.

Example 1: Tossing a Fair Coin

Here, $n = 2$, going by the above definitions. There are only two possibilities, i.e., Heads or Tails. Also, each Pri = 0.5 as it is a fair coin, and, therefore, Heads and Tails are equally likely.

Example 2: Probability of rolling a 5 on a fair die

Here, $n = 6$ because there are 6 sides on a die. The Pri = 1/6 as all the 6 outcomes are equally likely. Therefore, the probability of rolling a 5 on a fair die is 1/6.

essentially involves dealing with lotteries of some form. It is important to note that even though there are many outcomes listed in the lottery, only one outcome will actually occur. The other outcomes are simply alternate possibilities, all of which cannot be realized at the same time. The manager's problem is that at the time of making the business decision, it is not known to her the possibilities that will eventually occur. Therefore, the choice for the manager becomes probabilistic, and the manager has to carefully evaluate the probabilities of each of the event that may occur.

23-2 Expectations, Valuations, and Utilities of Lotteries

Managers are interested in the payoffs or returns from the realized outcomes of lotteries. Essentially, dealing with the lottery means figuring out how to ensure that the payoff is maximized from the potential uncertain outcome. There is a payoff associated with each possible outcome of a lottery.

Suppose there is a lottery with n possible events. Now assume that X_i denotes the payoff from the outcome when event 'i' occurs and given n events, "i" can take the value 1, 2, 3, ...n. So, the payoffs from each outcome are respectively X_1, X_2, X_3, ... X_n, but only one of these will actually occur.

23-2 a Expected Value

The **expected value** (EV) of the lottery is the probability-weighted average of all possible outcomes of a risky decision. It is the payoff you get on average if you could repeat the situation many times.

expected value is the weighted average of the payoffs from all possible outcomes of the lottery, with the weights being the respective probabilities of the outcome occurring.

So, for the lottery being discussed, the expected value is the sum of the payoffs in each possible outcome multiplied by the probabilities of those outcomes.

$$\textbf{Expected Value } (EV) = Pr_1 X_1 + Pr_2 X_2 + \ldots .\ Pr_n X_n$$

As an example, suppose you toss a coin and get nothing if Heads comes up and get ₹100 if Tails comes up. Then the expected value will be:

$$EV = Pr \text{ (Heads) * (Payoff if Heads)} + Pr \text{ (Tails) * (Payoff if Tails)}$$
$$= 0.5 * 0 + 0.5 * 100 = ₹50.$$

Box 23.2 Expected Values – Classroom Activity

Imagine given a choice between a sure option of ₹1 lakh or an option of a lottery that gives you a chance to win ₹3,00,002 with 0.5 probability and losing ₹1 lakh with 0.5 probability.

If you end up choosing the sure option, you are not alone. Millions of students worldwide would make the same choice. While this is the most common and natural, let us see what happened here. The expected value of the lottery was $0.5*(3,00,002) + 0.5(-1,00,000) = 1,00,001$, which is greater than the expected value of the sure outcome, which is 1,00,000 with probability 1. Clearly, majority of individuals choose an option with a lower expected value.

What will firms do? Will the manager choose the lottery? The chances are that the manager would also not choose the lottery but go with the sure outcome despite having a lower expected value. You may say that this is because the gain of 1 rupee in expectation is not worth it, but a similar result will appear even for larger sized gains.

This is because firms (and individuals and, therefore, managers) are not necessarily expected value maximizers. They are not choosing options to try and maximize expected value. But then what are they maximizing? Let us study this in the next section.

23-2 b Expected Utility

The fact that consumers and managers do not maximize expected values of lotteries does not necessarily imply that they are not rational. It just means that managers perhaps do not value money, per se, but instead value the utility that money brings them. This means that the value of money or wealth comes from what consumption that money can afford or buy.

The concept of utility we learnt in Chapter 21 can be adapted to decision-making under uncertainty. This revised version of utility is known as **expected utility**. It is nothing but the sum of the utility in each possible outcome, multiplied by the indicated probabilities of those outcomes.

expected utility is the value a decision-maker assigns to a risky option by averaging the utility or satisfaction and not the raw payoffs from each possible outcome weighted by its probability.

Using the similar logic as above for the expected value, the expected utility from the lottery in question can therefore be described as follows:

$$\textbf{Expected Utility } (EU) = Pr_1\, U(X_1) + Pr_2\, U(X_2) + \ldots.\, Pr_n\, U(X_n)$$

FYI The St. Petersburg Paradox

In the early 1700s, a Swiss mathematician by the name of Nicolaus Bernoulli came up with a problem, which later famously was known as the St. Petersburg Paradox. Although, the name (and often the solution) is credited to Nicolaus' cousin, Daniel Bernoulli, who was believed to be a resident of Saint Petersburg.

The game is as follows: a fair coin is tossed until the first Heads (H) comes up. If H comes up on the first flip, a payoff of 2 is received. However, if a T comes up the first flip, then it is tossed again. If H comes up this time, the payoff is $2^2 = 4$, but if T comes up, the game continues. So, if H comes up on the nth flip the player wins 2^n rupees. Notice, that the probability of H in the first flip is (1/2), that on the second flip is $(1/2)^2$, and so on up until nth flip where the probability is $(1/2)^n$. The EV of this lottery, if computed, is undefined and essentially is infinite. However, when offered as a bet, all gamblers are only willing to pay a bounded entry fee and not infinitely large amounts. People were initially surprised by this. But Bernoulli proposed the idea that it is not the wealth that matters but the valuation or perception of the wealth, the incremental value of which reduces as the wealth increases. This is what gave rise to the idea of diminishing marginal utility of income.

Here each $U(X_i)$ for all the n values of 'i' denote the utility from each specific outcome, sometimes known as the Bernoulli utility function. It is essentially putting a functional form to the pleasure or satisfaction derived from the realization of outcome 'i' and receipt of the associated payoff X_i.

Using the example of Box 23.2, while people were not maximizing EV when choosing the sure outcome over the lottery that yields a higher EV was perplexing, allowing for individuals to be expected utility maximizers resolves this dilemma. We can model the behavior observed as individuals and managers maximizing expected utilities and not expected values. Therefore, it must mean that for a specific functional form $U(.)$, the EU (Lottery) was smaller than the EU (sure outcome).

In other words, while comparing EVs we find:

$$0.5\ (3{,}00{,}002) + 0.5\ (-1{,}00{,}000) > 1{,}00{,}000$$

It must mean that for the decision makers here:

$$0.5\ U\ (3{,}00{,}002) + 0.5\ U\ (-1{,}00{,}000) < U\ (1{,}00{,}000)$$

This would mean that the weighted average of the utilities from the payoffs of each outcome (expected utility) is higher for the sure outcome than lottery, even though the expected value of the lottery is higher. In the following sections, we will formalize what such behavior implies and departures from such behavior.

Quick**Quiz**

1. Consider a lottery that yields ₹12, ₹7, or ₹1 (all in Lakhs) with probabilities 0.3, 0.5, and 0.2, respectively. Then the expected value of the lottery is:
   a. 5.9 b. 6.9
   c. 7.9 d. 8.9
2. Under expected utility, we average:
   a. Raw payoffs weighted by probabilities
   b. Utilities of outcomes weighted by probabilities
   c. Simple average of payoffs
   d. Simple average of utilities of outcomes
3. Expected value is
   a. Raw payoffs weighted by probabilities
   b. Utilities of outcomes weighted by probabilities
   c. Simple average of payoffs
   d. Simple average of utilities of outcomes

Answers are at the end of the chapter.

23-3 Risk Preferences

Risk preferences describe how decision makers trade-off higher average payoffs against the possibility of bad outcomes. Risk preferences reflect how your firm trades average return for downside exposure in the context of managerial economics. You may think of this as a bridge between mainstream microeconomic theory and managerial action.

In managerial economics, these principles guide operating decisions such as pricing strategies based on demand fluctuations, inventory management to mitigate stock-out risks, and hedging ratios for foreign exchange and commodities. Additionally, service-level commitments with penalties, capacity planning, and incentive compensation can influence team behavior, potentially encouraging risk-taking actions that might not be otherwise pursued by the firm. On the other hand, when faced with risky choices managers may adjust their strategy and decisions depending on their appetite and tolerance for risk.

It is with this premise that we will now model preferences for risk. Practically, knowing your organization's risk preference lets you choose among projects with the same expected margin but different downside, decide how much volatility to hedge, and design incentive plans that don't push teams into risks the firm wouldn't otherwise take.

23-3 a Characterizing Risk Preferences

Consider a choice that a manager faces between the following options:

Project A: *A safe project that yields a return on investment of ₹7 crore, for sure, in all states of the world.*

Project B: *A risky project that yields a return on investment of ₹18 crore if the project succeeds, but the firm may lose ₹4 crore if the project fails. Let us assume that the probability that the project will succeed is 50%.*

*In this case, the expected value of the return on the investment is: 0.5 * 18 + 0.5 * (–4) = ₹7 crore*

Essentially, the choice between projects A and B for the manager is a choice between two options that have the same expected value. One is a sure option, whereas the other is a risky option. Defining various types of risk preferences requires us to compare between a safe and a risky option such that both have the same expected value. It is important to remember that these definitions are laid out under this important premise of comparison and may not hold meaningfully if comparing options with different EVs.

risk-averse
people prefer the sure payoff to a risky lottery with the same EV as the sure payoff.

A **risk-averse** person or manager will be defined by the fact that such an individual when faced with a choice between Project A and Project B above will always choose Project A. These are the managers that dislike risk and hate dispersion. Essentially, they lack the taste for risk, and hence their preference towards risk is characterized by the fact that they prefer the sure payoff to any gamble with the same expected value because losses hurt more than equivalent gains benefit them.

Managerial Insight: In practice, risk aversion in firms shows up as managers that end up choosing stable margins over volatile but higher-EV bets, paying to insure tail risks, accepting forward contracts that shave a little off the mean to tighten outcomes, and valuing supplier terms that cap penalties or provide quantity-flex bands.

risk-loving
person prefers the riskier payoff to a sure payoff even when the EV of the risky lottery is the same as that of the sure payoff.

However, if a manager chooses Project B over Project A, then he or she will be known as a **risk-loving** person. Sometimes, this is also interchangeably known as ***risk-seeking behavior***. This implies that such managers (and firms) like dispersion and have a strong appetite for risk. A risk-loving manager prefers more spread for the same mean and will be disproportionately attracted to the upside even when it comes with downside. This is rare as a corporate policy but can appear in start-up settings, tournament-style incentives, or when managers chase option-like payoffs (e.g., breakthrough R&D, blockbuster bids for mergers and acquisitions, etc.).

Managerial Insight: Firms should be cautious here because risk-seeking preferences at the individual level can misalign with shareholder interests. As a result, boards often cap downside (stop-losses), tie pay to risk-adjusted metrics, or structure staged investments.

risk-neutral
person cares only about expected value and is indifferent between a sure value and a gamble with the same EV as the sure option.

A **risk-neutral** manager is the one who will always care about the expected value and therefore remains indifferent between a sure payoff and a lottery with the same means. Essentially, such managers, when faced with the above choice, would be indifferent between Project A and Project B and wouldn't care which one is chosen. They will accept variance if (and only if) it doesn't change the EV, which makes unbiased hedges irrelevant and focuses attention on NPV maximization and the cost of capital.

Managerial Insight: Managerially, you'll often assume risk neutrality for large, repeatable decisions (law of large numbers and portfolio effects) or when a firm has deep pockets and good diversification. Firm-level choices will reflect this. Consequently, we expect managers to pick the higher EV project even if it's bumpier, hedge only to reduce transaction costs or meet covenants, and evaluate contracts on their expected contribution margin without extra penalty for dispersion.

23-3 b Why are Managers Risk-Averse?

In general, the idea of risk aversion can be linked to the theory of diminishing marginal utility. However, since preferences here are defined over wealth or money, in essence, we need to think about the **diminishing marginal utility** of income or money.

diminishing marginal utility of income as income rises, utility from the income or wealth also rises but at a diminishing rate.

This means that every extra rupee earned in the bad state of the world, or when income is low, is valued more than the extra rupee earned in the good state or when the income is high. This would mean that the utility function for the manager, defined over income or wealth, is concave. It rises with higher income but at a lower rate, and therefore the slope keeps falling. Consider the following utility function over income. We plot income on the horizontal axis and utility from that income on the vertical axis.

The Risk-Averse Manager's preferences are represented by a concave utility function with the property of diminishing marginal utility over wealth. The horizontal axis measures the income levels, and the vertical axis measures the actual utilities from these corresponding incomes. For a risk-averse individual, the expected utility from a risky gamble is always lower than the sure utility from a sure payoff, which is equal to the expected value of the risky gamble. Therefore, the EU < U(EV), as depicted in this figure.

Clearly, the concave shape of the utility function indicates that the utility from income is increasing but the rate at which it is higher is decreasing. For instance, if we move from income of 40 to 41, the utility increases by a larger magnitude than when we move from 80 to 81.

Figure 1

Risk-Averse Manager

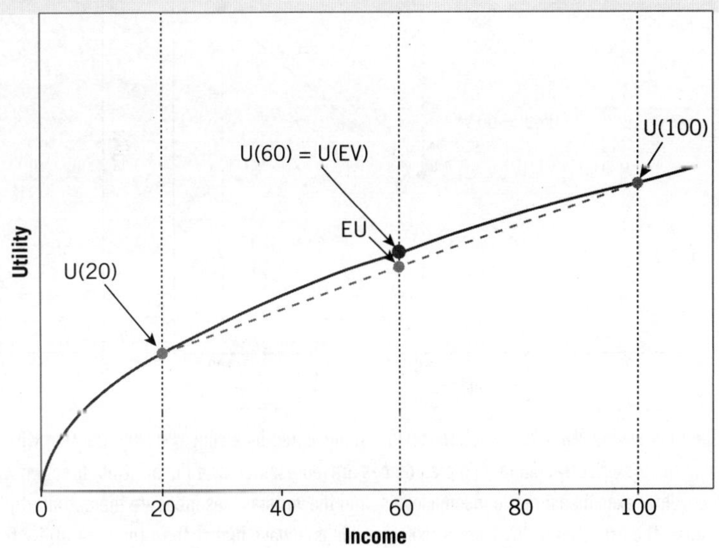

Now, consider a decision as discussed in the previous section. Suppose the choice is between a project that yields ₹60 crore for sure and another riskier one. Then, the utility from this sure project is measured as *U* (60) in the graph in Figure 1. For the risky project, suppose with probability of 0.5, it yields ₹20 crore and, with probability of 0.5, it yields ₹100 crore. When either of these is realized, the firm and the manager derive utility of either *U* (20) or *U* (100), as marked in the Figure. However, only one of these outcomes will be realized and due to uncertainty, when the manager is making the decision, he or she is unsure of which will occur. If the good state occurs, *U* (100) is higher than *U* (60), and therefore the risky option would have been better, but if the bad state occurs, *U* (60) from the risky trumps the U (20) from the lottery. A priori this makes managerial decision-making challenging.

If the manager computes the expected value of this lottery, the *EV* = ₹60 crore (0.5 * 100 + 0.5*20). This is exactly the same as the sure payoff. So, the same point on the utility curve can denote both the utility from the sure payoff, i.e., *U* (60) and also the utility from the expected value of the lottery *U* (*EV* = 60). Given this property, we

Box 23.3 Risk-Neutral and Risk-Loving Managers

Using similar logic, we can characterize risk-neutral and risk-loving behavior. Given a choice between a safe outcome and a risky outcome with same expected value as the safe outcome, a risk-loving manager will always choose the risky project, as discussed before. This must mean that for this manager, the *EU* (risky) > *U* (Safe = *EV*). This can be depicted by a convex utility function, representing increasing marginal utility of income, as in Panel A of Figure 2 below. Similarly, the risk-neutral manager is indifferent between these choices, implying that *EU* (risky) = *U* (safe *EV*) for this person, and therefore this manager is simply interested in maximizing expected value and does not have a distaste for risk. This is depicted by a linear utility function as in Panel B of Figure 2 below. Such a utility function implies that marginal utility of income is constant for all levels of income.

Figure 2

Risk-Loving and Risk-Neutral Manager

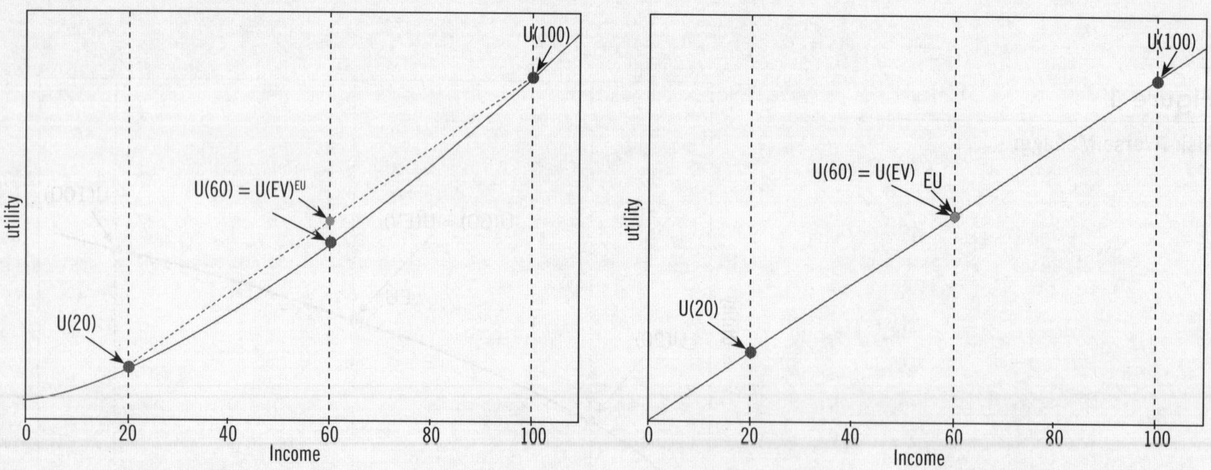

The Risk-Loving Manager's preferences are represented by a convex utility function with the property of increasing marginal utility over wealth, whereas the Risk-Neutral Manager's preferences are represented by a linear utility function with the property of constant marginal utility over wealth. The horizontal axes measure the income levels, and the vertical axes measure the actual utilities from these corresponding incomes. For a risk-loving individual, the expected utility from a risky gamble is always higher than the sure utility from a sure payoff, which is equal to the expected value of the risky gamble. Therefore, the EU > U(EV), as depicted in Panel A. For risk-neutral person, EU = U (EV), indicating neutrality towards risk and indifference about the dispersion.

can compare the sure payoff to the lottery in terms of risk preferences. This means that we can now analyze why managers are risk-averse when they have such a utility function, depicting diminishing marginal utility of income.

The manager's choice boils down to comparing the utilities of the payoffs in both situations: one where a sure income of ₹60 crore happens and the other where in expectation of ₹60 crore can be earned but the actual realization is either 20 or 100 crores. This is essentially comparing the following:

Utility from Sure: $U(60)$ *or* $U(0.5 * 100 + 0.5 * 20)$ *or* $U(EV)$
Utility from Risky: $0.5 * U(100) + 0.5 * U(20)$ or EU

The point EU, therefore, represents the utility from the risky or the expected utility from this gamble. The dotted line joining the two utilities denotes that it is a convex combination or average of the two utilities. From Figure 1, it is clear that **$U(EV) > EU$**. In other words, the utility from the sure outcome, which is same in value as the expected value of the lottery, is larger than the expected utility from the risky project or the average of the utilities from each of the possible outcomes. Consequently, faced with this choice, a manager should choose the safe option.

This indicates that the manager is risk-averse, because she is choosing a safe option over a risky gamble that has the expected value equal to the safe payoff. Therefore, concave utility functions of this form can be used to characterize risk aversion. This means a risk-averse manager is the one who has preferences that can be depicted by such a utility function. Conversely, if any individual has preferences over income that represents a concave function with the property of diminishing marginal utility over income, then that person is a risk-averse person.

23-3 c Certainty Equivalent and Risk Premia

Consider a risk-averse manager who prefers a sure return over a risky project that has the same expected return as the sure outcome. However, is there a sure income level that would make this manager indifferent between that sure return and this risky project?

This sure value is known as the **certainty equivalent (CE)** of the lottery or gamble. This means, if the choice for the manager was between the certainty equivalent value and the risky gamble, the manager would be exactly indifferent between the two. In fact, for every sure amount below CE, the utility of that sure amount is less than the lottery's expected utility, so the risk-averse manager strictly prefers the lottery. For any sure amount above CE, the risk-averse managers prefer the sure amount over the risky gamble.

certainty equivalent is the sure amount of money that makes the decision-maker indifferent between accepting a risky project and taking this sure amount.

In utility terms, this means the following:

$$U(CE) = EU(\textit{risky project})$$

Managerial Insight: As discussed, certainty equivalent (CE) is the amount of sure money that leaves a decision-maker indifferent between receiving that sure amount and facing a particular risky payoff. It translates a gamble into a single cash number that reflects both the average outcome and the decision maker's attitude toward risk. If a project could earn ₹10 lakh with 60% chance and ₹2 lakh with 40% chance (EV – ₹6.8 lakh), a risk-averse manager might judge that a sure ₹5 ₹5.5 lakh feels just as good as taking the gamble; that sure amount is the CE.

The gap between expected value and certainty equivalent is known as the **risk premium (*RP*)**:

$$RP = EV - CE.$$

Risk-averse managers have positive risk premia, implying that they have to give up some expected returns to avoid volatility. In practice, CE is what you compare

Figure 3

Certainty Equivalent and Risk Premium

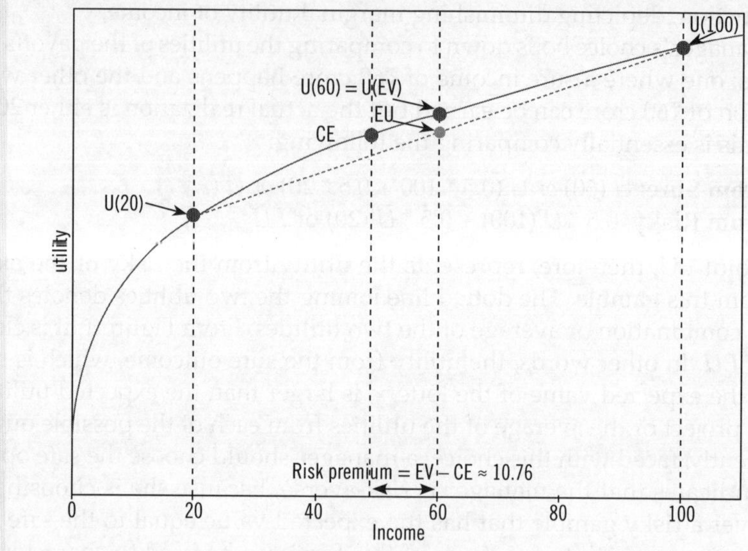

across options when variability matters. For example, deciding whether to buy insurance/hedge, whether to accept a fixed-price contract instead of a volatile spot price, or whether to pilot a rollout to shrink downside before scaling. A hedge or insurance policy is worthwhile when the increase in CE from a tighter distribution of outcomes exceeds the premium or hedge cost, even if expected value falls slightly.

Essentially, *RP* is the answer to question: "What is the maximum amount that a manager will be willing to pay to get rid of all the risk?' Practically, once the manager has an idea of the CE of a project and can easily calculate the expected value, she can back out the risk premia using the above relationship. The CE is what a firm would accept for a guaranteed outcome, while the RP is what they would pay to insure/hedge instead of facing the uncertain payoff. In the context of a risk-averse manager, facing a choice between a sure outcome and a risky project gamble, the CE and RP can be depicted as in Figure 3.

Quick**Quiz**

4. For a risk-averse manager, the certainty equivalent is always:
   a. Greater than the expected value of the lottery
   b. Same as the expected value of the lottery
   c. Smaller than the expected value of the lottery
   d. Same as above
5. Risk premium is:
   a. The excess of CE over EV
   b. The expected value of a lottery
   c. The difference between expected utility and CE
   d. The difference between EV and CE
6. If the expected utility from a gamble is higher than the utility from the expected value of the gamble
   a. The individual is risk-loving
   b. The individual is risk-averse
   c. The individual is risk-neutral
   d. Cannot say conclusively
7. Risk-neutral individuals
   a. Have a convex utility function over income
   b. Have a linear utility function over income
   c. Have a concave utility function over income
   d. Exhibit diminishing marginal utility of income

Answers are at the end of the chapter.

The Risk-Averse Manager will be indifferent between taking up the risky project if the choice is between the project and a sure outcome, which yields a payoff equal to the certainty equivalent (CE). Originally, the manager preferred the sure outcome of 60 because $U(60) > EU$, but if the sure payoff instead of ₹CE, then $U(CE) = EU$, which makes her indifferent. To avoid all the risk from the lottery, the manager is willing to pay a premium, such as insurance premium, up to the maximum value of EV – CE. This value is known as the risk premium.

23-4 Conclusion

This chapter showed how to turn uncertainty into prudent managerial choices. It is useful to think of risky decisions as lotteries and summarize them by expected value (the average). However, managerial decision-making essentially deals with maximizing expected utility over lotteries.

The chapter highlights concepts of certainty equivalent and risk premium, which translate risk attitudes into cash numbers. We linked risk preferences to the curvature of utility and used that to speculate how projects, contracts, and hedges on a like-for-like, risk-adjusted basis can affect decisions within the firm. In managerial terms, uncertainty is not something to "eliminate" but to strategize and design around.

Chapter in a Nutshell

- Managerial decision-making under uncertainty and risk can often be represented as choice between lotteries of various kinds.
- Managers generally maximize the expected benefit or satisfaction from their options and not merely expected values.
- When faced with a choice between a sure payoff project and a risky project that has the same expected payoff as the sure one, if a manager chooses the sure project, she is known as a risk-averse individual, whereas if the risky project is chosen, she is a risk-loving manager. A risk-neutral manager is indifferent and only cares about maximizing expected payoffs.
- If a risk-averse manager is indifferent between the risky project and a sure value project, then that sure value is the certainty equivalent of the gamble. This manager will be willing to pay a risk premium, such as insurance premium, up to the difference between the expected value of the lottery and the certainty equivalent to avoid taking the risk or neutralizing the risk from the project.

Key Concepts

Questions for Review

1. What are various ways to characterize risk appetites of managers?
2. Define certainty equivalent and risk premium.
3. What is expected utility? Why do managers maximize expected utility and not expected value?
4. Why is a risk-averse utility concave? Explain why such utility functions depict risk-averseness?

Problems and Applications

1. Suppose, Pratik derives utility from doing economics courses, core as well as electives, in his MBA program. Suppose his utility function is $U = X^{1/2}$, where X is the number of economics electives he takes. Suppose, he plans to pass in 10 economics courses, but there is a 30% chance that he may fail a course.
   a. What is the expected value of the gamble of taking economics courses in terms of how many he might pass?
   b. What is the expected utility?
   c. Is Pratik risk-averse, risk-neutral, or risk-loving over economics courses?

2. Shekhar is carrying 18 quail eggs from Mumbai to Thane in the local train. Making trips back home is costless because he has a free rail pass. He, however, faces an issue with transportation such that either all eggs reach Thane safely or all eggs break in transit. There is a 50% chance for each of these scenarios.
   a. Is Shekhar's utility function over number of eggs, X, defined as $U = X^{1/2}$? Is he risk-averse?
   b. Draw Shekhar's utility function over eggs.
   c. Should Shekhar make one trip back home or two trips?
   d. How would you answer for all the above change if the utility function is instead $U = X^2$

3. The CEO of Indian Patriots Ltd., Mr. Gautam is making a choice between two projects. Project Bharat requires investing ₹100 crore but will yield ₹200 crore in return. Project Hindustan also requires the same investment but can either yield ₹1000 crore with 10% chance or yield ₹111.11 crore with 90% chance.
   a. Suitably round up to calculate the EV of the gamble in Project Hindustan.
   b. Suppose Indian Patriots' risk preferences are given by concave utility functions. What can we say about risk appetite of Mr. Gautam in this case?
   c. Which project will Gautam choose?
   d. What is that value that will make Gautam indifferent between Projects Bharat and Hindustan?

4. Consider a risk-neutral firm by the name of ***OkWithRisk***.
   a. What does this imply about the risk appetite of the managers of OkWithRisk? Will it ever attempt to enter a M&A deal?
   b. Name some mathematical functional forms which might represent such utility.
   c. Do you think the concept of risk premium is relevant for OkWithRisk? Explain your answer.

5. Suppose Mankiw and Chatterjee are partners in a publishing firm. They must decide whether to publish a new edition of an existing book, which will yield profits of ₹100 lakhs, or commission and write a new book, which will yield a profit of ₹160 lakhs if it goes well but will only give a profit of ₹40 lakhs if it is less popular than their existing book. The chance of it being more popular is 50%.
   a. Compute the expected value from publishing each book.
   b. Will Mankiw and Chatterjee maximize this expected value, and how will they choose a book project?
   c. If Mankiw and Chatterjee have a preference over a project represented by square root utility function, then what do we know about their choice?
   d. Calculate the certainty equivalent and risk premium for the projects.

6. Suppose the utility over wealth for Nagma is denoted by $W^{1/3}$.
   a. Will Nagma like a lottery with a win probability of 20% for a prize of ₹10,000 (and 0 if she does not win) or a sure cash transfer from the state government of ₹2,000?
   b. For what sure value will Nagma be willing to go for the lottery?
   c. For what sure values will Nagma only take the sure payoffs?
   d. If Nagma wants to buy lottery insurance, how much premium will she pay?

QuickQuiz Answers

1. b 2. b 3. a 4. c 5. d 6. a 7. b

Chapter

24

Appendix: Data in Managerial Economics

"Data! Data! Data!" Sherlock Holmes once cried. "I can't make bricks without clay." As usual, the fictional detective was right: To solve a mystery, or to understand any other aspect of the world, we need data. Theories and principles are critically important, but only after observing what's happening around us can we be sure we know what is true and what is not.

The term **data** refers to factual information that provides the basis for reasoning and discussion. In economics, data are often quantitative, such as a person's income, a firm's profit, the market price of ice cream, the amount of ice cream sold, or a nation's gross domestic product. Data allow us to attach real numbers to the conceptual variables found in economic theory.

data
factual information, often quantitative, that provides the basis for reasoning and discussion

Data analysis is increasingly central to modern economics. Over the past half century, advances in computing power have enabled economists to analyze ever larger data sets, and research based on data has become increasingly important. Compared with economists of the past, modern economists base their beliefs and policy advice less on pure theory and casual observation and more on the hardheaded analysis of data.

econometrics
the subfield of economics that develops tools to analyze data

A subfield of economics, called **econometrics**, is devoted to developing tools for data analysis. In essence, econometrics is the study of the statistical methods that are useful for understanding the economy. Many colleges offer courses in econometrics, and students majoring in economics are often required to take one as part of their training. This appendix chapter offers a brief introduction.

We address three issues. First, we consider the kinds of data that economists use. Second, we discuss what economists aim to achieve through data analysis. Third, we examine some of the challenges that arise when drawing inferences from data and the methods that econometricians have devised to meet those challenges.

24-1 The Data That Managers Could Gather and Study

Let's begin by discussing the sources and types of data that economists use most often.

24-1a Experimental Data

randomized controlled trial
an experiment in which a researcher randomly divides subjects into groups, treats the groups differently, and compares their outcomes

Sometimes data come from randomized controlled trials. A **randomized controlled trial** is an experiment in which a researcher randomly divides subjects into groups, treats the groups differently, and compares how the groups respond to their treatments.

For example, suppose a pharmaceutical company comes up with a new drug to treat a disease. Before regulators allow the company to market the drug, it must prove that the drug is safe and effective. The company's researchers start by recruiting a sample of, say, 200 people who have the disease. Half of the patients are randomly assigned to the **treatment group** and given the drug. The other half are assigned to the **control group** and given a placebo (a harmless but ineffective pill that looks like the actual drug). The researchers then follow the health of the two groups. If the patients in the treatment group fare better than those in the control group, the drug is deemed safe and effective. Otherwise, the drug is declared unsafe, ineffective, or both.

experimental data
data that come from a researcher running a randomized controlled trial

Data gathered from randomized controlled trials are called **experimental data**. In many cases, controlled trials are the most reliable way to draw inferences about things we want to learn. If the number of trial participants is large enough and the assignment to the treatment and control groups is truly random, we can be sure that the only important difference between the two groups is their exposure to the treatment.

Randomized controlled trials are sometimes used in the social sciences. (The case study below presents an example.) But their usefulness is limited in economics. The problem is often one of feasibility. Experiments can be expensive to run, and policymakers may object to the unfairness of treating people differently. And sometimes, the economic cost of running the experiment would be too large. For example, to study the effects of monetary policy, a central bank could set its policy randomly from year to year and then observe the consequences. This experiment might advance the cause of social science, but it would have such an adverse impact on a nation's welfare that no one would seriously consider conducting it.

Case Study

The Moving to Opportunity Program

An important example of experimental data comes from the Moving to Opportunity Program, which the U.S. Department of Housing and Urban Development ran in the 1990s. The goal was to study the effects of living in high-poverty neighborhoods.

The researchers recruited several thousand low-income families living in neighborhoods experiencing high levels of poverty to participate in the experiment. By lottery, the families were divided into a treatment group and two control groups. Families in the treatment group received vouchers that subsidized rent if they moved to more affluent neighborhoods. In one control group, families received rental vouchers without any restriction on where they could live. In the second control group, families received nothing at all. The researchers compared the subsequent life outcomes, such as earnings and educational attainment, for the family members in the three groups.

Some of the results were disappointing. Even though many in the treatment group used the vouchers to leave high-poverty neighborhoods, the adults in the three groups did not exhibit significant differences in economic outcomes. The average incomes of the adult family members were about the same in the treatment and control groups, though health outcomes were somewhat better for those in the treatment group. Similarly, there were no significant differences in the measured life outcomes for older children (ages 13 to 18) in the treatment group.

Yet the program had a significant, positive impact on children who were below the age of 13 when their families received the vouchers. Younger children in the treatment group did not perform better in school than those in the control groups, as measured by test scores in reading and math. But later in their lives, they had significantly higher rates of college attendance, lower rates of single motherhood, and higher incomes as adults. These results show that young children enjoy long-term benefits if their families leave high-poverty neighborhoods. ●

24-1b Observational Data

Because experimental data are not always available, economists often rely on **observational data**, which are obtained not from conducting an experiment but from simply observing the world as it is. Observational data can come from surveys of households and firms and from administrative records, such as tax returns. Compared with experimental data, observational data have the advantage of being more easily produced and more widely available, but they present two challenges to data analysts.

observational data
data that come from a researcher observing the world as it presents itself

The first is the problem of confounding variables. A **confounding variable** is a variable that is omitted from the analysis but, because it is related to the variables being measured and studied, can lead the researcher to an incorrect conclusion.

confounding variable
an omitted variable that can mislead the researcher because it is related to the variables of interest

For example, suppose you want to know whether reducing class size in grade school improves learning. You might be tempted to estimate the impact of class size by comparing the average test scores of students in large and small classes. That strategy would be fine if students and teachers were placed into the classes randomly, as is the case with experimental data. But with observational data, it actually is. The benefits of parental education could be incorrectly attributed to class size. Or perhaps school principals assign less-experienced teachers to smaller classes. If teacher experience affects student performance, it is a confounding variable that makes the impact of small classes appear smaller than because the placement of students and teachers is probably not random, other variables related to class size may enter the picture and bias the results. Small classes, for instance, might be more common in towns with better-educated and higher-income populations. If parental education affects student performance, it is a confounding variable that makes the impact of small classes seem larger than it actually is. The disadvantages of having a less experienced teacher could mask the benefits of small classes. Because many variables can be correlated with one another in observational data, researchers need to carefully distinguish the effects of one variable from the effects of another.

reverse causality
a situation in which a researcher confuses the direction of influence between two variables

The second challenge presented by observational data is the problem of reverse causality. **Reverse causality** describes a situation in which a researcher believes that one variable influences a second variable, when, in fact, it is the second variable that influences the first.

For example, suppose you observe that the quantity consumed of some food is positively correlated with a person's body mass index (BMI), an indicator of obesity. Should you conclude that the consumption of that food causes an increase in BMI? That inference would be correct if food consumption were set randomly, as in a controlled trial, but problems can arise with observational data. If the food in question were ice cream, the direction of causality might indeed run from food consumption to BMI: Eating a lot of ice cream may cause weight gain. The positive correlation does not prove this, but the hypothesis is at least plausible. On the other hand, if the food were diet soft drinks, a different interpretation might be in order. Maybe people with a high BMI are trying to lose weight and therefore choose to consume diet soft drinks. That is, rather than the consumption of diet soft drinks causing a high BMI, a high BMI may cause the consumption of diet soft drinks. This example illustrates a general lesson: Sorting out what is cause and what is effect is often tricky when using observational data.

Despite these problems, observational data can be useful if the data analyst is careful. Later, this chapter introduces some of the methods econometricians have devised to deal with confounding variables and to determine causal effects.

24-1c Three Types of Data

Whether data are experimental or observational, they can come in three types: cross-sectional, time-series, and panel.

cross-sectional data
data that present information about multiple subjects (such as people, firms, or nations) at a given time

time-series data
data that present information about a single subject (such as a person, firm, or nation) at various times

panel data
data that present information about multiple subjects (such as people, firms, or nations) at various times

Cross-sectional data show the characteristics of multiple subjects (such as people, firms, or nations) at a given time. For example, we might survey a group of workers and ask each of them to report their wage, education, age, experience, profession, race, gender, and so on. We can use these data to see how these variables are related to one another. For example, we can examine how much wages differ by race or gender after adjusting for differences in education, age, experience, and profession.

Time-series data show the characteristics of a single subject (one person, firm, or nation) at various times. For example, we might measure a nation's unemployment rate (the percent of the labor force that is jobless) and its GDP (gross domestic product, a measure of production and income) every year over a 60-year period. We can use these data to study how fluctuations in unemployment and GDP are related.

Panel data combine the elements of cross-sectional and time-series data to show the characteristics of multiple subjects (such as people, firms, or nations) at various times. This type of data, also known as **longitudinal data**, is useful for examining how changes in one variable affect another. For example, we could study how winning the lottery affects a person's labor-force participation by comparing the changing behavior over time of lottery winners and losers.

Quick**Quiz**

1. In a randomized controlled trial, subjects are placed into treatment and control groups based on
   a. willingness to pay.
   b. income.
   c. estimated benefit from treatment.
   d. chance.

2. Observational data has the advantage of
   a. solving the problem of reverse causality.
   b. being widely available.
   c. avoiding confounding variables.
   d. coming from randomized controlled trials.

Answers are at the end of the chapter.

24-2 What Researchers and Consultants Do with Data

Having seen how economists gather data (from experiments or observations) and the types of data they gather (cross-sectional, time-series, or panel), let's consider what economists hope to achieve through data analysis.

24-2a Describing the Economy

Economic data are often interesting in themselves as quantitative descriptions of the world. For example:

- You may have heard that most people devote a large fraction of their spending to housing, but you might not know how large it is. The data show that average consumers in the United States spend 42 percent of their budgets on housing.
- You know that, by definition, a household at the 90th percentile of the U.S. income distribution has higher income than a household at the 10th percentile, but you might not know how different their incomes are. The data show that the rich household has about 12 times the income of the poor household.
- You probably know that the United States has higher income per person than Mexico, but you might not know how much higher it is. The data show that average income per person in the United States is about three times that in Mexico.
- You may have read that spending on healthcare has risen as a share of total spending in the economy, but you might not know by how much. The data show that U.S. healthcare spending has risen from 5 percent of GDP in 1960 to 18 percent in 2019.

These kinds of facts are useful to know. As we develop theories to understand how the world works and consider policies to improve it, keeping an eye on the data gives us a better sense of the world as it is.

24-2b Quantifying Relationships

Economic theory often suggests that certain variables are related, but it rarely tells us how strongly they are related. Often, we need a sense of those magnitudes. That is, we need estimates of a model's **parameters**, the numerical values that govern the strength of the relationships among variables.

parameters
the numerical values that govern the strength of the relationships among variables in a model

Consider an example. Suppose policymakers are considering a tax on luxury cars. They might want to know whether the burden of the tax will fall more on the buyers or the sellers of the cars. The incidence of a tax depends on the price elasticities of supply and demand, which measure the responsiveness of quantity supplied and quantity demanded to changes in the good's price. If demand is more elastic than supply, sellers bear most of the burden; if supply is more elastic than demand, buyers bear most of the burden.

This theoretical conclusion takes us only so far. To answer the policymakers' question, we need estimates of the parameters, which here are the price elasticities of supply and demand. To come up with those estimates, researchers would collect data on the luxury car market. A careful analysis of the data can establish quantitatively the determinants of quantity supplied and quantity demanded. In particular, it would yield estimates of the price elasticities, which can be used to project the incidence of the proposed tax.

24-2c Testing Hypotheses

Economic theories attempt to describe the world in which we live. Like all theories in science, an economic theory is just a hypothesis, an educated guess about how the world works. To confirm or refute the hypothesis, we need to turn to data.

For example, consider the impact of schooling on wages. Economist Betsey thinks that education is a great way to increase a worker's wage. She believes that the human capital produced in school makes workers more productive, and more productive workers are paid more. Economist Justin thinks education is a waste of time. He believes that most things taught in school are useless in most jobs and that people are better off getting job experience than wasting time in the classroom.

No amount of theorizing can settle the debate between Betsey and Justin. Their disagreement is **empirical**: It can be addressed only by the facts, not by sheer logic. In this case, we need to turn to data on wages, education, and job experience to decide which of their hypotheses is correct. (Spoiler alert: Most economists side with Betsey.)

24-2d Predicting the Future

"It's tough to make predictions, especially about the future." Yogi Berra was a wise man, yet economists are often asked to predict the future. A microeconomist might be asked how the upcoming merger between two firms will affect prices in the market for their products. A macroeconomist might be asked how quickly a sudden spike in inflation will subside.

Sometimes, you can make forecasts simply by finding patterns in the data and extrapolating them into the future. For example, suppose you observe that when married couples trade in their compact cars for minivans, they usually have a new baby a few months later. If your neighbors come home with a minivan one day, you might reasonably predict that a baby is on the way. Economists call this relationship between minivans and babies an **empirical regularity**, and it might be useful for forecasting for a while. But the relationship is not reliably stable. If a car company introduced a new line of family-friendly SUVs, for instance, minivan purchases might become a less useful tool for predicting births.

To make reliable predictions, economists often turn to models, which are mathematical representations of the forces at work in a given situation. For a model to be useful in making quantitative predictions, economists need to quantify each relationship within it. They do so using the relevant data to estimate the model's parameters. Once the estimated model is in hand, they can use it to make predictions.

QuickQuiz

3. Economists use data to
   a. describe the economy.
   b. estimate parameters.
   c. test hypotheses.
   d. All of the above.

Answers are at the end of the chapter.

24-3 The Methods of Data Analysis

Having discussed the kinds of data that economists use and what they hope to achieve using the data, let's consider some of the methods that econometricians have developed for data analysis.

24-3a Finding the Best Estimate

According to the theory of human capital, when workers become more educated, they become more productive, and their wages increase. That statement is **qualitative**: It addresses the nature of the relationship between education and wages but not the strength of it. Suppose you wanted to go beyond this qualitative statement and ask the **quantitative** question, "By how much does an extra year of schooling increase a worker's wage?" This question is empirical. You can only answer it using data.

You begin by surveying a number of workers and collecting data on their wages and education. It would look like Table 1. (You would likely want your sample to include more than seven workers, but for purposes of illustration, seven is sufficient.) The data in Table 1 are an example of cross-sectional data.

As you look over the data, you see that more educated workers do, in fact, tend to earn more. The two workers with 12 years of schooling, presumably high school graduates, earn an average of ₹25 an hour. The two workers with 16 years of schooling, perhaps college graduates, earn an average of ₹40 an hour. And the two workers with 18 years of schooling, who may have done some study in graduate school, earn an average of ₹45 an hour.

Yet wages do not always rise with education. Chloe has four more years of schooling than Brooke, but they earn the same wage. Emma has two more years of schooling than Flynn, but she earns ₹10 per hour less than he does. Education may be one determinant of a worker's wage, but there must be other important factors as well.

One way to start understanding these data is to graph them, as in Figure 1. Each point represents one observation. The figure shows the positive correlation between wages and education: Points to the right (indicating more years of schooling) tend to also be higher in the graph (indicating higher wages). Yet the points do not lie along a straight line or even a simple curve. They resemble a cloud, suggesting that there are factors beyond years of schooling that affect wages.

To determine how much each year of schooling increases a worker's wage, an economist will turn to a **statistical model**—a mathematical representation of the process that generates the data. The simplest such model is the following:

$$WAGE_i = \beta_0 + \beta_1 \times SCHOOL_i + {}_i$$

where β_0 and β_1 are parameters that measure how the variables are related. According to this model, person i's wage ($WAGE_i$) depends on years of schooling ($SCHOOL_i$) and is influenced by a random variable ($_i$). The variable on the left-hand side, $WAGE_i$, is called the **dependent variable**; it is the variable being explained. The

Table 1

Data on Wages and Education

Worker	Wage (₹/hour)	Years of Schooling
Andy	20	12
Brooke	30	12
Chloe	30	16
Diego	40	14
Emma	40	18
Flynn	50	16
Gina	50	18

measured variable on the right-hand side, $SCHOOL_i$, is called the **independent variable**; it is the variable taken as given. The term $_i$ is called the **residual**. It represents the many forces, such as experience and cognitive ability, that influence wages but are excluded from the model. The residual is assumed to be zero on average and uncorrelated with the independent variable. (We will discuss the role of this assumption later, but for now, let's just go with it.)

linear regression
a statistical model in which the dependent variable is linearly related to one or more independent variables plus a random residual

This statistical model is called a **linear regression**. In essence, this model draws a line through the cloud of points, as shown in Figure 2. The line shows the best guess of a worker's wage based on years of schooling. The residual represents the deviation of the actual wage from the wage predicted by the line, acknowledging that the model will not fit the data perfectly.

The key parameter of interest is β_1, which tells us how much each year of schooling increases a person's wage. The other parameter, β_0, determines the intercept of the line. Taken literally, β_0 would be the average wage for a person with zero years of schooling. But because our sample does not include anyone with no education at all, it is best to avoid that literal interpretation. Our focus is on β_1.

Figure 1

A Scatterplot of the Data

Plotting data on wages and education shows the positive correlation between these two variables. That is, they tend to move in the same direction.

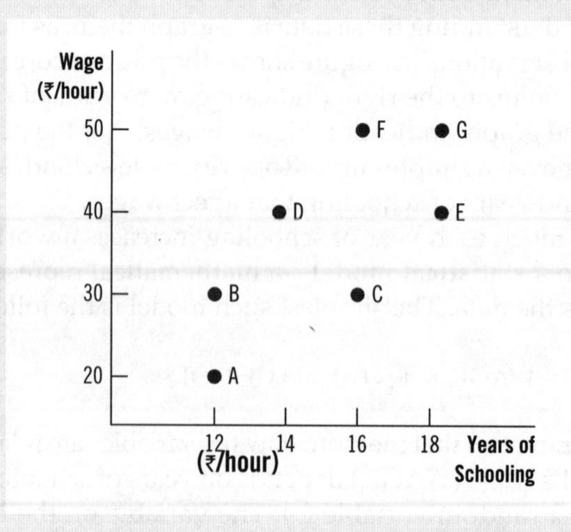

Figure 2

Estimating the Best-Fitting Line

A statistical model posits that wages are a linear function of education plus a residual representing other random influences on wages. The parameters of the model (β_0 and β_1) can be estimated by ordinary least squares (OLS), which yields the line that fits best as gauged by the sum of squared residuals.

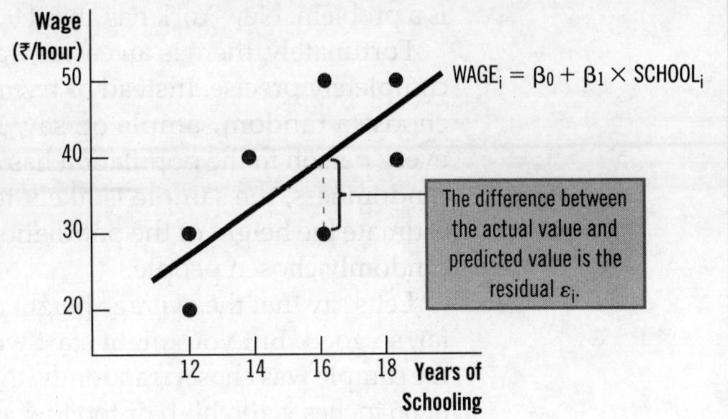

The question we now face is how to best estimate the parameters from the data we have. We could just try to draw a well-fitting line through the cloud of points by hand, but that approach is too inexact (and not easily generalized to more complex cases discussed in a moment). The standard method for finding the best-fitting line is called **ordinary least squares**, or OLS. We won't go into the details of OLS in this chapter, but the intuition is simple. OLS aims to determine the parameters (β_0 and β_1) representing the line that is closest to the data points. Closeness here is measured by the squared residuals. Squaring the residuals ensures that both positive and negative residuals are deemed to detract from the goal of closeness. OLS finds the parameters that minimize the sum of squared residuals.

ordinary least squares
a statistical method for estimating parameter values by minimizing the sum of squared residuals

When OLS is applied to the seven data points in Table 1, it yields the following result:

$$\text{WAGE}_i = -10.7 + 3.16 \times \text{SCHOOL}_i.$$

According to the estimated model, each year of schooling increases a worker's wage by ₹3.16 per hour. That is the answer to our question.

This example illustrates a general lesson: Economists often want to go beyond qualitative theoretical insights (education increases wages) to quantitative conclusions (how much each year of schooling increases wages). This leap requires data. The economists find the data relevant for the issue at hand, posit a statistical model that can plausibly explain the data, and estimate the model's parameters using a method such as ordinary least squares. Using the estimated model, they can reach quantitative conclusions.

24-3b Gauging Uncertainty

Economists use data to estimate key quantities (such as the wage benefit of a year of schooling in the previous section). Often, they want to know not only the best estimate but also how reliable that estimate is. That is, they want to know whether their estimate is precise or a rough guess.

Before returning to our model of wages and education, let's take a detour to consider a simpler example. Suppose you are interested in the height of the average person in New York City. One way to find that number is to get data on the height of every New Yorker. You then compute the average (also called the **mean**) by adding up all their heights and dividing by the number of people. Because your calculation includes the entire population, you arrive at the precisely correct answer. But there is a problem: New York has about 9 million people, so this approach is not practical.

Fortunately, there is an easier way if you are content with an answer that is not completely precise. Instead of trying to get data on the entire population, you can choose a random sample of, say, 100 people. The meaning of "random" is that every person in the population has an equal chance of being chosen. Because of the randomness, the sample is likely to be representative of the population. You can estimate the height of the population by computing the average height of these 100 randomly chosen people.

Let's say that the average height of the 100 people in your sample is 66 inches. So far, so good. But you might start wondering how reliable this estimate is. Because the sample was chosen randomly, there is no reason to think that the sample average of 66 inches is too high or too low an estimate of the average height of the population. But it could be either. You could have gotten unlucky by randomly choosing a sample with a few more tall people or a few more short people than normal. This uncertainty comes from what statisticians call **sampling variation**—the variability that arises because different random samples lead to somewhat different estimates.

Statisticians have developed ways not only to estimate parameter values but also to gauge the uncertainty associated with parameter estimates resulting from sampling variation. The details of this process are beyond the scope of this chapter, but the basic idea can be gleaned from our example. Here is how it works.

First, after computing the mean height of the 100 people in your sample, you compute the standard deviation of heights. The **standard deviation** is a measure of variability across observations, and you may have learned about it in a math or statistics class. In our example, let's say you compute that the standard deviation of heights is 4 inches.

What is a standard deviation? Technically, it is the square root of the average squared deviation from the mean. That is a mouthful, but there is a more intuitive way to think about it. For a normal bell-shaped distribution, about 95 percent of observations fall within two standard deviations of the mean. In our example, the mean is 66 inches, and the standard deviation is 4 inches (making two standard deviations 8 inches). So, if you pick a New Yorker at random, the probability that this individual's height lies between 58 and 74 inches is 95 percent.

standard error
a measure of the uncertainty associated with a parameter estimate that results from sampling variation

Next, using the standard deviation and the sample size, you can compute a measure of your estimate's reliability called the **standard error**. According to a formula developed by statisticians, the standard error of the sample mean as an estimate of the population mean is the standard deviation divided by the square root of the sample size. In this case, the standard error of your estimate is $4/\sqrt{100} = 4/10 = 0.4$. This number can be used to gauge the degree of sampling variation in your estimate. Just as the standard deviation measures the variability in the height of individual New Yorkers, the standard error measures the variability in the mean height of samples of New Yorkers.

Here is a useful rule of thumb: The true value of a parameter lies within two standard errors of the estimated value about 95 percent of the time. In this example, the estimate is 66 inches, and the standard error is 0.4 inches. Two standard errors equal 0.8 inches. So you can be 95 percent confident that the true mean height of the population is between 65.2 inches and 66.8 inches.

Based on this rule of thumb, twice the standard error is sometimes called the **margin of error**. Journalists often use this term when reporting results from public opinion polls. For example, you might hear that, according to a poll of 400 people,

57 percent favor a particular candidate, with a margin of error of 5 percent. That means you can be 95 percent confident that the true support for that candidate lies between 52 and 62 percent.

Standard errors are useful not only in simple examples like estimating a population mean but also in other contexts. Depending on the circumstances, the formulas to calculate standard errors can be complex. Fortunately, most statistical software used to produce parameter estimates automatically gives the standard errors associated with the estimates.

For the data on wages and education in Table 1, the estimated equation produced by Microsoft Excel, along with the standard errors in parentheses, is the following:

$$WAGE_i = -10.7 + 3.16 \times SCHOOL_i.$$
$$(20.7) \quad (1.35)$$

It turns out that the estimate of ₹3.16 for each year of schooling is not very precise. Two standard errors are $2 \times 1.35 = 2.70$. Thus, we can be 95 percent confident that the true wage benefit of a year of schooling lies between ₹0.46 and ₹5.86. That is a large range. But we should not expect much precision when estimating a parameter using only seven data points. If we had 700 data points similar to these, the standard error would be 0.135, and the 95-percent confidence interval would lie between ₹2.89 and ₹3.43, which is a smaller range. Estimated parameters become more precise with larger samples.

24-3c Accounting for Confounding Variables

In many situations, the dependent variable is a function of more than one other variable. Wages, for example, depend not only on education but also on experience, cognitive ability, job characteristics, and so on. If data analysts are not careful, they can mistakenly confuse the effects of one variable with the effects of another. Fortunately, statistical methods are available to help avoid this problem of confounding variables.

As an example, let's continue with our statistical model of wages and education:

$$WAGE_i = \beta_0 + \beta_1 \times SCHOOL_i + \varepsilon_i.$$

Earlier, we assumed that the residual ε_i had a zero mean and was uncorrelated with the independent variable $SCHOOL_i$. The assumption of a zero mean is not crucial: If the mean is not zero, it will alter only the estimate of the constant term β_0. Because the constant term is not the key parameter of interest, we are not led astray.

The assumption that the residual is uncorrelated with the independent variable, however, is fraught with potential problems. The residual reflects all the forces that influence wages other than years of schooling. If those other forces are correlated with schooling, OLS will yield an incorrect estimate of the effect of schooling on wages. The problem is one of confounding variables.

For example, suppose that some people are simply smarter than others. Cognitive ability is another plausible determinant of a worker's wage. If ability is unmeasured, it will be reflected in the residual. That is not a problem as long as ability and schooling are not correlated. Estimating the model above would, on average, give the correct estimate of the benefit of schooling. In the language of statistics, the estimate of β_1 would be **unbiased**.

But suppose that people with greater ability get more years of schooling than people with less ability. In this case, the residual (which includes ability) would be positively correlated with the independent variable (schooling). The value of β_1

estimated by OLS would reflect not only the effect of schooling but also, to some degree, the effect of cognitive ability. In other words, OLS would confound the effect of the independent variable, schooling, with the effect of a related omitted variable, ability. As a result, the estimate of β_1 would be **biased upward**. That is, it would indicate that schooling has a more powerful effect on wages than it really does.

What is to be done? One approach is to find some way to measure the confounding variable. Suppose we return to our seven workers and find that, as children, they each took an IQ (intelligence quotient) test, a measure of cognitive ability. Table 2 shows the expanded data. As expected, IQ and schooling are positively correlated: Higher IQ workers tend to have more years of schooling. If IQ might have its own direct effect on wages, beyond its indirect effect through schooling, then our previous estimate of β_1 is suspect.

All is not lost, however. We can expand our statistical model as follows:

$$\text{WAGE}_i = \beta_0 + \beta_1 \times \text{SCHOOL}_i + \beta_2 \times \text{IQ}_i + \varepsilon_i.$$

In this new statistical model, a worker's wage depends on education and ability as measured by IQ. Because this statistical model has more than one independent variable, it is called a **multiple regression**.

multiple regression
a linear regression model with more than one independent variable

We can again apply ordinary least squares to estimate the model's parameters. OLS will now choose β_0, β_1, and β_2 to minimize the sum of squared residuals. OLS yields unbiased estimates of the parameters as long as the residual is uncorrelated with all the independent variables (schooling and IQ in this example). And the results will be reliable even though the independent variables are correlated with each other. In this case, a multiple regression estimated by OLS lets us sort out the relative importance of schooling and IQ in determining wages.

Estimating this model using the data in Table 2 yields the following results (with standard errors to gauge parameter uncertainty in parentheses):

$$\text{WAGE}_i = \underset{(29.5)}{-49.1} + \underset{(1.41)}{1.86} \times \text{SCHOOL}_i + \underset{(0.35)}{0.57} \times \text{IQ}_i.$$

As we expected, once we control for IQ, the estimated effect of schooling decreases. The new estimate suggests that each year of schooling increases a worker's wage

Table 2

Data on Wages, Education, and IQ

Worker	Wage (₹/hour)	Years of Schooling	IQ
Andy	20	12	90
Brooke	30	12	100
Chloe	30	16	90
Diego	40	14	105
Emma	40	18	105
Flynn	50	16	100
Gina	50	18	120

by ₹1.86 per hour rather than ₹3.16 per hour as estimated when we did not include IQ in the model.

To sum up: When an omitted variable (ability as measured by IQ in our example) directly influences the dependent variable (wages), and the omitted variable is correlated with the independent variable (schooling), OLS yields misleading results. The OLS estimate confounds the effect of the independent variable with the effect of the omitted variable. One way to deal with this problem is to include the previously omitted variable in a multiple regression.

Multiple regression, however, is not the only way to handle the problem of confounding variables. The next section considers another approach.

24-3d Establishing Causal Effects

Data analysts are often interested in the causal effect of one variable on another. For instance, if workers get one more year of schooling, what change in their wages will that cause? If people double their intake of a particular food, what change in their body mass index will that cause? The estimation of causal effects using observational data is difficult due to both the potential omission of confounding variables and the possibility of reverse causality.

Sometimes, these problems can be addressed by exploiting a **natural experiment**. A natural experiment is a chance event that generates variation in the data as if a randomized controlled trial had been conducted.

natural experiment
a chance event that causes variation in the data similar to that generated by a randomized controlled trial

Consider an example. Imagine that one day, Phyllis Philanthropist gives a talk at a high school and makes a surprise announcement: Phyllis will pay four years of college tuition for all the students who graduate from that school and go on to college. This is great news for those students, more of whom will likely continue their education. Across town, there is another high school, much the same as the first but without a generous philanthropist. This situation offers a natural experiment. The first high school is the treatment group, and the second is the control group. By comparing the years of schooling and subsequent wages of the two groups, we can measure the causal effect of extra schooling.

Economists have developed a statistical approach to measure causal effects in data from natural experiments like this one and in similar situations. It is called the **instrumental variables** method, and you will study it if you take a course in econometrics. The key to this method is to find some random variable, called the **instrument**, that meets two conditions:

1. The instrument is correlated with the independent variable of interest.
2. The instrument does not affect the dependent variable other than through its effect on the independent variable.

In our example, the instrument is Phyllis's generosity in the first high school and its absence in the other. This random act increases the schooling of those in the treatment group (condition 1), but it does not affect their subsequent wages other than by increasing their schooling (condition 2). Under these conditions, we can use the instrumental variables method to identify the causal effect of schooling on wages.

For a numerical example, let's return to the workers in Table 1. Suppose Chloe, Emma, and Flynn attended the high school that received Phyllis's offer, while Andy, Brooke, Diego, and Gina attended the high school that did not. Simple calculation shows that the treatment group (Chloe, Emma, and Flynn) has average schooling of 16.7 years and an average wage of ₹40 per hour, while the control group (Andy, Brooke, Diego, and Gina) has average schooling of 14 years and an average wage of ₹35 per hour. Apart from exposure to the treatment (Phyllis's generosity), the two high schools are assumed to be the same. Because the treatment group has 2.7 more years of schooling and earns ₹5 per hour more than the control group, we estimate that each year of schooling increases wages by ₹5/2.7, or ₹1.85 per hour.

The use of natural experiments always raises thorny questions about whether the experiment is as random and easily interpreted as it seems. In our example, the key question is whether the two high schools really are the same aside from Phyllis's offer. In reality, the students might not have been sorted into the two schools randomly. Maybe student placement was based on residence, and one side of town has a richer and better-educated population than the other. Maybe Phyllis made her offer to the one school because its students seemed especially hardworking or especially in need. Such differences could bias the results. Whenever researchers rely on natural experiments, they need to consider whether the process generating the data differs from a randomized controlled trial and whether these differences could contaminate their findings.

Despite these caveats, finding a natural experiment is often the best way to estimate the causal effect of one variable on another, as the following case study shows.

Case Study

How Military Service Affects Civilian Earnings

What is the effect of a period of military service on a person's subsequent earnings as a civilian? This question is important both for personal decision making and for public policy toward the military.

There are plausible arguments in both directions. One might argue that civilian earnings would be higher for those with some military service on their résumés because the military teaches discipline, teamwork, and valuable job skills. Alternatively, one might argue that civilian earnings would be lower for those with military service because the military takes time away from the private-sector experience and on-the-job training that a civilian job would provide. Either of these hypotheses could be true. Only the data can decide.

Consider how we can use data to address the issue. A starting point might be to compare workers with past military service and those without. The difference between the average earnings of the two groups might be taken to be the effect of military service.

That approach, however, has a problem. The difference in earnings might result from the personal characteristics of people who join the military rather than from a causal effect of military experience. Perhaps people who join the military are already more disciplined and good at teamwork than those who forgo the experience. In this case, those with military service would earn more even if the military service had no effect. Or perhaps those who join the military do so because they don't have the skills for well-paid civilian jobs. In this case, those with military service would earn less even if the military service had no effect. Because there are many omitted variables, military service cannot be interpreted as the cause of the difference in average earnings between these groups.

So how can we answer the question? A randomized controlled trial would do the trick. We could randomly divide the population into two groups: one that is forced into a period of military service and one that is prohibited from it. We then compare the subsequent civilian earnings of the two groups. The difference must reflect the causal effect of military service because the randomization ensures that the two groups are otherwise the same.

We cannot conduct exactly that experiment, but historically, the U.S. government has done something close. In the early 1970s, during the Vietnam War, young men were drafted into the military based on a lottery. If a young man had a low lottery number, he was likely to be drafted. If he had a high lottery number, he would likely avoid military service. To be sure, the lottery number was not the only determinant of military service: The rich and well-connected could more easily avoid the draft, and those with high lottery numbers could nonetheless volunteer. But the lottery number itself was completely random.

In an important study, the economist Joshua Angrist noted that the draft lottery number is an ideal variable for applying the instrumental variables method. The lottery number satisfies the two conditions discussed earlier. It affected military service (condition 1). And it did not affect subsequent earnings other than through its effect on military service (condition 2).

What did Angrist learn from studying this natural experiment? Here is his bottom line: "In the early 1980s, long after their service in Vietnam had ended, the earnings of white veterans were approximately 15 percent less than the earnings of comparable nonveterans." Serving your country in the military can be a noble act, perhaps even more so once we recognize the long-term economic cost to many of those who serve.

In 2021, Angrist won the Nobel Prize for his "methodological contributions to the analysis of causal relationships." ●

Quick**Quiz**

4. Ordinary least squares is a statistical technique to
   a. find the best fitting parameters.
   b. avoid the problem of reverse causality.
   c. identify the smallest rectangle that includes all the data.
   d. turn observational data into experimental data.
5. Standard errors are used to
   a. categorize common mistakes.
   b. gauge the reliability of estimates.
   c. avoid confounding variables.
   d. provide more accurate forecasts.
6. Multiple regression is used
   a. to avoid the problem of reverse causality.
   b. to avoid the problem of large standard errors.
   c. when a statistical model has two or more independent variables.
   d. when a statistical model has two or more dependent variables.
7. The technique of instrumental variables is used
   a. to avoid the problem of reverse causality.
   b. to avoid the problem of large standard errors.
   c. when there is an excessive amount of data.
   d. when there is an insufficient amount of data.

Answers are at the end of the chapter.

Data Sources for Managerial Economics Applications

Listed below are various sources of data that managers in Indian firms can rely on for conducting valid empirical analyses to inform their managerial decision making. The sources of data are listed by topics.

1. **Macro, Prices, and Public Finance**
   - **MOSPI National Accounts / Economic Survey / Union Budget** : GDP, sectoral GVA, investment, subsidies/taxes.
     Use: market sizing, top-down demand forecasts.

Note: frequent base-year changes; always match series.

- **RBI Database on Indian Economy (DBIE)** — interest/exchange rates, credit aggregates, state finances.
  Use: pricing capital, FX exposure, working-capital planning.
- **CPI / WPI / CPI-IW (MOSPI and Labor Bureau)** — inflation by category.
  Use: price indexation, input-cost pass-through.

2. **Labor, Households and Welfare**
   - **PLFS / NSS (MOSPI)** — employment, unemployment, consumption.
     Use: labor availability, wage benchmarks, consumer segmentation.
     Note: recall periods & urban/rural splits matter.
   - **NFHS / NHA / HMIS (Health)** — health usage, OOP, insurance.
     Use: health-sector demand, payer mix, targeting.
   - **EPFO Payroll / e-Shram** — formalization indicators, worker registration.
     Use: hiring plans, state comparisons.
3. **Firms and Corporate Finance**
   - **MCA-21** (corporate filings; via paid providers)/**CMIE Prowess / Capitaline** — firm financials.
     Use: competitor benchmarking, profitability norms, leverage.
     Note: private firms' coverage uneven; watch restatements.
   - **BSE/NSE** — prices, shareholding, disclosures.
     Use: event studies, market expectations.
4. **Trade, Logistics and Industry**
   - **DGCIS / ICEGATE** — HS-code exports/imports by product & partner.
     Use: export strategy, tariff shock analysis, market entry.
   - **DPIIT IIP / ASI** — industrial production; plant-level manufacturing (ASI).
     Use: capacity planning, cluster targeting.
     Night-lights
     Use: climate shocks, local demand proxies, electrification.
   - *Note:* ASI microdata access is controlled; lagged.
5. **Agriculture and Rural**
   - **AgMARKNET** — mandi prices & arrivals.
     Use: commodity pricing, procurement windows.
   - **DAC&FW crop cuts/CCE, e-NAM** — production & digital auctions.
     Use: supply risk, hedging triggers.
6. **Energy, Environment and Transport**
   - **CEA / POSOCO** — generation mix, demand, outages (daily).
     Use: plant siting, time-of-day pricing, load shifting.
   - **CPCB / SAFAR** air-quality dashboards.
     Use: compliance risk, ESG targeting.
   - **VAHAN / NHAI FASTag (summary releases)** — vehicle stock, traffic.
     Use: auto demand, logistics time variability.
7. **Digital Economy and Payments**
   - **NPCI (UPI, NETC, RuPay)** — transaction volumes/values by state.
     Use: digital adoption, fintech product design.
   - **Aadhaar / AEPS and Account Aggregator (ecosystem notes)**
     Use: credit rails, KYC frictions, funnel design.
8. **Education & Skills**
   - **UDISE+ / AISHE** — school/college coverage & outputs.
     Use: campus recruiting maps, training market sizing.
   - **PMKVY / NAPS dashboards** — skilling & apprenticeships.
     Use: talent pipeline planning, CSR alignment.
9. **Open Data and Geospatial / High-frequency**
   - **data.gov.in (OpenGov)** — multi-ministry datasets.
     Use: rapid prototyping, joins across domains.
   - **IMD rainfall / temperature**
     Use: climate shocks, local demand proxies, electrification.**; VIIRS/ DMSP**

24-4 Conclusion

This chapter has been a whirlwind tour of the large and often technical field of econometrics. It discussed the kinds of data that economists use, what they aim to achieve with their data analysis, and how various statistical methods help in drawing reliable inferences from the data. But to feel ready to apply the tools of econometrics yourself, you will need to take a full course on the topic. The brief introduction in this chapter provides a foundation for that future study.

Chapter in a Nutshell

- Economists use two kinds of data to study how the world works: experimental data obtained from randomized controlled trials and observational data obtained from surveys and administrative records. Interpreting observational data requires extra care due to the problems of confounding variables and reverse causality.
- There are three types of data. Cross-sectional data present information about multiple subjects (such as people, firms, or nations) at a given point in time. Time-series data present information about a single subject over time. Panel data present information about multiple subjects over time.
- Economists usually have one of four goals when using data: describing the economy, quantifying relationships among variables, testing hypotheses, or predicting the future.
- To quantify relationships, statistical methods are used to find parameter estimates that best fit the data. One such method is ordinary least squares.
- Statistical methods not only estimate parameters but also determine the uncertainty associated with those estimates that arises from sampling variation. An estimate's standard error is a measure of that uncertainty.
- Data analysts can be led astray if a confounding variable is correlated with the independent variable and omitted from the statistical model. One approach to dealing with this problem is to add the confounding variable to the model and use multiple regression to estimate the true effect of the independent variable of interest.
- To estimate the causal effect of one variable on another, data analysts need to be careful about confounding variables and reverse causality. One approach is to look for natural experiments.

Key Concepts

Questions for Review

1. Explain the difference between experimental and observational data.
2. Why don't economists always use experimental data?
3. What two problems arise in the analysis of observational data?
4. Explain the difference between cross-sectional data and time-series data, and give an example of each.
5. How does ordinary least squares choose the parameter values of a statistical model?
6. What does the standard error of a parameter estimate measure?
7. Explain the problem of confounding variables, and describe two methods for solving the problem.

Problems and Applications

1. Choose the right words to complete this summary of a hypothetical research project.
   a. Ellie, an economist, wants to study how population growth affects national income. She collects data on 50 countries, measuring each country's population growth rate and national income per person. This is an example of [cross-sectional, time-series] data.
   b. She posits a statistical model in which national income depends on population growth. She plots the data and draws the best-fitting line through the points using [randomized controlled trials, ordinary least squares].
   c. There is a negative relationship: Countries with higher population growth tend to have lower incomes. She concludes that this finding is not

due to sampling variation because she has a small [sample size, standard error].

d. Ellie recognizes that her data is [experimental, observational]...

e. ...because it was not generated by a [randomized controlled trial, multiple regression].

f. She worries that a country's average educational attainment might affect both its income and population growth, leading to the problem of [confounding variables, linear regression].

g. She finds data on educational attainment in each country and adds it to her statistical model using [panel data, multiple regression].

h. Ellie also worries that the level of income may affect the availability of birth control and thereby population growth, leading to the problem of [reverse causality, standard errors].

i. She learns that some countries benefited from a UN program disseminating birth control while others did not and that the choice of countries enrolled in the program was random. She recognizes that this policy provides a [natural experiment, linear regression].

j. She can now estimate the causal impact of population growth on income using the technique of [ordinary least squares, instrumental variables].

Quick**Quiz Answers**

1. **d** 2. **b** 3. **d** 4. **a** 5. **b** 6. **c** 7. **a**

Glossary

A

ability-to-pay principle the idea that taxes should be levied on a person according to how well that person can shoulder the burden

absolute advantage the ability to produce a good using fewer inputs than another producer

accounting profit total revenue minus total explicit cost

adverse selection the tendency for the mix of unobserved attributes to become undesirable from the standpoint of an uninformed party

affirmative action those explicit policies that expand access to education, jobs, and other opportunities to historically marginalized and underrepresented groups through quotas and mandated reservations.

agent a person who performs an act for another person, called the principal

Arrow's impossibility theorem a mathematical result showing that, under certain assumed conditions, there is no method for aggregating individual preferences into a valid set of social preferences

average fixed cost fixed cost divided by the quantity of output

average revenue total revenue divided by the quantity sold

average tax rate total taxes divided by total income

average total cost total cost divided by the quantity of output

average variable cost variable cost divided by the quantity of output

B

behavioral economics the subfield of economics that integrates the insights of psychology

benefits principle the idea that people should pay taxes based on the benefits they receive from government services

budget constraint the limit on the consumption bundles that a consumer can afford

business cycle fluctuations in economic activity, such as employment and production

C

capital the equipment and structures used to produce goods and services

cartel a group of firms acting in unison

circular-flow diagram a visual model of the economy that shows how dollars flow through markets among households and firms

certainty equivalent the sure amount of money that makes a decision maker indifferent between accepting the risky project and taking the sure amount.

club goods goods that are excludable but not rival in consumption

Coase theorem the proposition that if private parties can bargain without cost over the allocation of resources, they can solve the problem of externalities on their own

collusion an agreement among firms in a market about quantities to produce or prices to charge

common resources goods that are rival in consumption but not excludable

comparative advantage the ability to produce a good at a lower opportunity cost than another producer

compensating differential a difference in wages that arises to offset the nonmonetary characteristics of different jobs

competitive market a market in which there are many buyers and many sellers so each has a negligible impact on the market price

competitive market a market with many buyers and sellers trading identical products so that each buyer and seller is a price taker

complements two goods for which an increase in the price of one leads to a decrease in the demand for the other

Condorcet paradox the failure of majority rule to produce transitive preferences for society

confounding variable an omitted variable that can mislead the researcher because it is related to the variables of interest

constant returns to scale the property whereby long-run average total cost stays the same as the quantity of output changes

consumer surplus the amount a buyer is willing to pay for a good minus the amount the buyer actually pays for it

corrective tax a tax designed to induce private decision makers to take into account the social costs that arise from a negative externality

cost the value of everything a seller must give up to produce a good

cost–benefit analysis a study that compares the costs and benefits to society of providing a public good

cross-price elasticity of demand a measure of how much the quantity demanded of one good responds to a change in the price of another good, calculated as the percentage change in the quantity demanded of the first good divided by the percentage change in the price of the second good

cross-sectional data data that present information about multiple subjects (such as people, firms, or nations) at a given time

D

data factual information, often quantitative, that provides the basis for reasoning and discussion

deadweight loss the fall in total surplus that results from a market distortion

demand curve a graph of the relationship between the price of a good and the quantity demanded

demand schedule a table that shows the relationship between the price of a good and the quantity demanded

diminishing marginal product the property whereby the marginal product of an input declines as the quantity of the input increases

discrimination the offering of different opportunities to similar individuals who differ only by race, ethnicity, gender, age, religion, sexual orientation, or other personal characteristics

diseconomies of scale the property whereby long-run average total cost rises as the quantity of output increases

dominant strategy a strategy that is best for a player in a game regardless of the strategies chosen by the other players

E

econometrics the subfield of economics that develops tools to analyze data

economic profit total revenue minus total cost, including both explicit and implicit costs

economics the study of how society manages its scarce resources

economies of scale the property whereby long-run average total cost falls as the quantity of output increases

efficiency the property of society getting the most it can from its scarce resources

efficiency the property regarding a resource allocation of maximizing the total surplus received by all members of society

efficiency wages above-equilibrium wages paid by firms to increase worker productivity

efficient scale the quantity of output that minimizes average total cost

elasticity a measure of the responsiveness of the quantity demanded or quantity supplied to a change in one of its determinants

equality the property of distributing economic prosperity uniformly among the members of society

equality the property of distributing economic prosperity uniformly among the members of society

equilibrium a situation in which the market price has reached the level at which the quantity supplied equals the quantity demanded

equilibrium price the price that balances the quantity supplied and the quantity demanded

equilibrium quantity the quantity supplied and the quantity demanded at the equilibrium price

excludability the property of a good whereby a person can be prevented from using it

expected utility the value a decision-maker assigns to a risky option by averaging the satisfaction levels from each possible outcome weighted by its probability of occurrence.

expected value the weighted average of the payoffs from all possible outcomes of a lottery, with the weights being the respective probabilities of the outcomes occurring.

experimental data data that come from a researcher running a randomized controlled trial

explicit costs input costs that require an outlay of money by the firm

exports goods produced domestically and sold abroad

externality the impact of one person's actions on the well-being of a bystander

externality the uncompensated impact of a person's actions on the well-being of a bystander

F

factors of production the inputs used to produce goods and services

fixed costs costs that do not vary with the quantity of output produced

free rider a person who receives the benefit of a good but avoids paying for it

G

game theory the study of how people behave in strategic situations

Giffen good a good for which an increase in the price raises the quantity demanded

H

horizontal equity the idea that taxpayers with similar abilities to pay taxes should pay the same amount

human capital the accumulation of investments in people, such as education and on-the-job training

I

implicit costs input costs that do not require an outlay of money by the firm

imports goods produced abroad and sold domestically

in-kind transfers transfers given in the form of goods and services rather than cash

incentive something that induces a person to act

income effect the change in consumption that results when a price change moves the consumer to a higher or lower indifference curve

income elasticity of demand a measure of how much the quantity demanded of a good responds to a change in consumers' income, calculated as the percentage change in quantity demanded divided by the percentage change in income

indifference curve a curve that shows consumption bundles that give the consumer the same level of satisfaction

inferior good a good for which, other things being equal, an increase in income leads to a decrease in demand

inflation an increase in the overall level of prices in the economy

internalizing the externality altering incentives so that people take into account the external effects of their actions

L

law of demand the claim that, other things being equal, the quantity demanded of a good falls when the price of the good rises

law of supply the claim that, other things being equal, the quantity supplied of a good rises when the price of the good rises

law of supply and demand the claim that the price of any good adjusts to bring the quantity supplied and the quantity demanded of that good into balance

liberal contractarianism the political philosophy according to which the government should choose policies deemed just, as evaluated by impartial observers behind a "veil of ignorance"

libertarianism the political philosophy according to which the government should punish crimes and enforce voluntary agreements but not redistribute income

life cycle the regular pattern of income variation over a person's life

linear regression a statistical model in which the dependent variable is linearly related to one or more independent variables plus a random residual

lump-sum tax a tax that is the same amount for every person

M

macroeconomics the study of economy-wide phenomena, including inflation, unemployment, and economic growth

marginal change an incremental adjustment to a plan of action

marginal cost the increase in total cost that arises from an extra unit of production

marginal product the increase in output that arises from an additional unit of input

marginal product of labor the increase in the amount of output from an additional unit of labor

marginal rate of substitution the rate at which a consumer is willing to trade one good for another

marginal revenue the change in total revenue from an additional unit sold

marginal tax rate the increase in taxes from an additional dollar of income

market a group of buyers and sellers of a particular good or service

market economy an economy that allocates resources through the decentralized decisions of many firms and households as they interact in markets for goods and services

market failure a situation in which a market left on its own does not allocate resources efficiently

market power the ability of a single economic actor (or small group of actors) to have a substantial influence on market prices

maximin criterion the claim that the government should aim to maximize the well-being of the worst-off person in society

median voter theorem a mathematical result showing that if voters are choosing a point along a line and they all want the point closest to their own optimum, then majority rule will pick the optimum of the median voter

microeconomics the study of how households and firms make decisions and how they interact in markets

monopolistic competition a market structure in which many firms sell products that are similar but not identical

monopoly a firm that is the sole seller of a product without close substitutes

monopsony a market that has only one buyer

moral hazard the tendency of a person who is imperfectly monitored to engage in dishonest or otherwise undesirable behavior

multiple regression a linear regression model with more than one independent variable

N

Nash equilibrium a situation in which economic actors interacting with one another each choose their best strategy given the strategies that all the other actors have chosen

natural experiment a chance event that causes variation in the data similar to that generated by a randomized controlled trial

natural monopoly a type of monopoly that arises because a single firm can supply a good or service to an entire market at a lower cost than could two or more firms

negative income tax a tax system that collects revenue from high-income households and gives subsidies to low-income households

normal good a good for which, other things being equal, an increase in income leads to an increase in demand

normal good a good for which an increase in income raises the quantity demanded

normative statements claims that attempt to prescribe how the world should be

O

observational data data that come from a researcher observing the world as it presents itself

oligopoly a market structure in which only a few sellers offer similar or identical products

opportunity cost whatever must be given up to obtain some item

ordinary least squares a statistical method for estimating parameter values by minimizing the sum of squared residuals

P

panel data data that present information about multiple subjects (such as people, firms, or nations) at various times

parameters the numerical values that govern the strength of the relationships among variables in a model

perfect complements two goods with right-angle indifference curves

perfect substitutes two goods with straight-line indifference curves

permanent income a person's normal income

political economy the study of government using the analytic methods of economics

positive statements claims that attempt to describe the world as it is

poverty line an absolute level of income set by the federal government for each family size below which a family is deemed to be in poverty

poverty rate the percentage of the population whose family income falls below an absolute level called the poverty line

price ceiling a legal maximum on the price at which a good can be sold

price discrimination the business practice of selling the same good at different prices to different customers

price elasticity of demand a measure of how much the quantity demanded of a good responds to a change in its price, calculated as the percentage change in quantity demanded divided by the percentage change in price

price elasticity of supply a measure of how much the quantity supplied of a good responds to a change in its price, calculated as the percentage change in quantity supplied divided by the percentage change in price

price floor a legal minimum on the price at which a good can be sold

principal a person for whom another person, called the agent, performs some act

prisoners' dilemma a particular "game" between two captured prisoners that illustrates why cooperation is difficult to maintain even when it is mutually beneficial

private goods goods that are both excludable and rival in consumption

producer surplus the amount a seller is paid for a good minus the seller's cost of providing it

production function the relationship between the quantity of inputs used to make a good and the quantity of output of that good

production possibilities frontier a graph that shows the combinations of output that the economy can possibly produce with the available factors of production and production technology

productivity the quantity of goods and services produced from each unit of labor input

profit total revenue minus total cost

progressive tax a tax for which taxpayers with high incomes pay a larger fraction of their income than do taxpayers with low incomes

property rights the ability of an individual to own and exercise control over scarce resources

proportional tax a tax for which taxpayers at all income levels pay the same fraction of income

public goods goods that are neither excludable nor rival in consumption

Q

quantity demanded the amount of a good that buyers are willing and able to purchase

quantity supplied the amount of a good that sellers are willing and able to sell

R

randomized controlled trial an experiment in which a researcher randomly divides subjects into groups, treats the groups differently, and compares their outcomes

rational people people who systematically and purposefully do the best they can to achieve their objectives

regressive tax a tax for which taxpayers with high incomes pay a smaller fraction of their income than do taxpayers with low incomes

reverse causality a situation in which a researcher confuses the direction of influence between two variables

risk aversion a dislike of uncertainty

rivalry in consumption the property of a good whereby one person's use diminishes other people's use

S

scarcity the limited nature of society's resources

screening an action taken by an uninformed party to induce an informed party to reveal information

shortage a situation in which the quantity demanded is greater than the quantity supplied

signaling an action taken by an informed party to reveal private information to an uninformed party

social insurance government policy aimed at protecting people against the risk of adverse events

standard error a measure of the uncertainty associated with a parameter estimate that results from sampling variation

statistical discrimination discrimination that arises because an irrelevant but observable personal characteristic is correlated with a relevant but unobservable attribute

strike a collective refusal to work organized as a form of protest

structural transformation the reallocation of resources among different sectors of an economy resulting in changes in the sectoral composition of the gdp, usually through a switch from less productive to more productive sectors

substitutes two goods for which an increase in the price of one leads to an increase in the demand for the other

substitution effect the change in consumption that results when a price change moves the consumer along a given indifference curve to a point with a new marginal rate of substitution

sunk cost a cost that has already been committed and cannot be recovered

supply curve a graph of the relationship between the price of a good and the quantity supplied

supply schedule a table that shows the relationship between the price of a good and the quantity supplied

surplus a situation in which the quantity supplied is greater than the quantity demanded

T

tariff a tax on goods produced abroad and sold domestically

tax incidence the manner in which the burden of a tax is shared among participants in a market

time-series data data that present information about a single subject (such as a person, firm, or nation) at various times

total cost the market value of the inputs a firm uses in production

total revenue the amount paid by buyers and received by the sellers of a good, calculated as the price of the good times the quantity sold

total revenue the amount a firm receives for the sale of its output

Tragedy of the Commons a parable that illustrates why common resources are used more than is desirable from the standpoint of society as a whole

transaction costs the costs that parties incur during the process of agreeing to and following through on a bargain

U

uncertainty a state of incomplete knowledge in which future outcomes and their probabilities are not well defined.

union a worker association that bargains with employers over wages and working conditions

utilitarianism the political philosophy according to which the government should choose policies to maximize the total utility of everyone in society

utility a measure of satisfaction

V

value of the marginal product the marginal product of an input times the price of the output

variable costs costs that vary with the quantity of output produced

vertical equity the idea that taxpayers with a greater ability to pay taxes should pay larger amounts

W

welfare economics the study of how the allocation of resources affects economic well-being

welfare government programs that supplement the incomes of the needy

willingness to pay the maximum amount that a buyer will pay for a good

world price the price of a good that prevails in the world market for that good

Index

Page numbers in *boldface* refer to pages where key terms are defined.

V

W

X

Y

Z